THE NEW OXFORD HISTORY OF ENGLAND

General Editor · J. M. ROBERTS

.

Finding a Role?

THE UNITED KINGDOM,

1970–1990

BRIAN HARRISON

CLARENDON PRESS · OXFORD

OXFORD

UNIVERSITY PRESS

Great Clarendon Street, Oxford OX2 6DP

Oxford University Press is a department of the University of Oxford.
It furthers the University's objective of excellence in research, scholarship,
and education by publishing worldwide in

Oxford New York

Auckland Cape Town Dar es Salaam Hong Kong Karachi
Kuala Lumpur Madrid Melbourne Mexico City Nairobi
New Delhi Shanghai Taipei Toronto

With offices in

Argentina Austria Brazil Chile Czech Republic France Greece
Guatemala Hungary Italy Japan Poland Portugal Singapore
South Korea Switzerland Thailand Turkey Ukraine Vietnam

Oxford is a registered trade mark of Oxford University Press
in the UK and in certain other countries

Published in the United States
by Oxford University Press Inc., New York

© Brian Harrison 2010

The moral rights of the authors have been asserted
Database right Oxford University Press (maker)

First published 2010

British Library Cataloguing in Publication Data

Data available

Library of Congress Control Number: 2009939957

Typeset by Laserwords Private Limited, Chennai, India
Printed in Great Britain
on acid-free paper by
Clays Ltd, St Ives plc

ISBN 978-0-19-954875-0

1 3 5 7 9 10 8 6 4 2

Preface

This is the second of two self-contained volumes on British history since 1951. The first, *Seeking a Role: The United Kingdom 1951–1970*, similarly structured, was published in 2009, and introduces all the major themes discussed in this volume. The acknowledgements and dedication in *Seeking a Role* apply with equal force here. David Coleman and Alex May were as generous with their comments on chapters in this volume as on chapters in its precursor; Alvin Jackson rescued me from errors in my discussion of Northern Ireland; and Shelagh and Walter Eltis commented most helpfully on Chapter 5. At this point I take pleasure in acknowledging the quiet patience, resourcefulness, diplomatic skills, and efficiency displayed by Matthew Cotton and Christopher Wheeler, both of the Oxford University Press. They got both volumes through the press despite being lumbered with an author who caused them more than a spot of bother. As before, I take full responsibility for any mistakes which remain, and will be grateful to readers who can draw them to my attention.

Brian Harrison
Corpus Christi College, Oxford

May 2009

Contents

List of Plates

All the plates are collected in a single sequence in the middle of the book. The page references supplied here identify where in the text each plate is relevant.

Illustrations

Abbreviations

ABCA	Army Bureau of Current Affairs
ANC	African National Congress
BBC	British Broadcasting Corporation
BPF	D. E. Butler *et al.*, *British Political Facts* (8 edns. 1963–2000)
BST	A. H. Halsey (ed.), *British Social Trends since 1900* (London and Basingstoke, 1988)
BT	British Telecom
CAMRA	Campaign for Real Ale
CBI	Confederation of British Industry
CCTV	closed circuit television
CEGB	Central Electricity Generating Board
CHOGM	Commonwealth heads of government meeting
CND	Campaign for Nuclear Disarmament
CPGB	Communist Party of Great Britain
CPRS	Central Policy Review Staff
CPS	Centre for Policy Studies
DHSS	Department of Health and Social Security
DT	*Daily Telegraph*
Econ	*Economist*
EEC	European Economic Community
EETPU	Electrical, Electronic, Telecommunications and Plumbing Union
EMS	European Monetary System
ERM	Exchange-Rate Mechanism
EU	European Union
FT	*Financial Times*
G	*Guardian*
GCHQ	Government Communications Headquarters
GCSE	General Certificate of Secondary Education
GLC	Greater London Council
HC Deb.	*House of Commons Debates*
HL Deb.	*House of Lords Debates*

HMC	Headmasters' Conference
IAPS	Incorporated Association of Preparatory Schools
IEA	Institute of Economic Affairs
IMF	International Monetary Fund
Ind	*Independent*
INF	Intermediate-Range Nuclear Forces [Treaty]
IOS	*Independent on Sunday*
IRA	Irish Republican Army (but applied to the 'Provisional Irish Republican Army' after 1972)
ISIS	Independent Schools Information Service
ISTC	Iron and Steel Trades Confederation
ITV	Independent Television
IVF	in vitro fertilization
LEA	Local Education Authority
LSE	London School of Economics
MIRAS	Mortgage Interest Relief at Source
MSC	Manpower Services Commission
NATO	North Atlantic Treaty Organization
NEDC	National Economic Development Council
NHS	National Health Service
NS	*New Statesman*
NUM	National Union of Mineworkers
NUPE	National Union of Public Employees
NUS	National Union of Students
NVQ	National Vocational Qualification
O	*Observer*
ODNB	*Oxford Dictionary of National Biography*, online version
OECD	Organisation for Economic Co-operation and Development
PFI	Private Finance Initiative
PLP	Parliamentary Labour Party
PLR	Public Lending Right
RSPCA	Royal Society for the Prevention of Cruelty to Animals
RSPB	Royal Society for the Protection of Birds
SAS	Special Air Service
SDLP	Social Democratic and Labour Party (Northern Ireland)

SDP	Social Democratic Party
SNP	Scottish National Party
Spec	*Spectator*
ST	*Sunday Times*
STel	*Sunday Telegraph*
STOPP	Society of Teachers Opposed to Physical Punishment
T	*Times*
TBS	A. H. Halsey (ed.), *Trends in British Society since 1900: A Guide to the Changing Social Structure of Britain* (London and Basingstoke, 1972)
TCBH	*Twentieth Century British History*
TCBST	A. H. Halsey (ed.), *Twentieth-Century British Social Trends* (London and Basingstoke, 2000)
TGWU	Transport and General Workers' Union
THES	*Times Higher Education Supplement*
TLS	*Times Literary Supplement*
TRHS	*Transactions of the Royal Historical Society*
TUC	Trades Union Congress
VAT	Value Added Tax
VHF	Very High Frequency
WEA	Workers' Educational Association
YOP	Youth Opportunities Programme
YTS	Youth Training Scheme

Introduction

1970 does not mark a major break in British history. 'The sixties' as a cultural and even demographic development had by no means ended in 1969,[1] the 'cold war' as yet showed no sign of melting, Northern Ireland's 'troubles' had already begun to escalate, the UK's entry to the EEC was still uncertain, and Edward Heath's election victory did not mark a significant transition even in politics, let alone elsewhere. A sharper political break would have required a major shift in significant opinion, and this had not yet occurred. Besides, his aim was not to repudiate the wartime corporatist settlement[2] but to make it work better. The terminal date for this book's detailed coverage of events, 1990, is more firmly grounded. In that year remarkable developments within the USSR and Eastern Europe ended a pattern of international relations that for decades had shaped British diplomacy. 1990 also terminated attitudes and structures that had pervaded British domestic institutions and politics since 1945. Somewhat paradoxically, 1990 was also the year in which the prime minister most overtly resolute in resisting Soviet Communism was driven from office after her three successive governments had transformed the terms of domestic debate. The corporatist settlement was superseded: government's economic role was curbed, the taxation structure was transformed, trade union power was greatly curtailed, and employers enjoyed greater freedom from the state. And yet she departed.

If such is the period under discussion, what of the area? When introducing his volume in the 'Oxford History of England', A. J. P. Taylor in 1965 felt the need to explain at some length what a historian of 'England' could be expected to discuss. It is an index to changed attitudes after 1970 that this book alone among the more recent volumes in the 'New Oxford History of England', fits somewhat awkwardly with the title of the series. Already in 1949 the British Broadcasting Corporation (BBC) was warning its variety producers, in its 'green book' policy guide for broadcasters, not to give offence by using the word 'English' where 'British' was correct,[3] and by 1970 such sensitivities had grown still more delicate. To foreigners the notion of nationality within the UK is very confusing: there exists no word other than 'British' to describe the UK's inhabitants collectively, but by 1970 they were increasingly choosing to describe themselves as 'English', 'Welsh', or 'Scottish' instead of, or in parallel with, the

---

[1] As argued in B. Harrison, *Seeking a Role: The United Kingdom 1951–1970* (Oxford, 2009), 520–31.

[2] The settlement is fully discussed ibid., pp. xvii, 41.

[3] BBC 'green book' quoted in B. Took, *Laughter in the Air: An Informal History of British Radio Comedy* (1st publ. 1976, rev. edn. 1981), 90.

term 'British'. All the more need, then, to carry forward Taylor's discussion here. If space were distributed according to land mass, England would receive 53 per cent of this book's coverage, Scotland 32 per cent, Wales 8 per cent, and Northern Ireland 6 per cent. If population were the criterion, these figures would in 1970 become 83, 9, 5, and 3 per cent, respectively.[4] Yet to assign space on that principle would be greatly to understate Scotland's role within the union. On the other hand, to discuss each component of the UK separately would run against the fact that in most respects up to 1990 Wales, Scotland, and England shared economic, demographic, cultural, environmental, social, and even political experience; in these areas the United Kingdom was still for practical purposes united. Northern Ireland's culture differed markedly from the UK's other three components, yet in one respect it was becoming after 1970 even more fully integrated into the United Kingdom, given the gradual move in 1969–72 towards the direct rule from Westminster that persisted (with only short intervals) till 2007. So where the history of England, Northern Ireland, Scotland, or Wales is distinctive, it will be treated separately in this book; otherwise the focus will rest on their shared experience. This double perspective explains why the last three areas are so prominent in the index. When the UK's four component parts are discussed collectively, the terms 'UK' or 'Britain' will be used, but when this area is discussed without Northern Ireland, the phrase 'Great Britain' will be substituted.

The main body of this book follows the same structure as *Seeking a Role*, with seven chapters focusing on the following fields of inquiry: changes in the world setting, the face of the country, the social framework, family and welfare structures, economic patterns, education and culture, politics and government. The chapters' arrangement and approach is analytic rather than chronological, since no single chronology can unite these disparate areas of British life. Even Chapter 7, on politics and government, will be concerned, not with a political sequence, but with analysing how Britain's political institutions were evolving. At pp. 550–91 a threefold chronology of events from 1970 to 1990 caters for readers who seek a timetable for the three areas that it covers; it outlines the separate chronologies the fields of inquiry require and sets them side by side. Chapter 8 rounds off the book, like Chapter 10 of *Seeking a Role*, by drawing together the past and the present. After surveying the hopes and disappointments attending the socialist advance up to the 1970s and its free-market alternative thereafter, it points towards the setbacks for both after 1990, and concludes by discussing the fate of the several possibilities earlier held out for Britain's role in the world.

If this book focuses less on the politicians and civil servants than is customary, this in no way reflects disrespect for their role. By their mistakes as much as by

[4] Central Statistical Office, *Annual Abstract of Statistics 1976* (1976), 7.

their successes, politicians and civil servants can—in peace, and still more in war—profoundly affect the lives of millions. Politicians should be credited as much for what they avert as for what they initiate. The journalist Peter Jenkins perceptively cheered himself up in December 1975 by noting all the unpleasant predictions that had proved unjustified during the past year: the economy and the political system had not collapsed, Britain did not vote herself out of the European Economic Community (EEC), the trade unions did not veto the incomes policy, and so on.[5] In the 1970s and 1980s politicians helped to ensure that substantial immigration occurred without prompting wholesale violence, that the cold war did not become hot, that class war was a fading vision, that Northern Ireland did not become a Lebanon, and that the United Kingdom held together. And although they failed to find a role for the UK,[6] their failure reflected the doubts of the people they represented.

In discussing Britain since 1970 it is particularly necessary to stress the politicians' importance and achievement, given that their difficult and delicate art—integral to democracy—was after the 1960s more depreciated and misunderstood than for at least a century. In an irreverent age they also experienced a constant fire of criticism that was often cynical, irresponsible, and ignorant. Yet for two reasons they could not adequately defend themselves. First, conflicting pressures made reticence almost as necessary for them as for that equally misunderstood public figure, the civil servant. But, second, their task was growing increasingly complex, and less easily explained. Both political and administrative worlds were beset with ever-crowding short-term deadlines and with distractions from ever-mounting publicity, so that any long-term sense of direction was easily blurred. In a democratic society which is not at war, politicians' freedom of manœuvre is very limited, and throughout this book their continuous interaction with public opinion and with social and economic change is emphasized. Politicians know, or should know, their own limitations better than most. Theirs can never be a straightforward, constructive, linear, and purely personal achievement. Not for them the historian's luxury of dividing events into distinct categories: politicians, especially when in government, must grapple with the major problems as they arise, seldom easily separable, and often crowding inconsiderately and simultaneously for attention. Politicians' successes are inevitably collaborative, often ephemeral, and frequently most lasting when unseen. Theirs is a world as much of means as of ends, a world of uncertainties, accidents, nuances, moods, and conflicting pressures, and their constituents' bright-eyed sincerity must for them be a luxury rarely enjoyed.

The political sequence can usefully be outlined briefly here. 'Corporatism', in the weak variant gaining ground in the UK after 1945, required the state to

---

[5] 'Seasoned Cheer', *G* (24 Dec. 1975), 8.   [6] See below, 546–9.

shape the economy in a democratic and participatory manner: it was a system of economic planning that enlisted trade unions and employers' organizations voluntarily and continuously behind government. Harold Wilson's Labour governments of 1964–70 sought economic prosperity by carrying corporatism to a higher power on the basis supplied by Labour's long-standing alliance with the trade unions. In so doing, they were beset by difficulties: an abandoned 'National Plan' (1965), an unwanted devaluation (1967), insufficient revenue to meet the UK's extensive overseas responsibilities, a failing incomes policy, and an ambitious trade union reform advocated in 1969 by a prime minister whose cabinet deserted him. The Conservative leader, Edward Heath, took office in June 1970 with 330 MPs to Labour's 253 and at first adopted a less interventionist stance, but his attempt to reform the trade unions without consultation created major difficulties when combined with the need to contain inflation, and in 1972 he was forced into a 'u-turn' towards an incomes policy even more ambitiously corporatist than Wilson's. Without trade union cooperation, however, it was bound to fail, and when Heath did not prevail at the general election of February 1974, Wilson took office in a minority government which he soon skilfully turned into a majority government when at the general election in October he won 319 MPs to the Conservatives' 277; he remained in office till April 1976, then resigned and was succeeded by Callaghan, his Foreign Secretary. Heath had at least attained his main objective: getting the UK into the EEC in 1973, an achievement consolidated by the two-to-one majority endorsing the change in the referendum of 1975. The Labour governments of 1974–9 then again found themselves drawn into an incomes policy which dominated their period of office; after initially appearing to succeed, it collapsed in the so-called 'winter of discontent' of 1978–9 amidst a trade union revolt. The years 1970–9 possess a certain corporatist unity, unlike the period from 1979 to 1990 when Margaret Thatcher as Conservative leader won three elections in a row and shifted the political agenda towards the free market. In this she was helped by a secession from the Labour Party into the Social Democratic Party (SDP) which divided her opponents. Despite presiding over massive privatization, cumulating curbs on trade union power, and notable cuts in higher-level tax—measures that no Conservative government had dared implement since the war—she was defenestrated in 1990 as leader by a rebellion within her own party, leaving her successor John Major to win the general election of 1992 with 336 seats to Labour's 271.

Several trends of the time cut across most chapters and receive sustained discussion in one: secularization, professionalization, and specialization, for example; the gradual fragmentation of the British elite; the growing salience and pervasiveness of the media; mounting concern about threats to cultural standards; the vitality of voluntarism; the combination of newly diverse lifestyles and privacy with pressures towards standardization and conformity; and the individual's simultaneous exposure to an atomized isolation and to new patterns of community and friendship. But other cross-cutting motifs receive no sustained discussion, and are at risk of getting lost in the text, though not in the index. *Seeking a Role* drew attention to eight of these,[7] and their continued relevance to this volume testifies to the continuity, and perhaps also to the conservatism, of British life. The motifs are, first, the equivocal legacy of the Second World War, which united on the one hand pride at having 'stood alone' in 1940, and at having later emerged on the victorious side, with a slowly growing recognition of the national self-deceptions thereby fostered.[8] The second motif concerns the UK's combination of growing insulation from the wider world (through the decline of empire and of any pretensions to 'world' status) with its opening up to the world (through immigration, mass tourism, economic globalization, and a new and closer European alignment). Third, there is the motif of almost continuously growing private affluence conjoined with persistent anxiety about the economy in public debate. This links to a fourth motif: the complex interaction between time-saving technology and the pace of daily living. Flowing from this is the fifth motif: the strain imposed by the UK's growing and secularized materialism on the values and structures that had grown up within a predominantly Christian society. The increasing prominence of two developments, environmentalism and terrorism, rendered this motif still more relevant after 1970. The sixth motif juxtaposes the major changes in social relationships since 1951 with the UK's unusually stable political framework. Seventh, there is the constraint on politicians' power that reflects their dilemma: they must continuously seek consensus for what they see as necessary changes, sometimes statist in nature, yet they must also simultaneously respond to opinion within a strongly voluntarist society. Interacting with this is the final motif, whereby the UK allegedly seeks an overt role while its citizens covertly resist any coordination behind it. As in *Seeking a Role*, these motifs will not receive dedicated chapters or even sections of chapters, but their occasional breaking above the surface of events reflects a continuous presence beneath, which is advertised in the index's subject-entries. The index's biographical entries briefly identify people not introduced in the text.

---

[7] See *Seeking a Role*, p. xx.   [8] For these ibid. 543, 545.

CHAPTER I

The United Kingdom and the World

In the 1970s and 1980s 'globalization' hit the UK at several levels. In this chapter's first section its cultural impact will be briefly outlined before the second section tackles the accelerated tightening of the international economy. The last three sections will move to the more formal relations between states, beginning with the UK's entry into the EEC—in retrospect more like a half-entry. There follows a section on the prolonged unwinding of the British imperial connection, and the chapter ends with the USSR's implosion, totally unexpected even by the experts in its suddenness but also in its relatively peaceful outcome. Its implications for the UK in its domestic as well as international politics after 1990 were profound.

1. A SHRINKING WORLD

After 1970 the world could be photographed from such a distance that nation-states seemed interdependent, for two reasons. First, when the world was viewed in this way, people were much more frequently reminded of its physical than its political attributes: national boundaries were invisible unless they followed natural features. But secondly, when the world was so frequently seen in the round, even the largest nations seemed vulnerable to the shared problems of population growth, nuclear pollution, and 'global warming'—a phrase first used in the 1970s. In that decade there was much talk about the need to internationalize control of the sea, given the environmental problems created by overfishing and by ever larger oil tankers. One well-informed commentator in 1973 saw the impending United Nations conference on the law of the sea as 'mankind's second chance', the first being the creation of the United Nations: 'we are now contemplating ... the end of practical practising nationalism'.[1] Threats to environment and health through migration, tourism, and new technologies forced all governments to think increasingly in global terms. When Eisenhower told Khrushchev in 1955 that the USA and USSR could between them wipe out the entire northern

[1] Lord Ritchie-Calder, *HL Deb.* 11 July 1973, cc. 767, 769.

hemisphere from nuclear fallout alone, Khrushchev immediately agreed: 'we get your dust, you get our dust, the winds blow and nobody's safe'. In 1987 the Chernobyl disaster amply bore him out; as the Environment Secretary Michael Heseltine put it in 1990, 'the wind and the tide know no man-made frontiers'.[2]

By the 1990s the solar system was revealed as in itself huge, but also as but one component of a universe whose size baffled human comprehension. Perhaps this is why public interest in astronomy did not advance in parallel with these researches. If given the choice between expenditure on space programmes and tackling problems nearer home, Gallup's respondents in February 1971 favoured the latter by 69 to 23 per cent.[3] Space research brought practical benefits, though. The major advances of the 1960s in weather forecasting as the computer supplanted the slide-rule[4] made two-day forecasts practicable in the 1970s. By 2003 six- to ten-day forecasts were feasible, and the forecasts' television presenters gradually became national personalities in their own right.[5] Even the ufologists, less in the public eye after 1970 than before,[6] were organizing themselves more professionally.[7] In 1981 a quarter of Gallup's respondents claimed to 'believe in flying saucers', and the Ministry of Defence in 1978–81 received an annual average of 563 reported sightings.[8] A more specific reason for the otherwise surprising loss of interest in the night sky was 'sky glow'; first identified by astronomers in the mid-1970s, it obscured the stars at night. Floodlit sports grounds, security lights, headlamps, streetlamps, illuminated monuments, and all the paraphernalia of affluence were to blame. By the 1990s satellite pictures showed much of night-time Britain ablaze with blocks of light. The Scottish Lowlands, the north-east, and the urban area from Lancashire to London, the south-east and the Severn estuary were all lit up, and in Europe only the Netherlands and Belgium were brighter than Britain. With the advance of affluence and urbanization came 'light pollution'.[9]

Britain's share of the world's population was shrinking: down from 2.0 per cent in 1951 to 1.4 in 1970, 1.0 in 2001.[10] The British birth-rate was relatively low, and there was a continuing outflow of emigrants, so the 'Pacific rim'

[2] Khrushchev over dinner at the Geneva summit, quoted in M. R. Beschloss, *Mayday: Eisenhower, Khrushchev and the U-2 Affair* (1986), 102. M. Heseltine, 'Co-operation, not Federation', *FT* (20 Nov. 1990), 21.

[3] G. H. Gallup (ed.), *The Gallup International Public Opinion Polls: Great Britain 1937–1975* (New York, n.d.), ii. 1126.   [4] Harrison, *Seeking a Role*, 124.

[5] For an interesting account of them, see *T* (10 Jan. 2004), 17.

[6] Harrison, *Seeking a Role*, 71.

[7] S. McIver, 'Ufology in Britain: A Sociological Study of Unidentified Flying Object Groups' (York D.Phil. thesis, 1983), 11–12.   [8] Ibid. 185, 193.

[9] *DT* (26 Nov. 1996), 10. *T* (26 Nov. 1996), 7.

[10] A. Maddison, *The World Economy: Historical Statistics* (Paris, 2003), 258. I owe this reference and the next to generous help from my late colleague, Andrew Glyn, Corpus Christi College, Oxford.

was advancing for demographic as well as economic reasons. Of the world's gross domestic product, Britain's percentage fell from 6.5 in 1950 to 4.2 in 1973 to 3.2 in 2001; and of the world's exports, Britain's percentage fell from 10.3 in 1950 to 5.1 in 1973, and remained at that figure in 1992.[11] If only from self-preservation, Britain's involvement with other nations proceeded apace, accelerated by the escalating improvement in global communications and the dwindling differential between the cost of domestic and international phone-calls. In 1998 Britain came third in the world for the number of minutes it devoted to outgoing international phone-calls, outclassed only by the USA and West Germany.[12] In its number of telephone-lines per person, Britain by 1990 was thirteenth among nations, surpassed mainly by affluent countries with populations more dispersed. But in its number of mobile-phone subscribers in that year Britain came second only to the USA; the take-up of both per head of population was about the same, but well below Japan's.[13] After the USA (with 19 per cent of Britain's outgoing minutes of telecommunications traffic), Europe took priority, with Germany at 11 per cent, France at 9 per cent, Ireland at 7 per cent, and Italy at 5 per cent.[14] Growing international communications meant growing resort to the 24-hour clock, and in 1996 an enthusiast for rendering British summer time permanent cited in support of the change the Edinburgh bankers' need for an extra hour's trading on the Tokyo market.[15]

Travel was becoming so much faster and easier that ephemeral fashions in clothing, language, and sport swept the world with bewildering speed. Twentieth-century air travel, like nineteenth-century rail travel, had its implications for British fiction. With the James Bond novels as exemplars, globally flitting authors warmly embraced international themes such as espionage and international finance.[16] Britain was a massive net exporter of books, with the English-speaking nations dominant in 1984–7: the USA took 20 per cent of UK book exports, Australia 11 per cent, with the Netherlands next (5 per cent).[17] In the fashion for global publishing many UK publishers were bought up in the 1980s.[18] Some British national newspapers, having transcended regional boundaries during the nineteenth century, now aimed to transcend national boundaries, most notably the *Economist* and *Financial Times*. So global

[11] Ibid. 261 (GDP). Maddison, *Monitoring the World Economy 1820–1992* (Paris, 1995), 234, 238.

[12] *FT* (8 June 1990), 4.

[13] G. C. Staple (ed.), *Telegeography 1992* (n.pl., 1992), 61–2. Using the population statistics in *Whitaker's Almanack* (1997), the UK take-up is (in millions) $1177/5647 = 0.020844$, cf. USA $5300/259681 = 0.0204096$, Japan $4300/124764 = 0.034465$.

[14] Staple (ed.), *Telegeography 1992*, 100.

[15] John Butterfill, *HC Deb.* 19 Jan. 1996, c. 995.

[16] For a good discussion see J. A. Sutherland, *Fiction and the Fiction Industry* (1978), 56–61.

[17] Publishers' Association, *Quarterly Statistical Bulletin* (Mar. 1983), 45; (Dec. 1988), 31.

[18] *The Bookseller* (12 Apr. 1991), 1100.

was the press empire of the Australian media tycoon Rupert Murdoch that the only British opinion he needed to cultivate was that of his readers.[19] Behind all this lay the growth of English into a world language. This was largely because the language was prominent in the rapidly growing areas of international travel and business, natural science, information technology, popular music, and diplomacy. Together with Spanish and Chinese, English was driving out the smaller languages, greatly easing Britain's path into the cultural dimension of internationalism. Although by the late 1980s more people spoke the Han version of Chinese, English was increasingly chosen as the world's second or third language, and was spoken by a fifth of the world's population.[20]

Teaching English had become prominent among Britain's invisible earnings: by the late 1980s 600–800 schools in the UK taught it as a foreign language, most of them in London and the south-east.[21] English-speaking was radiating out in three circles: the first and core circle, where English was the first language, consisted of the USA, the UK, and the colonies once British; the second and wider circle embraced the colonies of non-white settlement, where English was often the second language; the third circle, whose population was growing fastest, embraced countries like China, Greece, and Poland with no British colonial inheritance, for whom the language was learnt simply because it was useful.[22] Writers in ex-colonial territories were in a dilemma: the literature of traditionalist nationalism focused on what was distinctive: the land, the people, and the local languages. But this limited its impact even within their country, let alone worldwide. The literature of modernizing nationalism incurred the reverse difficulty: English was often the only language which could both unite the country and reach out towards world influence.[23]

These worldwide developments modified how English was spoken and written within the UK. The flexibility of English interacted with Britain's long-standing world trading role to accept many new words, especially after the sixties had overturned earlier notions that there was such a thing as 'proper English'.[24] The *Oxford English Dictionary* published in 1989 included 5,000

[19] A. Sampson, 'The Crisis at the Heart of our Media', *British Journalism Review*, 7/3 (1996), 43–4, 50.

[20] *DT* (27 Jan. 1989), 4. B. McCallen, *English: A World Commodity. The International Market for Training in English as a Foreign Language* (1989), 1.   [21] McCallen, *English*, 35.

[22] D. Crystal, *English as a Global Language* (Cambridge, 1997), 54.

[23] For good discussions of this see B. King, *The New English Literatures: Cultural Nationalism in a Changing World* (London and Basingstoke, 1980), 53, 57, 149. B. King (ed.), *Literatures of the World in English* (1974), 137. Crystal, *English as a Global Language*, 115.

[24] The Prince of Wales's phrase, when complaining about the new linguistic trends in 1995, *T* (24 Mar. 1995), 2.

more words than its precursor in 1933.[25] In the 1980s a wave of new words, phrases, and grammatical forms derived from the American computer manual swept over the English language, and pedants had to go along with one-time solecisms such as 'to access' and 'to input' simultaneously with the spread of Americanized business-school jargon. European linguistic imports were relatively insignificant, though in the 1960s American sociology acclimatized intellectuals to clumsy Germanic formulations, and in the 1980s at higher administrative levels a pretentious and somewhat Frenchified 'Eurospeak' became pervasive enough for Thatcher to counter-attack by robustly defending plain English usage;[26] towards the end of the decade deconstructionism brought another French infusion, with its paraphernalia of 'sub-texts', 'discourses', and the like. Reinforcing such changes were the new speech-forms that non-European immigrants brought to the UK, and the powerful pressures to simplify English so as to make an international language easier to learn. Furthermore, because more people were speaking English overseas than in Britain, the language's centre of gravity began to shift—especially towards American English—and this reacted back on British usage. When talking films had first entered Britain from the USA, many found their American accent unintelligible, but the problem faded away;[27] the influence of American English was already powerful enough by 1947 to evoke comment from Orwell.[28] Greater ease of communication between English-speakers worldwide helped to prevent the language from fragmenting. So did a second and much-predicted development: the emergence of two versions of English. The first, 'local alternative', was informal and colloquial for local day-to-day use; the second, 'world standard spoken English', was relatively formal, and was used for official and international purposes.[29]

Joining the EEC in 1973 did not generate any British boom in modern-language study. Entries for French at O level in England and Wales declined markedly between 1951 (18.4 per cent of the total) and 1976 (5.6 per cent), and those for German from 2.4 to 1.6 per cent. At A-level, too, the take-up was falling: for French from 9.4 per cent of the total to 4.5 per cent, and for German from 1.9 to 1.5 per cent.[30] Grumbles about declining educational standards were the outcome, yet the child's curricular choice was quite rational.

[25] C. Barber, *The English Language: A Historical Introduction* (Cambridge, 1993), 226.

[26] H. Young, *One of Us* (1st publ. 1989, final edn. 1993), 408.

[27] P. Trudgill, *The Dialects of England: Studies in Grammatical Variation* (Oxford, 1990), 10.

[28] 'The English People' (1947, though largely written in 1943–4), in *Complete Works*, ed. P. Davison, xvi (1998), 220–1.

[29] Crystal, *English as a Global Language*, 137. R. McCrum, W. Cran, and R. McNeil, *The Story of English* (1986), 373.

[30] Calculated from Department of Education and Science, *Education in 1951*, 116–19; DES, *Statistics of Education 1976*, 44–7. See also *DT* (31 July 2000), 14.

Heath when negotiating for entry into the EEC did not attack the dominance of French there, but the Irish and Danes ensured its demotion, and English steadily advanced thereafter. Even in the Channel Isles, the role of French had by the 1980s retreated almost entirely to formal functions.[31] What with this, with the advance of English as a global language, and with the continuous evolution of new and important subjects for study (the social sciences, business and computer studies, to name only three), the young understandably invested their energies elsewhere.

Between 1970 and 1990 Britain experienced waves of overseas influence in every area of national life: from Italy and France on approaches to planning and on the film industry; from Japan on manufacturing methods; from Singapore on social discipline; from European clubs on football; from Scandinavia on welfare issues and public administration; from Denmark and the Netherlands on sexual liberation; from the USA on free-market economics, civil liberties, and feminism. British opinion could not be insulated from overseas influence, as British governments discovered when they failed in the 1960s to curb pirate radio. And in diplomacy the more open governments set the pace for the closed, as witnessed Thatcher's failure in the late 1980s to limit the sales of Peter Wright's *Spycatcher*. Yet institutionally, political internationalism lagged behind: the United Nations made surprisingly little headway with British opinion after 1970. Governments held back from bypassing it, but the high hopes at its launch in 1945, kept alive by Labour up to 1964, had wilted. British governments held tight to the UK's permanent representation on the Security Council; there were flurries of Foreign Office alarm in 1993 at an American suggestion that it could hardly be retained if Japan and Germany were excluded.[32] But the United Nations was becoming a mere arena within which national interests were promoted. Nor could the Commonwealth provide an alternative international base for UK interests: by the 1970s its interests had become too diverse for that. The UK's only option was to participate fully and pragmatically in specialist international structures, and to promote the national interest through the customary diplomatic means. Given international trade's high proportion of her gross national product, given that trade requires international stability, and given that the UK could not single-handedly promote such stability—her continuous involvement in international structures was inevitable. The British left's hostility towards multinational companies in the early 1970s reflected the inability of national governments to control them: economic internationalism was far outrunning political. The political foundations of the new international world order therefore seemed likely to grow only out of regional political mergers; until then, political internationalism could rest securely only upon internationalism of the cultural and economic variety.

---

[31] G. Price, *The Languages of Britain* (1984), 213.   [32] *Ind* (28 Jan. 1993), 1.

2. A GLOBALIZING ECONOMY

The UK after 1970 was drawn even more deeply into the international economy than before. Imports of goods and services rose as a proportion of gross national product from 20 per cent in 1964 to 27 per cent in 1988, exports from 19 to 24 per cent.[33] 'The world economy has to be seen as a whole', said the summit meeting of the seven leading non-Communist industrial nations in 1977; '—it involves not only cooperation among national governments, but also strengthening appropriate international organizations'.[34] Callaghan had been particularly impressed as Labour's Chancellor of the Exchequer (1964–7) with Britain's inability to control its own economic fate,[35] but decided in 1967 that the risks involved in floating sterling outweighed the somewhat less tangible gains.[36] In 1971, however, the dollar was in effect floated, and other currencies followed, enhancing the role during the 1970s of the finance ministers' international consultations. Like heads of state, finance ministers tended to develop a fellow-feeling: 'as untouchables' in domestic matters, Denis Healey recalled, 'we developed a friendly freemasonry which transcended our economic differences'.[37] Callaghan as prime minister (1976–9), keen to get the depression lifted through international cooperation, found international gatherings of heads of government not only enjoyable in themselves, but useful for coordinating economic policy. These gatherings, he recalled, 'took on an existence of their own', in which 'we educated one another' into collaboration.[38] Coordination proceeded further in the 1980s, when the existence of a world market in currency became obvious; this profoundly influenced economic management within the nation-state. As Conservative Chancellor of the Exchequer from 1983 to 1989, Nigel Lawson became increasingly aware that international economic cooperation could curb inflation and unemployment, especially if the major countries' central banks were freed from day-to-day governmental control;[39] international collaboration was needed to smooth out the currency fluctuations stemming from the 'twenty-four-hour global market place where capital flows . . . rather than trade flows, dominate'.[40]

The government's direct control over the economy eased slowly during the 1970s under governments of both parties, with a retreat from import quotas

---

[33] A. Cairncross, 'Economic Policy and Performance, 1964–1990', in R. Floud and P. Johnson (eds.), *The Cambridge Economic History of Modern Britain*, iii. *Structural Change and Growth, 1939–2000* (Cambridge, 2004), 91.   [34] *T* (9 May 1977), 4.

[35] R. J. Lieber, *British Politics and European Unity: Parties, Elites and Pressure Groups* (Berkeley, Calif., 1970), 263 n. 50.   [36] Harrison, *Seeking a Role*, 75.

[37] D. Healey, *The Time of my Life* (1st publ. 1989, paperback edn. 1990), 419. The international community of finance ministers is excellently discussed in his ch. 20.

[38] J. Callaghan, *Time and Chance* (1987), 476–81, 497. See Callaghan's comments on discussions with President Carter in *T* (25 Mar. 1978), 1.

[39] N. Lawson, *The View from No. 11: Memoirs of a Tory Radical* (1992), 422.

[40] Ibid. 1023, cf. 1025.

and deposits, from hire-purchase restrictions, and even from managing demand through the budget. When the major economies' currencies were floated in 1972–3, exchange control was no longer needed to support a fixed parity,[41] and restrictions were relaxed in the stronger economies, though those in the Organization for Economic Co-operation and Development (OECD) did not make the move until the UK led the way in 1979. The UK's relaxation of controls over international investment began in 1977–8 as a requirement of EEC membership. Given the growth during the 1970s in Britain's oil resources, the pound strengthened, enhancing the arguments for going further and abolishing the exchange controls that had been in force since 1939. Even the Callaghan government had contemplated this reform, though fear of the Labour Party's response eventually deterred it.[42] Without abolition, British manufacturing competitiveness would suffer unduly from the pound's appreciation on becoming a petro-currency, whereas enhanced outflows of private capital for UK investment overseas would ease the situation. By 1979 most top people in the Bank of England and some in the Treasury wanted this to occur.

Free-market Conservatives inclined likewise: in 1977 Lawson in his maiden speech as a Conservative spokesman on economic affairs argued for 'a substantial relaxation of exchange control'.[43] The powerfully argued and timely monograph *Exchange Control for Ever?*, published by John Wood and Robert Miller with the Institute of Economic Affairs (IEA) in February 1979, reinforced the determination of key Conservative politicians—Lawson, John Biffen, Geoffrey Howe, and John Nott (with Thatcher a late convert)—to push through the reform.[44] Libertarian in aim, encouraging to invisible exports, administratively easy to implement, and undermining governmental secrecy and excessive bureaucracy, the reform's attractions were irresistible. Nonetheless, implementing the change 'was the only one of my decisions which gave me a sleepless night', Howe recalled twenty years later.[45] It had been too sensitive a subject to raise in the Party's manifesto in 1979, and only a tiny minority of the British public understood the issues. Howe first tested the market in his June budget with some small-scale reductions in control, and there were further relaxations in July, but no further changes could occur without complete abolition, which was announced on 23 October 1979. At that point Howe ended the entire apparatus of controls which the revolution in world communications had anyway by then rendered difficult to police. All controls

[41] For its peacetime continuance in 1946 see Harrison, *Seeking a Role*, 40.
[42] David Lipsey in *ST* (5 Feb. 1984), 62.
[43] *HC Deb.* 10 Nov. 1977, c. 983; see also c. 831.
[44] Howe, *Conflict of Loyalty* (1994), 141. D. Kynaston, 'The Long Life and Slow Death of Exchange Controls', *Journal of International Financial Markets: Law and Regulation*, 2/2 (May 2000), 42.
[45] *FT* (22 Oct. 1999), 7.

over British residents' use of foreign currency for travel, loans, or investment overseas ceased, and all rules hindering outward or inward investment were lifted; an entire department of the Bank of England, employing 750 people in 1979, could then be disbanded.[46]

By no means all abolition's consequences were predicted. The pound soared higher and for longer than had been hoped, placing British exporters in serious difficulty; it did not plunge till 1982. Offshore financial centres in the Channel Islands and Isle of Man were not undermined as far as predicted; indeed, between 1979 and 1991 their combined bank deposits rose more than eightfold in nominal terms.[47] On the other hand, British overseas travellers could now use foreign currency for any purpose, with no record in their passports about what currency they took on journeys abroad. Abolition also removed the barriers between the City's (relatively inward-looking and protective) domestic and its (relatively open) overseas aspects. The change thus exposed the British economy more fully to international competition, and introduced incentives to domestic productivity that were far less overtly political, far less restrictive, and much more powerful than anything that corporatist planning could offer. Shareholders now free to invest abroad would insist on a good rate of return before investing at home, and foreign investors would invest in Britain only if tempted. All this made it easier to erode trade union power, revive the profitability which had fallen so low in the 1970s, and fund extensive privatization. There followed a sharp rise in Britain's total external assets and overseas investments, and these in turn produced dividend and interest payments to offset Britain's trade deficit. A virtuous circle was thus created whereby the government could use revenue from North Sea oil to cut the budget deficit, thus freeing still more funds for investment overseas. The City of London's role as international financial centre was enhanced, and within four years Britain's total investment overseas had more than doubled.[48]

Salutary also was abolition's impact on financial services, accelerating the deregulation of banks, building societies, hire-purchase, and the stock exchange.[49] After 1979 it became much easier to buy gold and property overseas, and Britain rapidly joined Switzerland as by far the largest overseas investors in the USA. Overseas ownership of UK equities quadrupled from 4 per cent of the total in 1981 to 16 per cent in 1993, with the USA taking the lion's share.[50] Between 1979 and 1982 the nominal value of UK overseas portfolio investment, mostly by large pension and insurance funds, rose more

[46] FT (23 Oct. 1989), 22.
[47] R. Roberts, 'Setting the City Free: The Impact of the U.K. Abolition of Exchange Controls', Journal of International Financial Markets: Law and Regulation, 2/4 (Aug. 2000), 136.
[48] ST (5 Feb. 1984), 62.   [49] N. Lawson lists these in his View from No. 11, 626.
[50] FT (2 Dec. 1994), 9. See also Central Statistical Office, Share Ownership: A Report on the Ownership of Shares at 31st of December 1994 (1995), 8.

than threefold, and the nominal return from these investments in dividends and profits rose nearly fourfold.[51] By late 1988 the UK's net external assets reached a fifth of gross domestic product, a higher ratio than that of any other major country, even including Japan.[52] Britain's improved invisible trade balance returned British Chancellors of the Exchequer to a pre-1914 world where they no longer needed to worry about the impact of transactions outside their control on a balance of payments that had once more become self-correcting.[53] So by the late 1980s the UK could afford, whilst confidence remained, a balance of payments deficit unthinkable before 1979. The old stop–go balance-of-payments crises had come to an end, and by resuming her inter-war status as a large international creditor, Britain was building up a nest-egg for the time when North Sea oil ran out. The oil revenues, instead of being channelled by the politicians towards state-directed projects, were being voluntarily applied by individual investors towards building up overseas investments which would generate revenue for the country as a whole. However preoccupied Thatcher might be with national boundaries in other spheres, on economic matters she was an internationalist.

English as a world language was a growing asset for the City, together with its unique situation in a time-zone between its two main rivals, New York and Tokyo: unlike them it could deal with both the Far East and New York during a single (admittedly extended) working day. Add to these advantages London's cultural and traditional linkages with EEC, America, and Commonwealth, and the spontaneous flexibility of the City's financial institutions. London's growing role in international finance continued apace in the 1970s. Given that none of the OPEC countries had well-developed banking systems which could handle their new-found wealth after the 1973 oil crisis, the City was well placed to recycle the flow of petrodollars from creditor to debtor countries.[54] The nervous corporate investor, recruited further in the 1970s by the oil crisis and the growing volatility of the currency markets, still sought refuge in London's foreign exchange market. Exchange control's abolition in 1979, by placing Britain in the forefront of liberalization, accelerated the City's pre-eminence in providing specialist and complex financial services. The Conservative government's privatizations[55] brought the City more new business, given that the share offers, often unprecedented in size, required extensive overseas marketing. This expertise, once acquired, was a service which could be exported to countries seeking to follow suit, and associated professions such as lawyers and accountants gained international

---

[51] *ST* (5 Feb. 1984), 62.

[52] S. Brittan in D. Kavanagh and A. Seldon (eds.), *The Thatcher Effect* (Oxford, 1989), 15.

[53] Lawson, *View from No. 11*, 857–8.

[54] For a good discussion see J. Plender and P. Wallace, *The Square Mile: A Guide to the City Revolution* (1985), 14.   [55] See below, pp. 335–42.

business too. The number of banks reporting details of their international business to the Bank of England trebled in 1965–75, and in 1975–85 rose by another 50 per cent. The Japanese banks welcomed (among other things) the relative flexibility of regulation in the London market, and by December 1985 accounted for a third of the British banks' international liabilities, easily surpassing the Americans (with a sixth), and the combined banks of continental Europe (with only an eighth).[56] Five hundred and twenty-one foreign banks were directly represented in London by 1989, more than twice as many as in any other financial centre.[57] 'Popular capitalism is nothing short of a major world revolution', wrote the Conservative free-marketeer John Redwood in 1988, discussing the banks' readiness to facilitate it overseas: 'The politicians who try to resist it will be tossed aside like trees in a hurricane.'[58]

In 1992 foreign-owned companies generated more than a fifth of the output and nearly a third of the investment in British manufacturing; they paid on average higher wages than British companies and obtained higher productivity,[59] contributing almost a third of the improved productivity that stemmed from changes in work practices between the mid-1980s and the mid-1990s.[60] To this the Thatcher governments' policies contributed, for to the earlier strategies of EEC membership and development areas they added relatively flexible labour markets, better industrial relations, low corporate taxation, and good communications systems. By 1981 the Japanese and the EEC had begun to challenge the USA as Britain's prime inward investors; of the overseas stock of investments in the UK, the USA had 64 per cent in 1971 but only 56 per cent in 1981, whereas the EEC's had risen from 13 to 15 per cent and Japan's from nil to 2 per cent.[61] By 1987 Japanese investment in Britain accounted for nearly a third of their investment in Europe as a whole. In gross terms the Japanese impact was inevitably small by comparison with that of longer-standing investors like the USA, and in 1986 American-owned companies produced almost an eighth of Britain's manufacturing output.[62] But Japanese-owned firms were not content with producing manufactures whose cheapness and quality forced their way into British markets: they viewed Britain as a springboard for diving into European markets, and Japan's economic importance extended far beyond inward investment. Runcorn's UK Fasteners Ltd,

[56] A. Lamb, 'International Banking in London, 1975–85', *Bank of England Quarterly Bulletin* (Sept. 1986), 368, 371. R. J. Walton and D. Trimble, 'Japanese Banks in London', *Bank of England Quarterly Bulletin* (Nov. 1987), 524.

[57] R. C. Michie, *The City of London: Continuity and Change, 1850–1990* (London and Basingstoke, 1992), 93.   [58] J. Redwood, *Popular Capitalism* (1st publ. 1988, paperback edn. 1989), 157.

[59] *FT* (12 June 1996), supplement on 'Britain: The Rogue Piece in Europe's Jigsaw', ii.

[60] *FT* (13 May 1997), 10.

[61] J. Stopford and L. Turner, *Britain and the Multinationals* (Chichester, 1985), 5.

[62] *FT* (19 Apr. 1989), 24.

established in 1969 to make zip-fasteners, was the first manufacturing affiliate of a Japanese company to set up in Britain after 1945. The revolution
in electronics soon produced many more, and by 1982 Japanese companies
making colour television sets had captured nearly a third of the UK market.
Britain in the 1980s was quick to embrace the computer in its business practice,
and overseas investment in the early 1980s enabled it to become the leading
European producer of microchips. Over 400 Japanese companies were operating in the UK by the end of 1983, and there was a marked acceleration in
1984.[63]

Much more significant as an influence was the Japanese approach to employees. The pace-setters for best practice in British industry had been the USA
in the 1940s, West Germany in the 1950s, and to a lesser extent France,
Sweden, and Italy thereafter, but Japan swept all before it after the 1970s,
especially in the motor and electronics industries. Trade unions at first disliked the 'beauty contests' organized within this unfamiliar world: that is,
trade unions' pursuit of members through competing for 'feudal and alien'
exclusive deals which would improve labour relations.[64] But on a greenfield
site at Washington near Sunderland on 8 September 1986 Thatcher opened
Nissan's British car factory, where Japanese working practices were introduced
under a single-union no-strike agreement with the Amalgamated Engineering
Union.[65] Its innovations included team-working, standard uniforms for all
staff, all of whom used the same canteen, flexible working through multiple
skilling, and authority deployed through frontline supervisors instead of shop
stewards; there were even suggestions of early-morning pep talks and organized physical exercise.[66] Whereas Japan had imported technical expertise from
the late Victorian north-east, it was now exporting its management expertise,
with major implications for the entire British car industry; the Washington plant's success encouraged further Japanese investment elsewhere, from
Honda in Swindon and from Toyota in Derby. Japan's relatively classless
work relations and novel manufacturing methods spilled over into the British
manufacturers of car components, as well as prompting imitation from the
longer established UK car firms. Between 1980 and 1987 the British vehicle
and parts industry shed nearly half its workforce, massively improving productivity even at Ford's in Dagenham.[67] The word 'Japanization' seems first
to have been used in 1986 to denote the Japanese impact on British manufacturing.[68] Devolved responsibility within the factory, flexible assignment

[63] J. H. Dunning, *Japanese Participation in British Industry* (1986), 6, 15, 20, 140.
[64] Ken Gill, of the general technical union MSF, *FT* (7 Sept. 1991), 1.
[65] For the agreement see *G* (24 Apr. 1985), 12.   [66] *T* (23 Apr. 1985), 1.
[67] *FT* (20 Apr. 1995), 25.
[68] N. Oliver and B. Wilkinson, *The Japanization of British Industry* (Oxford, 1989), pp. xi–xii (Brian
Towers, foreword), cf. 2.

"We'd like something not made in Japan!"

Fig. 1. 'Jak', *London Standard* (9 Apr. 1987).

of duties within the workforce, continuous preoccupation with productivity, and closer control of quality in both what entered and left the factory were the aims; multi-skilled, better motivated, and better-trained workers were the means. Thus were entire areas of British manufacture rejuvenated.[69] Japan's influence on Britain after 1970 was, however, much narrower than America's: Britain had little knowledge of, and small temptation towards, Japanese political structures, and the language barrier precluded much cultural impact. Britain was relatively unimportant among recipients of Japan's outward telecommunications traffic as at 1990—well below the USA, Korea, Taiwan, and the Philippines.[70]

In opening up Britain's relationship with the world economy, the Thatcher governments aimed to expose the British labour market more fully to world

---

[69] For good discussions see *ST* (20 Dec. 1987), 41; *FT* (19 Apr. 1989), 24; *FT* (18 July 1996), supplement on 'Inward Investment into the U.K.', ii.　　　[70] Staple (ed.), *Telegeography 1992*, 119.

pressures, though without the accompanying logical consequence: the free flow of peoples across British frontiers. By cutting taxation and leaving wage-levels to the market, they assumed that people, too, would move. Refugees from high-tax regimes would arrive and British tax exiles would return. In 1955 Noel Coward had been one of Britain's most famous early tax exiles, and was so severely attacked for it in the press that the Queen Mother made a point of condoling with him two years later.[71] Tax exiles soon became commonplace, making the fortune of the Channel Islands as a tax haven; by the late 1970s there were said to be 150 millionaire residents in Jersey alone.[72] Britain adopted a low-tax policy after 1979 partly from economic principle, but partly because it was no longer possible to enforce a high-tax regime which had been devised when communications were relatively poor, populations relatively static, and firms largely confined within national boundaries. In all this Thatcher's Britain acted as exemplar to the world, though after 1984 the prize for bold innovation along these lines under governments of both parties was carried off by New Zealand, which strikingly exemplified how rapidly a country with regulatory traditions could open up its economy and scale down the role of the state.[73]

Incomes policies in controlling differentials during the 1960s and 1970s had always run up against the existence of an international market for labour, given that (other things being equal) the wealthy society poaches talent from the less wealthy. Money alone does not determine where people choose to live: Britain's relative political stability and libertarian traditions had long attracted Europeans, just as its relative cultural affluence had attracted Commonwealth citizens. But integral to the Thatcher policy revolution of the 1980s was the belief that tax-cutting helps to attract talent from abroad. The Thatcher governments, with no incomes policies, lost inhibitions about allowing the market to widen pay differentials at home. In his budget of 1988 Lawson felt the need to react to recent overseas tax cuts at higher income levels, and reduced the top rate of income tax from 60 to 40 per cent. 'Excessive rates of income tax', he claimed, 'destroy enterprise, encourage avoidance, and drive talent to more hospitable shores overseas', with the unintended effect of reducing the revenue raised.[74]

When Barbara Castle as Labour's transport minister wanted the businessman Peter Parker to head British Rail in 1967 he was keen to help, but (like Beeching a few years before) he stood out for a salary comparable with private industry: 'as a life-long Socialist I believe we simply can't make public ownership work by starving it of talent'.[75] There was paradox in the fact that before

[71] *The Noel Coward Diaries*, ed. G. Payn and S. Morley (1982), 296 (12 Dec. 1955), 357 (23 June 1957).   [72] *T* (17 Apr. 1978), 2.
[73] *FT* (27 Sept. 1996), survey on 'World Economy and Finance', xi.
[74] *HC Deb.* 15 Mar. 1988, c. 1012. See also Lawson, *View from No. 11*, 815, 817, 819.
[75] B. Castle, *The Castle Diaries 1964–70* (1984), 322 (13 Nov. 1967). Harrison, *Seeking a Role*, 141.

privatization the Thatcher governments were readier than previous Labour governments to pay the worldwide going rate when recruiting managers for nationalized industries—most notably and controversially getting the Scottish-born American Ian MacGregor to chair the British Steel Corporation. Feathers were ruffled in 1980 when the government generously compensated his former employers Lazard Frères, and paid a substantial headhunter's fee. When Alan Walters was tempted back from America to advise Thatcher on economic policy in 1980, he received about double Whitehall's going rate.[76] At several key moments in the 1980s tough assignments in British manufacturing were taken up by managers from America and the Commonwealth,[77] and other non-British managerial talent arrived through the multinational corporation. By the early 1980s one in seven British workers were employed in foreign-owned companies, which were on average more profitable, more productive, and bigger exporters than domestic firms.[78]

At the same time, more British people were temporarily working abroad, many of them in the 1970s chasing the opportunities Middle East oil wealth had opened up for craftsmen of all kinds. Better organized for political influence at home were the growing numbers working in Europe. The Thatcher government in 1985 enfranchised British citizens who had been abroad for less than five years (raised to twenty years in 1989 and cut to fifteen in 2000) and intended to return—that is, 500,000 of the three million living or working overseas. By July 1986 the 'Conservatives Abroad' structure had identified 110,000 of them, and had established twenty-eight local branches,[79] of which the largest were in the EEC. Holidaymakers, too, were mobilized: they became eligible for a postal vote in 1985. There was also voting traffic the other way, with Italian consulates encouraging British Italian expatriates to vote in Italian elections for the European Parliament, but potentially more significant in the longer term was the British-Italian population, whose influence could reinforce the British European alignment.[80] Of much greater long-term political significance, though, were the immigrants who were still arriving in Britain in substantial numbers after 1970, and whose predecessors were beginning to exert their voting power.

Immigration into Britain after 1970 must be seen in a European context, where Britain's experience was widely replicated. Although Britain's foreign-born population rose almost threefold between 1950 and 1980, in the same period

[76] M. Halcrow, *Keith Joseph: A Single Mind* (1989), 153–5, 161.   [77] See below, pp. 334–5.

[78] Stopford and Turner, *Britain and the Multinationals*, 4–5.

[79] *FT* (12 July 1986), 1. *T* (18 Aug. 1986), 10. Curtice in V. Bogdanor (ed.), *The British Constitution in the Twentieth Century* (Oxford, 2003), 489.

[80] T. Colpi, *The Italian Factor: The Italian Community in Great Britain* (Edinburgh, 1991), 227, 258; cf. *DT* (8 Oct. 2007), 17 for Polish politicians in Polish elections pursuing potential supporters within the UK.

foreign residents rose eightfold in West Germany and sixfold in the Netherlands; and if in Britain the minority population's share rose almost threefold in these years, in West Germany it rose sixfold.[81] In Britain the balance of population movement in the 1970s and 1980s involved a net outflow to Australia, Canada, and the USA and a net inflow from the African and Asian Commonwealth.[82] Between 1970 and 1991 those born in Ireland and the Caribbean Commonwealth were falling in their share of Great Britain's overseas-born population; those born in Europe, America, and the 'Old Commonwealth' were rising slowly; and those born in South Asia were rising quite fast.[83] The rich diversity of Britain's immigrant mix is immediately apparent. The impulse to immigration and the date of arrival varied both between and within each group, each group of newcomers helping to bed in its predecessors. The Jewish immigrant group continued to decline, partly because 'marrying out' had become common, though the Jewish shrinkage was less marked in London than in the provincial cities.[84] In 1991 the Old-Commonwealth-born numbered less than half the European-born residents in Britain. Almost all had English as their first language and were particularly prominent in the cultural and media worlds; they could easily disappear into the British white population.[85] The white proportion of the British population was falling, but in 1994 still made up 94 per cent. Furthermore, the 3.2 million in ethnic minority groups were highly fragmented, about half drawn from South Asia and a sixth in the black Caribbean category.[86]

The impulse to immigration changed significantly after the 1960s. Overall numbers were smaller, and the economic motive became less prominent than the political, so that immigrants tended to arrive in successive waves prompted by actual or anticipated faraway political events. 28,000 East African Asians arrived in 1972, 3,000 Chileans in 1973,[87] over 16,000 Vietnamese (many rescued from small craft at sea by British ships) in 1979–82,[88] and numerous immigrants from Hong Kong thereafter; by 1983 about 100,000 people of Chinese ethnic origin were living semi-permanently in Britain.[89] The Conservatives, as the

[81] S. Castles, *Here for Good: Western Europe's New Ethnic Minorities* (1984), 87–8.

[82] *Social Trends* (1995), 23.

[83] J. Haskey, 'Population Review: 8: The Ethnic Minority and Overseas-Born Populations of Great Britain', *Population Trends*, 88 (Summer 1997), 16.

[84] S. Waterman and B. Kosmin, *British Jewry in the Eighties* (1986), 7, 12, 20–1.

[85] Haskey, 'Overseas-Born Populations', 15. See also Lord Donaldson, *HL Deb.* 26 Feb. 1969, c. 1164.

[86] J. Haskey, 'The Ethnic Minority Populations of Great Britain: Their Estimated Sizes and Age Profiles', *Population Trends*, 84 (Summer 1996), 33.

[87] S. E. Hale, 'The Geography of Vietnamese Secondary Migration in Britain' (Swansea Ph.D. thesis 1991), 88–9.

[88] P. R. Jones, *Vietnamese Refugees: A Study of their Reception and Resettlement in the United Kingdom* (1982), 1–3.

[89] House of Commons, Home Affairs Committee, *The Chinese Community in Britain: Second Report from the Home Affairs Committee, Session 1984–85. Report together with Proceedings of the Committee, Minutes of Evidence and Appendices* (HC102-III, 1985), p. x.

self-consciously patriotic party, were less likely than other parties to welcome immigrants, but as the one-time party of empire they felt a special obligation towards immigrants from former colonies, and by extension to the Vietnamese refugees whose first destination had been Hong Kong. At the party conference in 1972, Home Secretary Robert Carr defended admitting East African Asian refugees, saying that 'we have our imperial heritage and obligations, and to these we shall stick'; Heath as prime minister led cabinet colleagues in a standing ovation backed by a majority on the floor.[90] At the party conference in October 1980, however, Home Secretary Whitelaw thought it time 'to dispose of the lingering notion that Britain is somehow a haven for all those whose countries we once ruled',[91] and the Nationality Act (1981) withdrew all remaining commitment to residents of former colonies. The humanitarian impulses to admission persisted, however, especially for refugees from Hong Kong: in 1989 Douglas Hurd as Foreign Secretary described the decision to allow up to 250,000 to claim British citizenship as 'just about the last main chapter in the story of this country's empire', adding that 'I am rather keen . . . that that last chapter should not end in a shabby way'.[92]

After 1970 the number of temporary migrants to Britain—that is, tourists—rose fast. With the Wilson governments' encouragement, the British hotel industry from the 1960s built larger hotels and merged them into ever larger chains. In the 1980s these chains bought into overseas hotels as well, so that by 1990 three of the leading international hotel brand names were under British ownership.[93] The smaller British proprietary hotel, also flourishing at this time, reached national prominence with the television serial *Fawlty Towers*, broadcast in twelve episodes in 1975 and 1979—memorable for John Cleese's strenuously surreal performance as the Towers' frenetic proprietor Basil Fawlty. The manufacture of historic spectacles, special tourist museums, and 'theme parks' became a growth industry in the 1980s, with York in a pioneering role. The tourist trade's employees rose fast in the 1980s, and had reached 1.47 million by June 1993.[94] Flying in to occupy the new hotels were hordes of overseas tourists, doubling in number between 1965 and 1970, and more than doubling again between 1971 and 1991. Tourists arriving from EEC countries rose threefold between 1971 and 1991, and those from non-EEC European countries and from all countries combined more than doubled.[95]

[90] *T* (13 Oct. 1972), 6, reporting debate on 12 Oct.
[91] Quoted by Harvey Proctor in *HC Deb*. 28 Jan. 1981, c. 997.
[92] *HC Deb*. 20 Dec. 1989, c. 368.
[93] D. A. Stewart, *Hoteliers and Hotels: Case Studies in the Growth and Development of U.K. Hotel Companies 1945–1989* (Glasgow, 1996), 25–6, 29–30, 37.
[94] British Tourist Authority, *Digest of Tourist Statistics*, 13 (Aug. 1989), 17; 17 (Dec. 1993), 17, including those employed in hotels, restaurants, pubs, nightclubs, and recreational services.
[95] *Digest of Tourist Statistics*, 3 (Nov. 1972), 14–15; 10 (Oct. 1982), 18; 13 (Aug. 1989), 22; 17 (Dec. 1993), 22.

Competition for UK space between British and foreign tourists was not total: British holidaymakers made for seaside resorts and the West Country, whereas foreign tourists made for London and cultural centres in the south-east. The overseas tourist presence in places such as Stratford-on-Avon, Bath, Windsor, Oxford, and Cambridge or in localities such as the Cotswolds or the London theatres became striking. Tourists of both types, however, converged on country houses and historic sites such as the Tower of London, Windsor Castle, or Stonehenge[96]—so much so, that they now spoiled what they had come to see. The Dean and Chapter of Westminster Abbey were by 1980 'extremely concerned' about tourist noise, emphasizing that 'a church is primarily a place of worship and not a museum'.[97] It was perhaps unreasonable to expect foreign tourists in the 1980s to conform to the time-worn and civilized British habit of queuing for buses in London, but eminently understandable was the response in 1997 of Cambridge undergraduates, almost continuously distracted from studying in their rooms by the booming commentary on tourist buses: Japanese tourists found themselves rained upon by tomatoes.[98]

British holidaymakers grew in cultural and economic importance after 1970. The number going away for four nights or more rose continuously between 1951 and 1990, doubling between those dates; up to the mid-1970s the number taking holidays within Britain also rose continuously but then tailed off. Its dynamic transferred to holidays abroad, which more than doubled between 1975 and 1990.[99] Those who took holidays anywhere between 1967 and 1992 (and a fairly steady two-fifths did not) took more of them.[100] In the early 1960s France, until then the most popular destination for one or more nights, was overtaken by Spain—thereafter by far the most popular British tourist destination in Europe.[101] In 1991 74 per cent of UK travellers abroad were going to EEC countries, 9 per cent to non-EEC countries in Western Europe, 7 per cent to Canada and the USA, and 9 per cent to the rest of the world.[102] Many of these British tourists overseas were escaping from the British weather, especially in the winter. A world tourist market was developing, whose flexible tariffs aimed to fill hotel accommodation all year round. Only the elite had gone skiing before 1945, but by the late 1960s the tour operators enabled the masses to join them, sometimes on a second holiday to complement their summer break.[103] The airlines, increasingly free from government control, seized their opportunities. Among the most enterprising was Laker Airways,

---

[96] For figures on individual buildings visited in 1980, see *T* (29 June 1981), 3.
[97] Archdeacon Edward Knapp-Fisher in *T* (1 Sept. 1980), 17.
[98] *T* (17 June 1997), 3; (23 June 1997), 21 (William Davies).
[99] *Digest of Tourist Statistics*, 3 (Nov. 1972), 66; 17 (Dec. 1993), 69.
[100] *Digest of Tourist Statistics*, 10 (Oct. 1982), 49; 17 (Dec. 1993), 71.
[101] *Digest of Tourist Statistics*, 3 (Nov. 1972), 71; 17 (Dec. 1993), 75.
[102] *Digest of Tourist Statistics*, 17 (Dec. 1993), 48.   [103] See Andrew Leigh in *O* (6 Sept. 1970), 11.

run from 1966 to 1982 by the ebullient entrepreneur Freddie Laker (Plate 1), who anticipated Ryanair and Easyjet with his no-frills cheap flights across the Atlantic.

Destinations were becoming ever more exotic, with a growing late twentieth-century taste for cruises and safaris; these often took British holidaymakers to the colonies their parents had once governed. After 1970 Europe's motorways were linking up to form an international network, British restrictions on travel currency were easing, and the EEC was killing off European frontier posts. Whatever British views on the EEC might be, British tourists were ranging more widely in Europe with their cars, and then began buying up Spanish apartments, French farmhouses, and Tuscan villas as second or retirement homes. Whereas immigrants from southern Europe in the 1950s had taken urban jobs in Britain, British emigrants in the 1980s were buying rural retreats in southern Europe. There they realized the long-standing British dream of owning a place in the country, with sun as a bonus. Earlier retirement, British–European house-price differentials, easier travel, and a freer market in house purchase ensured that the tourists of the 1960s and 1970s became the semi-permanent expatriates of the 1980s and 1990s. Already by 1990 Britain was sixth among EEC nations for the number of its citizens residing in France, after a growth-rate since 1982 which exceeded all but Denmark's and the Irish Republic's.[104] The number of UK residents in Spain more than doubled between 1983 and 1995, and grew much faster than Spain's German and French expatriates, though British expatriates in Italy remained fewer and were not rising. There was good reason in later life for returning to the UK, yet during the 1980s the number of pensioners drawing UK benefits while living abroad rose by 9 per cent a year. Most of the 763,000 UK pensioners living abroad by 1997 were in English-speaking countries: 24 per cent in Australia, 17 per cent in Canada, 14 per cent in the USA, and 11 per cent in the Irish Republic, but Spain attracted 5 per cent of them, Italy 3 per cent, and France 2 per cent.[105]

Young people were travelling too: in the 1980s the phrase 'gap year' came to denote an interval between school and university during which students interrupted their formal education, often for overseas travel. In English novels after 1945, 'abroad' (especially France) served yet another function, as 'somewhere you go for sexual adventure'.[106] Liberal Dutch attitudes to sexuality ensured that tracks from UK to Amsterdam were well trodden, and by the end of the century sex was added to sun and sea as an attraction of the many package holidays now targeted at young people. Here again the late twentieth century

[104] H. Buller and K. Hoggart, *International Counterurbanization* (Aldershot, 1994), 44.

[105] R. King, T. Warnes, and A. Williams, *Sunset Lives: British Retirement Migration to the Mediterranean* (Oxford, 2000), 24–5. I am most grateful to Professor Keith Hoggart, King's College London, for generous help on this subject.

[106] D. J. Taylor, *After the War: The Novel and England since 1945* (1993, paperback edn. 1994), 51.

was extending to the masses opportunities that had long been available higher up. International travel did not invariably promote internationalism, however: many British travellers were disappointed when standard British dishes were absent from foreign menus. Cosmopolitanism hit British football geographically at this time, but not culturally: their teams might be increasingly multinational, their fixtures increasingly overseas, but the fans who followed them were often coarsely chauvinist. Britain's late twentieth-century reputation in Europe was not enhanced by boorish and even hooligan episodes. Perhaps the nastiest occurred at Heysel Stadium, Brussels, on 29 May 1985, when thirty-nine fans, none British, died after a wall collapsed in the wake of a fight between Liverpool fans and Italians supporting Juventus. Meanwhile the UK, in its attitude to the EEC, was energetically squandering what was left of the abundant European goodwill which had flowed towards it immediately after the war.

3. EURO-EQUIVOCATION

The interaction between UK party politics and relations with the EEC was complex, and its sequence first needs outlining.[107] Greeted at its origin with indifference from both parties, the EEC after 1959 increasingly interested Macmillan, Conservative prime minister, as a new and growing world to redress the balance of a Commonwealth world that now seemed old and declining. Key Foreign Office officials were beginning to move, but not in a mood of humility: a new alignment, said Con O'Neill in 1966, 'could give the country as a whole a focus around which to crystallise its hopes and energies. Entry into Europe might provide the stimulus and the target we require.'[108] Macmillan got his party to agree in 1961 that entry should be sought, but failed to carry Labour's leader Hugh Gaitskell with him, and also failed to persuade the French President, de Gaulle, that Britain was 'ready' for the change. Labour's prime minister Harold Wilson reapplied in 1967, this time with all-party support, but de Gaulle remained adamant. As part of the Labour Party's reaction against the Wilson government when in opposition after 1970, there was a powerful left-wing move against any further application; Heath's support for entry as Conservative prime minister remained staunch, however, and with some breakaway Labour support he secured British entry on 1 January 1973. Wilson belatedly recognized the referendum as a useful device for holding his party together while keeping Britain in, and this tortuous process secured in 1975 a two-to-one majority for continued but modestly renegotiated membership.

[107] The sequence up to 1970 is discussed in Harrison, *Seeking a Role*, 114–21.

[108] Quoted in H. Parr, 'Gone Native: The Foreign Office and Harold Wilson's Policy Towards the EEC, 1964–67', in O. Daddow (ed.), *Harold Wilson and European Integration: Britain's Second Application to Join the EEC* (2002), 89.

Yet instead of ready all-party acceptance of membership thereafter, important elements within the Labour Party remained hostile, and for much of the 1980s committed the Party to departure. As for the Conservatives, they were less enthusiastic for the EEC connection than might have been expected, especially once Thatcher had replaced Heath as leader in 1975. Her strident campaign in the early 1980s for a fairer financial relationship with the EEC eventually succeeded, but generated much illwill, and though she agreed in 1985 to a single European market, she grew increasingly hostile later in the decade, and her Bruges speech crystallized her new position in 1988. Thatcher's criticism alerted Labour to the EEC's hitherto unperceived opportunities, and by the late 1980s Labour was beginning to find the EEC's statism promising. Britain therefore entered the 1990s with the Labour Party increasingly warming to the European link, but with Major's task as Thatcher's successor seriously complicated by deep Conservative divisions on the matter. These culminated in debates on the Maastricht Treaty of 1993, after which the EEC was officially renamed the European Union, with the UK remaining a rather unenthusiastic member. Blair as Labour prime minister from 1997 began with more enthusiasm, but in practice delivered little more than Major.

Flesh can now be put on these bones. Why did the third application in 1970–2 to enter the EEC succeed? De Gaulle's death in November 1970 made it easier for Pompidou, his successor as French President, to be more helpful. Furthermore, the enthusiasm for the European ideal felt by Heath and his close associates was by the early 1970s matched within the Foreign Office, in the Liberal Party, and at the highest levels in both Labour and Conservative parties. Some commercial interests and progressive middle-class opinion groups also thought Britain's economic problems might more easily be solved indirectly within a European context rather than directly through confronting them at home. The balance of Britain's trade had been shifting from the Commonwealth towards Europe for some time before Britain joined the EEC. In 1960 the Commonwealth took 41 per cent of British exports and provided 39 per cent of British imports; the EEC's Six plus Denmark and Ireland took 19 per cent of British exports and provided 20 per cent of British imports. By 1977 this situation had reversed: the EEC then took 36 per cent of UK exports and provided 37 per cent of UK imports, whereas the Commonwealth's equivalent had fallen to 15 and 13 per cent, respectively.[109] France and West Germany were four times more important as destinations for British exports in the mid-1980s than in the mid-1950s.[110] The interaction between economic strength and international influence was now increasingly clear. An influential

---

[109] *T* (1 Feb. 1977), 6.
[110] D. Sanders, *Losing an Empire: Finding a Role. British Foreign Policy since 1945* (London and Basingstoke, 1990), 152–4.

Central Policy Review Staff (CPRS) report of 1977 recommended a drastic cut in, and changed role for, British overseas representation. 'National revival requires, amongst other things, a switch of emphasis from what we can teach foreigners to what we can learn from them', it pronounced; 'a more realistic and modest concept of the UK's role in the world would contribute to this.' There was much publicity two years later for a leaked valedictory despatch, trenchant and wide-ranging, from the retiring British ambassador in Paris, Sir Nicholas Henderson: 'you only have to move about western Europe nowadays', he wrote, 'to realise how poor and unproud the British have become in relation to their neighbours. It shows in the look of our towns, in our airports, in our hospitals and in local amenities.'[111]

Britain's cultural affinities with Europe were growing: in 1971 Benjamin Britten, Mary Quant, Alec Guinness, and Yehudi Menuhin were among the many artists and intellectuals who signed a full-page advertisement in *The Times* declaring their support for EEC entry.[112] And although the Church of England had stronger links with the English-speaking peoples, European links for British nonconformists and Roman Catholics were relatively strong.[113] Intellectuals and artists hostile to British entry—who included Amis, Tynan, Osborne, Pinter, and F. R. Leavis—were quick to retaliate.[114] The mounting opposition had several components. Britain had less reason than 'the Six' to share the enthusiasm and idealism present in the EEC from its beginnings. Its central impulse was to end the hatreds fuelling two disastrously destructive world wars, and with these hatreds the UK was less deeply entangled. Geography had enabled her to 'stand alone' against Hitler in 1940, and her wartime experience of destruction and humiliation did not compare with that of 'the Six'. For them the EEC's creation and early success had snatched triumph out of wartime humiliation, whereas for Britain accession would be a confession of defeat, of failure to replicate in peacetime the wartime success of 'standing alone'. There was an institutional dimension, too: the attitudes and structures involved in building up a federation from the bottom up might seem suitable for the colonies, but jarred with the UK's unitary structure. Powerful as a precedent in Europe was Germany's zollverein; there, economic union had gestated political integration, whereas whatever might occur within individual colonies, the British empire as a whole had followed no such model.

Party politics fuelled hostility after 1970. For decades after 1961 there was enough public hostility in Britain to the European connection, and enough awkwardness of fit between Europeanism and the outlook of both major

[111] Central Policy Review Staff, *Review of Overseas Representation* (1977), 10. Henderson, *Econ* (2 June 1979), 30.   [112] *T* (22 July 1971), 5.
[113] G. Davie, '"An Ordinary God": The Paradox of Religion in Contemporary Britain', *British Journal of Sociology* (Sept. 1990), 417–18.   [114] *T* (30 July 1971), 15.

political parties, for opportunism to push each towards Euroscepticism when in opposition.[115] There were only three exceptions: Heath's backing (in opposition in 1967–8) for the second attempt at entry; Thatcher's growing Euroscepticism in government in 1988–90, which carried forward into backbench Conservative opposition to Major's government; and Labour's growing enthusiasm for the European Union (EU) when in opposition in the 1990s. Labour's Euroscepticism in 1970–4 was reinforced by a 'socialist' desire to repudiate the Wilson government and all its works, whereas Wilson had long before correctly seen the EEC's pedigree as Cobdenite Liberal rather than socialist.[116] For Labour's left, no international association so fervently recommended by a Conservative prime minister could be anything other than a capitalist device: just as in the late 1930s Labour would not accept rearmament from Neville Chamberlain, so in the early 1970s it would not accept EEC membership from Heath.

All this made it easier for Labour to go along with the little Englandism of its working-class following in the guise of pursuing 'socialism in one country'. The EEC, an embodiment of 'white bourgeois nationalism', was allegedly a rich men's club whose employers did not have the interests of British trade unionists at heart. For the polemical Marxist historian E. P. Thompson, the EEC was not a high-minded cause at all: it was 'about the belly'. He saw the 'eurostomach' as 'the logical extension of the existing eating-out habits of Oxford and North London', adding that 'once replete, the eurostomach will want to euronate. The present idea is to do it on the British working class.'[117] Labour's Eurosceptics exploited widely held sentimental ties with the English-speaking peoples worldwide, strengthened by memories of wartime collaboration and by the UK's long-standing reliance on Commonwealth food imports. Commonwealth enthusiasms may have been of secondary importance for Labour, but not for its leader.[118] The crusade against EEC entry was infused with all the zest of a battle for power inside the Labour Party, for here the left thought it had the advantage over Roy Jenkins, Wilson's heir-apparent as leader, and his modernizing, middle-class Gaitskellite followers. The Jenkinsites took a principled line, making a virtue of rejecting Labour's new-found scepticism about the EEC by repudiating the cynical politics of manoeuvre and party interest.[119]

Among the Conservatives, Enoch Powell was from the back benches playing rather a similar game against Heath, though with less support from within his party. He complained in 1971 that Heath's tactics resembled Macmillan's: once

---

[115] For the sake of conciseness I apply the term 'European' to those who were enthusiastic for closer integration with the EEC and later the EU. But of course 'Europe' even now is much larger than the area covered by the Union, as the 'Eurosceptics' (a term from the 1990s which I use throughout to denote the opponents of the 'Europeans') often emphasize.

[116] A. Morgan, *Harold Wilson* (1992), 204.   [117] *ST* (27 Apr. 1975), 32.

[118] Harrison, *Seeking a Role*, 7, 118.   [119] e.g. in Jenkins's speech at Worsley, *O* (12 Mar. 1972), 2.

the details had been settled, surprise would be expressed when anyone objected to the principle.[120] Powell was perhaps the most forthright in articulating one further ingredient of Euroscepticism: nationalism. 'Independence, the freedom of a self-governing nation, is in my estimation the highest political good', he pronounced, 'for which any disadvantage . . . and any sacrifice, are a cheap price'. Jenkins by contrast, did not see the nation-state as 'the ultimate good in politics': indeed, it had caused the First World War.[121] Those who opposed entering the EEC made much of the need to uphold sovereignty at two levels: of Britain as a whole, but also of parliament within Britain. Its longevity and paramountcy, said Powell in 1971, bound it more closely than other European national parliaments into the national self-image.[122] He and the Labour backbencher Michael Foot had been the most prominent among the backbenchers who had successfully resisted House of Lords reform in 1969; for them the reform would unduly promote executive power, and it was no coincidence that in 1972 they were both Eurosceptics.[123] Labour's backbench suspicions were accentuated by what Foot called the 'kind of lawyer's conjuring trick', whereby the government hoped to rush the Bill through the House of Commons by making it unexpectedly brief, and by Heath's elaborate extra-parliamentary staging of the case for it.[124]

For Jenkins, internationalism was 'quite fundamental to socialism', and John Mackintosh reminded the Party's special conference on the EEC in 1975 that the Party's song was 'The Red Flag', not 'Land of Hope and Glory'.[125] Labour's Eurosceptics by contrast, emphasized the narrowness of the EEC's 'Europe', and claimed that their wider internationalism embraced Eastern Europe and the underdeveloped countries. So it was not enough for British 'Europeans' merely to counter nationalism with internationalism: sovereignty as a concept needed refining. From the 1960s onwards they knew that, given the modern world's economic interdependence, the nation-state must choose between different types of subordination: to stand alone would consign its fate to private discussions among EEC powers, whereas to join would involve sacrificing some nominal sovereignty for influence within a larger collective. For Jenkins, British sovereignty had vanished. In 1971 he told parliament how as Chancellor at two financial summits he had been excluded from the talks held by the ministers of the Six, and had been reduced to chatting and

---

[120] *T* (18 Jan. 1971), 5 (speech at Banbridge, Co. Down).

[121] Powell, speech to Stockport luncheon club on 8 June 1973, reported in *T* (9 June 1973), 3. Jenkins in radio debate with Powell reported in *Listener* (19 July 1973), 75.

[122] Speech to the Association des Chefs d'Entreprises Libres on 12 Feb. in *T* (13 Feb. 1971), 10.

[123] Powell in *HC Deb.* 13 July 1972, c. 1925, noted the lack of paradox involved in this second cross-party collaboration.

[124] *T* (27 Jan. 1972), 5. See also *G* (13 July 1971), 18; M. Cockerell, *Live from Number 10: The Inside Story of Prime Ministers and Television* (1st publ. 1988, paperback edn. 1989), 173–6, 190.

[125] Jenkins, *Listener* (19 July 1973), 75. Mackintosh, *ST* (27 Apr. 1975), 4.

eating meals with the Secretary of the United States Treasury; he added, to cheers, that 'he did not wish to see a continuation of the position in which the Six decide . . . matters which are crucial to this country and all that we can do is to have a little chat with the Americans'. As a future Chancellor pointed out on a memorable occasion, the European enterprise should not be seen as 'some kind of zero sum game'.[126] Interaction between EEC states involved mutual persuasion within a continuing set of relationships: sovereignty could not be equated with virginity, in the sense that 'now you had it, now you did not'.[127] Sovereignty within the EEC was pooled; any one nation lost some control over its own affairs but at the same time gained some control over the affairs of partner nations. The EEC was, said Heseltine, 'a *political* market place—a process of wheeling and dealing—as well as an economic market'.[128]

The arguments were quite finely balanced, and in letters to *The Times* on 22 October 1971, 154 university teachers in economics thought EEC entry more likely to damage British interests than otherwise, whereas 142 thought Britain might gain.[129] Gallup polls showed public opinion wavering: in 1961–7 an overwhelming majority favoured applying to join, opinion was more evenly divided in 1967–9, in 1970–1 it turned strongly against applying, but in 1971–2 it grew more evenly balanced. When asked between April 1973 and March 1975 whether it had been right to join, opinion turned again, and a consistent and sometimes large majority thought not.[130] The battle inside the Labour Party in the early 1970s was fierce, if only because Labour's Europeans seemed to be propping up a Conservative government that Labour particularly disliked for other reasons. Furthermore, as emerged from the balance of parliamentary voting and from the referendum results later, hostility to entry increased the further away from Europe one moved within the UK: support for the EEC was strongest in the south and east, weakest in Scotland, Wales, and Northern Ireland.[131] The only areas where a majority of the voters were 'noes' in the referendum of 1975 were Shetland and the Western Isles. Labour's traditionalist heartland lay within the

---

[126] Quotations from *HC Deb.* 22 July 1971, c. 1703; Geoffrey Howe, 13 Nov. 1990, c. 463; cf. 20 Nov. 1991, c. 306. See below, pp. 447, 490.   [127] *HC Deb.* 20 Nov. 1991, c. 306.

[128] *FT* (20 Nov. 1990), 21.

[129] *T* (22 Oct. 1971), 4; 184 would answer only a confidential questionnaire, of whom 91 said they were undecided.

[130] *Gallup International Public Opinion Polls* (New York, n.d.), i. 599, 602, 609, 613, 626, 647, 654, 656, 660, 665; ii. 807, 813, 817, 824, 835, 840, 847, 850, 854, 863, 866, 872, 877, 884, 890, 895, 900, 908, 910, 917, 926, 930, 936, 946, 948, 953, 959, 997, 1051, 1056, 1064, 1091, 1095, 1099, 1102, 1107, 1115, 1122, 1132, 1134, 1136, 1139, 1147, 1157, 1161, 1166, 1173, 1179, 1187, 1197, 1201, 1215, 1219, 1239, 1247, 1254, 1263, 1268, 1277, 1286, 1296, 1318, 1328, 1335, 1342, 1371, 1386, 1391, 1398.

[131] For the breakdown of MPs' votes in the division on 28 Oct. 1971 see *Econ* (6 Nov. 1971), 4. For the referendum result regionally analysed see D. E. Butler and U. Kitzinger, *The 1975 Referendum* (1976), 266–7.

hostile areas, but its potential new support lay in areas where 'European' sympathies were strong. Westminster's holes and corners now witnessed significant but secret cross-party deals. Labour's Europeans refused to prevent Heath from getting Britain into the EEC, and their secret discussions with the government eased the Bill through parliament with help from the free vote which William Rodgers had privately requested, but which Heath had not originally wanted.[132] Labour's sixty-nine rebels and twenty abstainers helped to produce the government's majority of 112 for entry in the key division on 28 October 1971.

When Heath returned to Downing Street after parliament had endorsed British entry, he had cause for satisfaction. His courage, political skill, and sheer determination had secured a success which had never been certain, given the obstacles presented by the French, the Labour Party, and Eurosceptic politicians. He sat down to play to a few close friends Bach's first prelude and fugue for the well-tempered clavier on his clavichord. His Euro-enthusiasm was not widely shared. At the moment of entry, the *Guardian* captured the situation well with its headline: 'Britain Slips Quietly into Europe'. It went on to report the event almost as though it were a death: 'Britain passed peacefully into Europe at midnight last night without any special celebrations.'[133] A celebratory fifty-pence piece was minted, but the combined controversy and apathy about British entry made the musical and cultural 'Fanfare for Europe', organized to celebrate British entry, seem somewhat incongruous, even elitist, and it fell rather flat.[134] Labour remained decidedly Eurosceptic, and several discussions between Wilson and Powell in the House of Commons lavatory edged Powell into declaring for Labour at the general election of February 1974.[135]

Wilson was now adroit choreographer to a deft performance, with Foreign Secretary Callaghan as prima ballerina: it confirmed British membership on modestly renegotiated terms without splitting the Labour Party. The casting was shrewd, for Callaghan seemed quintessentially English, applying his practical common sense to getting a fair deal. Two unfamiliar devices made the show constitutionally memorable. The first was an announcement, once new terms of entry had been negotiated, that cabinet ministers would agree openly to differ on the issue until the matter was settled through employing the second device: a referendum. A genuinely democratic impulse had probably inspired the prominent Labour politician Tony Benn, the referendum's originator: in 1968 he was already predicting that within a generation 'electronic referenda'

---

[132] J. Prior, *A Balance of Power* (1986), 86. P. Whitehead, *The Writing on the Wall: Britain in the Seventies* (1985), 67.   [133] *G* (1 Jan. 1973), 1.

[134] J. Campbell, *Edward Heath: A Biography* (1993), 405, 556.

[135] B. Pimlott, *Harold Wilson* (1992), 611. But Joe Haines's account diverges in his *Glimmers of Twilight: Harold Wilson in Decline* (1st publ. 2003, paperback edn. 2004), 74.

would help to broaden popular participation in government.[136] The referendum was the slender hope of minorities in all three parties after 1968, and was at first unpopular within Labour's shadow cabinet after 1970. All this changed in March 1972, when President Pompidou announced a referendum in France on whether the EEC should be enlarged: a UK referendum suddenly became more feasible.[137] *The Times* directed a leader against the idea, Wilson showed no initial enthusiasm for it, and in 1972 Jenkins's distaste for it edged him further towards resigning as deputy leader. The conventional arguments against referenda resurfaced: they were the weapon of pseudo-democratic dictators and atavistic causes, they threatened the cohesion of government policy, their questions could not be framed fairly and clearly, they threatened parliamentary sovereignty, and so on.[138] As late as September 1974, Jenkins remained 'profoundly unhappy'[139] about using a device which had become the Eurosceptics' weapon. Yet the EEC's advocates soon turned it neatly against their opponents: it became a device for redirecting a united Labour Party towards Europe.

Wilson's handling of the issue after 1970 loaded the decision in favour of entry in several ways. Before taking office in 1974 he had focused Labour's objections to entry on the terms the Heath government had obtained. On Labour's taking office, in a rerun of Macmillan's tactics in 1961, discussion focused entirely on the newly negotiated terms, and once agreed upon they carried the government's endorsement. What with this and the fact that Britain was already in the EEC, 'safety first' shaped the referendum's outcome. Within the British two-party system, the Europhiles then benefited from the sort of centre coalition against the extremes that was familiar enough within Western Europe's multi-party systems, and which many Europhiles would have liked to replicate in Britain. The Eurosceptics, by contrast, were seriously divided, and one of their leading supporters (Benn) even refused to appear on the same platform as another (Powell). The referendum as used in 1975 had for Labour the double merit of uniting the party at the same time as seeming democratic and progressive. After taking office in 1974, Labour ministers wore down their Eurosceptic opponents in the cabinet's 'European Strategy Committee'. Pragmatism gradually supplanted principle as the prevailing mood, civil-service resources were marshalled behind continued membership, and the Eurosceptics

---

[136] Speech at Llandudno, *G* (27 May 1968), 2. His ideas evoked an unperceptive and jaundiced response in *The Diaries of a Cabinet Minister*, iii. *Secretary of State for Social Services 1968–70* (1977), 80 (27 May 1968). For a useful account of how the referendum became Labour Party policy, see David Wood, *T* (28 Apr. 1975), 13.

[137] V. Bogdanor, *The People and the Party System: The Referendum and Electoral Reform in British Politics* (Cambridge, 1981), 39–41. T. Benn, *Office without Power: Diaries 1968–72*, ed. R.Winstone (1988), 414 (16 Mar. 1972). D. Wood in *T* (28 Apr. 1975), 13.

[138] See *T* (1 Aug. 1970), 13 (leader) in response to Douglas Jay's advocacy. For Jenkins, see *T* (11 Apr. 1972), 4.   [139] B. Castle, *The Castle Diaries 1974–76* (1980), 182 (16 Sept. 1974).

were overborne by sheer weight of detail.[140] Benn claimed in cabinet in March 1975 that 'we are at the moment on a federal escalator, moving as we talk, going towards a federal objective we do not wish to reach'.[141] But in cabinet in December 1974 Wilson had said that economic and monetary union was 'as dead as mutton': a mere form of words, a pious aspiration not to be taken seriously. In vain did Castle declare, at the cabinet's key meeting in March 1975, that she opposed membership because 'we were asking the British people to remain in an organization in whose principles we said we did not believe'.[142]

On 5 June 1975, out of a total electorate of 40,456,877, 'yes' votes were cast by 17,378,581 people—in an overall turnout of 65 per cent, excluding the service vote (Plate 2). Of the civilian votes cast, 67 per cent were 'yes', or 43 per cent of registered voters, whereas only 21 per cent voted 'no'.[143] It was a major defeat for the more traditionalist, class-preoccupied Labour left: a severe shock for party activists who had hitherto thought themselves more closely in touch with opinion than the leaders they criticized. A demoted Benn was still nursing his wounds on 31 December when looking back over the year: it was 'a far bigger defeat for the Left—and for me in particular—than I had realised'.[144] The referendum was perhaps beneficial by confirming continued membership through harnessing to the decision an exceptional display of public participation. Educationally, though, it was defective, if only because the debate's two sides were ill-balanced. The 'yes' pressure groups drew heavily on elite connections; the 'noes', however, responded to popular but less expert sentiments relatively distant, geographically and psychologically, from the centres of power. 'Yes' campaigners in 1975 were backed by a majority of the cabinet, and almost unanimously by the press and by the larger interest groups except the trade unions.[145] The 'yes' camp spent eleven times as much as the 'noes', more than any political party had hitherto spent centrally on any general election,[146] and even the Europhiles were embarrassed that high-pressure advertising techniques dominated their campaign.[147]

Party interest ensured that the campaign was brief, and the European alignment's full implications were not advertised. Benn's complaint in cabinet was plausible: that during the campaign 'the real case for entry has never been spelled out, which is that there should be a fully federal Europe in which we become a province'. He claimed that 'it hasn't been spelled out because people

---

[140] For a good discussion see *ST* (9 June 1974), 17.
[141] T. Benn, *Against the Tide. Diaries 1973–6*, ed. R.Winstone (1st publ. 1989, paperback edn. 1990), 346 (18 Mar. 1975); cf. Castle, *Diaries 1974–6*, 342 (18 Mar. 1975).
[142] Quotations from Castle, *Diaries 1974–6*, 249 (12 Dec. 1974), 342 (18 Mar. 1975).
[143] Butler and Kitzinger, *1975 Referendum*, 263–4.   [144] Benn, *Diaries 1973–6*, 485 (31 Dec. 1975).
[145] Butler and Kitzinger, *1975 Referendum*, 95, 171.
[146] Ibid. 85–6, 95; see also *G* (8 Oct. 1975), 24.   [147] *T* (2 June 1975), 2.

would never accept it'. From Macmillan onwards, the EEC's supporters had chosen to emphasize membership's economic benefits while playing down its political implications; far from sounding a crusading note, they encouraged the idea that accession would not change anything very much. Heath and Jenkins did not conceal their belief in ultimate political union, but they saw it as a distant prospect to be duly scrutinized when the time came; the economic union now under discussion, they claimed, did not pre-empt the larger decision. The judge Lord Denning said later that, with accession, European would encroach on British law 'like an incoming tide. It flows into the estuaries and up the rivers. It cannot be held back',[148] but nobody spoke publicly like that at the time.

After so decisive a referendum result, Britain might have been expected to commit itself firmly to Europe rather than to USA or Commonwealth, especially as the Foreign Office now saw British interests as tied up with the EEC's closer union. Yet the French scholar André Siegfried thought England could be likened 'to a ship which, though anchored in European waters, is always ready to sail away'.[149] Although the majority for continued British membership was large in 1975, it was hardly enthusiastic, and given that the EEC was continuously evolving, this was ominous. Two factors combined after 1975 to erode within the UK even such Euro-enthusiasm as had existed: a government whose attitude to the EEC was entirely utilitarian, and a press and public wary of statist instincts in Brussels. The Labour Party's acquiescence in the referendum result was at best grudging. In 1976 overwhelming votes were cast in Labour Party conferences against direct elections to the European Parliament, and a divided cabinet was slow to legislate for them in 1977; it relied heavily on Conservative support to get the measure through. All this eventually fuelled the SDP's secession from Labour in 1981. As early as January 1971 Benn suggested to Jenkins that the EEC issue might split Labour and create a broad European centre party flanked by left- and right-wing Eurosceptic groupings.[150] Jenkins later came to see the British Europeans' all-party referendum campaign of 1975 as foreshadowing the end for the two-party divide; free momentarily to work with sympathizers from other parties, he felt 'a considerable liberation of the spirit'.[151] By December 1976, battered by his experience in a Labour Party that still seemed moving left and against Europe, Jenkins expressed himself weary of Westminster's gladiatorial politics[152] and soon retreated to Brussels as President of the European Commission.

---

[148] Benn, *Diaries 1973–6*, 346 (18 Mar. 1975). Denning, quoted in H. Young, *This Blessed Plot: Britain and Europe from Churchill to Blair* (London and Basingstoke, 1998), 250.

[149] A. Siegfried, *England's Crisis*, tr. H. H. and D. Hemming (1st publ. 1931, rev. edn. 1933), 244.

[150] Benn, *Diaries 1968–72*, 324 (13 Jan. 1971).

[151] R. Jenkins, *A Life at the Centre* (1991), 424.   [152] *Listener* (16 Dec. 1976), 775.

The general public was easily upset after 1975 by small episodes that seemed to symbolize the meddling inclinations of Brussels, and especially by tax and currency issues. The new Value Added Tax (VAT) was introduced amidst much bureaucratic upheaval on 1 April 1973 to replace the selective employment and purchase taxes. It caused much consternation and disruption among small businesses and retailers, and by 1976 required 11,000 people to administer it.[153] Decimalization was so unpopular that successive governments showed a 'pusillanimous attitude', prolonging the pain with 'each in turn giving way to the temptation of simplistic populist appeal'.[154] An appearance of continuity was preserved through orienting the new system round the pound sterling, and calling the smaller unit the 'new penny'; it was estimated in 1972 that no fewer than 12 million slot machines would need converting.[155] Not until March 1974 did Ordnance Survey maps abandon the inch for decimal distance measures,[156] and not until 1982 was petrol sold by the litre. By summer 1980 Labour's Europeans were on the defensive, and in June three members (Williams, Owen, and Rodgers) of the SDP's future 'gang of four' issued a statement deploring the revived threat to leave the EEC.[157] In October 1980 the Labour Party conference ignored Owen's plea and voted overwhelmingly to take Britain out without a referendum. Not surprisingly, the SDP listed securing 'international cooperation' among its twelve tasks in March 1981, with Britain playing a full role in EEC and North Atlantic Treaty Organization (NATO).[158]

Meanwhile the Conservatives in 1975 had acquired a leader who drew from the Second World War lessons quite different from Heath's. As prime minister, Thatcher showed no enthusiasm for EEC ideals, consistent impatience with EEC politicians and their style, and uncompromising hostility to European political union. Eurosceptic politicians were probably more in tune with public opinion than Heath and Jenkins, both sidelined in British politics after 1975. British parties were relatively inactive at Euro-elections, and turnout was scarcely more than half that for any other European country and lower than in British local government elections; this was partly because, uniquely in the EEC, Britain's Euro-elections replicated its simple-majority voting system—a system entirely defensible for elections to Westminster, but not for electing MEPs in relatively large constituencies to a non-governmental assembly. After Thatcher became prime minister, the Common Agricultural Policy's anomalies were the backdrop for her chauvinist tub-thumping quest to get 'our money back' in the form of a rebate. Of the great Foreign Secretary Lord Salisbury, his daughter wrote that 'his own conception of a perfect diplomacy

---

[153] For a good summary of the outcome see *T* (2 Apr. 1976), 19.

[154] *HL Deb.* (31 Jan. 1980), c. 1048 (Lady White, Lord Orr-Ewing's deputy on the Board for four years); cf. *T* (30 Apr. 1975), 21; *O* (28 Mar. 1976), 5.

[155] C. Emmins, *Automatic Vending Machines* (Princes Risborough, 1995), 28.

[156] *G* (8 Mar. 1974), 7.   [157] *T* (9 June 1980), 2.   [158] *T* (27 Mar. 1981), 2.

was always of one whose victories come without observation'.[159] Not so for Thatcher. It is doubtful whether such small financial gain as her methods secured was worth the substantial loss of goodwill. By linking her case for financial restructuring with national self-assertion, she made it more difficult to secure concessions because other European governments also had domestic publics to cultivate. Her approach may even unintentionally have united her opponents, who collectively wearied of her approach. But the unity which primarily concerned Thatcher was that of her own party at home, and in approaching European matters thus she could more easily unite the followers of Powell to those of Heath. Her stance exemplified the British tendency within the EEC to see everything in terms of national rather than collective interest. Even before Thatcher came to power the British ambassador in Paris thought British conduct since joining the EEC 'grist to the mill of those in France who see our intentions as being those of wreckers from within',[160] and still more so afterwards. An opinion poll in 1984 showed the British far more sceptical about EEC membership than any other EEC country, all of whose citizens when polled saw Britain as its least constructive member.[161] In a poll of French opinion in May of that year, only the USSR outclassed Britain in unpopularity among fifteen leading nations assessed, and among world leaders only Colonel Gaddafi and the Ayatollah Khomeini surpassed Thatcher in unpopularity.[162]

Still, as long as the EEC saw itself as a community of nation-states it could provide an enlarged free market for British goods, and Thatcher could go along with membership. 'My own vision of Europe can be summed up in two words', she said in November 1990. 'It should be *free*, politically and economically. And it should be *open*.' This vision of the EEC as an enlarged market enabled Britain in the 1980s to contribute usefully towards improving collaboration within it. In the late 1980s some even saw the single market, to be introduced in 1992, as an opportunity for 'the Thatcherization of Europe'.[163] Britain had much to gain from curbing corruption and excessive subsidy in the Commission's expenditure, from removing trade barriers and restrictions on free competition in the service sector, from a collaborative foreign and defence policy, and from better communications. Although Thatcher had little time for the Heath government's big state-promoted engineering projects, she backed the building of the Channel Tunnel in 1987. Her position was entirely consistent: the work

---

[159] Lady G. Cecil, *Life of Robert Marquis of Salisbury*, ii (1921), 232; cf. D. C. Watt's letter in *T* (4 Dec. 1979), 13.

[160] N. Henderson, *Mandarin: The Diaries of an Ambassador 1969–1982* (1994), 209 (14 July 1978).

[161] Marplan sample of over 5,000 in the seven member countries, *G* (19 Mar. 1984), 4.

[162] Sofrès poll of 1,000 people in May, reported in *T* (9 June 1984), 1.

[163] Quotations from M. Thatcher, 'My Vision of Europe: Open and Free', *FT* (19 Nov. 1990), 17. *T* (11 Mar. 1989), 4 (Secretary of State for Trade and Industry).

on it had been terminated in 1975 by the Wilson government for lack of funds, but this revived Anglo-French venture was privately funded. The Tunnel promised to maximize the trade benefits of British membership, and defence objections to it had diminished. The decision to go ahead was made public early in 1986, the first test shafts were begun later that year, the first people crossed the Channel by foot in 1990, and the world's longest under-sea tunnel opened in 1994.

How was it, then, that Thatcher moved from sceptical pragmatism on the EEC to overt hostility? The Single European Act (1986) committed all EEC members to extending 'qualified majority voting': abandonment of their veto on major issues in the event of a two-thirds majority 'weighted' according to population. It attracted little attention in Britain, whose politicians did not take its preamble's federalist tendency seriously. Thatcher was unembarrassed by it because it overcame protectionist barriers (especially French) to the free movement of goods and services within the EEC, which she favoured. Several developments in the 1980s, however, caused her to shift. First, the contrast between a free-market Britain and an interventionist EEC progressively widened as Thatcher's domestic economic revolution took shape, whereas the EEC simultaneously moved steadily forward from free trade area towards economic and then political union. She came to see the European Commission as a malign and scheming body with a statist agenda. British Eurosceptics came to see 'federalism'—an entirely respectable democratic concept concerned with the fragmenting of government power, and frequently applied by the British in ex-colonial contexts[164]—as a Brussels-promoted statist bogey. In 1991 the President of the Commission Jacques Delors stressed that federalism is 'a word you should speak out loud. It's not a pornographic word.'[165] Add to this the fact that the USSR's newly exposed inefficiencies confirmed Thatcher's distrust of large impersonal administrative structures. The USSR's growing weakness also undermined one of the EEC's major attractions for her: as a bulwark against Communism. And given Labour's weakness in the 1980s, Conservatives found it less useful to accentuate Labour divisions by playing up their own support for the EEC. Furthermore, Thatcher's experience in the 1980s highlighted the attractions of Britain's worldwide role: she relished the striking though inevitably ephemeral 'chemistry' of her personal relationship with Reagan and Gorbachev. By this route the 'special relationship' underwent a notable revival, together with reversion to the idea prominent in the 1950s of Britain as broker between the superpowers. Victory in the Falklands war evoked, on a rather small stage, memories of Britain's imperial past. By comparison with this, the European arena seemed small indeed.

---

[164] As Heath twice pointed out, *HC Deb.* 26 Jun. 1991, c. 1036; *G* (9 Oct. 1991), 9.
[165] *T* (9 Dec. 1991), 1.

Hence Thatcher's Bruges speech on 20 September 1988, which shocked many at the time by firmly espousing a Europe consisting of a community of sovereign nations, and by rejecting 'some sort of identikit European personality'.[166] Her relations with Jacques Delors, President of the European Commission, had been cool after she had inadvertently ignored him at a press conference in 1986. Still worse, his acceptance of the invitation from the Trades Union Congress (TUC) to address it earlier in the month, with its strong endorsement of Brussels interventionism, both clashed with Thatcher's economic outlook and seemed unduly to interfere in British domestic politics. The Foreign Office tried unsuccessfully to tone down her speech, whose abrasiveness was enhanced by the press briefing from her press secretary Bernard Ingham.[167] The speech only spelt out what had been implicit in her home and overseas policies since 1979. 'We have not successfully rolled back the frontiers of the state in Britain', she said, 'only to see them re-imposed at a European level, with a European super-state exercising a new dominance from Brussels.'[168]

The parties now began to change sides on the EEC. Just as some Conservatives in the 1970s espoused it as a defence against socialism, so some Labour leaders now espoused it as a defence against Thatcherism.[169] With the accession of Greece (1981), Spain and Portugal (1986), the EEC also had the attraction for the British left of consolidating democracy within countries hitherto authoritarian in tendency. In December 1989 Labour went further, and for European reasons abandoned its support for the closed shop. The EEC's proposed social charter endorsed the right to take a job without being required to join a trade union, and only by changing its stance could Labour plausibly attack the government for failing to endorse the charter. By this time Thatcher was losing a sequence of important ministers—Heseltine, Lawson, and (most damagingly of all) Howe—who disliked her new anti-European stance. She now saw herself as being swept off in a European train with no desire to reach its destination. Prominent Conservatives disagreed. The British economy was integrating steadily with the world economy, and even faster with that of the EEC; the latter supplied 17 per cent of British imports in 1964, 44 per cent in 1988; it took 20 per cent of British exports in 1964, 45 per cent in 1988.[170]

Like all EEC countries, Britain had entered the European Monetary System (EMS) in March 1979; this aimed to promote monetary stability in Europe by encouraging member states to cooperate on monetary policy. Britain had not, however, joined the Exchange-Rate Mechanism (ERM). Set up at the same

---

[166] M. Thatcher, *Collected Speeches*, ed. R. Harris (1997), 319.

[167] Comments of Geoffrey Howe and Charles Powell in the BBC2 television programme 'The Poisoned Chalice: 4: Nemesis', 30 May 1996. [168] *Collected Speeches*, 319–30.

[169] As Benn was already detecting in his *The End of an Era: Diaries 1980–90*, ed. R.Winstone (1992), 421 (21 Sept. 1985). [170] Cairncross, 'Economic Policy and Performance, 1964–1990', 91.

time as the EMS, it was a mechanism for minimizing currency fluctuations among the states which volunteered to join it, with procedures for realignment if the mechanism failed. From 1985 Lawson as Chancellor and Howe as Foreign Secretary privately pressed Thatcher to join the ERM. Their enthusiasm for it reflected, not Europhilia, but a pragmatic concern for the national self-interest. The increasingly public battle between Lawson and Alan Walters (Thatcher's adviser on economic matters), however, eventually prompted Lawson's resignation. 'The constant rubric of the Thatcher era', wrote Lawson, 'had been that we would join when the time was right: it turned out to be a recipe for joining when the time was wrong'—that is, in 1990 during the recession.[171] Howe felt that if Thatcher had responded earlier to her cabinet colleagues' pressure, the boom–bust cycle of the late 1980s would have been restrained, and British participation in the ERM would have been more successful.[172] By 1990, however, only the Greeks did worse than the British when the EEC nations ranked their fellow-members on how far they could be trusted.[173] Thatcher's outlook was beginning to cause concern in the City, for Britain's financial services had everything to gain from closer integration with Europe. It was this that provided ammunition against Thatcher both in Howe's damaging resignation speech on 13 November and in Heseltine's challenge to her leadership. 'How on earth could the Conservative Party—of all parties—risk the future of the City of London?', Heseltine asked the Conservative Party conference in 1992: 'Our invisible earnings are a priceless asset.'[174]

In the narrative so far, public opinion's limited role in Britain's EEC debate is striking. General elections did not centre upon the issue, and the EEC inspired only one referendum. This was partly because at each of Britain's three bids to enter or remain in the EEC—in 1961–3, 1967, and 1970–5—the prime minister's overriding concern had been to avoid splitting his party, and so he curtailed public discussion. The need to discover public attitudes to the EEC gave a boost to UK opinion polls in the early 1960s,[175] but the polls did no more than provide the politicians with their raw material. Britain's Europhiles never needed to mount sustained campaigns because at every stage in the EEC's advance governments took the initiative: Macmillan (prompted by civil servants, by desire for an up-to-date image, and by the need for an election-winning issue) in 1961, Wilson (seeking a distraction from serious setbacks on Rhodesia and the economy) in 1967, Heath (responding to personal conviction and prior party commitment) in 1970–3, Wilson again (having

[171] Lawson, *View from No. 11*, 1024; cf. his interview with C. Fildes in *Spec* (7 Nov. 1992), 18–19.
[172] Howe, *Conflict of Loyalty*, 689.
[173] Polls averaging 1,000 people in each of the 12 member states, *DT* (14 July 1990), 2.
[174] *Ind* (8 Oct. 1992), 6; cf. his comments in *FT* (20 Nov. 1990), 21, and Howe, *HC Deb.* 13 Nov. 1990, c. 463.   [175] D. E. Butler and A. King, *The British General Election of 1964* (1965), 205.

negotiated revised terms) in 1975, Callaghan (amidst strong opposition within his Party but with Conservative support) moving forward to direct elections for the European Parliament in 1977, Thatcher (somewhat apprehensively, after getting safeguards) acquiescing in the Single European Act (1986) and then reluctantly entering the Exchange-Rate Mechanism in 1990, Major withdrawing from it in 1992 only because market pressures precluded continued membership, and in 1992–3 (again after winning concessions) narrowly getting the Maastricht Treaty through parliament without seeking the endorsement from the referenda that were thought necessary in Denmark and France. With some justification it was claimed that 'European integration cannot happen by stealth, by closet agreement among governments. It must be with the people's consent', and that 'for any European policy to work it must enjoy the consent of the people'.[176]

Surprising, too, is the EEC's limited impact on Britain up to 1990. Western Europe influenced Britain between 1970 and 1990, as before, mainly through the direct influence of individual states. From the late 1950s West Germany provided guidance on how economic growth was best achieved, and when after 1972 corporatism seemed to need more ambitious planning structures, West Germany seemed also to exemplify how industrial relations were best managed.[177] When in the early 1970s Labour sought to improve on nationalization as a way to integrate government with industry, Italy's corporatist traditions had their charms: its Industrial Reconstruction Institute was the model for the National Enterprise Board that Labour established in 1975. Scandinavia had always strongly influenced Labour, and the Swedish example was in Healey's mind as Chancellor when he sought in 1976 to discover how permanently to ensure counter-cyclical investment.[178] As late as 1982 Healey was still telling the Labour Party conference that 'we must find a way in Britain, as they have found a way in Scandinavia and Austria, of controlling inflation which leaves real scope for collective bargaining'.[179] West European countries became far less relevant as exemplars under Thatcher, who wanted ideas to flow in the opposite direction. Towards the very end of the 1980s, however, her ministers were attracted by the idea of defeating inflation through making the Bank of England independent, and there Germany provided the precedent.[180]

The EEC's collective impact on Britain was neither rapid nor substantial, partly because British membership was so reluctant. When 'the Six' had first shown signs of strengthening their economic links in the mid-1950s, British politicians had initially responded by hoping that nothing would come of it.

---

[176] Quotations respectively from Blair, addressing businessmen in Brussels, *FT* (11 Jan. 1995), 1; manifesto of the eight Conservative rebels, *G* (20 Jan. 1995), 6.   [177] See below, p. 303.
[178] *T* (7 Apr. 1976), 4.   [179] *T* (1 Oct. 1982), 4, reporting conference on 30 Sept.
[180] Lawson, *View from No. 11*, 1059.

Then, when the links were created, Britain tried to erect the European Free Trade Association as a rival economic entity. When that failed, it was decided at the highest levels to join the EEC from national interest rather than from Euro-idealism. Likewise with the British decision in 1975 to remain within the EEC. Both Labour and Conservative parties were slow to affiliate with their equivalents in the European Parliament,[181] nor were European parties' traditions easily assimilated. The German social democrats pioneered socialist acceptance of new class relationships, but Labour was slow to follow. And few converts were made by the speech, despite its warm reception, of the West German Chancellor Helmut Schmidt at Labour's special conference on the EEC in November 1974, when he insisted that 'your comrades on the Continent want you to stay'.[182] Britain stayed in only because public opinion outflanked the labour movement. As for the Conservatives, their flag-waving component did not make for instant Euro-empathy, and European conservative parties were by contrast more coalitionist, less secular, and less distant from parties of the left.

The EEC's pioneers had hoped that British politicians might foster European parliamentarism. Before direct elections were instituted, MEPs were chosen from the members of national parliaments. When the British MPs belatedly arrived in the European Parliament they were at first keener to teach than to learn, and felt specially qualified to suggest improvements.[183] Even Jenkins, when first appearing in January 1977 before the EEC press corps in his new role as President of the European Commission, refused to speak in French.[184] Thereafter the British and European parliaments remained at arm's length, partly out of institutional jealousy, partly because their roles differed, partly because West European statist tendencies made British politicians wary: West European countries delimited less clearly the roles of civil servant and politician. Furthermore, the EEC in two significant respects threatened the Westminster parliament's sovereignty. Some MPs saw European precedents on the referendum as undermining their role;[185] and the EEC in transcending the nation-state showed some signs of releasing for a new Europe-wide role peoples hitherto subsumed within the nation-state. After 1973 it seemed that the Scots and Welsh might join Corsicans, Bretons, and Basques in a nationalist upsurge that would bypass London, Paris, and Madrid. The Irish-American lobby for conciliating the Catholics in Northern Ireland also had high hopes from the EEC link: Ulster Unionism did indeed seem an exotic plant at Strasbourg.

---

[181] On this see Castle, *Diaries 1974–6*, 436–7 (26 June 1975). N. Ashford in Z. Layton-Henry (ed.), *Conservative Party Politics* (1980), 119–20.   [182] *T* (2 Dec. 1974), 4.

[183] *T* (17 Jan. 1973), 1.

[184] For a useful discussion of languages at Brussels see *T* (20 Jan. 1977), 14.

[185] B. Harrison, *The Transformation of British Politics 1860–1995* (Oxford, 1996), 391, 400, 402.

After 1973 agricultural, environmentalist, humanitarian, and feminist groups often bypassed the House of Commons and operated directly in Brussels,[186] where more money and support could be won than at Westminster. The human rights lobby benefited, too. The European Convention on Human Rights had grown out of the Second World War and antedated the EEC, but the European connection after 1973 raised the profile in Britain of the European Court of Human Rights at Strasbourg: in the 1970s it helped to restrain repressive army techniques in Northern Ireland and curbed caning in schools. And despite rejecting the railwaymen's case for the closed shop in 1981, the Court championed civil liberties in Britain during the 1980s when the government party was unsympathetic. A kindred cause which also benefited from the UK's EEC/EU link was the campaign for electoral reform, championed partly with European precedents in mind by the Liberals, by the SDP, by some Conservative politicians under Heath, and by some Labour politicians under Neil Kinnock, Labour's leader from 1983 to 1992. British opposition parties after 1979, frustrated at being unable to oust the Thatcher governments, discovered a new charm in proportional representation. Besides, Europhile enthusiasm for the EEC easily elided into enthusiasm for European political institutions.

Britain's mounting integration with Europe ultimately entailed a less direct involvement with her old allies, USA and Commonwealth, but this is not how it seemed at the time. Heath told the Americans in 1970 that on taking office he had been disturbed at how the earlier easy two-way Anglo-American communication 'had deteriorated sadly'; he was, he said, determined to restore it.[187] Nonetheless, a separate North American desk was created at the Foreign Office to indicate a more conventional Anglo-American relationship, and Heath was keen to convince the EEC that Britain's new commitment was sincere. Welcoming the idea of monetary union during discussions with President Pompidou in May 1971, he claimed that the British did not 'feel sentimental' about retaining the pound. As for the 'special relationship' with the USA, there 'could be no satisfactory partnership . . . between two powers one of which was barely a quarter the size of the other', whereas the EEC's participating countries would be comparable in size.[188] Besides, as he noted in his speech at the White House when a guest of President Nixon in 1970, the phrase risked offending America's other allies, whether in Europe or in Latin America: it was no more than 'a natural relationship, the result of our common history and institutions, which nobody could take away from us'.[189] Given American encouragement of

---

[186] P. Dunleavy, A. Gamble, I. Holliday, and G. Peele (eds.), *Developments in British Politics*, iv (1993), 59–60, 172, 273.

[187] Interview for an American magazine, just before leaving for an official visit to Washington, *T* (14 Dec. 1970), 1. [188] *DT* (25 July 2005), 10.

[189] E. Heath, *The Course of my Life: My Autobiography* (1998), 472.

Britain towards the EEC, there was no conflict between the two alignments, but so overt and sustained a commitment to the EEC as Heath's was a novelty for Britain,[190] and Heath's Euro-enthusiasm was influential only till 1975, and never caught on widely, least of all with his successor as Conservative leader. He and Thatcher were both radical prime ministers, but on foreign policy Heath was the radical and Thatcher the traditionalist.

4. IMPERIAL AFTERMATH

On the Commonwealth there was much more continuity between Thatcher and Heath. By 1970 the gulf between UK and Commonwealth interests was widening. The Commonwealth was embroiling Britain in far-off conflicts, complicating her bilateral relations with some of its individual members, and perpetuating national notions of faded grandeur; people were beginning to ask what British purposes the Commonwealth now served.[191] Heath was particularly alert to its drawbacks because although it had never become an effective political, economic, or defensive entity, its interests had been deployed against the regional grouping that seemed likely to assume all three roles: the EEC. We have already seen how trade was shifting from Commonwealth to EEC well before Britain's accession in 1973. Race issues widened the gulf further: the Heath government's decision in 1970 to resume arms sales to South Africa prompted protests from the churches and a fierce argument between Heath and Kenneth Kaunda, President of Zambia, at a dinner party in 10 Downing Street.[192] In his Guildhall speech in November, Heath said the Commonwealth must 'accept that our right to take decisions in pursuance of British interests is no less than theirs to pursue the policies which serve their interests'.[193]

South Africa divided the Commonwealth throughout the 1970s and 1980s. Disagreement was not about the apartheid regime, which all repudiated, but about how best to end it. British Conservatives tended to argue that apartheid would eventually collapse from its internal contradictions: the free market was, in the long term, incompatible with apartheid's restraints on opportunity for talent, quite apart from apartheid's huge administrative and policing costs. If the UK neglected her defence and economic interests, they claimed, even black South Africans would not benefit, and sanctions (even if enforceable) would strengthen the Afrikaner's siege mentality and weaken the relatively enlightened influence that Britain could exert in South Africa. 'South Africa should not be

[190] Campbell, *Edward Heath*, 341–2, 351. T. Hames in A. Adonis and T. Hames, *A Conservative Revolution? The Thatcher-Reagan Decade in Perspective* (Manchester, 1994), 126.

[191] e.g. M. Beloff, 'Does Britain Need the Commonwealth?', *T* (10 Aug. 1970), 7.

[192] For the churches see *T* (26 Oct. 1970), 1; (27 Oct. 1970), 1. For the dinner, *T* (19 Oct. 1970), 1.

[193] *T* (17 Nov. 1970), 4. See also A. Douglas-Home, *HC Deb.* (22 July 1970), cc. 1711–12.

ostracised . . .', said the Foreign Secretary in July 1970, 'but . . . her territory should be opened up to the civilising influences of the outside world'.[194] The Labour Party and some Commonwealth states favoured boycotts and sanctions, if only as moral gestures. Labour also claimed that Britain, by implicating herself in the South African economy, propped up apartheid while simultaneously jeopardizing its economic interests elsewhere in Southern Africa. Kaunda in 1971, for instance, said that the Zambian government intended to hold back million-pound deals 'until we know whether we are dealing with an honest Britain or a dishonest one'.[195] Furthermore, Southern Africa's frontline states thought Britain exaggerated its military impotence on the Rhodesia issue.

Things were not made easier by the format and tone of the Commonwealth prime ministers' meetings. Like Britain in the EEC, Commonwealth countries were now participating individually in appropriate regional groupings, and the earlier affinity between the colonies of white settlement was waning. It became difficult informally to develop a common mind within the Commonwealth, and still more difficult when it was so selective in the racism that it condemned. Because decolonization brought more heads of state to these meetings, they became shorter and at times ill-tempered, most notably London's in 1966 and Singapore's in 1971. The first meeting held outside the UK was in 1966 at Lagos, adjourned to London. Thereafter they grew larger and leakier to the press, and from 1971 were renamed Commonwealth Heads of Government Meetings (CHOGMs), given that many member countries were now headed by executive presidents. The Commonwealth Secretary-General headed a secretariat that was increasingly international in nature, its staff doubling between 1968 and 1989.[196] By the 1980s more than forty delegations regularly attended the meetings. Seeking in 1957 to define what it was that unified the Commonwealth, Nehru alighted upon democracy. He admitted that the term 'was used now in . . . such a variety of ways that almost it might be said to have lost all meaning', yet there was 'such a thing as the temper of democracy. It is a temper of peaceful discussion', of majority rule moderated by the need to allow for minority feelings.[197] On no definition could General Idi Amin's regime in Uganda be described as democratic, still less as humane, as the 40,000 Ugandan Asians expelled in 1972 could testify; President Nyerere of Tanzania told the Commonwealth conference in 1973 that 'racism is racism no matter who practises it'.[198] In 1976 Britain was obliged for the first time to break off relations with a Commonwealth country, yet it proved

[194] Sir A. Douglas-Home, *HC Deb.* (22 July 1970), c. 585.   [195] *T* (12 Jan. 1971), 1.

[196] W. D. McIntyre, *The Significance of the Commonwealth* (Basingstoke and London, 1991), 60—a book to which this paragraph owes much.

[197] A. F. Madden (ed.), *Imperial Constitutional Documents, 1765–1965: A Supplement* (1st publ. 1953, 2nd edn. Oxford, 1966), 101.   [198] *G* (10 Aug. 1973), 12.

impossible to get unanimous condemnation from the London conference in 1977.

Meanwhile the long decolonizing process had proceeded so far that by the 1970s and 1980s, apart from Rhodesia, only staging-posts and Caribbean or Pacific islands had yet to become independent. Rhodesia was one problem too many, and Thatcher wanted it out of the way. Although her instincts favoured the white settlers, and she had publicly backed the recently established power-sharing regime with the relatively moderate black Bishop Muzorewa, world opinion would accept no such settlement, and her pragmatism was invoked. Armed with a large pair of dark glasses to ward off the acid that she feared would be thrown in her eyes,[199] she flew to the Commonwealth conference in Lusaka in August 1979 and found the African leaders more congenial than she had expected. In the familiar sequence where right-wing regimes are best placed to implement seemingly progressive reforms, she acquiesced in pursuing a more comprehensive settlement which would bring in the two black guerrilla leaders Joshua Nkomo of ZIPRA and Robert Mugabe of ZANU. After forty-seven plenary sessions at the Lancaster House talks from September to December 1979, the combination of international pressure with the energy and commitment of her Foreign Secretary Lord Carrington framed a settlement, an outcome still in doubt till a very late stage. With the electors' endorsement thereafter, Mugabe began his long reign as President in the renamed one-party state of Zimbabwe. Justifying in 1965 their declaration of independence, the white settlers claimed to have 'seen the principles of western democracy and responsible government and moral standards crumble elsewhere' in Africa, and some British commentators thought Zimbabwe's prospects 'predictably gruesome'.[200] For the moment, however, attention could turn elsewhere.

Given Britain's worldwide retreat from empire, Argentina understandably supposed that the Falkland Islands would be no exception, especially as Britain had privately said it would surrender sovereignty if the Islanders' interests were preserved. In the cabinet's discussion of 1968 Callaghan had 'asked solemnly whether the Falkland Islands were any use to us'; only fear of a parliamentary row deterred the government from reaching an agreement. 'Really', wrote Castle in her diary in 1968, 'the problem of winding up the last outposts of empire is almost ludicrously difficult'.[201] The Foreign Office's discussions with Argentina sketched out acceptable deals involving a leaseback arrangement, and British defence cutbacks of 1981 seemed implicitly to confirm Argentine hopes. Yet British governments could not brave themselves to resist the Islanders'

[199] Henderson, *Mandarin*, 296 (6 Oct. 1979).
[200] Quotations from Madden (ed.), *Imperial Constitutional Documents*, 113. Peregrine Worsthorne, *STel* (20 Apr. 1980), 16.   [201] *Diaries 1964–70*, 520 (24 Sept. 1968); see also 413 (28 Mar. 1968).

well-organized parliamentary pressure, and the relevant junior ministers before and after 1979 failed to whip up sufficient support for bipartisan concession to Argentina from prime minister, cabinet, or public.[202] In December 1981 General Galtieri took power, and—with India's successful invasion of Goa in 1961 as a precedent—Argentina invaded the Falkland Islands on 2 April 1982. Advice from her Defence Minister that the Islands, once seized, could not be retaken presented Thatcher with a situation she found 'totally unacceptable'; she sought and obtained contrary advice from the Chief of the Naval Staff, and personally authorized him to assemble a task force.[203]

A small event on the world's stage, this was on the British domestic stage a very large event indeed. House of Commons fury exploded in a debate on 3 April 1982 which launched the war on a non-party basis, fuelled by distaste for General Galtieri's undemocratic regime in Argentina as well as by anger at his insult to the UK. Sending out the task force was a huge risk, but Thatcher did not hesitate. Already 'outraged and determined' by the affront to national pride, she also knew that her premiership, highly controversial since 1979, could survive only if the campaign succeeded. Even as it was, she soon had to sacrifice her Foreign Secretary, who honourably acted as scapegoat by resigning to appease furious Conservative backbenchers. Self-preservation was by no means her sole motive. 'My passion is my country', she had said, in a radio broadcast earlier in the year.[204] She was inspired by what in more sophisticated circles then seemed a rather old-fashioned patriotism. Her outlook owed much to her memory of Britain's role in the Second World War and to her admiration for Churchill. Her earliest campaign speeches had breathed a faith in Britain's 'greatness', and in 1956 she had thought that the Suez venture, once embarked upon, should have been completed.[205] In the committee of cabinet which ran the Falklands war, she was in complete command and showed none of her colleagues' hesitation. A warrior herself, she hardly wavered in her trust of the service chiefs. As a woman her situation was highly paradoxical: in military matters, at least, she was as happy as any Victorian anti-feminist to accept military decision-making as a male sphere, and showed considerable admiration for soldiers. She felt no zest for war as such. Distressed at the news that thirty-two Welsh Guards had been killed at Bluff Cove, 'she sat there, absolutely silent, for two or three minutes, with tears rolling down her cheeks'.[206] The

---

[202] I. Gilmour, *Dancing with Dogma: Britain under Thatcherism* (1992), 242; Young, *One of Us*, 260. See also the well-informed discussion in *Econ* (27 Nov. 1982), 27.

[203] M. Thatcher, *The Downing Street Years* (1993), 179.

[204] Quotations, ibid. 179. *T* (11 Jan. 1982), 20.

[205] J. Campbell, *Margaret Thatcher*, i. *The Grocer's Daughter* (1st publ. 2000, paperback edn. 2001), 91. P. Cosgrave, *Margaret Thatcher: A Tory and her Party* (1978), 112.

[206] Michael Havers (then Attorney-General) quoted in G. Turner, 'The Warrior Prime Minister', *STel* (30 Apr. 1989), 14.

Argentines surrendered on 14 June, and within three days General Galtieri had been ousted as President. Two hundred and thirty-six British servicemen died in the campaign, eighteen civilians, and 750 Argentines.[207]

The UK's Falklands campaign was far from faultless: British bombs were ill-targeted, and HMS *Sheffield*'s destruction on 4 May revealed the navy as almost defenceless against the French-built 'exocet', or rocket-propelled short-range guided missile. Argentine troops were courageous, their air force expert. Yet on the British side the war was a triumph of strategy, planning, and professionalism, given the need to coordinate air, sea, and land forces with such extended lines of communication, in such terrain, and amidst all the complexities of ousting Argentine troops without killing the Islanders whom the troops were there to defend. The war cost £3,500 million at contemporary prices, including replacement and increased garrison costs,[208] yet was funded without any extra taxation or disturbance in the money markets. Victory entailed considerable long-term expenditure, however, if the Islands were to be defended against future attack. The Falklands economy showed signs of revival after the war, but a peaceable settlement was long delayed, and the war's implications for British trade and influence in South America were not obviously beneficial. Given that in 1980 there had been only 1,849 Islanders (95 percent British, and three-quarters born on the Islands),[209] there could be no utilitarian justification for spending money and lives on such a scale.

Yet the war brought benefits at several levels: militarily, diplomatically, and above all (for the Conservative Party, and especially for Thatcher) politically. The British army, toughened by its long experience in Northern Ireland, was invaluably supported by the harrier jump jets and helicopters. Its professional standing had already been advertised in May 1980 when the Special Air Service (SAS) ended terrorists' siege of the Iranian embassy in London's Knightsbridge with only two of the twenty-six hostages killed.[210] Britain by the early 1980s was a society increasingly distanced from any direct experience of war: the world war generations were ageing, national service had long gone, and the schools had for some time been offering alternatives to cadet training, partly because so few teachers had experienced active service.[211] But the army, like the police, was recruited from volunteers whose professionalism gained from specialization. Their intellectual calibre and skill with the media were increasingly apparent: they were among the few late twentieth-century British institutions undamaged by irreverent criticism. The war enriched the English vocabulary in two

---

[207] L. Freedman, *Britain and the Falklands War* (Oxford, 1988), 1. The British killed in action are listed in L. Freedman, *The Official History of the Falklands Campaign*, ii. *War and Diplomacy* (2005), 774–7.   [208] Freedman, *Britain and Falklands War*, 89.

[209] Ibid. 14–15. For a detailed breakdown which includes reconstruction expenditure up to 1987/8 see Freedman, *Official History*, ii. 672.   [210] *T* (6 May 1980), 4.

[211] M. Durham, 'Soldiering on at School', *DT* (30 May 1988), 12.

significant respects: it gave extended and colloquial application to the noun 'exocet', meaning a devastating attack; but it also launched the verb 'yomp' to denote the prolonged marching with heavy equipment over difficult terrain to which the British success owed so much.

Diplomatically, the war upheld the international rule of law, as well as advancing democracy within Argentina. New friends in the EEC were revealed as unreliable: the Irish Republic, for example, was particularly unhelpful within the United Nations.[212] On the other hand, the value of Britain's traditional allies was highlighted. American intelligence, supplies, and diplomatic support in the United Nations may well have enabled Britain to snatch victory from defeat.[213] The Commonwealth's value was also revealed. As British representative at the United Nations in 1982–3, Sir Anthony Parsons 'suddenly found that we could rely more on the Commonwealth than we could, for example, on many of our European partners'. Although the war evoked far-off imperial echoes, it could have no long-term imperial significance, given that almost all Britain's colonies had by then gone. But 'all of a sudden', wrote the diplomat Charles Powell in May 1982, 'thoughts and emotions which for years have been scouted or ridiculed are alive and unashamed'. The British people 'have discovered that they have a self, which the older among them supposed had been lost forever, and the younger, who never knew it, have nevertheless recognized for theirs'.[214] The emotional scenes on HMS *Invincible*'s arrival at Portsmouth on 17 September (Plate 3), with the Queen participating, were culturally important. The UK suddenly rediscovered patriotism as a respectable subject for academic enquiry, right-wing suspicions of the BBC were fuelled by its refusal to label the British forces as 'ours' or the Argentine as 'the enemy', and the somewhat half-hearted victory celebrations further soured relations between the government and the churches.[215]

The war's overriding significance therefore lay in British domestic politics. Thatcher's political fortunes may have been improving before the Falklands invasion, but the SDP's advent made outright victory in 1983 or 1984 unlikely,[216] whereas the invasion's defeat transformed her prospects. In her cabinet reshuffle of summer 1981 she had asserted her claim to authority over cabinet colleagues, but now her claim seemed vindicated. Not only was proof provided of her capacity—and, for that matter, the capacity of women in general—for wartime leadership: her party's hold on broad sections of opinion

---

[212] Prior, *Balance of Power*, 236–7.

[213] For more detail see J. Dickie, '*Special' No More: Anglo-American Relations. Rhetoric and Reality* (1994), 2–9.

[214] Quotations from 'Out of the Midday Sun?', BBC Radio 4 programme on 23 July 1993 (Parsons). 'This New Unity that our Leaders Must Not Betray', *T* (14 May 1982), 10 (C. Powell).

[215] N. Tebbit, *Upwardly Mobile* (1988), 196. For the churches, J. Amery in *T* (27 July 1982), 1; C. Longley, *T* (28 July 1982), 8.

[216] J. Campbell, *Margaret Thatcher*, ii. *The Iron Lady* (1st publ. 2003, paperback edn. 2004), 125.

was demonstrated, despite Labour's overwhelming support for the war. In this situation Thatcher had little need, at the general election of 1983, overtly to capitalize upon the victory. The SDP's massive growth since 1981 ensured that the Conservative vote was down by 685,000, but Labour's was down by 3,100,000. Given the operation of the simple-majority electoral system, this meant that the Conservatives, with 339 seats in the old House, had 397 in the new. Thatcher's political revolution of 1979 no longer seemed ephemeral. And though the Foreign Office was right to have initial doubts, which history may eventually vindicate, there was no doubt at all about the short and medium term: from Argentina's point of view, General Galtieri had played his hand disastrously.

Given Thatcher's patriotism, the salience of her wartime memories, her relatively lukewarm attitude to the EEC, and the empire's one-time centrality to Conservatism, she might have been expected to be keener than Heath on the Commonwealth, yet some close associates thought she disliked it even more than the EEC.[217] 'Right to the end', wrote Howe, she 'persisted in her often ill-concealed antipathy towards most of our Commonwealth partners as also towards the Foreign and Commonwealth Office and all its works'. As loose unions, both EEC and Commonwealth could be held together only by vague aspirational statements and blurred decisions, and these Thatcher could not abide. She was above all a practical politician, impatient with time-wasting, pretentious, and empty formulations, unafraid to confront an assembly of critics. Self-righteous herself, she had no time for self-righteousness in her critics, and still less for gesture politics. For her, as for Lawson, the Commonwealth was 'the smile on the face of the Cheshire cat which remains when the cat has disappeared',[218] and sentimental nostalgia should not distract Britain from pursuing her own interests. Thatcher's hostility to socialism worked in the same direction, given the influence of socialist and even Marxist ideas within many Commonwealth countries, some of which had cultivated close relations with the Labour Party.[219] In international as in class relations, guilt and apology were not Thatcher's style: whoever traduced the British people, whether inside or outside the Commonwealth, would receive short shrift. Where British national and Commonwealth interests and opinions conflicted, she knew where her priorities lay.

After 1979, as before, Commonwealth controversy centred on South Africa. At the Nassau CHOGM of 1985, Thatcher agreed only to what she later called 'gesture sanctions',[220] and then gave great offence afterwards by publicly belittling their extent. In the following year her isolation within

[217] Young, *One of Us*, 484.
[218] Quotations from Howe, *Conflict of Loyalty*, 500. Lawson, *View from No. 11*, 511.
[219] Harrison, *Seeking a Role*, 108.   [220] *T* (25 Oct. 1989), 8.

the Commonwealth on sanctions was beginning to provoke rumours of its impending break-up, and of sanctions being used against Britain.[221] During his diplomatic mission to the frontline states, Howe as Foreign Secretary (1983–9) displayed a remarkable capacity for turning the other cheek when publicly exposed to a stream of abuse in Zambia, but Conservatives and also allegedly the Queen were beginning to get alarmed. Compromises were eventually found, but in the acrimonious CHOGM at Kuala Lumpur in 1989 Thatcher was once more embattled, and again infuriated participants by signing a statement whose importance she almost immediately played down in public.[222] She was not alone during the 1980s in failing to perceive Nelson Mandela's affinities with Western, and even with her own, values, and in preferring the Inkatha party led by Chief Buthelezi to a supposedly Communist African National Congress (ANC). Buthelezi shared her hostility to sanctions, but she did not grasp that the apartheid regime was arming him against the ANC, nor did the anti-apartheid movement know that she was privately but continuously pressing President Botha to release Mandela and stop bombing ANC camps.[223]

However misguided and undiplomatic Thatcher's Commonwealth tactics might be, they probably did not weaken her rapport with British saloon-bar opinion, which felt diminishing emotional attachment to the Commonwealth, least of all to its African members. By the mid-1980s even Conservatives were beginning to complain that the Queen's close identification with the Commonwealth distanced her from the British people.[224] Britain's loss of empire and diminished influence within and through the Commonwealth evoked surprisingly little resentment in the UK. Helpful was the fact that the change coincided with the UK's rising living standards. Changing defence priorities severely hit garrison towns such as Aldershot or naval centres like Portsmouth and Plymouth, but the shedding of colonial responsibilities removed a hindrance to enhanced UK prosperity. Furthermore, the sterling area had arguably hindered British industry by shielding it from foreign competition; the associated interest-rate policy, with its stop–go accompaniments, had unduly complicated economic growth; and empire and Commonwealth had diverted investment away from Britain and towards Australia, South Africa, and the Middle East.[225] The domestic impact of the empire's decline was also moderated by the politicians' skill or obtuseness saying so little about it. Their readiness to brand foreign-policy realists after 1951 as 'appeasers' was in the long term harmful because misleadingly self-indulgent; in the short term, however, it moderated wounded national pride by masking the diminished national influence which the National Government had rightly identified as early as

[221] *DT* (6 Aug. 1986), 6.   [222] *T* (25 Oct. 1989), 8.

[223] For a good discussion see Campbell, *Thatcher*, ii. 318–34.

[224] See e.g. Powell's speech at Leicester, *DT* (21 Jan. 1984), 8. Worsthorne's leader in *STel* (20 July 1986), 20.   [225] Sanders, *Losing an Empire*, 204–5.

the late 1930s. Furthermore, the substitution of the term 'commonwealth' for 'empire' made it possible to present unexpected setbacks as planned opportunities: as natural outcomes of the liberal strain within British imperial traditions. Imperial decline could even be plausibly presented as expansion and diversification. With fifty member states by 1990, the Commonwealth was only one state smaller than the United Nations at its foundation; it comprised over a quarter of the world's population and nearly 30 per cent of the United Nations membership.[226]

The lack of public debate on the UK's colonial role from the 1950s onwards[227] persisted into the 1980s. As Foreign Secretary. Howe wanted a forward look from the Foreign Office which would enable him to assess how efficiently British resources were being deployed to attain specified international objectives. The review somehow never materialized: 'whether from the Treasury or from the Foreign Office, it always seemed impossible to open up to objective analysis the thought processes of the Ministry of Defence'. Such reticence damaged the diplomats' own cause because without the backing that could have been accumulated through public debate, they regularly found themselves embarrassed by a recurrent British need for unexpected and sudden retreats. Politicians could even convert the diplomats into scapegoats, while regaling the public with asides about the UK's need to avoid the indignity of becoming a Sweden or a Switzerland. Thatcher, drawing the wrong lessons from the Falklands war, merely postponed the national recognition of reality. More surprising was the fact that Labour governments, despite the Party's nonconformist and pacifist traditions, were at least as evasive. Not until 1993 was a (Conservative) Foreign Secretary prepared publicly to emphasize how overstretched British military resources now were: 'obviously', said Douglas Hurd, 'we cannot be everywhere and we cannot do everything'.[228]

Although between 1970 and 1990 the winding up of the British empire was almost complete, the story did not end there. The empire, having grown by evolving from informal influence to formal control, reverted in its decline from formal to informal—retaining many of its original cultural, economic, and demographic features. Nearly twice as many people born in the 'Old' Commonwealth had chosen to settle in Great Britain by 1991 as in 1951, and their number had been steadily increasing with each decade, though nothing like as fast as the 'New Commonwealth' immigrants.[229] The empire's relatively peaceful demise ensured that its slowly fading cultural palimpsest persisted long after formal imperial structures had vanished. Telecommunications traffic, as measured in minutes, highlights the ongoing links as at 1991: in Australia's

[226] McIntyre, *Significance of the Commonwealth*, 1, 7.
[227] See Harrison, *Seeking a Role*, 532–5, 543.
[228] Quotations from Howe, *Conflict of Loyalty*, 319. Hurd, *Ind* (28 Jan. 1993), 1.
[229] Haskey, 'Overseas-Born Populations', 15.

and South Africa's hierarchy Britain came highest of all, in Canada's second only to the USA, in New Zealand's second equal with the USA, in India's third equal with the United Arab Emirates, and in the USA's third after Canada and Mexico.[230] The imperial legacy also brought humanitarian responsibilities. The post-war growth of international aid owed much to European relief operations immediately after 1945, but it also reflected the sense of stewardship for power and wealth that had never been absent from the British imperial idea. OXFAM had 430 giftshops by 1972 and by 1998 its 840 shops had made it Britain's fifth largest retailer.[231]

British politicians' enthusiasm for taxpayer-funded overseas aid waned somewhat amidst Britain's economic troubles of the 1960s and 1970s. 'I am nauseated by the cynical way in which Harold [Wilson] plays ducks and drakes with this whole question of overseas aid', wrote Castle in June 1975, regretting its waning governmental salience—surprising, given Wilson's enthusiasm in the 1950s for such concerns.[232] Thatcher's advent saw the scaling down of such relief being justified rather differently. For her, Third World aid conflicted with self-help, and she dismissed the Brandt Commission's notion of redistributing world resources between north and south. She thought poverty best relieved through creating wealth rather than redistributing it.[233] There was even the danger that 'disaster pornography' would degrade the intended beneficiaries.[234] For some time economists had been asking whether in famine relief the emphasis should shift from relatively indiscriminate handouts towards a more precisely targeted aid that would foster self-help; less channelled through central planning, less prone to politicize the economy, it would aim rather to foster indigenous entrepreneurship. Peter Bauer's *Dissent on Development* (1976) was influential here, and Thatcher ensured that he became a life peer in 1982.[235] Thatcher advocated voluntarism at home as well as abroad, and the 1980s witnessed a notable outburst of recreational voluntarist idealism. The sixteen-hour 'Live Aid' concert at Wembley and Philadelphia in 1985, for example, attracted 72,000 people to Wembley, including the Princess of Wales, who sat next to its organizer, the pop singer Bob Geldof; a world television audience of 1,500,000,000 helped to raise £25 million for starving Africans.[236]

In 1970 the British people had hardly begun the long process of reassessing their empire's significance. Films of the 1970s with imperial themes helped to prompt reflection, and there was much anger in the House of Lords on

---

[230] Staple (ed.), *Telegeography 1992*, 76, 79, 112, 114, 117, 124.
[231] *T* (6 Oct. 1972), 14. *G* (15 Dec. 1998), 15.
[232] Castle, *Diaries 1974–6*, 415 (11 June 1975); cf. Harrison, *Seeking a Role*, 108.
[233] Thatcher, *Downing Street Years*, 169.
[234] A. de Waal 'Compassion Fatigue', *NS* (17 Mar. 1995), 15–17.
[235] Obituary, *DT* (6 May 2002), 21.   [236] *STel* (14 July 1985), 1.

6 July 1972 at the BBC's television series on the empire. Lord Ferrier's shocked comment was also rather poignant: having served in India like his father before him, he felt that he 'owed it to my forebears, to my old colleagues and my old comrades, both British and Indian, to monitor these Indian programmes'. Lord Gridley complained that they had not captured 'something mystical and perhaps even something spiritual about the Empire', and for Lord Auckland the programmes had set out to 'knock' it.[237] By the 1980s revaluation was well under way, and Kipling experienced a revival. His following was very diverse: when Benn in December 1975 quoted Kipling in a cabinet discussion about EEC passports, Wilson immediately recited some lines, saying 'you can't teach me anything about Kipling'. Thatcher had been fascinated by Kipling when in the top class at her primary school, and had often asked her parents for a Kipling book at Christmas: 'like the Hollywood films later, Kipling offered glimpses into the romantic possibilities of life outside Grantham'.[238]

A sequence of films with imperial themes in the 1980s proved controversial: many thought their portrayal of the British prejudiced and even a caricature. For the *Sunday Telegraph*, Richard Attenborough's widely discussed *Gandhi* (1982) was 'a piece of straight political propaganda for India, at the expense of his own country's imperial past which is grossly traduced'. The historian John Grigg thought the film did no service to its subject (who himself owed much to British traditions) by portraying the British authorities as nincompoops when they were 'for the most part, intelligent and sensitive men'.[239] Post-colonial British governments, unlike the French, did surprisingly little to nurture Britain's ongoing cultural empire. 'No one else will ever again live the kind of life that I have lived or see what I saw', wrote M. M. Kaye, author of the 1,000-page best-selling epic *The Far Pavilions* (1978).[240] Born in 1908 into a family deeply involved in the Raj, she set out to describe its nineteenth-century operation, helping to prompt the wave of nostalgia for the lost world of Anglo-India (nourished by India's wonderfully televisual scenery) which swept over British television in the 1980s. Her agent Paul Scott's influential epic about expatriate life, *The Raj Quartet* (1966–75), owed much to her, and was filmed for television in 1982 as *The Jewel in the Crown*. Anglo-India, though by no means whitewashed, was viewed more sympathetically there than in E. M. Forster's *A Passage to India* (1924), and it was Kaye who suggested the expatriate theme of Scott's most famous novel, *Staying On* (1977). With the empire safely distanced in the past, nostalgia could be indulged, if only as an escape from the UK's domestic gloom.

[237] *HL Deb.* (6 July 1972), cc. 1521 (Ferrier), 1527 (Gridley), 1530 (Auckland).
[238] Castle, *Diaries 1974–6*, 579 (4 Dec. 1975). M. Thatcher, *The Path to Power* (1995), 17.
[239] Quotations from 'Oscars Won by Knocking Britain', *STel* (17 Apr. 1983), 18. *STel* (10 Apr. 1983), 18.   [240] Quoted in obituary of Kaye, *DT* (31 Jan. 2004), 29.

5. COLD WAR IMPLOSION

The entire framework of British foreign policy was determined after 1970, as before, by the so-called 'cold war'. Its salience emerges from an incident trivial in itself, but revealing. The then Permanent Secretary to the Treasury Sir Douglas Wass recalled 'one terrible moment in 1976' when sterling was under attack, and when Healey as Chancellor was struggling to get the cabinet to accept the terms prescribed by the International Monetary Fund (IMF) for a loan: 'we were both extremely worried, and I said to him "well, Chancellor, it could be worse: we could be invaded by the Russians". And suddenly we both felt "yes, let's keep a sense of proportion" '.[241] The massive run-down in the British armed services[242] continued after 1970, though more slowly. In 1988 at 194 independent and 60 state-maintained schools about 42,000 youngsters were still receiving military training, but with regular soldiers dwindling from 196,000 in 1970 to 159,200 in 1990, upper-class career choices were unsurprisingly shifting: the editor of *Burke's Peerage* noted in 1999 'the enormous drop' in the tradition of pursuing an army career.[243]

Yet for the armed forces, small—far from meaning worse—meant an invigorating professionalism. Military history was rising in scholarly status after 1970, and Sydney Bidwell's *Modern Warfare* (1973) was by no means the only important book on strategy published in these years. The army had good publicists, too, and the careers of Michael Carver (chief of the defence staff) and of General Sir John Hackett falsified any notion that the intellectual and the military life were antithetical. Carver, whom Healey pronounced 'the ablest intellectual in the Services—and one of the best brains I have ever encountered in public life',[244] surprised many in his retirement by declaring against the UK independent nuclear deterrent: it would be suicidal to use it, nor could he conceive how it could ever be used independently of NATO. It would be cheaper and more sensible, he thought, to spend the money on boosting Britain's conventional defence forces. As for Hackett, he retired from the army in 1968, and from then till 1975 was a successful Principal of King's College London; he acted as President of the Classical Association in 1971, became something of a media personality, and in 1978 published his influential *The Third World War: A Future History*. Adorned with photographs, maps, and documents, it portrayed an end to the cold war far more frightening than soon occurred, and conveyed a message similar to Carver's: in his fictional narrative, democracy precariously triumphed in 1985 through a cold war that had grown hot, with Birmingham and Minsk among its nuclear

---

[241] Sir Douglas Wass, interview with Mary Goldring on Radio 4 on 2 Nov. 1983.
[242] Harrison, *Seeking a Role*, 93–5.
[243] *Burke's Peerage* (106th edn. 1999), p. xxxi. See also *DT* (30 May 1988), 12. J. Baynes, *No Reward But Honour? The British Soldier in the 1990s* (1991), 24–8.   [244] *Time of my Life*, 266.

casualties. Reissued in 1982, the book sold over three million copies in ten languages.[245]

The Anglo-American connection remained central to British overseas policy after 1970. Sheer economic power, reinforced by a shared language, ensured that between 1970 and 1990 the USA was the greatest political, cultural, and economic influence on Britain. The USA's priority in economic growth ensured that it was usually the first to experience the problems associated with affluence. With motels, supermarkets, and hypermarkets America long preceded Britain, and by the 1960s the freeways and clover-leaf road-junctions which had earlier seemed only to reflect America's unique combination of space and wealth—were crossing the Atlantic. The USA profoundly influenced British politics. The political parties rapidly absorbed American ideas on how to influence the electors: Macmillan with his advertising techniques in the 1950s, Wilson in planning party broadcasts for the general election of 1970, and Conservative Party chairmen organizing election victories in the 1980s.[246] American presidential campaigns influenced Labour, too, especially in 1964 and in the 1990s—less through setting technical precedents than through the overall tone of the Kennedy and Clinton campaigns. For all their capitalist associations, American libertarian and democratic ideas could attract the British left in such areas as open government, press freedom, parliamentary committees, the Irish question, and decolonization. As for Thatcher, she deliberately deployed American individualist and democratic ideas in her anti-socialist crusade after 1975, declaring herself in 1990 'an undiluted admirer of American values and the American dream'.[247]

After 1975 Thatcher earned her Soviet sobriquet 'iron lady' because fearless in resisting Communism; strategically but also ideologically robust, she spurned earlier Conservative leaders' more diplomatic tone. Nor was her anti-Communism a mere pose. On seeing the Berlin wall for the first time in 1982, she thought it 'horrifying, absolutely horrifying', adding 'with tears in her eyes, and a break in her voice' that 'it was even worse than I imagined'.[248] As a teenager she had been deeply influenced by 'a fantastic book on Communism', *Out of the Night* (1941), a vivid and sometimes shocking autobiographical work by the German-born R. J. H. Krebs ('Jan Valtin'); as a Soviet double agent, he had experienced the worst of both Communism and Nazism, ending as an American citizen and critic of both.[249] She once described *A Time for Greatness* (1942) as the most important single book she had ever read. This urgent and somewhat disorganized political preachment by the American author Herbert

[245] P. A. G. Sabin, *The Third World War Scare in Britain: A Critical Analysis* (Basingstoke and London, 1986), 1.

[246] See Cockerell, *Live from No. 10*, 157; K. Baker, *The Turbulent Years: My Life in Politics* (1993), 305–6, 324.   [247] To the Aspen Institute on 5 Aug. 1990, *T* (6 Aug. 1990), 8.

[248] *T* (30 Oct. 1982), 1.   [249] *STel* (20 Feb. 1983), 17.

Agar aimed to shake conservatives out of defeatism: if they shed cynicism, class warfare, and moral relativism, the English-speaking peoples would perceive their clear choice between good and evil. Then, energized by their belief in freedom, they would prevail over 'that cruel abstraction, the State' and defeat Fascism. Thatcher's fear of the state was nourished, as for several leading British politicians at the time, by reading Solzhenitzyn's *The First Circle* (1968), and as Conservative leader she turned for advice about the USSR to the fiercely anti-Communist Robert Conquest.[250] As prime minister she liked to say that it was from the Communist states, not from the democracies, that refugees fled,[251] and in March 1980 she braved opposition from Heath, the Duke of Edinburgh, and many Labour MPs by arguing for and obtaining a British boycott of the Olympic Games in Moscow as a protest against the USSR's invasion of Afghanistan.[252] All these influences, together with the mythology of 'appeasement' in the 1930s,[253] her Anglo-American alignment, and her distaste for the left's wishful thinking required her to confront Communism only from a position of strength: that is, through competitively building up armaments. She insisted that one-sided disarmament was destabilizing, that Labour had retreated from its earlier Gaitskellite stance, and that 'we are the peace-keeping party'.[254]

Her close personal rapport with Reagan began well before he became President in 1981. The very unequal Anglo-American 'special relationship' was complemented by a much more equal personal relationship, for Reagan respected Thatcher's intelligence. With shared, somewhat nostalgic, hopes for the future, they liked one another, and saw themselves as jointly crusading against an overmighty establishment in their two countries to promote traditional free-market and libertarian values against Communism's 'evil empire'. There was occasional Anglo-American friction, but neither was a fair-weather friend, and each took risks for the other: Reagan in the Falklands and Northern Ireland, Thatcher in condoning American ventures in El Salvador and Libya.[255] Thatcher needed to feel comfortable with a foreign leader before she could establish close relations with his country, and her Englishness distanced her from most European leaders. Besides, she worshipped power, and diplomats noted that in the presence of Reagan and Gorbachev she became almost coquettish.[256] Gorbachev seems first to have appeared on her horizon at one of the seminars where she formulated policy: at Chequers on 8 September 1983, in a discussion

---

[250] Quotation from Young, *One of Us*, 405; see also 170.
[251] e.g. on 4 Jan. 1981 in her New Year interview on BBC Radio 4.
[252] For Heath see *HC Deb.* 28 Jan. 1980, cc. 968–9. For the Duke of Edinburgh see *T* (24 Apr. 1980), 1.   [253] See Harrison, *Seeking a Role*, pp. xix, 534.
[254] Speech at Harrogate, *G* (27 May 1983), 2.
[255] For a good discussion see Young, *One of Us*, 257, 289, 475–7.
[256] H. Young and A. Sloman, *The Thatcher Phenomenon* (1986), 100.

with academics, he was drawn to her attention as a rising man with an open mind. He was urged to visit Britain, and on 16 December 1984, on his first visit, she found him a man she could do business with. 'He smiled, laughed, used his hands for emphasis, modulated his voice, followed an argument through and was a sharp debater . . . I found myself liking him.'[257]

The Campaign for Nuclear Disarmament (CND) had not gone away. In decline since the early 1960s, it revived after Thatcher's victory in 1979 for several reasons. It was a good platform for uniting her various opponents—all the more necessary given her forceful views about the USSR, and given her government's decision to deploy 160 Cruise missiles on British soil. CND also chimed in well with growing feminist and environmentalist concerns, and by autumn 1980 it could mount a Trafalgar Square demonstration reminiscent of CND's great days.[258] Its growth was accelerated by the Soviet invasion of Afghanistan in December 1979, by Reagan's advent as American President, and by Foot's as Labour leader in November 1980. From 1981 protests were mounted encircling the Greenham Common air-base near Newbury, where the largest number of cruise missiles was located. Out of these grew the women's peace camp, whose long-lived non-violent protest became a significant episode in British feminist history. CND's critics often stressed the democracies' handicap: the fact that the USSR's protesters were 'behind the wire and not linking arms outside it'.[259] Yet CND's sister organization, European Nuclear Disarmament, carried its appeal to both sides of the iron curtain, and did not alienate support as the Committee of 100 had done in the early 1960s. CND's resumed decline after the early 1980s owes much to the general election of 1983: to its revelation that Thatcher must be taken more seriously, and to the enervating disputes inside the Labour Party. Furthermore, the Falklands war had demonstrated the occasional need, however regrettable, to deploy physical force in international relations, at the same time as surprising the left by advertising the survival in the UK of the old-fashioned patriotic virtues. Besides, Thatcher's very different approach to the cold war seemed now to be paying dividends.

She seems really to have influenced Reagan, both on nuclear defence and on 'doing business' with Gorbachev. 'I was always glad to see her coming', US Secretary of State George Shultz recalled, '. . . and . . . I was shameless in saying "now Mr. President, here's what Margaret Thatcher says on that subject . . . and so you'll hear me out on this"'.[260] Thatcher never made

---

[257] Thatcher, *Downing Street Years*, 461. See also R. Harris, 'The Queen of the Kremlin', *O* (5 Apr. 1987), 10, and A. H. Brown, 'The Change to Engagement in Britain's Cold War Policy: The Origins of the Thatcher–Gorbachev Relationship', *Journal of Cold War Studies*, 10/3 (Summer 2008), 3–47.

[258] *G* (27 Oct. 1980), 1; cf. (26 Oct. 1981), 1 for an even larger meeting.

[259] Hurd, *HC Deb.* 15 Dec. 1982, c. 349.

[260] *The Downing Street Years*, BBC1 television programme 3 Nov. 1993.

Macmillan's and Wilson's mistake of thinking that the UK could act as broker between the superpowers: she saw herself simply as an intermediary or facilitator. Through such relationships, she could extend Britain's world influence for a decade longer than British economic strength merited. She exploited her successes in foreign policy to win elections, cultivating the image of the doughty fighter who advances British interests by worsting the foreigner, and who moves influentially among the powerful. At the general election of 1983 she had deployed the news film showing her with President Reagan at the world summit in Virginia. The Liberal Party's vote in September 1986 against nuclear weapons split the Liberal/SDP alliance wide open, and constituted an important moment in the Conservative pre-election recovery.[261] As Labour leader, Kinnock could gain little from visiting Reagan, but Thatcher was quick to exploit her semi-regal visit to Gorbachev. A montage of her foreign trips, with triumphal music composed by Andrew Lloyd-Webber, featured in her election campaign.[262]

As CND resumed its decline after the mid-1980s it forsook its more public campaign and again risked alienating opinion by reverting to direct action which non-violently disrupted the activities of the state.[263] With the signing of the Intermediate-Range Nuclear Forces (INF) Treaty in 1987, the USA and USSR agreed to remove all ground-based, medium-range nuclear missiles stationed in Europe, and these included the USA's Cruise missiles at Greenham Common. British peace groups lit beacons all over Britain on the day the Treaty was signed. The outcome owed little to their efforts, much to the process anticipated as early as 10 October 1957 by Macmillan when writing to President Eisenhower: by pooling 'the efforts of the free world we can build up something that may not defeat the Russians but will wear them out and force them to defeat themselves'. There were Conservative cheers in parliament on 9 March 1987 when Callaghan said that only the West's determination to deploy nuclear weapons had forced the USSR to negotiate, and he urged on his Party the 'lesson' that the Russians 'will pocket any concession and give nothing in return'; the nation 'should not give up Trident for nothing'.[264] Accordingly the Labour Party, as part of its long preparation for resuming power, moved away in the late 1980s from its earlier unilateralist stance. For all that, Thatcher's and Reagan's had been an extremely dangerous game, as students of the First World War's origins knew. The hazards were enhanced by the nature of the weapons involved, and by the danger that they might be let loose by accident. The idea of a nuclear war without winners was almost

---

[261] *FT* (11 Oct. 1986), 8.   [262] Cockerell, *Live from No. 10*, 280, 319–20.

[263] D. Maguire, 'When the Streets Begin to Empty: The Demobilization of the British Peace Movement after 1983', *West European Politics*, 15/4 (Oct. 1992), 85–8.

[264] Macmillan quoted in S. Greenwood, *Britain and the Cold War 1945–91* (London and Basingstoke, 1999), 167. Callaghan, *HC Deb.* (9 Mar. 1987), cc. 53–4.

universally accepted by the 1980s in defence circles.[265] The advocates and opponents of nuclear weapons at this time were aiming at the same objective, and diverged only on how best to get there. But the experts on Soviet Russia did not all agree that the Communist system was as severely strained as in retrospect it turned out to be. Peter Wiles was one of the few Sovietologists who from an early date penetrated the official statistics and grasped the truth.[266]

Thatcher helped to accelerate liberalization behind the iron curtain with visits to several East European countries. In Hungary in 1984 and in Poland in 1988, for instance, she preached human rights and cultivated trade relations with the West, thereby also usefully reminding people that the EEC did not comprise the whole of Europe. And then the Soviet empire collapsed—less predictably but faster than the British empire, and from the same combination of lost impetus at the centre and restiveness at the periphery. In August 1989 Poland's first non-Communist prime minister was elected; in September Hungary opened its Austrian border, allowing many East German refugees to flee to the West; in November the Berlin wall was breached; and December saw the Romanian revolution and the election of Czechoslovakia's first non-Communist president for forty-one years. Thatcher's Ostpolitik rested on a shared Anglo-Russian distrust of the Germans. Lawson thought her 'gut anti-German mode . . . never far from below the surface'.[267] When the Berlin wall came down she made a brief attempt to decouple the question of German unity from freedom for eastern Germany, but confessed in her memoirs that 'if there is one instance in which a foreign policy I pursued met with unambiguous failure, it was my policy on German reunification'.[268] Partly because Nicholas Ridley knew she shared his anti-German views, he felt able in 1990 to discuss them freely with a journalist; when he was obliged to resign on their publication[269] she lost one of her closest cabinet allies. Chancellor Kohl thought Thatcher's anti-German attitudes in the late 1980s fanatical. She was furious that Germany might reunite once the Berlin wall had fallen: 'we've beaten the Germans twice. Now they're back!'[270] Here her Second World War memories were all too lively, and relations with the German Chancellor Helmut Kohl had long been poor. In October 1990 Germany reunited; in September 1991 the Baltic States won their independence; in October Bulgaria acquired its first non-Communist president since 1944; and in December the Ukraine declared itself independent, the Commonwealth of Independent States was formed, and the USSR at last came to an end.

---

[265] Sabin, *Third World War Scare*, 36.   [266] Obituary, *T* (31 July 1997), 21.
[267] Lawson, *View from No. 11*, 656; cf. 900.
[268] Thatcher, *Downing Street Years*, 813; see also 792.
[269] Lawson, *View from No. 11*, 900. For German disgust see *T* (14 July 1990), 3
[270] *G* (3 Nov. 2005), 18.

An informed observer of British international relations in 1970 would have been surprised by several aspects of the UK's situation in 1990: first, by the scale of the UK's absorption into more integrated international cultural and economic structures, but also by the persistence of imperial linkages and influences, and perhaps also by the slowness of British integration into the EEC. In this chapter all eight motifs[271] have featured. The second, the ongoing tension between a hermetic and receptive response to worldwide influences, appears first—with Live Aid and the 'big bang' in the City exemplifying receptiveness, but Anglo-German footballing rivalry and UK Europhobia exemplifying its opposite. With the Second World War's ongoing equivocal impact, powerful enough to fuel both sides in the debate on EEC membership, we see the first motif in action. The explosion of tourism and leisure opportunities, which owed so much to faster and cheaper travel, exemplified the fourth motif: the tension between time-saving and time-using changes, and (together with mass immigration) constituted another threat (the fifth motif) to traditional Christian structures and priorities. Conservative economic strategy after 1979 impinged on three further motifs. For all the unemployment of the early 1980s, the earlier contrast between public gloom about, and private enjoyment of, material wealth (the third motif) almost went into reverse after the early 1980s, with Conservative politicians optimistic about the trends, and the general public less so. And for all the political disruptions associated with 'Thatcherism', the economy was at last being approached in such a way as eventually to moderate the strains on politicians operating within a voluntarist climate (the seventh motif). The free market's diminished expectations of the political system exposed the politician less frequently to testing situations. This, together with the EEC's small impact on the British political system, testified to its stability—actual, but also potential—amidst substantial change (the sixth motif). As for the UK's search for a role (the eighth motif), the Commonwealth, far from providing a secure platform for an international role, increasingly prompted controversy, not least about how best to combat racism; only with difficulty could the UK now pose as exemplar of the multi-racial society. As for the EEC, it seemed to evoke no consistent or constructive strategy from the UK at all, and in the Falklands, the UK's defence of democracy against Fascism was simultaneously counteracted by difficulties in upholding democracy and stability in Northern Ireland. These decades did not see British parliamentarism as readily exported as some had hoped, and only with reservations could the UK be seen as worldwide champion of democracy and exemplar of stable government.

[271] See above, xix.

CHAPTER 2

The Face of the Country

In the 1970s and 1980s attitudes to the environment changed as rapidly as changes on the ground. This chapter's first section reveals major shifts in policy on agricultural practice and in approaches to the natural world. The substantial transport changes in these decades are the theme of the second section. The third section, on controversy over architecture and urban life, resembles the first in witnessing a major shift in outlook. Out of the first three sections grows the theme of the fourth—community—for patterns of living in town, suburb, and countryside were profoundly influenced by the environmental, transport, and architectural shifts earlier discussed. The one area of the UK where 'community' could hardly be said to exist was Northern Ireland, the subject of the fifth and final section. There tragedy occurred because in Northern Ireland there was not one tight-knit community but two, each forced to live side by side with the other, and each apparently irreconcilable. As at 1990 there were all too few signs of resolution.

I. A FRAGILE LANDSCAPE

Both in the mind and on the ground, the UK after 1970 was almost imperceptibly changing shape; the northern section of Orford Ness, for instance, was by the late 1990s shrinking on average by a metre's width a year, while growing at its southern end by fifteen metres.[1] Elsewhere such reshaping was often deliberate. Foreshores were being continuously extended through landfill; the Channel Tunnel, for instance, added 73 acres to Britain's land mass (Plate 4),[2] though ambitious plans of the 1970s to reclaim Foulness for an airport came to nought. There was mounting concern about coastal erosion. Free of its Ice Age burdens, Scotland might be rising out of the sea, but England was slowly sinking, especially its east coast. In the 1980s the notion of erecting defences against the sea had not yet been abandoned, and more than a tenth of the

---

[1] National Trust, *Orford Ness* (c.1998), n.p.
[2] *FT* (6 May 1994), supplement on 'The Channel Tunnel', p. iv.

British coast was being defended,[3] but it was increasingly realized that any such defence had to be widely coordinated, otherwise defence in one area would prompt erosion in another. The threat from global warming, now becoming more apparent, made matters worse, and the Thames barrier was an early response. Such a barrier had been recommended in the aftermath of the storm surge in 1953,[4] but not until 1970 was agreement reached on a retractable barrier at Woolwich, not till 1975 did construction begin, and not till 1982 was it operational. With more than a million people living or working below the highest recorded water level, there was understandable all-party concern when parliament debated the scheme in 1972, one MP pronouncing it 'a splendid scenario' for an 'echo of doom' book.[5] Four years later Richard Doyle obliged by luridly portraying it in his novel Deluge. A storm could also do much damage inland: on the night of 15–16 October 1987 the storm in south-east England, the most serious in the home counties since 1703, blew down an estimated 15 million trees, including the equivalent within the affected counties of four to five years' normal production of conifers and six to seven years of hardwoods;[6] it was a pruning of the weakest trees more drastic than any landscape manager would have contemplated.

Interest in the foreshore and seabed, accelerating earlier,[7] continued apace after 1970. Increasing concern for fish stocks and mounting extraction of oil made the North Sea an area of intense political and economic interest, raising important issues of national sovereignty. Offshore drilling had become a vast new industry in its own right, and drillers and oilmen were now specializing between work on land or sea. North Sea oil raised Scotland's economic status by comparison with England, as well as creating a demand for oil rigs which brought desperately needed work to Clydeside shipbuilders. Potential fish and oil stocks lent a sudden interest to Rockall, an uninhabited lump of rock in the Atlantic; an order in council of 1974 incorporated it fully into the UK. Nearer to the Scottish mainland, fish farming's huge potential was being recognized by the mid-1970s; the term 'aquaculture' was coming into regular use, and it was increasingly realized that the fish farmer's legal redress against poachers and vandals must be upheld. Because fish farming made trout cheaper, and because cod was becoming scarce, trout and chips had hopes of becoming a popular dish. After pioneering research in the 1970s, salmon farming took off in the

[3] See figure 33 in A. S. Goudie and D. Brunsden, *The Environment of the British Isles: An Atlas* (Oxford, 1994). I am most grateful to Professor Goudie for generous help on this subject.

[4] Harrison, *Seeking a Role*, 124–5.

[5] David James, *HC Deb.* 5 June 1972, c. 132; see also c. 113 (C. Tugendhat).

[6] A. J. Grayson (ed.), *The 1987 Storm: Impacts and Responses* (Forestry Commission Bulletin, 87; 1989), pp. vi, 25. Dept. of the Environment, Ministry of Agriculture, Fisheries and Food, and Forestry Commission, *The Effects of the Great Storm* (1988), 11.   [7] Harrison, *Seeking a Role*, 125–6.

early 1980s, with its production increasing fivefold in five years, though even that figure could not match Norway's. Smoked salmon was going the same way as poultry: a one-time luxury was becoming commonplace. When John Noble launched his oyster-farming business in Loch Fyne in 1977, creating what soon became a restaurant chain,[8] even more dramatic possibilities opened up.

The oil industry encouraged divers to venture ever deeper, which made more under-sea wrecks accessible; most notable among them was the pride of Henry VIII's fleet, the *Mary Rose*, sunk in the Solent in 1545 and raised by a huge floating crane on 11 October 1982. The amateur diver was the under-water equivalent of the land-based hobbyist wielding his metal-detector. Both in some ways hindered archaeology, given that they usually sought treasure rather than scholarly knowledge; by 2003 metal detecting had damaged at least ten important battlefields.[9] Still, the newly developed very low-frequency metal detectors, which caused hobbyists' numbers to peak in the late 1970s, exposed a wealth of hitherto unknown sites and artefacts, though by no means always with adequate information on provenance. The magazine *Treasure Hunting* launched in 1977 reported a circulation of 10,000. To take only one instance of the outcome, between 1970 and 1995 the number of known Icenian coins rose from 1,150 to 12,946.[10]

Major changes in agricultural policy occurred after 1970. Post-war high farming had greatly enhanced British food production,[11] and by the end of the 1960s the national farm's net output at constant prices was double its pre-war level.[12] EEC subsidy in the 1970s encouraged a dramatic expansion in home-grown oilseed rape, so that by the mid-1980s it took up more of the country's arable area than any crop except wheat or barley.[13] Also during the 1970s massive drainage schemes were undertaken in the cereal-farming areas of southern and eastern England, but also in areas of intensive dairy farming further north and west. About a tenth of the agricultural land in England and Wales was drained in the 1970s—as much as in the three previous decades, and often resuming drainage work undertaken in the Victorian era of high farming.[14] The necessary massive investment concentrated ownership further. By 1979 the really big landowners were institutional rather than individual; only one of the top ten was a private individual. The size of farm varied markedly. More than half the holdings supplied less than a tenth of the output in 1988; in that year 70 per cent of UK farms were wholly or mainly

---

[8] M. Smith, 'How the Scots Learnt to Harvest Salmon, the King of Fish', *FT* (27 Dec. 1985), 10. *Scotsman* (19 Feb. 2002), 15 (Noble obituary). [9] *Ind* (22 Sept. 2003), 3.
[10] C. Dobinson and S. Denison, *Metal Detecting and Archaeology in England* (London and York, 1995), 61; see also 4–6. [11] In Harrison, *Seeking a Role*, 128–30.
[12] T. Beresford, *We Plough the Fields: Agriculture in Britain Today* (Harmondsworth, 1975), 80.
[13] D. Grigg, *English Agriculture: An Historical Perspective* (Oxford, 1989), 61.
[14] M. Robinson and A. C. Armstrong, 'The Extent of Agricultural Field Drainage in England and Wales, 1971–80', *Transactions of the Institute of British Geographers* (1988), 22.

owner-occupied, and more than half provided less than enough work for one full-timer.[15]

Livestock and livestock products accounted for three-fifths of British agriculture's revenue by 1988,[16] but the farming industry was diversifying. Glasshouse cultivation was high-yield, and during the 1980s clustered in small areas such as the Lea Valley in Essex, the West Sussex coastal plain, and Lincolnshire (Holland).[17] Also in the 1980s the acronym PYO ('pick your own') was imported from America, and by 1979 about half the country's raspberry crop and about a quarter of its strawberry crop were being gathered in this way.[18] Town-dwellers seeking rural bargains gradually advanced from the picking fields to patronize the growing number of farm shops which aimed to bypass the supermarkets. Garden centres continued to flourish, with help from the presenters of televised gardening programmes, who became national personalities; and in the 1990s the British horticultural industry's turnover grew by 40 per cent.[19] New glossy gardening manuals appeared almost as frequently as cookery books. Nonetheless, by 1982 agriculture accounted for a much smaller share of the British gross domestic product and of its workforce than in eight leading industrial countries.[20]

In improving their productivity, British farmers were almost too successful for their own good, for their employees' voting power was continuously declining. By 1970 agriculture could not claim as much as a third of the labour force in any UK constituency, and in only eight seats could it claim even as much as a quarter.[21] Enoch Powell in 1970 warned farmers above all to 'keep as far away from my profession as possible',[22] and in the 1970s their one-time political allies began to turn against them. The EEC's system of contributions aimed to prop up agricultural systems far less efficient than Britain's, and well before Thatcher wielded her handbag the EEC's redistributive system seemed highly anomalous when set beside overall national wealth.[23] British farmers' productivity was much higher than in several EEC countries, and helped to enlarge the Community's huge food surplus. This would in itself have given pause to policy-makers, even if conservation groups had not been spontaneously springing up for other reasons. Unsurprisingly, British agricultural policy changed course in the 1980s. The long-term trend for agriculture to encroach on other types of land-use had reached its peak in the late nineteenth century, and then (with a brief interruption in the Second

---

[15] H. Newby, *Green and Pleasant Land? Social Change in Rural England* (1979), 41–3. B. Hill, 'Agriculture', in P. Johnson (ed.), *The Structure of British Industry* (1988), 2, 5, 6.
[16] Hill, 'Agriculture', 3.
[17] J. G. S. and F. Donaldson with D. Barber, *Farming in Britain Today* (1969), 175.
[18] *DT* (20 July 1979), 6.   [19] *Ind* (17 Jan. 2000), 5.   [20] Hill, 'Agriculture', 1.
[21] D. E. Butler and M. Pinto-Duschinsky, *British General Election of 1970* (1970), 417.
[22] Speech to Shropshire branch of the National Farmers' Union on 16 May, *O* (17 May 1970), 3.
[23] As Prime Minister Callaghan complained in Paris on 12 Mar. 1979, *DT* (13 Mar. 1979), 1, 36.

World War) fell back from about 87 per cent of the late-Victorian land surface in England and Wales to about three-quarters of Great Britain's land mass by 1981.[24] It then began falling back further.

Britain now ceased to pursue national self-sufficiency in food through subsidies and tax concessions, if only because a European war now seemed much less likely. Instead, British farmers were encouraged to cut production, and imports from Commonwealth countries were discouraged in favour of their less efficient European rivals. The EEC supplied 12 per cent of Britain's agricultural imports in 1972, 35 per cent by 1987.[25] Food prices went up, planning restrictions on rural activities other than farming were relaxed, and 'set aside' payments rewarded farmers for carrying out their hitherto subordinate and incidental role as guardians of the countryside.[26] Britain's tilled land declined by 4 per cent between 1984 and 1990, and barley crops fell by a third.[27] The EEC connection changed the appearance even of the land that was tilled: the diminished need for cereals entailed the advance in the 1980s of bright yellow oilseed rape, followed in the 1990s by blue linseed, whose acreage soared tenfold between 1988 and 1992.[28] By 1990 7 per cent of Great Britain's land mass was urban or suburban, 21 per cent tilled land, 27 per cent managed grassland, 8 per cent woodland, with the rest consigned to uncultivated marsh, moorland, mudflats, and the like—though the balance varied markedly in different regions, with a far higher proportion of uncultivated land in Scotland and Wales than in England.[29]

The late twentieth century saw the conservationists gradually overtaking the farmers as the most significant rural lobby. The agriculture correspondents, still prominent in the serious newspapers of the 1970s, were twenty years later confined to subsections of press coverage on the environment as viewed from the towns. A fourth phase now seemed to be succeeding the three earlier phases in the evolution of British attitudes to poverty. The first, up till the industrial revolution, had assumed that poverty was inevitable. In the second, from about 1850 to 1950, poverty had seemed removable through a combination of personal reform and public welfare. In the third phase, from 1950 to about 1985, it was assumed not only that poverty was removable, but that overall wealth would steadily increase, and that concepts of poverty should now be 'relative' rather than absolute. During the fourth phase, however, from about 1985, it was increasingly realized that human demands on the world's resources were infinite, and that once a family had acquired one home or car they

[24] R. H. Best, *Land Use and Living Space* (1981), 45, 47.

[25] B. Burkitt and M. Baimbridge, 'The Performance of British Agriculture', *Rural History* (Oct. 1990), 265, 273.   [26] See e.g. Waldegrave, *FT* (20 Feb. 1987), 6.

[27] Dept. of the Environment, *Countryside Survey 1990: Summary Report* (1993), 8.

[28] D. Brown, 'How Blue is My Valley (Also Available in Red or Yellow)', *DT* (13 July 1992), 30.

[29] *Social Trends* (1995), 196.

would want two. The threat from global warming was perceived so slowly because its time-scale was so long: each generation accepted as natural what it inherited, without realizing how greatly that inheritance had moved on from its precursor's. Perceived deterioration in the quality of modern urban life crept up in a similar way, though rather faster. In attitudes to poverty the fourth phase's advance owed much to a sequence of environmental disasters worldwide: the Torrey Canyon oil spillage (1967), the serious accident at the nuclear power plant on Pennsylvania's Three Mile Island (1979), the world's worst industrial disaster with Union Carbide's gas leak at Bhopal in India (1984), and the world's worst nuclear power accident at Chernobyl in the Ukraine (1986). The fourth phase also owed something to books: to the Club of Rome's *The Limits to Growth* (1972) and E. F. Schumacher's *Small is Beautiful* (1973). A plainer lifestyle and a simpler technology were coming into vogue.

The late twentieth-century conservationist pedigree extended at least as far back as the concern felt by the eighteenth-century aristocrat and the nineteenth-century humanitarian for balance and proportion, especially between town and country. The Victorians wielded powerful environmentalist arguments against industrialization, and in Britain the expectation that material wealth must increase annually dates only from the 1950s. Changing priorities prompted a changed vocabulary. By the early 1970s environment had acquired a capital 'E'. The Department of the Environment was the first such department in Europe, and at a *Times* environment conference in 1972 its minister claimed that this governmental regrouping gave Britain 'a unique opportunity' to lead Europe in this policy area.[30] It was somewhat apprehensively concerned with the very broad context within which people's lives were lived: with air, water, sound, temperature, weather. 'In my totally ineffectual way', the diarist and conservationist Lees-Milne noted with surprise when discussing the population/pollution problem on 15 January 1972, 'I have been labouring on about this very subject, only to be considered a crank. Now letters are written almost daily to the *Times*.'[31] Late twentieth-century conservationism was a secular variant of earlier doom-laden millennial movements, a new manifestation of middle-class moralism, a new witness to the ongoing vitality of middle-class conscience and organizational zeal. Enthusiasts for recycling infused small purposive suburban gatherings with a new zest, and lent middle-class thrift and evangelism new outlets. Though not always without friction, late twentieth-century environmentalism united preservationists rural and urban, old and new: civic and amenity organizations like the Society for the Protection of Ancient Buildings and the Council for the Preservation of Rural

---

[30] P. Walker, *T* (29 June 1972), 4.
[31] J. Lees-Milne, *A Mingled Measure: Diaries 1953–1972* (1994), 195 (15 Jan. 1972).

England to ecologically aware newcomers like Greenpeace and Friends of the Earth.[32]

Of all environmentalist pressure groups, the Royal Society for the Protection of Birds (RSPB) grew fastest, uniquely combining hobby with crusade. By 1981 it had become Europe's largest voluntary wildlife conservation body. By then its adult membership had risen from 5,000 at the end of the Second World War to 350,000—the latter figure surpassing the Labour Party's individual membership by 83,000;[33] it went on growing for the rest of the century. It was reinforced by the EEC's 'birds directive', which became law from 1979: of the forty-six species nesting or wintering in the UK and listed for protection before 1993, twenty-three were recovering by 2007, including the kingfisher, osprey, and peregrine.[34] The National Trust's membership began to escalate in the 1970s, and reached 2.4 million by 1998. Friends of the Earth and Greenpeace were relative newcomers, with smaller memberships. Originating in America in 1969, the Friends soon began pressing drinks manufacturers to receive non-returnable bottles. Moving rapidly into recycling, animal conservation, and attacks on nuclear power, they owed little to charismatic leadership, much to their reasonable and well-informed campaigns and to energies spontaneously thrusting up from within the community.[35] Professional in a double sense, they owed much to their middle-class membership, which united expertise to self-interest, given that the professional person's home often abutted upon an environment that was worth preserving. 'Not in my backyard' became a catch-phrase of the 1980s, and self-interested suburban concern about the green belt readily became high-toned. Those who did not want London's third airport at Cublington, for instance, had before 1971 appointed a public relations officer, paid legal fees to counsel when giving evidence, and spent over £700,000 partly on promoting Foulness as an alternative.[36] Such pressure crowded out the trade union and working-class support for the much-needed local jobs that an airport at Cublington would have brought. On such issues, genuine clashes of interest during the 1970s were often muted in public discussion by trying to attach notional figures (sometimes seen as 'magic incantations') to the costs involved.[37]

During the 1980s the environmental movement, with rapidly rising and often enthusiastic membership, comfortably overtook the trade union movement (whose membership was steadily declining and often passive) in financial

---

[32] For a useful discussion of rural pressure groups see R. Sanders, 'Voices in the Wilderness', *Country Life* (17 Feb. 1994), 54.

[33] *FT* (13 Aug. 1981), 7. For the Labour Party see *BPF* (8th edn.), 159.   [34] *DT* (10 Aug. 2007), 9.

[35] For a good survey see C. Moorehead, 'Where to Now for Friends of the Earth', *T* (1 Oct. 1980), 9. For membership statistics of environmentalist organizations see *TCBST* 610–11.

[36] *T* (5 Apr. 1971), 1, 4; (26 Jan. 1971), 2.

[37] P. Self, 'Nonsense on Stilts', *Political Quarterly* (1970), 259.

power; membership of environmental organizations no doubt often overlapped, but when the members of fifteen 'green' organizations were aggregated in 1989 they totalled nearly four million.[38] By the 1970s the unobtrusively middle-class environmental causes were also competing with organized labour at the radical edge of policy. An increasingly ethical tone was imported into commercial discussion by customers worried about the treatment of animals, by depositors concerned about patterns of investment, and by shareholders preoccupied with the environment. Perhaps the best known among the commercial projects that such pressures frustrated was Concorde. Organized by Richard Wiggs from the front room of his suburban house in Letchworth, the Anti-Concorde Project owed some of its inspiration to his Quaker ancestry, and grew out of the *Observer*'s correspondence columns in 1966. By 1973 this articulate movement of the intellectuals rather than the masses had supporters in thirty countries,[39] but arrayed against it were a widespread national pride in what was an undoubted technological achievement, the governments' desire to conciliate the French during EEC entry negotiations, and the temptation for it to throw good money after bad.

For a brief moment in the 1980s the greens even seemed poised to transform party politics in Britain as substantially as in West Germany. At the Labour Party conference in autumn 1969 the new vocabulary of concern for the environment and the quality of life allegedly demoted the old class preoccupations.[40] Environmental issues embarrassed Labour in several ways.[41] Not only did they divide Labour's middle-class progressive from its working-class traditionalist followers; they also tilted the political agenda from concern with the prevalence of poverty towards alarm at the perils of affluence. The Liberals had much to gain from this, given that their predominantly rural base made a 'green' alignment instinctive. The Conservatives too, with their strong suburban affinities, could hope to benefit. They could advertise the large tracts of urban land that Labour had subjected to 'planning blight' or rendered unavailable by reluctance to modernize: derelict railway sidings, redundant hospitals, superfluous mines, under-used docks and ill-sited cattle markets. 'If you enter any major city in this country by train and look out of the window', said Viscount Ridley, complaining in 1971 about the railways' reluctance to vacate unused land, 'you see very much the seamy side of that city: filthy sidings, derelict, deserted lines and stations'. The Prince of Wales seized the moment: in 1983 he publicly backed organic food production, and among other things established a bottle bank at Buckingham Palace.[42]

---

[38] For useful figures see *T* (5 June 1989), 6; *Ind* (17 Jan. 1991), 19.
[39] 'Scourge of Concorde', *O* (18 Feb. 1973), 11.   [40] J. Margach in *ST* (5 Oct. 1969), 8.
[41] As C. A. R. Crosland was quick to perceive, *NS* (8 Jan. 1971), 40.
[42] Ridley, *HL Deb.* 17 Nov. 1971, c. 704. See also J. Dimbleby, *The Prince of Wales: A Biography* (1994), 311–12.

The conservationists after 1970 focused upon at least four aspects of rural life: hedgerows, afforestation, water, and wild life. High-productivity farming substituted prairie-like monocrop cultivation for the traditional patchwork pattern. This had involved grubbing up hedgerows in the 1960s at the rate of 10,000 miles a year, as well as draining numerous ponds and flood meadows; a quarter of Britain's remaining hedges disappeared between 1984 and 1990.[43] Ever larger fields demanded ever larger farm machinery (its purchase fostered by tax relief), so that parts of eastern England began to resemble American Mid-West prairie. By the 1970s hedgerows were increasingly seen as natural habitats worth conserving. Even trimming the hedgerows damaged the environment, tidiness being the death of young trees. The removal of dense undergrowth helped to oust nightingales from a third of their breeding sites between 1972 and 1991: their European frontier was contracting southwards.[44] Intensive farming and forestry also threatened the butterfly; by the end of the century, five of the sixty species native to Britain had become extinct, the latest being the large blue in 1979, and by 2002 a quarter of the marsh fritillaries, once common, were disappearing annually for lack of wildflower meadows.[45] On the other hand, by the 1990s the warmer climate was tempting some southern species northwards: the Essex skipper was now found in the Midlands, and the comma and speckled wood butterfly had spread from their few southern locations throughout England and Wales.[46]

On forestry issues after the 1960s the conservationist camp bifurcated. Some turned away from the Forestry Commission's afforestation policy which involved the mass planting of conifers. Imported from Germany to Britain and its empire early in the twentieth century, this policy aimed to save imports, avoid wartime shortages, and meet urban needs. The Commission's critics pointed out, however, that Britain's needs were changing, that not all types of afforestation benefit the landscape equally, and that afforestation policy had helped to destroy more native woodland in the thirty years since 1945 than in any other thirty years since the Norman Conquest.[47] A new emphasis on conserving broadleaved woodland would, they claimed, gear in with conservationists' growing perception that Britain's ancient woods (overlapping, but not identical) were ecologically important. By the 1980s the critics were reinforced by free-marketeers, who thought state-run bodies no more alert than private owners to longer term priorities.[48] Forests' share of

---

[43] *G* (17 Jan. 1976), 10 (leader). Dept. of the Environment, *Countryside Survey 1990*, 11.

[44] *Ind* (16 Apr. 1998), 11 (British Trust for Ornithology census).

[45] *Ind* (7 Aug. 2002), 7. See also *Ind* (2 Mar. 2001), 9.   [46] *Ind* (10 June 1999), 13.

[47] R. H. Grove, *The Future of Forestry: The Urgent Need for a New Policy* (Cambridge, 1983), 47–8. Once again I gratefully acknowledge the generous help I have received on forestry matters from Dr Peter Savill, of Oxford University's Dept. of Plant Sciences.

[48] R. Miller, *State Forestry for the Axe: A Study of the Forestry Commission and De-Nationalisation by the Market* (Institute of Economic Affairs Hobart Paper, 91; 1981), 16, 21–2.

the UK land mass rose from 6.7 per cent in 1947 to 9.4 per cent in 1980, and during the 1980s productive woodland grew much faster under private owners than under the Forestry Commission.[49] The Commission's 'broadleaves policy' adopted in 1985 launched a reversal of strategy that gained momentum thereafter—felling and thinning the conifers in ancient woods that half a century earlier had been expensively cleared to make way for them. By the late 1980s the Commission's critics had become self-confident enough to deploy the defence of ancient woodland as an argument against building new roads.[50] By 2000 the balance between broadleaf and conifer plantations had shifted markedly towards broadleaf, whose woods had grown by more than a third since 1980. Entirely unexpected and unplanned, however, was the demise of the English elm after the 1960s. Once a distinctive feature of the English countryside, tall in their lines or clusters, elms succumbed before Dutch elm disease, an imported fungus spread by the bark beetle. First observed near Tewkesbury in about 1965, the disease spread throughout southern England, and within thirteen years 86 per cent of its elms were dead,[51] though small enclaves survived in the Brighton area and parts of Scotland. England, with about 1.3 billion trees in 2000, remained well below the West European average in trees' share of its land mass.[52]

Water evoked growing concern in the second half of the twentieth century. Because domestic demand through the mains supply was growing steadily, with demand greatest in the south where it rained least, shortage was becoming serious. Industry met its needs, much larger than domestic, partly from its own resources. The Water Act (1963) established river authorities and set up a national Water Resources Board to coordinate their plans. The national plan for water was published in 1973, and coordination was greatly eased in that year by integrating numerous river and sanitary authorities under ten Regional Water Authorities organized round river catchments. The Kielder Reservoir, the largest man-made lake in Western Europe, was opened in 1982, an early outcome of regional water planning. It formed part of the UK's first regional water grid, making it possible to switch supplies between regions.[53] Nonetheless, there were serious droughts in 1976, 1984, and 1995 as well as scarcity in the late 1980s and early 1990s.[54] The conservationists' prime concern was with the water's quality. Heseltine in 1982 pronounced the Mersey, the most polluted estuary and river system in the UK, 'an affront to the standards a civilized

[49] H. F. Marks, *A Hundred Years of British Food and Farming: A Statistical Survey*, ed. D. K. Britton (1989), 96–7.

[50] O. Rackham, *Trees and Woodland in the British Landscape* (1st publ. 1976, rev. edn. 1990), 200.

[51] P. Jones, 'The Geography of Dutch Elm Disease in Britain', *Transactions of the Institute of British Geographers*, 6/3 (1981), 329.   [52] *G* (22 Nov. 2001), 2.

[53] J. Hassan, *A History of Water in Modern England and Wales* (Manchester, 1998), 103, 123, 132, 134.

[54] Ibid. 6, 195.

society should demand of its environment'.[55] From the late 1970s, however, the concentrations of zinc, lead, and copper in British rivers and lakes had begun to fall.[56] Otters were a success story. The pesticide Dieldrin, introduced in 1957, was thought to stop them breeding and a voluntary ban was introduced a decade later; otters could be hunted till 1978, but had almost become extinct, confined to a fastness in the north-west Highlands of Scotland. Then designated a protected species, they were thereafter introduced in many places, helped by the decline in river pollution. By 2003 they were more numerous than at any time since the Second World War. Flourishing especially in Wales, Scotland, and the south-west of England, they were advancing eastwards.[57]

In the fifteen years up to 1994, however, nine animals and plants disappeared from Britain, including the greater mouse-eared bat, the first mammal to disappear since the wolf in the mid-eighteenth century, though a single specimen was unexpectedly sighted in 2002. By the 1990s the dormouse, the pine marten, the red squirrel, and the otter were by no means secure, and many species of bird had suffered by the drainage of wetlands, the reclaiming of heathlands, and the conversion of grassland to arable since 1945.[58] On the other hand, wild-boar farming repaired a gap left since the early 1660s. Some boar escaped into the wild during the hurricane of 1987 and bred on the border of Kent and Sussex; an escape of 1996 led to another wild grouping in West Dorset, and probably also in Herefordshire, and in all three areas wild boar were still breeding in 2004.[59] Intensive farming was driving mammals from the countryside, and several species were moving into the suburbs: hedgehogs, voles, roedeer, shrews, dormice, hares, muntjac, foxes, and badgers.[60] The badger was among several species benefiting from animal programmes on television. Ernest Neal, 'the badger man', broadcast a film on them in 1954, became a regular broadcaster, and campaigned for their protection. The Badger Act (1973), the first protective measure, tightened up in 1991, helped to reverse the badger's downward trend.[61]

Plants, too, gave rise to concern. The Wildlife and Countryside Act (1981) extended protection to wild plants, and incorporated a schedule of endangered species updated at five-yearly intervals. By 1980 the ten national parks covered nearly a tenth of the land mass in England and Wales, but none had been established since 1956; none were in the farmed countryside of lowland England most vulnerable to agricultural change. Localities designated 'areas

[55] Dept. of the Environment, *Cleaning up the Mersey: A Consultation Paper on Tackling Water Pollution in the Rivers and Canals of the Mersey Catchment, and Improving the Appearance and Use of their Banks* (1982), 1, 3.   [56] *Social Trends* (1995), 194.

[57] Wildlife Trust survey, *T* (18 Nov. 2002), 9. *T* (12 May 2003), 9. *Ind* (26 June 2001), 9.

[58] *T* (28 Mar. 1994), 6.

[59] M. J. Goulding, G. Smith, and S. J. Baker, *Current Status and Potential Impact of Wild Boar (Sus Cofa) in the English Countryside: A Risk Assessment* (1998), 11. *Ind* (26 Jan. 2004), 3.

[60] Mammals Trust survey, *ST* (21 Mar. 2004), pp. i, 11.   [61] *T* (9 June 2001), 16.

of outstanding natural beauty' were more widely dispersed but less well protected. They included Dedham Vale ('Constable country'), which the architect Raymond Erith indignantly struggled to protect against advancing ugliness: 'if Dedham Vale is not worth keeping', he wrote, 'nothing is worth keeping'.[62] In 1988 the Norfolk Broads gained a status similar to that of a national park, and at the end of the decade there was hope for an environmental 'peace dividend' when the Ministry of Defence's reduced need for training grounds coincided with farmers' reduced need to colonize them. As late as 1994 the Ministry owned an area the size of Surrey,[63] not to mention all the barracks, arsenals, and dockland sites that became available in the 1990s as 'heritage' homes for owner-occupiers.

Pressure groups often aim to maximize their political influence by forming a political party. The People Party founded in 1972 soon became the Ecology Party, and then in 1985 the Green Party. With the success of West Germany's Greens as a precedent, the total vote for green candidates in Britain more than doubled between 1979 and 1987, as did the number of candidates; their number doubled again in 1992 to 254.[64] The Greens' advance as a distinct party was obstructed by the UK's two-party system, which strongly encouraged all three established parties to purloin any of the greens' practicable ideas, and protected two of the three with a high electoral threshold from which to fend off intruders. The Labour Party, becoming less statist in mood, began reaching back to its green pioneers Owen and Ruskin, and Thatcher went characteristically on to the offensive. She received the 'green' spokesman Jonathon Porritt at 10 Downing Street, holding a seminar and putting much effort into a speech on the subject, as well as issuing a green paper, *This Common Inheritance*.[65] 'A good environment and a strong economy are dependent on each other', it pronounced: a prosperous community both generates the resources to improve its environment and needs to do so if it is to attract talent. Government cannot do everything, and voluntary involvement must be encouraged, operating in a free-market context: 'the oldest and best way of controlling the pace at which we use up natural resources is to let the market work. If one resource is in short supply, its price goes up, and somebody develops alternatives.' On the principle that 'the polluter must pay', the green paper continuously stressed the importance of natural science in combating natural hazards.[66] But Thatcher's departure, together with the depression's onset, downgraded environmental concerns among the electors' priorities. Idealistic and wary of strong leadership,

---

[62] R. Erith, 'How to Ruin the Constable Country', *Spec* (8 Jan. 1965), 38.
[63] *Ind* (11 Aug. 1994), 16.
[64] D. E. Butler and D. Kavanagh, *The British General Election of 1987* (1988), 344; *BPF* (8th edn.) 173.
[65] See e.g. *ST* (10 Dec. 1989), 1; *DT* (26 May 1990), 1.
[66] Dept. of the Environment, *This Common Inheritance: Britain's Environmental Strategy* (1990), 114, 33, 37.

the environmental movement was riven in the early 1990s by disputes; these denied it impetus when the general election arrived in 1992.[67]

2. MORE PEOPLE MOVING FASTER

After 1970, as before, more people were communicating with one another over longer distances, whether by moving about, or by remaining stationary and using new electronic media. The overriding story was one of ever-growing travel by road, with governments of whatever party deferring to the motorist. The number in Great Britain qualified to drive rose by 52 per cent between 1975/6 and 1991/3; by then two-thirds of the population aged 17 or more were qualified, and the number of women drivers doubled.[68] The car's persisting male image was bizarrely reflected, however, in modes of suicide: men were more likely to use a car's exhaust fumes for the purpose.[69] Sixty-one per cent of British households owned a car by 1981, and 15 per cent had the use of two or more; in parts of the home counties one household in three ran a second car. Two-vehicle families increased threefold in Britain between 1972 and 1995.[70]

In an affluent society where people had run out of things to buy, they bought experiences instead, including travel as a recreation in itself. Driving was enjoyable in the motorways' early years. The UK system's overall length rose threefold between 1970 and 1990, to 1,919 miles.[71] Improved car technology made journeys faster and safer, and in the 1970s a growing proportion of cars exceeded the 70 mph speed-limit.[72] By 1975 a basic motorway system had come into existence, with linkages between the M1, M6, M5, and M4; by 1981 the network was almost complete, including the trans-Pennine M62; and by 1986 the jigsaw was complete when London's outer ringroad, the M25, was finished. By 1979 cars and taxis constituted three-quarters of motorway traffic, other goods vehicles nearly a fifth,[73] and in the following year over half the UK population lived within 25 miles of a motorway; among major cities, only Aberdeen and Norwich now remained beyond easy reach of the system, which accounted for about a tenth of the total traffic mileage on British roads and a quarter of all goods-vehicle traffic mileage.[74] The archaeologist J. N. L. Myres in 1985 recalled how walking, riding, and sailing sixty years earlier had helped him

---

[67] For useful accounts, see *ST* (30 Aug. 1992), ii, 5; *THES* (17 Sept. 1993), 17.

[68] *Social Trends* (1995), 205.

[69] *Voluntary Euthanasia Society Newsletter*, 58 (Sept. 1996), 12.

[70] *DT* (1 Oct. 1986), 2; (20 Mar. 1997), 4.

[71] P. and R. Baldwin (eds.), *The Motorway Achievement*, i. *The British Motorway System: Visualisation, Policy and Administration* (2004), 182.

[72] G. Charlesworth, *A History of British Motorways* (1984), 240.   [73] Ibid. 237.

[74] T. P. Hughes in Institution of Civil Engineers, *Twenty Years of British Motorways: Proceedings of the Conference Held in London 27–28 February, 1980* (1980), 6, 11.

grasp what England had been like when the Romans departed; yet now the scale of road traffic made long-distance walking intolerable, and the motorways often cut across the natural grain of the country instead of following it, bypassing the towns instead of going through them. 'My generation of historians was perhaps the last for whom it was comparatively easy to identify and appreciate the meaning of these traditional patterns', he wrote, 'unhampered by the physical distortions now imposed on them by the requirements of motor transport'.[75]

Tourism exploited the 'romance of travel'. British Rail at first forbade steam excursions over its tracks, but the 1960s saw steam railway preservation societies become well established,[76] and in 1972 it approved five stretches of lightly used line for steam trains, and more later. Private-railway mileage rose eightfold between 1970 and 2005, three-fifths of it on track once run by British Rail.[77] A railway preservation society would form a limited company to buy track and equipment; with help from the parent society, it would then run the railway, often using privately owned locomotives.[78] In 1970 Lionel Jeffries's production of E. Nesbit's *The Railway Children* revealed an additional source of income: film revenue, which in that instance benefited the Keighley and Worth Valley Railway. In 1975 the National Railway Museum opened at York; by the following year some 30,000 people had joined railway preservation societies; and by 1997 Britain's heritage railways were carrying about eight million passengers a year.[79] The National Trust was a major beneficiary of recreational travel. Its membership shot up from the late 1960s, rising ninefold between 1970 and 1990,[80] with associated gains in acreage owned and full-time staff employed. In the early 1990s England accounted for 90 per cent of listed buildings and conservation areas in Great Britain, 90 per cent of the historic properties in the UK, and 80 per cent of the scheduled monuments in Great Britain, with a heavy concentration on the south-east.[81] Like medieval places of pilgrimage, each tourist location advertised its own distinctive claim on tourist expenditure, sometimes putting at risk the attraction and even the survival of the site itself. The historic buildings attracting more than 200,000 paying visitors in 1980 included some in quite small communities: Chatsworth with 250,000, for instance, or the Brontë parsonage in Haworth with 205,000.[82] Tourism after 1970 transformed the local economy of such places.

---

[75] 'Introduction' to his *The English Settlements* (Oxford, 1986), p. xxviii.
[76] Harrison, *Seeking a Role*, 142–3.   [77] I owe these statistics to Mr Dennis Dunstone.
[78] For a useful discussion see P. N. Grimshaw, 'Steam Railways: Growth Points for Leisure and Recreation', *Geography* (Apr. 1976), 86.
[79] C. Loft, *British Government and the Railways, 1951–1964: Beeching's Last Trains* (2004), 137.
[80] *TCBST* 611.
[81] B. Casey, R. Dunlop, and S. Selwood, *Culture as Commodity? The Economics of the Arts and Built Heritage in the United Kingdom* (1996), 153.   [82] For a complete list see *T* (29 June 1981), 3.

After 1951, with help from containerization, freight massively transferred from railways to roads, with a smaller growth in transport by pipeline and (after the 1960s) by water.[83] With such opportunities, and by international standards lightly regulated, British motorway freight transport became in effect an enterprise zone in the 1970s, with self-employed owner-drivers to the fore.[84] Relaxation of weight limits in 1955, 1964, 1966, 1972, 1983, and 1988, together with ever-larger commercial firms, ensured ever larger vehicles.[85] Containerization fostered new cross-country routes for the juggernauts, and by 1972 Tilbury was second only to Rotterdam among European container ports. Juggernauts highlight the first among the motorways' several drawbacks, only gradually apparent, and often the products of their success. The juggernauts caused much noise and disruption on leaving the motorway, especially as larger lorries did not seem to entail fewer.[86] By the mid-1970s the Sheffield Polytechnic lecturer John Tyme had become well known for appearing at numerous motorway planning inquiries to challenge the road lobby on environmental grounds.[87] Inspired by the equation 'truth + courage + numbers = invincibility', he saw democracy as needing continuously to be fought for. Alarmed at amenity destroyed, land wasted, communities disrupted, and deploring the motorways' sheer cost, he claimed that 'the more highways we build, the more we generate traffic to fill them'.[88] His *Motorways and Democracy* (1978) both exaggerated the cohesion of the motorways' advocates and understated the widespread support for them. He saw himself and colleagues as plain but determined citizens asking awkward and unanswered questions of expert but undemocratic, wily, self-interested, and conspiratorial authorities powered by the 'technological imperative'. Protests like his increased the cost of further motorway extensions, and culminated in the intense but ultimately failed attempt to prevent the M3 motorway from being driven through Twyford Down—a development authorized by the Department of Transport in 1991.

A further and highly paradoxical difficulty after 1970 with all types of road, more intractable than any other, lent some credence both to the motorways' critics and to their advocates. Technology initially presented as saving time tempts its user to cram yet more activity into the time saved. In traffic terms this meant living further from work, and holidaying further from home, thus drawing the authorities into what Tyme condemned as 'dispersal planning'.

---

[83] See the striking graph in *FT* (27 Oct. 1994), 12.   [84] J. Wardroper, *Juggernaut* (1981), 44.

[85] For statistics see B. A. Frith, *Trends in Road Goods Transport 1983–1991* (Crowthorne, 1994), 4, 12. See also D. Starkie, *The Motorway Age: Road and Traffic Policies in Post-War Britain* (1982), 107–10.

[86] As Albert Booth complained in *HC Deb.* 9 Dec. 1981, cc. 922–3.

[87] For a portrait, see *G* (27 Sept. 1976), 7.

[88] J. Tyme, *Motorways versus Democracy: Public Inquiries into Road Proposals and their Political Significance* (London and Basingstoke, 1978), 14, 1.

Life in such circumstances became if anything still more pressured. It also became less interesting because local contrasts were ironed out, removing at least one of the incentives to travel. Motorway travel gradually became less enjoyable: because motorways were used much more intensively than other roads, they became so crowded and so sorely in need of repair that their traffic slowed down. In 1980 they constituted less than 1 per cent of Britain's road network, but carried about a tenth of all motor-traffic mileage and a quarter of all goods-vehicle traffic mileage.[89] The word 'contraflow', in relation to road traffic, entered the language in the 1970s, and gained special currency round about 1981 during a severe bout of repairs to the M1.[90] Driving on crowded roads, like living in crowded towns, made people cross: the phrase 'motorway madness' to denote irresponsibly fast driving became current round about 1971, and was joined in the mid-1990s by the American phrase 'road rage'.[91] Motorways generated more traffic on all types of road, forcing planners to find ways round the bottlenecks, so that the entire system grew almost of its own accord. 'Road pricing', the free-market alternative to the queue, might have been expected to attract the Thatcher governments, but was left for a much later Labour government seriously to advance.

Road travel's most obvious drawback was the level of accidents, but here the motorways appear in a better light. The speed, weight, and number of vehicles involved produced some spectacular and much-publicized motorway accidents, but without motorways accident levels would have been very much higher; rates of injury and deaths per mile driven were far lower on motorways than on other types of road. Better roads, better vehicles, and better training had been reducing British accident levels throughout the century, so that by 1985 the death rate in relation to vehicles owned (let alone to miles driven) was lower than at any time for sixty years, except for 1948 when petrol rationing had temporarily reduced car usage. Yet the deaths were numerous enough: in 1985 0.8 per cent of all deaths at all ages, and 35 per cent of all deaths between the ages of 15 and 24.[92] Prevailing values were illuminated in that year with the absence of outcry when 76,145 people were killed or suffered serious injury on British roads.[93] The road lobby did not preclude ever tighter controls on motorists. In 1960 the Ministry of Transport decided to impose an annual test of vehicles ten or more years old as a condition of licensing; the testable vehicle age fell steadily to three years by 1967, with many subsequent elaborations of what soon became known as the MOT test. Introduced in 1967, breathalyser tests rose threefold between 1968 and 1980; the number of convictions for

[89] Institution of Civil Engineers, *Twenty Years of British Motorways*, 6.   [90] *T* (20 July 1998), 8.
[91] *DT* (14 Sept. 1971), 2; (21 May 1996), 4. *G* (21 May 1996), 16.
[92] Sir R. Doll, 'Major Epidemics of the Twentieth Century', *Journal of the Royal Statistical Society*, series A, 105 (1987), 388.
[93] Dept. of Transport, *Transport Statistics: Great Britain 1976–1986* (1987), 122.

drinking and driving also rose threefold, to 79,000, much faster than the rise in car-miles travelled.[94] By 1988 the UK had the lowest road accident rate in the world except for Norway, Sweden, and Japan, and driving had become much safer than in the 1930s. Despite the huge increase in traffic in the interval, fewer pedestrians were killed on the roads per vehicle in 1987 than sixty years before.[95]

Of the other seven widespread ways of moving about—walking, cycling, motor-cycling, travelling by water, by rail, by communal road transport, and by air—urban walking was in decline. The car deterred others besides its passengers from walking by making streets noisier, smellier, and more dangerous. Safety considerations pushed pedestrians into trudging up footbridges and down subways, yet this did not deter 70 per cent of the adult population in 1980 from spending 46 minutes of an average day walking for just over a mile, often to shop.[96] Pleasanter ways of segregating pedestrians from road traffic were being found. The hypermarket, an American expansion of the supermarket, reached Britain in the early 1970s, and provided out-of-town parking facilities; it differed from the Victorians' covered market primarily in being owned by a single firm, and also in being located too far from the city centre to be approached solely on foot. More accessible to pedestrians were the pedestrian precinct and the shopping mall. More than a third of London's 168 precincts as at 1981 dated from before 1939, and nearly a tenth of the UK's 1,304,[97] but from the 1960s their number rose. As for the shopping mall, it was the Victorians' arcade in glossier and larger format, and advanced fast after the success of Chester's Grosvenor-Laing Centre (opened in 1965). Huge malls opened at Brent Cross (1976), Milton Keynes (1980), Dudley (Merry Hill, 1986), Gateshead (Metrocentre, 1986), Sheffield (Meadowhall, 1990), and Thurrock (Lakeside, 1990). These innovations may help explain why the average numbers of pedestrians killed annually in British traffic accidents fell from 2,879 in 1970/4 to 1,380 in 1990/4; there was an even more striking fall in deaths per vehicle mile.[98] Little credit accrues, however, to the Pedestrians Association, with a mere 1,000 members in 1998 as against the Automobile Association's 9.3 million.[99] Rural walking, defended by the Ramblers' Association, was in better health.[100] The Association was growing fast: its 10,000+ members in 1952 had become 50,000 in 1986 and 100,000 in 1994. Responsible for this were growing

[94] T. R. Gourvish and R. G. Wilson, *Brewing Industry 1830–1980* (Cambridge, 1994), 569–70.

[95] D. A. Coleman and J. Salt, *The British Population: Patterns, Trends, and Processes* (Oxford, 1992), 269.   [96] J. E. Todd and A. Walker, *People as Pedestrians* (1980), 20.

[97] J. Roberts, *Pedestrian Precincts in Britain* (1981), 29, 32.

[98] Dept. of Transport, *Transport Statistics: Great Britain 1996*, 184–5.   [99] *FT* (31 Aug. 1998), 5.

[100] This paragraph has benefited from its admirable website, www.ramblers.org.uk/news/media/ramblers-history.html, consulted 26 June 2005.

leisure, increasing concern with fitness, and legislation to defend rights of way. In 1958 the Ordnance Survey was persuaded to show public rights of way in England and Wales on its popular maps, and Britain's first long-distance footpath, the Pennine Way, dates from 1965. Three years later the Countryside Act required county councils in England and Wales to signpost footpaths and broadened the definition of open country to include woods and river banks.

The bicycle's long decline was arrested in the 1970s, and in the 1980s even began tentatively to revive. It profited from growing concern about health and the environment, and from new designs, most notably the 'mountain bike' (robust, fat-tyred machines pioneered in California); in 1979 more bicycles were built in Britain than in any year since the war.[101] Local authorities increasingly set about reviving that long-neglected thoroughfare, the cycleway. Sustrans (a Bristol group founded in 1977), aided by employment-creation schemes, began to build up what became the twenty-first century's national cycle network, drawing disused railway lines and canal towpaths into the system. Still, the bicycle's overall share of passenger-miles travelled never rose above 1 per cent between 1970 and 1995, and the motor-cycle's trajectory was very similar;[102] declining numbers and the earlier adoption of helmets did not prevent almost three times as many motor-cyclists as pedal-cyclists from being killed annually in these years.[103] The resemblance did not stop there: bicycling and motor-cycling had alike begun with an elite image, but had moved between the wars towards a routine commuting role. Then slowly from the 1950s both gave way to the privately owned car, and by the 1960s had acquired a down-market image, only later recouped by an enhanced recreational role. During the 1950s the motor-cyclist who had bought his vehicle to get him to work, adding a side-car on marriage, was acquiring a car instead, and by 1995 the AA's research showed that 51 per cent of motorcyclists also owned a car. Associated during the 1960s with 'rough' teenage tearaway 'bikers', motor-cycles were forced on to the defensive, but their image partially recovered when motor-cycling became a largely leisure pursuit: middle-aged and even middle-class motor-cyclists moved enthusiastically about the country in the 1980s on their expensive machines, increasingly vigorous in self-defence through the British Motorcyclists' Federation.[104]

With three other modes of travel—canals, communal road passenger travel, and railways—there were stronger signs of revival. The canal's great strength, its leisurely pace, lent it a new recreational role from the 1960s. By 1973 at least

---

[101] *G* (26 Aug. 1980), 3.   [102] Dept of Transport, *Transport Statistics: Great Britain 1996*, 178.
[103] *TCBST* 460.
[104] S. McDonald-Walker, 'Driven to Action: The British Motorcycle Lobby in the 1990s', *Sociological Review* (May 2000), 188–90; 'Fighting the Legacy: British Bikers in the 1990s', *Sociology* (May 1998), 388–90.

twenty-eight restoration schemes were in progress and about sixty clubs and societies were directly associated with reviving the inland waterways.[105] One of the most impressive, the Kennet and Avon Canal, had been partly closed in the 1950s, but became navigable again from Bristol to Reading after the Queen had reopened it in 1990. The motorway from the 1960s greatly boosted the coach and lorry, enabling them to compete directly with the railways over short and long distances except where commuting congestion gave railways the edge. Thatcher claimed that 'if a man finds himself a passenger on a bus having attained the age of 26, he can account himself a failure in life'.[106] There must still have been many failures in Britain in 1979, when buses and coaches contributed 1 per cent of the vehicles on motorways,[107] though their number had been falling steadily since the 1950s, and still more their share of passenger miles—down from 15 per cent in 1970 to 7 per cent in 1990.[108] More damaging to the railways was the fourfold increase in the transport of freight by road between 1952 and 1992.[109] The railways' unimportance for industry by 1982 was exposed by the lack of pressure to end the strike in that year, for British Rail's freight by then carried only about a tenth of total British tonnage.[110] In the 1970s more than half personal expenditure on rail transport came from the richest fifth of the population, and only 5 per cent from the poorest—an upward slant still more marked when it came to expenditure on season tickets.[111]

Railway passenger miles and railway mileage open to passenger traffic hardly changed between 1970 and 1990, but the railways' share of total passenger miles fell from 9 to 6 per cent.[112] Important moves were made to improve British Rail's long-distance role. The 17 per cent of the track that had been electrified by 1970 rose to 30 per cent of a somewhat smaller track in 1990/1.[113] British Rail first used the term 'inter-city' in 1966 to describe its first full electric service from London to Liverpool and Manchester, and the system reached Birmingham in 1967, Glasgow in 1974. Timetables were improved, and experiments were conducted with new types of passenger train. The High Speed 125 train broke the world speed record for diesel trains in 1973, though the coach-tilting Advanced Passenger Train had to be abandoned because of discomfort on curves at high speed. Government-planned phased staff cuts, together with a decentralized and clearer management structure, ensured that

---

[105] R. W. Squires, *Canals Revived: The Story of the Waterway Restoration Movement* (Bradford-on-Avon, 1979), 115.   [106] Quoted in *O* (26 July 1998), 3—a reference I owe to Amanda Root.
[107] Charlesworth, *British Motorways*, 237.
[108] Dept. of Transport, *Transport Statistics: Great Britain 1996*, 178.
[109] Royal Commission on Environmental Pollution, *18th Report: Transport and the Environment* (Cm 2674; 1994), 10.   [110] *FT* (19 July 1982), 4.
[111] Loft, *Government, Railways and Modernization*, 139–40.
[112] Dept. of Transport, *Transport Statistics: Great Britain 1996*, 178.   [113] Ibid. 186.

train miles per staff member rose by 42 per cent between 1982 and 1989; by then British Rail received a lower level of public support than railways in any other EEC country.[114] As for the suburban commuter, there were important developments in the 1980s, with the first stretch of the Tyne and Wear metro system launched in 1980, and the first stretch of the Docklands Light Railway opened in 1987. Both made extensive use of earlier British Rail lines, both were innovative and successful, and both added substantial extensions later. Built cheaply so as rapidly to open up the newly developing docklands area in East London, the Docklands Light Railway operated with driverless trains and unmanned stations. Meanwhile, London Transport went into a serious decline. Once among the capital's major assets, this one-time pace-setter in design decayed sadly in cleanliness and amenities; by 2000 graffiti caused its rolling stock to resemble the mobile dustbins that New York's subway cars had by then become.

Air transport, within the UK as elsewhere, followed the pattern set by international travel: crowding its passengers into ever larger groups. It was growing continuously in absolute and relative terms between 1970 and 1990. Passenger-miles travelled by air on domestic flights, including Northern Ireland and the Channel Isles, rose by 160 per cent in these years, though even by 1990 domestic air flights accounted for only 0.8 per cent of total passenger transport within the UK.[115] Escalating international air travel[116] prompted pressure for a third London airport. Out of the controversy in the early 1970s came Cublington as initial choice after exhaustive cost-benefit analysis; then it was rejected on environmental grounds in favour of reclaimed land at Maplin in a scheme later dropped. Quieter and larger aircraft ('jumbo jets') soon destroyed the case for any new London airport, though by 1990 London Heathrow had become the busiest airport in the world.[117] So air travel diverged from the pattern established in the earliest days of flight: instead of encouraging passengers to fly directly between destinations, it required them increasingly to fly only where many other people wanted to go—with all the noise, congestion and delay that accompanied the ever larger planes and airports required. There were hints of an alternative line of development. The trend already established for greater use of helicopters before 1970[118] persisted. And for recreation, in the air as on the ground, the combination of speed and silence was ever more seductive: parachutes, hang-gliders, microlights, wind-surfing, water-skis, and balloons, and any combination of all these, were gaining ground. The 'new aviation',

[114] Loft, *Government, Railways and Modernization*, 141.
[115] *Transport Statistics: Great Britain 1996*, 178.
[116] Harrison, *Seeking a Role*, 84–5; see also pp. 17–20 above.
[117] W. D. Rubinstein, *Capitalism, Culture, and Decline in Britain 1750–1990* (1993), 39.
[118] Harrison, *Seeking a Role*, 144.

the collective term applied to this cluster of interlinked sports, democratized the art of flying by making it cheaper and simpler, yet also more adventurous. The 'Bristol Belle', the first modern hot-air balloon built in Western Europe, received its test flight on 9 July 1967, and prompted the growth of a Bristol firm that by the late 1970s was manufacturing more than 100 balloons a year, later becoming the world's largest constructor. The microlight, though lacking the attraction of silence, had the great advantages of cheapness and closer control, and grew so fast after the 1970s that there were 500 in Britain by the end of 1981.[119]

Changes after 1970 in British telecommunications were dramatic. Only a fifth of British households had a telephone in 1965, four-fifths twenty years later.[120] People were using their phones more freely, too: the number of local calls more than doubled in both the 1960s and 1970s, and long-distance calls within the UK escalated even faster. Postal traffic grew far more slowly: letters delivered grew by only 34 per cent between 1970 and 1990, and both parcels and telegrams declined.[121] Commerce required a delivery service more responsive to the customer, whose needs by the 1980s were increasingly met by revived courier services dependent upon young male motor-cyclists speeding between urban destinations. The Thatcher government split off telephones from the Post Office in 1981, and privatized them as 'British Telecom' in 1984 so successfully as to boost the entire privatization process. Thereafter the mobile phone revolution gradually gathered pace. Vodafone's precursor was set up in 1985, with 700,000 subscribers by 1991.[122] The mobile phone demonstrated its political potential in 1990 when campaigners against the poll tax used it to mobilize supporters. In his budget speech of March 1991 the Chancellor of the Exchequer Norman Lamont half-humorously referred to 'one of the greatest scourges of modern life, the mobile telephone'.[123] With affluence comes the private facility: by the end of the century the mobile telephone had become so ubiquitous as to send the public phone-box into the sort of decline that had earlier hit the public lavatory. Mobile phones were immensely convenient for people in mobile occupations, and like other contemporary electronic revolutions enabled a simultaneous geographical dispersal of firms and of employees within firms. People now had less need to travel in order to do business, and had less need to cluster in London. Britain's transport revolution had no terminus: it was continuous and ongoing.

[119] I am most grateful to Chris Finnigan, Chief Executive of the British Microlight Aircraft Association, for most generous guidance on this important subject, and especially for his interview on 5 Sept. 2005.
[120] S. Bowden and A. Offer, 'Household Appliances and the Use of Time: The United States and Britain since the 1920s', *Economic History Review*, 47 (1994), 744.   [121] *TCBST* 444–5.
[122] Obituary of Sir Gerald Whent, *DT* (24 May 2002), 31.
[123] *T* (26 Mar. 1991), 13 (leader); cf. *Ind* (26 Mar. 1991), 18 (leader).

3. URBAN UTOPIA ABANDONED

The implications of transport change for town life were serious. The juggernaut's environmental impact on small towns straddling trunk roads could be devastating. As for larger towns, the priority their maps gave to street plans indicated that they were becoming places to get through rather than arrive at or live in. Front gardens were sacrificed to free the streets from parked cars,[124] and street-parked cars were unsightly, created congestion, and worsened the litter problem. Streets gradually ceased to be places for trading and recreation. The travelling fairground's periodic descent upon city centres prompted what was perhaps the most frontal among the growing conflicts between the street as social centre and as traffic conduit; by 2000 many fairgrounds had vacated the central streets for the suburbs.[125] In such circumstances the community sense that had nourished Victorian pride in city centres was at risk; indeed, the traffic's demands in the 1960s caused Birmingham's progressive city council to rip out the heart of a community that had epitomized Victorian civic pride. The cities which between the wars had turned themselves inside out by moving residents from centre to periphery were by the 1980s (in Britain as in America) moving out the big shops as well—a pattern not replicated in European countries stronger in civic culture and weaker in their bucolicism. The proportion of new retail floorspace in Britain assigned to out-of-town sites rose from a seventh in 1960–81 to more than half in 1982–92, more than doubling the overall number of superstores; out-of-town locations accounted for 5 per cent of retail sales in 1980, 37 per cent by 1992.[126] Out of working hours many city centres were becoming little more than leisure zones for the young, offering cafés, late-night bars and clubs, but not much else.[127] From the late 1960s, however, a counter-revolution on urban transport policy began: pedestrian precincts extended,[128] and London in 1968 substituted a cap on parking provision within authorized buildings for its earlier requirement that new commercial buildings should provide their own parking space. More importantly, the only section of London's so-called 'motorway box' of inner-city motorway that was built, the high-level extension of the A40 across North Kensington opened in 1970, got no further. The success of well coordinated local protest against it had implications for similar schemes elsewhere.

Urban frustrations inspired a leader headed 'Are we getting more bloody minded?' in *The Times* on 25 August 1970, and the resulting correspondence targeted planning regulations, growing taxation, services unsupplied, overcrowding, traffic jams, and exhaust fumes. Pollution of the ground, of the air,

---

[124] See e.g. *DT* (4 Nov. 2002), 9.   [125] *FT* (6 June 2000), 3.

[126] Defined as 25,000 square feet in area or more: Royal Commission on Environmental Pollution, *18th Report*, 16.   [127] 'Reclaiming the Night', *Econ* (12 Aug. 2000), 37.

[128] Harrison, *Seeking a Role*, 136–7.

and of silence had already prompted concern before 1970.[129] The pollution stemming from burning coal in urban homes and factories had declined markedly since the 1950s, and by the early 1990s sulphur emissions had halved in the preceding twenty years, compelling many farmers to add sulphur as a top dressing to improve their yields.[130] Urban pollution reappeared in the guise of vehicle exhaust, and differential taxation introduced in 1987 ensured that by 1992 the market-share of unleaded petrol had risen from nil to half.[131] Less tractable was road traffic's pollution of silence. Cities had never been entirely silent, but their noise in public places had been relatively intimate and human in scale—generated by bells, street cries, animals, entertainers, salesmen, fair-grounds, and the like. Secularization drowned out church bells, and inhuman levels of noise complemented urban buildings fashionably inhuman in scale. Although individual older vehicles had been much noisier, the growing bulk of motor traffic ensured that its collective noise continued to creep up after 1970. Street noise escalated like conversation at a party. Emergency vehicles on the ground (ambulances, police cars, fire engines) substituted sirens for bells and were forced to use them more often, at the same time as escalating crime spawned burglar and car alarms. The increasingly congested traffic tempted the affluent into noisy helicopters, and growing air-traffic noise of all kinds depreciated house values across wide urban swathes. By the early 1990s England's tranquil areas had contracted markedly since the early 1960s: noise spreading out from the conurbations and motorways confined tranquillity to the Pennines, the Lake District, the Welsh borders, Cornwall, and parts of East Anglia.[132]

Noise segregated the generations: young people in their music after the 1960s cultivated decibel levels that evoked pained medical comment and complaints from the old. Electronic innovation—amplifiers, microphones, cassette-recorders, car radios, 'ghetto blasters'—were eagerly embraced, and by the 1980s some shops even deployed noise-levels to pre-select their customers by age. Technology does not inevitably escalate noise; the advent of the Walkman cassette-player from the 1980s, for example, enabled people to consume their own noise. The problem lay rather in the uses to which technology was put. Noise was not a problem solely of volume. Many people were more concerned about the prevalence of continuous background noise, and by the 1980s fewer town-dwellers embraced an aural version of W. H. Davies's injunction to stand and stare. Protected from the dark by artificial light, they were now protected from silence by 'musak'. Widely used by the 1950s, it was a device often used to ward off suspicion or fear: loosening shoppers' purses or soothing airline passengers at their moment of greatest danger.

[129] Harrison, *Seeking a Role*, 147–50.   [130] *FT* (28 Feb. 1995), 31.
[131] B. W. Clapp, *An Environmental History of Britain since the Industrial Revolution* (1994), 63.
[132] See the maps in *TCBST* 455.

Between 1967 and 1992 complaints to local authorities about noise rose steadily from 976 to 111,515. In the 1980s complaints rose threefold when related to population, and a third of those surveyed in 1991 said that noise to some extent spoilt their home life.[133] Public authorities could respond with at least three strategies: curbing noise at source, separating it from people, or (if all else failed) insulating people against it. All three strategies gained from the Noise Advisory Council, appointed in 1970 in response to growing dissatisfaction with the Noise Abatement Act (1960). The Council's combination of lay and expert opinion seems to have worked well.[134] To curb noise at source, government could (and, under the Civil Aviation Acts of 1968 and 1971, did) specify flight times for aircraft, as well as maximum noise-levels on take-off and landing. On curbing motor-vehicle noise, the government's powers had been gradually strengthening since 1912: by 1970 horns could not be sounded at night, noise limits had been set for vehicles in use, with lower limits prescribed for new vehicles; by 1973 prosecutions for noisy vehicles were running at the level of 14,000 a year.[135] In British car factories noise was 'a remorseless enemy of quality everywhere', if only because it hindered employees from listening for defects.[136] By no means all curbing of noise was planned. Its export to foreign eardrums was for the UK an incidental benefit of allowing late twentieth-century British heavy industry to decline, for instance, and it was changing technology (the word-processor) that freed office-workers and printers from clattering typewriters and typesetting machines.

For the second strategy, separating people from noise, the plans of the 1970s for motorways and new airports, environmentally harmful from some points of view, were beneficial; this was one impulse behind the government's scheme for a third London airport at Maplin, for example. On road traffic, the Wilson Committee saw traffic planning as a remedy, and favoured creating residential precincts excluding all but very local traffic.[137] The Advisory Council took up the 'noise abatement zone' concept on the analogy of the successful smoke-free zones, and the idea was incorporated into the Control of Pollution Act (1974). But such zones were difficult to designate and police, and of the fifty-eight designated since 1976, only eighteen were still being enforced in 1995.[138] As for the third strategy, insulation, government grants were available from 1966 for sound-proofing homes affected by aircraft noise and public works, and the Factory Acts incorporated powers to ensure employees' insulation against noise at work. The research of William Burns and D. W. Robinson

---

[133] HC Deb. 16 Feb. 1996, c. 1252. Social Trends (1996), 189, 191.
[134] Lord Sandford, HL Deb. 14 Mar. 1973, c. 367.
[135] Lord Sandys, HL Deb. 14 Mar. 1973, c. 357.   [136] G. Turner, The Car Makers (1963), 167.
[137] Sir A. Wilson (Chairman), Committee on the Problem of Noise, Final Report (Cmnd. 2056; 1963), 30, 133.
[138] C. N. Penn, Noise Control: The Law and its Enforcement (1st publ. 1979, 2nd edn. 1995), 114.

on noise's impact on health, published in their *Hearing and Noise in Industry* (1970), made it easier to focus such legislation, and for the first time in Britain a court in 1971 awarded damages for deafness caused by noise at work.[139]

The sheer complexity of urban planning should now be clear, yet it was a highly paradoxical post-war disappointment that British town life was in some respects impoverished by the people keenest to improve it: the planners and the architects. Enthusiasts for modernity with their philosophy of demolition, they complemented Hitler's bombs by laying waste large urban tracts. By 1970 the 'new town' ideal was in decline, though Milton Keynes retained its centralized road system, small-neighbourhood plan, and enclosing boundary.[140] By then the conservationists were up in arms about what the planners had done to Bath: Lord Clark was 'amazed to see' its municipal authority colluding to destroy 'the most beautiful city in England'.[141] Lees-Milne's diaries at this time deplored well-intentioned vandalism not only in Bath, but in Edinburgh's Royal Mile and in Shropshire's small towns.[142] Alison Murray, on leaving Northam station in Margaret Drabble's *The Ice Age* (1977), found that its façade and nearby shops had been knocked down, and she 'was confronted by an enormous roundabout, the beginning of a flyover, a road leading to a multi-storey car park, and an underpass'. After 'she had struggled along for a few hundred yards, in the stink of carbon monoxide, shuffling through litter, walled in by high elephantine walls, deafened and sickened, she was feeling extremely cross . . . This was no improvement: this was an environmental offence as bad as a slag heap.' What Betjeman called 'a devastating book',[143] lavishly illustrated, *The Rape of Britain* (1975), juxtaposed on the one hand unplanned but varied and pleasant groups of buildings, human in scale, that were destined for demolition; and on the other hand the standardized and awful car parks, tower blocks, and widened roads that replaced them. The part-time conservationist seemed to have little chance when confronted by full-time promoters of corporate greed conspiring in their committees.

Nonetheless, comprehensive redevelopment did eventually succumb before conservation as the planning mood of the 1970s, with a new valuation for human scale and local identity. Britain is 'pensioning off the bulldozer', Environment Secretary Peter Shore announced in 1976. No longer would redevelopment be comprehensive or clearance large-scale; instead there would be gradual renewal

---

[139] *HL Deb.* 14 Mar. 1973, c. 352 (Summerskill).

[140] S. E. Rasmussen, in D. Walker, *The Architecture and Planning of Milton Keynes* (1982), 3.

[141] Letter in *T* (18 July 1972), 13.

[142] Lees-Milne, *Mingled Measure*, 216 (17 Mar. 1972), 225 (21 Apr. 1972), 230 (1 May 1972), 256 (30 June 1972) on Bath; 138 (5 Oct. 1971) on Edinburgh; *Ancient as the Hills: Diaries 1973–1974* (1997), 9 (19 Jan. 1973).

[143] M. Drabble, *The Ice Age* (1st publ. 1977, paperback edn. 1978), 168. Betjeman, preface to C. Amery and D. Cruickshank, *The Rape of Britain* (1975), 7.

and rehabilitation.[144] Conservation as a concept was opening out from concern for individual buildings to safeguarding their immediate surroundings, and from there to conserving the local, then the national, and then the world environment. From outsider-protest against architects and planners, conservationists were becoming insiders incorporated into the planning process: 'the economics of conservation', said Viscount Esher in 1973, 'must in principle boil down to this: to conserve by planning so as to avoid having to conserve by spending'.[145] Between 1967 and 1973 conservation areas grew from nil to 2,288, and civic societies affiliated to the Civic Trust doubled. By 1973 the government was subsidizing four national amenity societies: the Society for the Protection of Ancient Buildings, the Georgian Group, the Victorian Society, and the Ancient Monuments Society—'an astonishingly rapid turnabout in opinion'.[146] This was a time when conservationists of many varieties participated with ultimate success in the long-drawn-out battle to preserve London's vacated Covent Garden market area from comprehensive redevelopment. In an alliance with the *Evening Standard*'s editor Simon Jenkins, Betjeman campaigned against London's further desecration, and as a long-standing enthusiast for trips to Southend he helped launch the National Piers Society in 1979. A further landmark in London preservationism was the rejection by the inquiry appointed in 1985 of a scheme for a posthumous Mies van der Rohe tower block near the Mansion House.

By 1973 the listing of buildings was advancing by 20,000 a year, having risen in six years from 100,000 to 170,000.[147] This was partly because protection's chronological frontier was ever extending. In 1980 Trafalgar House property developers hastily demolished the Firestone building on the Great West Road in advance of its consideration for spot-listing,[148] thus highlighting the need to preserve inter-war art deco factories. This was to the Thirties Society what the Euston Arch's destruction had been to the Victorian Society eighteen years before. In 1970 Pevsner, a crusader for modernism, had left non-modernist gaps when recommending inter-war buildings for preservation: the Thirties Society now sought to fill them, but from the start the Society addressed itself to the entire period after 1914, rechristening itself the Twentieth Century Society in 1992. Commercialism redeemed itself with conservationists in that year, however, by one striking piece of altruism, the relatively well-mannered Sainsbury extension to the National Gallery; and by one notable success in reconciling public and private interest: Tesco's restoration of the remarkable art deco Hoover Building in Perivale. Till 1988 government excluded from listing all buildings erected after 1939, but conservation bodies then got the

[144] *T* (4 June 1976), 7; cf. (15 May 1976), 2.   [145] *HL Deb.* 11 Apr. 1973, c. 655.
[146] Earl Jellicoe, *HL Deb.* 11 Apr. 1973, cc. 670, 674.   [147] *HL Deb.* 11 Apr. 1973, c. 668.
[148] S. Jenkins, 'Downfall of a Workingman's Palace', *O* (31 Aug. 1980), 2.

Department of the Environment to consider all buildings up to thirty years old. By the following year the UK's listed buildings totalled 434,000, and in 1991 the Department agreed to list its newest building, the Willis Faber office building in Ipswich, completed in 1975. By the early 1990s one in forty of the country's total stock of buildings was listed as of 'special architectural or historic interest', nearly all of them privately owned.[149]

During the 1970s the reaction against the modern style, already revving up in the mid-1960s,[150] went into full throttle. Economic setbacks bring benefits if they hold back a relatively expensive, insensitive, and taxpayer-funded architectural style. By 1982, when the Barbican Centre for Arts and Conferences opened, the doubts about spending so much on so inaccessible and intimidating a set of buildings had been vindicated.[151] The Prince of Wales won much publicity through telling the Royal Institute of British Architects that the initial proposal for the National Gallery's extension in 1984 was 'a kind of vast municipal fire station . . . like a monstrous carbuncle on the face of a much loved and elegant friend'; he questioned whether architects and planners 'have the monopoly of knowing what is best about taste, style and planning'. He remained on the attack: deploring the planners' destruction of the London skyline; likening Colin St John Wilson's British Library to 'an academy for secret policemen'; proclaiming Birmingham's famous Bull Ring development as possessing 'no charm, no human scale, no character except arrogance . . . a planned accident'; championing the ideal of a 'community architecture', more human in scale; and defending the layman against the professions' pretensions. 'The professionals have been doing it their way, thanks to the planning legislation, for the last 40 years', he said in 1987. 'We, poor mortals, are forced to live in the shadow of their achievements.'[152] Informing the attack on high-rise was a changed concept of space: whereas high-rise's early champions owed much to the ideal of the city in a park, their successors were already by the early 1960s acknowledging the less windswept attractions of the small enclosed open-air private area, earlier dismissively associated with the slum. The relationship between public and private was being more subtly appreciated: neighbourliness did not necessarily benefit from making all open space accessible to all.[153]

Hoping in December 1987 for a rebuilt London skyline, the Prince told the annual dinner of the Corporation of London's planning and communications committee that property developers and design consultants had been more

[149] *This Common Inheritance*, 132. *Ind* (29 July 1992), 4.   [150] Harrison, *Seeking a Role*, 153–60.
[151] B. Appleyard, 'The City's Dated Dream of Urban Bliss', *T* (22 July 1981), 15.
[152] Quotations from Dimbleby, *Prince of Wales*, 316–17. Paul Vallely, interview with Wilson, *Ind* (3 Nov. 1997), 13. *FT* (13 Dec. 1990), 8. *T* (2 Dec. 1987), 24.
[153] M. Glendinning and S. Muthesius, *Tower Block: Modern Public Housing in England, Scotland, Wales and Northern Ireland* (New Haven and London, 1994), 143–4.

destructive than the Luftwaffe.[154] With their pride wounded and their tone defensive, the architects' counter-attack was feeble.[155] Their impulse had been their desire to give more people better housing, and their success at first seemed patent. After all, each house now offered better facilities for fewer occupants, and the proportion of the population sharing or lacking baths, hot-water supply, or lavatories steadily declined to a tiny proportion.[156] Nonetheless, high-rise architects had simultaneously armed Conservatives with a weapon against the sixties, and by implication against planning and progressivism generally. Heseltine in 1980 was already linking planning with dreary and standardized architecture.[157] In 1987 Thatcher reminded the Conservative Party conference of the planning disasters of the 1960s: 'the schemes won a number of architectural awards. But they were a nightmare for the people . . . they made people entirely dependent on the local authorities'.[158] The Thatcherite mansion consigned to its doghouse state-funded architects together with academic economists, sociologists, trade unionists, and socialists. The publicly financed building of the 1960s was discredited partly because of the scandals flowing from its funding,[159] but mainly because the experience of occupying it revealed how poor was its execution, how ill-suited it was to the British weather, and how inadequately its open-plan interiors catered for occupants' desire to conserve fuel and privacy. The graffiti that spread over any available urban flat surface in the 1980s, from Canberra to Chicago, as well as in large British cities, represented an inarticulate protest against what the sixties had done: they were a visual equivalent of the 'musak' and disc-jockey babble with which increasing numbers adorned their silence. Some even saw them as introducing a human dimension to those grey concrete surfaces.

All the more reason, then, to destroy these concrete monsters. In 1992 the nineteen-storey towers of the Department of the Environment's twenty-one-year-old Marsham Street buildings were so unloved, so ruinous to Westminster's skyline, internally so inconvenient and so urgently needing repair that it was decided to demolish them within five years. On demolition day the Environment Secretary was eager to push the plunger. 'We have decided to knock it down', Heseltine announced.[160] So complete was the reaction against the modern style that preservationists began campaigning late in the 1980s to protect some of what many then saw as its ugliest manifestations before it was too late. The Queen Elizabeth Hall, embedded inside

---

[154] *ST* (24 Dec. 1989), 4.   [155] See e.g. Lasdun's defence of Le Corbusier, *ST* (12 Apr. 1987), 17.

[156] *BST* 374, 380–1.   [157] Speech at the British architects' annual conference, *T* (19 July 1980), 4.

[158] M. Thatcher, *Speeches to the Conservative Party Conference 1975–1988* (1989), 128; cf. Major at the party conference in *DT* (9 Oct. 1993), 10.

[159] For an obituary of John Poulson see *T* (4 Feb. 1993), 19.

[160] *Ind* (7 Feb. 1992), 3; cf. M. Cassell 'Nightmare on Marsham St', *FT* (17 Dec. 1993), 18, and leader in *T* (7 Jan. 1991), 9.

the faceless concrete wilderness with which the sixties had squandered its major opportunity on the South Bank site, was defended as anticipating 'the architecture of services'—an approach carried so much further, and far more imaginatively, in Richard Rogers's Lloyd's Building.[161] By 1993 the schools and university buildings erected since 1945 had begun to win listed status, and the candidacy even of high-rise office and residential buildings was being touted.[162]

The architects could not now maintain a united front. Cracks were already appearing in the modernists' professional edifice by 1961, the year when Pevsner, champion of the modern style, condemned 'what I regard as an alarming recent phenomenon': the return of some modernist architects to historicism, and the associated apostasy from modernism, forsaking the pure reflection of function in form. If architects' personality-cults were reintroducing 'funny turns', the modern style could no longer be seen as uniform, rational, and appropriate to modern living.[163] Pevsner detected heresy in Gowan and Stirling's influential engineering building at Leicester University (1959–63), and disliked Stirling's combination of personal rudeness with his professional pursuit of ugliness.[164] By the 1970s Pevsner's *Buildings of England* had become a national institution, and some of his pupils, most notably David Watkin, were beginning to turn against him. Late twentieth-century modernists divided into late moderns (exponents of hi-tech such as Norman Foster and Richard Rogers, memorably at the Lloyd's Building in 1986 and the Pompidou Centre in 1971–7), and post-moderns such as James Stirling (whose influential extension to the Staatsgalerie in Stuttgart opened in 1984 and combined modernity with tradition). The reaction against the modern style, especially in its monumental aspects, represented a loss of professional self-confidence, a shock to professional status, not paralleled elsewhere in the late twentieth-century fine arts. Reversion to a somewhat populist post-modernist pastiche and parody marked the end of any whiggish notions of progress through professional leadership, and substituted the search for security through harnessing the experience of earlier generations.

Architectural tradition had never been abandoned by a small group of decidedly serious architects who belonged to neither camp. The erection of Sir Thomas Pilkington's country house, King's Walden Bury, in 1971 seems a turning point only in retrospect. This English evocation of Palladio's Italian villas by the lifelong classicist Raymond Erith and his former apprentice Quinlan Terry, partners since 1966, was seen by its creators as proceeding on a plane quite distinct from modernism, faithful to the traditional skills, materials,

[161] By Alexander Chablo in his letter to *T* (11 June 1991), 19.   [162] *IOS* (24 Jan. 1993), 10.
[163] N. Pevsner, 'Modern Architecture and the Historian, or the Return of Historicism', *RIBA Journal* (Apr. 1961), 230. S. Games (ed.), *Pevsner on Art and Architecture: The Radio Talks* (2002), 277.
[164] M. Girouard, *Big Jim: The Life and Work of James Stirling* (1998), 147; see also 300, 301, 307.

and classical scholarship which modernists so enthusiastically repudiated. 'All my life I have been waiting for the revival of architecture...', said Erith in 1971, two years before he died; 'how wonderful it would be. The world could be beautiful again.'[165] Terry carried classicism forward in the 1980s into many new buildings, including Heseltine's summerhouse at Thenford in 1979 and the Riverside development at Richmond from 1985—solid, predictable, reassuring, scholarly. There was an associated revival of the skills involved in conservation: picture restoring, carving, plasterwork, and the like—not to mention the quietly accumulating historical scholarship that owed so much to the magazine *Country Life*. Its architectural editor Christopher Hussey wrote a long series of scholarly articles on individual houses, and his successors as architectural editor (Mark Girouard, John Cornforth, Marcus Binney, and Clive Aslet) were all influential in the same sphere. Binney in 1979 founded Save Britain's Heritage, and Aslet in 1979 became secretary to the Thirties Society.

The reaction against high-rise public housing prompted a resort to relatively densely packed medium-rise substitutes, but also helped to discourage local-authority building for rent altogether. Many problems about high-rise flats that now seem obvious enough emerged only through experience. 'Heaven help me, high blocks', Keith Joseph replied in 1973, when asked how he had won his first ovation at a party conference in 1962.[166] During the 1980s housing like unemployment was downgraded as a political issue: much of the statist strategy for dealing with both had been abandoned. Joseph's renewed enthusiasm for free-market ideas began when he read Alfred Sherman's two articles attacking social engineering in the new towns and in public transport. Sherman noted that enthusiasts for the new towns did not choose to live in them, and claimed that the social engineers had in such places 'destroyed older communities without producing new ones', their casualties including the extended family.[167] In 1979 Birkenhead blew up two high-rise blocks built only twenty-one years earlier, and Salford followed suit in 1990 by blowing up five within an estate of eight nine-storey flats. Frank Allaun, Labour MP for Salford East and author of *Heartbreak Housing* (1966), had felt proud of the estate at first, but 'families wanted their own front door. Mothers wanted a little bit of garden for their children to play in.'[168] When confronted in 1985 with a reproachful Church of England report on the inner city's plight, *Faith in the City*, Conservative ministers did not apologize: public expenditure and ambitious planning under governments of both parties had themselves caused some of the problems the

[165] J. M. Robinson, *The Latest Country Houses 1945–83* (1983), 156. See also R. Hewison, *The Heritage Industry: Britain in a Climate of Decline* (1987), 74.   [166] *G* (12 Nov. 1973), 13.

[167] The articles were in the *DT* (10 and 29 Aug. 1973). See R. Cockett, *Thinking the Unthinkable: Think-Tanks and the Economic Counter-Revolution 1931–1983* (1994), 233.

[168] *G* (15 Oct. 1990), 1. See also *DT* (1 Oct. 1979), 21.

report highlighted, whereas the welcome growth in private ownership pointed to a remedy.[169]

Trends in housing tenure between 1971 and 1990 are clear. In 1971 half the 18.8 million dwellings in Great Britain were owner-occupied, 30 per cent rented from local authorities, and 20 per cent privately rented; of the 22.8 million dwellings in 1990, the equivalent shares were 67, 22, and 8 per cent, but a new category, the 'housing association', accounted for another 3 per cent.[170] Private tenancies shrank continuously in their share, and from the mid-1970s council-house starts made up a declining proportion of total housing starts.[171] Behind these figures lie several major changes. The growing share of owner-occupiers continued an existing trend, which accelerated in the 1980s. More significant was the new prominence of the housing association: a non-profit organization building new homes or improving existing ones which were then rented to the needy. Traditionally it had focused on the needs of particular groups: the elderly, young singles, and people for whom the local authority could not cater; hence much of its housing stock was initially too small for the larger families in the councils' waiting lists. Its role was transformed by reintroducing free-market and voluntarist structures which many had only recently assumed would never return. At the end of the 1980s housing associations were beginning to supplant the local authority in meeting the social need for rented accommodation. The major change was privatization. The Heath government re-echoed Macmillan's zeal for a property-owning democracy with a marked acceleration in council-house sales. These declined markedly under the last Wilson government, but the house-privatizing concept was being seriously considered behind the scenes even then,[172] and under Callaghan's government, sales rose fast.[173] Trends in housing tenure did not change in 1979: they accelerated, because to Labour's acquiescence in a consumer-led demand was added Conservative zeal. The Conservatives took up the case of John Graham, school-crossing supervisor in Manchester. He had tried to buy his council house when the Conservatives controlled the local authority, but its policy was changed under Labour and he lost the chance. He mounted a local protest, appeared in a party-political broadcast, and bought his house when the Housing Act (1980) gave local-authority tenants a statutory right to buy.[174]

Simultaneously with the growth in owner-occupation in the 1980s, council-house rents were forced up to market levels. A combination of carrot and stick

[169] e.g. K. Baker, *HC Deb.* 11 Dec. 1985, cc. 938–45.

[170] J. Newton, *All in One Place: The British Housing Story 1971–1990. A Compilation of Housing Statistics* (1991), 18.   [171] Calculated from figures in *T* (12 Dec. 1984), 15.

[172] J. Haines, *The Politics of Power* (1977), 96, 98, 109–11. B. Donoughue, *Prime Minister: The Conduct of Policy under Harold Wilson and James Callaghan* (1987), 106, 108.

[173] K. Young and N. Rao, *Local Government since 1945* (Oxford, 1997), 167.

[174] *ST* (2 Feb. 1997), i, 7.

ensured that by 1989 1.5 million rented homes (nine-tenths of them previously owned by the local authority) had been sold to their tenants in England and Wales;[175] no less than 43 per cent of receipts from privatization between 1979 and 1989 came from selling publicly owned housing.[176] Thatcher herself participated in the ceremony whereby the millionth council home sold under the Housing Act (1980) was handed over in 1986; by then nearly two-thirds of British homes were owner-occupied.[177] Between 1979 and 2001 a third of Britain's 2.1 million council houses were sold to their tenants.[178] Housing associations' stock, small at the outset, was shrunk further by the Housing Act (1980); its statutory 'right to buy' provision transferred 22,000 association houses into the owner-occupation category between 1981/2 and 1990/1.[179] Yet the Act gave the associations a new role of major long-term importance, and already by 1990 they were building more houses (18,671) than the public sector (4,106), though both totals remained well below that of the private sector (135,252).[180] The long-term decline in slum clearance caused a marked decline in planned annual housing losses throughout the period—almost to vanishing point by the end of the 1980s.[181] So the inter-war balance between local-authority and owner-occupier housing completions was reappearing, with local authorities in 1980–4 building only half as many houses as the private builder in England and Wales. The number of new mortgages taken out annually in Great Britain from building societies was more than twice as high in 1972 as in 1960, and by 1984 more than three times as high.[182] Given the tax incentives to house purchase, this trend is hardly surprising. Not till 1974 was a limit set on the size of the loan whose interest could be set against tax. Mortgage interest relief at source (MIRAS) was in effect a state subsidy on house purchase: it diverted resources from industry and the tax-collector, and even accentuated booms and slumps. Thatcher, so hostile to subsidies elsewhere, ensured that it survived all challenges, even from Lawson, her Chancellor of the Exchequer.

Privatizing council housing in the 1980s advanced several of Thatcher's aims. By encouraging middle-class people to buy into what had hitherto been 'council estates', government policy could prompt self-generating urban improvement. Council houses built for large early twentieth-century working-class families were suitable for the smaller late twentieth-century middle-class families whose self-interest swelled the urban gentrifying tide. Privatization also weakened Labour-controlled local authorities, dispersed power and wealth within the community, and extended to lower social levels the inheritance of

[175] G. C. Baugh, 'Government Grants in Aid of the Rates in England and Wales, 1889–1990', *Historical Research* (1992), 229.   [176] Kavanagh and Seldon (eds.), *Thatcher Effect*, 219.
[177] J. Doling, 'British Housing Policy: 1984–1993', *Regional Studies*, 27/6 (1993), 583.
[178] *Econ* (5 May 2001), 33.   [179] Newton, *All in One Place*, 23.
[180] Doling, 'British Housing Policy', 585.   [181] For useful figures see Newton, *All in One Place*, 22.
[182] *BST* 384 (useful table), 392.

wealth through the family; the Conservative manifesto of 1987 pointed out that owning a house was 'the first step most people take towards building up capital to hand down to their children and grandchildren'.[183] Owner-occupiers were less likely than council tenants to find themselves trapped in one locality for fear of losing their home, and to that extent the labour market became more flexible. The wage incentive for people to move house could be enhanced by eroding nationwide wage-bargaining and by abolishing incomes policies: 'the working population must choose', said Keith Joseph (oversimplifying in 1974 the choice each individual faced), 'between narrow illusory job security in one place propped up by public funds or the real job security based on a prosperous dynamic economy'.[184]

The entire housing market became more flexible. The large council house might still be needed for the diminishing number of large working-class families, but social change now enhanced the demand for smaller houses from equally needy groups: the one-parent family, the divorced, the aged, and the infirm living alone or in sheltered accommodation—especially now that the old were no longer being prematurely institutionalized. Smaller families, higher expectations, second homes, and longer life ensured that the number of households grew faster than the population. The one-person household's share of all households rose steadily from 7 per cent in 1931 to 24 per cent in 1985, included the growing number of young single and old widowed people living alone, and reflected among other things the twentieth century's diminished fertility. The aged, the divorced, the unmarried, and the childless were more likely to live on their own, and by 1983 nearly a quarter of Great Britain's households consisted of only one person.[185] Whereas in 1951 families shared homes in a fifth of households in England and Wales, thereafter the inter-war trend towards one family per household resumed, and by 1991 only 3 per cent of homes in England were shared. There was a growing twentieth-century tendency for houses to be detached (a fifth of those built in 1945–64, but more than a half after 1980), though built on smaller plots.[186] Owner-occupied houses could vary in size with the life-cycle. The owner-occupier could begin with a one-bedroom 'starter home', an American term which had arrived in Britain by 1980. The well-known British housebuilder Lawrie Barratt[187] promoted the concept in the 1980s; his homes for the mass market were advertised on television; his starter homes tempted the young into the housing market by providing everything built-in and a 100 per cent mortgage. The owner-occupier once launched could move on to a three-bedroom town-house or semi-detached house, then aspire to a detached and gardened home if affluent.

[183] I. Dale (ed.), *Conservative Party General Election Manifestos 1900–1997* (2000), 317.
[184] Speech on 14 Dec. 1974, *T* (16 Dec. 1974), 2.   [185] *BST* 20, 119.
[186] *TCBST* 483–4, 481.
[187] For portraits of Barratt see *DT* (31 July 1991), 17; *O* (28 Sept. 1997), business section, 9.

All these were rungs in what was increasingly seen as a housing ladder which during the life-cycle was first climbed, then descended. In later life retirement income could be boosted by downshifting, perhaps even to the extent of buying a permanent plumbed-in caravan home. By 1975 between 170,000 and 200,000 people were living in caravans,[188] with 'sheltered accommodation' (a term which came into use in the mid-1970s) as the final owner-occupied destination for the newly abundant 'fourth generation'.

Builders eagerly catered for the owner-occupiers' demand. Brand-new suburban estates with pennants flying and brightly coloured billboards sprang up on the edge of cities, tempting the passer-by to savour their pseudo-Georgian bow-fronts and their bogus Tudor gables. Barratt sold the Thatchers an up-market variant behind security gates and walls in Dulwich. For devotees of the bauhaus style this was a nightmare, and yet these pastiche homes responded to a deep-rooted British bucolicism and pride in ownership: once a nation of shopkeepers, the British people had become, unusually in Europe, a nation of house-owners. Owner-occupation emancipated the householder from council regulation, and encouraged the housing stock's continuous and spontaneous improvement. Social advancement occurred through buying a new house, but also through improving the old. In the century's concluding three decades, second cars shuttled between do-it-yourself-stores and freezer-centres, converting the up-market suburban home into a cross between warehouse and factory. In a continuously busy pursuit of home design and home improvement, today's luxuries became tomorrow's necessities, with indoor lavatories, pinch-pleat curtains, wall-to-wall carpets, built-in wardrobes and cupboards, showers, patio doors, minibars, second bathrooms, satellite dishes, television aerials, conservatories, double garages, and swimming pools chasing one another through the decades as symbols of status. All this nourished Conservative values and Conservative voting.

If the Thatcher governments could have responded merely to instinct, their free-market philosophy would have led them vigorously to revive the housing market's privately rented sector. Its relative prosperity helped to render American labour geographically much more mobile than British, and encouraged better-off Europeans to pursue an urban lifestyle. But in this area of policy, as so often, the Thatcher governments gathered momentum only slowly. With rent reform, as with industrial relations, an obvious policy had to be pursued cautiously so as to ward off confrontation and ensure that further elections were won: it was not politically feasible to end rent control, or even to channel housing subsidy neutrally according to need as between owner-occupiers on the one hand and privately renting tenants on the other. The Housing Act (1980) introduced two new types of tenancy, shortholds and assured tenancies, in the

---

[188] *HL Deb.* 22 May 1975, c. 1508.

hope of attracting private investment, but still the privately rented sector did not revive. Late in the 1980s there was at last an arrest to its long-term decline: for all new lettings, and with due safeguards, the Housing Act (1988) freed landlords from the fair rents system of the Rent Act (1965).

The Conservatives' substantial housing reforms of the 1980s left at least three problems behind. The first was short-term, but alarming for those involved. Government subsidy of the owner-occupier had seduced people into buying their own houses, and not till the early 1990s was the real value of mortgage interest relief allowed to fall. By then the economy's downturn had caused house prices to fall, trapping in negative equity many of those skilled and semi-skilled manual workers who had earlier been tempted to buy; many now also lacked the jobs which had earlier enabled them to keep up their mortgage payments. The total of UK borrowers who were at least six months behind with their mortgage payments rose from over 70,000 in 1985 to over 350,000 in 1992.[189] A second problem was the fact that expanded owner-occupation did not loosen up the labour market as much as had been hoped. Already by 1973 there were more houses than households in England, but they were not always in the right places: the surplus lay in the East Midlands, West Riding and north-east, whereas the need lay elsewhere.[190] By the early 1980s only 29 per cent of the English population lived in state housing, whereas the equivalent figure for Scotland was 58 per cent; high-rise building in the 1960s rendered Glasgow 'the foremost exponent of high-rise living in Europe'.[191] The new owner-occupiers were usually in the areas of fullest employment, mostly in south-eastern England; there prices became so high as to ward off intruders from less prosperous areas where rented accommodation was simultaneously scarce. Even those unemployed people in the north who wanted to move could hardly have afforded to do so without staying in cheap hostels during the week and travelling home at weekends—as, indeed, some did. So in its housing dimension, Thatcher's policy unintentionally accentuated the north–south divide.[192] Insult seemed added to injury when Edwina Currie, a newly promoted social security minister, carried from the south to the twentieth-century north the self-help preachment that the north had carried to the nineteenth-century south. Denying any simple link between ill-health and poverty, she told northerners that their health lay largely in their own hands: they should smoke and drink less and lace their diet with healthier food.[193]

---

[189] Doling, 'British Housing Policy', 584.　　　[190] HL Deb. 21 Mar. 1973, c. 847.

[191] I. H. Adams in C. M. Clapperton (ed.), Scotland. A New Study (Newton Abbot, 1983), 165–6.

[192] For figures see Seldon and Kavanagh (eds.), Thatcher Effect, 220. C. Hamnett, 'The Political Geography of Housing in Contemporary Britain', in J. Mohan (ed.), The Political Geography of Contemporary Britain (Basingstoke and London, 1989), 218–19.

[193] G (24 Sept. 1986), 1. T (6 Oct. 1986), 2.

There was, thirdly, a significant long-term consequence of Thatcher's housing policy: it segregated the 'underclass' geographically.[194] With her third successive general election victory behind her in 1987 she set about rejuvenating the inner cities, and was famously photographed in September walking—in a smart suit and 'sensible shoes' complete with handbag and every hair in place—into weed-ridden derelict land in Teesside where an engineering works had once stood (Plate 5).[195] Unemployment was rife in the area, and hers was a two-pronged assault: on social need, but also simultaneously on Labour's heartland. 'Nowhere are the damaging effects of dependence and socialism seen more clearly than in some of our inner cities', she emphasized.[196] With council and private rents gradually pushed up to market levels, and with the best council houses sold off, the authorities now had to make the less attractive council houses saleable, and encourage their tenants to buy them. This was difficult, given that remaining 'council estates' were at risk of entering a downward spiral: the far-sighted and the provident moved out, diminishing numbers chose to move in, empty properties were vandalized, petty crime and graffiti proliferated, and councils found the remaining properties unsaleable and even uninhabitable. By the early 1990s such places witnessed vendettas between the police and unemployed male youths.[197] The Meadow Well estate in North Shields became notorious in 1991. For Heseltine, then promoting his City Challenge scheme whereby urban authorities competed for inner-city regeneration funds,[198] the estate was 'one of the most disgraceful examples of local authority-managed estates I have ever seen'; the local authority 'should be ashamed of themselves', he added, for dumping problem families there and then deserting them.[199] When launching her crusade for the inner cities, Thatcher admitted that she had no new policies to offer, and was merely seeking to make the old policies succeed.[200] The complexity of the problems involved, the onset of the depression, and the difficulty of getting the relevant civil servants coordinated all explain why the crusade achieved less than had been hoped.[201]

By the 1970s it was assumed that almost all adults wanted a permanent home; even young people pursuing a migrant lifestyle in the 1960s claimed to be seeking one. The squats of the 1960s culminated with the non-violent occupation in 1973 of Centre Point, which had lain empty for nine years, 'the symbol of everything rotten in our society'.[202] Young runaways to London

---

[194] For more on this see Harrison, *Seeking a Role*, 213, 329; and pp. 175–83 below.
[195] *DT* (17 Sept. 1987), 13. See also *Ind* (13 June 1987), 6.   [196] *DT* (25 June 1987), 1.
[197] For a good discussion see the Joseph Rowntree Foundation's *Findings*, 116 (June 1997).
[198] *FT* (1 Aug. 1991), 16.
[199] *FT* (14 Nov. 1991), 9. *T* (14 Nov. 1991), 2. See also *FT* (14 Sept. 1991), 6.
[200] For the launch see *FT* (8 Mar. 1988), 8.   [201] *FT* (7 Sept. 1990), 22. G (6 Mar. 1991), 25.
[202] Jim Radford, director of Blackfriars Settlement and leader of the demonstration, *T* (19 Jan. 1974), 1. Peter Walker in June 1972 had promised that, unless the practice ceased, he would legislate to

and occupants of cardboard boxes on the Thames embankment evoked much concern. 'Voluntary vagabondage' was becoming 'an ever-increasing aspect of the youth life of the great cities', said Lord Soper in 1973, claiming that the young accounted for about half London's 11,000 homeless people.[203] The television programme *Johnny Go Home* (1975) highlighted the problem of young people arriving anonymously in London, with immediate risk of sexual exploitation. There was growing preoccupation with so-called 'new age travellers'. Their migrant habits, their unkempt appearance, their trespassing on farmland, and their eagerness to claim welfare benefits seemed to threaten domesticity's entire value-system. The Home Secretary in 1986 likened them to 'a band of mediaeval brigands',[204] and there were much-publicized confrontations with the police. Fears were accentuated by the travellers' mixing with young middle-class enthusiasts for rave music and drugs at the many open-air music festivals then springing up like mushrooms, for 'travelling' had a mixed pedigree: partly in gypsies and fairground people, partly in the hippies of the 1960s seeking an alternative lifestyle.[205] Thatcher's housing policy did, however, bring at least one eye-catching purely local payoff. As chief executive of Teesside Development Corporation, Duncan Hall was by February 1991 presiding over the regeneration of 'Teesdale', the renamed derelict area where Thatcher had been photographed walking in 1987. Offices, houses, shops, leisure facilities, and new waterways were by then conveying a 'Venetian feel', and in him at least, she had won a significant admirer: 'her visit here', he said, 'was the best thing that ever happened to us'.[206]

4. COMMUNITIES OLD AND NEW

Many of the trends so far discussed threatened the town's community sense. With middle-class residence and even commercial activity decanted to the sub-urbs, with streets dividing rather than uniting neighbourhoods, with transport and recreation increasingly privatized, and with urban homes turning in upon themselves, there was far more scope within the public sphere for vandalism, petty crime, and violence. The family car might bring cohesion to the family, but at the expense of cohesion in the wider community. The advance of anonymity and standardization symbolized the local community's erosion. The sheer size of modern cities had long been weakening their corporate feeling, and the single-city parliamentary constituency had been disappearing since the 1880s. From the late 1960s the Post Office encouraged letter-writers to use

---

prevent non-ratepaying property companies from holding London office blocks empty while their value appreciated, *HC Deb*. 26 June 1972, cc. 1094–5.

[203] *HL Deb*. 16 Apr. 1973, cc. 993, 995.   [204] *DT* (4 June 1986), 36.
[205] For a good discussion see 'The Travellers' Club', *Econ* (15 Aug. 1992), 19.
[206] *G* (4 Feb. 1991), 6.

an impersonal postcode, and in 1969 John Ticehurst, for one, in a letter to *The Times*, claimed that postcodes could never be remembered like the old districts: 'I for one will never sink so low as to sully the envelopes I use with such absurdities.' Nonetheless, by the finance-year 1970/1 71 per cent of all mail specified the postcode correctly.[207] Telephone numbers were going the same way. Until the 1960s they had reflected locality: Londoners dialled MAYfair or ABBey, for instance. In 1965, however, this ceased for two reasons: many exchanges by then had no recognizable geographical connection, and Subscriber Trunk Dialling increased the pressures on the system, so more codes were needed than the old only partially numeric system could offer. For Betjeman in 1975 the culmination of urban anonymity was the redevelopment scheme: 'places cease to have names, they become areas with a number. Houses become housing, human scale is abandoned.'[208]

This relatively anonymous and increasingly meritocratic society either lacked or spurned the personal knowledge earlier thought necessary for assigning people to jobs, and required substitute specialisms, occupational and even electronic. The 'headhunter', for example, could prosper only in a society which attached less importance to personal connection and long-term loyalty. This American concept crossed the Atlantic from the early 1980s: too much well-paid talent was eager to move for 'placing' through the traditional informal structures to be feasible.[209] Changes in the marriage market carried the loss of community to its ultimate. Family, locality, and 'background' had once been central to selecting a partner, with contacts promoted through the community's integrating social institutions. Now partners were increasingly chosen within national and even international firms, universities, and professions. Matchmaking periodicals such as the *Matrimonial Times* (which survived till 1961) emerged, together with marriage bureaux, of which by 1980 there were between 60 and 100 in Britain. A *Sunday Times* survey in that year was not impressed with the fifteen it contacted: 'very few seemed able to deliver on their promises. Behind all the comforting phrases, all too often we found a one-room postal address, a depressingly small list of prospective partners and the hand of an entrepreneur making profit from the shuffling of human loneliness.'[210] From the 1960s, however, the computer was livening things up: the phrase 'computer dating' arrived in Britain from the USA in the mid-1960s, and by 1966 Britain had three computerized introduction agencies,[211] either owning their own computers or hiring time on them.

---

[207] *T* (20 June 1969), 9 (Ticehurst). J. F. Raper, D. Rhind, and J. Shepard, *Postcodes: The New Geography* (Harlow, 1992), 49.　　[208] Preface to Amery and Cruckshank, *Rape of Britain*, 7.
[209] For a useful discussion see *FT* (6 July 2000), 23.　　[210] *ST* (28 Dec. 1980), 9.
[211] H. S. Pearce, 'Contemporary Matchmaking: A Sociological Study of Dating Agencies and "Lonely Hearts" Columns' (Bedford College London Ph.D. thesis, 1982), 59, 152–3. See also H. Jenner, *Marriages are Made on Earth* (Newton Abbot, 1979), 140.

The urban population remained almost stationary in absolute and proportionate terms after 1951. In 1981 it accounted for nine-tenths of the population in England and Wales, and filled a steadily rising proportion of its land mass: one-seventh by that year.[212] In 1985 the Archbishop of Canterbury's report on urban priority areas publicized the declining urban sense of community. Subtitled 'a call for action by church and nation', the report was ecumenical in tone, and was compiled by churchmen, sociologists, and laymen. It emphasized that any social polarization in Britain was not between north and south, but within both: that is, between urban-priority and other areas. 'It is now the large housing estates in the inner ring or on the fringes of the cities', it declared, 'that present the most pressing urban problem.' It claimed that 'migration has been selectively reversed, and the inner city is increasingly the territory of those left behind in the scramble for comfortable survival', with the less affluent inner-city residue afforced by successive waves of immigrants. Such areas all too often became 'in effect "separate territories" outside the mainstream of our social and economic life'. They could be identified by the burglar alarms and sirens to ward off car theft that were so often heard in such places. The report deplored middle-class flight; even clergymen got their children educated elsewhere, privately if necessary.[213] When inner-city areas were assessed in 1984 against criteria of deprivation (levels of unemployment, broken families, overcrowded housing, population decline, ethnic background, and so on), London boroughs contributed ten of the twelve worst cases in England, headed by Hackney, Lambeth, and Brent.[214]

Even in the suburbs the middle-class refugee found a community less vibrant than twenty years earlier, if only because birth control, home mechanization, the new media, and mass car ownership made suburban homes smaller, more secluded, and more self-sufficient. Children were being more carefully shielded against new or newly perceived hazards, and women's advance into the labour market now denied the suburb its social cement: the daytime presence of wives and mothers bringing up their children and operating suburban networks. On the suburban weekday there was often nobody at home. The shared communal accoutrements of neighbourly urban and suburban life—churches, chapels, pubs, tea-shops, coffee mornings, bridge afternoons, public lavatories, public baths, public transport, public phone-boxes—were all in decline. Only slowly did it become apparent that these communal facilities had merely filled the transitional gap between no facilities at all and facilities becoming available within every home. Conservatives were by no means unconcerned at the situation, and the Merseyside task-force was launched as a short-term response

---

[212] *BST* 325–6.

[213] Quotations from *Faith in the City: A Call for Action by Church and Nation. The Report of the Archbishop of Canterbury's Commission on Urban Priority Areas* (1985), 176, 8, 175; see also 131.

[214] *BST* 343.

to the Toxteth riots of 1981. Within five years Glasgow had become the model for inner-city task-forces,[215] and it was increasingly recognized that a locality's visual impact and cultural opportunities, as well as its labour relations, were what drew in talent and funds. Refurbished waterfronts and marinas could be integral to such developments: Liverpool's huge Albert Dock complex was the most striking example, but Leeds, Birmingham, and Manchester were among the cities whose urban waterway vistas, hitherto concealed, now opened up. Nonetheless, Conservative self-help led ineluctably towards owner-occupation and the suburbs, and the growing ease of travel ensured that towns steadily encroached on the countryside. 'Wherever I drive in southern England today', said Heseltine in 1988, 'the place is being torn up and torn apart.' The problem the high-rise planners had earlier rightly identified, suburban sprawl, was worsened by the synthetic Tudorbethan and even Victorian subtopias of the 1980s. By 1988 the leading architectural historian Sir James Richards was arguing for a return to the human scale of the eighteenth and nineteenth centuries' more compact urban planning.[216]

People's growing taste for moving within the UK emerges from the mapping of surnames, which had been fixed in the fifteenth century. So great were subsequent movements in population that surnames with a regional origin had by the 1980s almost completely dispersed.[217] Geographically remarkably static at first, surnames slowly spread out from their heartlands. Easier, cheaper, and faster travel had long been eroding loyalty to locality, and the Isle of Man exemplifies the trend, accentuated later by its offshore financial status: the proportion of Manx-born inhabitants fell steadily with each census from 1841, and in 1991 was for the first time overtaken by the elsewhere-born, with 51 per cent.[218] Middle-class social mobility prompted their relative geographical mobility, especially when after 1945 universities moved towards recruiting nationally rather than locally.[219] Reinforcing dispersal after 1970 were changes in family patterns. This mobility had implications for community at all levels from neighbourhood to city to county to region and even to nation. Far fewer MPs now had any residential connection with their constituency,[220] and the county, once such a significant political unit, no longer carried much resonance. The merging of town and country was acknowledged in the local government reform of 1972 in England and Wales, which designated six conurbations (Greater London, the West Midlands, South-East Lancashire,

[215] *G* (3 Feb. 1986), 2. For the riots, see below pp. 525–6, 529–30.
[216] Heseltine, *DT* (14 Mar. 1988), 5. Richards, *T* (20 May 1988), 17, and rejoinder from W. Thomas (3 June), 17. See also S. Gardiner, 'No Place like Home', *O* (8 Nov. 1981), 35.
[217] Coleman and Salt, *British Population*, 214.
[218] J. Belchem, *A New History of the Isle of Man*, v. *The Modern Period 1830–1999* (Liverpool, 2000), 421, 426, 432.   [219] Harrison, *Seeking a Role*, 360, and the website www.surnameprofiler.org.
[220] S. A. Walkland (ed.), *The House of Commons in the Twentieth Century: Essays by Members of the Study of Parliament Group* (Oxford, 1979), 87–8.

West Yorkshire, Merseyside, and Tyneside) as metropolitan counties. Such large administrative units were inevitably impersonal, and could never attract the loyalty once harnessed by their component cities. Constituency boundary change had been decanting Conservative voters from city centres to the suburbs since the 1880s, and a century later all the conurbations in England and Wales were losing population. By 2000 they accounted for more than a third of the population in England and Wales, but this was a smaller proportion than at any other twentieth-century period; between 1961 and 1991, for example, London lost 16 per cent of its population, Merseyside 18 per cent.[221]

Add to all this the temporary mobility stemming from new patterns of recreation. Second homes, of which there were more than 180,000 in England and Wales in 1970, mostly in coastal or rural areas and in Wales,[222] arguably involved pursuing two communities rather than one, but an inevitably diluted commitment to each. Second homes were less continuously built into the seasonal routines of British households (only 3 per cent of which owned them in 1980) than in Sweden (20 per cent) and France (18 per cent);[223] three-quarters of British second-home owners in 1972 used them for holidays, but a tenth had earmarked them for eventual retirement. Although many East End families had owned them between the wars, second-home owning, in the 1970s as earlier, was a predominantly middle-class trait.[224] By the end of the decade their number was growing at the rate of 25,000 a year, with inhabitants of conurbations in the Midlands and north-west temporarily migrating to second homes predominantly in Wales and the south-west of England.[225] By the 1970s the trend had fully begun towards self-catering in British holidays; more than two-fifths of holiday nights in Britain in 1976 were spent in this way,[226] and more and more 'mobile homes' were shuttling between suburban driveways and caravan parks. Tourism also had the effect of converting some British communities into recreational non-communities, hosts for fluctuating tides of short-term visitors. British equivalents of Bruges and Florence appeared in Oxford, Stratford-on-Avon, and Cambridge, and London like all European capital cities accommodated more and more late twentieth-century visitors. Quietness, the environment, and whole ways of life were endangered thereby.

The success of Norfolk's 'Singing Postman', Allan Smethurst, with his record of the dialect song 'Hev Yew Gotta Loight, Boy' (1964), showed the continued potential of dialect for comedy, and the stir caused in parliament by

[221] *TCBST* 419.

[222] C. L. Bielckus, A. W. Rogers, and G. P. Wibberley, *Second Homes in England and Wales* (Wye College Studies in Rural Land Use, Report 11; Dec. 1972), 39.

[223] A. D. King (ed.), *Buildings and Society: Essays on the Social Development of the Built Environment* (1980), 194.   [224] Bielckus, *Second Homes*, 43, 51.

[225] C. Bollom, *Attitudes and Second Homes in Rural Wales* (Cardiff, 1978), 1.

[226] *T* (22 Aug. 1977), 3.

Thatcher's use of the Lincolnshire dialect word 'frit' in 1983[227] demonstrated the continued dominance there of 'received pronunciation'. Nonetheless, a regional accent was becoming fashionable by the 1980s, and the academics endorsed the new linguistic egalitarianism by claiming that no one dialect or accent was culturally superior, thus rendering the elocutionist redundant. Within England after 1970, and with men setting the pace, regional accents gained ground over the south-east's 'received pronunciation' to such an extent that an Americanized equality of status between all educated regional accents seemed imminent.[228] There was significant cultural change in Wales, too: the Welsh language's enhanced status in education and government ensured that by the 1980s Welsh-speaking was no longer confined to north Wales, but was reviving among young people further south and east.[229] There was also a notable late twentieth-century resurgence of non-metropolitan culture. Environmental change after 1970 was slowly outdating the tenacious fictional stereotype of the contrast between north and south. Examples of major cultural developments outside London after 1970 include the notable contributions to British literature made from the universities of Hull and East Anglia, to popular culture by Liverpool, to architectural conservation by the refurbishment of Glasgow and Newcastle, and to imaginative tourist provision by York's much-imitated Jorvik Viking Centre, which emerged in 1984 out of local archaeological discoveries. Glasgow's self-rejuvenation also involved displaying its Burrell collection in a new building, and launching its annual Mayfest arts festival in 1983.[230]

Improved communications and the integration of the economy, however, flattened out much regional distinctiveness, from shops to humour: southern humour might not have travelled well in the north during the 1940s, but television subsequently had the effect of standardizing comedy.[231] With no maximum wage after the 1960s, footballers slowly lost their localism: they were now drawn from the entire nation and increasingly from overseas.[232] In more fundamental ways, London's dominance persisted with, if anything, greater force. The spread of new universities with nation-wide recruitment might temporarily distribute talent throughout the country, but it was in the south-east that graduates tended to pursue their careers.[233] As for economic life, only a seventh of the fifty largest companies in 1973 had a head office outside London.[234] Privatization had a less decentralizing impact than might have been expected:

---

[227] HC Deb. (19 Apr. 1983), c. 159.   [228] For more on this see Barber, English Language, 266.
[229] C. H. Williams, 'New Domains of the Welsh Language: Education, Planning and the Law', Contemporary Wales, 3 (1989), 42–4. H. Carter, 'Patterns of Language and Culture: Wales 1961–1990', Transactions of the Honourable Society of Cymmrodorion (1990), 273–4.
[230] R. Hewison, Culture and Consensus: England, Art and Politics since 1940 (1995), 280.
[231] R. Wilmut, Kindly Leave the Stage! The Story of Variety 1919–1960 (1985), 169.
[232] Harrison, Seeking a Role, 79, 386–9, 545.   [233] FT (16 July 2001), 4.
[234] C. M. Law, British Regional Development since World War I (Newton Abbot, 1980), 159.

the long-term tendency towards larger commercial enterprises continued, and many of the head offices returned to London. Firms' growing dependence on research tended to draw them towards the south of England, with its good communications, closeness to government, proximity to Europe and cultural and environmental attractions.[235] Perhaps the most notable attack on provincial community loyalties occurred during the miners' strike of 1984–5, when highly distinctive neighbourly networks were destroyed at London's behest.

These and other changes cumulated to blur still further[236] the once clear distinction between town and country. By 1977, 99.5 per cent of the UK population could receive BBC1 television and 98.7 per cent Independent Television (ITV) on Very High Frequency (VHF); and 99.3 per cent could receive VHF broadcasts of Radios 2–4.[237] In December 2005 the last community in the UK was linked to the national grid: a group of farmhouses in the Nedd Valley, in the Brecon Beacons, free now to discard their generators, candles, and flickering lamps.[238] At the same time as businesses were moving to the country in search of cheap land and labour, agricultural concerns were becoming ever more commercial, with their glasshouses, their new warehousing for mass storage, and their mass-production of animals for food.[239] By the early 1990s even in rural areas only a seventh of the population worked in agriculture.[240] More and more country-dwellers went to the towns for their schools and shops, while townspeople travelled in the opposite direction to pick their own fruit. By the very end of the century, new office technology (fax machines, mobile phones, computer modems) enabled people to pursue urban occupations from rural homes. Larkin noted in 1974 how all his friends seemed to live in homes called 'the old mill', 'the old forge', or 'the old rectory';[241] these friends were not countrymen but transplanted townsmen.

All this had profound implications for the culture of the countryside, much of which had somehow survived industrialization's onslaughts. Already by the 1840s the Conservative Party could no longer win elections without cultivating the towns. In 1970 its hold over suburban and rural areas remained strong, as was Labour's over the major cities, but Conservatives could no longer risk championing any rural cause that endangered their urban vote. Urban enthusiasm for the natural world owed much to high-quality television programmes on animals in the wild, and the countryside was increasingly seen

[235] C.M. Law, *British Regional Development Since World War 1*, 161, 163–4. R. J. Buswell and E. W. Lewis, 'The Geographical Distribution of Industrial Research Activity in the United Kingdom', *Regional Studies*, 4/3 (Oct. 1970), 299, 302.

[236] This trend before 1970 is discussed in Harrison, *Seeking a Role*, 164–8.

[237] Committee on the Future of Broadcasting, *Report* (Chairman Lord Annan, Cmnd 6753; 1977), 370, 372–3.   [238] *G* (2 Dec. 2005), 6; cf. Cwm Brefi, *Ind* (4 June 2003), 8.

[239] M. J. Healey and B. W. Ilbery (eds.), *The Industrialisation of the Countryside* (Norwich, 1985), 1–19.   [240] Coleman and Salt, *British Population*, 537.

[241] *The Selected Letters of Philip Larkin, 1940–1985*, ed. A. Thwaite (1992), 502.

as a recreational resource for townspeople whose values pervaded rural lifestyles ever more deeply. Many town-dwellers knew animals only as pets: although Britain came only seventh among fifteen industrialized countries surveyed in 1984 for number of dogs per person, and eleventh in the league for cats, it was a nation of animal-lovers.[242] After 1945 several sources of friction arose between humanitarians and the food industry on the treatment of animals, and by 1973 parliament was restive at exporters' methods.[243] In the growing movement for 'organically grown' foods and herbal remedies, an attempt was made from the Prince of Wales downwards to harness commercial interest behind a humane environmentalism, given that a combination of medical, humanitarian, and ecological influences enhanced the charms of vegetarianism, especially with the young. The two leading vegetarian organizations amalgamated in 1969 and their joint membership doubled in the 1970s to about 8,000, but the total number of practising vegetarians was already far larger.[244]

Urban humanitarianism seemed to threaten rural values all the more because the proportion of the population directly involved with producing food or exposed to nature's harshness was still shrinking. The affinity between conservationists and animal-lovers had never been total; huntsmen, for instance, were as fond of animals and as keen on conserving the countryside as any town-dweller, but they diverged on how best to contain the number of foxes. This was one of several growing points of potential friction, and from the 1970s animals' defenders displayed a new zeal and sharpness of tone; they soon became entangled in all the paradoxes that violent tactics entail for a self-proclaimed humanitarian movement. The Animal Liberation Front, founded as the Band of Mercy in 1972, originally targeted hunting, but soon prompted arson attacks on pharmaceutical companies, raids on laboratories and fur farms, and (from the mid-1980s) the fire-bombing of department stores.[245] Selective in membership, the Front's diffuse and decentralized structure, characteristic of terrorist organizations, was designed to head off the police.[246] Scientists engaged in vivisection were now in personal danger, and in 1986 a London University professor told the British Association that after letter-bombs had recently been sent to scientists he was taking 'a calculated risk' in speaking out.[247] Controversy among humanitarians about such tactics reached a new height in 1990 with bomb attacks on animal researchers.[248]

[242] *Econ* (26 Apr. 1986), 44.

[243] See the debate on the export of live animals, *HC Deb.* 12 July 1973, cc. 1799–1862.

[244] J. Twigg, 'The Vegetarian Movement in England, 1847–1981: With Particular Reference to its Ideology' (LSE Ph.D. thesis, 1981), 306–7.

[245] For chronologies of activity see *T* (24 Feb. 1989), 11; *DT* (12 June 1990), 21.

[246] For an interview with Ronnie Lee, a founder member, see *G* (23 Apr. 1983), 4. See also *T* (6 Feb. 1987), 3.   [247] Professor Jeffrey Gray, *T* (6 Sept. 1986), 18.

[248] *Ind* (12 June 1990), 2.

Willingness to deploy consumer power behind moralistic causes had already forced Barclays Bank to withdraw from South Africa in 1986, and similar pressures hit vivisection and the Anglo-American cosmetics, pharmaceutical, fur, and whaling trades.[249] Courageous, serious-minded, acutely conscious of pain and often self-sacrificing (even self-sabotaging) in seeking to curb it, these humanitarians were direct descendants of the progressive individualists so powerfully marshalled in the nineteenth-century Liberal Party. To their opponents they seemed one phalanx within a humourless 'new puritanism' that united feminists, homosexuals, blacks, and ecologists in an anti-political mood of intolerant and sometimes millenarian distaste for their times and for many of their fellow citizens.[250] The new puritans attacked rural recreations as well as rural sources of livelihood. The prolonged war of attrition fought by an alliance between the Royal Society for the Prevention of Cruelty to Animals (RSPCA) and the League against Cruel Sports shifted in the mid-1980s towards combating the national network that promoted illegal badger-baiting and dogfights, events embellished with substantial betting and video-films. In May 1985 the RSPCA and the police broke into a disused barn in Enfield to find a bloodstained fighting ring with several bull-terriers and spectators drawn from many parts of southern England.[251]

The atomization of the citizen, the long-term decline in civic pride, the decay of the inner cities, the decline in local loyalties, the cultural friction between town and country, and the decline in overt cohesion within the UK[252] could lead pessimists into detecting an overall decline in community sense within the UK as a whole. Indeed, the late-twentieth-century advance of terrorism[253] was the ultimate in the demise of community, though sometimes in the name of transnational loyalties. The aristocratic and middle-class paternalism and the working-class cohesion which had once held so many communities together was in decline, and advancing secularization and specialization left little leisure or hope for realizing Thatcher's middle-class dream of reviving the Victorian spirit of municipal altruism. The 'burgeoning civic pride' she yearned for[254] rested on a set of religious values now departed, and it was never clear how Victorian voluntarism could thrive in a secular and much more specialized society with no social class identified by its leisure. Yet this is to over-simplify: new communities were arising to replace or supplement the old.

New technologies, structures, attitudes, and insights ensured that by 1990 the family in its newly diversified forms was becoming much more of a community than its unduly cramping and standardized precursor. Relations between the

---

[249] See the leading article in *FT* (25 Nov. 1986), 14.
[250] A. Hartley, 'The New Face of Puritanism', *ST* (7 Aug. 1988), 14.
[251] *T* (30 July 1985), 3; (1 Aug. 1985), 3; cf. (7 June 1986), 4.
[252] Harrison, *Seeking a Role*, 14, 137, 147, 166, 174, 334.   [253] See below, pp. 102–20.
[254] *Ind* (24 Nov. 1987), 2.

sexes, between people of the same sex, and between parents and children lent a new richness and flexibility to family structures.[255] Social contacts, place of residence, lifestyle, and decisions on career were opened up for both sexes. Nor did the late-twentieth-century family lack supportive communal institutions; they simply took a new or newly popular form. Restaurants catered for the family eating out, suburban supermarkets encouraged family shopping expeditions, garages serviced the family car in its role as the home's detachable mobile room, caravan parks housed the family's mobile second home. In the age of the telephone and the car, distance between relatives and friends did not necessarily mean separation, only a freer choice of association, with the concept of community spreading over a much wider area.[256] In the mid-1960s a tenth of Great Britain's population had moved house within or between local authority areas in one year, nearly a third within five years.[257] Formal types of neighbourhood group spontaneously emerged to reinforce the household: play-groups and childminding organizations, nursery schools, consumer groups, 'neighbourhood watch' schemes, sheltered accommodation. Still more important, the media were developing community at the national level in an entirely new guise: the 'virtual' community, into which they drew many who had hitherto been seriously isolated by geography and the weather. For the old, this was a special boon. The media ensured that public figures were much better known. Partly as a result, an extraordinary number of people were now doing the same things at the same time of day in their leisure time. National media personalities such as Brian Redhead, John Timpson, and Jack DeManio sprang into existence; political leaders were regularly scrutinized by electors within the family circle; and even the royal family became in this sense more accessible.

In so far as politicians had the power to encourage a community sense, their diverse remedies were in some ways complementary. Thatcherite Conservatives favoured scaling down the size of economic and social units: breaking up the welfare state into the hospital trust and the self-governed state school, and the corporate economy into privatized units run by entrepreneurs operating within a small state. Their hope lay in mobilizing the volunteer, the consumer, the parent, and the owner-occupier in a combination of self-defence and self-interest from which they hoped the larger good would emerge. The Liberals favoured devolution and the 'community politics' that grew out of the new pressure-group politics of the 1960s. For Labour the decline in community was particularly serious because the Party's earliest successes had grown out of working-class shared sociability. Some thought it worth revitalizing the concept

---

[255] See below, pp. 216–19, 228–31, 240–1.
[256] See the discussion in P. Willmott and M. Young, *Family and Class in a London Suburb* (1960), 80.
[257] *TBS* 26, 36.

of 'citizenship', a principle of union between the classes which industrialization had prised apart, and which had inspired Tawney and Attlee.[258] Others sought alternatives to social class as routes towards mobilizing support: the interest group and the ethnic minority might enable the Party to manufacture an electoral majority from an array of separate groups.

The new pressure groups extended new types of community. Alongside the all-male sporting and drinking communities there sprang up women's groups to tackle the practical problems emancipation presented, most notably within the one-parent family.[259] The spread of paid work for women, the diminished need for heavy machinery on the shop floor, and the typewriter's disappearance from the office, enabled the workplace to recover some dimensions of community lost elsewhere: even something of the conversational workshop community once prevalent in the days of craft labour. Environmentalists, ethnic minorities, and age-specific groups were mobilizing for practical purposes and sometimes also for political impact.[260] Such groups could tap into the electronic 'virtual' communities that began to cater for minority requirements with a new-found completeness. Business firms, too, were creating more closely targeted consumer communities, using the 1.5 million postcodes for the purpose;[261] census enumerators and political parties also found them useful. And for all the computer dating agency's anonymity, its marital hypermarket was both more efficient and more randomized than its precursors: it carried to the ultimate the long-term trend towards enlarging the gene pool. Though by no means always innocuous, the internet's 'virtual' communities from the 1990s brought together international groupings of hobbyists, interest groups, experts, and minority causes of every kind. Such was community's continuous capacity for spontaneous self-regeneration.

5. IRISH TRAGEDY

There was an important exception to the flexibility of community in the UK in an area where community was if anything too lively: Northern Ireland. The problem there was less absence of community than the simultaneous presence of two distinct and close-knit communities unable to live in harmony with one another but with nowhere else to go. This was the one area of the UK where communal violence was endemic. The UK had last felt the need to distinguish between tactical or 'stunt' and 'mass' violence (though without using the terms) in the Edwardian period, when a media-conscious militant

---

[258] R. Plant, *Citizenship, Rights and Socialism* (Fabian Tract, 531; 1988), 1–2.
[259] See below, pp. 235, 242.   [260] Harrison, *Seeking a Role*, 132–6, 219, 285, 485.
[261] The system is clearly explained in D. Diamond and R. Edwards, *Business in Britain: A Philip Management Planning Atlas* (1975), 18–19.

minority of suffragettes distracted the authorities by attempting to simulate the mass violence that its leaders knew they could not deploy. The two types of violence differ in their relationship with government. Politicians manœuvre continuously to ward off both, but because mass violence is potentially far more damaging to themselves and others, it seems safer to side-track rather than repress. Stunt violence, by contrast, challenges the democratic politician's right to exist; if only for that reason it cannot be allowed to prevail. Mass violence is unpredictable, rarely planned in advance, and in relation to the media is more manipulated than manipulating, whereas stunt violence simulates mass violence by aiming at newsworthy targets, and is carefully planned and media-conscious. Given that its activists constitute only a small minority, they can be contained by authorities who combine persuasion of the public with repression of, and perhaps also covert negotiation with, the stunts' organizers.

When stunt violence in Germany and Italy took the form of radical intellectuals pursuing ill-defined objectives, it could be eliminated through deploying against it mass anti-intellectualism and skilfully ruthless policing, for the terrorists had no hope of mass support. The UK's Angry Brigade[262] had even less rapport with the general public, and was quickly suppressed. Sectarian violence in Northern Ireland was different because it combined violence of both types. When operating in Great Britain it displayed the Angry Brigade's weakness, but within Northern Ireland it came close to resembling mass violence, for two reasons. Republican violence emerged from the long Irish Catholic tradition of resisting British rule, and could rely on much tacit support from within the nationalist community. Furthermore, unlike the Basques, Northern Ireland's Irish nationalists had the advantage of abutting on a fully fledged sympathetic and sovereign state which could unofficially supplement the many safe havens nearer home; Irish militants could also draw upon ill-informed Irish-American backing. The militant nationalists inflamed the fracture within the Province's deeply divided community, generating a continuous and often bloody gang warfare whose vendettas the order-keeping forces tried to damp down but could not conclusively defeat. Politicians must make terms with sustained mass violence, and in southern Ireland had already done so, but to the stunt violence further north their resistance had to be more protracted, but could also be more tenacious—given that Ulster Unionism was so intense in its defensive loyalties. Such circumstances invalidated European parallels whereby smaller nations won a measure of autonomy or even independence.

The republican terrorist campaign in Great Britain outside Ireland had ended in 1939, but resumed in 1972, petered out in the mid-1970s, but re-emerged in 1981–4, and again in 1988. Protestant violence helped in the late 1960s to entrench the Provisional Irish Republican Army (usually labelled

---

[262] Harrison, *Seeking a Role*, 503–4.

the IRA) within Catholic communities as their means of self-defence. As the crisis intensified, long-standing sectarian vendettas hardened into mutually reinforcing terror gangs. Protestant killings of Catholics were less disciplined and more random than IRA killings within the security forces, and between 1969 and 1989 produced 705 deaths, three-quarters of them uninvolved civilians.[263] Loyalist and republican murders followed a broadly similar chronological pattern, rising to a peak in the early 1970s and then tailing off; loyalist murders in these years were far fewer than republican overall.[264] In no year after 1972 did the level of political killings in Northern Ireland (467 in that year) rise so high, and by the 1980s their average annual number had fallen to a plateau of 78.[265] As for IRA violence in Great Britain, by February 1996 bomb blasts in London had killed 45 people and injured 1,204.[266] There were far more killings in Northern Ireland: a total of 2,863 loyalist and republican killings between 1969 and 1990, of whom 68 per cent were civilians, and 33,003 injured, of whom 66 per cent were civilians.[267] Feuds between nationalist factions and the randomness of IRA bombing campaigns ensured that its victims included many of the 1,543 Catholics who died during the troubles.[268] Total security forces in Northern Ireland reached their peak in 1978, after which there was a decline in both the security forces' total and in the share the British army contributed to it.[269]

Given that in 1972 civil war in Northern Ireland seemed all too likely, why did Belfast not become a Beirut? All the necessary ingredients were present. Within a deeply divided community, the dominant Protestant group had a long tradition of stubborn refusal to compromise. Their republican Catholic and American critics often branded Ulster Unionists as agents of a colonial power. 'There are those who tell us that the British government will not be moved by armed struggle', said the Sinn Fein MP Gerry Adams in 1983. 'The history of Ireland and of British colonial involvement throughout the world tells us that they will not be moved by anything else.'[270] Tony Benn shared his view, pointing out in 1989, in an Irish context, that 'the history of Britain is a terrorist ending up having tea with the Queen at Buckingham Palace as a world statesman'.[271] British soldiers implicitly drew the analogy when, patrolling Belfast's streets after 1969, they vigorously applied techniques learnt in colonial situations to the 'bogwogs', their contemptuous label for the Belfast Catholics. Yet in Northern Ireland the colonial analogy was far too crudely drawn and for

---

[263] S. Bruce, *The Red Hand: Protestant Paramilitaries in Northern Ireland* (Oxford, 1992), 277.
[264] See the graph ibid. 295.
[265] Calculated from S. Elliott and W. D. Flackes, *Northern Ireland: A Political Directory 1968–1999* (1st publ. 1980, 5th edn. Belfast, 1999), 681.   [266] *DT* (20 Feb. 1996), 2.
[267] Calculated from Elliott and Flackes, *Northern Ireland*, 681, 684.   [268] *T* (17 Apr. 1999), 15.
[269] For a useful table see Bruce, *Red Hand*, 297.   [270] *G* (14 Nov. 1983), 1.
[271] *DT* (19 June 1989), 2.

several reasons only superficially plausible. First, the alleged colonists had been there for so long—far longer than most settlers in the USA. Their indigenous culture had therefore distanced them not only from the Irish nationalists, but from the alleged colonial power. They might deploy the union flag on every possible occasion to symbolize their loyalty—reinforced by bowler hats, brass bands, and umbrellas—but they were loyal to an anti-Catholic British regime that had long gone. All the more, then, was Northern Ireland their homeland: they had no other home. Their culture was strengthened by the bond between religion and social status that was not replicated elsewhere in the UK. As a journalist noted in 1971, Protestant housewives kept everything spotless: 'this they attribute directly to their religion . . . Every day I was plied with countless examples of Roman Catholics who bred greyhounds in their baths, kept coal in their washbasins, burnt the doors of their new council houses for firewood and used lifts as public urinals.'[272] So if there was a colonial analogy at all, it was with Cyprus, Palestine, Ceylon, and India, where a British departure gave free rein to long-established indigenous hatreds.

The colonial analogy was implausible for a second reason: the alleged colonial power was not at all keen to embrace its alleged role. Opinion polls and general elections repeatedly demonstrated British indifference to, or even impatience with, Northern Ireland's problems; in 1970, as so often later, British voters showed 'an almost total lack of any sense of involvement' in the issues of Northern Ireland, the justification for whose quarrels seemed merely antique.[273] Nor were British politicians much keener on the connection, for Ulster Unionism had grown apart from the British political parties, whether Conservative or Labour. Reginald Maudling articulated the outlook of many prominent Conservatives when returning to London after his first visit as Home Secretary there in 1971: 'what a bloody awful country!'[274] Besides, Ulster Unionist priorities frequently cut across the wider and more pressing concerns of British political leaders—most notably the need (for economic reasons) to limit the army's commitments and (for power-political reasons) to cultivate good relations with the USA and with the EEC, and therefore with the Irish Republic. Democratic considerations complicated the colonial analogy with a third difficulty. Britain's style of colonial retreat was infinitely varied, and whereas it often seemed undemocratic to remain in the face of anti-colonial pressure, in Northern Ireland it could plausibly be said that the local 'freedom fighters' had access to democratic institutions, however imperfect; with help from a sympathetic government based in Great Britain, gradual non-violent improvement was feasible. Furthermore, democracy entails some degree of

---

[272] Christopher Walker, *T* (8 Apr. 1971), 14.

[273] C. Serpell, 'An Absence of Foreign Affairs', *Listener* (18 June 1970), 816.

[274] Quoted in Campbell, *Edward Heath*, 425.

respect for minorities, and no modern democratic state could conceivably have coerced a million reluctant Protestants into a united Ireland—a geographical concept that, rightly or wrongly, they detested. 'Why should Ireland be united just because it was an island?' asked Lord Brookeborough in 1971: the only reason people expected it 'was that it would make a tidier looking shape on the map'.[275]

A combination of Protestant fears and Catholic hopes caused Northern Ireland's 'troubles' to escalate in the late 1960s. 'The most perilous moment for a bad government', wrote Tocqueville, 'is one when it seeks to mend its ways.'[276] Terence O'Neill, Northern Ireland's Unionist but reforming prime minister from 1963 to 1969, stirred Protestant worries by opening up contact with the Republic in 1964, and on 14 January 1965 the two Irish prime ministers (O'Neill and Lemass) held their historic encounter at Stormont. The reforming climate fuelled the hopes of Northern Ireland's growing Roman Catholic middle class, but also their resentment at continuing discrimination. With a Labour government at Westminster unsympathetic to Unionism, the Protestants needed to hone their publicity skills. They had many assets. Links with the churches and political parties in Great Britain, amply exploited by Unionists when threatened with home rule between 1886 and 1922, were now less useful, but there were many descendants of Ulster Protestant settlers waiting to be mobilized in Canada and the USA. Memories could have been stirred on the wartime contrast between the response to Hitler shown by Unionists and the Republic, nor should it have been difficult to deploy the IRA's terrorist outrages as a formidable Protestant weapon. Yet the Ulster Unionists squandered these assets by taking up a consistently defensive and parochial stance which made no converts. They were law-abiding, hard-working people with a strong sense of mutual obligation and personal responsibility, but their public image did not reflect their private virtues.

Unionist leaders did not appreciate even the need for widespread British support until shocked into it by Heath's unexpected introduction of direct rule in 1972. James Molyneaux, the Ulster Unionist Party's leader from 1979 to 1995, though tactically astute, was intellectually unresourceful—a quiet man with no aptitude for swaying opinion outside his hermetic Protestant world. As for the Democratic Unionists who split off from the Ulster Unionist Party in 1971, their leader Ian Paisley topped Northern Ireland's poll for the European Parliament in all four of its elections between 1979 and 1994. As Benn later pointed out, in private he differed totally from his public image: he was 'an

---

[275] T. Coleman, *The Scented Brawl: Selected Articles and Interviews* (1978), 105.

[276] A. de Tocqueville, *The Ancien Regime and the French Revolution*, tr. S. Gilbert (paperback edn. 1966), 196.

attractive old rogue really'[277] and a decent family man with a strong case; yet he threw it away by clothing it with an anti-Catholic bluster that in relatively secularized Britain seemed truly antique. Energized by all the simplicity that springs from a black-and-white view of the world, Paisley imagined conspiracies and betrayals everywhere. His almost Churchillian hunched shoulders and large frame came to symbolize, not the courage and determination he undoubtedly possessed, but coarse bigotry. His bellowing rhetoric and populist humour was the Unionist voice that the British people heard most often, and it was not congenial. The Protestants never even began to match the nationalist skill in cultivating the media: they had no hotline to Hollywood, and all too few connections with the fine arts. They too were freedom fighters, but self-defence could radiate far less of the drama and romance that nationalists in their films and plays could deploy.[278]

In the early 1960s the Irish Republican Army's recent burst of violence was de-escalating, and the Stormont government released the last batch of republican prisoners in 1961. For a time it seemed that republicanism in Northern Ireland might forsake violence, take a welfarist direction and seek mass support. Shortly before violence erupted in 1969 only about sixty men in Belfast and only about ten in Londonderry saw themselves as IRA members, often for social rather than terrorist reasons.[279] Nor did the IRA's revival thereafter seem likely to last longer than its ephemeral bombing campaigns of 1939 and 1956–62, or provide more than a vehicle for Northern Ireland's long familiar exchange of provocation and counter-provocation. What falsified such expectations was the impact on Catholic assertiveness of the American civil rights movement. The Northern Ireland Civil Rights Association was formed in 1967, and in October 1968 its second march encountered a much-publicized police baton charge. Unionists felt still less secure when the Wilson government, without getting directly involved, pressed Stormont for concessions to the Catholics.[280] The civil rights movement was soon taken over by Irish republicans, and Unionist moderates felt the ground shifting beneath their feet. After violence in Londonderry's Bogside area in August 1969, the British army was for the first time deployed on the streets of Northern Ireland to protect the Catholics against Unionist intimidation, and so was at first welcomed by Catholics. 'They're going to be there for seven years at least', Wilson privately predicted.[281]

Since Stormont was then still responsible for law and order, the army inevitably drifted into executing Unionist orders. Lasting resentment was caused

---

[277] Benn, *Diaries 1991–2001*, 220 (25 Jan. 1994).
[278] See D. McKittrick's important 'Hungry for a Voice', *Ind* (31 Oct. 2008), arts and books supplement, 17.   [279] P. Bishop and E. Mallie, *The Provisional IRA* (1987), 67, 73.
[280] Castle, *Diaries 1964–70*, 648 (8 May 1969), 696 (30 July 1969), 700 (19 Aug 1969). Crossman, *Cabinet Diaries*, iii, 719 (6 Nov. 1969).   [281] Pimlott, *Wilson*, 549.

when suspect Catholics were exposed publicly to humiliation and privately to treatment hardly distinguishable from torture. The British in Northern Ireland, as in colonial wars, subjected prisoners to the techniques pioneered in the USSR and China after 1945; these operated through psychological disorientation rather than physical pain—with hooding, and loss of sleep, warmth, water, and personal dignity. Televised battles in Belfast streets stirred up sympathy for the Catholic cause outside the UK, especially in the Republic and in the USA. In December 1969 the need to defend Belfast Catholics more vigorously prompted a split in the IRA between 'officials' and 'provisionals', formalized on 11 January 1970. As late as August 1969 Crossman privately wondered whether the United Nations could be invited to mediate in Northern Ireland,[282] but events moved rapidly on. Heath as Conservative prime minister publicly attacked the Irish Republic's prime minister in 1971 for threatening to support passive resistance north of the border, and introduced internment without trial. This strategy, ineptly executed, helped gain the provisionals the community backing that terrorists require. They could now brand the 'Brits' as an army of occupation, and see themselves as protecting the Catholic population against it. In February 1971 the provisionals killed their first British soldier. Thirteen Catholic marchers were killed in Londonderry on 30 January 1972 (henceforth labelled 'bloody Sunday'), and the Republic withdrew its ambassador from London. In the House of Commons on the following day the republican Bernadette Devlin, present at the march, struck the Home Secretary, whom she denounced as 'that murdering hypocrite'.[283] In March the British government prorogued the Stormont parliament and Whitelaw became Secretary of State for Northern Ireland. 'I believe increasingly', Wilson told parliament, 'that there can be no political solution without a united Ireland';[284] such an assertion from the leader of the opposition merely helped to polarize the situation by accentuating Catholic hopes and Protestant fears.

There was now a real danger of civil war, and because Protestants and Catholics were closely intermingled, massive population movements would have resulted; Roman Catholics constituted 28 per cent of Belfast's population in 1971, for example.[285] In 1973 the Irish Republic's prime minister claimed that if the British troops left Northern Ireland 'there would be an immediate and frantic attempt by both communities to consolidate their positions and clear out pockets of "opposition", and this . . . seems to be a prescription for civil war'.[286] Given that the Stormont government now lacked authority with

[282] Crossman, *The Diaries of a Cabinet Minister*, iii. *Secretary of State for Social Services 1968–70* (1977), 619 (14 Aug. 1969).   [283] Heath, *T* (20 Aug. 1971), 2; Devlin, *HC Deb*. 31 Jan. 1972, c. 41.
[284] *HC Deb*. 1 Feb. 1972, c. 321.
[285] See P. Compton, 'The Demographic Background', in D. Watt (ed.), *The Constitution of Northern Ireland: Problems and Prospects* (1981), 78–9, for useful tables and maps.
[286] Speech in London on 2 July, *T* (3 July 1973), 1.

a significant section of its population, Heath decided to suspend it and assume direct control, as announced on 24 March 1972. The provisionals called a ceasefire on 26 June but withdrew from it on 9 July, and on 21 July detonated twenty-two bombs within forty-five minutes in Belfast's city centre, killing nine and injuring 130; thirty years later they publicly admitted that such indiscriminate slaughter had been mistaken.[287] The IRA cease-fire, by contrast, proved lasting: in their political emphasis, which involved moving closer to Sinn Fein, it was anticipating the strategy to which the provisionals turned only in the 1990s. In the short term, however, those who kill for the cause all too readily gain status through their daring, their self-sacrifice, and their seemingly superior zeal. With their deeply rooted historical consciousness and their long memory for anniversaries, the provisionals saw themselves as carrying forward the Irish republican tradition, though without the democratic legitimacy of the Irish Republic's creators. The provisionals' shift towards violence soon lent them dominance within the republican movement—so much so, that thenceforward when most people spoke of the IRA they meant the provisionals and not their ongoing non-violent parent body. This narrative will henceforth do the same.

On the night of 30 July—for Heath 'one of the worst of my life'—the troops went in to free areas of Londonderry from IRA control, and at 5 a.m. Whitelaw told him by phone that the objective had been achieved with only two civilian deaths.[288] Heath's Foreign Secretary Alec Douglas-Home, in a secret note of 1972, opposed direct rule for Northern Ireland: 'I do not believe they are like the Scots or the Welsh, or ever will be. The real British interest would be best served by pushing them towards a united Ireland . . . Our history is one long story of trouble with the Irish.'[289] Heath thought Ireland would eventually be united for all practical purposes through Britain's shared involvement with the Irish Republic in the EEC, but he also seriously considered redrawing the border between Northern Ireland and the Republic, a strategy also favoured in the 1970s by prominent soldiers. Many British soldiers would have survived, for instance, if the Boundary Commission's recommendation in 1925 for transferring South Armagh to the Republic had been acted upon. In July 1972 Heath secretly considered but rejected a plan for shifting a third of Northern Ireland's population—most of Fermanagh and Tyrone and parts of Londonderry, Down, and Armagh—into the Republic so as to render the shrunken Protestant enclave more defensible.[290] In the outcome, the army enforced the existing frontier at great cost by erecting in South Armagh much-resented symbols of continued British authority: hilltop watchtowers with high-tech equipment to monitor traffic between Crossmaglen and the

[287] G (17 July 2002), 6.   [288] Heath, Course of my Life, 438.   [289] Quoted in G (1 Jan. 2003), 1.
[290] Quoted in T (1 Jan. 2003), 11.

border, complemented by weird and somewhat sinister urban structures to protect police stations and barracks (Plate 6). However effective these ugly utilitarian barbed-wire and corrugated-iron structures might be in the short term, their psychological impact in the long term was counter-productive: they merely enhanced the alien image that the British army had begun to acquire.[291]

A devolved political structure involving power-sharing seemed the best intermediate solution. In the referendum of March 1973, on a 58 per cent turnout, 591,820 voted for the Province to remain within the UK, and only 6,463 wanted it united to the Republic. In June 1973 a new 78-member Northern Ireland Assembly was elected by single transferable vote and backed the idea of a power-sharing executive. Subsequent talks were held between the Assembly's executive designate (composed of the mainstream Catholic and Protestant politicians but not the terrorists, and including the prime ministers and senior ministers from UK and Republic); Ian Paisley was not invited, but nonetheless presented himself and was refused admission. The talks culminated on 9 December in the so-called 'Sunningdale Agreement'—for Heath 'one of the proudest moments of my premiership'.[292] This confirmed the idea of an assembly elected by proportional representation, likely to produce an outcome more balanced than the discontinued Stormont parliament. Its eleven-person executive was also to be elected proportionately, to reflect balance between the main parties in the assembly, and there was a provision (never implemented) to set up a Council of Ireland which would stimulate ongoing cooperation between Republic and Province. In January 1974 a power-sharing executive took office, but many Unionists shared the view of Lord Brookeborough in 1971: that having Catholics in the cabinet would be 'exactly like the British Government, during the last war, having a German in the Admiralty and a German in the War Office'.[293] IRA violence remained serious, and in such a climate the Agreement had little chance. Unionists organized themselves at the general election of February 1974 to maximize opposition to power-sharing within the new assembly, leaving its supporters divided. The executive collapsed in May after a strike by the Ulster Workers' Council; it skilfully exploited the media and shut down the electricity grid which the army could not operate. On no occasion was the cultural gulf between Northern Ireland and Great Britain more vividly displayed than when the TUC's General Secretary Len Murray during this strike led 'a pitifully small procession of 200 men and women' on a back-to-work march amidst loyalist obscenities and throwings of stones and eggs.[294]

---

[291] For excellent photographs see J. Olley, *Castles of Ulster* (Belfast, 2007).
[292] Heath, *Course of my Life*, 444.   [293] Coleman, *Scented Brawl*, 106.
[294] *G* (22 May 1974), 6.

Ephemeral the Sunningdale agreement might seem in the short term, but as a source of constitutional innovation it had in retrospect a rather longer life. Its referendum on the border, its introduction of proportional representation at local government and Assembly level, and its repudiation of Westminster's adversarial model were all innovations which could later be slotted into the pedigree for constitutional innovation throughout the UK after 1997.[295] Nonetheless, by June 1974 opinion polls revealed that the British public were much keener on withdrawal from Northern Ireland than on staying, a situation which prevailed for the rest of the decade.[296] Wilson as new prime minister accused the Province of 'sponging' on the British taxpayer and then rejecting democratic methods; Ulster Unionists took great offence, and sported pieces of sponge in their buttonholes.[297] Wilson at this time was secretly considering several radical options, convinced that 'we must not get into a Vietnam'. Boundary change was one, but so was 'the unmentionable': withdrawal, with some sort of Dominion status for Northern Ireland.[298] In a memorandum of 30 May, of which only four numbered copies were made, Wilson asked civil servants to draft a four-month withdrawal plan for what he called the 'Doomsday scenario'.[299] The civil servants, however, mounted a strong counter-offensive against withdrawal,[300] and the Labour governments muddled on with what was becoming a familiar combination of repression and overt or covert negotiation with the IRA. In 1986, however, Callaghan still favoured his own suggestion of 1981: that Britain should withdraw from Northern Ireland after a predetermined period, offer British citizenship to all who wished to retain it, and leave the Province to become an independent state.[301]

Henceforth anyone in Northern Ireland identified with the Sunningdale power-sharing experiment of 1973–4 was tainted as a moderate, for influence now lay with extremists on both sides; continued direct rule was the option least unacceptable to both. With the Stormont parliament disbanded, the Northern Ireland Office increasingly resembled the Scottish Office in its structure,[302] but the Secretary of State for Northern Ireland after 1972 was more like a colonial governor, and was there to preserve order rather than represent the local population. Nonetheless, British politicians soldiered on with attempts to revive self-government in Northern Ireland. In 1975 the Labour government

[295] V. Bogdanor, *The New British Constitution* (Oxford, 2009), 24–6.
[296] See the useful table in R. Rose and I. McAllister, *United Kingdom Facts* (London and Basingstoke, 1982), 121, where the figure for June 1974 is misinterpreted.
[297] H. Wilson, *Final Term: The Labour Government 1974–1976* (1979), 76–7. Pimlott, *Wilson*, 634.
[298] B. Donoughue, *Downing Street Diary: With Harold Wilson in No. 10* (2005), 124 (20 May 1974); see also 129 (29 May 1974).   [299] *DT* (1 Jan. 2005), 11; cf. *T* (1 Jan. 2005), 24.
[300] Donoughue, *Downing Street Diary*, i (2005), 130–1 (29 and 31 May 1974).
[301] Callaghan, *Time and Chance*, 500.
[302] For a useful organizational chart see P. Hennessy, *Whitehall* (1st publ. 1989, paperback edn. 1990), 471.

introduced a seventy-eight-member constitutional convention, but it failed in the following year. When the Queen visited Northern Ireland in August 1977 the Province's polarization was at once apparent, for only in Protestant areas were there decorations; even Gerry Fitt, leader from 1970 to 1979 of the Social Democratic and Labour Party (SDLP), refused to participate in the celebrations, and the overseas press showed much interest in the security precautions.[303] Northern Ireland's polarized situation produced many political casualties. The sociable and somewhat bibulous Fitt was among the bravest. Hit by a policeman's baton during a civil-rights march in 1968, he found himself eight years later fending off IRA intruders into his house with a pistol at 4 a.m. Bombed, floodlit, and armour-plated, the house survived till 1983, when it was set on fire. Fitt's willingness to compromise made him a politician with whom the British government could do business, and after Adams had defeated him in the general election of 1983 he received a life peerage. From 1982 to 1986 Prior as Secretary of State for Northern Ireland introduced 'rolling devolution'; this involved a seventy-eight-seat assembly, again based on proportional representation, whose role was at first confined to scrutiny, debate, and advice, but with the hope that it might later acquire legislative powers. Because only the Unionists took their seats, many even of them not staying for long, the assembly had to be disbanded.

These moves were but one dimension of a fierce and wearisome contest between British governments and the IRA, which now developed a terrorist structure more formidable than any in Europe. Whereas Italy had successfully tackled the Red Brigades, Germany the Baader Meinhof gang, France Action Directe, and Spain had managed at least to contain ETA, Britain by the 1990s seemed unable to achieve more than stalemate with the IRA.[304] From the late 1960s the latter felt able to make new claims on long-standing loyalties within republican families, but also to break new ground with the young male Catholic working class: it could exploit resentments at injustices perpetrated by the Protestants, the police, or the British army, and could politicize its recruits later, sometimes in prison. Its strategy was so to weary British electors with its violence that their 'troops out' sentiment would eventually shift British government policy. From the Fenians in the 1880s onwards, London had been the main nationalist terrorist target, though not till 1972 did Irish-based terrorism subject ordinary citizens in Great Britain to the sort of continuous threat that Northern Ireland's inhabitants experienced after 1970. High-profile republican murders thereafter included Airey Neave, opposition spokesman on Northern Ireland, on 2 April 1979 (by the Irish National Liberation Army); Earl Mountbatten on 27 August 1979; five prominent Conservatives in the Grand Hotel Brighton on 12 October 1984

---

[303] *T* (11 Aug. 1977), 2.   [304] As Heath complained in *HC Deb.* 8 June 1993, c. 167.

when the IRA tried to blow up the entire cabinet at the party conference; and Ian Gow on 30 July 1990. 'We do not expect these things to happen in this country,' said Thatcher on Neave's death, 'but somehow they have happened here.'[305] At the same time the IRA sought to distract the police and retain the headlines by continually varying its targets and methods, and to intimidate the politicians directly by threatening their lives. 'Today we were unlucky', it declared after its Brighton bomb of 1984, 'but remember, we have only to be lucky once; you will have to be lucky always.'[306] With the rocket attack on 10 Downing Street while the cabinet was in session in February 1991, this aspect of their strategy reached the depths of futile daring.

To brand the terrorists as 'mindless' involved wishful thinking: as Thatcher pointed out, although terrorism may attract some psychopaths, it involves 'the calculated use of violence—and the threat of it—to achieve political ends'.[307] In court during 1980, Brian Keenan, a highly intelligent and articulate television engineer, carefully presented the image of innocent family man, yet was thought to be the IRA's Director of Operations and responsible for some horrific killings and maimings.[308] Funds from racketeering and American sympathizers made weapons available, especially the collapsible Armalite rifle so well-suited to urban terrorism, and arms were conveniently stored in terrorist hide-outs inside the Irish Republic. Semtex, the relatively stable putty-like explosive invented in 1966 in Czechoslovakia, reached the IRA via Libya, and deadly explosions could then be perpetrated in Northern Ireland, in Great Britain, and in strategic locations overseas. As with the suffragettes and CND's Committee of 100, the need to organize illegal acts of violence necessitated for the IRA by the mid-1970s a decentralized and tight cell-like structure; it was impenetrable to the authorities because any one member knew only the three or four other members of his cell. The trial of the four Balcombe Street bombers provided a brief glimpse in 1977 of the cool and committed way in which the IRA ran its 'active service units' in Great Britain. During their sixteen months in London before arrest in 1975 the unit carried out up to fifty bombings and shootings in the London area and killed at least sixteen people. Its anonymity was preserved through disciplined discretion and carefully avoiding known republicans.[309] Then on 27 August 1979 the Prince of Wales recorded in his diary the 'mixture of desperate emotions' that swept over him when his beloved 79-year-old great-uncle, Earl Mountbatten, was blown up and killed with three others at Warren Point. The IRA explained that as the British government

[305] *HC Deb.* 2 Apr. 1979, c. 907.   [306] *T* (13 Oct. 1984), 3.
[307] Thatcher, *Downing Street Years*, 383.
[308] For a full report of the trial see *G* (26 June 1980), 17.
[309] *G* (10 Feb. 1977), 11; see also *Ind* (24 Apr. 1998), 2.

persisted 'with the oppression of our people and the torture of our comrades in the H-Blocks . . . we will tear out their sentimental, imperialist heart'.[310]

To combine the mounting of terror with milking it for publicity value was a feat indeed: the more shocking the methods, the higher toned the advertised idealism needed to be. The IRA successfully deployed the moral advantages of being seen as an oppressed minority, and like the Ulster Unionists made no attempt to win support within Great Britain. But whereas the Ulster Unionists looked only to their own kind, the IRA sought simultaneously to ventilate its hatred, and to bid for support primarily among the large Catholic Irish public in southern Ireland and the USA. The Republican engine from the late 1960s was fuelled by a powerful ideological concoction of Marxism, nationalism, and liberationism. It was all the more effective for being able to exploit the Catholic cult of martyrdom, for alternately presenting its political and its violent profiles as circumstances required, and for lacking any democratic obligation to conduct its affairs in public, while at the same time setting its own agenda for public discussion. Each side in Northern Ireland, while arming against the other, strove to present itself as working for peace, but the IRA with Orwellian ingenuity turned to its own purposes the well-intentioned but often naive efforts of humanitarians and peace-lovers. Its frequent schisms usefully enabled it to present different faces to different publics, while leaving its fragmented structures and their mutual relations impenetrable. IRA maimings and killings aimed to inflate the impression of the movement's numerical strength, thereby demoralizing or exhausting governments and public in Great Britain. The City of London , as a great financial centre, was particularly vulnerable, as were all public figures. The IRA's search for symbolic targets reflected its skill at manipulating the media. As the Foreign Secretary pointed out in 1993, 'the camera is an actor': selective in topic, vivid in impact, and favouring dramatic action more than patient diplomacy.[311] The IRA's dependence on what Thatcher called 'the oxygen of publicity' ensured that journalists rarely received death threats, and at important republican funerals journalists often found a tiered stand and scaffolding made conveniently available.[312]

Here, then, was a formidable adversary. The authorities countered it simultaneously at several levels, and the CID's so-called 'bomb squad' achieved notable successes in the 1970s not only against the Angry Brigade, but against the IRA.[313] There was first the need to curb street violence without making things worse. By the late 1960s CS gas was being used in Northern Ireland

---

[310] Dimbleby, *Prince of Wales*, 266. R. English, *Armed Struggle: The History of the IRA* (2003), 220.
[311] D. Hurd, 'The Power of Comment', talk at the Travellers Club, 9 Sept. 1993, typescript, 7, 9.
[312] For a good discussion see J. Dettmer, 'Oxygen Supply in Trouble', *T* (5 Apr. 1989), 33.
[313] For an obituary of CID Commander Roy Habershon see *DT* (28 Mar. 1992), 15.

somewhat hesitantly, given that it was not being used in Great Britain,[314] but 10,000 such canisters were thrown during order-keeping operations of 1970. The contrast was advertised by a man who threw two CS gas canisters on to the House of Commons floor on 23 July 1970 and shouted 'now you know what it's like in Belfast'.[315] In the same year rubber bullets were introduced into Northern Ireland to help keep order, and by December 1974 more than 55,000 had been fired; plastic bullets were introduced as an alternative to live ammunition in 1973, but were not generally used till 1976.[316] By mid-decade there was some concern that police access to submachine guns threatened the tradition of unarmed policing even in London.[317] Then there was the gruesomely escalating contest between terrorism and counter-terrorism: knee-cappings and shootings that made Belfast hospitals particularly expert at repairing damaged brains and knees;[318] and increasingly sophisticated bombs, whose anti-handling devices demanded increasingly sophisticated detecting and defusing equipment. Of the 106 IRA men who died between 1969 and 1973, 44 were blown up by their own bombs, which prompted the incorporation of safety circuits.[319] To prevent booby-trapped IRA bombs from killing soldiers who tried to defuse them, the wheelbarrow robot was invented in 1972 and destroyed more than 400 bombs.[320] Then in the early 1980s 'time and power units' enabled the IRA to prime a bomb long before it was due to go off, as with the Brighton hotel bomb of 1984.[321] Technical skill had to be complemented by assiduity in protecting those at risk. As a trial run for the Queen's jubilee visit to Northern Ireland in August 1977, Princess Anne in the preceding March was helicoptered into a Hillsborough that was swamped by troops and policemen.[322] The homes of British government ministers involved with Northern Ireland had to be floodlit at night and their gardens patrolled,[323] and at the general election of 1979 leading politicians were distanced from the electors by an unusual array of bodyguards and by not pre-announcing their movements.[324]

[314] Crossman, *Diaries of a Cabinet Minister*, iii. 570 (15 July 1969).

[315] *T* (24 July 1970), 1; a 26-year-old labourer James Anthony Roche was later charged with the offence.

[316] R. Faligot, *Britain's Military Strategy in Ireland: The Kitson Experiment* (1983), 139, 143.

[317] *HC Deb.* 5 Apr. 1984, cc. 1108–9.

[318] See W. A. Hadden, W. H. Rutherford, and J. D. Merrett, 'The Injuries of Terrorist Bombing: A Study of 1532 Consecutive Patients', *British Journal of Surgery* (Aug. 1978), 525–31, eloquent in the horrific injuries photographed, but perhaps still more eloquent in its cool, factual prose. I am most grateful for generous help in this area to Professor Alvin Jackson of Edinburgh University, Sir Peter Froggatt, and to Professor R. J. S. Clarke (Hon. Archivist to the Royal Victoria Hospital Belfast). For head wounds see *T* (29 June 2009), 48 (obituary of Derek Gordon).

[319] Bishop and Mallie, *Provisional IRA*, 149.

[320] *T* (6 Sept. 2006), 62 (obituary of its inventor, Lt. Col. Miller).

[321] G. Esler, 'Explosive Developments: The IRA's Bomb Technology', *Listener* (19 June 1986), 10.

[322] *T* (24 Mar. 1977), 2.   [323] e.g. Roy Mason in *DT* (9 Oct. 1979), 1.

[324] *Econ* (28 Apr. 1979), 21. *STel* (29 Apr. 1979), 17.

'To all the people of the Province of Ulster', Thatcher told her party conference in 1979, 'I repeat this pledge: we do not forget you, we will not abandon you.'[325] Her relations with the Unionists were often strained, but her Nonconformist background, her commitment to democracy, her patriotism, and her 'Victorian values' ensured much shared ground. Here, as elsewhere, she was adept at the timely gesture. Already by August 1979 she was wearing a flak jacket in the heart of IRA country at Crossmaglen, and during her second visit on Christmas Eve she accepted a red beret from a paratrooper in Armagh and wore it for the rest of the day.[326] She visited Northern Ireland more often than other prime ministers, and made a point of doing so after major terrorist incidents such as the Ballykelly bombing of 1982.[327] On 8 November 1987 eleven people were killed and more than sixty injured when an IRA bomb was detonated without warning during a Remembrance Day commemoration at Enniskillen. After some delay, IRA regrets were expressed, and Thatcher pushed the propaganda advantage home by braving all security risks in order unexpectedly to attend the postponed ceremony there on 22 November.[328]

In September 1979 the Pope's direct appeal at Drogheda 'in language of passionate pleading' to politicians and terrorists to end the violence[329] did not prevent the IRA in 1980 from resuming a long republican tradition and turning the Catholic cult of the martyr to secular purposes. In the early 1980s the centrality of the prison experience in terrorist self-education moved gradually into focus. Jenkins as Home Secretary in 1974 had abandoned the force-feeding of hunger strikers, two of whom died in 1974 and 1976. Thereafter, the IRA prisoners' struggle for political status prompted escalating levels of protest: from going 'on the blanket' (refusing to wear prison clothes) to the so-called 'dirty protest', whereby prisoners smeared their cell walls with excrement. By summer 1978 the latter had involved between 250 and 300 republican prisoners.[330] Visiting their cells at the Maze prison in 1979 was not pleasant: with excrement on cell walls and urine poured under the cell doors, Nicholas Henderson hovered outside 'overcome by the stench' as the Governor entered the cells.[331] The death in May 1981 of Bobby Sands, elected MP while in prison, was widely publicized; his letters written on lavatory paper were smuggled out of prison and published in a booklet. Ten men died from hunger-strikes within seven months without securing any government concession. The republican leadership was now at risk of being decimated, and decided to end the strikes later in the year.

[325] Thatcher, *Party Conference Speeches*, 57.   [326] *DT* (30 Aug. 1979), 1. *T* (27 Dec. 1979), 2.
[327] *DT* (23 Dec. 1982), 1.   [328] *G* (23 Nov. 1987), 1.   [329] On 29 Sept., *O* (30 Sept. 1979), 3.
[330] Bishop and Mallie, *Provisional IRA*, 280.   [331] Henderson, *Mandarin*, 275 (8 July 1979).

Throughout all this, Thatcher risked her own life by adopting an uncompromising stance, denouncing the 'calculated cynicism' of a movement which worked on 'the most basic of human emotions—pity—as a means of. . . stoking the fires of. . . hatred', with its members more useful dead than alive.[332] Patrick Magee, closely watched by the police for years, was a dedicated terrorist and former prisoner whose mission took him all over Great Britain and the continent.[333] It was he who bestowed on Thatcher's extraordinary premiership one of its most dramatic moments in 1984 during the Conservative Party conference—by planting the bomb at the Grand Hotel, Brighton, whose killings on 12 October almost included Thatcher herself (Plate 7). When the restored hotel was reopened in 1986 she had at first intended only to send a congratulatory telegram, but 'last minute impulse' led her to attend. Recalling the event during which he had been seriously injured and his wife permanently paralysed, the Conservative cabinet minister Norman Tebbit described with characteristically wry humour how 'room service was rather slow on that night—I had to wait three and a half hours before anyone came'.[334]

Counter-insurgency techniques may have worked well in Malaya, but they were less suited to urban contexts. More importantly, in Northern Ireland they were unacceptable. The black-and-tan episode of 1920–1 was a standing warning on how sensitive British opinion could be on such matters: to destroy homes and forcibly relocate British citizens would be a cure worse than the disease. So in tackling terrorism close to home, the army had one hand tied behind its back, and its physical force merely angered Catholic opinion without intimidating it. The IRA was not winning either: it had merely fought the army into a stalemate, and in retrospect Danny Morrison's rhetorical question at Sinn Fein's convention on 31 October 1981 was historic: 'will anyone here object if, with a ballot paper in this hand, and an Armalite in this hand, we take power in Ireland?'[335] The republican shift towards political participation for whatever purpose worked with the grain of opinion in Northern Ireland. To judge from the five elections (by proportional representation) to the European Parliament, its people were eager to vote, for their turnout was far higher than in Great Britain. And though turnout in six of the eight parliamentary elections between 1970 and 1997 was lower than in Great Britain, the SDLP could usually attract at least a fifth of the votes cast. If only the Catholic voters could be fully mobilized and united, they might at least come close to the Unionist vote, which rarely constituted more than half the votes cast. The difficulty had hitherto been that whereas Paisley's Democratic Unionist Party acted as a sort of ginger group for the Ulster Unionist Party, the IRA had fragmented the Republican impact by cutting across the SDLP's non-violent

---

[332] Speech in Ulster, *T* (29 May 1981), 2.   [333] For a portrait see *G* (12 June 1986), 4.
[334] *DT* (29 Aug. 1986), 2.   [335] Quoted in English, *Armed Struggle*, 225.

strategy. When in 1983 Sinn Fein for the first time contested seats in the British parliamentary election, all this changed, and British politicians felt an even greater need to give the SDLP voters some hope that the ballot box would deliver results.

Thatcher recalled that her Irish policy 'was always...determined by whatever I considered at a particular time would help bring better security'.[336] With this in view, she developed one of those personal relationships with individual statesmen that were so important in shaping her foreign policy—with the Irish prime minister Dr Garret FitzGerald, whom she learnt to trust. In 1985 'Dr FitzGerald and I', a phrase she frequently came to employ, brought off with great difficulty the Anglo-Irish Agreement, whose main impulse was to assist the SDLP within the republican movement. The Agreement was important less for its precise proposals, which were not substantial, as for the change of mood in the two governments which had made it possible, and for its vision of the directions that political progress could usefully take. Both governments declared that Northern Ireland's constitutional position should remain unchanged while the majority so wished, and an intergovernmental conference of ministers with a permanent secretariat was set up for organizing regular meetings to discuss matters of shared interest.

In retrospect the Agreement anticipated the more substantial Anglo-Irish Declaration promulgated in 1993. Unionist hostility to the Agreement was predictable, and Unionist politicians had to respond to it for fear of losing control. Paisley had already in 1981 conjured up the memories of Carson and the Covenant by inviting pressmen to witness a secret display of Unionist fighting capacity on a windswept mountainside.[337] Unionists did not show themselves sufficiently united or resolute to destroy the Agreement, whose overwhelming endorsement at Westminster exposed them as vulnerable there too. The SDLP now gained ground over Sinn Fein, whose share of the votes cast declined from 13.4 per cent in 1983 to 11.4 in 1987 and 10.1 per cent in 1992. Mounting influence accrued to John Hume, SDLP leader since 1979; his resolute pursuit of what he called 'a healing process' in Northern Ireland accelerated the approach towards peace in 1993–4.[338] On the other hand, the Agreement's undermining of the Protestant politicians may help to explain the growing salience of more desperate Protestant methods: their share of sectarian killings rose from 15.4 per cent in 1980–4 to 29.9 per cent in 1985–9 to 47.2 per cent in 1990–4.[339] The sustained pressure on the IRA from both sides of

---

[336] Thatcher, *Downing Street Years*, 384.

[337] C. Seton, 'Paisley Men Rally on a Windswept Mountain', *T* (7 Feb. 1981), 3.

[338] For FitzGerald's more detailed list of what the agreement had achieved see his letter in *T* (7 Oct. 1987), 17.

[339] Malcolm Sutton's updated (Oct. 2002) statistics at http://cain.ulst.ac.uk/sutton/book/#append, consulted 21 July 2007.

the border that Thatcher hoped for did not materialize, and the Agreement did not advance power-sharing or widen the scope of Anglo-Irish collaboration as rapidly as had been hoped.

Through all this, Westminster's all-party consensus on Northern Ireland did not crack, nor were British troops withdrawn, nor did the IRA give up. Its process of forming policy should not be over-intellectualized. Skill at killing people and at manipulating the public response to killings does not bring success unless the strategy is right, and there lay the IRA's major weakness, for its hatreds and conspiratorial outlook denied it the breadth of perspective that could be secured only through open debate. It was prison that gave IRA leaders from the late 1970s the opportunity and the leisure for much-needed reflection, given that IRA prisoners were left remarkably free to associate with one another, and to establish a semi-military structure. For Magee, the Maze prison offered a first-class degree with the Open University and a doctorate on how the troubles had influenced the popular novel. Others engaged in research, writing, and thought about their movement at a more practical level, for here was a terrorist university—or, rather, a university for drawing its students away from terrorism. Coolest of all, perhaps, at least to British eyes, for he was popular enough among his own people, was Gerry Adams, President of Sinn Fein from 1983. Articulate, intelligent, and invariably well-groomed, he had been born into the republican purple, and combined charisma and ruthlessness with skill at presenting indefensible actions in the best possible light. A brave man, who eventually risked assassination from his own side by making overtures of a sort to the enemy, he never seemed to lose his temper, despite four years of internment, despite having been shot in the chest and neck by 'loyalists' in 1984, and despite being obliged heavily to fortify his semi-detached house in Belfast against unwanted visitors.

Secret meetings between leading British politicians and republican leaders had been frequent in the early 1970s, and contacts of a sort were maintained at intervals thereafter. Wilson met republican leaders secretly in Dublin in 1971 and again in 1972 in England, and Whitelaw as Secretary of State for Northern Ireland met them secretly in Chelsea in 1972. Senior officials met Sinn Fein leaders regularly near Belfast in 1974–5, and in 1978 Hurd met Adams in Belfast. Such high-level talks, embarked upon with the best of motives, carried the risk of polarizing Northern Ireland still further, for they enhanced the IRA's credibility among its followers, and simultaneously boosted republican hopes and Unionist fears. So much so, that governments in the Irish Republic, which repudiated any contact with terrorists, felt undermined and exasperated with UK governments.[340] In the longer term, however, these contacts gave republican leaders confidence that a conciliatory approach would not be rebuffed. Helpful,

---

[340] See Garret FitzGerald's forcible complaints in *Ind* (13 July 1996), 17.

too, at the end of the 1980s were unexpected international developments, and
to these the nationalists had long been more alert than the Ulster Unionists.
Gorbachev's remarkable achievement in presiding over the peaceful break-up
of the Soviet empire was followed by a wave of peaceful and democratic
revolutions in Eastern Europe. These advertised how powerful the critics
of unpopular governments could be if they could substitute even the threat
of mass violence for the reality of stunt violence. Thereafter, long-standing
disputes need no longer be inflamed by entanglement in the cold war, and
a most unexpected peaceable settlement followed in South Africa. Television
advertised the massive suffering that resulted from failure to compromise,
most notably in Yugoslavia. By 1990, then, the pieces were moving into
place for further progress towards a peaceable Irish outcome—though by
blowing up Thatcher's close associate, the Conservative MP Ian Gow in
1990, and by organizing massive destruction of property in the City of
London in the early 1990s, the IRA demonstrated the distance still to be
travelled.

The untold suffering stemming from the inhumane direction politics in
Northern Ireland had taken after the late 1960s has already been touched upon.
Families and friendships were torn apart by deaths, imprisonments, and sheer
intensity of feeling. The consequences of the killings and the maimings (physical
and mental) long outlasted 'the troubles', and public apologies for unintended
outrages such as Black Friday (1972) offered small comfort. The terrorists also
discussed the publicity setback involved in other incidents—the accidental
killing of British children, for instance[341]—but only behind the scenes. The
decline in the quality of life in Northern Ireland was serious enough to
accelerate Protestant migration to Great Britain, which in turn accentuated
Ulster Unionist defensiveness. Although in the 1940s and 1950s the Catholics
had left for Great Britain in disproportionate numbers, the relatively high
Catholic birth-rate had long encouraged Unionist speculation about when there
would be a Catholic majority in Northern Ireland.[342] Terence O'Neill explained
in 1969 that 'the basic fear of Protestants in Northern Ireland is that they will
be outbred by Roman Catholics. It is as simple as that.' Protestant worries
about the mounting loss of Protestant university students to Great Britain were
reinforced when the census of 1991 showed an acceleration in the Catholic
proportion of Northern Ireland's population. Some statisticians specified 2025
as the year when numbers in the two subgroups would equalize,[343] though two
assumptions were often mistakenly made: that the Catholic birth-rate would be

---

[341] In their secret oral contact with the government on 22 Mar. 1993 the IRA claimed to accept
responsibility 'with total sadness' for accidentally killing two children in Warrington, *DT* (30 Nov.
1993), 12.

[342] F. S. L. Lyons, *Ireland since the Famine* (1971), 745. P. Buckland, *History of Northern Ireland*
(Dublin, 1981), 24.   [343] *G* (13 Oct. 1993), ii, 16.

unaffected by affluence, and that Catholics would necessarily favour integration with the Republic.

The substantial growth of public welfare in Northern Ireland after 1945 had been one factor accentuating the divide between north and south,[344] and in economic planning at the regional level the Northern Ireland government pioneered several approaches introduced into Great Britain after 1964.[345] Given the cheapness of houses in Northern Ireland, its public employees on British pay-scales were relatively prosperous in real terms. In the early 1990s Northern Ireland's private-sector output was 64 per cent of Great Britain's, yet British subsidies ensured that consumption there ran at 82 per cent of Great Britain's.[346] The 'troubles' from the 1960s seriously damaged the economy in Ireland north and south, most notably by discouraging inward investment and tourism: whereas the number of UK visitors to eight European countries was shooting up between 1971 and 1986, to the Irish Republic visitors hardly increased at all.[347] The troubles were also a drain on Great Britain through defence costs and transfer payments. They enhanced the Province's dependence on British subsidy, given that they discouraged private investment and extended government employment, especially in security. Taxpayers paid huge sums in security costs, in compensation for damage to property and person, and in welfare benefits to people who would not otherwise have been injured or unemployed.[348] Terrorism lowered the quality of life for millions in the UK and the Republic. The public grew accustomed in Northern Ireland to being frisked on entering stores, and both there and elsewhere to keeping their baggage with them at all times, to unpredictable disruptions of commuter trains, and to the lack of litter bins and post boxes in prominent places, not to mention the hours of tedium for the police involved in preventive and protective work.

In London, as in Belfast, people went phlegmatically about their business, routinely coping with the risks of terrorism, just as commuters struggled to work through the strikes, and travellers at airports trooped uncomplainingly through the metal detectors designed to prevent hijacking. Given that IRA atrocities in Great Britain from the 1970s onwards were so ruthless and random, the lack of British resentment against the many Irish-born settlers in Great Britain is surprising; between 1961 and 1981 about half settled in the south-east (with sizeable Irish enclaves in London), and an eighth in the Midlands, both areas where atrocities occurred.[349] Some hostility was generated

---

[344] Lyons, *Ireland since the Famine*, 731.   [345] V. Bogdanor, *Devolution* (Oxford, 1979), 65.
[346] *Econ* (6 Nov. 1993), 22.
[347] British Tourist Authority, *Digest of Tourist Statistics*, 10 (Oct. 1982), 33; 13 (Aug. 1989), 42; 17 (Dec. 1993), 48.
[348] For attempts to quantify the economic cost see *T* (4 Nov. 1983), 1. *FT* (16 Nov. 1985), 7. *Ind* (22 May 1990), 4.   [349] *BST* 573.

by particular incidents,[350] and the mental health of some Irish-born settlers in Great Britain suffered as a result,[351] but much more significant was the ill-treatment and unjust imprisonment[352] of Irish-born people suspected of perpetrating the IRA atrocities of 1974; they languished in prison for years after the IRA had denied their involvement. In this the IRA did the British judicial system a somewhat backhanded favour, exposing the need for reform. In further distancing governments from governed in Great Britain, however, the IRA did British democracy no favours at all. The authoritarian structures that terrorist organizations require tend to prod governments into generating their equal and opposite. The threat of assassination after 1970 distanced British politicians from British voters:[353] hotels in Blackpool and Brighton became fortresses during the party conference season, and steel gates blocked off 10 Downing Street from the general public. Terrorism was one among several impulses to the growth in telephone-tapping and threats to media independence; the latter culminated in government's attempt from 1988 to 1994 to deny terrorists the glamour of publicity by excluding the IRA from radio and television.[354]

What significant benefit emerged from all this? An incidental gain was architectural in nature, for if Belfast had shared in British cities' late twentieth-century prosperity, many of its stately Victorian and Edwardian buildings would have been bulldozed to make way for unworthy successors, whereas many survived intact to enhance the city's image once peace had been restored. As for UK relations with the Republic, the British government had never seen partition as precluding a united Ireland, as witnesses the proposal in the Government of Ireland Act (1920) for a council of Ireland elected from its two parliaments. Unionists did nothing to promote it before 1969, however, and from the Catholic point of view the Stormont regime before 1970 was far from ideal. The civil-rights protests of the late 1960s gave a new salience to Catholic opinion, and both tourist revenue[355] and cross-border collaboration showed signs of advance before 1970. If both had continued thereafter in conjunction with shared membership of the EEC, a gradual moderation of old enmities might have been expected, with all the attendant prosperity. As it was, the killings and maimings still further postponed such prospects, though they also had the effect (unintended by both Protestant and Catholic terrorists) of bringing the British and Irish governments closer even than their shared participation in the EEC would have effected; politicians on both sides of the border detested terrorism. Nor could the violence arrest the ongoing cultural and social integration of Southern Ireland into the UK, a long-term process

---

[350] See e.g. responses to the Ideal Home Exhibition bombs, *T* (2 Apr. 1976), 15. *G* (2 Apr. 1976), 1.
[351] *G* (9 Feb. 1998), 2.   [352] See Ch. 7.   [353] See Ch. 7.
[354] For chronologies of these threats see *T* (1 Aug. 1985), 2. *Ind* (28 Nov. 1990), 21.
[355] For figures from the 1960s see Lyons, *Ireland since the Famine*, 679.

not at all desired by unionist or nationalist militants in Northern Ireland. The number of tourists from the Republic to the UK rose almost threefold between 1975 and 1995;[356] across the Irish Sea, as elsewhere in the world, communications between independent nations were tightening not loosening. In minutes of telecommunications traffic, the UK in 1991 took 70 per cent of the Republic's outgoing traffic, with the USA (10 per cent) as nearest competitor.[357] But the greatest failure of Northern Ireland's unionist and nationalist causes has yet to be mentioned. The inexcusably inhumane methods espoused by some of their advocates were not only counter-productive: they permanently discredited causes once dignified.

This chapter has shown how the 1970s and 1980s witnessed a major retreat from the agricultural strategy so central to British policy during and after the war, and how this coincided with EEC membership and a newly aroused environmentalism. Yet at the same time transport's demands on the environment continued to escalate. Not only did they rake over the face of the country: they threatened urban peace and amenity. The towns fought back, preventing further damage from urban motorways, exposing in architecture the practical drawbacks of the modern style, and displaying a new awareness of the need for architectural conservation while at the same time rapidly extending owner-occupation. We have also seen how, if the speed of economic and social change threatened many aspects of the traditional community, new technologies were in many respects drawing town and country together, and were simultaneously drawing minorities into new communities that could not earlier have existed. As for Northern Ireland's special circumstances, few indeed by 1990 had any hope that its two deeply entrenched communities might eventually merge, if only because so much had occurred since 1970 to prise them apart.

All eight motifs have once more featured in this chapter. Environmentalism presented the first frontal challenge to the post-war materialist agenda, thereby accentuating the contrast between the anxious tone of public economic debate and the quietly private enjoyment of affluence (the third motif). Relatively alert to the drawbacks of faster travel, the environmentalists chimed in with those who recognized how complex was its link with the pace of daily living (the fourth motif). These recreational and materialistic priorities put further strain on religious institutions (the fifth motif), though less in Northern Ireland than elsewhere. The most notable motif to surface in this chapter, however, is the seventh: how heavily the politicians depended upon opinion to generate effective change, not only on environmental issues throughout the UK, but on community issues in Northern Ireland. Where consensus did not

---

[356] *Digest of Tourist Statistics*, 17 (Dec. 1993), 20; 20 (Dec. 1996), 20.
[357] Staple (ed.), *Telegeography 1992*, 94.

already exist within the community, the politicians with the best of intentions could not create it. Northern Ireland also highlights the remaining motifs, though the sixth (political stability persisting amidst social change) only by contrast, for there social change was slow indeed, whereas political change was recurrent yet ineffective. Given the impact of American, European, and Irish Republican encouragements to the nationalists, the second (hermetic/receptive) motif also features. The Unionists, on the other hand, neglected their own interests by carrying the UK's hermetic tendencies to an extreme. Northern Ireland's implications for the eighth motif (the UK's pursuit of a role) were considerable, for 'the troubles' severely embarrassed any UK worldwide claim to exemplify democratic practice. Nor could the UK claim any distinctive role on environmental issues, which by definition and in practice readily crossed national boundaries. The Second World War's equivocal influence (the first motif) was in Northern Ireland unhelpful, given its prominence in Ulster Unionist mythology. Yet the Unionists' fading rapport with UK opinion reveals the limits to the war's impact on current UK issues, and in agriculture the UK made remarkably little fuss about completely reversing one of the war's most substantial domestic achievements.

CHAPTER 3

The Social Structure

The social-class hierarchy in the UK, while far stiffer than in the USA, had never been as rigid as in some European countries, and in the 1970s and 1980s continued to display its flexibility in the face of strongly meritocratic and even demotic pressures. This chapter's first section will discuss how surprisingly unaffected was the monarchy's standing in the face of the apparent aristocratic decline that is discussed in the second section, though that decline masked a remarkable capacity for unobtrusive survival. The third section focuses on the middle-class capacity for sustained expansion through fragmentation and evangelism, moving on in the fourth section to the painful transition made by the trade unions during these decades. Erosion at its upper boundary showed signs of shrinking the working class into what the Victorians would have called a 'residuum', discussed in the chapter's fifth section: a miscellaneous, unintegrated grouping of the deprived and the underprivileged to which social-class categories could scarcely apply. Still less did they apply to the theme of the chapter's sixth and final section: the ethnic minorities. Their advent has been discussed in Chapter 2's second section: here the discussion turns to their patterns of settlement.

I. THE MONARCHY IN TROUBLE

British society's meritocratic, irreverent, and even egalitarian tone from the 1960s posed a special threat to monarchy. Reticence and respect, formality and precedent, were integral to its current role; dignity and ceremonial implied social distance, and the Queen kept her own counsel. Yet all British institutions were now being required to explain and justify themselves. Furthermore, mid-century incomes policies lent a new sharpness to the public discussion of class relations, from which in an inflationary situation the monarchy could not long be shielded.[1] The tradition in the British radical press for sniffing out scandal in high places began to transcend the gossip column (whose methods had been

---

[1] As noted in Benn's speech to a co-operative and trades union conference on 27 Jan. 1974, *G* (28 Jan. 1974), 4.

ruthlessly exposed by Penelope Gilliatt in the early 1960s), and to pervade the
late twentieth-century media with a knowingly irreverent tone. Undeterred by
discouragements from the rich and powerful, investigative journalists—Bruce
Page, Tom Bower, and Paul Foot—found much that was worth exposing,
concurrently with Robin Day's forthright style when interrogating public
figures on television. Press and political elite, hitherto locked in mutual wary
respect, now (like so many other segments of public life) began to go their
separate ways. Milestones along this road were the slow emergence of the truth
about the Suez venture in 1956, the *Sunday Times*'s campaign in the 1960s for
justice to thalidomide victims, the example set in the early 1970s by American
investigative journalists exposing President Nixon, and the appointment of
Kelvin MacKenzie as the *Sun*'s editor in 1981. In that year the Queen's Press
Secretary invited editors of the national newspapers to a meeting where he
asked them to allow the Princess of Wales more privacy; alone among editors,
MacKenzie did not attend.[2] By the 1990s the Queen could no longer rest secure
at the apex of an accepted social hierarchy graded continuously from top to
bottom, nor could she assume that her dealings with press and public would
operate within an unspoken gentlemanly code of conduct. In 1992 MacKenzie
even stole a march on other papers by breaking the embargo on the advance
publication of her Christmas message.[3] Boisterous lapses of taste and earthy
headlines poured out from this energetic and influential journalist, whose pert
pinpricks could as readily puncture MPs as monarchs.[4] Yet in probing relations
between the Prince and Princess of Wales, for example, the journalists in their
early brushed-aside warnings were often later vindicated.

   In her taste for country pursuits the Queen resembled her parents and a
wide section of the British upper class. Throughout her reign she accumulated
expertise on horses and racing by regularly resorting to *Sporting Life*; to relieve
the tensions inevitably accompanying her role, says her biographer, 'horses
remained her refuge'.[5] But after 1970 the decline in its props of aristocracy
and empire exposed the monarchy to the full blast of egalitarian fashion, and
few now chose publicly to defend the hereditary principle, however willing
they might be to act upon it in their own lives. Furthermore, for all her
institutional traditionalism, Thatcher in her peculiar variant of Conservatism
did not encourage traditionalist deference, and in the 1990s the inexpensive
and relatively informal styles of the Scandinavian and newly revived Spanish
monarchies seemed relatively attractive. The British monarchy was not yet in
danger, but it was moving into waters more stormy than any experienced for two
generations. Nor was it easy at a time of waning and diversifying religious faith

   [2] *T* (9 Dec. 1981), 1.   [3] *T* (24 Dec. 1992), 1. *G* (24 Dec. 1992), 20.
   [4] See his evidence before the Heritage select committee in *DT* (22 Jan. 1993), 11.
   [5] B. Pimlott, *The Queen: A Biography of Elizabeth II* (1996), 361.

for the Queen to combine her role as head of the established church with her other responsibilities. Modern monarchy can survive the decline of aristocracy only if it can perform a triple balancing act: through upholding tradition without seeming archaic, through preserving dignity without seeming to lose touch, and through appearing approachable while still seeming special. Shrewd republicans disclaimed any hostility to the Queen herself and instead attacked the monarchy's powers and revenue:[6] forty-seven MPs voted against a royal pay-rise in December 1971, eighty-nine in February 1975. The parliamentary voice of British republicanism was not weighty: Willie Hamilton was a miner's son who became a hard-working parliamentarian, but was a publicity-seeker more than a serious threat. After the civil-list settlement of 1971, public funding was placed on a new basis, and the monarchy's return on expenditure was henceforth subject to frequent and unprecedented public review. Republicanism became fashionable in some middle-class circles late in the 1980s, but it found no powerful advocate or publicist, and never transcended its negative tone. The Queen had little to fear from such scrutiny, but not so her family.

For her children's problems the Queen, like any parent, was partly respons-ible, and in dealing with family matters she seems to have been less adroit than in handling the more public aspects of her role—showing something of her mother's reluctance to get involved. But her family problems had their institutional dimension. There was first the difficulty for monarchy of com-bining the romantic love concept with the persistence of inherited status. In 1936 Edward VIII could not marry the divorced woman of his choice and remain King, nor twenty years later could Princess Margaret as the Queen's sister retain her status if she married the commoner Peter Townsend.[7] Royal relationships were complicated further by the intense strain of living in the public eye. For example, press intrusiveness now precluded the informal mar-ital 'arrangements' once widespread in upper-class circles. 'The man should sow his wild oats and have as many affairs as he can before settling down', Earl Mountbatten advised his great-nephew Prince Charles in 1974, 'but for a wife he should choose a suitable, attractive and sweet-charactered girl *before* she met anyone else she might fall for'.[8] Such attitudes did not harmonize well with media as intrusive as they had now become. Yet by 1978 attitudes had relaxed sufficiently for there to be no fuss when Princess Margaret's marriage to Anthony Armstrong-Jones was dissolved, and little success for the subsequent attempt to work up public indignation when she holidayed in Mustique with the pop singer Roddy Llewellyn.[9] Nor did Princess Anne's separation from Captain Mark Phillips in 1989 weaken the rising esteem she won through her

---

[6] e.g. Benn, *Diaries 1980–90*, 142 (29 July 1981).   [7] Harrison, *Seeking a Role*, 180, 296.
[8] Quoted in P. Ziegler, *Mountbatten: The Official Biography* (1985), 687.
[9] *T* (3 Apr. 1978), 1, 13. For a substantial obituary of Townsend see *DT* (21 June 1995), 31.

charitable work.[10] In one respect these broken marriages made the royal family more representative in a society whose families were changing fast. Its example-setting role, highlighted by Bagehot in his classic text on the constitution, had never entailed much more than reflecting, after a discreet interval, the family values of the day.

Old enmities were eased skilfully away when the Queen visited the Duke of Windsor for the first time in 1972, and when she invited his widow to stay at Buckingham Palace for the Duke's funeral ceremonies.[11] But there was a distance, and even a coolness, between the Queen and her eldest son, and her failure to get her husband's relationship with him on to a sounder footing was in the long term damaging, personally and institutionally. Reflective, well-intentioned, and versatile, the Prince of Wales lacked the application to seize his chance in the late 1970s of getting a better grasp of public affairs, and was overfastidious in feeling 'so unsuited to the ghastly business of human intrigue and general nastiness'.[12] The outcome was all too often the sort of yearning but petulant and frustrated ineffectuality which Alan Clark memorably observed during a lunch held at Highgrove in 1988 to promote one of the Prince's many good causes.[13] The Prince was too shy to relish the publicity into which he was born, too impatient and imaginative to see his indeterminate role as anything other than a 'great problem in life'.[14] On the other hand, the Prince's Trust carried the long-standing association between monarchy and philanthropy to new heights, and Prince Charles like his father showed courage in opening up new issues for public debate.

Princess Anne's limited social connections and brusque manner with the press were at first unhelpful, but her image greatly improved through her dedicated and highly professional work for the Save the Children Fund. Prince Andrew, the Queen's second son, helped to ensure that in the early 1980s the monarchy participated fully in the rediscovery of patriotism that flowed from the Falklands war. During the highly emotional scenes when the aircraft carrier HMS *Invincible* was welcomed back to Portsmouth (Plate 3) in September 1982, the Queen was observed to be in tears on the bridge when greeting the Prince, whose role as a helicopter pilot had been much publicized.[15] The subsequent extravagance of his domestic arrangements, however, highlighted the rising cost of supporting an expanding royal family, and Prince Edward in his early adult years was no help at all. Wth his mother's consent he mounted a royal version of the popular television competition programme *It's a Knockout*.

---

[10] See the interesting leader 'Daylight upon Magic', *T* (1 Sept. 1989), 13.
[11] *T* (19 May 1972), 11; *G* (29 May 1972), 1.
[12] As he told a friend in a letter written in 1992 when his marriage was in real trouble, quoted in Dimbleby, *Prince of Wales*, 488.   [13] A. Clark, *Diaries* (1993), 235 (20 Dec. 1988).
[14] Speech at Cambridge University, Nov. 1978, quoted in Dimbleby, *Prince of Wales*, 225.
[15] *T* (18 Sept. 1982), 1, 18.

Broadcast on 19 June 1987 from a muddy Staffordshire field on a damp day, with royal teams dressed in medieval costume and reinforced by media stars, it raised about £1 million for charity, but the programme was thought to have chosen the wrong route towards making the monarchy more accessible. Still less helpful were the Prince's media ventures in the 1990s, and his petulant response to their failure.

The monarchy's survival during this difficult period owed much to public inertia, but much also to a widely felt national need for institutionalized dignity, continuity, and impartiality amidst declining international influence, rapid social change, and sharp party controversy. The monarchy's customary expertise at organizing and even enhancing formal ceremonial persisted. Pageantry at the jubilee celebrations of 1977 was as splendid and meticulous as ever, and was enhanced by the unexpected issue of a silver jubilee medal to 30,000 recipients on the following day to people who had been connected with the jubilee or who had given service throughout the Queen's reign.[16] Yet there were some awkward juxtapositions. It was pointed out at the time that Princess Anne's wedding in 1973 occurred only two days after a national state of emergency had been declared owing to the miners' ban on overtime, and that the night before the Prince of Wales's wedding in 1981 had seen the worst night's rioting in Liverpool during the past month.[17] 'Day of romance in a grey world' was the headline on *The Times*'s wedding souvenir number.[18] On the other hand, the monarchy was making itself more approachable. The royal walkabout, pioneered as early as 1957 in the USA, was revived in Malta in 1967 and in New Zealand in March 1970; in the UK it was first applied at Coventry three months later. On the Queen's silver wedding anniversary in 1972 the royal family lunched in the Guildhall and then spent fifty minutes talking to passers-by.[19] The criteria for invitation to Buckingham Palace garden parties had gradually broadened, so that 35,000 a year were being invited by 1983, and by then the masses were invading the Palace interior: in 1962 its rebuilt chapel was opened to the public as an art gallery, and from 1993 tourists were admitted to parts of the Palace itself.[20]

It's a Knockout was by no means typical of the monarchy's media ventures in these years. The Queen's embracing of the media was not universally welcomed, but the critics never explained how the monarchy could survive without exploiting the most modern and effective means of communication, nor did they recommend any practicable alternative. Princess Anne ventured further by giving the press a ninety-minute interview before her wedding in

[16] *T* (8 June 1977), 1, 4; (9 June 1977), 1.
[17] *T* (15 Nov. 1973), 1; (30 July 1981), 6; cf. W. Hamilton in *T* (25 Feb. 1981), 2.
[18] *T* (30 July 1981), 1; cf. 3 (the Archbishop of Canterbury's address).
[19] Pimlott, *The Queen*, 284, 397; E. Longford, *Elizabeth R: A Biography* (1983), 266; *T* (21 Nov. 1972), 1.   [20] Longford, *Elizabeth R*, 209–10. *Ind* (30 Apr. 1993), 1.

1973, and in September 1985 she became the first member of the royal family to participate in a radio phone-in.[21] The close interaction between monarchy and media was patent during the Prince of Wales's wedding in 1981, when people on the processional route followed the procession and the service on their portable television sets while the streets behind them were almost empty because people were clustering round their screens at home.[22] The national pattern of demand for electricity coincided closely with the service's details, producing surges at the dull moments after the couple had made their vows at the altar, when the register was being signed, when the procession arrived at Buckingham Palace, and when the couple had left Waterloo for their honeymoon. These reflected the decision to put on the kettle, turn on lights and ovens, or visit the loo.[23] The monarchy did not confine its innovations to mere presentation. New roles were embarked upon. The trend established in the 1920s by the future Edward VIII for combining overseas visits with promoting British trade fairs and other business contacts was pushed much further.[24] And although the royal family were conservative in their social connections and recreations, the Duke of Edinburgh and later the Prince of Wales were imaginative and even courageous in causes espoused: encouraging nature conservation, new approaches to architecture and estate management, enterprise among businessmen and youth, and a healthy scepticism about professional pretensions in the arts, medicine, education, and the media.

Yet the prime reason for the monarchy's survival lay with the Queen herself. Sheer longevity, good health, and accumulated experience helped, but her contribution lay deeper than that. Addressing the Guildhall lunch in honour of her silver wedding anniversary in 1972, she revealed two of her major assets. 'I think everybody really will concede', she said, 'that on this, of all days, I should begin my speech with the words "My husband and I"'.[25] She was highlighting the fact that in her married life she continued, slightly but suitably behind the times, to set the example which Bagehot a century before had included among monarchy's major functions. At the same time she gave the public a rare glimpse of the light vein of humour so relished by her intimates. When receiving Nicholas Henderson before he was posted as ambassador to Washington, she briefly revealed her unusual combination of qualities. She might in formal situations seem rather stiff, yet on other occasions she could be 'extremely natural', and Henderson thought this 'one of her outstanding qualities coupled with great self-discipline'. On this occasion she 'was obviously wanting to find something to laugh about', and 'when she laughs her whole face creases', a feature 'particularly noticeable because otherwise it is very

[21] *T* (12 Nov. 1973), 6; (4 Sept. 1985), 3.   [22] *T* (30 July 1981), 4.
[23] M. Dickson, 'The Power Behind the Royal Wedding', *FT* (31 July 1981), 30.
[24] On this see O (26 Oct. 1969), 6.   [25] *T* (21 Nov. 1972), 17.

composed'.[26] The jubilee tours of 1977 revealed a personal popularity far greater than had been expected a year earlier;[27] a habit of organizing street parties then began (Plate 8) which in many places continued for years afterwards. The monarchy gained immeasurably from the revived interest in the national 'heritage' which grew out of expanding tourism from overseas and growing access to leisure at home. When the Prince of Wales's engagement was announced in February 1981, shares rose appreciably in companies making souvenirs and in hotel chains benefiting from tourism.[28] In 1982 Roy Strong described how the Queen handled the distribution of honours, with no sign of boredom, and with a 'always a word . . . a lot of nods, the face composed with momentary understanding and concern, then always released into a happy smile'.[29] She was shrewd enough to know when and how to change in order to preserve, and as the years passed, the unconsciously cut-glass accent of her early speeches slowly and probably unconsciously evolved into southern 'received pronunciation'.[30] Conventionally feminine yet authoritative and dignified, she had intuitively discovered how a major institutional transition could be brought off smoothly and with quiet style.

2. THE COUNTRY HOUSE REVIVED

At Harold Macmillan's memorial service in 1987 Alan Clark felt depressed. When Macmillan had enlisted in 1914 Britain had been 'at the very height of her power and dominion', with 'the habitual bearing, stoicism, self-sacrifice, sense of "fair play"; the whole *tenu* of the English upper class . . . in place and unquestioned, looked up to and copied everywhere. Now look at us—and them!'[31] Clark was focusing on appearance rather than reality: after 1970, as before, the British upper-class instinct for self-preservation survived. They displayed the same flexibility at their class frontier, and the same mix of qualities: lineage and title, wealth and lifestyle, personal merit and power. Each now requires consecutive discussion.

Whereas the nineteenth century had slowly decoupled honours from owning a landed estate, the twentieth century slowly decoupled honours from owning property of any kind. This happened gradually, unobtrusively, and in characteristic British fashion; outward forms changed far less than inner realities. Wilson as prime minister continued to broaden admission to honours

---

[26] Henderson, *Mandarin*, 272 (16 June 1979).
[27] See the editorial 'The Jubilee Achievement', *T* (13 Aug. 1977), 12.   [28] *T* (25 Feb. 1981), 2.
[29] R. Strong, *Diaries 1967–1987* (1st publ. 1997, paperback edn. 1998), 313 (9 Mar. 1982).
[30] As Australian researchers revealed in 2000: *T* (21 Dec. 2000), 1;*G* (21 Dec. 2000), 21. For a *tour de force* of technicality making the same point, see J. Harrington, 'An Acoustic Analysis of "Happy-Tensing" in the Queen's Christmas Broadcasts', *Journal of Phonetics*, 34/4 (Oct. 2006), 439–57.
[31] Clark, *Diaries*, 158 (10 Feb. 1987).

by abandoning hereditary honours and curbing the numbers awarded to civil servants. Some felt that his resignation honours list of 1976 carried the trend almost to the point of farce,[32] but the inclusion of 34 people in sport, entertainment, and culture among the 619 awarded honours in June 1982 demonstrated the all-party impulse behind decoupling honours from the class system and aligning them with merit and even with celebrity.[33] This was not what had at first been expected from a Conservative government after 1979. Thatcher revived political honours, which Labour had discontinued between 1966 and 1970 and again between 1974 and 1979. In this she was backed by the Liberals, and 56 of the 702 New Year honours in 1980, none of them for Labour, were political.[34] Thatcher was far readier than Heath to keep her backbenchers in line through deploying knighthoods, nor did she rule out hereditary honours, though these, she said, 'would have to be for something of very great distinction'.[35] The first hereditary peerage since 1964 was created for her right-hand man in cabinet, William Whitelaw, who became a viscount in 1983; as she once said, with unconscious humour, 'every prime minister needs a Willie'. In 1991 her husband acquired a hereditary baronetcy which, unlike Whitelaw's title, continued down the male line.

Thatcher's enthusiasm for entrepreneurship did not preclude a taxation policy which raised country-house hopes, and here she built upon significant changes that had occurred before she became prime minister. When Labour took office in 1974 country-house morale was at a low ebb. Labour's manifesto promised 'a fundamental and irreversible shift in the balance of power and wealth in favour of working people'; Healey as prospective Chancellor of the Exchequer had allegedly said that he would 'squeeze the rich until the pips squeak',[36] and the new government seemed ready to advance the Edwardian Liberal attack on landed wealth and the 'unearned increment'.[37] Public welfare's advance now involved developing the concept of 'the social wage'; furthermore, with incomes policies yoked to an undiminished faith in planning, wages seemed likely to be determined by publicly prescribed criteria. By 1974 incomes policies were leading Scottish miners to ask whether 'the dirtiest and most dangerous jobs' should be paid less than 'the lightest, most comfortable, least dangerous work'.[38] and governments' need for trade union cooperation on incomes policies

[32] For angry reactions see *T* (27 May 1976), 7; *ST* (30 May 1976), 17; George Hutchinson in *T* (29 May 1976), 14. For Wilson's policy on honours see Pimlott, *Wilson*, 686; J. Walker, *The Queen Has Been Pleased: The British Honours System at Work* (1986), 150–5.

[33] For useful analyses of honours awarded in June 1982 see Walker, *Queen Has Been Pleased*, 25–6.

[34] *T* (31 Dec. 1979), 1.

[35] *HC Deb.* 26 Nov. 1979, c. 883. For the honours she awarded see *FT* (14 June 1988), 16.

[36] Quotations from I. Dale (ed.), *Labour Party General Election Manifestos 1900–1997* (2000), 212–13. Healey, *Time of my Life*, 369, cf. 463; Healey later denied the claim, but what is significant is that at the time the claim carried conviction.   [37] H. Wilson's speech in *G* (8 Oct. 1974), 1.

[38] The Miners New Charter quoted in *T* (27 June 1974), 2.

lent force to such opinions. Benn thought it unreasonable to assume that in wage planning redistribution should occur only within the working class rather than between classes, and welcomed the fact that 'our class structure is at last being publicly discussed'. He had for some time perceived the growing conflict between shop stewards and the trade unions' national leaders, and knew which side he was on.[39] The Royal Commission on the Distribution of Income and Wealth, chaired by Lord Diamond, collaborated closely with government departments between 1974 and 1979 in illuminating this neglected area, and in June 1974 Benn favoured publishing all salaries, with built-in tax penalties for anyone with a salary more than ten times that of the firm's lowest-paid worker.[40] The fears voiced by Bagehot and the nineteenth-century opponents of a mass franchise seemed at last vindicated, with the miners acting as advance guard for the proletariat.[41]

In the House of Lords debate of 26 June 1974 on the wealth tax, some speakers emphasized the country house's importance to British cultural life and (through tourism) to the economy, but others stressed that such a tax would be unworkable and inequitable, given that wealth and country-house ownership were not correlated. It was also claimed that country-house treasures were a burdensome responsibility rather than props for an extravagant lifestyle, especially as art historians increasingly thought house and contents culturally inseparable. The Duke of Devonshire's mood in September was gloomy: 'if I am driven away from Chatsworth, which is likely, I shall never return, I shall never set foot in Derbyshire again'. In the following January, when the Labour majority in the Commons endorsed the tax, he saw it as 'an historic week, for it means the end of the country estate. It is the end of the English parkscape scene.'[42] Yet this was a turning-point. The landed classes had gained a new lease of life after 1945 by becoming farmer-pensionaries of a state which in peace as in war sought national self-sufficiency in food.[43] Labour's threat of a wealth tax pushed them into a further renewal by causing them to mobilize behind the Historic Houses Association, formed in 1973 to secure tax benefits for country-house owners willing to admit the public. Since the late 1930s the National Trust had been making it easier for owners to remain in the family seat while having it maintained: now the Association's campaign helped win acceptance for the idea that country houses deserved special tax concessions.[44] In 1975 the

---

[39] Benn, speech to a co-operative and trade union conference in London, G (28 Jan. 1974), 4. See also Benn, *Diaries 1968–72*, 285 (19 May 1970), 364 (30 July 1971).

[40] Benn, *Diaries 1973–6*, 165–6 (5 June 1974).

[41] As Benn enjoyed pointing out—see his *Diaries 1973–6*, 619 (5 Oct. 1976), 641 (10 Nov. 1976).

[42] Quoted in Lees-Milne, *Ancient as the Hills*, 192 (16 Sept. 1974). J. Lees-Milne, *Through Wood and Dale: Diaries, 1975–1978* (1998), 9 (25 Jan. 1975).

[43] Harrison, *Seeking a Role*, 128–31; see also pp. 58–60 above.

[44] F. M. L. Thompson, 'English Landed Society in the Twentieth Century. iii. Self-Help and Outdoor Relief', *TRHS* (1992), 19–22.

Victoria and Albert Museum's exhibition on 'The Destruction of the Country House, 1875–1975' consolidated the position. The Capital Transfer Tax Act (1975) exempted houses whose owners opened them to the public for at least sixty days a year. The owners of landed estates banded together to ward off taxation, and especially the threat of a wealth tax, through admitting the public more widely to their homes, through diminishing their tax liability by creating trusts to manage them, and through cultivating a public image for promoting tourism, providing film sets, and conserving national traditions and treasures.[45] Healey eventually concluded that a wealth tax could not be drafted 'which would yield enough revenue to be worth the administrative cost and political hassle'.[46]

So with the distribution of wealth as with educational opportunity,[47] Labour's threats of 1974–9 unintentionally prompted the adversary to regroup. The pace of country-house destruction slowed, and from 1976/7 the equalizing trend in income since the 1930s ceased. By the late 1970s the share of the richest 1 per cent in British personal wealth had fallen from two-thirds before 1914, and from over half in the late 1930s, to a fifth of the total. The share of the top 10 per cent had fallen too, from 85 per cent of the total before 1914 to only half by the late 1970s. If state and occupational pension rights are included, the downward shift in the distribution of wealth had been even more marked.[48] This equalizing trend ceased thereafter, partly because the Thatcher governments' income-tax reforms involved rejecting the idea that poverty is best attacked through equalizing wealth. This shift in attitude was one reason why by 1984/5 income in Britain was distributed almost as unequally as in 1949. The number of people liable to income tax stabilized at about 24 million from the mid-1970s till the end of the century,[49] and whereas by the 1970s the person earning ten times average earnings paid 70 per cent of total income in income tax and national insurance contribution, this had fallen by the 1990s to 38 per cent; gains on this scale were not made among the less wealthy.[50] Yet Conservative policy was only partly responsible for the shift. It was shortly before Thatcher took office that the tide turned, and it turned in several industrial societies, though Britain came second only to New Zealand in the subsequent pace of change.[51] Wage differentials widened in most developed countries after the 1960s, though nowhere faster than in Britain during the 1980s, when they became more unequal than at any time for at least a century.[52] What powered the shift in British wealth distribution was the ongoing growth

[45] Hewison, *Heritage Industry*, 68. Thompson, 'Self-Help and Outdoor Relief', 19.

[46] Healey, *Time of my Life*, 404.   [47] On this see below, p. 390.

[48] C. H. Feinstein, 'The Equalizing of Wealth in Britain since the Second World War', *Oxford Review of Economic Policy*, 12/1 (1996), 102–3.

[49] www.inlandrevenue.gov.uk/stats/taxreceipts/gto41htm, consulted 12 June 2002 (table T1.4).

[50] *G* (10 Mar. 2004), 25. See also *T* (11 Apr. 1997), 29.

[51] Joseph Rowntree Foundation, *Income and Wealth*, i (York, 1995), 13–14.

[52] *FT* (14 Feb. 1994), 19. See also C. Huhne, *G* (18 Dec. 1987), 2.

in home ownership and occupational pensions.[53] These pressures persisted into the 1970s and 1980s, accentuated by a rise in house prices (more significant for the assets of the less wealthy) faster than the rise in share prices (more significant for those of the wealthy).[54]

By 1990 the top 1 per cent of wealth-owners possessed 18 per cent of total marketable wealth, the top 2 per cent nearly a quarter, and the top 10 per cent nearly half.[55] 'New' money reinforced 'old' among the country-house owners of the 1980s: in 1970 George Harrison, the Beatle, bought Friar Park, a huge Victorian Gothic mansion near Henley with a staff of ten gardeners growing exotic flowers.[56] The boom of the 1980s in the City and in City salaries helped create for the first time a national market for country houses, boosted by and boosting the estate agents large enough to handle it: Savills, Chestertons, Cluttons, Lane Fox, Knight Frank and Rutley. It was the large, rural, and preferably listed house that was in demand, and as its price rose, the search for it extended progressively beyond south-eastern England.[57] Boosting the supply was the simultaneous erosion of local authority wealth: by the 1990s many country houses long occupied by institutions (often local authorities) returned to private ownership, sometimes even to the families which had once lived in them.[58] Where no single owner-occupier could be found for an unfurnished older country house, some were rescued and subdivided for multiple occupancy—Burley-on-the-Hill in Rutland, for example, or Callaly Castle in Northumberland—by Kit Martin, enterprising son of the architect Leslie Martin. Multiple occupancy in a rather different guise arrived when the distinction between the country house, the high-class hotel, and the restaurant became less sharp. Furthermore, in the second half of the twentieth century, a few new country houses, mostly neo-Georgian, were being unobtrusively built, by no means all replacing older houses destroyed.[59]

After 1970 the earlier trend continued towards viewing the country house, as well as its estate, as a source of income. In 1973, 9 per cent of the population owned 59 per cent of the land in England and Wales, and although estates might be smaller, they had been rationalized and were managed more professionally.[60] All this helps to explain how 2,250 family seats could survive into the 1990s,[61] and how old-established landed families could then still supply between a fifth and a quarter of the 200 wealthiest people—a proportion that had been stable at

[53] Harrison, *Seeking a Role*, 36, 161–4, 184–5, 265, 284, 318.
[54] Feinstein, 'Equalizing of Wealth', 104.
[55] www.inlandrevenue.gov.uk/stats/taxreceipts/-gto-41htm, consulted 12 June 2002 (table T13.5).
[56] H. Davies, *The Beatles* (1st publ. 1968, rev. edn. 1985), 455.
[57] A. Leyshon and N. Thrift, *Money/Space: Geographies of Monetary Transformation* (1997), 175, 177.
[58] For examples see J. Cornforth, *The Country Houses of England 1948–1998* (1998), 298–9.
[59] J. M. Robinson, *The Latest Country Houses* (1983), 6, 11, 197–234.
[60] H. Newby, *Green and Pleasant Land?* (1979), 40.
[61] J. Paxman, *Friends in High Places: Who Runs Britain?* (1st publ. 1990, paperback edn. 1991), 25–6.

least since the 1880s.[62] Country houses contributed about 1,500 of the 184,000 buildings in England which by 1974 had been statutorily listed as of special historic or architectural interest,[63] and of the 2,013 historic buildings in England open to the public in 1997, 44 per cent were privately owned.[64] These were supplemented by the National Trust: its seventeen significant houses owned in 1945 had become 230 fifty years later.[65] From 1974 historic parks and gardens joined houses in qualifying for grant aid, and during the 1980s English Heritage compiled its register of them, complete with plans and illustrations.

There was a scholarly dimension to the country-house revival, which coincided with a formidable mid-twentieth-century advance in the history of art and architecture. The architects Terry and Erith lent it tangible form with their quiet commitment to reviving the Palladian country-house style.[66] County record office archives were greatly extending understanding of the country house, and a network of expertise opened out from the upper classes into museums and sale rooms. It could not prevent the sale of Mentmore's impressive contents in 1977, but it left less excuse for stripping country houses of the contents around which so many had been built.[67] The Victoria and Albert Museum and the Furniture History Society were greatly improving guidebooks and catalogues, and were encouraging the linked scholarly study of house and contents. Likewise with that fast-growing new scholarly specialism: garden history. It, too, encouraged a fully rounded contextual view of the country house, and was fostered by the need to defend the gardens, not always successfully, against the motorway's intrusion.[68]

The country-house revival had its recreational aspect. The social calendar as at 1971 ran from the Badminton horse trials in April, to the Chelsea Flower Show and Queen Charlotte's Ball in May, to Ascot and Goodwood in June and July, to sailing at Cowes late in July, to shoots in Scotland after the Glorious Twelfth, and thence to hunting in the autumn and winter with the Heythrop or the Duke of Beaufort. The cost of sporting lets reached a new peak: 'the first thing new money wants', said Alan Clark, 'is to trail parties of people round an estate and pretend they've shot something'.[69] The newcomers bought country estates less as investments than because they liked the lifestyle, and most of their wealth was salted away elsewhere.[70] In its jet-set department, the social world also embraced Dublin, Monte Carlo, and Deauville in August, Venice in September, New York in November, the ski-slopes of St Moritz in

---

[62] F. M. L. Thompson, 'English Landed Society in the Twentieth Century. iv. Prestige without Power?', *TRHS* (1993), 1.   [63] *HL Deb.* 26 June 1974, c. 1490.
[64] Cornforth, *Country Houses of England*, 4.   [65] 'James Lees-Milne' in *ODNB*.
[66] On this see pp. 84–5 above.   [67] Cornforth, *Country Houses of England*, 117–18.
[68] For some failures ibid. 194–5.
[69] Quoted in G. Turner, 'New Life for Old Money', *STel* (26 Nov. 1989), 51.
[70] F. M. L. Thompson, 'English Landed Society in the Twentieth Century. ii. New Poor and New Rich', *TRHS* (1991), 19–20.

mid-winter, and the West Indies in January.[71] The country-house party had never died, and the country-house weekend was by now no longer an aristocratic monopoly, if only because the new motorways made it much easier to attend. The year 1971 also witnessed more than 250 private balls, each with between 400 and 800 guests—almost ten times as many as had been held annually in the 1930s.[72] Peter Townend, social editor of the *Tatler* from 1974, appointed himself unofficial and unpaid organizer of the London season in the 1960s and 1970s. Rich in genealogical expertise and a keen raconteur, he found in his later years opportunities for applying the epithet 'common' more frequently than was by then customary. Preoccupied with such topics as dress and manners, discreet yet gossipy, and beset by vendettas, he was a keen matchmaker, and few 'society' weddings eluded his presence. 'In his own way', wrote his *Telegraph* obituarist in 2001, 'he is quite irreplaceable'.[73] Even the political hostess lived on: Pam Hartwell, wife of the *Telegraph*'s chairman, held parties which in 1979 were still 'a traditional and enjoyable feature of elections', and she conducted 'with verve' a salon in London for journalists and politicians.[74]

With growing disposable income and enhanced awareness of its cultural and economic importance, 'old money' regained its self-confidence in the 1980s. The old word 'heritage' acquired a new resonance and political salience during the 1970s, and the 'country-house style' of interior decoration, with its profusion of rich chintz fabrics and hand-blocked wallpapers, made many converts. It had largely been the creation of John Fowler, co-founder of Colefax and Fowler. He decorated most of the major houses in England, including the Queen's audience room at Buckingham Palace and twenty-four major projects for the National Trust, for which he acted as principal adviser on decoration. The style was popularized during the 1980s through the textile firm Laura Ashley.[75] The media were quick to latch on to the country-house revival. In 1971 Joseph Losey's film rendering of L. P. Hartley's *The Go-Between* (1953), adapted by Pinter, brilliantly highlighted the class tensions lurking beneath the smooth surfaces of Edwardian country-house life. A class-conscious generation found 'false consciousness' especially intriguing, and several servants' memoirs became publishable.[76] Also in 1971 the popular costume series *Upstairs, Downstairs* viewed that same world from below stairs, won 15 million viewers in its second week, and ran for six years.[77] In the 1980s some even saw a revived domestic service as helping to cure

---

[71] M. Bowen, 'So What's Happened to the Season?', *ST Magazine* (17 Oct. 1971), 17–34.
[72] Ibid. 18.   [73] *DT* (18 July 2001), 27. See also *T* (18 July 1002), 17.
[74] Henderson, *Mandarin*, 265 (16 May 1979).   [75] Hewison, *Heritage Industry*, 77.
[76] e.g. Margaret Powell's *Below Stairs* (1968) and *Climbing the Stairs* (1969), and Rosina Harrison's *My Life in Service* (1975).
[77] J. Potter, *Independent Television in Britain*, iv. *Companies and Programmes 1968–80* (Basingstoke and London, 1990), 75.

unemployment.[78] In 1981 Granada Television's slow-moving but lush rendering of *Brideshead Revisited* was influential, its nostalgia enhanced by the exotic surroundings of Castle Howard, by Jeremy Irons's voiceover, and by the melancholy trumpets of Geoffrey Burgon's score. A similar rich and nostalgic tone informed the Merchant-Ivory films: drawing heavily on Henry James, E. M. Forster, and Ruth Prawer Jhabvala, they carried country-house nostalgia and England's pastoral image through the 1980s and well into the 1990s, reinforced by the richly evocative and poignant *The Shooting Party* (1985), filmed from Isabel Colegate's novel of 1980.

So in most spheres the 'establishment' remained in place in 1990, but politically it had been retreating for some time. Writing in 2004, the distinguished journalist Anthony Sampson claimed that in the early 1960s the establishment had still seemed in place, but that in the subsequent forty years 'the anti-Establishment' had supplanted it. Wilson, Thatcher, Blair, businessmen, sportsmen, and the media had collectively undermined its political and social power.[79] Under Labour governments such a development would be no surprise, but it continued even under Conservative governments from 1979 to 1997. For all Thatcher's endorsement of the hereditary principle, the essence of Thatcherism was a continuously churning society whose citizens—by saving, investing, inventing, and above all working—were ceaselessly moving up and down the social ladder. Her world could not accommodate a social group defined by its leisure and entrenched by birth and privilege; she had still less time for the languid urbanity of aristocrats in politics. In the free-market economy she espoused so much more enthusiastically than her predecessors, high position had to be earned, and was never secure. In a secular society exposed to decades of socialist rhetoric, she could not hope to provide the one-time moral and religious underpinning for wealth, even had she wished to. Without that, however, wealth's responsible and altruistic deployment could not be guaranteed, and if wealth became the qualification for social status, selfishness and greed would merely be enthroned. By the mid-1980s some were growing concerned that the pursuit of enterprise resembled 'bourgeois triumphalism', and that the long-standing link between wealth and public service was being disrupted.[80] According to the *Oxford English Dictionary* the 'yuppy' was 'a jocular term for a member of a socio-economic group comprising young professional people working in cities' that had originated in the USA by 1984; in his materialistic selfishness and greed the yuppy soon arrived in the UK, nor did there seem

---

[78] e.g. Peregrine Worsthorne, 'Why Domestic Service Should Not be Spurned', *STel* (22 Aug. 1982), 18. See also A. Root, 'Return of the Nanny', *New Socialist*, 22 (Dec. 1984), 16–17.

[79] A. Sampson, *Who Runs This Place? The Anatomy of Britain in the 21st Century* (1st publ. 2004, paperback edn. 2005), 357.

[80] See e.g. P. Worsthorne, 'Bourgeois Triumphalist Threat to Mrs Thatcher', *STel* (7 June 1987), 22, and her inadequate rejoinder, *STel* (28 June 1987), 23.

much limit to top management's wage-claims.[81] By summer 1989 Thatcher was herself concerned at these, which not only dwarfed her own salary, but hardly set the tone for employees whose wages her government then wished to restrain.[82]

Thatcher was the daughter of a provincial Methodist, and the essence of her respectability lay in repudiating values located at both social extremes. Until the 1880s both political parties had been aristocratic in their leadership; thereafter the parties of the left acquired an anti-aristocratic tone, but up to the 1980s the party of the right had remained sympathetic to aristocracy so long as this alignment was compatible with electoral success and growing support lower down. The transition in Conservative leadership in 1965 from the fourteenth Earl of Home to the lower middle-class Edward Heath was less significant for social-class relations than it seemed at the time. 'I am not a product of privilege', said Heath in 1974: 'I am a product of opportunities and individual effort.'[83] Yet his party had adopted meritocratic leaders before without changing its social basis, and Heath was no social revolutionary. Thatcherism, however, generated by the early 1990s a two-party system neither of whose components felt any special affinity with aristocracy. The knights of the shire were slowly dwindling on the Conservative back benches, and Thatcher's sympathies lay not with the landowners, nor even with the bankers and the professions, but with outsiders like the small entrepreneur, the self-made, and the upwardly thrusting working class.

After fighting successfully from 1975 to establish herself within her party against her patrician critics, she gradually outflanked as prime minister the so-called 'wet' advocates of compromise and the middle way. Her enemies were by no means only on the left, given that her untrumpeted aim was to transform her own party as well as Labour. In struggling early on as prime minister to reshape the Conservatives, she tended to ask whether someone was 'one of us': was he dependable when the going got rough? Because she applied the term 'wet' to Conservatives with no stomach for the fight, her supporters were labelled 'dry'.[84] 'Wets' were cautious, conciliatory, moderate, centrist, and self-consciously pragmatic. Their weakness within their party consisted in shortage of zeal and coordination, in lacking a leader, and in the suspicion that their supposed remedies had already been tried and had failed. They were more waspish from the wings than forcible on-stage. Shocked at his first cabinet to witness Thatcher's tone in rebuking a colleague, Christopher Soames (soon himself to be dismissed) said that 'I wouldn't even treat my gamekeeper like that.' By the time the Party's thoughts were being articulated

---

[81] *Oxford English Dictionary.*   [82] M. Wilkinson, 'Snouts in the Trough', *FT* (27 July 1989), 23.

[83] Opening the general election campaign on 11 Feb. 1974, *T* (12 Feb. 1974), 4.

[84] Critchley quoted in Young and Sloman, *Thatcher Phenomenon*, 54. Lawson, *View from No. 11*, 27.

in the lower middle-class tones of Tebbit, who entered the cabinet in 1981, and in MacKenzie's demotic headlines in the *Sun*—it was becoming clear how radical Thatcher's social revolution within her party really was. It was a party, said Healey, which she had 'hijacked . . . from the landowners and given . . . to the estate agents'.[85]

Thatcher's assault on the upper-class 'wets' worked with the grain of advancing political professionalism at Westminster; together with wider parliamentary recruitment, her assault further fragmented the UK's elite. The one-time integral link between the Oxbridge debating societies and recruiting the establishment was eroded by changes at both university and Westminster ends: the Oxford and Cambridge Unions were becoming more recreational in function, academic demands on the student were advancing, the political parties were broadening their image and recruitment, and Thatcher was aiming to divert talent from government into industry and commerce, and to diversify her party's recruitment. Oxbridge might contribute forty-one of the top hundred names in the City in 1993,[86] but this largely reflected recruitment in earlier decades from universities that even then were becoming meritocratic. In the 1990s the financial community as a whole was opening out in all directions, regionally within Britain as well as internationally. By the early 1990s half the chairmen of the top fifty UK companies by turnover had been educated at state schools.[87] The media—now fragmented between radio, television, and the press—were also recruiting more widely, and the press was dispersing from Fleet Street into other parts of London. And if, among Britain's 500 wealthiest people in 1994, clustering in the south-east of England, more than a quarter had inherited their wealth—they were being rapidly joined by Asian entrepreneurs and popular entertainers.[88]

Integral to the ideal of the English gentleman had been a willingness to volunteer for unpaid public service at local and national levels, yet after 1970 both were under serious threat. The phrase 'the great and the good' was increasingly used during the 1970s, slightly facetiously, to describe those who volunteered for high-profile public duties. Although the last Wilson government set about expanding the list, which by 1981 had reached 3,900 names,[89] Thatcher's repudiation of the royal commission as a policy-making device meant that they became less busy. Furthermore, enhanced professionalism felt less need for the upper-class volunteer. The House of Lords witnessed a growing disjunction between its membership and the honours system, a

[85] Soames quoted by Prior in BBC1 television programme *Thatcher: The Downing Street Years* (20 Oct. 1993). Healey quoted in Young and Sloman, *Thatcher Phenomenon*, 55.

[86] *ST* (14 Feb. 1993), iii, 3.   [87] Professor L. Hannah quoted in *FT* (10 Nov. 1993), 22.

[88] *T* (11 Apr. 1994), 3.

[89] P. Hennessy, *The Great and the Good: An Inquiry into the British Establishment* (Policy Studies Institute report, 654; Mar. 1986), 25.

widening divergence between heredity and status. The introduction of life peers in 1958 might have aimed to reform in order to preserve, but the long-term effect was for the life peers slowly to ease out the hereditaries. Up to the end of the century, under the Peerage Act (1963) seventeen peers (including Benn, Hailsham, and Home) disclaimed their titles, though five of their sons resumed them, and two remained in the House as life peers.[90] By the 1970s the hereditary peers were becoming less prominent in Lords business. In challenging the 'wets' within her own party—with their allies in the Foreign Office, the Church of England, the universities, and the professions—Thatcher was only pushing to its ultimate the long withdrawal of the privileged from their public responsibilities. By the end of the 1980s the Duke of Devonshire could describe his wealth as actually hindering political influence: 'if you have a title like mine, then you aren't taken seriously', he said. 'If you are as privileged as I am . . . then you must realize that the price you pay for that is that you cannot have influence.'[91] Still, if the old families no longer sought political power, they got along well enough without it. By the 1990s they encountered no great resentment or jealousy, partly because they were being so amply and recently recruited from below, partly because they were acquiring such useful new functions. There were now fewer distractions to prevent them from quietly conserving their resources: 'a few garden openings . . . otherwise they're just into tax avoidance and gossip columns'.[92]

3. MIDDLE-CLASS TRIUMPH

With the aristocracy tamed and the countryside urbanized, the tripartite class model was fast becoming unhelpful in the late twentieth century.[93] A 'middle class' required the presence of 'upper' and 'lower' classes, yet few now claimed to be in either category. In 1987 British Rail discarded even the two-class model, and embraced the class-neutral labels 'first' and 'standard' class. Left-wing militancy in the 1970s had so prolonged the rhetoric of class antagonism as to obscure the contemporary reality of a more subtly graded, less conflictual hierarchy, for these years saw the middle classes at last unobtrusively prevailing over their rivals. The early and mid-Victorian middle class had prevailed over a dominant landed aristocracy in a sequence of reforming movements whose anti-aristocratic purposes had been only half concealed; but its triumphs had been prudently muted after the 1870s by employers' and landowners' shared need to unite in defending property against a potentially subversive labour

---

[90] 'Reform by Erosion', *Econ* (6 Jan. 1973), 18. For disclaimed peerages see *BPF* (8th edn.), 231.

[91] Paxman, *Friends*, 29.

[92] Clark, *Diaries*, 159 (10 Feb. 1987); cf. F. M. L. Thompson, 'English Landed Society in the Twentieth Century. i. Property: Collapse and Survival', *TRHS* (1990), 10; 'New Poor and New Rich', 20.   [93] Cf. Harrison, *Seeking a Role*, 177–8.

movement. Then after a century's interval, the 1970s witnessed a Conservative partnership between Keith Joseph and Margaret Thatcher which could at last realize the middle-class ambitions of the mid-Victorian Liberal alliance between Cobden and Bright: the bluff of organized labour could now be called. The basis of middle-class power no longer lay, though, in manufacturing employment: the latter's peak occurred in 1966, with an almost continuous decline thereafter, so that total numbers employed in manufacturing had halved by 1990.[94] The middle classes gained from the blurring of their upper and lower frontiers. This eased their five-dimensional advance—through professionalization, education, owner-occupation, voluntarism, and political activism—each now to be discussed.

The service sector's proportion of the working population, rising throughout the twentieth century, had by 1960 gone further in the UK than in many industrial societies, though not as far as in America. In Britain the trend speeded up from the 1960s, but accelerated still faster in other leading industrial societies, so by 1984 the British service sector's proportion of total employment (65 per cent) was not by international standards as unusually large as before 1950.[95] In decline by 1971, not only in their share of the workforce but in absolute terms, were the employers, the owners of firms, and the manual workers; by contrast, the higher and lower professions, the managers and administrators, and the clerical workers were on the rise. An occupational structure that had earlier been dominated by manual work had now become divided fairly evenly three ways: between professional/managerial work, intermediary occupations, and manual work.[96] Between 1970 and 1990 the service sector contributed a rising share of gross domestic product in the USA, Japan, France, Italy, and Germany as well as in the UK.[97] Among the new occupations struggling to be born as professions were the many counselling occupations (often state employees) with links to psychology and social work, sometimes colonizing territory vacated by the religious professions.[98] Prominent, too, were practitioners within the highly mobile world of information technology. Even in 2000 the competing occupational structures within computing were too numerous and their expertise too fluid for any single set of professional standards to be enforceable: well under a tenth of the 500,000–600,000 who were by then employed in computing joined their largest organization, the British Computer Society.[99]

Passing examinations was integral to professional advancement, and education remained as pressing a middle-class preoccupation after 1970 as ever. The

---

[94] Cairncross, 'Economic Policy and Performance', 68–9.
[95] See the valuable table in R. Floud and D. McCloskey (eds.), *The Economic History of Britain since 1700*, iii. *1939–1992* (1st publ. Cambridge, 1981, 2nd edn. 1994), 335.   [96] *TCBST* 288–9.
[97] See the graph in *FT* (2 Mar. 1999), 8.
[98] For statistics see P. Halmos, *The Faith of the Counsellors* (1st publ. 1965, 2nd edn. 1978), 39, 41, 43.
[99] 'Is IT a Profession or Not?', *T* (12 Jan. 2000), 34.

traditional middle-class route to educational advantage had lain through the grammar schools, but the partially frustrated campaign to preserve them had the late twentieth-century effect of broadening access to the second of the three middle-class routes to smaller classes and better teaching: buying both at an independent school.[100] As for middle-class parents unable or unwilling to desert the comprehensivized state educational system, many were active in campaigning to improve it. The self-described 'black papers' of the late 1960s questioned prevailing educational trends and fuelled an assault in the 1970s on declining standards in state schools which helped to push Labour on to the defensive. Other middle-class parents ensured that their children took a third route to educational advantage by sending them to a state school that was already 'good'. This often required well-planned moves of the home, yoking middle-class educational aspiration to the other middle-class strategies—suburbanism and owner-occupation—already discussed.[101] Middle-class educational zeal operated in adult education, too. The Open University in the early 1970s recruited more than 30,000 students a year, and 6,000 of the 39,000 who graduated in its first decade lacked the necessary entry qualifications for university.[102] Yet for all its dreams of scooping up hidden and frustrated working-class talent through forsaking conventional entry requirements, the Open University, like the Workers' Educational Association (WEA) before it,[103] ineluctably approached a predominantly middle-class destination. Its typical recruit was 'a man, in his thirties, in a white-collar job . . . now apparently middle-class', though probably working-class in origin. Recruitment was relatively high in south-eastern England, teachers were by far the largest occupational category, and were reinforced by housewives and professional people.[104]

Propensity to volunteer was in 1987 far more widespread among people from professional, employing, and intermediate non-manual groups than among manual groups; the proportion rose with income and especially with high degree-level qualifications.[105] Furthermore, while in the early 1970s members of both 'service' and 'working' classes were particularly likely to join voluntary associations, the former chose types of association that were more diverse and less purely social.[106] Self-confidence, articulateness, relevant expertise, flexible working times and career patterns also guaranteed ample middle-class volunteers for participation in all political parties. Despite the class resonance

[100] See below, p. 388.   [101] Harrison, *Seeking a Role*, pp. 162–4, 200–1; see also pp. 88–9 above.

[102] A. Briggs, 'Ten Years of the Open University', *Trends in Education* (Spring 1980), 20.

[103] Harrison, *Seeking a Role*, 208, 362.

[104] N. McIntosh, Head of its Survey Research Dept., in J. Tunstall (ed.), *The Open University Opens* (1974), 54; see also 48.

[105] J. Matheson, *Voluntary Work: A Study Carried out on Behalf of the Home Office as Part of the 1987 General Household Survey* (1990), 9–10.

[106] J. H. Goldthorpe, with C. Llewellyn and C. Payne, *Social Mobility and Class Structure in Modern Britain* (Oxford, 1980), 188–9.

of the Labour Party's name, the two-party system did not in practice even in the 1970s reflect any clear polarity between employer and employee, middle class and working class, still less between capitalist and proletariat. Nor did the middle-class willingness to volunteer necessarily conflict with the ideals of public welfare. Middle-class activism was integral to the growth of the welfare state,[107] from which the middle classes gained both in jobs and benefits. Politically and in other ways, the late twentieth-century middle class was strong enough to support continuous and often quite sharp debate within its own ranks.

Faced with the industrial conflict of the 1970s, one middle-class option was to join what might otherwise have become an enemy camp, hoping thereby to render its policy safe. This did not reflect a narrowly tactical and self-interested outlook: the Labour Party's twentieth-century advent had not subverted the nineteenth-century middle-class radical belief in a progressive alliance between middle and working class. Labour could mobilize middle-class support through its meritocratic concern to extend political democracy into the economic sphere. Its rationalistic belief in state planning and its idealistic quest for unfulfilled working-class talent had a strong middle-class following. Hence the Party's enthusiasm until the 1960s for the grammar school, which enshrined what was then its approach to social engineering: equality of opportunity rather than of outcome. This alignment had been self-reinforcing: many grammar-school meritocratic pupils gravitated naturally to the Labour Party and into the types of service occupation, often state-run, that grew so fast during the twentieth century. But a Fabian gradualism and collectivist self-interest, already familiar to the British middle class, were also relevant here. The Association of Supervisory Staffs, Executives and Technicians (ASSET) had for some time been setting the pace through mergers and energetic recruitment, becoming by 1980 the fifth largest among the unions.[108] In the 1970s and 1980s its cocky and self-promoting one-time Communist General Secretary, the trade union entrepreneur Clive Jenkins, was viewed by colleagues as an intriguer, but he made it the fastest-growing union. At least as energetic in the 1970s, and at least as resented by rival unions, was the National Union of Public Employees (NUPE), which championed the low-paid; Alan Fisher, its General Secretary in the 1970s, was as quick in repartee as Jenkins, but far less arrogant. Middle-class trade unionists of this type had little reason to fear nationalization and state planning. In 1970 the National Union of Teachers voted overwhelmingly to affiliate to the TUC, whose role as vehicle of heavy industry was in decline:[109] by the early 1980s nearly half the country's trade unionists were

---

[107] Harrison, *Seeking a Role*, 200, 265–8.
[108] For a useful discussion see I. Bradley, 'New Militancy of Doctors and Social Workers', *T* (2 Jan. 1980), 4. See also Jenkins's obituary in *DT* (23 Sept. 1999), 31.   [109] *T* (31 Mar. 1970), 1.

white-collar workers, and they included a growing number of women and home-owners.[110]

Alertness to accent and language frequently accompanies shrewdness in assessing where power is thought (not always correctly) to lie. Middle-class people had long imitated working-class speech—half affectionately, half patronizingly—as their filter when admitting recruits from below and as a bridge towards their own move higher up. Such mimicking was now diminishingly facetious, however, and aimed to reduce rather than accentuate social distance. The proletarian style of the left-wing Oxford undergraduate in the 1930s and of the middle-class national serviceman in the 1950s served a temporary self-protective purpose within a localized power structure. But by the 1970s significant sections of the middle class, especially among the young, were ready to compromise more comprehensively on language and culture. Mike Leigh's television play *Abigail's Party* (1977), with his wife Alison Steadman taking the lead part as the obnoxious Beverly, unsympathetically though compellingly portrayed how the middle classes had traditionally consolidated their position—articulating upward-aspiring false values from behind suburban curtains. Yet in 1977 the play was already slightly out of date, given that significant middle-class groups had by then begun looking lower down for their cultural exemplars. Middle-class snobbery was becoming inverted.

Whereas earlier middle-class generations had hoped to educate their new (working-class) masters towards congenial voting habits and the mass adoption of high culture, sections of this new middle-class generation opted for a populist rejection of 'elitism' in favour of supposedly working-class accents, vocabulary, syntax, recreations, and attitudes.[111] By the 1970s influential sportsmen and media personalities were lending new force to middle-class linguistic populism, which was becoming entrenched with growing academic endorsement, and under male rather than female impulse.[112] So, unusually among linguistic trends, fashions set below were travelling socially upwards: acquired glottal stops and a colourful vocabulary now laced so-called 'estuary English',[113] the watered-down version of cockney that issued from more and more young middle-class mouths throughout England. Slowly the 'received pronunciation' of Oxford University and the BBC ceased to be the passports to career success, and even came itself to be seen as an 'accent'.[114] By the 1990s the English language was experiencing 'convergence in grammar and vocabulary

[110] R. Taylor, 'The Looking-Glass World of the Unions', *O* (12 Sept. 1982), 7. P. Kellner, 'Can the Brothers Ever be Wooed Back to Labour?', *T* (2 July 1984), 10.

[111] See Philip Howard, 'Elite Force in the War of Words', *T* (25 Aug. 1978), 10.

[112] J. C. Wells, *Accents of English*, i. *An Introduction* (Cambridge, 1982), 105.

[113] A phrase originating with David Rosewarne, 'Estuary English', *Times Educational Supplement* (19 Oct. 1984), 29.

[114] For more on this see Harrison, *Seeking a Role*, 161–2; see also above, pp. 96–7.

but divergence in phonology'.[115] Roy Jenkins and some of his followers were suspect within the labour movement in the 1970s as much for their plummy accents as for their Europeanism, and Crosland felt the need to compensate for his patrician tones by refusing as Foreign Secretary to wear a white tie at social functions.[116]

Thatcher's electoral success in 1979 did not immediately cause the middle class to forsake this type of compromise with and deference to organized labour. It was not then at all clear that the 1980s would be the decade when the middle classes ceased to apologize. An early sign of a middle-class breakout, however, was the split from the Labour Party in 1981 of the SDP, 'the middle class on the march';[117] its conferences were filled, said Healey, with 'the non-political professional and managerial middle class'.[118] It was the Conservative Party, however, which most forcibly sounded the middle-class trump. Provincial grammar schools in the 1930s had produced Harold Wilson and Roy Jenkins, and had despatched them to Oxford and thence into national politics; their grammar-school origins had deeply shaped their affinity with the left. A provincial grammar school in the 1930s had also produced Margaret Thatcher, and Oxford had claimed her also. A Conservative Party which—as under Thatcher—rejected corporatism offered the middle classes a clear alternative at last to the menu the Labour governments had been offering between 1964 and 1979. Conservative governments could now cater more effectively for the meritocratic ideals which with Labour did not always take pride of place. This new variant of Conservatism combined a frontal (though tactically astute) assault on trade union power with an unapologetic and resolute defence of middle-class individualism.

In view of the strident class rhetoric prevailing in the 1970s, the Conservatives' newly robust stance had to be carefully prepared. Thatcher's predecessor as leader, Heath, was described in March 1970 as 'the right-thinking, hard-working lad who is doing well for himself, making the best of his opportunities in a decent, law-abiding, tidy-minded, thoroughly British middle-class suburb'.[119] He did not set out to challenge the Party's more traditional leaders: instead he sought acceptance. Trained in the 1950s as right-hand man to the grouse-shooting Macmillan, he shared his party's reluctance to harp upon class divisions lest class recrimination should get out of control. As prime minister between 1970 and 1974 he was intellectually outflanked by Conservative dissidents within his own party and beleaguered by an aroused trade union movement. By January 1974 he was reduced to pleading with fellow citizens

---

[115] Author's collection: Professor Peter Trudgill to author, 31 July 1997.
[116] Professor John Honey in *T* (19 Aug. 1981), 8. Crosland, *NS* (19 Nov. 1976), 707.
[117] Simon Hoggart's phrase, *O* (11 Oct. 1981), 11.
[118] 'Consensus and the SDP', *New Socialist*, 2 (Nov.–Dec. 1981), 27 .
[119] Paul Johnson, *NS* (27 Mar. 1970), 433.

to 'remember their common citizenship'. Seeking a 'one nation' centrist set-tlement, he disliked raising class issues in the general election of February 1974,[120] whereas Thatcher in the following January, shortly before becoming party leader, rounded on critics of her suburbanity: 'if "middle-class values" include the encouragement of variety and individual choice, the provision of fair incentives and rewards for skill and hard work, the maintenance of effective barriers against the excessive power of the State and a belief in the wide distri-bution of individual *private* property, then they are certainly what I am trying to defend'. Middle-class apology was not to be her style: 'for a generation, the middle class was made to feel guilty about climbing the ladder of success', she said in 1987; 'this country can never be strong unless the most able are allowed to contribute to the full'.[121]

Conservative backbenchers had never unanimously or whole-heartedly endorsed the post-war centrist consensus, the welfare state, and an intervention-ist approach to the economy, if only because alert to their constituents' doubts. In Thatcher after 1975 they found their voice. Under her regime, feather-bedded farmers, sheltered professional people, smooth merchant bankers, statist busi-nessmen, and clubland paternalists took second place to entrepreneurs, people in small businesses, pensioners on fixed incomes, upwardly mobile working people, and anyone who felt that trade union power had harmed themselves or their country. The Party had always attracted widespread support at this and lower levels, and both Heath and Thatcher came from there; Thatch-er's achievement was to be unabashed in making this manifest. Beneath her banner she attracted those who had felt excluded by the corporatist estab-lishment and battered by its trade union barons: grammar-school meritocrats like her press secretary Bernard Ingham, self-made buccaneers like Jeffrey Archer, patriotic entrepreneurs like her policy adviser John Hoskyns and her minister David Young. And by extending the ownership of houses and shares, the Party reinvigorated those old Conservative slogans: a 'property-owning democracy' and 'popular capitalism'. Spreading out from their Barratt 'starter homes' and their privatized and refaced council houses adorned with coach lamps, minibar and ranch-style living room, new recruits to the middle class were advancing upon what had once been secure Labour territory. The saddest thing for me', Benn told a Nottinghamshire miners' gala in 1983, 'was to go along some council housing estates and find the famili-ar sign of a new front door and a brass knocker—and a Tory sign in the window.'[122]

[120] Quotation from speech at Eastbourne on the miners' dispute, *T* (19 Jan. 1974), 1. S. Fay and H. Young in *ST* (7 Mar. 1976), 34.

[121] Finchley speech on 31 Jan. 1974, quoted in Cosgrave, *Thatcher*, 69. Interview with Bruce Anderson, *STel* (28 June 1987), 23.

[122] Quoted in R. Butt, 'The Message of the Brass Knocker', *T* (16 June 1983), 8.

From 1974 Sir Keith Joseph was Thatcher's John the Baptist. In 1975 he welcomed the idea that the entire British population might soon display the traditional middle-class virtues: self-reliance, postponed gratification, independence from the state. His ideal was, he said, 'the artisan of Victorian days, who read serious literature, supported radical causes, was sober and self-improving'.[123] Eleven years later he recommended Samuel Smiles's *Self-Help* (1859) as 'a book for *our* times', a 'management classic', and a salutary corrective to the 'perceptible depressing limpness in individual attitudes' flowing from public welfare and high taxation. 'Only when we match the . . . moral qualities . . . of our more productive competitors abroad can we hope to employ all those here who seek work'.[124] If one sought 'a condition of society which would be the most civilized and the least barbarous and with the most scope for individual choice', Joseph argued in 1979, bourgeois society was 'the least bad yet invented'.[125] In one of his many significant semantic shifts,[126] he sought in 1975 to substitute the phrase 'market-orientated society' for Marx's pejorative 'capitalist society', so as to highlight aspects of the free market not captured by the earlier emphasis on patterns of ownership: 'the market, choice, democracy'.[127] Not that the word 'capitalism' was often uttered at this time even by Labour prime ministers: Benn thought it worth noting in his diary when Callaghan first used the word in cabinet (on 21 December 1976).[128] Given Labour's traditions, however, Callaghan was in no position publicly to declare (as did Thatcher in June 1978) that 'we have got to get every person a capitalist, so that they can save out of their income . . . so that they can start with nothing and end up with something'.[129]

Many of Thatcher's critics at first thought that her resolutely middle-class tone would divide the nation, but the dominant public rhetoric of the 1970s had misled them. The political salience of organized labour in that decade and the even greater moral and intellectual salience of economic and social interventionism were articulated by statist sections of the middle class: their sixties populism embodied a downwardly deferential cultural shift which underplayed the trade unionist's free-market instincts. In Labour circles, the term 'socialist' (not too precisely defined) had become a talisman, and to cross a picket line incurred widespread moral disapproval. In wider circles, the words

---

[123] K. Joseph, speech on 15 Jan. 1975 to Economic Research Council, in his *Reversing the Trend: A Critical Re-appraisal of Conservative Economic and Social Policies. Seven Speeches* (Chichester and London, 1975), 56. For more on his campaign see B. Harrison, 'Mrs Thatcher and the Intellectuals', *TCBH* 5/2 (1994), 211–20.
[124] Introduction to S. Smiles, *Self-Help* (1st publ. 1859, Penguin edn. Harmondsworth, 1986), 11, 16, 13.   [125] *G* (18 July 1979), 7.
[126] For more see below, pp. 265, 311–12, 319.
[127] Speech at Oxford, 14 Mar. 1975, in his *Reversing the Trend*, 68.
[128] Benn, *Diaries 1973–6*, 691 (21 Dec. 1976).
[129] Speech to Wales Conservative Conference, 10 June 1978, *T* (12 June 1978), 2.

'caring' and 'committed' had become vogue-words.[130] Still more distorting to perceptions of class realities at the time was the unprecedented level of inflation in the 1970s. 'Inflation . . . makes strikers of us all', wrote Sherman, by then Thatcher's aide, in a memorandum to Thatcher of December 1978. 'In a period of stable prices, many unions and their members will accept the status quo. In a period of inflation, no one can afford to be left behind; once they have tasted blood, even artificial blood, their appetite grows.'[131] Each group of employees struggled to stay ahead in an increasingly frenetic competition for finite resources: each sought both to frighten the enemy into concession, and to dress up its pluralistic self-defence as simultaneously altruistic and socialist. A rhetoric of class conflict lay readily to hand, a Labour government was in power, and intellectually the early Marx was still in fashion. Conflicts over small-scale differentials between groups of workers led frequently to strikes which were readily misinterpreted as indicating increased working-class consciousness. Thatcher earned her place in history by recognizing how completely the labour movement was misrepresenting social trends, and how seriously some trade union leaders were misrepresenting their members' aspirations.

The Conservatives could not of course hope to mobilize the entire middle class. So dominant was it by the 1970s that it could safely afford internally to bicker. Indeed, it was a class born to bicker: entrepreneurs competed for advantage, professions elbowed for position, suburban neighbours jockeyed for status advantage. At the general election of 1979, 40 per cent of the support for the Labour and Conservative parties combined came from voters who opposed the party which might be thought to articulate their class interest.[132] By then the Callaghan government had alienated many middle-class interests, especially with its incomes policies: doctors whose wage claims and status lost out to the most militant sections of organized labour, for instance, or the many professional groups resenting intrusive public scrutiny.[133] Labour's public employee, idealist, and planner confronted the Conservatives' entrepreneur, practical man, and volunteer.

Thatcher throughout the 1980s readily confronted middle-class opinion when necessary. In 1984 she said she wanted her governments remembered for liberating the country from 'vested interests': trade unions, nationalized industries, local authorities, and monopolistic professions.[134] Her free-market policies were unpopular with many middle-class employees of state-run concerns: after 1979 the career civil servant's worst nightmares were successively realized, for example, and teachers were early among the professional groups

[130] G. Frost, 'A Social, Caring, Relevant Guide to Labspeak Situation', *DT* (23 Apr. 1979), 16.
[131] Quoted in Cockett, *Thinking the Unthinkable*, 269.
[132] D. E. Butler and D. Kavanagh, *The British General Election of 1979* (1980), 350.
[133] Donoughue, *Prime Minister*, 117–19.
[134] To centenary lunch of the parliamentary lobby journalists, *FT* (19 Jan. 1984), 10.

exposed to governmental target-setting and subsequent monitoring. Curbs on advertising among the professions were lifted: customers were freed to shop around for their spectacles, and architects were exposed to owner-occupiers far less tractable as clients than local authorities had been. Thatcher shared Heseltine's doubts about accountants' contribution to the economy; he had failed his accountancy exams in the 1950s, and thought Britain needed fewer accountants, but more of the technicians who were relatively abundant in France and Germany.[135] There were of course limits to what could be achieved. Challenges to the welfare state's beneficiaries could antagonize quite wide sections of the middle class, forcing Thatcher more than once to back off. Restraints on Sunday shopping were enforced by a powerful alliance between churchgoers and trade unionists. Nigel Lawson long saw the legal profession as 'a particularly ripe subject for critical scrutiny', but when Lord Hailsham (then Lord Chancellor) was outvoted in a cabinet committee on the monopolies of barristers and solicitors he banged his walking sticks on the table and stormed out. Only after Hailsham was no longer Lord Chancellor did Lawson feel free to move; James Mackay, effectively Hailsham's successor, found it easier as the first member of the Scottish Bar in the post to champion the English legal system's reform, but even he needed to dilute considerably his initial proposals of 1989 for attacking monopoly within the system.[136] Skill at harnessing the many middle-class enemies made by Conservative governments since 1979 contributed much to Labour's election victory in 1997.

4. TRADE UNIONS ON THE DEFENSIVE

'We were the first working-class heroes in England to ever get anywhere without changing their accents', said John Lennon, reflecting in 1972 on Beatle history.[137] Both culturally and politically, the working class seemed by then to have entered into its inheritance, and in June 1979 Prince Charles became the first member of the royal family to address a trade union assembly.[138] In 1968–76 the trade union movement experienced one of its periodic leaps forward in membership—to new heights;[139] the labour correspondents of London newspapers until 1979 enjoyed high status in their profession and dined with cabinet ministers.[140] Some trade unions chose as their headquarters

[135] Heseltine, *FT* (6 Feb. 1993), 1, 22; (11 Feb. 1993), 12.

[136] Lawson, *View from No. 11*, 620–4; see also N. Ridley, *'My Style of Government'. The Thatcher Years* (1st publ. 1991, paperback edn. 1992), 28. For Mackay's efforts see *T* (17 Feb. 1992), 13; *FT* (21 July 1989), 10. Lord Havers was briefly Lord Chancellor between Hailsham and Mackay.

[137] Quoted in J. Lahr, *Prick up your Ears: The Biography of Joe Orton* (1978), 298.

[138] To the ISTC annual conference, *FT* (21 June 1979), 11.

[139] Harrison, *Seeking a Role*, 205, 211–12.

[140] R. Harris, *Good and Faithful Servant. The Unauthorized Biography of Bernard Ingham* (1st publ. 1990, paperback edn. 1991), 40.

country houses vacated by the aristocracy, and in the early 1980s Benn visited several. In 1980 Whitehall, the mansion built near Bishop's Stortford on the profits of Gilbey's gin, became ASTMS's country club, and boasted saunas, swimming baths, and fine lawns. It was 'like an executive mansion for the chiefs of multinational companies to relax in'.[141] The General and Municipal Workers Union headquarters at Claygate in Surrey was an old manor house surrounded by a crenellated Victorian castle with a swimming pool.[142] When Benn visited Clive Jenkins in 1979, his family occupied a house made from four cottages that before the war had housed forty-one people,[143] and when the National Union of Mineworkers (NUM) held its conference in Jersey in 1979, Arthur Scargill (soon to become its leader) complained about meeting in 'a millionaires' paradise and playground that has nothing in common with working miners'.[144] Unionization was stronger the closer its links with government and the larger the firm; there was as yet no reason to think that either government employment or the firms would shrink. Under-unionized groups—agricultural workers or bank clerks, for example—seemed likely either to decline further, or to unionize where work units grew larger.

Official and unofficial strikes in the early 1970s were damaging, were much publicized, and often verged on the political, especially when mounted against the Conservatives' Industrial Relations Act of 1971. They should be set in perspective: days lost in strikes, and days lost per worker, were far lower in the 1970s than earlier in the century, though far higher than they became during the 1980s;[145] and whereas in 1984 the UK lost 27.1 million working days because of strikes, it lost more than 350 million through illness.[146] Strikes were regionally very patchy: whereas in 1971–3 Sussex lost a tenth as many days per thousand workers from strikes as the national average, Merseyside lost two-and-a-half times as many.[147] In 1964–6 British strike levels, when measured in terms of stoppages per 100,000 employees, were lower than in five of the fifteen other comparable industrial countries. They were considerably worse, however, than in another five; furthermore, unofficial strikes overwhelmingly predominated in the UK, and were spreading by comparison with official.[148] The official statistics seriously under-recorded the scale of disruption, let alone the continuous managerial effort required to avert it.[149] By 1971/3 the strike-prone industries centred on mining, shipbuilding, and heavy industry—especially in the lowlands of Scotland, the Midlands,

---

[141] e.g. Benn, *Diaries 1980–90*, 10 (15 June 1980); see also 5 (13 June 1980).
[142] Ibid. 190 (15 Jan. 1982).
[143] Benn, *Conflicts of Interest: Diaries 1977–80*, ed. R. Winstone (1990), 527 (26 Aug. 1979), cf. 580 (12 Feb. 1980).   [144] *DT* (5 July 1979), 1.
[145] *BST* 195–6.   [146] Johnson (ed.), *Structure of British Industry*, 349.
[147] *Econ* (4 Dec. 1976), 122; cf. *FT* (27 Dec. 1978), 3.
[148] Royal Commission on Trade Unions and Employers' Associations 1965–1968, *Report* (Chairman Lord Donovan, Cmnd. 3623; 1968), 95–8.   [149] *FT* (16 Jan. 1987), 12.

Merseyside and the north-west. Their employees—in car factories, docks, mines, shipyards, and steelworks—were slowly going the same way as the textile workers. It was in the large and predominantly state-run establishments that the unions were most firmly entrenched.[150] The strikes might centre upon a few plants in Britain—two-thirds of all days lost in strikes between 1966 and 1973 came from 5 per cent of plants, whereas in 98 per cent of firms strikes were very rare[151]—but because they seriously hampered major industries with high profiles, Britain's image abroad suffered. So did the trade unions' image within Britain, for strikes mobilized the organized and the organizable against the rest; the latter included the old, the sick, and the unemployed, who depended far more than the rich on the services the strikers withdrew.[152] Helen Arbuthnot told *The Times* during a strike in February 1971 that she was retired and unable substantially to increase her income. For her the strike was 'no longer a useful defensive weapon against an oppressor but . . . an out-dated and anti-social offensive weapon against the powerless': it had become 'a sort of demonstration or even a blackmail against the public'.[153] By May 1979 a strike by 200 people manning two computers could render £126 million inaccessible to people who wanted to withdraw money from their National Savings accounts.[154]

During 1964 the Conservatives had detected a change in public attitudes to trade unions that might justify their moving on from the consensual approach pursued since 1945. Without consulting the trade unions, and following American precedents, they responded to pressure from the Society of Conservative Lawyers, and decided to restrain trade union power through invoking the law. This strategy ran full tilt against the non-interventionist orthodoxies of the Confederation of British Industry (CBI), the personnel managers, the trade unions and the industrial relations experts. By May 1965 the Conservatives had agreed on requiring trade unions to register, and on monitoring this through an industrial court. Their manifesto of 1966 promised 'new industrial policies, involving major reforms of both management and unions',[155] but the (Donovan) Royal Commission on Trade Unions and Employers' Associations appointed in 1965[156] did not regard American precedents as relevant in the UK, and in retrospect Castle's proposals of 1969 for trade union reform might have secured all-party consensus; James Prior later thought the Conservatives should have backed Castle, and had made 'a major tactical error' in preferring short-term

---

[150] On this see R. Price and G. S. Bain, 'Union Growth Revisited: 1948–1974 in Perspective', *British Journal of Industrial Relations* (1976), 341–2, 348.
[151] *FT* (27 Dec. 1978), 3. *Econ* (4 Dec. 1976), 122.
[152] See Joseph, *HC Deb.* 21 Jan. 1974, c. 1225; cf. Paul Johnson, 'A Brotherhood of National Misery', *NS* (16 May 1975), 654.   [153] *T* (1 Feb. 1971), 11.
[154] *DT* (2 May 1979), 2.
[155] Dale (ed.), *Conservative Manifestos*, 165.   [156] Harrison, *Seeking a Role*, 457–60.

party advantage.[157] Heath's government, however, backed by its manifesto's precise proposals, felt able to push through the Industrial Relations Act (1971). It established the National Industrial Relations Court with authority in industrial disputes to impose cooling-off periods and require a strike ballot, to fine unions practising 'unfair industrial practices', and to enforce collective agreements when legally binding. Unions were required to register (to their financial benefit) with a Registrar of Trade Unions and Employees' Associations, but must ensure that their rule books safeguarded the rights of the individual worker, especially his right not to join a union.

Ominous for the authorities at this time was the gradual advance of 'secondary picketing'. This phrase, American in origin, denoted strikers' attempts to mobilize employees in related businesses beyond their own. It flourished on hopes of working-class solidarity, and benefited by the greater mobility that stemmed from motorways and mass car ownership, especially among Yorkshire miners from the mid-1950s. 'Flying pickets', another phrase gaining currency in the 1970s, could henceforth be used to spread a strike from one coalfield to another and engineer a national strike without requiring a national ballot. Their best-known advocate was Arthur Scargill, the former Communist whose steady rise up the NUM hierarchy worried his critics. He made his name by mobilizing secondary picketing on an unprecedented scale at Saltley's huge coke depot during what was politically a crucial episode: the national coal strike in February 1972. In what he saw as a 'class war', he got the Yorkshire miners to coordinate secondary picketing on 'the vulnerable points'. Backed by other unions, the pickets in their thousands forced the police to close the gates, thereby compelling the Heath government to climb down (Plate 9). Standing atop a urinal, Scargill pronounced this event 'living proof that the working class had only to flex its muscles and it could bring governments, employers, society to a total standstill'. Three years later he rightly claimed that 'they were scared out of their skins by what took place at Saltley'.[158] Many civil servants at the time likened the situation to Britain's plight in the aftermath of nuclear attack: without food, power, sewerage, communications, and public order.[159] Twenty-six years later Heath saw it as 'the most vivid, direct and terrifying challenge to the rule of law that I could ever recall emerging from within our own country'.[160]

It soon became clear that the Industrial Relations Act had attempted too much, if only because it could not win the necessary collaboration from trade unions and even from employers. In September 1972 the TUC suspended thirty-two trade unions with 500,000 members for refusing to deregister under

---

[157] Prior, *Balance of Power*, 48, cf. 72, 156. For Castle's proposals see Harrison, *Seeking a Role*, 458–9.
[158] Scargill interviewed in 'The New Unionism', *New Left Review*, 92 (July–Aug. 1975), 13, 19, 20.
[159] See Brendan Sewill's recollection in *T* (22 Nov. 1979), 3.   [160] Heath, *Course of my Life*, 351.

the Act.[161] Not only did the Act fail to cut strike levels:[162] it accelerated the earlier trend towards political strikes. Unfamiliar phrases now gained currency: 'industrial action', for example, which was neither 'industrial' (it spread far beyond industrial concerns) nor 'action' (it could succeed only through inaction).[163] Those who had opposed entangling industrial relations with the law seemed entirely vindicated when the Act produced all sorts of unintended results. Law-breaking London dockers yearning for martyrdom in 1972 had to be rescued (much to their disgust) from being sent to prison by obscure stratagems difficult to justify to the public. 'It's a bloody liberty', said Mr. Turner. 'They had no right to do it. We were quite ready to go to jail.'[164] Communists were prominent in union militancy less because their followers shared their political outlook than because Communists' beliefs made them tough bargainers: among the 'politically motivated men' whom Wilson condemned for their role in the seamen's strike of 1966,[165] among the workers in Upper Clyde Shipbuilders who in summer 1971 'worked in' rather than accept redundancy,[166] among the shop stewards who resisted Michael Edwardes's reorganization of British Leyland after 1977,[167] and above all among the miners. The bluff but pragmatic Joe Gormley, who like several other trade union leaders of the time had been a Special Branch informer,[168] was greatly concerned about growing intimidation by demonstrators.[169] As the NUM's National President from 1971 to 1982 he thought it worth staying on for an extra year in 1981–2 to ensure that the Communist Mick McGahey would be too old to qualify as a candidate to succeed him.[170]

Heath's response to the setbacks of 1972 was to resume the corporatist strategy which his government had initially half-abandoned, complete with an incomes policy.[171] This merely stored up further trouble with the miners, whose pay-claim of 1973 not only breached the policy's limits, but was pushed home by discontinuing overtime working. The resultant fall in coal stocks led the government to introduce a three-day working week with effect from 1 January 1974. All further efforts to secure a settlement failed, and 81 per cent in the NUM ballot supported an all-out strike. Opinion polls from December 1973 to February 1974 showed no clear public endorsement for the government as against the miners,[172] but at that point the phrase went round Westminster that

---

[161] G (5 Sept. 1972), 1, cf. 6 for a list of the unions affected.
[162] For statistics see T (15 Feb. 1974), 14.
[163] Oxford English Dictionary's first citation is from T (17 Mar. 1971), 1.   [164] T (17 June 1972), 1.
[165] e.g. Bert Ramelson, DT (14 Apr. 1994), 21.
[166] e.g. Jimmy Airlie and Jimmy Reid, T (17 June 1971), 1; DT (11 Mar. 1997), 25 (obituary of Airlie).
[167] e.g. Derek Robinson, T (6 Feb. 1980), 14.   [168] T (24 Oct. 2002), 2.
[169] See e.g. his comments in G (6 Sept. 1977), 5.   [170] DT (15 June 1979), 1.
[171] For more on this see below, pp. 290, 308, 316.
[172] See tables 6.4 and 6.5 in R. Taylor, The Trade Union Question in British Politics: Government and Unions since 1945 (Oxford, 1993), 214.

'the miners have had their ballot and we must have ours'.[173] Heath's handling of the unions had so far been conciliatory, reverting to the 'one nation' tone of centrist Conservatism that he had only temporarily forsaken in 1970–1. After a month's experience of the three-day week he had been impressed by the 'remarkable' collaboration between employer and employee which occurred. 'Why, why, why', he asked parliament, 'does it require a crisis of this kind for the British to be able to work together in order to get an answer to our problems in the production of more goods?'[174] Yet early in 1974 Heath was reluctantly drawn into playing his last card: seeking to out-trump sectional opinion by appealing to the entire electorate at the general election of February 1974. If the electors had stoutly backed him, the essentials of his trade union legislation would probably have survived;[175] even as it was, the Conservatives won more votes than Labour, but Labour won more seats, and eventually took office.

Since 1970 Labour and Conservative had been competing for public support by offering rival strategies on industrial relations. Each strove to present the other as out of touch with public opinion, as more likely to provoke violence, and as mistaken in its view of liberty; each sought to ward off any extremist taint, and manœuvred to win the moral advantage. Labour harped upon the clumsiness involved in complicating a delicate set of relationships by introducing lawyers, and advertised the usefulness of the Party's direct links with the trade unions and its hold on long-established loyalties. The Conservatives harped upon Labour's timidity in the area, and cited evidence of trade union intimidation and undemocratic procedures. The Labour governments of 1974–9 pushed Heath's latter-day appeasement strategy still further when confirmed in power by a second general election in October. Industrial relations improved considerably in the short term, the country once more seemed governable, and Prime Minister Wilson's reputation for tactical shrewdness was much enhanced: 'he has come closer than any other politician in his time to an instinctive understanding of the British people', wrote the seasoned journalist Peter Jenkins.[176] The trade unions received much: the Industrial Relations Act (1971) was repealed, concessions on wages and subsidies were made, trade union participation in government extended, free collective bargaining was restored, and the Advisory, Conciliation and Arbitration Service was set up with power to recommend trade union recognition where refused by employers.

Yet the problems Heath tackled had not gone away. Mounting inflation in the mid-1970s advertised the attractions of an incomes policy, though Labour dared not make it statutory. Less obvious at the time were the dangers that the policy concentrated political and economic power, threatened individual liberty, and undermined the pressure group's capacity to represent its members.

[173] T (8 Feb. 1974), 2.   [174] T (15 Feb. 1974), 4. HC Deb. 22 Jan. 1974, c. 1450.
[175] As argued in Howe, Conflict of Loyalty, 685.   [176] NS (13 Mar. 1976), 311.

Trade union leaders' hostility to incomes policies is entirely comprehensible: such policies distanced them from their members, thereby entrenching the shop stewards. Nor did the Callaghan government's incomes policies prompt any significant national debate on the wage structure as a whole. The incomes policies of 1975–9 were used only for short-term crisis management, with Labour's leaders mobilizing the trade unions' loyalty to 'their' government in order to secure wage restraint; nor did the associated corporatist policies seem to be enhancing British manufacturing competitiveness. Furthermore, many manufacturing employees, especially from ethnic minorities, found that their choice lay, not between work on present or better terms, but between work on present terms and no work at all. So large-scale secondary picketing in 1977–8 at Grunwick, the photo-processing plant at Willesden, failed not only to compel the employer into recognizing trade unions, but even to prevent his employees from turning up for work.[177]

Much more significant in the longer term were the activities of the tough and bluff South African Michael Edwardes, who began his five-year term as Chairman at British Leyland in November 1977. He was keen to end the 'we and they' situation among its vehicle-manufacturing employees, and thought the distinction between white- and blue-collar workers on terms and conditions untenable.[178] Devolving power widely, clarifying through accounting reform where the losses were being made, making himself highly visible to the public and to employees, and above all communicating with them directly rather than through allegedly representative intermediate bodies, Edwardes with his no-nonsense messages and appeals for support was unconsciously pioneering within one company the techniques for assessing opinion that Thatcher later applied nation-wide. His success was far from immediate and always precarious. When the prime-ministerial Rovers needed replacing in summer 1978, only a British-made car would do; Callaghan as prime minister ordered two new Rover 3.5's, and after a long delay they were delivered with thirty-four mechanical faults. After they had been repaired and adapted to the prime minister's safety needs, Callaghan went out in one, felt the need for fresh air, pressed the relevant electronic button, and the window fell into his lap. He wanted to see no more of them, and grumbled that British Leyland must be broken up and parts of it closed, whoever won the next general election.[179]

In August 1977, however, there had been a spontaneous shopfloor rebellion against shop stewards organizing a strike for a 47 per cent wage-increase at the firm's Longbridge plant: 'listen to the lads who do the work for a change

---

[177] See J. Rogaly, *Grunwick* (Harmondsworth, 1977) for a detailed perspective mid-dispute.
[178] M. Edwardes, *Back from the Brink: An Apocalyptic Experience* (1983), 288.
[179] B. Donoughue, *Downing Street Diary: With James Callaghan in No. 10* (2008), 353–4 (Sept. 1978); 363 (14 Sept. 1978); 380 (26 Oct. 1978).

"YOUR VOTING FORM DID
COME, I'VE DEALT WITH IT . . .
YOU VOTED 'YES'!"

Fig. 2. Wife to British Leyland employee returning from work, in the context of recent direct appeals from management to workforce over the heads of trade unions. *Birmingham Evening Mail.*

instead of the bloody shop stewards', one employee Ron Hill told the press.[180] Assiduous attendance at committee meetings, early initiatives, and strategic locations taken up at plenary meetings—devices all choreographed by 'Red Robbo' Derek Robinson, the Communist leader of the joint shop stewards' committee—could no longer suppress employee opinion, and in November 1979 Edwardes gained nine-to-one support for his recovery plan from his employees in an 80 per cent poll, despite opposition from the firm's largest union and the need to axe more than 25,000 jobs and totally or partially close thirteen plants.[181] Although she publicly distanced the government from British Leyland when prime minister, Thatcher interested herself very directly in its

---

[180] *T* (27 Aug. 1977), 1. [181] *FT* (2 Nov. 1979), 1.

day-to-day running.[182] Output per man-year in British Leyland began rising fast, and the car industry was at last on its way to attaining new heights of production in the mid-1990s.[183] After five years Edwardes left the company with managers more accessible, employees better informed and better respected, and a new spirit prevailing.[184]

Sir Keith Joseph had uncompromisingly launched the Conservative reaction against Heath's industrial-relations strategy in 1974, a shift which involved what was then a startling inversion of language. Overmanning, strikes, and the consequent discouragement of investment made the trade unions, hitherto widely accepted at their own altruistic valuation, seem 'job destroyers' and poverty creators, responsible for what was now widely known as 'the British disease'.[185] By September 1977 Thatcher was inclining towards the referendum for resolving conflicts between unions and government if no general election was in the offing: 'let the people speak', she said, to applause at the party conference in the following month.[186] Public-sector unions' prominence in a sequence of strikes did not help their public image, and even enhanced privatization's attractions for the Conservatives. In 1977–8 the firemen held their first national strike ever, with no appreciable loss of life but substantial losses in property.[187] But it was the so-called 'winter of discontent'—the eruption of strikes in winter 1978–9—which gave the Conservatives their prize opportunity, and shocked some Labour politicians too (Plate 10). 'If it means lives lost, that is how it must be', said Bill Dunn, spokesman for the London ambulance drivers during their twenty-four-hour strike even against emergency cover in January.[188] Peter Shore, Secretary of State for the Environment, deploring the strike by Liverpool gravediggers in the same month, told MPs that 'some sense of common fellowship and decency between members of the same community ought to come across'.[189]

Both parties had now given the corporatist approach to industrial relations its chance, and it was on the basis of its perceived failure that new directions were now taken. Thatcher made it clear on assuming power in May 1979 that she would break the vicious circle in which 'income becomes something to vote for, or to strike for, but not to work for', and in his first budget speech her

[182] Young, *One of Us*, 362.

[183] P. Bassett, 'How BL Sought a Peaceful Recovery', *FT* (30 May 1984), 12.

[184] Edwardes, *Back from the Brink*, 288.

[185] *HC Deb.* 4 Dec. 1980, cc. 448, 452; cf. Tebbit at the 1982 party conference, *G* (8 Oct. 1982), 4, and Lawson at the 1984 party conference, *G* (11 Oct. 1984), 4. See also D. Metcalf, 'Trade Unions and Economic Performance: The British Evidence', *LSE Quarterly*, 3/1 (Spring 1989), 21–42 for evidence in support; I am most grateful to Professor Metcalf for giving me a copy of this article.

[186] Television interview, *G* (19 Sept. 1977), 1. Thatcher, *Party Conference Speeches*, 35; cf. *T* (15 Oct. 1977), 4.　　　　　　　　　　　　　　　　　　　　　　　　　　[187] *T* (12 Jan. 1978), 2.

[188] *DT* (20 Jan. 1979), 1; cf. its angry editorial 'What Rough Beast . . .' (2 Feb. 1979), 18.

[189] *HC Deb.* 31 Jan. 1979, c. 1476.

Chancellor dismissed 'the illusion that we can somehow strike our way to higher living standards'.[190] The trade unions did not immediately learn the lessons of the 'winter of discontent'. The Conservative Secretary of State for Social Services said that the issues in the engineers' unofficial strike, which prevented supplies from reaching cancer patients at Charing Cross Hospital in November 1979, 'pale into insignificance beside the sheer horror of seeing cancer patients wrapped up in blankets going down to the front gate and pleading with pickets to allow their treatment to continue'.[191] When the British Leyland management sacked 'Red Robbo' in the same month, there was minimal support for him at the protest meeting: instead there were insulting banners, much bad language, and 'a fusillade of rubber washers'.[192] Management's position was strengthened by growing unemployment, which ended the long rise in trade union membership. Longbridge's workforce had halved in recent years, aided by a management weapon whose power was repeatedly apparent in the 1980s: 'mention voluntary redundancies', said a Midlands trade union official in 1982, 'and you run the risk of being crushed in the rush for the door'.[193]

The industrial-relations climate was changing even before the Conservatives took office. Learning from Heath's mistakes, Thatcher's governments moved cautiously, thereby invalidating Labour's predictions that they would be led into u-turn. There was first Prior's Employment Act (1980) curbing the closed shop, outlawing most forms of secondary picketing, and offering government funds for trade union ballots. Then at the Department of Employment from 1981 to 1983 there was Tebbit, a critic of the trade unions since their closed shop had bullied him into membership as a 16-year-old journalist thirty-five years before.[194] He proved an unexpectedly successful minister; like Thatcher he lacked middle-class guilt, and positively revelled in abuse from trade unions. After the Act of 1982, unions could be sued for damages if officials called for unlawful industrial action; the Trade Union Act of 1984 required unions to hold a secret ballot before industrial action; and the Employment Act of 1988 carried further the earlier reforms, monitoring the closed shop and electoral procedures for trade union posts. This formidable package was further strengthened by the Employment Acts of 1989 and 1990.[195] Tactics alone cannot explain the government's success: the Labour Party was now even more deeply divided than in 1970–4, and Thatcher's governments had no need to cultivate the unions because unlike Heath's they had retreated from central planning of the

---

[190] Thatcher addressing the Conservative women's conference in London on 21 May, *T* (22 May 1980), 1. Howe, *HC Deb.* 26 Mar. 1980, c. 1489.
[191] Patrick Jenkin at a TUC conference on social security, *T* (28 Nov. 1979), 2.
[192] *G* (21 Feb. 1980), 24; cf. 10 for the leader, 'Exit Derek, Humiliated'. [193] *FT* (16 Aug. 1982), 1.
[194] Tebbit, *Upwardly Mobile*, 15; see also 116–17.
[195] A. Seldon and S. Ball (eds.), *Conservative Century: The Conservative Party since 1900* (1994), 534, conveniently summarizes this legislation.

economy and incomes policies. Enoch Powell had long ago dismissed the notion of 'responsible' trade unionism,[196] in the sense of collaborating in an ongoing planning regime: trade unionists could now act upon his vision and resume their traditional, congenial, fully representative, and free-market function of bargaining directly with employers.

They did not immediately do so, for in the early 1980s they were living in a private world, and the TUC's gathering in September 1979 was hardly likely to change that. Its delegates included all too few from growth areas in the work-force: women, ethnic minorities, young people, and Conservative voters.[197] So their initial response to Thatcher was to mount processions and demonstrations aimed at the predicted u-turn: 'we simply did not believe what Mrs Thatcher said she would do', the TUC's General Secretary recalled.[198] Supporters ebbed away, however, and a major setback was the bitter thirteen-week steel strike in 1980, defeated by massive imports of steel from Europe. Ian MacGregor, the Steel Corporation's rugged, laconic, and somewhat unsubtle Scottish-born chairman and chief executive, was a workaholic who from the government's point of view had earned his fee. The fact that Bill Sirs, General Secretary of the Iron and Steel Trades Confederation (ISTC), was a genuine democrat and no extremist did not prevent him from sharing Red Robbo's fate in being outflanked by management ballots of the workforce. A three-to-one employee endorsement of the plan for restructuring prevailed over its clear rejection on a much lower turnout in the preceding trade union ballot.[199] The trade union left incurred fur-ther blows in 1982 with important reforms in the make-up of the TUC general council, and with the run-down in public employment thereafter, together with privatization's cumulative build-up. Trade union strength rested on the public-sector unions, and powerful within the TUC were NUPE and the Confederation of Health Service Employees (COHSE). The twenty-one-week civil-service strike in 1981 was an expensive failure for all concerned, and Thatcher pro-nounced the National Health Service (NHS) strike in 1982 'totally contrary to the traditions of care and service which are a hallmark of the health service in this country'.[200] Together with the three rail strikes of 1982 it was defeated, and when the water workers mounted their first ever all-out national strike in 1983, Thatcher emphasized how seriously a monopolistic union was damaging the public-service ethic by denying essentials to a helpless public.[201] This was the government's first defeat, though but one episode in an ongoing battle.

In January 1984 the government held that the growing and more ruthless use of tactical strikes justified outlawing trade unionism at the Government

---

[196] E. Powell, *A Nation Not Afraid: The Thinking of Enoch Powell*, ed. John Wood (1965), 132–3.
[197] *O* (9 Sept. 1979), 4, 9.   [198] *O* (2 Sept. 1984), 9.   [199] *T* (17 Jan. 1981), 1.
[200] *T* (11 Sept. 1982), 2.
[201] *G* (29 Jan. 1983), 28. *HC Deb.* 24 Feb. 1983, cc. 1050–1. P. Bassett's 'The Pay Strategy Springs a Leak', *FT* (24 Feb. 1983), 22, usefully summarizes events.

Communications Headquarters (GCHQ) in Cheltenham on grounds of national security.[202] 'It shocked me: shocked me', was Len Murray's pained reaction to Thatcher's brusque way of rejecting the TUC's protest;[203] his aim of edging trade unionists towards 'new realist' moderation was greatly complicated thereby. The privatization of public-sector industries after 1983 entailed massive share-issues to employees and the general public, rendering large-scale change in the industrial-relations climate feasible. There were more trials to come. In 1984–5 the thirty-six-week strike of about 400 computer workers over shift payments and rosters in the Department of Health and Social Security (DHSS)'s computer centre at Longbenton, Newcastle, the longest in civil-service history, ended only after affecting benefit payments to 12 million people.[204] UK trade union density (its proportion of the employee workforce) had been falling, however, since its peak (54.4 per cent) in 1979, and between then and 1984 trade union membership had fallen by a sixth; by 1995 density had fallen to the levels of the late 1930s, thus unravelling the two major subsequent periods of trade union growth in the 1940s and 1970s.[205] Already by 1984 Roy Hattersley, Labour's spokesman on economic affairs, was envisaging diminished trade union influence within the Labour Party.[206]

Yet Thatcher's position remained precarious until the miners had tacitly accepted government's primacy over sectional pressures. Scargill was by no means the only labour leader since the 1960s to emphasize that 'all our freedoms and laws have been won as a result of people who, when conscience dictated, have been prepared to defy existing law'.[207] Even Callaghan referred, during the NHS strike in September 1982, to 'a contingent right' of law-breaking 'if the law is a bad law'—a view firmly rebutted by Thatcher at her party's conference in the following month.[208] Gormley, Scargill's predecessor as NUM National President, was a shrewd negotiator who thought Scargill doctrinaire and unrealistic in the demands he encouraged the Yorkshire miners to make.[209] Gormley knew that negotiation involved more than annual threats of class confrontation, whereas Scargill pronounced it 'the easiest thing in the world . . . to compromise one's principles. The most difficult thing is to stand firm.'[210] Scargill had reached high position very young, and could afford to wait. 'He is a young fellow', said Gormley in 1982: 'he will, I hope, grow into the job'.[211] As National President from 1982 Scargill was a workaholic with not

---

[202] For the subsequent legal judgements in favour of the government, see *FT* (7 Aug. 1984), 7. *T* (23 Nov. 1984), 23.   [203] *FT* (31 Aug. 1984), 18.
[204] *FT* (21 Jan. 1985), 8.   [205] *BST* 186–8; *TCBST* 310.
[206] Speech at Fabian Society centenary school, Oxford, *FT* (9 Jan. 1984), 1.
[207] At the TUC, *T* (2 Sept. 1980), 4; cf. E. Heffer, *O* (18 Feb. 1973), 10.
[208] Callaghan, *T* (7 Sept. 1982), 1. Thatcher, *Party Conference Speeches*, 85.
[209] e.g. the demand in 1975 for the £100 per week miner, *T* (8 July 1975), 1.
[210] Quoted in *ST* (15 Nov. 1987), 35; cf. Gormley on compromise, *DT* (3 July 1979), 1.
[211] *T* (25 Mar. 1982), 2.

the slightest intention of 'growing', and preferred martyrdom to betraying his class in what he saw as a class war. His beliefs may have obscured his long-term vision, but they lent him the courage and commitment a leader needs in the short term. He was far more deft with the media than MacGregor: with a quick turn of phrase to spice his interviews, this neatly dressed north-country card knew how to excite and intimidate media people while evading their questions, and his cocksure sense of fun and skilful mimicry went down well in the miners' clubs.[212] All this contrasted oddly with the intense seriousness of his beliefs, which inspired his passionate high-toned rhetoric before the large audiences he attracted in TUC and Labour Party conferences. Given the gulf between his own views and those of his rank and file, his achievement was remarkable. 'King Arthur' built up a devoted following among young miners, who carried their chant of 'here we go, here we go' from the football terraces into a contest with the government that was anything but a game. Everyone knew that Thatcher must eventually take on Scargill and defeat him.

Conservative preparations for doing so had already begun before 1979, with plans for building up coal stocks and imports, diversifying power stations' fuel requirements, removing state benefits from strikers, and establishing effective policing.[213] The government's defeat in 1972 had reflected a major failure of intelligence that was soon counteracted: 'secondary picketing' eventually generated 'aggressive policing'. The Home Office's inadequate Emergencies Committee was replaced by the Cabinet Office's Civil Contingencies Unit, a standing committee of ministers and civil servants organizing the defence of essential supplies.[214] Dockers driving from Hull to picket at Scunthorpe in August 1972 had been denied their weapons at road checks,[215] and by 1973 a central information room had been established in Scotland Yard to provide the police with coordinated information on illegal picketing.[216] Bristol riots in 1980 led the police to shed their decentralizing traditions still further, and operate through a 'national reporting centre' at New Scotland Yard, the mechanism used to defeat the miners in 1984–5.[217] Plans for maintaining order during a major confrontation were quietly laid in the early 1980s, and the cabinet committee MISC 57 began planning the build-up of coal stocks and the switch to oil-burning power stations in the event of a strike.[218] MacGregor at age 70 was not a man to shirk challenges, and moved on in 1983 to an even tougher three-year term as Chairman of the Coal Board, aiming to import a business

---

[212] See Robert Taylor's brilliant portrait in *O* (6 Dec. 1981), 9.

[213] For the Ridley report see *T* (4 Mar. 1985), 2.

[214] For a good account of how it worked see Peter Hennessy's two articles in *T* (13 Nov. 1979), 4; (14 Nov. 1979), 3.   [215] *T* (10 Aug. 1972), 1.

[216] *HC Deb.* 13 Nov. 1973, c. 261.

[217] D. Beresford, 'The Force to be Reckoned With', *G* (23 June 1984), 17. See also *ST* (25 Mar. 1984), 4.   [218] P. Hennessy, *Cabinet* (Oxford, 1986), 32.

culture. Tackling the NUM tested Thatcher's political agility to the full. She shrewdly executed move and counter-move against Scargill's activists, whom she labelled 'the enemy within', without ever risking undue public loss of face, and always chose her ground carefully. In 1981, when an opportunity for combat presented itself with miners' resistance to pit closures, discretion had for the moment been the better part of her valour.[219] Her right-wing critics should at the time have realized that through short-term tactical retreat she hoped to avoid Heath's mistake: she did not intend to entrench herself and then retreat into a u-turn which sacrificed personal and governmental dignity.

Thatcher and Scargill could hardly have differed more sharply in background and values, but in their determination and courage they were well matched. Unlike Thatcher, however, Scargill did not know when, or even how, to compromise. He had also drawn the wrong conclusion from Saltley, whose alleged mass working-class solidarity he assumed could be replicated in the quite different political and economic climate prevailing ten years later. Nonetheless, the outcome of Scargill's strike in 1984–5 was far less predictable at the time than it seemed in retrospect. Thatcher later recalled that, though ostensibly aloof from the dispute, she and Peter Walker, her energy minister, 'followed with constant anxiety every phase of the battle for public opinion'.[220] Strikes against MacGregor's plans for the latest round of pit closures began on 6 March 1984, and Scargill, instead of calling for a national ballot, resumed his earlier tactic of spreading the strike from its Yorkshire base through despatching flying pickets. His extensive knowledge of labour history had somehow not alerted him to the independent traditions of the Nottinghamshire miners. The Yorkshire pickets were too energetic for their own good, and those who got past Nottinghamshire's Chief Constable Charles McLachlan's large Methodist presence—and 164,058 presumed pickets in the first twenty-seven weeks of the strike did not—were so energetic as to drive the Nottinghamshire miners in summer 1984 to leave the NUM and set up the rival Union of Democratic Mineworkers.[221] In May Scargill openly admitted that the strike aimed to bring down the Thatcher government. The violence on both sides—especially at Orgreave, widely seen on television—was not a sight for faint hearts.[222] In comments which to his critics seemed evasive, to say the least, Scargill confined himself to attacking police violence. When later threatened with prosecution, he declared: 'I stand by my class, by my union—and if that means prison, so be it.'[223] The strike witnessed the largest ever policing operation, coordinated

[219] A. Raphael and R. Taylor, 'High Cost of Margaret's Danegeld', *O* (22 Feb. 1981), 15.
[220] Thatcher, *Downing Street Years*, 342; cf. 366.   [221] For McLachlan see *ST* (25 Nov. 1984), 10.
[222] For detailed chronologies of the strike see *FT* (31 Oct. 1984), 14; *T* (4 Mar. 1985), 2.
[223] *FT* (5 Oct. 1984), 40. See also *T* (2 Oct. 1984), 4 (speech at Labour Party conference on 1 Oct.). *FT* (2 Oct. 1984), 8.

from the National Reporting Centre; it was seen by many as an embryonic national police force, but since it had no budget of its own, did not give orders, and had no continuous existence, the Centre was in truth a substitute for centralization.[224] In June 77 per cent of those polled by MORI thought the police had handled the situation well, and 88 per cent thought the NUM should hold a national ballot.[225]

An intense community spirit now built up within mining communities, which with help from sympathetic trade unions and Labour local authorities became localized welfare states or even (in the eyes of some) miniature socialist utopias. Newly revealed organizational skills, women's action committees, belt-tightening, extended credit, and self-help got the striking miners through the summer, and at the time much was made of the solidarity and mutual help displayed.[226] Through 'Women Against Pit Closures' the miners' wives organized food, clothing, collections of money, and thus hope for the striking miners.[227] At least as much courage was required from the families of working miners,[228] for far from uniting the mining communities, the strike fomented bitter divisions between and within families, together with intimidation and fierce, long-lasting vendettas. The 10,372 criminal charges brought during the dispute included three of murder,[229] and by December 1984 thirteen deaths were being in some way attributed to the strike, including two suicides of intimidated working miners.[230] 'Scabs? They are lions', Thatcher told her party conference in October 1984.[231] One of them was the fictional Billy Elliot's father Jackie, whose militant son Tony is left speechless at seeing him on the strikebreakers' bus well on into the strike which Jackie had hitherto backed: 'you can't do this' said Tony: 'Not now. Not after all this time. Not after everything we've been through.'[232] Backed by a network of sympathetic barristers and solicitors, the working miners took legal action against the NUM on a scale unparalleled in trade union history.[233] The leaders of the Miners' Wives Back to Work Campaign secretly met Thatcher in Downing Street and provided useful intelligence; 'I was moved by the courage of these women', she later recalled.[234] 'The sheer viciousness of what was done', she wrote, 'provides a

---

[224] G (23 June 1984), 17. ST (25 Mar. 1984), 4.   [225] ST (10 June 1984), 1.

[226] e.g. P. Vallely, 'The Strike that Turned Wives into Warriors', T (4 Mar. 1985), 10. D. Goodhart, 'Strike Revives Community Spirit among Miners', FT (24 July 1984), 9.

[227] See G. Goodman, 'Betty Heathfield', G (22 Feb. 2006), 32.

[228] For a list of attacks on the person and property of working miners between Mar. and Sept. see T (6 Oct. 1984), 4.   [229] T (20 Mar. 1985), 2. See also T (17 July 1984), 2.

[230] T (1 Dec. 1984), 2.   [231] Thatcher, Party Conference Speeches, 105.

[232] L. Hall, Billy Elliot (2000), 78; screenplay written in 1999 for the highly successful low-budget film released in 2000, and later adapted as a musical launched in 2005.

[233] For more on this see G (27 Nov. 1984), 21; FT (31 Oct. 1984), 14; FT (4 Dec. 1984), 9; T (2 Mar. 1985), 2.

[234] Thatcher, Downing Street Years, 364. Irene McGibbon's reminiscences were broadcast on BBC Radio 4's programme 'The Thatcher Decade' on 11 Apr. 1989.

useful antidote to some of the more romantic talk about the spirit of the mining communities.'[235]

With the mines still partly open, the power stations had no need to close. Keeping its strategy secret, the Central Electricity Generating Board (CEGB) switched its resources between nuclear, oil-fired, and coal-fired power stations, as required; when denied rail facilities it was free to replenish its stocks by road, confident that the government would pay any strike-related extra costs.[236] Demand throughout the strike was satisfied by a combination of Midlands power stations and oil-fired plants in the south, together with a continued supply from nuclear power stations. As the CEGB's Chairman Sir Walter Marshall later pointed out, Scargill had made the case for nuclear power more eloquently than the Board could ever have done. After six months of the strike, Britain was still exporting more fuel than it imported.[237] When Gallup asked the public on five occasions during the strike whether they approved the miners' methods, those approving never rose higher than 15 per cent, and those disapproving never fell below 79 per cent.[238] By Christmas 1984 miners were slowly returning to work. The third who worked throughout the strike were likely to grow, given MacGregor's terms: redundancies were voluntary and were generously compensated. By 27 February 1985 more than half the NUM's members were back at work, Thatcher's 'magic figure',[239] and on 3 March the miners' national delegate conference voted by 98 votes to 91 for an organized return to work. Two days later the remaining strikers marched back to work behind their banners, a dignified but poignant sight (Plate 11), after a dispute which had lost more working days than any strike since that of the miners in 1926.[240] 'It was a huge victory', Kinnock recalled, 'much greater than [Thatcher] could ever have anticipated.' She did not want Scargill let down lightly: the militants could be tamed only though ensuring that they 'lost face'; but for all her tough talk, she remained throughout her premiership worried lest another strike should catch her unawares.[241]

Scargill had courageously and almost single-handedly conducted a long and complex battle against great odds. He had many allies, most notably middle-class guilt and the labour movement's mythology, traditions, and conscience. Socialists from outside the working class felt half-guilty, half-admiring at the men who had to work in such 'appalling conditions', as Benn put it—the 'blackened men who have to use the roadways and the corners for lavatories'.

---

[235] Thatcher, *Downing Street Years*, 353, 364. M. Wainwright, 'Tory Link with Strikebreakers', *G* (20 Jan. 2000), 14.
[236] M. Samuelson, 'How the CEGB Stopped the Lights Going Out', *FT* (1 Mar. 1985), 8.
[237] *G* (8 Mar. 1985), 36. *T* (28 Sept. 1984), 1–2.
[238] A. King (ed.), *British Political Opinion 1937–2000: The Gallup Polls* (2001), 337.
[239] Thatcher, *Downing Street Years*, 376.   [240] *BPF* (7th edn.), 371–2.
[241] Kinnock, interview with David Dimbleby in *The Lost Leader* (BBC2 TV broadcast on 5 Dec. 1992). Thatcher, *Downing Street Years*, 372. Lawson, *View from No. 11*, 718.

Jimmy Reid, veteran of the Upper Clyde sit-in and fiercely critical of Scargill, claimed that some within the labour movement seemed to think that people had a permanent right to labour 'like moles in the bowels of the earth'.[242] Kinnock felt unable to speak out against Scargill's tactics, and confined himself to describing the strike as 'a fight in the mining communities for survival'.[243] Privately he was more sceptical. The miners' disagreements, especially over the lack of a ballot, together with Scargill's refusal to condemn intimidation, hindered Kinnock from rationally presenting 'the case for coal'.[244] Thatcher capitalized on his apparent weakness, and Tebbit contemptuously dismissed him as crawling along 'like a puppy at Scargill's heels'.[245] Some years later Kinnock admitted that he would 'regret . . . to my dying day' his failure publicly to recommend a ballot,[246] yet if in 1984 he had done so, he would have bitterly divided his party, and would probably have destroyed himself as leader.

Why, then, did Scargill fail? Thatcher's determination, strategic skill, and access to superior resources cannot alone explain it. We have seen that she worked with the grain of public opinion; for David Owen as SDP leader in July 1984 the strike 'must be beaten in the name of economic and political sense'.[247] But opinion on such matters is volatile, and Thatcher was not confident of success till the very end. 'Lions led by donkeys' was the phrase applied to the troops at the Somme in the First World War. At the Labour Party conference in October 1985 the phrase was applied (amidst uproar) to Scargill's miners by Eric Hammond, successor to Frank Chapple as General Secretary of the Electrical, Electronic, Telecommunications and Plumbing Union (EETPU).[248] The audience which shouted him down knew he was right, for though Scargill might be intelligent and articulate, he was also egotistical and monumentally foolish. He began the strike at the wrong time of year, failing adequately to appraise the balance of power, and made the initial and fatal tactical mistake of not basing it on mass support through a national ballot. 'We had to act so that at any one time we did not unite against us all the unions involved in the use and distribution of coal', Thatcher recalled. 'This calculation had an enormous impact on our strategy.' Scargill created all the divisions she needed, and had made no effort to cultivate friends in the TUC. The EETPU overwhelmingly refused to back the NUM,[249] and in 1984 Bill Sirs refused

---

[242] Benn, *Diaries, 1977–80*, 536 (17 Sept. 1979). J. Reid, 'Barnsley's Lenin', *Spec* (13 Oct. 1984), 15.

[243] On 14 July 1984, when on the same platform as Scargill at the Durham miners' gala, *ST* (15 July 1984), 2.

[244] See Kinnock's address to the TUC, *T* (5 Sept. 1984), 4. See also *G* (6 Dec. 1984), 28.

[245] *HC Deb.* 1 Aug. 1984, c. 324; cf. Thatcher's reference to Kinnock's being described by a branch colliery president as 'a puppet' of those who favour extra-parliamentary tactics, *HC Deb.* 31 July 1984, c. 252.   [246] *G* (9 July 1993), 8.

[247] *FT* (14 July 1984), 4.   [248] *T* (3 Oct. 1985), 4.

[249] Quotation from Thatcher, *Downing Street Years*, 349. *FT* (11 Mar. 1983), 20 (Scargill). DT (20 Oct. 1984, 1 (EETPU).

to sacrifice the steelworkers' interests on Scargill's altar. When the TUC's new General Secretary Norman Willis urged Welsh striking miners to avoid damaging their cause with violence, their image was not enhanced when a hangman's noose was let down from the ceiling in front of him.[250] TUC leaders' dilemma was captured by the senior trade union leader quoted in September 1984: 'we don't want Arthur to win but we can't let the miners lose'.[251] Reid saw Scargill as a sort of ayatollah whose authoritarian style of leadership and refusal to condemn violent tactics were 'totally alien to the British Labour movement'.[252] Scargill's strong but romantic and sectarian sense of history blinded him to the world around him, and encouraged a pursuit of personal martyrdom which was tragic for his admiring but (as events turned out) collectively martyred followers. Courage and self-sacrifice, abundantly displayed within the mining communities, were exploited to promote a quite unnecessary trade union Dunkirk, thereby achieving the reverse of Scargill's underlying political objective. On every count, Scargill's strident quest for heroic defeat was no substitute for Gormley's unflamboyant but astute search for compromise.

Lawson provoked a parliamentary scene with his claim on 31 July 1984 that the strike, resulting from the government's decision not to subsidize uneconomic pits, 'even in narrow financial terms . . . represents a worthwhile investment for the nation'; unrepentant, his budget speech claimed in the following March that the costs 'both economic and constitutional, of submitting to this strike would have been infinitely greater than the costs that have been incurred in successfully resisting it'.[253] For Tebbit at Trade and Industry, money spent in resisting the strike was 'money well spent', and the coal industry's productivity now began rising fast.[254] Ever since 1957 the NUM's membership had been falling—by 1980 to 257,000, by 1990 to 90,000, and by 1998 to a mere 5,000.[255] If Scargill had compromised before or during the strike, the run-down would have been slower and far less painful.[256]

The miners' loss was the trade union movement's gain, for with the end of the strike the 'new realism' could resume. A TUC ban on accepting government funds for trade union ballots on pain of expulsion had hitherto nullified that aspect of the Employment Act (1980), but government was increasing its pressure on unions to democratize both elections to posts and their decisions on political affiliation and strikes. In November 1984 the EETPU was the first to break the TUC ban, and the AEU soon followed; it was no accident

[250] *FT* (3 July 1984), 10 (Sirs). *FT* (14 Nov. 1984), 1 (Willis).   [251] Quoted in *O* (9 Sept. 1984), 9.
[252] J. Reid, 'The Damage Scargill has Done to the Left', *O* (16 Sept. 1984), 8; cf. Reid's 'Barnsley's Lenin', *Spec* (13 Oct. 1984), 15.
[253] *HC Deb.* 31 July 1984, cc. 306–7; 19 Mar. 1985, c. 783 (budget speech).
[254] *FT* (2 Aug. 1984), 8 (Tebbit). *Econ* (16 Jan. 1988), 28.   [255] *BPF* (8th edn.), 394–5.
[256] As argued by Roy Hattersley, *G* (8 Mar. 2004), 20.

that both had pioneered the computerized central membership lists which the government favoured, and which enabled them to ballot their members directly.[257] By mid-decade the unions were increasingly cooperating with the government's new legislation, were offering employers no-strike agreements, and were even detecting advantages in the state-subsidized requirement that they should consult their members more extensively through postal ballots. This required unions to acquire new equipment, central membership lists, precise definitions of membership, and even accurate membership statistics.[258] Computers worked with the grain of Conservative legislation, though few trade union leaders were prepared (with Hammond) publicly to say of Thatcher that for this reason 'the entire trade union movement owes her a debt'.[259] The labour movement had been coerced into a direct democracy that had long been recommended by prominent sympathizers, and could have emerged from its own initiative.[260]

The strike's cultural aftermath was significant. The success of three outstanding films—*Brassed Off* (released in 1996), *The Full Monty* (1997), and *Billy Elliot* (2000)—owed much to their original plots, their fine acting, their richly varied emotions ranging all the way from comedy to tragedy, and their evocative recapture of a fast fading northern industrialism and community-based brass-band culture. They seduced their audiences by poignantly depicting courage, resourcefulness, and resilience in the face of larger forces well beyond the individual's control, with Thatcher as villain unseen. With their dramatic force enhanced by lacking any felt need for balance and context, these films massaged the middle-class conscience at the point when 'New Labour' was rising to its apogee. The governments responsible for, respectively, the anguished council estates of 'Grimley' during the pit closures of 1992, the derelict steelworks of Sheffield in the late 1990s, and the mining villages torn apart in Durham during 1984–5 were by implication heartless. Highlighted against the night sky in *Brassed Off*, and unlikely to fade from audiences' memories, was the horribly surreal writhing figure of Phil, the distraught young miner, attempting but failing to kill himself by hanging from a crane in the clown's gear he had worn while raising funds for his family at local children's parties.

The Conservatives' long-term image could hardly benefit from all this, yet for the Labour Party and labour movement there was no going back. The scene now shifted to Fleet Street, where the impulse for change came from the provinces. There tough small businessmen, many of them newcomers to the industry, were pioneering important innovations, including the freesheet.

---

[257] For a good discussion see *FT* (2 Aug. 1985), 7.
[258] For a good discussion see G. Hodgson, 'Computers Key to Successful Ballots', *FT* (2 Aug. 1985), 7.   [259] Quoted in G. Turner, 'Scourge of the Brothers', *STel* (4 Sept. 1988), 6.
[260] e.g. Michael Young, *The Chipped White Cups of Dover: A Discussion of the Possibility of a New Progressive Party* (1960), 18.

Christopher Pole-Carew in his Nottingham *Evening Post* was the first to breach trade union restrictions on using the new computerized print technology which had captured the American presses years before.[261] The most dramatic battle was fought from 1982 by the enterprising public-school-educated Anglicized Persian Eddie Shah, founder of Messenger Group Newspapers. He was readier than his rivals to invoke the government's new trade union legislation against the closed shop run by the National Graphical Association and National Union of Journalists, and with a loyal workforce he successfully braved secondary pickets at his Warrington plant. Shah then invaded Fleet Street with help from Freedom Association contacts; Hammond's EETPU in July 1985 offered him a single-union no-strike flexible-working agreement, thereby infuriating the printing unions, and in March 1986 Shah launched *Today* as the first national colour daily.

'Spanish practices' had long been rife in Fleet Street, and in the following January the tough Australian Rupert Murdoch of News International rose to Shah's challenge. Murdoch had arrived in Fleet Street in 1969 when he bought the *News of the World*, and soon afterwards acquired the *Sun*. With *The Times* also under his control from 1981, its last issue with any component produced by hot-metal composition appeared on 1 May 1982; thereafter it was the first national broadsheet set entirely by photocomposition and computer. Though by then the most powerful figure in Fleet Street, Murdoch could not get the printers' unions to allow the journalists to bypass the typesetters and enter their text directly. Audaciously sacking his 5,500 workers, he re-engaged none. Then, in a brilliantly planned ruse, which could not have occurred without Thatcher's trade union reforms, he moved all four of his national titles—*News of the World*, *Sun*, *Sunday Times*, and *The Times*, collectively accounting for a third of Fleet Street's circulation—to barbed-wired premises in the new docklands complex at Wapping, where the EETPU helped to recruit and train a new labour force. A bitter and prolonged dispute was the outcome, but because the printers' unions could not close the plant, there was no need to implement the contingency plan for the newly engaged employees to use a helicoptered escape-route behind closed fire-doors. As earlier with the miners, compensation payments slowly eroded opposition, and the strike ended early in 1987 after violent conflict between police and strikers in January. Murdoch could now shift his four titles into greatly enhanced productivity,[262] becoming still more hated on the left, as much for his management practices as for the tone of his papers. London's press geography was permanently transformed, with Fleet Street no longer at its heart: national newspapers raised funds by

---

[261] *Econ* (7 Apr. 1984), 23.
[262] For a good account of the ruse see J. Lloyd and H. Hague, 'Murdoch Wins First Round in the Battle over Wapping', *FT* (27 Jan. 1986), 8.

selling up and operating from cheaper areas of London. As for Shah, he could not afford to retain control over *Today* for more than three months after its launch; the paper never really took off, and closed almost ten years later.

Trade union membership was now falling, as in most industrial nations, but in Britain decline was accelerated by privatization, diminished government and manufacturing employment, hostile legislation, rising part-time work, and relatively high unemployment. Between 1980 and 1990 UK trade unions lost a quarter of their members. The annual average for working days lost in industrial disputes fell from 14.1 million in 1970–4 to 10.5 million in 1980–4 to 0.8 million in 1990–4; the figure for 1994 was the lowest since records began in 1891.[263] There was also a significant change of generation among trade union leaders. The plump and amiable but tragi-comic and almost inarticulate Norman Willis succeeded the slim and quietly efficient Murray as TUC General Secretary in 1984, and somehow remained in post till 1993. 'Every time Mr Willis clambered to his feet and pulled up his trousers for another verbal ramble', wrote one seasoned journalist of the TUC in 1987, 'an audible unease wafted across the hall'. Other new trade union leaders included Ron Todd (Transport and General Workers Union (TGWU)), Bill Jordan (AEU), and John Edmonds (General Municipal Boilermakers and Allied Trades Union), but the most distinctive among them was Eric Hammond (EETPU). Even in the mid-1970s Chapple had defended the free market, and in 1981 he had openly sympathized with the SDP's objectives, though not with its tactics. 'If you think I'm right wing', he allegedly said of his successor, 'wait till you see Eric'.[264]

Reserved and abstemious, Hammond had once been a Bevanite, and his impeccably working-class background made him all the more damaging as populist critic of Labour's left. In this he had much in common with Tebbit, yet he remained a consistent Labour voter, and at Labour Party and TUC conferences he relished puncturing the left's self-deception with his blunt home truths: 'I do enjoy it', he said in 1986, 'it gees me up. The blood rises once they start on me.' He was shouted down at the Labour Party conference in 1984 for condemning Scargill's handling of the miners' strike,[265] and when taking the same line at the TUC he gave as good as he got: 'Hitler would have been proud of you lot', he declared.[266] He brought free-market values overtly to the trade union world: for him, recruiting was going out to get business, though the CBI turned down his union's application for membership in 1984. Other unions disliked his no-strike deals and thought he poached their members, but he saw the EETPU's members as consumers who deserved to get good

[263] *BPF* (8th edn.), 401. *Social Trends* (1996), 91.
[264] Robert Taylor, *O* (13 Sept. 1987), 9 (Willis). *FT* (1 Feb. 1986), 8 (Chapple).
[265] *G* (29 Jan. 1986), 30. *FT* (2 Oct. 1984), 8.   [266] *FT* (4 Sept. 1984), 10.

value: extensive ballot-based consultation and a package of practical advantages, including the private health-care benefits with which he had outraged the TUC as early as 1979. 'I feel comfortable with business executives', he once told an interviewer.[267] In 1988, when the TUC expelled his union for organizing no-strike, single-union deals, he pronounced the TUC 'wholly irrelevant' to his members' needs, and denounced 'the sherry-party revolutionaries with their model resolutions and conference hall rhetoric'.[268]

Hammond was probably better attuned than his TUC critics to rank-and-file views. After all, the working population with bank accounts had risen from 51 per cent in 1976 to 75 per cent in 1983,[269] and many trade unionists now owned shares and houses and even voted Conservative. Kinnock at his party conference in 1987 argued that Labour could no longer depend solely on the dispossessed; he went on to mimic a slightly peeved TGWU General Secretary Ron Todd on how to recruit a docker on £400 per week who owned his own house, microwave, car, video, and holiday home near Marbella: 'you do not say, let me take you out of your misery, brother'.[270] Alert Labour Party and trade union leaders now began to wonder whether both would benefit from semi-detachment.[271] The trade union leaders so prominent at the TUC were white, employed, male, uniformly Labour-voting, favoured unilateral disarmament and nationalization, and apparently owned no shares. They had become 'a peculiar people',[272] at risk of losing touch not only with the public, but with their own members. Their resistance to Thatcher's further assaults on corporatism—to more privatization, to the government's training initiative in 1988, to the Dock Labour Scheme's abolition in 1989—was counter-productive because so easily defeated.[273] By 1989 restrictive practices had reduced employment in the forty Scheme ports to only 70 per cent of dock work: business had moved elsewhere, from Liverpool and London to non-Scheme ports such as Dover and Felixstowe.[274] Research showed that, although union membership brought members a wage premium of about a tenth, unionization (especially when enforced by the closed shop) weakened productivity and profits, and so reduced employment in the longer term; as the *Sun*'s headline put it, 'Unions won you more money but got you sacked!'[275] As for the National Economic Development Council (NEDC), it was a survival from corporatist days, fostering what Benn in 1974 had called 'a mush of consensus',[276] and it became the trade unions' forum for attacking the government. Tebbit as Secretary of State for Employment had found

[267] *STel* (4 Sept. 1988), 6. For health benefits see *G* (5 Sept. 1979), 4.   [268] *Ind* (6 Sept. 1988), 8.
[269] R. V. Brown, *Banking in Britain* (Banking Information Service, n.pl., 1984), 19.
[270] *G* (30 Sept. 1987), 4.   [271] Hattersley was early in the field: *FT* (9 Jan. 1984), 1.
[272] Robert Taylor's phrase, *O* (13 Sept. 1987), 9; cf. John Edmonds, *FT* (10 Sept. 1987), 11.
[273] *G* (3 Sept. 1988), 18 (leader). *FT* (16 Sept. 1988), 13; (2 Aug. 1989), 9.
[274] *DT* (7 Apr. 1989), 19.
[275] Metcalf, 'Trade Unions and Economic Performance', 21–42. *Sun* (20 Sept. 1988), 6.
[276] Benn, *Diaries 1973–6*, 119 (11 Mar. 1974).

its meetings 'an agony of boredom',[277] and it began to meet less often, with ministers increasingly sending their deputies. In summer 1987 the government unilaterally scaled down its role, and in January 1989 provoked the TUC by ending its right to select the Council's trade union members, and chose Hammond.[278] In 1992 the NEDC was abolished. By then the TUC had at last begun reluctantly to move with the times: in 1986 it supported the successful motion endorsing pre-strike ballots, and it was perhaps symbolic that on 23 May 1990, by arrangement with the Bank of Scotland, it launched its own credit card. [279]

We have seen how the social-class significance of trade union militancy was misunderstood in the 1970s. Politicians on the left (most notably Benn) often assumed that unionization signified class consciousness, but the motive was often simply instrumental.[280] Given that any one employer now commanded less of the employee's time and wielded waning influence over a household with at least two earners, workplace relations diminished as an influence on social and political attitudes generally. Furthermore, strikes were often fomented by structural factors. Because of their long history, British trade unions—uniquely in Europe—were powerful in each of the three categories: craft, industrial, and general. So an entire industry was rarely covered by a single union, and inter-union disputes were frequent.[281] In areas of unemployment, strikes could set worker against worker: the china-clay workers in Cornwall, for example, marched in their thousands to protest in 1972 when 108 dockers closed the ports on which their industry depended. On 27 May 1980 the police had to intervene when coaches took 1,400 members of seven unions to the Isle of Grain power station in Kent in a competition for work there.[282] Complexity was compounded by the growing importance in Britain of split-level bargaining, nationally and on the shopfloor, and by the resulting tensions between union headquarters and branch.[283] Plant bargaining was the major source of unofficial strikes, and it suited all parties to settle many issues locally, and therefore quickly and flexibly, in discussions between employer and shop steward.

Compounding all this was a temporary problem: the combination in the 1960s and 1970s of inflation with periodic incomes policies. These generated a continuously gnawing and navel-gazing anxiety about status differentials that was all too easily misunderstood as mounting class consciousness. The salaries of the socially adjacent prompted more anxiety than those of the socially remote, and the unionization and militancy of the 1970s merely showed trade unionists

[277] Tebbit, *Upwardly Mobile*, 193; cf. Lawson, *View from No. 11*, 714.

[278] *FT* (2 July 1987), 8. *T* (10 Jan. 1989), 6.   [279] *T* (2 Sept. 1986), 1. *FT* (24 May 1990), 11.

[280] Harrison, *Seeking a Role*, 210–12, 329, and above, p. 149.

[281] G. K. Ingham, *Strikes and Industrial Conflict: Britain and Scandinavia* (1974), 80.

[282] *T* (10 Aug. 1972), 2 (Cornwall). *T* (28 May 1980), 1 (Kent). See also J. Torode, 'The More the Murrayer for TUC', *G* (11 Sept. 1980), 19.   [283] Harrison, *Seeking a Role*, 457.

acting upon the individualist message that Heath had preached in 1970–1: they were standing on their own two feet. Once incomes policies were imposed, militancy became a mode of organizational self-defence so as to ensure full representation in national negotiations. With the growing state employment that accompanied interventionist policies, unionization automatically advanced. The British trade union movement had in its day-to-day activities long been predominantly free-market in its instincts,[284] and in focusing on the direct promotion of their members' wages trade union leaders were only delivering what their members paid them to deliver. After ten years of observing his constituents as MP for Leyton, Bryan Magee concluded that 'it is only middle-class socialists whose entrails are deeply stirred by the ideal of social equality'.[285]

For all the class rhetoric of the 1970s, the manual labour which had once lent it credibility was steadily ebbing away. From 1911 onwards there was a steady fall in the balance of occupations in the occupied population: the 1970s witnessed the crossover in Great Britain between the falling trend in manual employment and the rising trend in non-manual.[286] The change was not all one way. Visiting the North Sea oilfields in July 1975, Benn was impressed: 'it must be absolute hell to work there. It is a complete science fiction world', he wrote.[287] Nonetheless, the share of the British labour force employed in manufacturing, mining, construction, and public utilities in the early 1970s was (at 43 per cent) almost identical to what it had been in the mid-nineteenth century, but it had peaked at 46 per cent in the early 1950s, and by the end of the 1980s had fallen below 30 per cent. Manufacture's share of employment fell from 35 per cent in the 1960s to 31 per cent in 1975, to 26 per cent in 1984, to 20 per cent in 1993.[288] The same picture emerges from trends in sectoral employment: in Great Britain the decline in agriculture, energy (especially in the 1980s), metal manufacture, and mechanical engineering (especially since 1970) was marked, whereas there was a huge rise in recreational services from 1970, and in financial services in the 1980s, together with large rises in medical and other services.[289]

In reality, trade union hostility to Conservative legislation after 1970 was deeply conservative in mood: 'this was not a revolutionary England', wrote the *Economist*, commenting in February 1971 on the TUC's demonstration against the Industrial Relations Bill, 'but a tightly conservative one, seeking to hang on to the ways it knew'.[290] Whereas in the twentieth century the

---

[284] Ibid. 454, 458.

[285] B. Magee, 'Is Anyone Envious Enough These Days to Want Equality?', *G* (20 June 1990), 21.

[286] *BST* (1988), 9; 163; see also 20, 24, 162.   [287] Benn, *Diaries 1973–6*, 419 (16 July 1975).

[288] B. Supple, 'Fear of Failing: Economic History and the Decline of Britain', *Economic History Review* (Aug. 1994), 452.   [289] *TCBST* 284.

[290] *Econ* (17 Feb. 1971), 26.

middle class expanded (through professionalization, entrepreneurship, and privatization) by dividing, the working class contracted (through unionization, state planning, and nationalization) by uniting. Socialism could temporarily bypass, but could not prevent, the continuous growth in occupations that lay beyond the politician's reach. Given that Labour's heartland still lay in the areas of densely unionized heavy industry, the Party's delayed response to change was understandable. 'A lump comes to one's throat as one sees a lodge banner crowned with black crepe and knows that a worker in that pit has been killed during the past year', wrote Castle of the Durham miners' gala in 1968.[291] Wilson rebuked Crossman posthumously for being indifferent to this function, which Labour leaders in the 1960s assiduously attended. But the gala was, as Benn admitted in 1966, 'slowly turning . . . into a folk festival'.[292] Although Crossman as he surveyed the 60,000–70,000 people packed into Bedlington's wide street at the Northumbrian miners' picnic in 1969 'had a marvellous sense of the wonderful spirit of the miners', he at once noted how regularly even under a Labour government the mines were closing.[293]

Late twentieth-century Britain in some ways saw Labour's long-term class-reconciling objectives realized, though by somewhat unexpected and not always socialist routes. Absolute poverty was in slow long-term decline, and although the overall dispersal of wage-levels within the manual-labour category before 1970 had remained remarkably stable for more than eighty years,[294] average real earnings for male manual workers rose more than fivefold during the twentieth century: by the 1990s hardly any full-time workers had real earnings as low as even the average in 1914.[295] As for the Conservatives, Thatcher's dream of creating a share-owning democracy may not have been overtly realized, given that the share of total equity owned by individuals continued to fall—from 47 per cent in 1969 to 28 per cent in 1981 to 20 per cent in 1990—but this decline was more than counterbalanced by the pension funds' growing share, with 9, 27, and 32 per cent, respectively.[296] In July 1979 Keith Joseph pointed out that workers' pension funds now owned half the shares in the private sector; class-conscious workers restricting their labour, he added, 'injure themselves, their families, and everyone else in the country including the pensioners'.[297] To the Victorians the combination of mass deprivation with large working-class

[291] Castle, *Diaries 1964–70*, 492 (20 July 1968).

[292] H. Wilson, 'A Desire to Educate', *Listener* (5 Jan. 1978), 7. Benn, *Diaries, 1963–7*, 454 (16 July 1966).   [293] Crossman, *Cabinet Diaries*, iii. 517–18 (14 June 1969).

[294] See the table in P. Townsend, *Poverty in the United Kingdom: A Survey of Household Resources and Standards of Living* (1979), 139.

[295] See the interesting table in P. Johnson (ed.), *Twentieth-Century Britain: Economic, Social and Cultural Change* (1994), 6.   [296] Central Statistical Office, *Share Ownership*, 8.

[297] Discussion with Michael Charlton, Radio 4, on 30 July 1979.

numbers seemed potentially explosive, but the twentieth century saw both components of that alarming package slowly shrink.

5. FROM WORKING CLASS TO UNDERCLASS

Late twentieth-century Britain saw the surprising resurgence of concern about three types of individual earlier thought to be problems serious only for the Victorians: the feckless, the unemployed, and the criminal. Central to considering the feckless is the concept of the 'residuum', the Victorian term for the social groups in hopeless poverty and dependence. For Marx they were the 'lumpenproletariat'. For him the term incorporated political as well as moral disapproval because 'down and outs' were unlikely to promote his desired revolution. The mid-Victorian residuum was large enough[298] to present a political as well as economic threat. In the 1980s, by contrast, the socially deprived might periodically erupt from the inner-city backstreets,[299] but their threat was much less serious. The riots in Liverpool during 1981 weakened the local economy, but their destructiveness was not politically motivated. Liverpool's Professor of Politics felt that a more structured local protest would in some respects have offered more hope; as it was, 'capitalism has destroyed the social order in inner cities, much as Marx said in the Communist Manifesto, but . . . no real class identity has emerged'.[300]

'Lumpenproletariat' was a term unlikely to catch on within the UK, and late Victorian Liberal optimism had assumed that a discriminating philanthropy yoked to mass education would gradually draw the residuum towards respectability. There was a religious incentive and a tradition within the working class for doing so, together with well-established institutions for the purpose, but in a secularized society whose avenues out of the working class were so much broader, the late twentieth-century equivalent of the Victorian 'respectable artisan' was less likely to be active. A major impulse to the rise of the Labour Party had been the hope that collective philanthropy—that is, public welfare and planning—would spirit away the residuum, and for that reason (as well as because Latin had faded out of public debate) the term 'residuum' slowly disappeared. In 1969 Crossman credited Labour with having done much to eliminate poverty: it had been the country's 'astonishing achievement' to transform itself into a society 'where the majority are well off and the minority

---

[298] E. J. Hobsbawm, *Labouring Men: Studies in the History of Labour* (1964), 279, estimated that the 'labour aristocracy' comprised about 10% of the mid-Victorian male industrial workforce, though according to H. J. Dyos (ed.), *The Study of Urban History* (1968), 146, 148, this is an underestimate. On the whole subject see B. Harrison, 'Traditions of Respectability in British Labour History', in B. Harrison, *Peaceable Kingdom: Stability and Change in Modern Britain* (Oxford, 1982), 157–216.

[299] See below, pp. 525–30.

[300] F. F. Ridley, 'Will it Take an Away Match to Waken Downing Street?', *G* (13 July 1981), 7.

are poor', and 'if we can do that in thirty years, in the next thirty we can get rid of poverty among the minority'.[301] Poverty then seemed both curable and well on the way to being cured. Viewed from this perspective, the growing mid-century tendency to distinguish between the working class and the poor was but a staging post on the way to eliminating the 'working class' altogether: Richard Cobden's ideal of a dominant middle class seemed at last in prospect.

Sociologists in the 1960s found that moralism, though not of Marx's variety, still shaped British attitudes to those at the bottom of the heap: it was then widely assumed that the lowest social level was 'made up of deprived, undeserving or disadvantaged persons'. The sociologist Peter Townsend noted that the revived use of the term 'poor' was 'associated in the public mind with a largely workless (unsupported mothers, the aged, sick, and disabled) and supposedly small minority'.[302] In all essentials this minority resembled its Victorian precursor, and was likewise segregated. Its members, either by choice or ill-fortune, were too poor to participate in the affluent society's feast, and fell into the late twentieth-century category of the 'socially excluded'. At the same time the more successful or fortunate drew apart into suburban owner-occupied homes, leaving the poorest groups to council estates and privately rented inner-city accommodation. Yet disquietingly, the socially excluded did not seem to be dwindling. To the small minority who for whatever reason had always chosen a migrant lifestyle, the two world wars had added a new layer of unsettled veterans. Then, just as their numbers were waning from natural causes, the sixties added a younger group who deliberately chose to reject an affluent lifestyle; 'busking', no longer confined to the old, became familiar in the streets. Then in the 1970s and early 1980s came three significant social changes, all also unexpected, and all recruiting newcomers to the socially excluded: the growth of one-parent families,[303] the return of mass unemployment as a major social and political problem,[304] and the attempt to reduce it through cutting unemployment benefit for the young. The last of these may have driven some of the young into work, but it drove others to advertise their plight. Social commentators in the 1970s echoed the Victorians' Charity Organization Society in worrying about 'problem families', and about the 'cycle of deprivation' whereby poverty percolated down the generations. This was the problem Keith Joseph highlighted at Edgbaston on 19 October 1974.[305] So the new residuum was more diverse than the old: by

---

[301] Crossman, *Cabinet Diaries*, iii. 454 (24 Apr. 1969); cf. iii. 517 (14 June 1969); T. Dalyell, *Dick Crossman: A Portrait* (1989), 170.

[302] J. H. Goldthorpe *et al.*, *The Affluent Worker*, iii. *The Affluent Worker in the Class Structure* (Cambridge, 1969), 149. Townsend, *Poverty in UK*, 410.

[303] Harrison, *Seeking a Role*, 247–8, 295–6; see also below, pp. 221–4.

[304] See below, pp. 179–83, 357–63.

[305] See his 'The Cycle of Deprivation', in Pre-School Playgroups Association, *Playgroups in Education and the Social Services: Speeches at the PPA Conference for Local Authorities . . . 29/30 June, 1972* (1972), 1–9, for evidence of his humane and well-informed earlier interest in the cycle.

sex, region, and age. Poverty, said Crossman in 1969, had once affected whole communities, but now 'poverty in the midst of plenty . . . concentrated on those who are the weakest and least able to protect themselves; the chronic sick, the widows and deserted wives, the unmarried mothers and, above all, the 14 per cent. of the population who are over pension age'.[306]

Given the post-war collapse of the secondhand clothing trade and the growing overall levels of affluence by the 1970s, the unkempt homes of the socially excluded or self-excluded were by the 1970s usually more identifiably poor than their occupants. But respectability still sought to segregate itself (and especially its children) from uncongenial language, demeanour, and lifestyle: council houses and 'sink' schools were deserted for owner-occupation and better education while the going was good. The teacher remained in the frontline of the quest for respectability, with the police as last resort. Nigel Williams, in his two-act play with its deliberately ambiguous title, Class Enemy (1978), provided a memorably pessimistic and unsentimental portrait of likely new recruits for the residuum. The foul-mouthed 16-year-olds in the 'sink' class 5K of a south London comprehensive school find in violence and sex their only means of self-expression: 'I think if we put you lot in the Garden of Eden—in ten minutes you'd have it looking like a slum', a master tells them.[307] They frighten off their teachers, and yet when abandoned they dislike the neglect, and in staging their own five-minute 'lessons', they bleakly reveal their intellectual and emotional potential if only someone could draw it out. There were significant contrasts, though, between old and new responses to the residuum: teachers in their fight against it were now backed more by doctors and social workers than by clergymen and philanthropists, and late twentieth-century progressive opinion turned away from moralistic condemnation—even to the extent of criticizing moralizing as itself immoral. The socially deprived were no longer criticized for their personal qualities or lack of them: a morally neutral and preferably state-organized remedy was thought more appropriate. Philanthropy, if involved at all, was now not individual but collective, channelled through the voluntary organization or through public welfare. Changes in terminology seemed, as by magic, to have consigned the 'feckless' to oblivion.

By the end of the 1980s, the growing concern about British competitiveness in the global economy that was now emerging prompted doubts about whether even an affluent society could afford to subsidize the socially excluded, and there were growing worries about whether such subsidy might corrupt both them and wider groups: fecklessness might prove catching. At this point a replacement for Victorian terminology became available. The term 'underclass', first employed by the Swedish economist Gunnar Myrdal, had often been used since the 1960s in the American context of black deprivation as a weapon of the left,

---

[306] HC Deb. 19 Jan. 1970, c. 54.   [307] N. Williams, Class Enemy (1978), 38.

but during the 1980s the American social scientist Charles Murray exported the term to Britain as part of an attempt to avoid lumping all varieties of deprivation into the general category of 'the poor'.[308] The term reimported moralism into discussions of deprivation, and aimed to denote a type rather than a degree of poverty. It was only the latest term for welfare problems going back more than a century, moving forward from the mid-Victorian 'residuum' to the late Victorian 'undeserving poor', to the inter-war 'social problem group', to the post-war 'problem family', and to the 1970s 'cycle of deprivation'.[309] In the UK in the 1980s the term 'underclass' became a weapon of the right, a vehicle of disillusionment with the outcome of sixties welfare, which had allegedly taken too little account of the long-term impact on the conduct of its beneficiaries.[310] Rising illegitimacy and crime and family breakups led Murray to see the unemployed male youth as integral to a spreading underclass, ill-housed, ill-educated, and potentially violent.[311] The cultural, racial, social-class, and generational dimensions of comment on the underclass emerge in 1987 from Ralf Dahrendorf's discussion. He condemns 'a lifestyle of laid-back sloppiness, association in changing groups of gangs, congregation around discos or the like, hostility to middle-class society, peculiar habits of dress, hairstyle, often drugs or at least alcohol'. He saw this as a culture espoused by only 5 per cent of British society, but with a wider appeal, so that 'at times one feels that it is the only magnetic cultural style in our society'.[312] Preoccupation with the underclass accentuated, in short, the British reaction against sixties values and against the longer-standing welfarist tendency. Self-government, self-help, and self-discipline were returning into fashion as poverty's remedies.

The attack on dependency was central to Thatcherism, and informed her policies on tax and welfare. She favoured the polltax, for example, because it helped 'the very people who had always looked to me for protection from exploitation by the socialist state': the lower middle class. The tax aimed to ensure that 'a whole class of people—an "underclass" if you will—had been dragged back into the ranks of responsible society and asked to become not just dependants but citizens'.[313] In the late 1980s it was not yet clear that hers were anything other than right-wing sentiments, nor was the unsmiling aspect of 'New Labour' then predicted, though Frank Field was already setting out its agenda. In 1989 he claimed that in the 1980s privatization, means-tested welfare, growing unemployment, and a newly regressive taxation structure had fostered 'a psychological and political separation of the very poorest from

---

[308] C. Murray, *The Emerging British Underclass* (1990), 1–2.
[309] J. Welshman, *Underclass: A History of the Excluded 1880–2000* (2006), 127.
[310] D. J. Smith (ed.), *Understanding the Underclass* (1992), 1, 3.
[311] Murray, *Emerging British Underclass*, 13, 17, 22.
[312] R. Dahrendorf, 'The Erosion of Citizenship and its Consequences for Us All', *NS* (12 June 1987), 13.   [313] Thatcher, *Downing Street Years*, 658, 661.

the rest of the community'. Hence the 'drawbridge mentality', whereby those who had risen out of poverty prevented others from joining them. The Labour Party, he argued, needed to erode the underclass through mobilizing a combined working-class self-interest and altruism, thereby minimizing the divide between the working class and the one-parent family, the old-age pensioner, and the long-term unemployed.[314] Here were serious problems for 'New' Labour to tackle in the 1990s.

The second 'excluded' category, the unemployed, were worrying enough in themselves, especially when their number ineluctably increased from the late 1960s. They seemed all the more worrying because unemployment could well breed 'fecklessness'. Perhaps the most prominent among Conservative Party advertisements in the build-up to the general election in 1979 showed a long queue of people—employed members of the advertising firm Saatchi and Saatchi, as it turned out[315]—seeking work beneath the slogan 'Labour still isn't working'. We now know that mistaken policy caused the first Thatcher government at first even to exacerbate the problem.[316] The new right may have seen the shock of escalating unemployment in 1979–81 as salutary, but the shake-out of labour was less discriminating and more intense than intended.[317] Furthermore, whereas in 1961–79 the poorest tenth in the UK population increased their real income, between 1979 and 1992 that income fell, whereas it was the richest whose incomes gained most.[318] Here, then, was the basis for a formidably moralistic pilgrimage of passion against the first Thatcher government by a revived Labour opposition. Such a mood suited Labour's new and historically literate leader Michael Foot: the Jarrow March of 1936, Peterloo, and Tolpuddle all featured in his speech at the Trafalgar Square meeting to welcome the 40,000–50,000 people who joined the last leg of the People's March for Jobs in May 1981. This was largely a gathering of trade union and Labour Party supporters, and although in August 1975 there had been about seventy branches of the Claimants' Union throughout the country, the movement made less progress during the 1980s than might have been expected. When a mere 15,000–20,000 people from the People's March converged on Hyde Park in June 1983, their number disappointed the organizers.[319]

Why were the unemployed in the 1980s less active, and less able to find champions, than in the 1930s? Their protest's weakness cannot stem from the psychology of the unemployed person, for in both periods he was demoralized,

---

[314] F. Field, *Losing Out: The Emergence of Britain's Underclass* (Oxford, 1989), 3, 4.

[315] Max Madden, *HC Deb.* 1 Aug. 1978, cc. 233–4.   [316] See below, pp. 359, 525.

[317] As Lawson himself admitted in his *View from No. 11*, 980. See also S. Brittan in D. Kavanagh and A. Seldon (eds.), *The Thatcher Effect* (Oxford, 1989), 20–2.

[318] Joseph Rowntree Foundation, *Income and Wealth*, i. 15–16.

[319] *T* (1 June 1981), 2. Interview with the Union's founder Joe Kenyon, *O* (3 Aug. 1975), 2. *T* (6 June 1983), 5.

relatively apathetic politically, and isolated from fellow victims. Nor, in either decade, did rising unemployment necessarily knit together the employed and the unemployed. Trade unionists are almost by definition employed, and trade union leaders had to allow for their many members who ascribed their employed status to their own virtues: in both periods it was widely thought that work was readily available for those who really wanted it.[320] In both periods, too, mounting unemployment was accompanied politically by schism on the left and therefore by power for the right, yet such schism cannot explain protest's relative weakness in the 1980s because that weakness was already causing comment before Thatcher took office, and well before the most serious schism occurred.[321] Social situation may be relevant to the contrast, for the unemployed in the 1980s were ethnically and age-wise more diverse, and occupationally and regionally less concentrated than in the 1930s.

Yet there were also significant political/cultural contrasts between the two periods. Three relevant features of the 1930s were not present in the 1980s. First, the Communist Party of Great Britain (CPGB), a powerful inter-war goad to Labour's conscience, had lost its dynamic by the 1980s. On the other hand, unemployment's tenacity in the later period was more salient, if only because comparative statistical information about it was more accessible, and because modern economies were more obviously interlinked. British manufacturing supremacy, toppled earlier in the century by the USA and Germany, was in the post-war free-trade regime increasingly challenged (in common with several other Western industrial economies) by the lower labour costs prevailing in the Pacific rim. If majority Labour governments had achieved so little, perhaps the problem was less easily solved by political means than had been supposed. But, third, there had been in the interval a significant change in the type of palliative offered. Inter-war voluntarist effort for the unemployed was prodigious, and inter-war sociologists had interacted with social workers in church and community to promote relief schemes. No such voluntarist energy emerged in the 1980s, and this contrast might in itself have prompted resentment among the unemployed but for the fact that by then the palliatives had become more secular, professional, and paid. The Labour Party had now become a genuinely national party, less moulded by the dwindling number of single-industry manual-labour communities, and its statist instincts from the 1940s made it far more obvious in the 1970s than in the 1930s that government was doing its best through job-creation schemes and benefits systems to confront the problem.

On youth training the Thatcher governments were statist too, and pushed further the burgeoning training schemes of the 1970s.[322] The Manpower

[320] B. Jordan, *Paupers: The Making of the New Claiming Class* (1973), 27.
[321] e.g. R. Collins, 'The Jobless: A Nasty Smell under Society's Nose', *G* (21 Jan. 1976), 21.
[322] See below, pp. 361–2, 386.

Services Commission (MSC) was launched as an offshoot from the Department of Employment in January 1974 by the Heath government, which had been impressed by the Swedish Labour Board. By spring 1987 it was promoting no fewer than five ambitious schemes: the community programme, providing temporary work for the long-term unemployed (245,000 participants); the Youth Training Scheme (YTS), providing work experience and training for teenagers (362,000); the enterprise allowance scheme, helping the unemployed start their own business (110,000); the restart scheme, advising the longer-term unemployed on job and training options (700,000); and a new job-training scheme for unemployed people under 25 to provide at least six months' work experience and training with an employer.[323] In the 1930s it had been easy to blame unemployment on an economic system as yet unmoderated by majoritarian Labour governments, but in the 1980s the memory of two Labour majority governments' painful struggles to curb rising unemployment was decidedly green.

Welfare benefits were far more generous in the 1980s than in the 1930s, so more people registered for them, thereby simultaneously inflating the unemployment statistics and discouraging people from taking such jobs as were on offer; in 1980 young blacks in Liverpool, Manchester, and Wolverhampton, for instance, were readier than whites to remain unemployed or semi-legally employed rather than accept so-called 'shit work'.[324] Also in the later period, it seemed more acceptable for the older unemployed gradually to elide from failing to get work into retiring, especially as public welfare now cushioned retirement more generously.[325] Add to all this the impact made by the enhanced employment of women. In the 1980s men's special disadvantages in the labour market by comparison with women were much discussed, especially when the men were unskilled and aimed at full-time work. In the 1980s, as in the 1930s, it was women's suitability for the newly growing industries (light industry between the wars, the service sector in the 1980s) that made them more likely to get work when they sought it.[326] A difference between the two decades, however, lay in the secure presence of married women within the labour market, making the the double-income family a further cushion against unemployment. As the *Economist* put it, 'it is easier for dad to strike while eating mum's paypacket'.[327] Here again, unemployment statistics were boosted by more people (women) registering for benefit. The point should not be overdone. The number of workless households and of workless adults living in them quadrupled between 1969 and 1999, and jobs for women were

[323] *FT* (23 Apr. 1987), 11. See also A. Britton, *Macroeconomic Policy in Britain 1974–87* (Cambridge, 1991), 255.   [324] *T* (11 Aug. 1980), 2.
[325] Harrison, *Seeking a Role*, 35, 284; see also below, p. 277.
[326] J. Burnett, *Idle Hands: The Experience of Unemployment, 1790–1990* (1994), 273–4.
[327] *Econ* (3 Feb. 1979), 12. See also below, pp. 229, 324.

not necessarily correlated with lack of jobs for men. Work was distributed unevenly, and there was some polarization between the work-rich and the work-poor.[328]

For all these reasons unemployment slowly declined among political priorities from the 1970s, fragmenting rather than consolidating class loyalties in the 1980s. In 1975 Healey as Chancellor of the Exchequer rejected pressure 'to treat unemployment as the central problem' and deliberately to expand demand; instead, he lent priority to balancing the budget.[329] Callaghan wondered privately in September 1977 whether unemployment now mattered electorally very much, given that 'inflation affects everybody and unemployment comparatively few';[330] in March 1978 he admitted publicly that despite the government's doing more than any other in Europe to alleviate unemployment he could 'see no basic solution to the problem',[331] yet in the following month he privately claimed that 'beating inflation is *politically* more important than beating unemployment'.[332] Still, nobody in 1979 would have guessed that a Conservative government which even on its own estimates had presided over a rise in unemployment from 1,464,000 in July 1979 to 3,225,000 in January 1983[333] could have gone on to win three more general elections. Thatcher was worried enough about unemployment, but unlike Heath in 1972 she did not allow it to deflect her from her chosen line of policy. On 9 May 1981 a leader in *The Times* thought that 'the great mystery of the present administration is that it is not more unpopular'. When his deputy Jeffrey Archer claimed in 1985 that the Conservatives could not hope to win an election if the number of unemployed did not fall, Tebbit's response as Party Chairman was to say 'I do not altogether agree with him', and at the general election of 1987 the Conservatives did not do especially badly in constituencies with high unemployment.[334] By then it had become commonplace among her critics to say that Thatcher had coarsened public sensibility by depreciating social concern,[335] and had encouraged the majority in work to neglect the minority without it. On the other hand, her supporters saw the nation as at last ceasing to deceive itself, with a basis laid for significant long-term recovery. Those on right and left whose political outlook had been moulded by the reaction against the 1930s found this revolution in political priorities bewildering. In May 1988 Heath recalled cabinet discussions which

---

[328] P. Gregg et al., 'The Rise of the Workless Household', in P. Gregg and J. Wadsworth (eds.), *The State of Working Britain* (Manchester, 1999), 89.   [329] *HC Deb.* 15 Apr. 1975, c. 282.

[330] Benn, *Diaries 1977–80*, 214 (13 Sept. 1977), cf. 227 (11 Oct. 1977).

[331] At a joint meeting of cabinet and NEC on 13 Mar. 1978, *G* (14 Mar. 1978), 6.

[332] Donoughue, *Downing Street Diary*, ii. 307 (3 Apr. 1978).   [333] *BPF* (8th edn.), 401.

[334] Tebbit, *T* (7 Oct. 1985), 1. See also Butler and Kavanagh, *British General Election of 1987*, 266, 331–2.

[335] See e.g. Hugo Young, 'The Snares that Lie in Wait for Mrs Thatcher', *G* (31 Dec. 1985), 15; 'A System which Excludes 3 Million People', *G* (9 Sept. 1986), 23.

assumed that a million out of work 'was socially intolerable and politically unacceptable'.[336] No longer, apparently.

As for the third problem category, the criminal, Blair's phrase, coined in 1993, on the need to be 'tough on crime and tough on the causes of crime',[337] implied that here Labour would be more discriminating than the Conservatives. Violence and crime moved quickly up the political agenda after 1970, but progressive people had at first responded dismissively with references to 'moral panics', drawing parallels with the baseless fears and phobias pervading Victorian cities. True, the incidence of crime was not always viewed in due proportion. In 1983 40 per cent of Londoners thought it unsafe to go out at night, rising to 57 per cent among those over 60, yet there was no necessary correlation between the fear and the reality: although assaults on the relatively helpless seemed particularly shocking and reportable, it was the young and not the old who were most likely to be violently assaulted.[338] Violence in industrial disputes, street fighting, brutal sports, and election riots were much less common than in the nineteenth century. At the general election of 1964 the UK witnessed violence only in West Belfast, where republicans illegally displayed a flag and initiated three days of riot.[339] Violence occurred at Sussex and Essex universities during the general election of 1970 and in 1987 arson hit the Conservative campaign headquarters in Hackney North and Stoke Newington,[340] but this was small beer by Victorian standards. Levels of drunkenness in Britain after 1970 could not begin to compare with what Victorian cities had witnessed on a Saturday night, and at Cambridge in 1981 a bare-knuckle prize-fight was rare enough to get into the national press.[341] The discontented tend in any society to seek and receive disproportionate attention: for the historian, 'distress evidence' is a poor guide to day-to-day reality.

Nonetheless, in 1978 the former Metropolitan Police Commissioner (1972–7) Sir Robert Mark admitted that 'for the first time in this century the belief that the state can or even wishes to protect people effectively from burglary, breaking offences and theft should be abandoned, at least in the great cities'.[342] The gentleness of English life, which Orwell had emphasized in the 1940s,[343] seemed rather less secure thirty years later—somewhat paradoxically, given that the warlike virtues, brutal sports, and harsh punishments had by then fallen into eclipse. The persistence of crime even at its existing level

---

[336] Letter in *T* (19 May 1988), 13; cf. D. Wood, 'The Politics of Rise in Jobless', *T* (30 June 1980), 15.
[337] First uttered on radio, 21 Feb. 1993, quoted in J. Sopel, *Tony Blair the Moderniser* (1995), 157.
[338] *T* (19 Nov. 1983), 4; (8 Mar. 1984), 2.
[339] 'A Peaceable People', *Econ* (1 Mar. 1986), 27. Butler and King, *British General Election of 1964*, 222 n. 1.
[340] For these incidents see *G* (3 June 1970), 1 (Sussex); *T* (3 June 1970), 1 (Essex); *STel* (14 June 1987), 1.   [341] *T* (2 Feb. 1981), 4.
[342] *T* (18 Oct. 1978), 1.   [343] Orwell, 'English People', 200, 206.

into the relatively affluent and more fully employed society of the 1970s could hardly be dismissed as the outcome of a 'moral panic', and would have shocked anyone who had observed the marked improvement in public order that had occurred between the 1850s and the 1950s. In retrospect we can see that the early twentieth century's very low levels of crime in England and Wales were exceptional; the rapidly rising levels of homicide and other types of violent crime per head of population from the late 1950s did not even approach mid-Victorian levels. Even in 1990, when the police recorded twice as many murders (676) as in 1860, their incidence was far lower when the intervening rise in population is taken into account.[344]

By the 1970s, however, the high hopes of earlier decades were being disappointed. Crime persisted amidst affluence just as illness persisted amidst better health-care. Crime no longer seemed confined to a small, abnormal, and distinct group: it now seemed a tendency pervading the entire community. A third of males born in 1953 had acquired at least one criminal conviction for an indictable offence by the time they were 46.[345] Law and order, hardly mentioned by parliamentary candidates in their addresses of the 1950s, were discussed by more than two-thirds of candidates at the election in 1987. Particular episodes pushed crime up the political agenda. In 1973 an attempt to kidnap Princess Anne in the Mall led *The Times* to say that 'acts of casual terrorism . . . are part of the texture of our lives in the 1970s'.[346] In 1975 over 2,000 London busmen marched in the funeral procession for Ronald Jones, a black bus driver attacked while his bus was two-thirds full of passengers. Three years later the Bishop of Southwark, no illiberal figure, insisted that the victim received too little attention by comparison with the criminal: four priests in his diocese had been violently assaulted recently, and in many areas mugging now precluded winter-evening meetings.[347] The problem of crime and hooliganism was at its worst in the poorer housing estates in the 1980s, but however much the affluent might seek to protect themselves in their suburbs with their burglar alarms, their 'neighbourhood watch' schemes, and their fortified walls and gates, the criminals penetrated there too.

The politicians wanted to seem in control of events, but were not: nobody knew why affluence and public welfare had not curbed steadily rising crime, or how crime could be restrained. The political parties diverged somewhat on priorities and remedies. The labour movement tended to see crime as reflecting social injustice, the police as requiring close monitoring by the local authority, and the judicial system as class-biased, especially against trade unionists.[348]

---

[344] *T* (29 Mar. 1991), 3, reporting research by Simon Field.

[345] M. Maguire, 'Crime Statistics: The "Data Explosion" and its Implications', in M. Maguire, R. Moran, and R. Reiner (eds.), *The Oxford Handbook of Criminology* (3rd edn. 2002), 326.

[346] *T* (21 Mar. 1974), 15. See also D. E. Butler, *British General Elections since 1945* (Oxford, 1989), 88.

[347] *T* (30 Jan. 1975), 4; (14 July 1978), 4 (Mervyn Stockwood).

[348] e.g. at the Labour Party conferences of 1979 and 1985: *DT* (5 Oct. 1979), 36; *G* (1 Oct. 1985), 4.

There was 'nothing mystical about the law', the Labour MP Eric Heffer told a Labour Party meeting in 1973: laws reflect class relationships, are sometimes unjust, and do not necessarily deserve universal respect.[349] Some speakers at the Labour Party conference's law-and-order debate in 1978 still thought the subject better suited to a Conservative Party conference, or even to the National Front, but others disagreed, if only because crime was relatively rife in Labour's council-estate heartlands.[350] Here as elsewhere, Callaghan helped to draw Labour closer to the general public: 'I am rather in favour of dealing with teenage hooliganism', he told the Labour cabinet of September 1974, claiming that the Conservative manifesto gained over Labour's in this respect; 'Hear! hear!' was Healey's response.[351]

Crime's growing incidence was not a narrowly British problem, as British tourists overseas by the 1970s well knew. In the somewhat unfocused inter-party debate of the 1980s and early 1990s, all wanted to deter crime by reshaping the environment, but the Conservatives (ever sceptical about high hopes of human nature) were more preoccupied with its moral components, Labour and the Liberals with its social. A rare occasion on which Thatcher as a young MP had diverged from the party line was to favour birching young violent offenders: 'in the prevailing climate of opinion, this was a line which I knew would expose me to ridicule from the self-consciously high-minded and soft-hearted commentators', she recalled. 'But my constituents did not see it that way.' In consistently wanting hanging restored, she felt very much in tune with constituency opinion: 'civilised society doesn't just happen', she told her party conference in 1987: 'It has to be sustained by standards widely accepted and upheld.' To contain crime, 'the moral energy of society' and 'the values of family life' should be drawn upon.[352] She rightly dismissed any simplistic correlation between poverty and crime, pointing out that much lower levels of reported crime accompanied much greater levels of poverty in some present-day societies, and in Britain at earlier periods.[353] Besides, she thought it insulting to the unemployed to assume that they were more dishonest than the rest. For many Conservatives, the media seemed seriously to pollute the moral environment. Had not the Annan committee on the future of broadcasting in Britain reported in 1977 that the American child on an average day would see between twenty-five and twenty-seven violent incidents, far more than in real life?[354] Thatcher also condemned 'the culture of excuses' fostered by local authorities hampering the police in pursuing the criminal, by parents failing to discipline their children, and by 'the professional progressives among

---

[349] T (24 Jan. 1973), 2. O (18 Feb. 1973), 10.   [350] T (6 Oct. 1978), 6.
[351] Castle, Diaries 1974-6, 182 (16 Sept. 1974).
[352] Thatcher, Path to Power, 116–17. Party Conference Speeches, 130.
[353] e.g. HC Deb. 23 Mar. 1982, c. 793; 17 Mar. 1987, c. 812; 19 Mar. 1987, c. 1037.
[354] Annan Report on Future of Broadcasting (1977), 247.

broadcasters, social workers and politicians who have created a fog of excuses in which the mugger and the burglar operate'. Crime was, for her, 'not a sickness to be cured' but 'a temptation to be resisted, a threat to be deterred, and an evil to be punished'.[355]

She had a special reason for approaching crime moralistically. If, as she hoped, the state was to retreat, the community must resume the moral functions eroded by secularization, bureaucratization, and the big city's anonymity, and refurbish the moral basis of the UK's 'civil society'. The spontaneous inventiveness, investment, and care for the customer that the free market required meant that bargains must be kept and order maintained. All the more necessary was it, then, for the community to foster her prized 'Victorian values'. These had rested upon a moralistic but neighbourly consensus involving mutual respect and responsibility, yet some wondered, with Rowntree and Lavers in 1951, whether Britain was not now 'living on the spiritual capital of the past'. Hence 'Thatcherism' embroiled itself in its later years with the churches and with those of the social and behavioural sciences which (on Archbishop Runcie's admission in 1987) had undermined the sense of personal responsibility;[356] Kenneth Baker as Home Secretary held a series of lunchtime meetings with religious leaders on how crime could be curbed.[357] For Thatcher's opponents, however, it seemed only common sense to say that crime levels could hardly be improved by rising unemployment, and that better housing and social conditions might cause them to fall; indeed, there was a close correlation in the 1980s for males under 25 between the numbers unemployed and the number of burglaries.[358] Labour could also claim that in so far as crime stemmed from greed, Conservative individualism and the advertisers' acquisitive society undermined mutual responsibility and fostered selfishness.[359] On the other hand, there were signs early in the 1980s that Labour's outlook on crime was becoming more nuanced—moving on from criticizing the police, the prisons, and the legal system to suggesting wider police recruitment, more sophisticated diagnosis of crime, and more transparent procedures for dealing with it. By the early 1990s more reflective attitudes were gaining ground in both parties:[360] Blair as shadow Home Secretary laid increasing stress on fostering personal responsibility, and Conservatives became less strident in dismissing social-environmental diagnoses.

---

[355] Speech to Conservative Central Council, Buxton on 19 Mar. 1988, *Ind* (21 Mar. 1988), 5. Speech to the Conservative Party conference, *G* (13 Oct. 1990), 4; cf. Major to Conservative Party conference, *DT* (9 Oct. 1993), 10.

[356] B. S. Rowntree and G. R. Lavers, *English Life and Leisure: A Social Study* (1951), 372, cf. 227. Runcie interview with B. Levin, *T* (30 Mar. 1987), 10.   [357] Baker, *Turbulent Years*, 453.

[358] *Ind* (7 Jan. 1994), 1.

[359] See e.g. Hattersley in *FT* (12 Oct. 1988), 12; Blair in *Ind* (2 Oct. 1992), 6, and (20 Feb. 1993), 5.

[360] I. Taylor, 'Is Crime Here to Stay?', *NS* (12 Nov. 1982), 12–14; and see e.g. Clarke v Lilley in *T* (8 Mar. 1993), 2.

In retrospect, though, public debate about crime after the 1950s seems all too crude, and such research into it as was conducted often lacked practical value.[361] In the public arena, 'lumping' into the overgeneral categories 'crime' and 'criminal' was widespread, whereas correlations were useful only between subdivided categories. Often ignored was the distortion of trends by such factors as the insurance companies' reporting requirements, police numbers, their enforcement policy, or their reporting methods. The statistics could also reflect changing public sensitivity to some types of offence: to rape, homosexuality, domestic violence, and child abuse, for instance. Allowance was also required for temptation's changing incidence: an increasingly complex society creates more regulations to be broken and many new types of offence, especially traffic offences. Readier access to drugs generated new types of violence: unstructured, random, non-political, and sometimes bizarre. Furthermore, in an affluent consumer-oriented society, more consumer goods not only existed but were accessible, especially in the big cities, and by the 1980s few shops hid their goods securely behind counters. In Scotland, where shoplifting was first separately classified as an offence in 1980, offences recorded by the police rose inexorably from 24,100 in 1980 to 32,300 in 2000. Shoplifting offences in England known to the police in the three years 1974–6 were distributed very widely, but the areas of the three major urban police forces—Metropolitan, Greater Manchester, and West Midlands—claimed the most: 12.8, 6.4, and 5.1 per cent, respectively.[362]

6. 'MULTICULTURALISM'?

The shop was increasingly likely to be run by an immigrant, and one further alignment cutting across social-class and political-party loyalties in the 1970s and 1980s remains to be discussed: ethnic background. After 1970 Britain's European immigrants were becoming assimilated and therefore less visible. Between 1971 and 1991 the Irish-born share of overseas-born residents in Great Britain fell still further, to 18 per cent; the 'Old Commonwealth' group remained at 6 per cent; those born in Europe fell to 19 per cent, but the 'New Commonwealth' group rose further to 45 per cent.[363] Many of the Irish-born were returning to the booming Irish Republic, and those who remained made up nearly 2 per cent of Great Britain's population.[364] By 1981 the Irish-born in Britain were an ageing group by comparison with the UK-born, and almost half

---

[361] See D. Downes, 'Promise and Performance in British Criminology', *British Journal of Sociology* (Dec. 1978).

[362] *Annual Abstract of Statistics, 1987*, 81; *1996*, 95; *2005*, 179. D. P. Walsh, *Shoplifting: Controlling a Major Crime* (London and Basingstoke, 1978), 30.   [363] Haskey, 'Overseas-Born Populations', 16.

[364] L. Greenslade, *The Irish in Britain in the 1990s: A Preliminary Analysis* (University of Liverpool Reports on the 1991 Census, 1; 1993), 4, 6.

lived in the south-east of England;[365] settlers in Britain of Irish parentage were far more numerous. By 1981 the fertility of Irish-born mothers had fallen to British norms, and Irish immigrants were gradually diversifying from labouring into professional and skilled occupations. Although many of the Irish-born still clustered in low-paid occupations, especially in the building trade, they were moving up within that trade by setting up as contractors and subcontractors.[366] Britain's Jewish community, though also numerically declining, remained in the late 1980s the fifth largest Jewish community in the world—behind only the USA, Israel, the USSR, and France.[367]

Britain's links after 1973 with the EEC prompted no sudden incursion of immigrants born in its component countries. Taking those born in all European countries outside the Irish Republic, there were only 6 per cent more in 1991 than in 1971, whereas the number of immigrants born in the Old Commonwealth had risen by 30 per cent and the American-born by 29 per cent. The most striking increase among the immigrants born in EEC countries after 1971 was among those from Germany, whose total from East and West Germany rose by 37 per cent, though the rate of immigration was no faster after 1971 than before. The number of Italian-born immigrants, by contrast, actually fell after 1971, though it rose by 139 per cent between 1951 and 1991 overall; these settlers clustered in the Greater London area.[368] Immigrants born in France did not register any marked increase till the 1980s, and the Spanish-born rose substantially before 1971 but then levelled off. As for European countries then outside the EEC, the number of immigrants born in Hungary and Poland was also declining after 1971, and despite several waves of new Polish immigrants after 1951 the number of Britain's Polish-born residents fell steadily between 1951 and 1991. By the 1990s the sexes were better balanced within the group, and nearly a third lived in London, to whose better suburbs they had begun to move; they were well on the way to invisibility.[369]

New Commonwealth immigrants were much more visible, not just by colour, but by number and culture. Race-consciousness was even less likely than class-consciousness to develop among them, if only because each new wave of immigrants has the effect of bedding in its precursors. There was very little intermarriage even in the 1990s between different 'New Commonwealth' ethnic groups.[370] If it cannot be assumed that all immigrants within any one

---

[365] Coleman and Salt, *British Population*, 498–9.   [366] *BST* 97, 575. *TBS* 473–4, 503.

[367] G. Davie, *Religion in Britain since 1945: Believing without Belonging* (Oxford, 1994), 64.

[368] Haskey, 'Overseas-Born Populations', 15. R. King, 'Italians in Britain: An Idiosyncratic Immigration', *ATI: Association of Teachers of Italian Journal* (Autumn 1979), 9.

[369] Haskey, 'Overseas-Born Populations', 15. K. Sword, *Identity in Flux: The Polish Community in Britain* (1996), 77, 233.

[370] T. Modood and R. Berthoud (eds.), *Ethnic Minorities in Britain: Diversity and Disadvantage. The Fourth National Survey of Ethnic Minorities* (1997), 31.

category have much in common at any one time, still less can such identity be assumed among immigrants from different locations and at different times. For example, the New Commonwealth immigrants entered a society where public welfare had eroded the self-help required from their Irish and Jewish predecessors; those earlier traditions led some prominent British Jews to regret that self-education, self-provision, and hard work were neglected by the well-intentioned people who focused on later immigrants' social problems. The Jews had not pressed their cultural claims on the British people: they '*were quite content for Britain to remain "ethnocentrically" British*'.[371] By contrast, a culture of victimhood undermined any sense of responsibility.[372] Yet the new immigrants were not always eager for public welfare. Bangladeshis in Spitalfields instinctively turned to mosque and family for help,[373] and both they and Pakistanis were more likely than other ethnic groups in 2001 to provide unpaid voluntary care for more than twenty hours a week within the household.[374] As for Chinese settlers, their self-help inclinations combined with their distinct medical traditions (requiring scarce and purchased skills in using herbal medicine and acupuncture) to distance them from public welfare.[375] Besides, the Chinese feared 'losing face' by accepting help from outsiders or by declaring themselves unemployed, and so when in trouble they tended to rely on family rather than state help. Familiar with corrupt government, they preferred to remain unobtrusive, repeating to one another the injunction 'in this world, avoid entering the door of a government office, as in death, you would avoid entering hell'.[376]

Immigrants' fragmentation by place of origin was often compounded by distinctive religious and even dietary contrasts. New Commonwealth immigrants were even more disparate by place of origin than European immigrants after 1945.[377] Even those from the Indian subcontinent came from very different localities, including immigrants from the South Asian diaspora on the Indian Ocean's coasts. The latter arrived in three phases: before 1968, then the several thousand who arrived in that year to anticipate impending restrictive legislation, then those who arrived in 1972 when President Amin expelled them from Uganda. Immigrants' links with home were strengthened in some

---

[371] I. Jakobovits, *From Doom to Hope: A Jewish View on 'Faith in the City'* (1986), 7 (emphasis in the original), quoted in J. Torode, 'Self-Help is Better than State Help', *G* (11 Feb. 1986), 23; cf. A. Sherman in *T* (4 Feb. 1978), 15, and rejoinder by G. Mayers *et al*. T (7 Feb. 1978), 15.
[372] *T* (20 Oct. 2007), 9 (interview with Chief Rabbi Jonathan Sacks).
[373] A. J. Kershen, *Strangers, Aliens and Asians: Huguenots, Jews and Bangladeshis in Spitalfields 1666–2000* (2005), 128.
[374] H. Young, E. Grundy, and S. Kalogirou, 'Who Cares? Geographic Variation in Unpaid Caregiving in England and Wales: Evidence from the 2001 Census', *Population Trends* (Summer 2005), 29.
[375] House of Commons, Home Affairs Committee, *Chinese Community in Britain* (HC102-III, 1985), 173.   [376] Quotation ibid. 172. See also *Chinese Community in Britain* (HC102-II, 1985), 73.
[377] Harrison, *Seeking a Role*, 223–4, 230–1.

cases, as earlier with the Irish and Italian immigrants, by regular visits, or by a long-term aim to retire there. Elaborate chain-migration structures were set up for immigrants from Hong Kong whereby relatives organized passports, funding, and jobs (often in restaurants) in the UK; immigrants then sent money home, and often returned there for festivals and family occasions, and to marry.[378] Under pressure of shared experience after emigration, and sometimes also in self-defence, some of these cultural contrasts could wane—as between West Indian groups in the Notting Hill carnival,[379] though such mergers did not come easily. Among the younger generation of West Indian immigrants the distinct accents of the West Indian islands partially merged, leaving Jamaican Creole dominant, but where settlers from one island formed a cluster, other West Indian variants could persist.[380]

Immigrants shared patterns of settlement to the extent that they all at first preferred large towns, especially inner-city London. With each subsequent generation the immigrants moved ever further out into the suburbs, though the countryside remained overwhelmingly white British. There were well-intentioned efforts to aid assimilation by creating 'dispersed clusters' of between four and ten families; these had some success with Hungarian immigrants in the 1950s, but not with Asian refugees from Uganda later. The policy failed with the Vietnamese too, for the same reason: newcomers to Britain naturally gravitated towards their own kind for mutual help and for shared cultural and other facilities, and more than half the Vietnamese immigrants had by 1987 resettled in the large cities where compatriot clusters could be found.[381] In other regional respects, immigrant groups had little in common. British Jews, for instance, were not only urban but metropolitan, and became more so after 1951: their provincial urban settlements shrank, whereas by 1985 London had 61 per cent of the 330,000 Jews then identified as such in the UK. Many had by then moved out into the London suburbs or into seaside resorts.[382]

In the 1990s more than two-thirds of the South Asian, African, and West Indian minorities lived in large cities, especially London, but fewer than a third of whites. South Asian groups were more likely than Caribbeans to choose the East Midlands and conurbations in northern England, though inner London attracted a special concentration of Britain's Bangladeshi immigrants, nearly

---

[378] J. L. Watson, 'The Chinese: Hong Kong Villagers in the British Catering Trade', in Watson (ed.), *Between Two Cultures: Migrants and Minorities in Britain* (Oxford, 1977), 190, 209–10.

[379] A. Cohen, 'Drama and Politics in the Development of a London Carnival', in R. Frankenberg (ed.), *Custom and Conflict in British Society* (Manchester, 1982), 331.

[380] C. Peach 'The Force of West Indian Island Identity in Britain', in C. G. Clarke, D. Ley, C. Peach, and P. Paget (eds.), *Geography and Ethnic Pluralism* (1984), 226–7.

[381] Hale, 'Vietnamese Secondary Migration', 260. P. R. Jones, *Vietnamese Refugees*, 4. W. G. Kuepper, G. L. Lackey, and E. N. Swinerton, *Ugandan Asians in Great Britain: Forced Migration and Social Absorption* (1975), 75.   [382] S. Waterman and B. Kosmin, *British Jewry in the Eighties* (1986), 20–1.

a quarter of whom lived in the London borough of Tower Hamlets.[383] After 1971 the white population tended to move out from the inner cities, with immigrant minorities replacing them; this helped to reverse the decline in inner London's population during the 1980s. London like nineteenth-century New York and Boston had become a magnet for immigrants, and by 1991 housed 12 per cent of Britain's population but 45 per cent of Britain's ethnic-minority population.[384] By 1991 London's more recent ethnic minorities showed signs of moving into the suburbs. By then a higher proportion of Indians, Pakistanis, and East African Asians than whites had become owner-occupiers, despite relatively low incomes, and so were dispersing faster than the West Indians and Bangladeshis, who tended to choose local authority housing; during the 1980s owner-occupation was spreading within other ethnic minority groups as well. Where the Asians did move into the suburbs, they still tended to cluster, with Ugandan Asians choosing Hounslow and Ealing, Punjabis choosing Southall and Gravesend.[385]

Motives for immigration were very diverse. The earlier Black African immigrants had often come to study, and in 1991 were the best qualified ethnic minority, especially in the older age-groups.[386] Very different were the Afro-Caribbeans, whose motives (like those of the Chinese and the South Asians) were primarily economic. By the end of the century, educational under-achievement among boys of West Indian origin was well known, and it was noted in 2003 that whereas about 6,000 Afro-Caribbeans were studying for a degree, almost 10,000 were in prison.[387] Nonetheless, by the 1990s the male and female Afro-Caribbean participation-rate in the workforce was high—with West Indian male immigrants clustering in heavy industry and transport, and West Indian women in service occupations such as nursing and catering.[388] In self-employment there were significant ethnic contrasts, with Pakistani and Bangladeshi immigrants well above average in 1992 for self-employment.[389] Afro-Caribbean and white self-employment was widespread in the construction industry, whereas half the self-employed in minority groups were in retailing (for South Asians except Bangladeshis), and catering (Bangladeshis and Chinese).[390] Persecution was the impulse to East African Asian immigration, as for their European predecessors fleeing Communism and Fascism, or the Vietnamese later. Such a motive

---

[383] Modood and Berthoud (eds.), *Diversity and Disadvantage*, 186. C. Peach (ed.), *Ethnicity in the 1991 Census*, ii. *The Ethnic Minority Populations of Great Britain* (1996), 158.
[384] P. Ratcliffe (ed.), *Ethnicity in the 1991 Census*, iii. *Social Geography and Ethnicity in Britain* (1996), 201.
[385] Coleman and Salt, *British Population*, 492. Modood and Berthoud (eds.), *Diversity and Disadvantage*, 221–2; see also 199. Peach, 'West Indian Island Identity', 220.
[386] Peach (ed.), *Ethnic Minority Populations*, 56–7.
[387] Commission for Racial Equality, quoted in *DT* (15 Dec. 2003), 10.
[388] *TCBST* 147. *BST* 581.   [389] *FT* (20 May 1993), 9. See also *Social Trends* (1995), 69.
[390] Modood and Berthoud, *Diversity and Disadvantage*, 122, 124.

profoundly influenced conduct on arrival, given that the chances of returning were remote, that success could be attained only within a white-dominated society, and that entrepreneurship broke through prejudice more effectively than the 'Grunwick' alternative of accepting relatively low pay.[391]

In some occupations Asian or black recruitment was discouraged: in the army, for example, covertly well into the 1970s.[392] Yet no surviving prejudice within industry and commerce could withstand the immigrant's hard work, long hours, thrift, adaptability, mutual help within the kinship network, and entrepreneurship within the family as economic unit. A 'Jewish' future seemed to beckon some Indians and East African Asians, whereas the Afro-Caribbeans, Pakistanis, and Bangladeshis seemed heading for an 'Irish' one.[393] In Leeds by the late 1970s British Asians were following their Jewish predecessors into the same sorts of business in the same localities, and by 1996 British Asians owned half the country's independent shops; there were by then more than 300 British Asian millionaires.[394] With the Chinese as pioneers and with many Indians following them, the restaurant offered entrepreneurship in a rather different form.[395] Often originally catering for minority groups, these restaurants could become large concerns manufacturing food for all, as with Laxmishanker Pathak, a refugee from Kenya whose firm began by providing Indian restaurants with ready-made sauces and chutneys. In 1972 the Indian-born Anglophile curry magnate Gulam Noon set up his confectionery shop in Southall, and became head of the world's largest factory for ready-made Indian food.[396] The Bangladeshis, poorest among the UK's South Asian immigrants, contributed powerfully to the fivefold growth in the number of Indian restaurants between 1970 and 2000.[397] For the second generation, the professions and salaried jobs proved as tempting as earlier for the offspring of white businessmen. Though in 1991 the Chinese and Asian minorities included a larger proportion of high-status people than any other British ethnic group including whites, the Chinese only slowly overcame their reluctance occupationally to diversify.[398] Not so the Asians, especially the Indians: their self-employment in Britain was often a platform from which they hoped to regain their earlier professional status or to realize other aspirations that their emigration had (they hoped) only temporarily delayed. Whereas in 1997 South

[391] See above, p. 156.   [392] DT (4 Jan. 2005), 10.
[393] John Rex, BST 609. See also DT (4 Jan. 2005), 10.
[394] T. Forester, 'Asians in Business', New Society (23 Feb. 1978), 421. Ind (12 June 1996), 3.
[395] Harrison, Seeking a Role, 4, 86–7, 228, 230–1.
[396] Obituaries of Pathak in Ind (10 Apr. 1997), 18; DT (7 Apr. 1997), 23. For Noon see Ind (15 July 2006), 40–1.
[397] G. Dench, K. Gavron, and M. Young, The New East End: Kinship, Race and Conflict (2006), 129.
[398] TCBST 132, 166.

Asians made up less than 3 per cent of the British population, they contributed nearly a fifth of the hospital doctors, about a sixth of the general practitioners, and about an eighth of the pharmacists.[399]

Family and work patterns interacted, and the contrasts in sexual behaviour between the generations in any one ethnic minority were marked and often caused trouble. The broad overall contrast lay between two groups. On the one hand there were the West Indian, African, East African Asian, Chinese, and white populations with smaller families, fewer persons per household, and extended families relatively rare. On the other hand there were the Indian, Pakistani, and Bangladeshi populations diverging on all these counts.[400] Men were at first numerically more prominent among South Asian immigrants than among black West Indians, who had arrived earlier; it took time before the Asian women arrived, and longest of all for the Bangladeshi women.[401] Almost all Pakistani and Bangladeshi immigrants married, and earlier than most; Indians married rather later, and black Caribbean immigrants later still, if at all, for they were much more likely than South Asians to stay single, and (like whites) more likely to cohabit and separate.[402] All this had implications for household size. In 1985–7 multi-family households were nine times as frequent among ethnic-minority householders as among white. British South Asian households in 1985–7 were the most likely of all ethnic groups to live within extended families, whereas a fifth of black Caribbean households in 1991 were lone-parent families with dependent children, and much more likely to be headed by a woman.[403] Traditional attitudes—with a marked separation of spheres between the sexes, often accompanied by arranged marriages—abounded in Pakistani, Bangladeshi, and Chinese immigrant communities. Religious and cultural contrasts ensured that in 1997 Indian women were as likely to work (62 per cent) as white women, and much more likely to do so than Pakistani (22 per cent) and Bangladeshi (21 per cent) women.[404] Bangladeshi women's segregation was accentuated by their relative fertility, in an immigrant group that was on average younger than the rest. By the mid-1980s white families included 1.8 dependent children, East-African Asian and African 2.0, Indian 2.1, and Bangladeshi 3.3.[405] Among female Chinese immigrants with the husband as sole breadwinner, serious problems resulted from the wife's simultaneous loneliness and overwork, given the absence of the extended family that usually provided

[399] FT (10 Sept. 1996), 1, 17; cf. T (5 Jan. 2002), 6. B. Parekh, 'South Asians in Britain', History Today (Sept. 1997), 65.
[400] J. Haskey, 'Families and Households of the Ethnic Minority and White Populations of Great Britain', Population Trends, 57 (Autumn 1989), 19.   [401] TCBST 144.
[402] A. Berrington in D. Coleman and J. Salt (eds.), Ethnicity in the 1991 Census, i. Demographic Characteristics of the Ethnic Minority Populations (1996), 204–5.
[403] Haskey, 'Families and Households', 14, 19. TCBST 145.
[404] Parekh, 'South Asians in Britain', 67.   [405] Haskey, 'Families and Households', 12.

support in Hong Kong: 'they can become withdrawn within themselves and even housebound, not daring to venture out alone'.[406]

From 1984 more of the UK's 'Afro-Caribbean' people had been born in Britain than in the West Indies, but the age-balance within the groups of immigrants who arrived later in the cycle was inevitably younger: by the mid-1980s less then a fifth of the white, West Indian, African, and East African Asian populations were aged under 16, but more than two-fifths of the Pakistani, Bangladeshi, and mixed-race populations.[407] The second generation of any one ethnic minority was culturally cross-pressured more intensely than the first, even when originating in the same region. After 1971 the proportion of second-generation New Commonwealth immigrants was rising fast: 0.5 million by 1971 had been born in the UK, but rose to a million by 1981;[408] and to take one subgroup, those of Pakistani and Bangladeshi descent, the British-born constituted only 24 per cent in 1971 but 47 per cent twenty years later.[409] V. K. Edwards, whose knowledge of West Indian immigrants was close, was unsure in 1979 what to call their British-born children, as no generally accepted label had yet emerged: it would do so 'from the West Indian community itself in time', but, he added, 'for the present purpose "West Indian" is preferred'.[410] Many young second-generation West Indians, far from wishing to integrate, soon sought to reinforce their distinctiveness in speech, dress, and culture. Their schoolteachers observed that children who in primary school were not noticeably West Indian in speech became markedly so in secondary school, taking on a Jamaican intonation whether their parents had come from Jamaica or not. Creole culture lent these teenagers a group identity, a self-respect, and an insulation from what they viewed as an alien world. It also gave them a vehicle for frank and private communication: as circumstances required, they could move between Creole, Rastafarian jargon, and standard English speech. Teachers did not always grasp how complex was this linguistic situation, or the sophistication of Creole speech in itself; this may have educationally disadvantaged teenage boys of West Indian origin by comparison with second-generation immigrants from cultures whose first language was undeniably not English.[411]

Chinese immigrants' situation was in some ways similar and in some ways very different. By 1981 about a quarter of the Chinese living in Britain had been born there, and were in a position to translate and interpret English-language documents and speech for parents who did not speak English in the home.

[406] *Chinese Community in Britain* (HC102-III), 162; see also HC102-II, 105; HC102-III, 64.

[407] *TCBST* 143. Haskey, 'Families and Households', 10–11.   [408] Castles, *Here for Good*, 43.

[409] See the useful table in P. Lewis, *Islamic Britain: Religion, Politics and Identity among British Muslims* (1st publ. 1994, 2nd edn. 2002), 15.

[410] V. K. Edwards, *The West Indian Language Issue in British Schools: Challenges and Responses* (1979), 2.   [411] Ibid. 38–9, 61, 127.

Some Chinese settlers thought their culture far superior to European cultures, and attached great importance in the 1980s to the educational and social facilities available in their Chinese-run community centres.[412] So Chinese-born parents were keen to organize 'mother tongue classes' to perpetuate their language and culture within Britain; by 1984, in sixty self-funded classes, 480 part-time teachers were teaching 6,700 Chinese children.[413] Problems of the generation gap were accentuated because their parents—known as 'the faceless ones'—worked for such long and unsocial hours; in the late 1980s nearly nine-tenths of the UK's Chinese were employed in the catering trade.[414]

By 1990 there were growing signs of assimilation at a day-to-day level, so long as compatible with cultural diversity. Although in the 1980s and later South Asians were notably reluctant to choose white partners, people of West Indian origin were increasingly likely to do so, but this advance was admittedly from a very low base: both partners were white in 96 per cent of marriages, both from the same non-white ethnic group in 2 per cent, and in 1 per cent of cases white people chose a partner from a non-white ethnic group.[415] By the mid-1990s half British-born Caribbean men and a third of the women were living with a white partner. Mixed-race marriages accounted for almost one in ten of the total ethnic-minority population, and were spreading rapidly.[416] There were signs of recreational integration, too. In fashion, sport, and music, prejudice by the 1990s could not prevail against the younger black generation's attributes and expertise. London's Notting Hill carnival was marred in the 1970s and 1980s by friction with the police, but it attracted a huge multi-racial following, and by the 1990s was peaceful enough to acquire extensive sponsorship.[417] Afro-Caribbeans were advancing fast in football: with only 1.4 per cent of the population, they contributed 7.7 per cent of professional footballers in 1988,[418] whereas Asians were virtually absent from the game. English West Indians were not always eager for the home team to win when it came to cricket contests with the West Indies; in July 1973 they were jubilant at the West Indies' first victory in twenty test matches (Plate 12).[419] As late as 1990 Tebbit thought it worth applying a 'cricket test' on how far immigrants backed the team of the country they had joined: 'which side do they cheer for? . . . Were they

[412] J. L.Watson, *Emigration and the Chinese Lineage: The Mans in Hong Kong and London* (Berkeley and Los Angeles, Calif., 1975), 127. *Chinese Community in Britain* (HC102-I, 1985), p. xx.

[413] *Chinese Community in Britain* (HC102-III), 27; see also 85, 100, 126.

[414] *BST* 595. *Chinese Community in Britain* (HC102-I), p. xii.

[415] D. Coleman, 'Ethnic Intermarriage in Great Britain', *Population Trends*, 40 (Summer 1985), 5–9.

[416] *T* (22 May 1997), 6. Haskey, 'Ethnic Minority Populations of Great Britain', 33.

[417] For a more jaundiced view of the carnival see Joseph Harker, 'The Carnival is Over', *G* (26 Aug. 2000), 26.

[418] C. Critcher, 'Putting on the Style: Aspects of Recent English Football', in J. Williams and S. Wagg (eds.), *British Football and Social Change: Getting into Europe* (Leicester, 1991), 79.

[419] *G* (1 Aug. 1973), 1, prints a photograph (Plate 12) of a West Indian embracing a policeman at the Oval. See also *G* (31 July 1973), 1.

still harking back to where they came from or where they were?' Though a good-humoured and justified attempt to emphasize the importance of national identity for integration, this evoked angry Muslim comment.[420]

Nonetheless, a social platform, initially precarious, was coming into existence as a basis for implementing a multicultural ideal for Britain. This mid–century term was imported from abroad, and did not become widely current till the end of the century, though the ideal pervaded UK politicians' approach to race from the late 1960s. Roy Jenkins articulated it as Home Secretary in May 1966. Through waves of immigrants 'we have been constantly stimulated and jolted out of our natural island lethargy', he said; British businesses to a 'phenomenal extent' had been founded by people born outside Britain. The goal for him was 'not . . . a flattening process of assimilation but . . . equal opportunity, accompanied by cultural diversity, in an atmosphere of mutual tolerance'.[421] Hostility to ethnic groups was henceforth strongly discouraged, and even the transitional phase of good-natured humour at their expense was going out of fashion. Charlie Williams, the television comedian popular in the early 1980s with his catchphrase 'me old flower', was an intermediate figure comparable in race relations to the actors Frankie Howerd and Kenneth Williams in attitudes to homosexuality. Born in Britain, his father from Barbados, he pioneered the role of the black comedian and made a virtue of his distinctness, poking fun at colour and racial issues and unafraid to defend the golliwog.[422]

The immigrant's initial poverty and distance from the established church made him a natural recruit for parties of the left, whether Liberal, Communist, or Labour. Just as the Liberal Party had catered for nineteenth-century nonconformist, Irish, and Catholic opinion, so the Labour Party catered for twentieth-century Jews. With both Irish Catholics and Jews, the Liberal Party's free-trade and libertarian outlook, its internationalism, and its taste for cultural pluralism had encouraged the immigrants to set forth for Britain, defended them when they arrived, and provided political careers for those who sought integration by that route. Communist determination to confront the Fascists in the 1930s had attracted many Jews, and by 1951 the Jewish and Irish Catholic link with the British left was well established. The Jewish entrepreneurs who helped to fund Wilson's office after 1970 were rewarded in his resignation honours list of 1976,[423] and Callaghan's cabinet included two grandsons of Lithuanian Jews (Silkin and Lever). The Party's Irish and Catholic inheritance had by the 1970s delivered an abundance of political talent, from politicians like Callaghan (great-grandson

---

[420] Interview with *Los Angeles Times*, as reported in *T* (21 Apr. 1990), 1, cf. 4 for his comment on the 'Today' programme.
[421] Speech on 23 May 1966 to the voluntary liaison committees of the National Committee for Commonwealth Immigrants in R. Jenkins, *Essays and Speeches* (1967), 269, 267.
[422] Obituary in *DT* (4 Sept. 2006), 25.   [423] Pimlott, *Wilson*, 572. Morgan, *Wilson*, 383.

of an Irish weaver) and Healey (great-grandson of an Irish tailor) to trade union leaders like Bill Carron and Terry Duffy (presidents of the AEU). As for the Jews, the career of Gerald Kaufman, son of Polish-born tailors in Leeds, was not untypical; this hard-working, sharp-witted second-generation immigrant progressed through grammar school and Oxford to journalism and the Fabian Society. As a Leeds Jew he had almost instinctively joined the Labour Party in 1949 and by 1987 had become its shadow Foreign Secretary.[424]

Working-class hostility to New Commonwealth immigrants hindered Labour from enthusiastically helping to welcome them, and blacks were rare at Labour Party and trade union conferences in the 1970s and 1980s.[425] Such indifference jarred with Labour's role as heir to the Liberals—with its internationalism and concern for minority rights. The regional clustering of ethnic minorities, reinforced by the freedom of Commonwealth citizens to vote if resident in the UK, made the 'ethnic' vote worth cultivating. So Labour felt cross-pressured in 1968: it was divided at cabinet level and below between 'those who want to allow the coloured communities to remain foreign . . . and those who want full integration or assimilation according to the American pattern'.[426] A combination of age-balance and distance from the political system ensured that immigrant numbers did not carry proportionate political influence, but in so far as public expenditure on welfare helped assimilation, Labour was again the immigrant's first line of defence. Benn by 1980 was telling New Commonwealth leaders that 'we go down separately or we win together'. Much effort was side-tracked thereafter into controversy about whether Labour should form 'black sections', which would reserve black places on selection committees and short-lists. The strategy was overwhelmingly rejected at the Party's conference in 1987; the career of Bill Morris, General Secretary of the TGWU from 1991 to 2003, showed how an immigrant who had arrived from Jamaica in 1954 and who followed the Party's traditional career line, could acquire a key post. 'I was not the black candidate', he pointed out when elected Deputy General Secretary in 1985; 'I am the candidate who just happens to be black.'[427]

Governments of the 1950s had not hesitated to admit large numbers of immigrants from the Caribbean partly because of the Commonwealth connection, but also because of labour shortages. Furthermore, the Conservative Party was gradually assimilating much of the Liberal Party's free-market and individualist tradition. Here the Jews blazed a trail. The entrepreneurial thrust required to enable the immigrant or his offspring to get established created a

[424] 'The School Swot Who Made Good', O (6 May 1984), 7.
[425] As several observers noted, e.g. S. H. Beer, O (7 Oct. 1973), 12; R. Taylor, O (7 Sept. 1980), 11.
[426] R. H. S. Crossman, *The Diaries of a Cabinet Minister*, ii. *Lord President of the Council and Leader of the House of Commons 1966–68* (1976), 774 (10 Apr. 1968), discussing divisions within the cabinet.
[427] Benn, T (17 Nov. 1980), 3. See also T (4 June 1983), 4. Morris, T (18 Sept. 1985), 2.

natural affinity, more in practice than in theory, with the party of free enterprise. So well had Labour performed its assimilating role by the 1970s that some Jews were displaying the discriminating attitude to party that denotes a minority's full integration. For the fully integrated and prosperous British Jew with a recent immigrant background, Labour seemed a diminishingly obvious political home, especially when the Six Day War alienated some Labour supporters from Israel.[428] So whereas in 1945 not one Jew was returned to the House of Commons as an official Conservative MP, in 1983 the Jewish Conservative MPs for the first time outnumbered their Labour colleagues. Jews—Alfred Sherman, David Wolfson, Norman Strauss, and above all Keith Joseph—were central to pioneering Thatcherism within the Centre for Policy Studies (CPS) after 1974.[429] Jewish refugees from totalitarian regimes also helped to fuel Thatcher's robust challenge to Soviet Communism after 1975. A rising proportion of the substantial Jewish electorate in Thatcher's Finchley constituency supported her in the 1980s, and Macmillan quipped that her cabinet contained 'more Estonians than Etonians':[430] Lawson was grandson of a Latvian Jew, Rifkind the grandson of a Lithuanian Jew, Michael Howard son of a Romanian Jew, David Young and Leon Brittan sons of Lithuanian Jewish doctors. Thatcher felt 'enormous admiration' for the Jews' enterprising and self-help traditions; she promoted them, she said, because she 'just wanted a Cabinet of clever, energetic people'.[431] Shirley Porter, subsequently discredited, played a key role in Thatcher's local government reforms, and Thatcher's economic reforms attracted Jewish entrepreneurs like Alan Sugar.[432] She learnt much from Sherman, who in 1978 stressed the need for West Indian immigrants to follow the self-help trail that the Jews had pioneered; and she relished the company of Chief Rabbi Immanuel Jakobovits, who received a peerage in 1988, and who controverted statist attitudes in the Church of England's report *Faith in the City*. He thought 'many people in this country . . . work-shy', whereas in the Jewish view 'work itself ennobles; if we did more of it we would be competitive and flourishing'.[433]

The Conservative Party had good reason in the 1980s to expect much in the longer term from the New Commonwealth immigrants, particularly from entrepreneurs with a South Asian or East African Asian background. An analysis of adults in employment in 1981 in Great Britain revealed a far higher proportion in professional or managerial roles from the Indian subcontinent

---

[428] On this see G. Alderman, 'Converts to the Vision in True Blue', *THES* (10 July 1987), 15; *T* (14 Apr. 1970), 1; *NS* (13 Mar. 1970), 358.   [429] Halcrow, *Joseph*, 119, 125, 152.
[430] Alderman, 'Converts to the Vision', 15. Macmillan quoted in J. Ranelagh, *Thatcher's People: An Insider's Account of the Politics, the Power and the Personalities* (1st publ. 1991, paperback edn. 1992), 55.
[431] Thatcher, *Downing Street Years*, 509.
[432] J. Lloyd, 'Preaching in the Market Place', *FT* (18 July 1988), 15.
[433] Sherman letter in *T* (4 Feb. 1978), 15. See also Young, *One of Us*, 424. Jakobovits, *G* (29 Dec. 1988), 20.

than from the West Indies, and Indians contributed to the professional category in a far higher proportion even than whites. By 1981 Asian immigrants were more likely than others to own their own homes: in 1992–4 six out of ten Indian heads of household were buying their home with a mortgage, but only four out of ten white households.[434] By the 1970s the Conservatives were already making a special effort to recruit among the immigrant groups. The Party might resist further large-scale immigration, but it was keen to integrate those who had already arrived, and the latter could only benefit from the damping down of white fears.[435] By 1990 the Asian millionaires in Britain had strong interests in property, retailing, hotels, and textiles, and were headed by the Hinduja brothers, Britain's first Asian billionaires. By holding a dinner for Britain's Asian multi-millionaires at 10 Downing Street in November 1991, Major acknowledged their political significance.[436] Nonetheless, the ethnic minorities remained overwhelmingly Labour as voters, and in the five elections from October 1974 to 1992 the Conservatives were able to attract more than a tenth of them only in 1987. It was from the Asian group that the Conservatives had most to hope, given that (though from a low base) they were almost four times more likely than black voters to support them.[437]

Belief in multiculturalism was far from universal. By no means all ethnic minorities were integrating to vanishing point like the Huguenots, or were on the way towards doing so like the Irish, Jews, and Poles. We have seen that the Chinese did not even wish to assimilate. In their religious and dietary practices and language many immigrants chose to perpetuate the first generation's insulation from British culture; South Asian groups, for example, were slow indeed to lose their distinctive attributes.[438] White opposition to multiculturalism was noisier, and often stemmed less from Fascism than from practical problems.[439] Many complaints against immigrants arose from considerations only tangentially related to race: from their age-balance, for example, which was slanted markedly towards youth, and therefore towards that age-group's relatively heavy claims upon welfare and educational facilities. The youthful age-balance of immigrant communities specially exposed them to the customary friction between authority and inner-city male teenagers. Add to this the immigrant population's inner-city location, and the cultural disorientation of its younger members, together with the relative scarcity of work and leisure opportunities, and it is easy to see why blacks were three times as likely in 1975 to be arrested

[434] BST 584–5, 592. Social Trends (1996), 184.

[435] T (7 June 1976), 2; (17 Nov. 1977), 14; (18 Sept. 1978), 1.

[436] 'Asian Millions', T (25 Aug. 1990), 11 (leader). DT (2 Dec. 1991), 34.

[437] S. Saggar and A. Heath, 'Race: Towards a Multicultural Electorate?', in G. Evans and P. Norris (eds.), Critical Elections: British Parties and Voters in Long-Term Perspective (1999), 109. I owe this reference to Dr May.   [438] Harrison, Seeking a Role, 224–5, 227, and above, p. 193.

[439] Ibid. 219, 222.

for mugging (an old word now revived) than their proportion of London's population would justify.[440]

Particularly inflammatory were police attempts to curb illicit drug-dealing and the wide application of the 'sus' law, whereby a person could be arrested on suspicion of committing a crime. The police, in turn, resented being hampered by the 'race relations industry', and were concerned at the high proportion of London blacks involved in mugging offences. The drug culture made matters worse because it embroiled inner-city youth with a police force overwhelmingly white, so that some areas witnessed a trial of strength between black youth and white police. Effective policing needed to be sufficient to contain illegality, but not so heavy as to intimidate or provoke. In the mid-1970s the Notting Hill carnival advertised this friction. By 1976 robberies, drug-related and violent crimes at the carnival, now attracting huge crowds, were held to justify very heavy policing, but this in itself seemed provocative. After 325 police and 131 members of the general public had been injured in the carnival of 1976, Robert Mark announced that 'there are not going to be any "no-go" areas in the Metropolitan Police area'; nonetheless, in the following year the police adopted a lower profile, and less crime was evident, though this did not prevent 139 from being hurt in disturbances on 29 August, some (including a policeman) by knife wounds.[441] Tension was worsened by immigrants' reluctance to join the police; of 117,000 police officers in England and Wales in 1981, only 286 were black or Asian. Their reluctance was hardly surprising, given that racist attitudes pervaded informal police conversation, though if the Metropolitan Police in the early 1980s were at all typical, the rhetoric of their hostility exaggerated the reality. Recruited as they were from the 'respectable working class', London's white policemen were keen to distance themselves from people who they thought unrespectable, and whom they identified informally as 'slag' or 'rubbish': that is, from an underclass rootless, deviant, or delinquent, and more often black than brown, with the Asian immigrants seen as more devious than criminous.[442]

Although race and culture might often overlap, it is important to distinguish between them as components of hostility to ethnic minorities on practical grounds. It was a concern with cultural rather than race contrast that inspired Tebbit's 'cricket test': as he put it many years later, 'a multi-ethnic society can work as long as it is monocultural'.[443] Health-based objections to the immigrant were changing. The early twentieth-century fear about imported diseases was

---

[440] Blacks made up 4.3% of the Metropolitan Police area's population, but 12% of those arrested for mugging there. *T* (13 Apr. 1976), 14.

[441] Mark, *T* (1 Sept. 1976), 1; see also *G* (1 Sept. 1976), 1. For the following year see *T* (30 Aug. 1977), 1; (31 Aug. 1977), 1.

[442] Statistics *T* (14 Apr. 1981), 4. See also D. J. Smith and J. Gray, *Police and People in London*, iv. *The Police in Action* (1983), 109, 118, 127.   [443] Interview, *Times Magazine* (29 Sept. 2007), 37.

less often heard in its old form after 1970, partly because tuberculosis was now less feared, but mainly because immigrants as a group were relatively young and therefore relatively healthy.[444] Becoming more common was a new (and to a large extent imagined) fear: of their alleged cost to a National Health Service that in 1900 had not yet come into existence. Still, cultural diversity did present serious practical problems to the inner-city parents of white children whose schools had to focus so heavily on teaching the English language. Complaints on this score led Labour politicians instinctively to greet racial violence with promises to spend more on welfare. This too could cause trouble, given that the contrasts between ethnic groups in family size and marriage patterns were considerable. Irish precedents suggested, however, that these would dwindle over time; the contrasts were most tenacious among immigrants from South Asia.[445]

Opponents of racism, quick to allege parallels between Nazism in the 1930s and British hostility to immigration in the 1970s, did not always themselves exemplify reason and research on race issues. During the Labour cabinet discussion in 1968 on the wording of the forthcoming census, Michael Stewart pronounced it 'one of the basic principles of socialism that one should base one's policies on reliable information'. Powell, thirsting from the late 1960s for immigrant statistics, accused the authorities of concealing them, and on launching the census in 1971 the Registrar-General urged immigrants to cooperate, if only to scotch harmful rumours.[446] The immigrants and some of their champions in Labour cabinets feared that questions targeting immigrants would discourage their full integration and might even forearm their enemies.[447] During his lunchtime lecture in May 1973 on racial theory at the London School of Economics (LSE), H. J. Eysenck, a professor of psychology who did not rule out the possibility of congenital differences between the races, was physically assaulted by opponents of his alleged views. He thought the National Union of Students (NUS), in preventing specified speakers from addressing student meetings, was displaying a Nazi irrationalism in reverse.[448] Eysenck was not alone: student critics of Keith Joseph and Enoch Powell from the late 1960s were often reluctant to trust fellow students to reach their own views, and tried to silence such speakers.[449] When the census of 1981 was at the planning stage, the Commission for Racial Equality favoured inserting

[444] M. G. Marmot et al., *Immigrant Mortality in England and Wales 1970–78: Causes of Death by Country of Birth* (Office of Population Censuses and Surveys, Studies on Medical and Population Subjects, 47; 1984), 1.   [445] *BST* 96–9.

[446] For Stewart see Crossman, *Cabinet Diaries*, ii. 664 (6 Feb. 1968). For Powell see e.g. his speech at Brent on 7 Apr. 1973, *T* (9 Apr. 1973), 3. For Registrar-General, *T* (15 Apr. 1971), 1.

[447] Castle, *Diaries 1964–70*, 369 (6 Feb. 1968); *Diaries 1974–6*, 280 (16 Jan. 1975).

[448] J. Leishman, 'Students Condemn LSE Attack', *G* (9 May 1973), 24. Eysenck's letter in *G* (30 Apr. 1974), 16. See also *T* (14 Oct. 1978), 15 for his attack on obscurantism within the National Union of Teachers.   [449] See Joseph's letter in *T* (4 Dec. 1974), 17.

questions on ethnic origin, but a pilot survey showed that they would not be accurately or fully answered.[450] Special efforts were made to ensure that ethnic minorities participated fully in the census, leaflets urging this were distributed in appropriate languages, and community leaders' help was enlisted. Yet Lord Scarman, the distinguished judge who was very much their champion, could still complain in that year that precise information was lacking on their special problems.[451]

British hostility to immigrants sometimes went beyond concern about practical grievances. Anti-immigrant activism had Fascist connections, the National Front welcomed the allegedly racist views of Eysenck and the American educational psychologist Arthur Jensen, and the Smithfield meat porters who processed to the Home Office in protest at the impending 'invasion of Britain' in 1972 included Front members. It was strongest in London and parts of the Midlands, and in 1981 Richard Barnes, a Front sympathizer, received a life sentence for racist murder.[452] In the 1960s the term 'racism', American in origin, gradually supplanted the British term 'racialism' to denote the sort of belief in racial superiority which might foster hostility to other races. White electors in 1970 disliked voting for a coloured candidate, and the prospect in August 1972 of Ugandan Asians arriving in large numbers alarmed the Labour-controlled city council in Leicester, where New Commonwealth immigrants clustered heavily. When Gallup asked in September 1972 whether the Ugandan Asians should be allowed to settle in Britain, 32 per cent said yes, but 57 per cent no.[453]

The National Front put up fifty-four candidates at the general election of February 1974 and ninety in October. Though beset by internal disputes, the Front could deploy within the inner cities support that specially threatened Labour, and when it began marching provocatively in the streets, some opponents understandably but not always helpfully took to counter-marching instead of taking Roy Jenkins's advice and ignoring them.[454] The Front march through Lewisham in August 1977 brought out a quarter of the entire Metropolitan Police force on duty, with riot shields used in Great Britain for the first time;[455] a Lewisham hospital doctor witnessed 'the sort of scene you expect in Belfast or France—but I would never have believed I would see it in England'.[456] The Anti-Nazi League originated in 1977 with the counter-marching idea, and organized a colourful coalition of anti-Nazi

[450] DT (3 Sept. 1979), 2. For the answers see T (8 Dec. 1979), 2. G (21 Mar. 1980), 1.

[451] Office of Population Censuses and Surveys Census 1981, General Report: England and Wales (1990), 33. Lord Scarman, The Brixton Disorders 10–12 April, 1981: Report of an Inquiry (1st publ. 1981, paperback edn. 1982), 169.

[452] M. Walker, National Front (1977), 169. T (25 Aug. 1972), 2. For Barnes, see T (8 Dec. 1981), 4.

[453] Butler and Pinto-Duschinsky, British General Election of 1970, 408. For Leicester, T (25 Aug. 1972), 2. Gallup International Public Opinion Polls, ii. 1200.   [454] G (26 July 1976), 4.

[455] ST (14 Aug. 1977), 1; G (15 Aug. 1977), 20; O (14 Aug. 1977), 1.   [456] O (14 Aug. 1977), 1.

organizations at its carnival in Brockwell Park, south London, on September 1978.[457] Community leaders in the Bengali area of London's East End had already called for more police protection after 150 skinheads (shaven-headed self-consciously tough youth gangs prevalent from the 1960s) had gone on the rampage and damaged five shops and a car.[458] The League's supporters were too controversial, however, and its tactics too likely themselves to provoke violence; it faded away after the Southall riots of April 1979.[459]

There was renewed protest in 1979 when Thatcher's first government agreed to admit large numbers of refugees from Vietnam, 'a country with which we have no connections and towards which we have no obligations', as Powell put it; within eight years 19,000 had settled in Britain.[460] In March 1981 violence and looting from breakaway groups occurred as 3,000–4,000 West Indians marched through the West End. They were protesting against the police response to what the marchers saw as a racially motivated fire at Deptford in which thirteen people had died. Confrontation between a policeman and a young black man triggered the serious riots at both Brixton and Toxteth in 1981: the local context of mutual suspicion explained how this small incident was so easily inflamed.[461] As Lord Scarman had pointed out in 1978, 'we must legislate now not for the homogeneous society we have known for centuries but for a plural society'. When Mrs Cherry Groce was accidentally shot during a police raid at her house in September 1985, rioting, looting, and burning hit Brixton.[462] More sinister were events at Tottenham's Broadwater Farm estate in October, where Mrs Cynthia Jarrett had died following a police search of her home; riots nearby left one policeman (PC Keith Blakelock) dead and 232 injured. It was the first such death in Great Britain in modern times. The black Haringey councillor Bernie Grant (Labour MP for Tottenham from 1987 till his death in 2000) had for months been predicting violence, but his comment on the riots, that 'the police got a bloody good hiding', prompted much local indignation; more than a thousand of the council's trade unionist employees marched to the town hall demanding his resignation.[463] Behind this episode lay all the threats to the quality of urban life that have hitherto been discussed: race prejudice, distrust of the police, inner-city deprivation and unemployment, and award-winning but inept modern architectural planning. This grim system-built estate had been constructed in 1971 with a labyrinth

[457] For a vivid account, *T* (25 Sept. 1978), 2.   [458] *T* (12 June 1978), 1; cf. (27 June 1978), 18.
[459] *DT* (24 Apr. 1979), 1. *Econ* (28 Apr. 1979), 15.
[460] Powell, *HC Deb.* 18 July 1979, c. 1782. Statistics, *BST* 607.
[461] *T* (3 Mar. 1981), 2. 'How Britain's Riots Began', *Econ* (3 Apr. 1982), 36–7.
[462] Scarman, *HL Deb.* 29 Nov. 1978, c. 1345. Groce, *T* (30 Sept. 1985), 3.
[463] For employee protest see *T* (12 Oct. 1985), 1. For a portrait of Grant see *FT* (12 Oct. 1985), 6, and obituary in *G* (10 Apr. 2000), 20. See also *G* (10 Oct. 1985), 12 (leader); *T* (8 Oct. 1985), 1.

of walkways and underground passages. Water soon penetrated the concrete, the estate rapidly acquired a bad reputation, and by 1985 its concentration of young blacks was high.[464] Drug-dealers seem to have been prominent among the instigators of the riots in Handsworth, where intense hostility to the police was manifest in 1985; of the 315 arrested, 60 per cent were black and 11 per cent Asian. In these riots, as in others during the 1980s, Pakistani and West Indian minorities were by no means united against the police, and sometimes turned against each other; two Asian brothers died, for instance, when petrol bombs were thrown at their shop.[465]

'A riot is an event in search of a meaning', wrote one journalist in 1985, discussing recent occurrences. If such small events could trigger destruction on such a scale, there must be some deeper underlying cause, and Powell found in race his all-embracing explanation. Shortly after the Brixton riots in 1981 he expressed the hope in parliament that the government would bear in mind 'in view of the prospective future increase of the relevant population, that they have seen nothing yet'.[466] After the riots in 1985 he predicted that the local concentrations of New Commonwealth immigrants would eventually produce 'a Britain unimaginably wracked by dissensions and violent disorder, not recognizable as the same nation as it has been, or perhaps as a nation at all'.[467] Repatriation with government encouragement, organization, and incentives was his proposed remedy. The only other options were quietist segregation, violent separatism, and gradual integration. Given the pressures of British culture on the second-generation immigrants, segregation could hardly outlast the first generation, nor in the current climate was segregation likely to be quietist. Violent separatism could have succeeded only if immigrant groups had been regionally even more aggregated than they were, for whatever Powell might say, the immigrants were hopelessly outnumbered within the nation as a whole. For all its difficulties, and for all the temporary hindrances to it that violence presented in the 1980s, a 'multiculturalist' gradual integration into a more diverse multi-racial British society seemed the only feasible and likely destination.

How best, then, to get through the medium term? Enough politicians from all parties thought it would be helpful further to restrict immigrant numbers. The Conservatives at the general election of 1970 gained an extra 6.7 per cent of votes because seen as the party most likely to exclude immigrants.[468] The momentum for further legislation came from the government's agreement

---

[464] For useful descriptions see *FT* (8 Oct. 1985), 10; *G* (9 Oct. 1985), 2.

[465] *T* (20 Nov. 1985), 3; cf. (11 Sept. 1985), 1, where the chronology of events begins with an Asian shopkeeper being stabbed by a West Indian during an attempted robbery.

[466] Quotations from Peter Jenkins, 'The Riot Factor', *ST* (20 Oct. 1985), 16. Powell, *HC Deb.* 13 Apr. 1981, c. 25.

[467] 'My Challenge to Mrs Thatcher', *T* (21 Sept. 1985), 8; cf. speech at Stretford, *T* (22 Jan. 1977), 1.

[468] *T* (7 June 1976), 2.

to accept the Asian refugees from Uganda in 1972; even Powell thought humanitarian considerations justified admitting them so long as Britain's quota was no larger than that of any other world nation.[469] By the Immigration Act (1971) the Heath government substituted for the old distinction between aliens and Commonwealth citizens a new one between 'patrials' and 'non-patrials'. Broadly speaking, this conceded right of residence to the 'patrials'—that is, to people who had been born, or who had a parent or grandparent who was born, in the UK; non-patrials were placed on the same basis as aliens. This left the UK with two major commitments: to the wives and children of New Commonwealth immigrants who had settled before the Act came into force in 1973, and to the East African Asians who had been admitted on a voucher system from 1968.

We have seen how immigration boosted the National Front during the 1970s. Thatcher's aim to contain this prompted her much-criticized remark in January 1978: 'people are really rather afraid that this country might be rather swamped by people with a different culture'. Her critics saw her as racist, or at least as electorally exploiting the race issue, whereas she saw herself as providing the sort of reassurance that would contain racism and channel public concern away from the streets and towards parliament. 'If you want good race relations', she said, 'you have got to allay peoples' fears on numbers.'[470] The episode exposed the divisions between immigrant groups, for some Jews felt that the arrival of so many New Commonwealth immigrants fomented racism; two prominent Jews, Joseph and Sherman, endorsed Thatcher's stance.[471] The National Front stalled badly at the general election in 1979,[472] and the Nationality Act (1981) restricted British citizenship with full right of residence to people already settled in Britain or who had one British parent; thereafter, those born in Britain no longer had an automatic claim to British citizenship. If there is any link between Conservative legislation and the National Front's greatly diminished salience in the 1980s,[473] that had been Thatcher's intention. Grumbling doubts about multiculturalism persisted thereafter within Conservative constituency parties, often with Tebbit as spokesman. When in 1989 Hurd as Foreign Secretary was defending the admission of refugees from Hong Kong, Tebbit claimed that this would transfer to an opportunist Labour Party a key group of voters who would be much needed at the next election. 'Most people in Britain', he said, 'did not want to live in a multicultural, multiracial society, but it has been foisted on them.'[474]

[469] T (13 Sept. 1972), 4.

[470] T (31 Jan. 1978), 2; cf.Whitelaw on 7 Apr., T (8 Apr. 1978), 1 and Thatcher's speech to Conservatives on 8 Apr., O (9 Apr. 1978), 2.

[471] Halcrow, Joseph, 120. Sherman T (4 Feb. 1978), 15; (12 Jan. 1996), 17. Alderman, 'Converts to the Vision', THES (10 July 1987), 15.   [472] DT (5 May 1979), 8.

[473] As argued in C. T. Husbands, 'Extreme Right-Wing Politics in Great Britain: The Recent Marginalisation of the National Front', West European Politics (Apr. 1988), 76–7.

[474] G (22 Dec. 1989), 24.

Still, during the 1990s, race as an issue in British politics became much less salient than Powell had predicted in the late 1960s. In 1992 viewers preferred the black newscaster Trevor McDonald, born in Trinidad, to his white colleagues as ITN's anchorman for its *News at Ten* programme: research showed that he was 'not only very popular with viewers but also carries immense authority and credibility'.[475] How accurate, then, was Powell in his predictions of the late 1960s? Dismissively to juxtapose his lurid forecasts with the relatively mild long-term outcome would be unfair, for his critics' liberal optimism did not prove fully or rapidly justified either. Powell later saw inner-city riots as vindicating his earlier stance: 'the time of truth is coming at last for those who sit in the seats of authority', he intoned after the Handsworth riots in 1985, and on rereading his 'rivers of blood' speech twenty years later he claimed to have been 'struck by its sobriety'.[476] Had his forecasts helped to falsify liberal hopes, then? Politicians' forecasts can aim to invalidate fears as much as to realize hopes. Liberal-minded multiculturalists were often naïve about how race relations are best improved, and if the restrictive legislation of 1971 and 1981, by moderating fears, achieved anything towards falsifying Powell's nightmarish predictions for the longer term, his role had been constructive. Furthermore, his forecasts with their vivid imagery had aimed at two undeniably democratic outcomes: to prevent the voter from being denied important choices, and to uphold parliament's representative role. His concern had always been less with the total number of immigrants than with their regional clustering. Given the many variables involved and the lack of key statistics, it would have been surprising if predictions made in the late 1960s about ethnic-minority size thirty years later had been fully borne out,[477] but Powell was at least correct to highlight the importance of immigrants' regional concentration, and to predict in 1973 that Greater London's inner suburbs thirty years hence would be 'at the absolute theoretical minimum one third to one half coloured'.[478]

Against all this needs to be set the utter inadequacy of Powell's remedy: subsidized repatriation was diminishingly relevant with every year that passed, though in 1993 Bernie Grant backed its voluntary implementation.[479] The riots of the 1980s in British cities were by no means always inspired by racial hatred, or if race was involved, the dispute sometimes lay not between whites and immigrants, but between non-whites—in Birmingham's Handsworth in 1985, as later in the Lozells area in 2005.[480] Powell always exaggerated the cohesiveness of the 'New Commonwealth' category. We have seen that it was

---

[475] *DT* (14 July 1992), 4.
[476] 'My Challenge to Mrs Thatcher', *T* (21 Sept. 1985), 8; cf. *DT* (25 Apr. 1979), 1 (Southall riots). E. Powell, 'Fears that have Not Changed', *T* (19 Apr. 1988), 12.
[477] For a measured assessment of them see *Ind* (18 Apr. 1988), 5.
[478] Speech at Brent, *T* (9 Apr. 1973), 3.
[479] Powell, *DT* (5 Oct. 1976), 1. Grant, *DT* (6 Oct. 1993), 2.   [480] *DT* (26 Oct. 2005), 22.

divided not only by country of origin, but by motive for migrating, date of arrival, and location within each individual country; it was cross-cut further by religious, linguistic, generational, and even caste alignments.[481] Immigrants were further subdivided after settling in Britain, for the effect of the free market, which Powell championed, was to disperse them, like their Jewish predecessors, geographically by social status. On the other hand, immigrant groups could also constructively engage in mutual help: when appalled at the poor working conditions of the Bengalis in East London, the Prince of Wales persuaded rich Asian businessmen to respond generously.[482] There will always be debate, however, about three aspects of Powell's approach to race relations. Should he have deployed his considerable courage and intellect in a more overtly constructive way? Should he have used his status as MP to guide, rather than merely represent, his constituents? And did his very different approach ultimately do more harm than good? Controversy on these matters will long persist.

We have seen in this chapter how change in the social structure was at every level gradual and not advertised. With monarchy and upper classes it was change in order to preserve, but in both cases change accompanied a continuing retreat from any overt political role. At the middle-class level, change was masked by more compromises with organized labour than in retrospect seemed necessary, for we have seen how rapidly trade union influence crumbled after 1979. Meritocratic educational opportunity, the decline in manufacturing, the continued advance of home-ownership, and a further relaxing of social-class boundaries all eroded working-class self-consciousness and numbers. Politicians found themselves increasingly diverted to problems arising among old or new subgroups near the bottom of society. In this sphere as in others, they were exposed to the contrast between ongoing affluence and anxiety about the persistence of problems that had earlier been ascribed to its absence: rising crime, for instance, now moved up the political agenda, with associated worries about the impact of religious decline. The new ethnic minorities, still growing, were by no means all to be found among the subgroups: multi-dimensionally fragmented among themselves, they were now beginning to integrate with British society at every level, though not without transitional difficulties which severely tested the politicians' skills.

All but one of the eight motifs have surfaced in this chapter. The Second World War's equivocal legacy (the first) was exposed in the tensions over wages that from the late 1970s broke up the corporatist settlement. The corporatist demise incidentally advertised the third motif: the contrast between public economic anxiety and growing private affluence. Together with mass

[481] K. Thapar, 'No Such Thing as an Asian "Community"', T (24 June 1982), 3.
[482] T (2 July 1987), 20; (25 Aug. 1990), 22.

immigration it also advertised the sixth motif, the British political system's capacity to survive almost intact amidst major social change—Thatcher's aim all along. Mass immigration also highlighted the seventh motif: British politicians' heavy dependence on spontaneous voluntarist opinion, together with the ongoing need for their skills; only in Northern Ireland was the need for these more clearly apparent. The period may have seen a decline in upper-class voluntarism, but middle-class volunteers remained lively, very much with the royal family's encouragement. These years also saw the rise of working-class voluntarism to its trade union peak in 1979 followed by decline, as both parties found corporatism creating more problems than it solved. To represent the lowest social levels, the volunteers usually had to be drawn from altruistic groups higher up. Central to race issues was the tension between hermetic and receptive attitudes (the second motif), both within each ethnic group and between all of them and the general public. Such issues also exposed British institutions Christian in origin to serious strain (the fifth motif). Among the worldwide roles claimed for the UK (the eighth motif), no confident claim could yet be made to exemplify a successful multi-racial community.

CHAPTER 4

Family and Welfare

The revolution in attitudes to sexuality, well under way in the 1960s, continued after 1970, as did the associated changes in family structure. Such are the themes of this chapter's first two sections. They provide a basis for the four subsequent sections, which broadly follow through the life-cycle. These consider first childhood and adolescence, then the dynamic which grew up behind an expenditure on health and welfare which applied to all age-groups, but especially to the young and the old. The chapter's fifth section concerns changes in attitudes to and experience of old age, and the brief concluding section draws upon all sections to discuss post-war changes in friendship.

1. PERMANENT SEXUAL REVOLUTION

What in retrospect seems a remarkable private conversation occurred on 30 January 1979 between Jim Callaghan and colleagues. For all his wartime naval experience and worldly wise grasp of politics, the 68-year-old Labour prime minister claimed to have been completely unaware of homosexuality till well into adult life. He 'seemed surprised' when told that there were well-known homosexuals in parliament and even in his government. 'They say we are all suppressed homosexuals', he said, 'but it all puzzles me. There have always been so many attractive girls.'[1] The escalating knowledge and public debate about sexuality from the 1960s left little room in later generations for such innocence. The transatlantic impulse to greater understanding by no means ceased with Kinsey: that industrious research partnership, William Masters and Virginia Johnson, carried forward his firmly empirical approach, but shifted it in a more therapeutic direction with their *Human Sexual Response* (1966) and *Human Sexual Inadequacy* (1970). Their UK impact did not rival Kinsey's, but popularizers spread their gospel, with agony aunt Marje Proops perhaps the best known. Taboos tumbled, and earlier agony aunts' moralism and sentimentality succumbed to practical and common-sense advice about how to cope with numerous worries hitherto concealed. Substituting enjoyment for

---

[1] Quoted in Donoughue, *Downing Street Diary*, ii. 435–6; cf. 2.

Fig. 3. *Daily Express* (7 Feb. 1973).

agony, Proops's menu was that of Alex Comfort's influential best-seller, *The Joy of Sex* (1973), whose title echoed Irma Rombauer's best-seller *The Joy of Cooking* (1953).[2] These commentators held in precarious balance the passion of the romantic with the precision and reason of the natural scientist. They did not initiate the late twentieth-century revolution in personal relationships, international in scope, but their influence can only have accelerated it, and the exposure of each new area for public discussion set a precedent for more.

The UK's overall population trends received surprisingly little public discussion, given their importance. Despite the mid-century enthusiasm for central

[2] Proops's obituary, *T* (12 Nov. 1996), 21.

planning, population planning was left to the individual, unconstrained by concern for the general interest.[3] This was perhaps because the British birth-rate was declining spontaneously after the 1950s; population rose by only 18 per cent between 1951 and 2001.[4] Only a rapidly rising birth-rate could perhaps have justified the interference with privacy and freedom that population planning would have entailed.[5] The rate of increase in population had been declining throughout the twentieth century, and in 1977 the population fell in peacetime for the first time since the mid-eighteenth century.[6] Also deterring analysis was the compartmentalized nature of public debate: emigration, immigration, and indigenous growth or decline were not discussed as components of any overall population package. The first was little discussed except in the context of the 'brain drain', the second only episodically in the crisis-avoiding context of curbing race prejudice, and the third hardly at all. Sexual individualism was fuelled by a pervasive but seldom articulated belief in the privacy of the British bedroom, accentuated by revulsion at Nazi intrusion into German bedrooms. Eugenics for Labour seemed to promote a dangerous diversion from necessary reforms in living conditions towards class-biased restraints on freedom, and Conservatives suspected state control in any form. Keith Joseph's fate provided illustration enough of how readily initiatives in public demographic debate roused pejorative eugenic associations: when he even hinted in 1974 at solving welfare issues through encouraging birth control among problem families, his career suffered severely from the subsequent storm of abuse.[7] Nonetheless, by 1970 some wanted more government action. 'Family size is the business of the state', Douglas Houghton told a conference of doctors in 1969, recommending that the NHS provide voluntary sterilization and birth-control services.[8] Over-crowding in large parts of Britain, together with the affluent citizen's growing demand for personal space, could have justified a government strategy, and a select committee of the House of Commons expressed surprise in 1972 that the government had none. On 'population day' (12 May 1973) over a hundred processions were organized, one of which presented a 'call for action' to the prime minister.[9] Yet this initiative sprang from high-minded rationalistic progressive attitudes, not from widespread pressure, and revolution upon revolution within the British family therefore continued after 1970 without guidance from the centre.

The courtship sequence, and its relationship to childbearing, was transformed in these years. Until very recently there had been a regular pattern: a more or less chaste courtship, then a formal and public engagement, then a public

---

[3] Harrison, *Seeking a Role*, 244, 299.   [4] Calculated from *Annual Abstract of Statistics 2005*, 29.
[5] See the hostile leader 'A Policy for People?', *T* (10 Aug. 1972), 13.   [6] *BST* 103–5.
[7] Speech at Edgbaston, *T* (21 Oct. 1974), 3. See also below, p. 313.
[8] *T* (27 Sept. 1969), 1; cf. (20 Mar. 1970), 8.
[9] *T* (10 Aug. 1972), 1. For 'population day', *ST* (13 May 1973), 3.

wedding in church or registry office, with pregnancies usually beginning only nine months afterwards. Now the sequence was becoming much less formal, much less public, and children were produced in or out of wedlock at any stage in the sequence. Accessible and convenient contraceptives accelerated the long-term resort to birth control that had long been in progress. Retailers slowly edged forward: first refusing to supply, then supplying only surreptitiously, then displaying and selling openly. The state moved forward gradually from merely allowing birth-control advice on its premises in the 1930s to itself taking over birth-control centres in 1975. So acceptable had birth control become by 1974 that the time could be envisaged when family-planning clinics would be concerned more with conception than contraception. By the end of the 1950s 90 per cent of women were using some form of contraception within marriage;[10] by 1975 more than 1,400,000 people were attending birth-control clinics, and more than 17,000 vasectomies were performed annually in England.[11] Birth control was one reason for the ongoing and rapid fall in family size: the percentage of children living in families with three or more dependent children fell from 41 in 1972 to 27 in 1993. By the 1980s more than a quarter of women aged between 16 and 49 used no contraceptive protection at all; nearly a quarter were protected through male or female sterilization, and another quarter by the pill; other methods (the condom, cap, withdrawal, and the 'safe period') had markedly declined.[12] Birth-controlling evangelism had now to focus primarily on young unmarried adolescents.

Abortion can be viewed as a last-resort variant of birth control, but those who campaigned in the 1960s for the right to it nonetheless hoped that sex education and ready access to contraception would make it unnecessary. Their hopes were fulfilled to the extent that there was a consistent decline after 1970 in deaths from infanticide and from illegal abortion, with thirty-seven of the latter in 1970–2, one in 1979–81, and none in 1982–4. Less compatible with their hopes, however, were the 100,000 legal abortions being carried out annually by 1979; among women of childbearing age, one in ten had by then experienced a legal abortion after the Act had come into force in 1968, and by the end of 1989 over three million terminations had been carried out in England and Wales.[13] The proportion of abortions to live births rose fairly steadily in the 1970s, and by 1985 had reached one in five. It rose particularly fast among younger women, and during the Abortion Act's first twelve years of operation

---

[10] DHSS, *Report of the [Finer] Committee on One-Parent Families* (Cmnd. 5629; 1974), i. 34. *BST* 58.

[11] DHSS, *Health and Personal Social Services Statistics for England (With Summary Tables for Great Britain)* (1977), 125.

[12] B. Botting, 'Population Review (7): Review of Children', *Population Trends*, 85 (Autumn 1996), 25. *TCBST* 47–8.

[13] B. Botting, 'Trends in Abortion', *Population Trends*, 64 (Summer 1991), 19, 24. *DT* (14 July 1979), 1.

about 300,000 'shotgun marriages' were rendered unnecessary. David Steel, the Act's author, pointed out in 1981 that 'abortion is, I am afraid, being used as a contraceptive'.[14]

By extending doctors' discretion and allowing social reasons to justify abortion, the Act in practice advanced beyond its authors' intentions. It made Britain a haven for pregnant women beset by more restrictive laws elsewhere—especially in Ireland north and south, in the USA until New York state relaxed its law in 1970, and in several European countries until they too shifted.[15] The patients treated in England and Wales during the six years from 1970 to 1975 were very diverse: 29 per cent did not reside there, half were single, 2 per cent were under 16, and 19 per cent between 16 and 19. After rising fast in the early 1970s, the proportion of conceptions outside marriage that were legally aborted levelled off to a plateau of about a third.[16] This was too high for those among the Act's critics who tried to curb access to abortion, especially in pregnancy's later stages, but they encountered two powerful obstacles to further restriction: any such change would involve infringing the doctor's clinical discretion, extended under the Act,[17] and feminism had become strong enough in Britain to uphold the 'woman's right to choose'. The emphasis by the largely Roman Catholic Society for the Protection of Unborn Children on the supreme sanctity of human life, in a sequence of emotive confrontations during the 1970s,[18] could no longer mobilize the Labour Party's Catholic connection. Labour MPs were keen to extend to all women the control over their own bodies that only the better-off women had enjoyed before 1967, and now braved Catholic wrath.

Self-consciously progressive people had long viewed birth control's divorce between sexuality and procreation as integral to completing women's emancipation. On such a view, the nineteenth-century feminist attempt to raise male standards of sexual abstinence to female was a mere feminist staging-post before reliable birth-control methods could sexually emancipate both sexes. By 1970 this development, predicted by some inter-war progressives,[19] was occurring. Whereas the proportion of live births that occurred outside marriage in England and Wales fell sharply after the Second World War and stabilized at about one child in twenty, it started rising towards the end of the 1950s, rose faster in the 1960s, and shot up to unprecedented heights in the late 1970s. By the mid-1980s

---

[14] P. Bartram, *David Steel: His Life and Politics* (1981), 85. See also *BST* 60–1. *ST* (27 Jan. 1980), 6.
[15] For more detail on this see Botting 'Trends in Abortion', 19–21.
[16] *Health and Personal Social Services Statistics for England . . . 1977*, 186. Coleman and Salt, *British Population*, 154–5.
[17] J. Keown, *Abortion, Doctors and the Law: Some Aspects of the Legal Regulation of Abortion in England from 1803 to 1982* (Cambridge, 1988), 137–8, 158. S. Sheldon in E. Lee (ed.), *Abortion Law and Politics Today* (London and Basingstoke, 1998), 44.
[18] e.g. *G* (1 May 1972), 5 (at Liverpool); 26 Mar. 1973, 5 (at Manchester). *T* (20 Oct. 1975), 1 (in Hyde Park). [19] e.g. B. Russell, *Marriage and Morals* (1929), 13, 69, 73.

the UK was at the top of the illegitimacy league in Europe outside Scandinavia, with about one child in five born out of wedlock, rising to one in two by 1997; two years later *Burke's Peerage and Baronetage* felt able to include illegitimate children.[20] If traditional attitudes to legitimacy had persisted, these changes would have been disastrous for the children, but in reality they reflected only a change in attitudes to marriage, for although babies were still being born to teenage girls out of wedlock, many were now being born to older women in informal but long-term unions.

Solving one problem accentuated another: the spread of birth control, abortion, and the growing acceptance of extramarital conception meant fewer children available for adoption. UK adoptions rose in the 1930s to a peak in the mid-1940s, fell sharply to 1951, then rose slowly in the 1950s to a peak in the late 1960s. A sharp decline set in throughout the 1970s, slowing down in the 1980s; in 1968 there were 27,000 UK adoptions, in 1992 only 8,000.[21] If healthy babies for adoption were scarce in Western Europe and America, pressure built up to import them from elsewhere, as well as prompting more research on infertility.[22] For the latter, as earlier with artificial insemination, ethical guidelines had to be established and much opposition overcome, especially from Roman Catholics.[23] Relatively stringent ethical constraints in the USA helped to ensure that the breakthrough occurred in Britain: the world-famous partnership between the biologist Robert Edwards and the gynaecologist Patrick Steptoe produced the world's first 'test-tube baby', Louise Brown, on 25 July 1978. Thereafter, opinion moved fast: a Gallup poll in September 1982 found that of the 95 per cent of the public who were alert to the concept of test-tube babies, two in three approved, and in 2005 infertility treatment produced one in sixty-four of the babies born in the UK.[24] In 1990 Bernard Braine's reference in a parliamentary debate on embryo research to the 'awful example' of Nazi medicine evoked jeers from MPs: the force of that once-powerful argument was now waning.[25] Each liberation made it more difficult logically to hold the line against more. With birth control and artificial insemination conceded, masturbation could not lag far behind. Kinsey had fully documented both its widespread prevalence and its interaction with other sexual 'outlets', hetero-sexual and homosexual, and already in 1958 Glanville Williams had noted how sexologists were switching attention from the physiological harm masturbation

[20] *BST* 62–3. *Ind* (17 Mar. 1999), 10. J.Roll, 'One in Ten: Lone Parent Families in the European Community', in N. Manning (ed.), *Social Policy Review 1990–1* (Harlow, 1991), 172. For *Burke's Peerage* see *DT* (24 May 1999), 3.   [21] *Social Trends* (1995), 43.
[22] *T* (6 July 1970), 2; (21 Sept. 1970), 2.
[23] *T* (6 Apr. 1973), 21. For the Catholic lobby's energy see *G* (21 Feb. 1985), 12; (17 June 1985), 8.
[24] For Robert Edwards's obituary of Steptoe see *Ind* (30 Mar. 1988), 20. R. J. Wybrow, *Britain Speaks Out, 1937–87: A Social History as Seen through the Gallup Data* (Basingstoke and London, 1989), 28. *DT* (7 Dec. 2007), 16.
[25] *HC Deb.* 23 Apr. 1990, c. 54 (Sir B. Braine). For the jeers, see *Ind* (24 Apr. 1990), 6.

allegedly caused to the psychological harm done by ignorantly denouncing it. According to the former archbishop Robert Runcie, 'once the Church accepted artificial contraception, they signalled that sexual activity was for human delight and a blessing, even if it was divorced from any idea of procreation'.[26]

To homosexuals the Sexual Offences Act (1967) by no means brought full liberation; indeed, to the extent that the public reticence on homosexuality before the Act made the press less intrusive, homosexuals had in some ways been freer before their 'liberation' than after. After 1967 there remained much ill-informed moralistic criticism to controvert, and much need to take Kinsey's perceptions further by advertising how numerous, ill-defined, and diverse the 'homosexual' category really was; even in 1991 perhaps only a tenth of homosexuals had made a home together.[27] So the Act was only the beginning of a journey, and further legislation was needed to rectify anomalies—in the age of consent, for example. In 1988–91 there were more than 2,000 arrests for offences involving consensual sex with men under 21. When the Press Council condemned the *Sun* in 1990 for describing homosexuals as 'poofs' and 'poofters', the paper was unapologetic—indeed, indignant: 'we know a great deal more about how people think, act and speak... *What is good enough for them is good enough for us.*'[28]

No legislation could remove the day-to-day drawbacks of finding oneself unintentionally in this minority. Nick Guest, in his twenties the central character in Alan Hollinghurst's *The Line of Beauty* (2004), 'saw the great heterosexual express pulling out from the platform precisely on time, and all his friends were on it, in the first-class carriage—in the wagons-lit!'[29] Integral to homosexual emancipation was public confession: the process, often painful in the early years, of 'coming out' of the closet—to oneself, to other homosexuals, to friends and family, to the world. The analogy with the conscientious objector's wartime situation was less close (because prison was now unlikely for homosexuality as such) than with declaring oneself a teetotaler in the 1830s, a socialist in the 1890s, or a Communist in the 1930s: in all three cases friends were forsaken, relatives saddened, persecution likely, even livelihood risked. Survival required self-help. Looking back in 1994, the homosexual campaigner Peter Tatchell saw self-help as the prime source of liberation after 1967: help-lines, social centres, legal advice agencies, meeting places, periodicals, victim support networks.[30] Campaigning after 1967 to improve the public

---

[26] Runcie interviewed in Radio 4 programme (16 May 1996), 'The Purple, the Blue and the Red'. G. Williams, *The Sanctity of Life and the Criminal Law* (1958), 132.

[27] As estimated in Family Policy Studies Centre, *Family Change: A Guide to the Issues* (Family Briefing Paper, 12; 2000), 5.

[28] For arrests, *HC Deb.* 21 Feb. 1994, c. 76. *Sun* quoted in M. Leapman, *Treacherous Estate: The Press after Fleet Street* (1992), 214–15 (emphasis in the original).

[29] A. Hollinghurst, *The Line of Beauty* (2004), 65.   [30] *O* (19 June 1994), 21.

understanding of homosexuality posed numerous dilemmas. Homosexuals, unlike ethnic minorities or women, were less readily identifiable as a group than their critics supposed: quietism and self-concealment were usually an option. The homosexuals who had won the Act of 1967 included many who came out only with the aim of going back in: who asked only to be left unprosecuted in their private spaces. For them there were marked attractions in the middle-class caution and professionalism of the Homosexual Law Reform Society. Aiming as always primarily to win heterosexual allies, it renamed itself the Campaign for Homosexual Equality in 1971, and in 1973 held its first annual conference at Morecambe; seven years later it had 4,000 members, though many more had passed through it.[31]

Yet there was a case for supplementing the Campaign with a less reticent movement confined to homosexuals. Homosexuals who 'came out' felt some resentment against predecessors who had not: the 'three terrible men'—Coward, Maugham, and Forster—criticized in 1977 by Angus Wilson, for example. Their success (like Dirk Bogarde's) was built upon concealing their sexuality.[32] Some had even exploited it: homosexual comedians, for example—most notably Kenneth Williams and Frankie Howerd, whose camp humour allegedly hindered liberation by perpetuating the homosexual stereotype. The Gay Liberation Front—livelier, structurally less formal, with a younger membership—was co-founded by Bob Mellors on returning from New York in 1970, aiming at group self-advertisement. The Gay Pride festival, an occasion for collectively 'coming out', began in London in 1970 with a few hundred, and took off in the 1980s; in 1991 it attracted 40,000.[33] *Gay News*, founded in 1972, consolidated the homosexual community by supplying an information exchange; it was the last of the successful underground magazines that had flourished in the 1960s, and prompted a network of self-help structures, most notably the London Gay Switchboard in 1974.[34] *Him* first appeared in 1975, was rechristened *Gay Times* in 1984, and was joined by the weekly *Pink Paper* in 1987. Fewer homosexuals now sought sanctuary in polari, for which Gay Liberation felt no taste, so that old private language slowly fell out of use.[35] The Front's members, by collectively and very obviously 'coming out', could nerve themselves into taking what was still a courageous decision, build up their self-confidence, and simultaneously educate society on their numbers and diversity. The big cities set the pace for homosexual liberation, especially London; in 1992 men in London reported sexual experience with

[31] *G* (23 Aug. 1980), 3.　　[32] M. Drabble, *Angus Wilson: A Biography* (1995), 481.

[33] *Ind* (23 June 1995), 19.

[34] Its founder Denis Lemon died of an AIDS-related illness: see obituary, *T* (23 July 1994), 17. Lisa Power describes the Switchboard's origins in B. Cant and S. Hemmings (eds.), *Radical Records: Thirty Years of Lesbian and Gay History, 1957–1987* (1988), 145–6.

[35] P. Baker, *Polari: The Lost Language of Gay Men* (2002), 121.

the same sex in twice the proportion that happened anywhere else in Britain.[36] Booking Kensington Town Hall for a homosexual dance in December 1970 was in its day a major breakthrough,[37] and the NUS overwhelmingly backed the provision of university social facilities in 1973.[38] Homosexual public functions were helpful not just for advertising the minority's sheer size, but for extending the homosexual's social space. Commerce soon discovered a new and relatively affluent homosexual market, just as in the 1950s it had discovered new markets among teenagers and later (more slowly) among pensioners.

On the other hand, building up a homosexual lifestyle with its own facilities risked creating a ghetto. Well-known homosexuals, most notably Antony Grey, hoped—with the pioneering American author on homosexuality 'D. W. Cory'—that the male homosexual's freedom to be himself would destroy the effeminate and flamboyant homosexual stereotype. The Front's activists, by contrast, were often people with nothing to lose by publicity—self-indulgently histrionic and iconoclastic. This unhelpfully confirmed misleading effeminate stereotypes and misleadingly presented sexual orientation as central to personality. It also clumsily divided the world into 'gays' and 'straights' without allowing for infinite intermediate gradations. Not until the 1980s did the Anglo-American homosexual subculture become masculinized in its clothing, conduct, and image. The Front's pressure to 'come out' also antagonized many homosexuals and others because intolerant and even intrusive. Lesbians were initially active within the Front, but male dominance within it pushed many into the feminist movement.[39] The more aggressive campaigners for homosexual liberation mobilized in the direct-action pressure group OutRage; launched in 1990 to defend homosexuals against attack, it began 'outing' Anglican bishops.[40] The homosexual exhibitionist Quentin Crisp was so alienated as actually to reject homosexual liberation, labelling homosexuality an illness, and the Conservative MPs who had been so crucial to getting reform through parliament in 1967 held aloof from a movement which now courted radical connections.[41]

AIDS was first identified in the USA in 1981, and temporarily reversed the British trend towards eliminating death from infectious disease; by June 1991 there had been 2,787 AIDS-related deaths in Britain.[42] The vast majority of sufferers in the developed world were male homosexuals, drug addicts injecting drugs intravenously, and patients who had received intravenous injections of

---

[36] K. Wellings, J. Field, A. Johnson, and J. Wordsworth, *Sexual Behaviour in Britain: The National Survey of Sexual Attitudes and Lifestyles* (1994), 193.

[37] For a useful discussion see D. Fernbach, 'Ten Years of Gay Liberation', *Politics and Power* (1980), 169–72.　　　　　　　　　　　　　　　[38] *G* (5 Apr. 1973), 9; cf. *T* (19 Oct. 1973), 7.

[39] J. Weeks, *Coming Out: Homosexual Politics in Britain from the Nineteenth Century to the Present* (1st publ. 1977, rev. edn. 1990), 200, 213–14. Fernbach, 'Ten Years', 173–8.

[40] *T* (14 Mar. 1995), 5. *G* (14 Mar. 1995), 3.

[41] Crisp, *DT* (22 Nov. 1999), 23. See also A. Grey, *Quest for Justice: Towards Homosexual Emancipation* (1992), 184.　　　　　　　　[42] Coleman and Salt, *British Population*, 250 (probably an underestimate).

blood products. Of the 1,862 cases reported up to the end of October 1988, 1,532 were homosexual or bisexual men, 38 intravenous drug users and 123 haemophiliacs; only 69 were cases of heterosexual transmission.[43] The epidemic hindered the public understanding of homosexuality less than might have been expected. A century earlier the feminist reformer Josephine Butler had seen venereal disease as divine punishment for sin, and mounted a nationwide moral crusade for male abstinence as the alternative to state-regulated prostitution. It was perhaps a sign of how secularized British society had become, and also perhaps of how much less simplistically Christians now viewed disease, that in the 1980s AIDS prompted no such moralistic crusade.[44] On the contrary, the leading medical authorities, alarmed by 1985 at the spread of AIDS, pressed the government to educate the public about it.[45] Not only was this achieved, but the churches felt some pressure to recommend the use of condoms in same-sex relationships, and even the Catholic Church in England tacitly acquiesced in this.[46] The Church of England was already moving on further: two homosexual clergymen 'came out' at the General Synod in 1981, and in 1983 the Mothers' Union recognized the need to overcome prejudice on the subject.[47] The authorities, even under a Thatcher government, were so keen to avoid pinning blame that some homosexuals thought its health education insufficiently targeted towards themselves. 'The received view became to see the plight of victims not as a warning against vice but as a call for sympathy and solidarity in suffering.'[48] The epidemic carried much further the mutual help already promoted within the homosexual community. The Terrence Higgins Trust, founded in 1982, was named by his friends to commemorate Britain's first AIDS victim, who had died earlier in that year: it aimed to help his fellow-sufferers, and to advance the research and understanding of AIDS.

'D. W. Cory', writing in an American context in 1951, thought that homosexuality 'must inevitably play a progressive role in the scheme of things', strengthening freedom and democracy.[49] The Gay Liberation Front seems in practice to have accepted this view, and after 1967 any overt support for further homosexual liberation tended to come from the left. Jeremy Thorpe, the Liberal leader, when prosecuted for murder in 1979, did not turn his prosecution to liberal advantage by contesting the relevance of his private sexual activities to his effectiveness as a politician. His successor David Steel, however, was more alert to J. S. Mill's ongoing relevance, and publicly regretted Scarborough's refusal

[43] S. Garfield, 'Now it's the Real Thing', *G* (18 July 1996), ii, 3.

[44] See N. Fowler, *Ministers Decide: A Personal Memoir of the Thatcher Years* (1991), 253 for his regret, as Secretary of State for Social Security, that the churches mounted no such movement.

[45] e.g. *T* (23 Aug. 1985), 11.   [46] *T* (6 Dec. 1986), 1.

[47] *T* (28 Feb. 1981), 2. *G* (1 Aug. 1983), 2.   [48] Matthew Parris, *ST* (1 June 1997), viii, 2.

[49] 'D. W. Cory' [pseud. for E. Sagarin], *The Homosexual Outlook: A Subjective Approach* (London, 1963 edn.), 235.

to accommodate the Campaign for Homosexual Equality's annual conference in 1976; the Liberal Party, he said, would not hold its conference there either.[50] In 1977 Maureen Colquhoun alleged that her lesbianism had precluded her re-adoption as Labour candidate for Northampton North, and in 1983 Peter Tatchell, challenged as Labour candidate at Bermondsey by-election by a 'real Labour' candidate, lost the seat to a Liberal; he later became a key figure in OutRage.[51] When the Labour MP Chris Smith announced his homosexual orientation in 1984, he was the sole openly homosexual MP; Conservative homosexuals were still lying low, and the more populist Conservatives (especially Tebbit as party chairman[52]) included homosexual liberation among Labour's allegedly 'loony left' affiliations. When clause 28 in the Local Government Act (1988) forbade local authorities in any maintained school to teach that homosexuality could provide the basis for a family relationship, homosexuals were alerted to the importance not only of politics, but of political skills. The attempt to get the clause repealed prompted the creation in 1989 of the Stonewall Group and resumption of the all-party approach which had been pursued before 1967—with ultimate success in 2003, when repeal was secured.

This long-term shift in attitudes to homosexuality, important enough in itself, was but one dimension of further late twentieth-century shifts on sexuality. The barriers were weakening against publicly discussing another taboo subject, rape, where even victims had earlier been reticent. Several factors interacted during the 1970s to advertise the rape of women as a social problem. Rising concern about violence within the family familiarized the public with the idea of women's refuges, and in 1976 Women against Rape was established at roughly the same time as the USA exported the idea of 'rape crisis centres'. British feminists suspected the police of bias when dealing with rape's female victims, and this was a growing concern if only because freer movement was integral to women's emancipation. Two murder cases in the 1980s further alerted the public. Despite massive public cooperation the police took five years to catch Peter Sutcliffe, the so-called 'Yorkshire ripper'. His thirteenth murder in 1980 led to the formation of 'Women against Violence against Women', a pressure group which tried to reach the causes of male violence; its campaign to censor American films showing violence against women aligned it with a woman of more traditional views, Mary Whitehouse.[53] Public concern was revived by the mysterious disappearance of the estate agent Suzie Lamplugh on 28 July 1986 after she had arranged to see a client in Fulham; her body was never found. By 1990 the taboo against discussing male rape was now sufficiently vulnerable for Richie McMullen, himself a victim, to publish his survival manual entitled *Male Rape*. The predominantly heterosexual orientation of

[50] O (8 Aug. 1976), 3.   [51] T (28 Sept. 1977), 6. G (26 Feb. 1983, 4.   [52] G (13 Dec. 1986), 2.
[53] C. Dawson, 'Angry Women Fight the Violence', STel (21 Dec. 1980), 17.

male rapists often goes unrecognized, he argued, causing the offence to be even less frequently reported than the rape of women: 'male victims of rape must be one of the most silent and isolated groups of victimised people in the country today'.[54] Their bewilderment was hardly surprising, given that British law on rape then assumed that the perpetrator must be male and the victim female; the punishment for indecent assault was far lower. 'Male rape is a reality', McMullen concluded, 'and will have to be addressed and recognised in law sooner or later.'[55] This soon occurred: within a year the Criminal Justice Act (1994) had secured Britain's first conviction for attempted male rape.

Behind all these changes lay an overriding but rarely explicit shift in opinion: the slow abandonment of allocating everyone neatly into slots marked either 'heterosexual male' or 'heterosexual female', and of assuming that family structures must rest only upon a formal and lifelong alliance between one of each. The concept of transsexuality cut across such notions completely, and was slowly being refined in the 1950s and 1960s.[56] Fewer people now confused transvestism with transsexuality, and the 1970s saw a boom in transvestite stage performances: Barry Humphries gained an ever larger following for his unabashed impersonation of Dame Edna Everage, a surreal variant of the pantomime dame with her coruscating parodies of bad taste, and George Logan and Patrick Fyffe performed the more genteel cross-dressing double act of Hinge and Bracket.[57] The 1970s also saw the first non-sensational autobiographical British account of a sex-change operation. Its author, Jan Morris, had been contemplating the operation in 1972; by then more than 600 men and women had experienced it in the USA and perhaps another 150 in Britain.[58] Morris published *Conundrum* in 1974, and offered it to the public 'diffidently, like a confidence',[59] thereby rendering the account all the more attractive, and ensuring that it went into several editions.

2. NEW FAMILIES, NEW WOMEN?

Although Marx had long ago emphasized the responsiveness of family structures to social change, twentieth-century Britain still viewed 'the family' as a fixed entity. Indeed, the trend in early twentieth-century British families was to become more similar: in propensity to marry, age of marriage, health, size of family and house, and age of childbearing, retirement, and death,[60] as well as

---

[54] R. McMullen, *Male Rape* (1990), 128; see also 14, 21, 81, 83, 118.   [55] Ibid. 23, cf. 15.
[56] Harrison, *Seeking a Role*, 33, 243–4.
[57] Obituaries of Fyffe in *Ind* (14 May 2002), 18; *G* (15 May 2002), 18.
[58] J. Morris, *Conundrum* (1st publ. 1974, paperback edn. 2002), 110.
[59] Ibid., 1986 introduction to the Penguin paperback edn. 1987, 7.
[60] *TBS* 10. M. Anderson, 'The Emergence of the Modern Life Cycle in Britain', *Social History* (Jan. 1985), 86. Coleman and Salt, *British Population*, 158.

in cultural and recreational tastes. So at mid-century the two-parent, two-child family seemed likely to remain the norm. From the 1960s onwards, however, the standardized family 'package' began to diversify. The nuclear model of (heterosexual) husband, (heterosexual) wife, and two children (preferably one male and one female, abstaining from sex until marriage) all living in the same house and taking their meals together gradually succumbed. Self-designed family structures, like self-designed religions, were now being sought to reflect the full diversity of human circumstances and inclinations.[61] This late twentieth-century shift had the advantage of drawing more fully into the community those minorities whose earlier repression had often made them seem or feel regrettably eccentric. Yet it was often a change more in appearance than in reality: the earlier standardized family package had frequently itself been a construct, propped up by numerous surreptitious devices and hypocrisies, whereas now contraception's full implications for personal conduct could be acknowledged.

One outcome was that marriage became less popular. By the 1980s people were once more marrying later: the proportion of women between 18 and 49 who married fell from 74 per cent in 1979 to 51 per cent in 2000.[62] Households oriented round a married couple fell steadily in their share of British households from 68 per cent in 1971 to 45 per cent in 2001, by which time nearly a third of all adults were staying single.[63] Far from signifying any retreat from monogamous relationships, this indicated only that in Britain, as in most industrial societies, monogamy was occurring outside marriage. For the major change in British family patterns accelerating after 1970 was the spread of cohabitation, which frequently led to a long-term and publicly endorsed relationship. By 1979 one in ten of all unmarried women were cohabiting: that is, 330,000 women under 50 were living with a man to whom they were not married. By the early 1990s two-thirds of unmarried women were living with their future husband, whereas only one in twenty had done so thirty years earlier.[64] So when British family history is viewed over the very long term, the Victorian crusade to make marriage the precondition for motherhood, remarkably successful up to the 1960s, is an aberration. In 1981 *Debrett* in its guide to modern manners advised hostesses that unmarried couples need no longer be assigned separate rooms: indeed, it could often be 'a courtesy to put them together'. For a contributor discussing cohabitation in the *Guardian* that year, 'the sheer speed of the change in attitudes has been breathtaking'.[65]

All this transformed the wedding's social significance, and change even reached that deeply conservative area, surnames and titles. As late as 1976

[61] See also Harrison, *Seeking a Role*, 296–7, 300.
[62] See the interesting table in Coleman and Salt, *British Population*, 179. *G* (12 Dec. 2001), 7.
[63] *T* (14 Feb. 2003), 5.   [64] *T* (10 Dec. 1981), 5. *Ind* (14 June 1995), 5.
[65] E. B. Donald (ed.), *Debrett's Etiquette and Modern Manners* (1981), 248. *G* (4 Aug. 1981), 10.

the ranking of the first and second most common surnames—Smith and
Jones, respectively—had not changed since 1853.[66] The early twentieth-
century feminist hyphenation of male and female surnames after marriage,
never widespread, now revived; more commonly, the married woman retained
her earlier surname, at least for professional purposes, but surnames' long-
term destination was left unclear. More immediate were difficulties about
marital nomenclature: 'partner' eventually prevailed over such alternatives
as 'mistress', 'spouse', 'companion', and 'lover'.[67] The designation 'Miss' for
the adult unmarried woman gradually fell out of use, if only because the
unmarried woman could not now be assumed to lack a sexual partner. The
American 'Ms', favoured by feminists as freeing women from being categorized
by marital status, was first accepted by the Passport Office in 1974 and came
quite widely into use, though in Britain even among women it never quite lost
a pejorative association with militant feminism.[68] As for the terms 'bachelor'
and 'spinster', they fell gradually out of use: their sexual experience was
diminishingly likely to differ from that of husband and wife, or even father and
mother.

Divorce-law reformers after the 1940s hoped that relaxing the grounds for
divorce would lower the divorce rate by winkling out the unhappy marriages,[69]
and advocates of so-called 'trial marriage' hoped to curb divorce by ensuring
that the decision to marry was better-informed. Relaxations in the divorce law
were indeed followed by a rise in divorce levels as the backlog was digested, and
the Divorce Reform Act (1969) was no different. But reform had the unintended
effect of encouraging the idea that divorce was acceptable, even fashionable,
and the UK's divorce rate, far from stabilizing, had by the mid-1980s become
the highest in Europe, where divorce rates were everywhere rising, though
they were higher still in the USA.[70] Mounting divorce greatly diversified family
shape: the extended family, having declined in one form, re-emerged in another.
From mid-century the generations were increasingly living separately,[71] a trend
carried further after 1970. At the same time a household was more likely to
contain children with different parents. Whereas in the late 1960s 83 per cent
of marriages were first marriages for both partners, by the early 1990s over
40 per cent of weddings involved at least one formerly married person and
12 per cent involved two divorced persons.[72] Step-families had earlier been
formed to assist mutual support within a society without public welfare and
with separated roles for the sexes: they were now being formed for personal
fulfilment. By 1991 just under 7 per cent of all families with dependent children,

[66] *Econ* (7 Aug. 1976), 23.

[67] For interesting and astonished discussions of what was happening see B. Beck, 'Just Good Friends',
G (4 Aug. 1981), 10; F. Cairncross, 'How Marriage Went out of Fashion', *G* (25 May 1982), 8.

[68] *DT* (24 Mar. 1997), 5.   [69] Harrison, *Seeking a Role*, 295–6, 298.

[70] *BST* 83. Roll, 'One in Ten', 171.   [71] Harrison, *Seeking a Role*, 286.   [72] *TCBST* 64.

including one-parent families, were step-families.[73] Mounting divorce did not reflect widespread disillusion with monogamy, but monogamy energetically pursued in a more palatable form. After 1970, as before, rising divorce rates reflected higher expectations of marriage, especially among women. During the twentieth century up to the 1960s, mortality (which frees the survivor from a marriage to remarry) was falling, whereas divorce was not yet rising fast, so in those years remarriage had been uniquely rare.[74] With wider access to divorce thereafter, remarriage revived as a social relationship. By 1985 more than one wedding in three involved at least one person who had been married before: the first spouse had not (as earlier) died, but had divorced, for divorce was now supplanting death as the most important reason why marriages ended.[75]

Widening access to divorce had even broader implications: by no means all divorced people with children found a new partner. But family breakdown as the cause of single parenthood was overtaken in the 1980s by the decision of more women to bear children outside any long-term relationship, and the growing number of one-parent families led some people unsurprisingly to ask whether a family consisting of two same-sex 'parents' might not sometimes be preferable. The term 'lone parent' originated in the USA in the late 1940s; the phrase 'one-parent family', also transatlantic in origin in the late 1960s, was used synonymously with 'single-parent family'. The phrases had become sufficiently common in Britain by 1973 for the National Council for the Unmarried Mother and her Child to rechristen itself in that year the National Council for One Parent Families. This reflected the importance of Danish influences on the Council, and the imaginative impact made by Margaret Bramall, its energetic director from 1962 to 1979. She professionalized the Council, broadened its agenda and outlook to include all one-parent families, and with government help made their number statistically visible and documented. The Council combined providing information and services with acting as a pressure group on behalf of this new category. As it pointed out in 1973, 'all lone parents share one crucial characteristic: the responsibility of bringing up children single-handed in a society that is geared economically, socially and emotionally to two-parent families. It is this that makes them an identifiable social group.'[76]

By 1973 more than a million children under 16 were living in one-parent families, whose earned income was on average only half that of comparable two-parent families; five out of six lone parents were women, but lone parents of either sex were by 1991 more likely than others to be unemployed, usually

---

[73] J. Haskey, 'Step Families and Stepchildren in Great Britain', *Population Trends*, 76 (Summer 1994), 17.
[74] Coleman and Salt, *British Population*, 203.   [75] *BST* 82. Finer *Report*, i. 40–1.
[76] National Council for One Parent Families, *Annual Report Apr. 1972–Mar. 1973*, 1. For Bramall's obituary see *G* (17 Aug. 2007), 39.

involuntarily.[77] By 1990 the nuclear family consisting of two parents living in the same household with their children was only the third largest among household groups, accounting for 25 per cent of the total—outpaced by households containing married or cohabiting couples without children (36 per cent) and by households containing only one person (26 per cent).[78] The number of single mothers in Great Britain who had never shared their household with a partner was growing fast, from about 160,000 in 1981 to 430,000 ten years later; such women headed an eighth of all families with dependent children in 1994, by which time this group was attracting attention from ministers seeking welfare cuts.[79] This is hardly surprising, given that the number of lone parents on supplementary benefits more than doubled between 1971 and 1986, with a rising proportion willing to claim; and claims once begun tended to persist.[80]

Behind these changes lay a shift in moral attitudes which to older generations seemed remarkable—to some, even repugnant. The moralism which had once condemned deviant sexuality and unconventional family relationships was by the end of the century being transferred to the newly liberated outlook. By the 1970s the National Council for One Parent Families had shed its earlier censorious perspective together with the psychological approach that succeeded it, and had adopted an entirely pragmatic and utilitarian outlook. For the 'illegitimate' child and the 'unmarried' mother it substituted 'natural' child and 'single' mother. This was 'no mere change of words': it reflected a 'determination to cease using language that is offensive and wounding to a group of people who have enough disadvantages without suffering the indignity of being referred to in pejorative terms'. The word 'illegitimate', it claimed, 'is deeply hurtful to many people born out of wedlock, implying as it does that they are second-class citizens'.[81] When in 1993 two Conservative cabinet ministers urged a return to the two-parent family, they found the Archbishop of Canterbury publicly arrayed against them.[82] The Marriage Guidance Council had moved on by the 1970s from propping up existing marriages to smoothing over the consequences of their break-up, substituting 'marital counselling' for 'marriage guidance' in its aim to encourage self-help. Renamed 'Relate' in 1988, it saw 150,000 clients in 2008.[83]

[77] National Council for One Parent Families, *Annual Report Apr. 1973–Mar. 1974*, 3. J. Bradshaw and J. Millar, *Lone Parent Families in the United Kingdom* (Dept. of Social Security Research Report, 6; 1991), 47, 96.   [78] *FT* (4 Sept. 1992), 8; cf. *T* (15 Sept. 1992), 7.
[79] *Ind* (20 Nov. 1993), 10. Berthoud *et al.* in S. McRae (ed.), *Changing Britain: Families and Households in the 1990s* (Oxford, 1999), 354.   [80] Bradshaw and Millar, *Lone Parent Families*, 64–5.
[81] National Council for One Parent Families, *Annual Report Apr. 1973–Mar. 1974*, preliminary (unpaginated) page.   [82] *G* (12 Oct. 1993), 2.
[83] Home Office, *Marriage Matters: A Consultative Document by the Working Party on Marriage Guidance Set Up by the Home Office in Consultation with the Department of Health and Social Security* (1979), 4–6. Statistic kindly provided by Relate. See also http://www.relate.org.uk/aboutus/researchandstatistics/, consulted 25 Aug. 2009.

When the Street Offences Act had been going through parliament in 1959 there had been critics of the designation 'common prostitute', and a desire for some acknowledgement of moral equivalence between prostitute and customer. The late-century resurgence of feminism might have been expected to carry this further,[84] but of the feminists' twin objectives—sexual liberation and sexual equality—the former took priority. In the new climate of the 1970s the female prostitute was encouraged to 'come out', and even seek acceptance for her social role. In 1975 the energetic and voluble Helen Buckingham, herself a prostitute, launched PUSSI (Prostitutes United for Social and Sexual Integration), and campaigned to get prostitution decriminalized. Her movement gained much publicity in 1979 when she threatened to intimidate parliament by identifying highly placed clients: 'we want to be seen as competent, mature people who act as sex therapists and answer a social need', she said. She was echoing remarks made in parliament by the Labour MP Maureen Colquhoun,[85] whose Protection of Prostitutes Bill aimed to protect prostitutes from exploitation, and to end imprisonment for soliciting; it won 130 supporters as against 50 opponents, but was lost in the subsequent general election.

The implications of this sexual revolution for household size, and therefore for housing need, were considerable. The number of British households consisting of only one person rose throughout the twentieth century, but mounting divorce helps to explain why after 1971 the number of households rose faster than the British population: between 1971 and 2000 one-person households rose from 17 to 32 per cent in their share of all households.[86] After a marriage broke up, both parents tended to downsize their housing; the lone parent and offspring were more likely to move into council or owner-occupied accommodation, whereas the other parent lived alone or returned to accommodation that was shared—often with the offspring's grandparents.[87] Between 1977/8 and 1995/6 the number of people in the UK living alone almost doubled, to 1.9 million, and the number of single people buying their own homes rose threefold, to a million.[88] There was a growing tendency for young people and for men of all ages to live alone: between the 1970s and the mid-1990s men in their thirties moved from contributing the lowest to the highest percentage of all male groups living alone.[89] The young were more likely to get divorced, and the divorce-led demand for smaller houses worked with the long-term housing grain: newly built homes shrank by a third in floor-area between the 1920s and the end of the century, with lower ceilings and much smaller gardens, encouraged by

[84] As Mary Warnock noted, O (16 Nov. 2008), 29.
[85] O (11 Mar. 1979), 3 (Buckingham), cf. Colquhoun, HC Deb. 6 Mar. 1979, cc. 1095–6.
[86] Statistics, TCBST 77. See also G (12 Dec. 2001), 7.
[87] Bradshaw and Millar, Lone Parent Families, 93–4.
[88] G (9 May 1997), 7.   [89] DT (9 May 1997), 6.

the shortage of land and by government pressure to fill it with more homes.[90] Within both public and private sectors it became usual to have two or three bedrooms, but in both sectors one-bedroomed houses became increasingly common during the 1980s (for about a fifth of the overall total); four bedrooms or more were more common throughout the period in owner-occupied houses, rising to about a fifth of them in the 1980s.[91]

The UK's family revolution after the 1950s was replicated in other contemporary advanced industrial societies. Unplanned and rapid, it had been predicted by few, yet it was a revolution in British social arrangements fully comparable with and perhaps more lasting than the growth of class consciousness during the industrial revolution. It was all the more startling in Britain for the reticence and even puritanism that had moulded British public life since the evangelical revival. After the 1960s British institutions—the law, the taxation system, building societies, schools, churches, political parties—stumbled awkwardly in its wake. Women's welfare and freedom by no means uniformly benefited. British feminism's first three phases[92] up to the mid-1960s had been wary of commitment to women's sexual liberation—not just from tactics, but from the belief voiced by Mary Stocks (a key figure in third-phase British feminism) that 'a sex-dominated world is not going to be a good world for women'. Relaxing restraints upon male sexuality conjured up feminist fears of deserted wives and mothers. The fourth-phase British feminists who emerged in the 1960s were keener for women both to control their fertility and to enjoy sexual emancipation, whereas Stocks urged them to 'keep off sex'. She added: 'for goodness' sake, let there be no more burning of bras', for the more breasts were talked about, 'the more breast-conscious the mass-media will become'.[93] Even here, feminism had been but one among several causes of change: also at work was the combination of better access to birth-control techniques with a greater willingness to use them. In so far as this owed anything to campaigners, these had been the pioneer birth-controllers from earlier generations, whether feminist or not, and such earlier pioneers of sexual emancipation for both sexes as H. G. Wells, Marie Stopes, and Bertrand Russell.

Before and after 1970 feminists were no more than a minor influence in extending women's work opportunities, liberating as these were.[94] Women were by then deploying their control over fertility to render themselves more employable. In the late 1970s they began postponing childbearing from their twenties into their thirties, so that the couple could first build up the family's resources, or (if in a professional occupation) qualify fully for a double career.

[90] *DT* (9 Apr. 2003), 13.
[91] *BST* 388. See also the useful discussion in J. Burnett, *A Social History of Housing 1815–1970* (1978), 296, 305, 309.   [92] The first three phases are explained in Harrison, *Seeking a Role*, 30–1.
[93] Mary Stocks, 'Where do we Go from Here?', *Woman's Journal* (Sept. 1973), 49.
[94] Cf. Harrison, *Seeking a Role*, 30–1, 255.

This meant either a long gap between marriage and the first child's birth, or postponing marriage.[95] By 2000, mothers in Great Britain gave birth on average at age 29, three years later than in the early 1970s.[96] So far had married women advanced within the workforce by the late 1960s that they seemed to be hindering older men from getting work, especially in service industries such as cleaning, retailing, and the food industry, where part-time work was particularly in demand.[97] In 1975 about two-thirds of British women in their forties or early fifties were either working or seeking work, and more British women were returning to paid work after having children than in any other EEC country.[98] In each of the four periods 1960–73, 1974–9, 1980–9, and 1990–4 the proportion of British women aged between 15 and 64 who were in paid work surpassed the combined six-country average for USA, Japan, France, Italy, Canada, and the UK.[99] Only in the UK's dwindling number of heavy-industry communities, and in its peripheral and agricultural areas, were women likely to stay at home without taking paid work. In farming employment in the 1980s, for example, men remained dominant, and women did not become prominent (and then only at lower levels) except to supply part-time seasonal and casual labour.[100] Traditional lifestyles for women persisted for longest in areas such as Wales, the north-west Highlands, Cornwall, and Devon where farming was prominent, whereas inner-city West London was the area with most women in full-time paid work. If part-time work is included, there were by 1991 some parts of the country where more women than men were in paid work. In the Grampian region, centre of the North Sea oil industry, it is not surprising that men accounted for 57 per cent of the employees, but in East Sussex women accounted for 54 per cent, and for 52 per cent even in Merseyside.[101]

Yet in seeking paid work, women did not forsake their distinctive domestic role. By the 1980s more women and fewer men were in paid work than ever before, but in Great Britain jobs available after 1951 tipped markedly towards part-time. Proposals for formalized job-sharing were much discussed in the early 1980s,[102] but the job-splitting scheme of 1983, designed to curb unemployment, had by the end of 1984 caused only 1,000 jobs to be split; the necessary coordination was difficult indeed. Far more spontaneous and far more effective as an impulse to job-splitting was employers' creation of the

---

[95] See the graph in *T* (14 Apr. 2001), 5. Coleman and Salt, *British Population*, 151. *BST* 52–4.

[96] Family Policy Studies Centre, *Family Change*, 2. See also C. Jones, 'Fertility of the Over Thirties', *Population Trends*, 67 (Spring 1992), 10–11.

[97] Townsend, *Poverty in UK*, 682–3. For women's part-time work in service industries see the table in *Finer Report*, i. 417.   [98] *T* (12 Apr. 1977), 2.

[99] OECD, *Historical Statistics 1960–1994* (Paris, 1996), 41.

[100] Hill, 'Agriculture', in Johnson (ed.), *Structure of British Industry*, 8.

[101] S. Duncan, 'The Geography of Gender Divisions of Labour in Britain', *Transactions of the Institute of British Geographers* (1991), 428. Statistics, *Ind* (10 May 1993), 1.

[102] See e.g. *T* (6 Aug. 1981), 3.

supposedly new part-time jobs that were mostly taken up by married women hitherto absent from the unemployment statistics.[103] Whereas the part-timers' share of the male workforce rose steadily from a low base in 1951, the part-timers' share of the female workforce rose steadily from a high base. The really rapid increase in British women's employment occurred among part-timers, and then only in the 1970s and 1980s. By 1981 women made up 84 per cent of part-time employees, with married women constituting the vast majority of the female part-timers;[104] in 1991 there were four times as many female as male part-timers. These were high figures by comparison with other industrial societies.[105] The ratio of female employees and of part-timers was far higher in service than in manufacturing employment. Both sexes were far more likely to take part-time work in services than in manufacturing, but even in service industries, part-timers as a ratio of the employment in their sex were at least four times as numerous for women as for men. Indeed, the female part-timer virtually colonized some occupations: in 1981 four-fifths of school cleaners worked for twenty-one hours a week or less, and the school meals service was staffed mainly by women working for less than thirteen hours.[106] Whereas by the early 1990s two-thirds of women in professional and managerial jobs worked full-time, only a twelfth of unskilled women did so. Still, women part-timers, the vast majority of them married, tended to stay with their employers for as long as women full-timers. The women part-timers were much readier to emphasize the priority of the woman's household tasks, and seem to have been choosing to subordinate the satisfactions of higher pay and status for flexible and shorter working hours. The latter rendered feasible what they saw as a complementary partnership within the family; women's part-time jobs were not seen as fractions of full-time jobs that would have been preferred.[107]

Within each household, job-sharing of a sort came about informally and spontaneously through mutual give-and-take within the two-earner partnership. Between 1979 and 1999 the proportion of dual-earner families rose from 50 to 70 per cent. The partners' working hours were complementary: the more hours worked by one, the fewer worked by the other.[108] But it was the men whose paid-work hours were longest, beginning too early in the day for taking the children to school, even had fathers wished to do so; furthermore, fathers

[103] O. Robinson, 'The Changing Labour Market: The Phenomenon of Part-Time Employment in Britain', *National Westminster Bank Quarterly Review* (Nov. 1985), 28.
[104] O. Robinson and J. Wallace, *Part-Time Employment and Sex Discrimination Legislation in Great Britain: A Study of the Demand for Part-Time Labour and of Sex Discrimination in Selected Organizations and Establishments* (Dept. of Employment Research Paper, 43; 1984), 3.
[105] C. Hakim, 'The Myth of Rising Female Employment', *Work, Employment and Society* (Mar. 1993), 101, 103. C. Hakim, 'A Century of Change in Occupational Segregation 1891–1991', *Journal of Historical Sociology* (Dec. 1994), 439.   [106] Robinson and Wallace, *Part-Time Employment*, 4, 42.
[107] Hakim, 'Myth', 104–6. C. Marsh, *Hours of Work of Women and Men in Britain* (1991), 69. Robinson and Wallace, *Part-Time Employment*, 43.   [108] Marsh, *Hours of Work*, pp. x, 70.

spent only half as much time as mothers with their children under 16 and only a third as much time on household tasks.[109] Still, an EEC survey in 1979 showed that English men were readier than men in other EEC nations to help with domestic tasks; 85 per cent said they were prepared to help wash up, 57 per cent to clean the house, 30 per cent to change nappies, and 29 per cent to do the ironing. Although in all countries women reported that the men did less than they claimed, the English men claimed to do more in each of these four categories than men in any other EEC country.[110] Some sociologists even saw history as coming full circle. In the pre-industrial 'symmetrical family', they claimed, both sexes had collaborated in the home as a single economic unit; industrialization then took family members out of the home as individual wage-earners; now they were once more collaborating within a home that had become the unit of consumption.[111] What relieved the strain on the increasing number of double-income families after 1970 was less the sharing of domestic tasks between the sexes than the shrinking of those tasks by changes in fashion, technology, and retailing. Time-consuming and dreary tasks gradually gave way to home mechanization, new polishes and cleaners, new surfaces easily kept clean, and the sort of silver that required no polishing, and supermarket shopping as a family expedition supplanted the housewife's daily shopping expeditions.

Where male and female interests conflicted, retailers and restaurants took much of the strain. Home mechanization and better shopping facilities helped to reconcile the married woman's two roles, but they owed little to feminism and almost everything to commercial motive, changed patterns of transport, and women's felt need to supplement the family income. Clothes from the retailers Marks & Spencer swept away home knits and Singer sewing machines in a wave of creative destruction. Women's fashions now had to facilitate free movement and were less dominated by Paris, and meals' timing and preparation had to suit women's paid employment away from home. The major late twentieth-century shifts in food purchasing reflected the impact of overseas holidays (pasta, rice) and concern for health (low-fat milks, leaner meats), but also (and not always compatibly with the first two) convenience: fewer raw ingredients and basic foodstuffs such as sugar and flour, more prepared dishes, packaged fruit and vegetables. Family eating became less communal, especially during the working week, and was organized more to suit individual timetables and tastes. So the competitive values of Tesco, Marks & Spencer, and Sainsbury's helped to realize the collectivist dreams of pioneer feminists like the American Charlotte Perkins Gilman by an entirely unexpected route, and without making

[109] Ibid. 29. *T* (12 July 2001), 13.   [110] *Econ* (8 Sept. 1979), 53–4; cf. *BST* 22.
[111] M. Young and P. Willmott, *The Symmetrical Family: A Study of Work and Leisure in the London Region* (1973, paperback edn. 1975), 28–30.

impracticably feminist demands of men. Communal food preparation emerged, not from the specialization of function made possible by communal living and professionalized domesticity, but through the sale of commercially prepared food which individual households could prepare from microwaves and freezers.

Further evidence of employed women's continued domestic priorities, in the 1970s as in the 1990s, comes from their occupational choice. There was a long-term slow and tentative twentieth-century shift among employed women from secluded and segregated to public and unsegregated occupations, but their new occupations were more likely than men's to focus on personal relationships and small work-groups. Women tended to cluster in occupations that were seen as their speciality, whether inside the home or out: cleaning, preparing food, dressmaking, retailing, secretarial work, teaching, and welfare services, with men in control of heavy industry, transport, and manual labour.[112] In 1991 women contributed 99 per cent of employees in British secretarial and child-care occupations, but only 1 per cent of employees in the construction trades. This sex-segregation, though declining faster among full-timers than part-timers,[113] stemmed partly from legal restraints on the types and timing of work that women could take up. In 1979 the Equal Opportunities Commission wanted to remove such restraints—against excessive overtime, night and shift work, for example—but the TUC preferred attaining equality through extending equal protection to men. The restraints were eventually eroded by a combination of EEC feminism and free-market Conservatism, so that in 1988 the ban on women's night work was removed.[114]

Nonetheless, women were slowly transcending the occupational separation of spheres. Among the professions in 1966, women in England and Wales accounted for a majority only in schoolteaching and social-welfare work, whereas in some professions their contribution was tiny: they contributed only 5 per cent of barristers and solicitors, for instance, and only 2 per cent of surveyors and architects.[115] This soon changed, given that professional occupations were relatively compatible with childrearing: during the 1970s women's share of new recruits to accountancy, banking, and law rose fast, and in 1986 for the first time more women than men passed the solicitors' final examinations. Women's share of general practitioners rose from a tenth to a quarter between 1970 and 1990, though more than half the women so employed were part-timers.[116] In business,

---

[112] C. Hakim, 'Explaining Trends in Occupational Segregation: The Measurement, Causes, and Consequences of the Sexual Division of Labour', *European Sociological Review* (Sept. 1992), 135.

[113] Hakim, 'Century of Change', 451–2; 'Myth', 105–6; 'Explaining Trends', 133–5.

[114] *G* (5 Sept. 1979), 4. Marsh, *Hours of Work*, 2.

[115] Political and Economic Planning, *Sex, Career and Family* (1971), 23.

[116] *Econ* (12 Sept. 1987), 34. I. Loudon, J. Horder, and C. Webster (eds.), *General Practice under the National Health Service 1948–1997: The First Fifty Years* (Oxford, 1998), 53, 309.

free-market Conservatism pursued talent wherever profits might benefit: with Thatcher as role-model, the successful woman entrepreneur could create firms without glass ceilings; in the ten years after 1981 the number of self-employed women who employed staff rose by 49 per cent, but by only 14 per cent for men.[117] Laura Ashley, the fabric and fashion designer, who began printing fabrics on the kitchen table during her first pregnancy in 1953, is perhaps the most famous example, but to her should be added Anita Roddick, who opened the first Bodyshop branch in 1976, and the many prosperous feminist publishers of the 1980s, led by Virago.[118] So women were slowly gaining well-paid and powerful jobs, and by the 1980s held a growing share of professional and managerial posts.[119]

Better job opportunities for married as well as single women could only advance women's wealth and standing. Marriage to an older man was ceasing to be the younger woman's route to security and status: in 1963 15 per cent of married women married men younger than themselves, 26 per cent by 2003.[120] By 2003, estimates based on taxation figures showed that there were in the UK 314,000 men over 18 in the top two of seven wealth categories: that is, each with wealth exceeding £500,000 in net capital value. Women in these two categories (298,000) were much closer to the men in their number than in their aggregate wealth: the men in these categories possessed £452,520 million, the women only £287,994 million. In the next category down (each with between £200,000 and £500,000), there were far more women than men, with far more aggregate wealth than the men. In the lower four categories, the sexes did not significantly differ from one another either in number or in aggregate wealth.[121] The three exemplars for women seeking to break most comprehensively into what had hitherto been a male sphere included Castle, whose political career peaked when Secretary of State for Employment in 1968–70, acting in some respects as Joan the Baptist for Thatcher as prime minister from 1979 to 1990; Crossman in March 1968 thought Castle 'one of the great successes of the Government'.[122] She and Thatcher were joined in 1992 by Betty Boothroyd, first woman Speaker of the House of Commons. None of the three saw herself as feminist: still less did they identify with the women's liberation movement. Boothroyd urged MPs to 'elect me for what I am and not for what I was born', and Castle showed the customary Labour preference for collaboration between the sexes against deprivation: her objective, for women as for immigrants, was

---

[117] M. Kenny, 'Ladies of the Right', *Spec* (3 July 1993), 8–9. *FT* (20 May 1992), 9.

[118] *G* (29 June 1983), 8. Kenny, 'Ladies of the Right', *Spec* (3 July 1993), 8–9.

[119] For fuller detail see Hakim, 'Explaining Trends', 136–7.

[120] *T* (21 Feb. 2006), 29; cf. *FT* (12 Dec. 2003), 3.

[121] www.hmrc.gov.uk/stats/personal_wealth/13 2 delay mar 06.pdf, consulted 28 Jan. 2007. The late Andrew Glyn guided me to this table.

[122] Crossman, *Cabinet Diaries*, ii. 729 (21 Mar. 1968); cf. iii. 404 (9 Mar. 1969).

assimilation.[123] In 1972 she lectured American feminists on the triviality of their concerns, and argued that women would best be advanced by plunging into the sort of political crusading which would offer 'a cause bigger than themselves'. She was amused in 1975 to find herself cast in a feminist role 'after a lifetime in which I have hated the whole idea'.[124]

Until 1969 the future seemed to lie with Castle, but her star waned thereafter, leaving the field open to Shirley Williams and Margaret Thatcher, both seen in the mid-1970s as candidates for Britain's first woman prime minister. After 1974 Williams was increasingly at odds with the Labour Party, whose fortunes were about to wane, whereas Thatcher's party was recovering and had begun moving in her direction, so it was Thatcher who prevailed. To Castle, Thatcher's election as party leader in 1975 gave 'a sneaking feminist pleasure'.[125] She cast a half-awestruck woman's eye at Thatcher's professionalism: 'how *does* she keep her hair so unchangeably immaculate?', and did she really do all the housework herself?[126] There must also have been a touch of envy in Castle's comment about how 'blooming' Thatcher looked in the midst of her triumph: 'she is in love: in love with power, success—and with herself. She looks as I looked when Harold made me Minister of Transport.'[127] Thatcher was quite prepared to exploit her femininity in getting her way politically with men,[128] and throughout the 1980s the feminists grumbled about her. Her social policies harmed women, it was claimed, and she did too little to promote women politicians. She 'feels no guilt about women, because she is one', wrote the prominent journalist Polly Toynbee. 'She is that all too familiar creature, the Queen Bee. The one who makes it herself, and pulls up the ladder behind her.'[129] Toynbee and Williams agreed in disliking Thatcher's politics, yet in her Conservatism Thatcher marched in step with women, who between 1945 and 1992 were consistently more likely than men to vote Conservative.[130] Both commentators also confessed that Thatcher's career had incidentally despatched many half-concealed male prejudices—for example, laying to rest 'for ever the belief that women can't make decisions in the middle of the menopause'.[131]

From 1886 to the late 1960s the sex differential in earnings remained at about 64 per cent. The EEC's relatively advanced position on equal pay began to influence Britain even before British accession, and Gallup polls showed that

---

[123] Boothroyd, *FT* (28 Apr. 1992), 7. Castle, *Diaries 1964–70*, 373 (14 Feb. 1968). See also Castle, *Diaries 1974–6*, 278 (15 Jan. 1975); *G* (2 Oct. 1984), 10.

[124] *T* (16 Feb. 1972), 8. Castle, *Diaries 1974–6*, 388 (10 May 1975).

[125] Castle, *Diaries 1974–6*, 303 (4 Feb. 1975); cf. 309 (11 Feb. 1975).

[126] Ibid. 487; cf. 362 (5 Aug. 1975), 432 (23 June 1975), 518 (13 Oct. 1975).

[127] Ibid. 303 (5 Feb. 1975); cf. 518 (11 Oct. 1975).

[128] Prior, *Balance of Power*, 139. See also Young, *One of Us*, 306–7.

[129] P. Toynbee, 'Goodbye to All That', *G* (11 Aug. 1988), 16. See also *G* (20 Jan. 1986), 12; *O* (7 Oct. 1979), 64.   [130] See table 16.1 in Seldon and Ball (eds.), *Conservative Century*, 615.

[131] Williams, interview with Janet Watts, *O* (24 May 1987), 20.

in 1968–9 British opinion was moving strongly in favour of equal pay for equal work; nearly three-quarters of those polled favoured the principle.[132] Men had hitherto been paid 'a living wage' sufficient to support the entire family—that is, more than was paid to working women with no such responsibilities—but the differential had become insufficiently discriminating to seem justified. With the collapse of the 'living wage' concept, and with so many women working, Conservative Chancellors of the Exchequer thought it sensible to tax women as individuals rather than as adjuncts of the male as head of family, and moved significantly towards this in their budgets of 1971 and 1988.[133] On equal pay Castle told the cabinet in September 1969 that 'there would be a move to equal pay anyhow and it was far better that we [the Labour government] should control it and get credit for it'.[134] Wilson helped her promote the cause through the party conference, and the Equal Pay Act (1970) forbade employers to discriminate between men and women on pay and conditions when doing the same or similar work, work rated as equivalent, or work of equal value. With a five-year lead-in, the Act came into effect in England, Wales, and Scotland in 1975. In the early 1970s women's wages for like work rose sharply from 64 to 74 per cent of men's, but the differential then established stalled till 1987.[135] Partly responsible were high levels of unemployment, accentuated by public-sector cuts which specially hit part-timers (mostly women). Continued EEC pressure in the early 1980s to broaden the definition of 'equal work' in equal-pay legislation had some impact,[136] though not immediately on pay, but the Thatcher governments were less keen than their Labour precursors on government manipulation of wage bargaining, and not till 1987–92 did the differential narrow further, taking women's wages for like work from 74 to 79 per cent of men's.[137]

Mary Stocks highlighted the fourth-phase feminist's difficulty: 'the dark shadowy forces of anti-feminism' still persisted, but combating anti-feminism 'can't be embodied in a legislative programme for no law will touch it'. Feminists could combat it now only 'in their own lives'.[138] British feminism in its first three phases had secured the necessary political emancipation: this must now be pushed home through feminizing 'civil society'. The male and female stereotypes long persisted in Mills & Boon novels, and not till the mid-1980s were their heroines allowed sex before the inevitable marriage; safe sex did not arrive till 1993, and not till 1994 was a female character at last allowed a career of her own.[139] Nor was feminist advance uncontested in Britain in the 1970s.

---

[132] N. C. Soldon, *Women in British Trade Unions 1874–1976* (Dublin, 1978), 179. *Gallup International Public Opinion Polls*, ii. 1010, 1042.

[133] Barber, *HC Deb.* 30 Mar. 1971, c. 1377. Lawson, *View from No. 11*, 881–7. Howe, *Conflict of Loyalty*, 566. [134] Castle, *Diaries 1964–70*, 704–5 (4 Sept. 1969).

[135] Hakim, 'Myth', 107. [136] *T* (11 June 1981), 11; (10 Jan. 1983), 9.

[137] Hakim, 'Myth', 107. [138] Stocks, 'Where do we Go', 49.

[139] 'Alan Boon', *T* (9 Aug. 2000), 19.

The Labour government established the Equal Opportunities Commission in 1975 to implement the Sex Discrimination Act of that year, and to prevent discrimination, especially on sexual or marital grounds, but Enoch Powell opposed its establishment on principle. Condemning the current 'fashionable but foolish craze', the 'mania . . . in legislation for attacking discrimination, oblivious that all life is about discrimination, because all life is about differences', he thought any bureaucratic machine which even attempted to counteract 'life' would be intrusive and would ultimately fail. His predictions proved incorrect only because the Manchester-based Commission's aims were modest and its methods not seriously intrusive. It was not dominated by feminists, nor did it crusade: it preferred to operate behind the scenes, and specialized in legal cases; many feminists thought it too timid.[140]

It was still widely believed in 1980 that where jobs were scarce, married women should be discouraged from working—a view taken by 28 per cent of the women and 34 per cent of the men polled.[141] Furthermore, the domestic separation of spheres persisted, with men more likely than women to undertake household repairs, and (though moving into more shopping and cooking) spending much less time on household tasks. In 1983 a tenth of working wives still did not know their husband's income.[142] Diaries of how time was spent in 1961 and in summer 1983 illuminate how home-bound women still were, how continuous throughout weekdays and weekends their housework tasks remained, and how gardening and do-it-yourself occupied the male sphere.[143] Male superiority in 'physical force' had always been central to the anti-feminist case, and it remained salient in diverse areas. Husbands in 1980 were on average five and a quarter inches taller than their wives, and even in reported statistics, obscene telephone calls from men to women increased in England, Scotland and Wales from about 80,000 to 180,000 between 1971 and 1980—deterring women from identifying themselves as such in telephone directories.[144] Accident statistics revealed men as still relatively adventurous: in 1980, for instance, they took more risks when crossing the road.[145] Throughout the twentieth century in northern industrial towns the working-class recreational worlds of men and women were distinct, with the sporting hero and his mates exemplifying

---

[140] Powell, *HC Deb.* 26 Mar. 1975, c. 544. For the Commission see *G* (7 Dec. 1983), 12 (Frances Cairncross). Letter to *T* (15 Aug. 1984), 11. K. Whitehorn, 'The Watchdog that Lost her Bark', *O* (17 Nov. 1985), 57.

[141] *NS* (7 Nov. 1980), 11, MORI survey (Aug.–Sept.) of 1,041 working men and women aged 18 and over throughout Great Britain.

[142] *Social Trends* (1995), 32–3. Poll of 1000+ over 16, *T* (18 May 1983), 2.

[143] BBC Audience Research Dept., *The People's Activities* (1965), 1.5, 1.7, 1.24, 1.25. BBC Broadcasting Research Dept., *Daily Life in the 1980s* (1984), ii. 115–23, 232–7, 346–51.

[144] I. Knight, *The Heights and Weights of Adults in Great Britain: Report of a Survey Carried Out on Behalf of the Department of Health and Social Security Covering Adults aged 16–64* (1984), 7. Obscene calls, *T* (21 Dec. 1983), 11.   [145] Todd and Walker, *People as Pedestrians*, 67.

allegations of female unreason. Wielding an inexplicable power, she seemed able to intimidate the prime minister; indeed, from her subordinate post she had no other leverage against him. According to Haines, 'even on the most mundane level, humiliation of him was her constant aim'.[157] Widespread gossip assumed in the 1960s that she added a second among women's traditional roles to her first, but it emerged in 1974 that the father of her two children was not Wilson but the journalist Walter Terry.[158]

What, then, did organized feminism contribute to British women's late twentieth-century advance? In its third phase up to the mid-1960s it had lost impetus.[159] That phase's final achievement had been to guide the politicians in sounding out women's opinion. Heath set up the Women's Consultative Council in 1962 to spread information about the EEC, and out of that grew the Women's National Commission, created in response to the Wilson government's need for a forum to coordinate the pressures, not necessarily feminist, on women's issues.[160] The impulse for fourth-phase feminism came from the USA, with an agenda more strident in tone and less reticent in content than British feminism had been in its three earlier phases. Moving much more boldly into the sexual sphere, American feminism played down women's physique as hindering their emancipation, and dwelt instead on acquired cultural hindrances, substituting the word 'gender' for 'sex'. It was not till the late 1960s that the new impetus was felt in Britain even by the public, let alone by governments. Not till March 1970 did Caroline Benn read what for her husband was 'a book called *The Feminine Mystique* about the Women's Liberation movement which is beginning to develop strongly in the States and even in Britain'. Even within that progressive household Betty Friedan's influence lay primarily through the wife's traditionally indirect route: through her husband, who in this instance had great confidence in her judgement, and consistently discussed things with her.[161]

Even sympathetic British opinion was puzzled by American feminist priorities, and Castle in her robustly common-sensical way declared that if she had fussed about replacing 'Mrs' and 'Miss' with 'Ms', she would 'never have worked up to the good neuter title of Minister'.[162] The first national demonstration by women's liberation did not occur till 1971, when about 2,500 women—in a procession reminiscent of CND's Aldermaston marches—walked from Speaker's Corner to Trafalgar Square.[163] Stocks in 1973 urged her successors to 'avoid joining in processions and demonstrations which include anarchists, Maoists, Trotskyites, gay people, student bodies, strikers and other such irrelevant groups, which do no good to their "image"'. Politically less shrewd

[157] Quotations from Haines, *Glimmers of Twilight*, 12, 142.   [158] Pimlott, *Wilson*, 522–3.
[159] Harrison, *Seeking a Role*, 31.
[160] Castle, *Diaries 1974–6*, 141 n. 1 (10 July 1974). *T* (22 July 1969), 3.
[161] Benn, *Diaries 1968–72*, 257 (29 Mar. 1970); cf. *Diaries 1980–90*, 177 (6 Dec. 1981).
[162] *T* (16 Feb. 1972), 8.   [163] *O* (7 Mar. 1971), 1.

than their predecessors, fourth-phase British feminists could not even hold together in a national movement. 'There was no "movement" ', Polly Toynbee recalled. 'There were some dazzling feminist stars . . . There were slogans and myths . . . There was precious little unity. There were, to be honest, precious few women involved at all', and 'that "great movement" of ours was a small, eccentric, fissiparous group of warring tribes'.[164]

It was not British fourth-phase feminism that produced the major emancipation involved in the growth of jobs for married women after 1945: that had begun when British feminism (in its third phase) was at its weakest. Besides, British feminism in its first three phases, to the extent that it was concerned with jobs at all, had focused primarily on the needs of single women. Its first concern had in effect been to pare down women's major attraction to employers by promoting equal pay, equal terms of employment, and equal promotion prospects. Wider opportunities for women's paid work in the 1950s owed everything to collectively commercial and individually domesticated motives. The driving force lay in the combination of a tight post-war labour market whose industrial growth was powered by new technologies with little need for heavy labour, and with much need for a weakly unionized workforce flexible on hours and pay.[165] The Sex Discrimination Act (1975) applied in England, Wales, and Scotland, and prohibited sex discrimination against individuals of either sex and of any age in employment, education, and trade; it also forbade discrimination in employment against married people. But by then the major changes in women's employment had already occurred, and had been enhanced by an ongoing separation of domestic roles which ensured for the economy's growing areas a labour-force as flexible as was required.[166]

British feminists after the 1960s understandably focused on mobilizing women, and showed little interest in the roots of male anti-feminism, which they did little to subvert; indeed, its prevalence seemed conveniently to validate the feminist position. For some feminists, women's liberation had 'delivered the aspirations without delivering the goods', for despite the success of networking, women at work had progressed only slowly towards equal pay, and often found themselves pursuing two roles in place of one.[167] Yet this was too gloomy a view. Menstruation and the menopause were still rarely discussed in public, and were not prominent in the medical literature,[168] but after 1970 they were diminishingly seen as disabling. Women's entry into so many new occupations, not least into that of prime minister, and their growing sporting prowess, at

[164] Stocks, 'Where do we Go', 49. Toynbee, G (6 June 2002), ii, 8.
[165] E. J. Mishan, 'Was the Women's Liberation Movement Really Necessary?', Encounter (Jan. 1985), 9, 19.   [166] See the interesting article 'Restaurants and Radiology', Econ (26 July 1975), 27.
[167] Polly Toynbee, G (11 Aug. 1988), 16.
[168] S. M. and J. B. McKinlay, 'Selected Studies of the Menopause', Journal of Biosocial Science, 5 (1973), 534; cf. K. Dalton, The Menstrual Cycle (1969), 11 (menstruation).

least got these contrasts with men into proportion. Late twentieth-century women world-wide were breaking new frontiers even in sporting achievement. Women's records in endurance sports, for instance—marathon, cycling, and swimming—were steadily approaching the men's. By the early 1980s women were overtaking men in long-distance swimming; women held the non-stop record for English Channel swims in either direction, and had achieved eight of the ten fastest swims.[169] Here as elsewhere, women had moved into a virtuous cycle whereby greater self-confidence prompted greater achievement, which advanced self-confidence still further. If fourth-phase British feminism could not claim credit for women's progress in all its dimensions after 1970, and may sometimes have hindered it, such progress owed much to British feminism's three earlier phases, and was substantial: fewer women trapped in loveless marriages, fuller control over fertility and therefore better health, more chance of sexual fulfilment, much wider choice in lifestyle and career, and much more freedom of movement.

Such gains did not come without losses. Society adjusted only slowly to the quietly gradual disappearance of the leisured woman: her many lubricating social and family roles had often gone unacknowledged in the past because unobtrusive and unpaid, yet her absence was soon felt. There were losses even for women themselves, especially as family and welfare structures adapted so slowly to rapid social change. These included the stresses arising from women's enhanced freedom of choice. Lynne Reid Banks, so enthusiastic in *The L-Shaped Room* for the freedom of lone parenthood, later had three sons of her own; in 1984 she recalled that she had begun 'to realize unromantically what bringing up children was all about', and claimed that any woman who embarks on single motherhood deliberately 'must be mad'.[170] In the 1980s women were still travelling far less than men, especially from their twenties onwards, and when driving were still far more likely to be a passenger, but they were driving much more than in the past, and so their share of total road accidents rose.[171] Women's accelerating late twentieth-century emergence from the private sphere may also explain their narrowing advantage over men in life expectancy. Already by the 1970s teenage girls were likely to smoke as heavily as boys, and late twentieth-century women drank more and were more subject to stress.[172] The number of women in prison began rising fast in the early 1990s,

---

[169] E. Cashmore, 'Women's Greatest Handicaps: Sex, Medicine and Men', *British Journal of Sports Medicine*, 33/2 (Apr. 1999), 76. K. F. Dyer, *Catching up the Men: Women in Sport* (1982), 168.

[170] Interview in *T* (13 Aug. 1984), 7; cf. Harrison, *Seeking a Role*, 247.

[171] *TCBST* 457–8. P. E. H. Hair, 'Deaths from Violence in Britain: A Tentative Secular Survey', *Population Studies* (Mar. 1971), 9. Office of Population Censuses and Surveys, *Trends in Mortality 1951–1975* (1978), 31.

[172] For smoking, 'The Life and Death of Ms Solomon Grundy', *Econ* (4 Jan. 1975), 60–1. *T* (29 July 1981), 3. For drinking, *T* (23 June 2003), 3.

though it remained far below that of men, and drug-related offences were far more frequently the cause.[173] Still, in 1990 as in 1951, the experiences of men and women remained very different, as Jan Morris was specially qualified to know: 'we are told that the social gap between the sexes is narrowing', she wrote: 'but I can only report that having, in the second half of the 20th century, experienced life in both roles, there seems to me no aspect of existence, no moment of the day, no contact, no arrangement, no response, which is not different for men and for women'.[174]

3. A BETTER LIFE FOR THE YOUNG?

How far were the adults, in these major changes, pursuing self-fulfilment at the expense of their children? Birth control's advance ensured that in Britain there were proportionately fewer of them: 24 per cent of the UK population were under 15 in 1971, but only 19 per cent in 1994, as compared with a third in the world as a whole. There were proportionately more children, though, among Britain's ethnic minorities; children in 1994 made up (for example) half Britain's Bangladeshi immigrant population.[175] More British women were postponing childbirth or not having children at all: about a quarter of women born in 1961 had borne no child by age 35.[176] The decision to be childless had by 2000 become so widely accepted that there was an outcry in that year when the Bishop of Rochester pronounced the deliberately childless 'self-indulgent and incomplete'. For the many adults who were involuntarily childless, infertility treatment was gradually improving; by 2002 in vitro fertilization (IVF) had produced more than 68,000 British babies, and about a million in the world as a whole. More than half the world's IVF treatments were by then being conducted in France, Germany, and Britain, with an average success-rate above one in five.[177]

The humane approach to children cultivated in schools by inter-war psychologists and educationists, influential in the 1950s, now went further.[178] Parents' growing control over fertility ensured that their children were more likely to have been wanted. Their number and the timing of their arrival, but not their sex, had become more predictable—though in the 1980s postponing childbirth combined with IVF treatment to generate a sharp and unintended rise in the small number of multiple births.[179] Childhood, instead of being seen as a mere stage on the road to adulthood, was increasingly prized for its own sake, as

---

[173] *T* (26 Nov. 2001), 4.   [174] Morris, *Conundrum* (2002 edn.), 130; see also 132, 134.

[175] Botting, 'Review of Children', 25. Modood and Berthoud (eds.), *Diversity and Disadvantage*, 20, defining 'child' as 15 and below.   [176] *TCBST* 45.

[177] For the Bishop see *STel* (12 Mar. 2000), 38 (leader). For IVF see *Ind* (22 Oct. 2002), 6. *DT* (28 June 2000), 13.   [178] Harrison, *Seeking a Role*, 51–2, 350.

[179] For statistics see A. Macfarlane, B. Botting, and F. Price, 'The Study of Triplet and Higher Order Births', *Population Trends*, 62 (Winter 1990), 26.

an experience to be relished and shared with adults, who now took a much more serious interest in children's literature—though Roald Dahl's success as a writer for children owed much to his siding with them against the adults. Yet in some ways the child's situation worsened after 1970: mothers in paid work were often absent at key moments, and social institutions adjusted only painfully to the spread of divorce and extramarital childbirth. It was concern for the children that helped draw Thatcher into the minority who voted in 1968 against making the 'irretrievable breakdown' of a marriage a ground for divorce.[180] By the early 1990s three times as many children were living in one-parent families than twenty years before. 'Social' as distinct from 'biological' parenting was becoming more common: already by 2004 17 per cent of men born in 1970 had become stepfathers, double the percentage among men born in 1958.[181] If the divorced parent formed a new relationship, older offspring were not necessarily happy, or even welcome, within the new grouping. Not only did the child need to acclimatize itself to new parents: it must also adjust to step-siblings or half-siblings. By 2001 one in five children in step-families were leaving home after failing to cope with the new relationship; by age 16, one in nine young people had left home from all types of family.[182]

The subcategories of childhood which had been evolving at mid-century[183] were consolidated further after 1970. The early twentieth-century emphasis on the need for better baby-care had by the 1980s helped render a child's death from disease an unusual tragedy. Perinatal mortality in England and Wales continued to fall: from 28.2 per thousand live births in 1964 to 8.6 in 1996. The pre-school child was growing healthier: in 1900 a quarter of all deaths in the UK population occurred in the first year of life, falling to 1 per cent in the 1990s.[184] Improved diet and sanitation, reinforced by immunization, ensured that fewer late twentieth-century children caught infectious diseases, which antibiotics from the 1940s anyway rendered less dangerous. Immunization of children against diphtheria, whooping cough, polio, tetanus, measles, mumps, and scarlet fever continued apace in the 1970s and 1980s;[185] in 1978 for the first time on record there were no notifications of diphtheria, and in 1988 no deaths from whooping cough.[186] The apparent late twentieth-century spread of autism and dyslexia was an illusion stemming from more widely recognizing and more broadly applying the terms for these conditions; by 1991 there

---

[180] Thatcher, *Path to Power*, 151.

[181] Botting, 'Review of Children', 25. I. Stewart and R. Vaitilingham (eds.), *The Seven Ages of Man and Woman: A Look at Life in Britain in the Second Elizabethan Era* (Swindon, 2004), 22.

[182] *T* (23 Mar. 2001), 17.   [183] Harrison, *Seeking a Role*, 256–63.

[184] C. Webster, *The National Health Service: A Political History* (Oxford, 1998), 136. *TCBST* 98.

[185] *Social Trends* (1995), 124. Doubts about the whooping-cough vaccine, however, prompted a marked decline in vaccination's take-up for this and other diseases in the 1970s; see C. Webster, *The Health Services since the War*, ii. *Government and Health Care. The National Health Service 1958–1979* (1996), 680.   [186] Coleman and Salt, *British Population*, 246.

were more than eighty local associations mobilized in the British Dyslexia Association.[187]

Pre-school children were spending more time away from their parents, fewer now thought the mother should stay at home, family allowances were now in effect marginalized,[188] and even Thatcher did not seek to reverse the trend. Nor did she favour conceding to working mothers tax relief which would offset the extra cost of caring for their children: the family's double income should suffice, she thought, and single-income families should not be required to supplement it.[189] By European standards, Britain did little to promote state nursery schools; so in the care of the pre-school child more than anywhere, self-help became central to British women's networks after 1970, and huge efforts were made. A survey of 1984 showed that among those who cared for the child when the mother went to work, grandmothers accounted for 34 per cent of the cases, and were surpassed only by the father with 47 per cent. By 1982 parents were organizing playgroups for 500,000 children in England and Wales;[190] in the UK between 1970 and 1990 the number of day-care places for the under-5s more than doubled, and the number in nursery schools almost doubled.[191] Between 1981 and 1991 the number of places with registered childminders more than doubled, so that by 1991 nearly two-thirds of UK families with children under 5 used some form of child-care away from home: nursery schools, unpaid family or friends, voluntary or local authority facilities, or paid childminders.[192]

'Childhood' filled the long stretch from the start of schooling (usually at 5) into teenage, and populism rather than any substantive change inspired the growing tendency after 1970 for children to be designated as 'kids'. The death-rates for children under 9 declined markedly in the 1970s and 1980s,[193] yet the longer-term nutritional trend was ominous. From 1971 local authorities were no longer required to provide milk for children older than 7; the schools health service staff in England and Wales declined by more than a fifth between 1974 and 1986;[194] and during the 1970s state schools retreated from promoting nutritional education through school meals. The proportion of children aged 5 to 14 who consumed school meals in the maintained and local authority schools of England and Wales rose from a half to two-thirds between 1950 and 1970, but the take-up declined thereafter. Local authorities tried to reverse the trend by introducing multi-choice menus, but by 1979 school meals were being

---

[187] *DT* (6 Sept. 2002), 11 (autism). A. M. Scott, *1966–1991: An Account of Events and Achievements during the Twenty Five Years since the Foundation of the first Local Dyslexia Association* (n.pl., n.d.), 17.

[188] Harrison, *Seeking a Role*, 250.

[189] Thatcher, *Downing Street Years*, 630–1; cf. *Ind* (23 Nov. 1990), 6.

[190] *T* (31 May 1984), 3. B. Crowe, *The Playgroup Movement* (1st publ. 1973, 4th edn. Hemel Hempstead, 1983), 79.   [191] *Social Trends* (1995), 46. *TCBST* 192–3.

[192] *Social Trends* (1995), 46. Botting, 'Review of Children', 27.

[193] For statistics see Botting 'Review of Children', 28.

[194] B. Harris, *The Health of the Schoolchild* (Buckingham, 1995), 215.

eaten by fewer than half the pupils in England and Wales. In the following year nutritional standards for meals were abandoned, with menus left to local authority discretion; thenceforward both the numbers taking school meals, and the meals' share of educational expenditure, fell sharply. In 1992/3 the diet of 4-year-olds—with worse bread, fewer vegetables, and more sugar—was less nutritious than in 1950.[195]

Adults found it difficult to monitor children's media recreations, if only because of peer-group pressure, the widening choice of programmes, time-shifting, and the presence of more television sets within the home. Children's programmes proliferated greatly from the 1950s to the 1990s in absolute terms, though not in their overall share of television output, and by the 1970s they were spreading beyond their earlier afternoon location. Saturday morning children's television began in the 1970s; it accounted for a fifth of overall children's output in 1976, for more than a third in 1996, and with a similar growth in children's Sunday morning programmes in the 1980s and 1990s. The nine-o'clock watershed was gradually introduced in the 1960s, after which time the seriously adult programmes became more accessible,[196] but in 1978 BBC1 launched its series *Grange Hill*, based on the realistic portrayal of an East London comprehensive school. The programme was stranded between children who thought it too tame and parents who thought it too tough. Among the latter was Princess Anne, who banned her daughters from watching it, and wondered aloud in 1999 'why on Earth such a programme should be on television, particularly on that station'.[197] As with all new media, commentators worried about television's underlying impact: did its inherent lack of reticence undermine age-related intellectual and other hierarchies? Did its instant accessibility foster passivity, thereby subverting literacy and the steadily cumulative learning process essential to growing up? Was it drawing adults and children together by infantilizing the adult and destroying childhood?[198] Her religious impulse, her populism, and her narrowly moralistic concerns deterred Britain's most vigorous critic of the media, Mary Whitehouse, like Reith before her, from venturing far into these important questions.

Progressive views in Britain combined in the 1960s with the influence of the American civil-rights movement to promote the idea of children's rights (Plate 13), and to prise apart and weaken the community's mutually supportive disciplinary structures (police, teachers, neighbours) which had once informally

---

[195] *BST* 486. *TCBST* 204, 535. C. J. Prynne *et al.*, 'Food and Nutrient Intake of a National Sample of Four-Year-Old Children in 1950: Comparison with the 1990s', *Public Health Nutrition* (Dec. 1999), 537–47.
[196] D. Buckingham, H. Davies, K. Jones, and P. Kelley *et al.*, *Children's Television in Britain: History, Discourse and Policy* (1999), 92–5. For the 'watershed' ibid. 152.   [197] *T* (24 Apr. 1999), 21.
[198] Arguments proffered in an American context by N. Postman, *The Disappearance of Childhood* (1st publ. 1983, paperback edn. 1985), 74, 80, 82–4, 88, 101–2.

helped parents to monitor their children.[199] On disciplinary issues, parents were in a serious dilemma. The dangers—from drugs, traffic accidents, sexual disease, and violence—seemed greater than ever before. So parents needed to supervise their children more closely, especially by regulating television programmes watched, hours kept, places visited, company kept. The average distance from home where children played shrank from 840 metres in 1970 to 280 by 1997, and the percentage of children aged 7 and 8 who travelled to school without adult supervision fell from 80 to 10 per cent between 1970 and 1990. No doubt such restraints help to explain the massive decline in traffic accidents to child pedestrians between 1971 and 2005.[200] Yet to keep the child continuously supervised was to risk its social isolation and even to incur the child's ultimate sanctions of suicide or running away. By 1976 the problem of runaways from the provinces to London had become serious enough to inspire the television programme *Johnny Go Home*. Social workers worried about teenagers attracted to the amusement arcades near London's Piccadilly, and then recouping their funds through prostitution. Several charities sprang up to cater for children's anxieties, most notably Childline, founded in 1986, which fielded 200,000 calls in its first year.[201]

The balance of the law's priorities was shifting away from children's abuse of adults (through juvenile delinquency) towards adults' abuse of children (through physical and sexual abuse). The Children Act (1975) no longer assumed that the interests of child and parent coincided, viewed the child's welfare as paramount, and provided for its separate representation in court hearings. Emphasis on personal responsibility was reviving: in explaining child cruelty, the adult's personal defects received growing emphasis by comparison with the social conditions earlier stressed. The American paediatricians who developed the idea of the 'battered baby syndrome' from the 1940s claimed that adult cruelty to children could begin early, and concern about it reached Britain through the medical press in 1963. The National Society for the Prevention of Cruelty to Children took up the syndrome idea, which was advertised in 1973 by the notorious case of 6-year-old Maria Colwell, killed by her stepfather. Figures from London and Oxford—in 1973 and 1975, respectively—showed that a seventh of children seen in routine hospital medical practice were victims of non-accidental injury or abuse, with children under 2 especially vulnerable.[202] Prior warnings failed to protect Maria,[203] and the issue was kept alive by the

---

[199] *T* (9 Apr. 1976), 3. See also Harrison, *Seeking a Role*, 34, 263.

[200] *T* (4 Aug. 2007), 7. *G* (6 Feb. 2001), 6 (travel to school). *T* (4 Aug. 2007), 7 (accidents).

[201] *T* (5 Aug. 2000), 4.

[202] Select Committee on Violence in the Family, *Violence to Children: First Report* (1977), p. viii; cf. its *Evidence*, 161.

[203] *British Medical Journal* (21 Dec. 1963), 1558–61. For a helpful overview see N. Parton, *The Politics of Child Abuse* (Basingstoke and London, 1985), 49–53.

death in 1984 of 4-year-old Jasmine Beckford from starvation and violence at her stepfather's hands. By then the phrase 'child abuse' was being more widely used in the UK to denote physical, psychological, and sexual cruelty.[204]

Parents' retreat from the disciplinary beating of children was an international movement, with Britain by no means in the forefront.[205] Two-thirds of Nottingham mothers surveyed in 1985 smacked their one-year-old children when necessary, and were more likely to do so the lower their social location. In all social classes smacking became more common at age 4, when only a quarter of the parents sampled were smacking less often than once a week. This punishment tailed off as their children grew older, and was less frequent with girls than with boys; still, a fifth of 7-year-olds were being struck by their mother with an implement.[206] The film *If . . .*, with its beating scene, was made in the year that the Society of Teachers Opposed to Physical Punishment (STOPP) was founded. Single-minded and practical in strategy, factual and shrewdly diplomatic in tactics, skilful with the media and run throughout by parents and teachers, STOPP worked fruitfully with the grain of European opinion. Once Britain had joined the EEC, STOPP found the going easier, and the European Court of Human Rights forced the government's hand by ruling in 1982 that a parental objection to beating must be respected. While teachers in inner-city state schools worried at first about losing a weapon against teenage pupils, 'many of them daunting in stature',[207] reformers tended abstractly and idealistically to deploy many of the arguments that had earlier ended hanging. Corporal punishment, which STOPP renamed 'child beating', soured the school's atmosphere, they claimed, and teachers using the cane would gain respect neither for themselves nor for study. STOPP claimed advisedly in 1981 that 'a quarter of a million beatings' occurred annually in England alone, with a beating in England and Wales 'once every nineteen seconds' in 1983. In 1986 on a free vote, parliament banned corporal punishment from state schools, with the ban supported by some Conservatives and by even more from the other parties.[208]

Attention was already moving on in the 1980s to an escalating and at times simplistic concern with the adult sexual abuse of children—a concern which continued well into the next century. To judge from a poll in 1984, this was no small problem: one in ten adults claimed to have been sexually abused as children, four-fifths within their own family. Given Kinsey's documented

---

[204] *A Child in Trust: The Report of the Panel of Inquiry into the Circumstances Surrounding the Death of Jasmine Beckford* (London Borough of Brent, 1985), 20.

[205] For a useful chronology see P. Newell, *Children are People Too: The Case against Physical Punishment* (1989), 131–40.

[206] J. and E. Newson, *The Extent of Parental Physical Punishment in the UK* (1989), 1, 4, 5, 9, 10, 14; the Nottingham sample of 1985 was based on interviews concerning 700 children.

[207] I. G. H. Walker, letter in *NS* (6 Dec. 1968), 788.

[208] Newell, *Children are People Too*, 119. For a good discussion of how the reform came about see *Ind* (24 Nov. 1988), 21; *G* (4 Nov. 1986), 15.

emphasis on childhood sexuality,[209] the escalating eagerness to demonize the adult abuser was surprising. When overzealous paediatricians in 1987 brought accusations against hundreds of Cleveland families, most of which were later proved false, the escalation ceased, providing a salutary warning against deferring unduly to the professions. Much more serious were the revelations from the mid-1980s about the nightmarish sexual abuse by adults within some public institutions, sometimes over many years.[210] The fate of Alison Taylor, ultimately vindicated in exposing paedophile rings at Welsh children's homes, illustrated the courage and persistence whistleblowing often requires.[211] It was sometimes essential to take children into care—the 6,510 children in England and Wales whose parents were officially homeless or living in poor housing conditions in 1971/2, for example—but the abuses subsequently exposed in care homes reinforced the grounds for abandoning institutionalization. In the late 1970s more than 90,000 children were in care, but only 50,000 by 1996. Fewer than a fifth even of those were by then institutionalized; the rest were in foster homes.[212]

Childhood was commercialized earlier in the USA than in Britain, but in both societies its effect was to push the market for toys to ever younger age-groups while promoting precociously adult teenage tastes. The post-war revival in the British toy industry proved short-lived, and in the 1950s encountered the relative decline, familiar elsewhere, when confronted by foreign competition. American toy retailing was more aggressive than British, and with every store of 'Toys R Us' opened in the 1980s, eight independent toyshops closed; the firm had been founded in Washington in 1948, and by 1991 had thirty-three British outlets.[213] Teenagers from the 1980s were exposed increasingly to computerized Japanese video games. Teenage was the peak time for crime in both sexes, and boys' relatively high crime rate[214] reflected the adventurousness which also shaped accident patterns. By the 1970s, however, war-related and uniformed recreation for children was out of fashion, and the semi-religious civic culture which had infused the scouts, the brigades, and the youth clubs, together with the volunteers who ran such organizations, was threatened by 'Saturday jobs', secularization, the growing attractions of home-based recreation, and the advance of women's careers. As one Brownie leader put it, discussing the shortage of volunteers in 1995, 'you kind of rock from one crisis to another'.[215] Segregation of the sexes, too, was falling out of fashion, and a more knowing

---

[209] MORI poll, cited in *T* (20 Oct. 1986), 17. See also P. Robinson, *The Modernization of Sex: Havelock Ellis, Alfred Kinsey, William Masters and Virginia Johnson* (1976), 88, 92.

[210] *G* (22 Mar. 1986), 1.

[211] See S. Laville, 'I Had the Proof But they Wouldn't Listen', *DT* (16 Feb. 2000), 5; cf. *T* (16 Feb. 2000), 6.   [212] *HL Deb.* 21 Mar. 1973, c. 816. *FT* (15 June 1996), 6.

[213] K. D. Brown, *The British Toy Business: A History since 1700* (1996), 152–3, 161, 169, 227.

[214] 'Ms Solomon Grundy', *Econ* (4 Jan. 1975), 60–1.

[215] Elaine Ellis, quoted in *DT* (16 Oct. 1995), 7.

generation was anyhow wary of single-sex structures, yet to integrate teenage children of both sexes in adventurous exploits was problematic indeed.

The ethos of youth organizations involved bridging the gap between the generations while teenage culture was drawing them apart. Hence the phrase 'boy scout' was being used by some as a term of mild insult. 'It sounds like a Boy Scout code', was Austin Mitchell's response when Callaghan explained how he expected ministers to handle civil servants: 'what is wrong with the Boy Scouts?' was the rejoinder.[216] Youth organizations' rapid growth-rate in the first half of the twentieth century was not maintained thereafter. UK membership of the Combined Cadet Force and the Boys' Brigade declined from a shared peak in 1960, but the former stalled at a much lower plateau for the rest of the century, whereas the latter went into continuous and sharp decline. Youth-club membership and Girl Guides declined from their shared peak in 1980. The Boy Scouts showed some resilience, renaming the Wolf Cubs 'Cub Scouts' in 1966 for boys under 11, and in 1982 carving out from them the new category of 'Beaver Scout' for boys aged 6 to 8; nonetheless, the movement's membership declined after reaching a peak in 1990.[217] The Prince of Wales shared his father's belief in the adventurous outlet for adolescents who, as he told the House of Lords in 1975, 'have excess energy to spare and need adventure, excitement and a challenge of one sort or another'. The Outward Bound movement revived in the 1980s partly as a result of the Duke of Edinburgh's award scheme, which by 1990 was making 40,000 awards a year;[218] by 1999 nearly three million young people had participated in the scheme.[219]

Several factors now blurred what had earlier seemed a clear frontier between adolescence and adulthood. Adolescents were physically maturing earlier: by the 1970s males were reaching their maximum height at between 17 and 18, as compared with about 26 half a century before. For girls the average age at menstruation fell by eight months between 1969 and 2000, and by the late 1990s a tenth were menstruating while at primary school.[220] A further problem for youth organizations was growing competition from paid part-time work for adolescents, which enhanced their independence from parents and provided a bridge from teenage to adulthood. There were growing efforts after 1970 to link education and employment through 'work experience' schemes, vacation jobs for university students, and 'Saturday jobs' for teenagers. The minimum age for working part-time out of school hours was not raised concomitantly with rises in the school-leaving age, and in 1970 about one in four 13-year-olds took

[216] Quoted in Hennessy, *Whitehall*, 491.   [217] *TCBST* 612–13.
[218] *HL Deb.* 25 June 1975, c. 1419. Table 17.20 in *TCBST* 613. Mr Ian Lawson of Forres provided most generous help on this subject.
[219] Duke of Edinburgh's Award, Fact Sheet, *General Information* (1999).
[220] W. A. Marshall and J. M. Tanner, 'Puberty', in A. J. Davis and J. Dobbing (eds.), *Scientific Foundations of Paediatrics* (1974), 146. Menstruation *T* (19 June 2000), 3. *T* (15 June 1999), 12.

regular paid jobs; by 1991 students and teenagers held a tenth of all part-time jobs.[221] The integration of education with work through apprenticeship schemes attracted 39 per cent of male and 8 per cent of female school-leavers in the mid-1970s, but accounted for only 4 per cent of all employees in 1981, and was most prevalent in the engineering, timber, and furniture trades.[222]

After the 1960s governments grew more interested in training young people for work, initially to relieve shortages of skilled workers, but later to tackle youth unemployment. The state coordinated its increasingly professionalized efforts with employers in an all-party strategy which boosted the number of qualified training officers from 1,532 in 1965 to 3,148 in 1978.[223] Youth training was the MSC's main role, and with 22,500 employees by November 1977 the Commission's boundaries with the education and labour ministries were becoming controversial.[224] This was an area of state activity which even Thatcher favoured, if only to demonstrate her governments' concern about rapidly mounting unemployment in the early 1980s among this vulnerable group. The combination of the baby boom of the early 1960s and the depression of the early 1980s ensured that by then many of the unemployed were young, especially as the post-war narrowing of age-differentials in pay had denied the young their major asset of cheapness within the labour market. During the 1970s young people's proportion of the unemployed was rising fast in Belgium, Germany, France, and Italy as well as in Britain. In summer 1985 unemployment for 16- and 17-year-olds in Britain was running at 24 per cent, and at 26 per cent for 18- and 19-year-olds, but at only 9 per cent for adults between 35 and 55.[225] The Youth Opportunities Programme (YOP), launched in 1978, brought together work experience, training, and employment subsidy programmes, and in 1983 was integrated with the YTS. Influenced by German precedents, the Scheme began in 1981 as a one-year programme for school-leavers which combined work experience with further education; and by 1983 the government was guaranteeing, for each 16-year-old not in full-time work or education, a place on a programme of training and work experience for one year, extended in 1985 to two. By 1986 nearly a third of all school-leavers were joining a YTS scheme.[226] To some extent YTS replaced apprenticeships, whose take-up continued to decline in the early 1980s despite rising youth unemployment, and in 1988 the MSC was reabsorbed into the Department of Employment.

[221] *HL Deb.* 4 May 1972, c. 883. Hakim, 'Myth', 112.
[222] *Econ* (19 Apr. 1975), 76. P. G. Chapman and M. J. Tooze, *The Youth Training Scheme in the United Kingdom* (Aldershot, 1987), 93–4, 96–7.   [223] Ibid. 30.
[224] D. Hencke, 'The Rise and Rise of the Government's Job Machine', *G* (7 Nov. 1977), 23. For the Commission's later evolution see *FT* (23 Apr. 1987), 11; *THES* (8 July 1988), 8–9.
[225] Table in *T* (17 May 1977), 5. M. Prowse, 'The High Tide of Unemployment', *FT* (17 July 1985), 22.
[226] C. Wallace and M. Cross, 'Introduction', in Wallace and Cross (eds.), *Youth in Transition: The Sociology of Youth and Youth Policy* (1990), 4.

There was much concern in the 1980s about the plight of the young unemployed and unskilled male in a society which needed to tilt the workforce away from manual labour and towards the educated employee, but labour direction was impossible in a free society. For adults this had seemed justified only in wartime emergency, and the Attlee government had quickly abandoned it under trade union pressure. The Thatcher government's caution even with unemployed teenagers emerged from the very tentative ideas floated by Prior as Secretary of State for Employment in July 1980 for encouraging them into voluntary social work. There were immediate trade union protests against 'conscription', Prior had publicly to deny that he intended to require work in exchange for benefit, and the Prince of Wales failed to persuade politicians to take up the idea of compulsory community service.[227] Still, it was slowly becoming politically more feasible for governments of both parties to press the unemployed to take work, trying out on teenagers strategies later applied to adults. In a parliamentary confrontation with Callaghan in 1980, Thatcher infuriated Labour by saying that unemployed young people in Wales should consider moving towards work rather than expecting the work to come to them.[228] Between 1980 and 1993 there followed a sequence of cuts in benefits for students on vacation and for the young unemployed, especially for those who refused job offers.[229] In December 1984 Lord Young, soon to be Secretary of State for Employment, publicly cited Beveridge to the effect that 'for boys and girls there should ideally be no unconditional benefit at all; their enforced abstention from work should be made an occasion of further training'. Thatcher echoed him in the same month: 'young people ought not to be idle. It is very bad for them. It starts them off wrong.' In its manifesto of 1987 her party promised to withdraw benefits from those under 18 who chose to remain unemployed.[230] From April 1988 unemployed teenagers between 16 and 18 were denied entitlement to benefits and income support, and were removed from the unemployment register.

Adolescence was not clearly demarcated from adulthood in law or legislation. As at 1983, young people could be convicted of a criminal offence at 10, be deemed capable of sexual relationships at 14 (if male) and at 16 (if female), and leave school at 16, but not buy an alcoholic drink, vote, or engage in armed combat till aged 18.[231] Other anomalies included regional discrepancies: legislation in 1963, for example, raised the age of criminal responsibility to 10 in England, Wales, and Northern Ireland, but left it at 8 in Scotland. Such

[227] Prior, *T* (10 July 1980), 2. Dimbleby, *Prince of Wales*, 371–2.

[228] *HC Deb.* 24 July 1980, cc. 762–3.

[229] These measures are conveniently listed in K. Roberts, *Youth and Employment in Modern Britain* (Oxford, 1995), 16. See also *T* (2 Sept. 1983), 9. Tebbit, *Upwardly Mobile*, 189, 191.

[230] *Social Insurance and Allied Services: Report by Sir William Beveridge* (Cmd. 6404; 1942), 58. Young quotes Beveridge in *T* (5 Dec. 1984), 12; cf. (6 Dec. 1984), 17 (leader). For Thatcher, *T* (18 Dec. 1984), 2 (BBC interview, 17 Dec. 1984). See also Dale (ed.), *Conservative Manifestos*, 328.

[231] M. D. A. Freeman, *The Rights and Wrongs of Children* (1983), 7.

discrepancies undermined respect for the law, and enhanced the attractions of winning peer-group status by breaching it. The coincidence between marriage and leaving home was probably closest in the 1960s, when people were marrying younger and housing was less scarce, but thereafter the years of education extended, cohabitation spread, and housing costs rose.[232] Britain's young men became by European standards stay-at-homes because in Britain the rented sector, so suited to young single people on the move who were short of capital, was relatively small, and because single people rarely qualified for council housing. Britain's proportion of single-person households whose occupants were under 35 was the lowest of the major European countries in 1989; as at 1982, in the male age-group from 20 to 24, 58 per cent were still living with parents, and far fewer lived alone than in four other West European countries surveyed.[233]

Confusion and change at the adult frontier were nowhere more rife than on the age of consent for sexual relations. Decision on this entailed weighing up the relative importance of the age of majority (18 for both sexes from 1969), the ages of physiological and psychological maturity, and the age when sexual orientation could be seen as determined. On the last two, opinion differed, as well as on whether the same age suited both sexes. To complicate matters further, all public discussion of legislative change had to bear in mind what a shifting public opinion would tolerate. Birth-control clinics had been advising girls under 16 for some time, and in 1985 a decision was reached in the important case brought unsuccessfully by Victoria Gillick, who claimed that doctors could not legally supply contraceptive advice to a girl under 16 without parental consent. The judges, disagreeing, argued that parental authority existed 'not for the benefit of the parent but for the child'. They did not think parental authority ended suddenly at the age of consent: it tailed off gradually according to circumstances; 'social customs changed, and the law ought to . . . have regard to such changes when they were of such major importance'.[234] Levels of teenage abortion were higher in British cities than elsewhere, and highest of all in big cities. In the 1970s the UK birth-rate among women aged 15 to 19 replicated a Europe-wide decline, but in the 1980s the British rate went up whereas the European rate continued to decline, and the UK's rate of conceptions leading to legal abortion rose from 14.3 per thousand female teenagers in 1971 to 24.6 in 1990—a year whose teenage fertility rate in England and Wales was second only to the USA when sixteen Western industrial societies were compared. A fairly steady annual average of 3,000 legal abortions were performed on girls

---

[232] K. Kiernan, 'Leaving Home: Living Arrangements of Young People in Six West-European Countries', *European Journal of Population* (Oct. 1986), 178–80.

[233] Coleman and Salt, *British Population*, 226. Kiernan, 'Leaving Home', 182.

[234] Lord Fraser, *T* (18 Oct. 1985), 25.

under 16 in the 1970s and 1980s, but on women aged 16 to 19 the average rose from 22,000 to 36,000.[235]

Well before 1970 the idea of either partner seeking parental permission to marry, and even the idea of formal engagement, were falling out of fashion. This change reflected a marked freeing up of the marriage market and the final triumph of romance over more practical motives for marriage, and was associated with young people's freer movement beyond parental supervision. To parents such freedom seemed particularly alarming in the late 1980s when rave parties were organized in obscure locations with drugs and dancing. Freedom's perils were advertised by two sets of serial murders, both leading ultimately to the murderer's life imprisonment. Much discussed was the prosecution in 1983 of Dennis Nilsen, a dull and apparently meek north London jobcentre clerk, 'the lonely murderer who preyed on young drifters'. His victims were homeless without close family connection who, if they escaped, were coy about their homosexual leanings; between 1978 and 1983 he murdered fifteen young men.[236] The trial of Rosemary West in 1995 received even more publicity, partly because the torture and murder of an unknown number of young women in the house she shared with Fred West in Gloucester went on for so long, and because the local authorities had done so little to coordinate relevant information about the Wests. In both cases the police failed to exploit leads supplied by escaped victims, and both illustrated how vulnerable were young people of either sex when far from their parents. Thirteen of Nilsen's fifteen victims between 1978 and 1983 had not even been reported as missing, and many of the Wests' victims were unknown.

4. A WELFARE DYNAMIC

After 1970, as before, the pressures to spend more on health and welfare were continuous, well-informed, emotionally powerful, and therefore politically influential, especially in a competitive two-party system. Both political and economic cycles incorporated a welfare ratchet effect. Restraints on welfare expenditure might tighten once a party gained power, but they weakened during the run-up to a general election as each party bid up the other. NHS expenditure rose fairly continuously, regardless of the government's party complexion: each party reproached the other for not doing enough to improve the NHS, and each carefully avoided precise commitments about spending on it. But whereas Conservative governments continued the steady upward trend,

---

[235] P. Babb, 'Teenage Conceptions and Fertility in England and Wales, 1971–91', *Population Trends*, 74 (Winter 1993), 13, 15. *TCBST* 50.
[236] Headline in *T* (5 Nov. 1983), 3. For a full summary of the case see *G* (5 Nov. 1983), 3.

Labour governments tended to begin by escalating it, only to rein it sharply back later in their term.[237] In its share of gross domestic product, government expenditure rose under a sympathetic Labour government from 37 per cent in 1964 to 42 per cent in the late 1960s; Heath's u-turn of 1972 and its aftermath had pushed the share up to 49 per cent by 1975/6, though the IMF helped to rein in the share to 43 per cent in 1977/8.[238] Current decisions did not always inspire such increases: many resulted from routinely implementing earlier decisions in response to demographic change, and some were incidental or even unintended. 'It is in the nature of the public services', said the Treasury in 1984, 'that demands are literally limitless, because they are not restrained by the price mechanism which forces those making demands to balance them against costs.'[239]

Planning and state intervention before 1970 owed much to information painstakingly accumulated. More and more questions were asked in the decennial census of population, and by the 1970s many planners were pressing for a five-yearly census.[240] The number of pages of tables in the census rose threefold between 1951 and 1971, its real cost fivefold.[241] The census of 1971 was a huge operation, requiring 8,224 administrators and 96,741 enumerators.[242] This helped seriously to hold up publication of the results—for more than three years in 1971. Buttressing the census were royal commissions, whose functions varied from pushing controversial subjects off the immediate political agenda to continuously providing necessary information and virtually merging with government departments. The Diamond Commission on the Distribution of Income and Wealth, which collected data from 1974 to 1979, exemplifies royal commissions of the latter type, and was preparing the ground for a wealth tax. Medical research continued to drive up NHS costs after 1970. Pharmaceutical firms were continually marketing new drugs: psychotherapeutic drugs in the 1950s, oral contraceptives, beta blockers, and anti-inflammatory medicines in the 1960s. Not till 1984 did government bring cost-pressures to bear by introducing a 'limited list' of the cheapest suitable drugs which doctors could prescribe, though only after making concessions to a furious pharmaceutical industry in 'an unholy alliance with the medical profession and the Labour Party'. Norman Fowler, the minister responsible, thought it 'as fierce and nasty a little campaign as I can remember'.[243] Hi-tech medicine was often

[237] Webster, *Health Services since the War*, ii. 760, 764–5, 803–4.   [238] *T* (1 Dec. 1994), 12.

[239] Green paper on 'The Next 10 Years', *FT* (14 Mar. 1984), 24.

[240] S. Tendler, 'Why the Pressure is Growing for a Five-Yearly Census', *T* (2 Dec. 1974), 14. See also Harrison, *Seeking a Role*, 266–7, 268.

[241] General Register Office, Census 1951, England and Wales, *General Report* (1958), 28. OPCS, Census 1971 England and Wales, *General Report, Part 2: Administration, Fieldwork, Processing* (1983), 98, 113. RPI figures from *BPF* (8th edn.), 411.

[242] OPCS Census 1981, *General Report: England and Wales* (1990), 23.

[243] S. Letwin, *Anatomy of Thatcherism* (1992), 214. Fowler, *Ministers Decide*, 194.

involved, and by the end of the 1980s 'spare part surgery' had become routine in Britain, with 1,800 kidney transplants, 35,000 hip replacements, and 10,000 knee replacements each year. In 1980 Britain's best-known heart-transplant surgeon, Magdi Yacoub, performed his first heart transplant at Harefield Hospital, and at his hospital alone 2,000 had been performed by 1996.[244] The NHS workforce grew accordingly: between 1973 and 1997 staff medical and dental, scientific and technical, each more than doubled. As for UK general practitioners, there were 24,239 in 1969 and 29,684 in 1985; doctors per patient rose steadily between 1961 and 1991, and the number of prescriptions dispensed doubled.[245]

Once policy on grants and benefits was decided in any area—whether on old-age pensions, investment grants or agricultural support—costs were bound to reflect the numbers qualifying for payment. Quite apart from rising expectations in the population as a whole, governments felt they must honour their commitment to meet the growing welfare claims of an ageing population. The 'dependency ratio' (persons under 15 and over 65 expressed as a ratio of those aged between 15 and 64) in England and Wales reached a low point in the 1930s, rose until 1971 and then fell back.[246] In 1960–75 increases in overall expenditure stemmed less from demographic factors than from raising benefits in health, education, pensions, and unemployment. This situation reversed in 1975–81:[247] the mounting unemployment and ageing of the population in the 1970s and 1980s left politicians free to do no more than tinker at the margins, given that improved or more accessible benefits might prompt unpopular tax increases. Total welfare expenditure rose autonomously after 1970 even without any legislative change; this was because the rising welfare cost of an ageing population more than counterbalanced the impact of schooling fewer children.[248] Demographic change shifted the balance of treatments required towards the relatively expensive diseases of later life—arthritic, cancerous, and pulmonary—whereas, for example, by 1984 the 19,008 deaths from pulmonary tuberculosis in 1946 had fallen to a mere 375.[249] In 1985 nearly half the deaths in England and Wales stemmed from failure of the heart and blood vessels, nearly a quarter from cancer, and a tenth from failure in the respiratory system;

---

[244] J. Charlton and M. Murphy (eds.), *The Health of Adult Britain 1841–1994*, ii (1997), 123, 151. Yacoub, *T* (10 June 1996), 14.

[245] C. Webster, 'Caring for Health in the UK 1974 to 2001', in Webster (ed.), *Caring for Health* (3rd edn.), 205. For GPs, Johnson (ed.), *Structure of British Industry*, 333. *Social Trends* (1995), 138.

[246] Coleman and Salt, *British Population*, 544–5. M. Anderson, 'The Social Implications of Demographic Change', in F. M. L. Thompson (ed.), *Cambridge Social History of Britain 1750–1950*, ii. *People and their Environment* (1990), 46–8.

[247] See P. Johnson's interesting table in Floud and McCloskey (eds.), *Economic History of Britain since 1700*, iii (2nd edn.), 295.

[248] As Castle pointed out in cabinet, *Diaries 1974–6*, 593–4 (14 Dec. 1975), to which she could have added the rising costs of higher education.   [249] Johnson (ed.), *Structure of British Industry*, 106.

the contribution of infectious diseases was tiny by comparison.[250] Between the 1970s and the 1990s deaths from heart disease were falling across all age-groups, but more slowly for women than for men. Deaths from stroke, only half as prevalent as heart disease, were declining fast, and even faster for women than for men. Between 1971 and 1992 the death-rate from stroke and lung cancer almost halved for men under 65. Cancer's changing incidence among men differed between sites—declining in the bladder, lung, stomach, pancreas, and rectum, but rising in the prostate, colon, and oesophagus.[251]

Changes in lifestyle and occupation supplemented demographic change as unpredictable influences on health patterns. Faster and more frequent travel was associated with spinal problems, not to mention the consequences of violent collision. Shifts in office technology (the electric typewriter in the 1960s, the word-processor in the 1980s) brought repetitive strain injury to the wrist and elbow, though as late as 1993 Judge Prosser felt able to dismiss this type of injury as psychosomatic.[252] Governments could, however, enforce regulations to curb accidents; they had long been keeping a close eye on national accident statistics, modifying the regulations accordingly. Partly as a result, accidents overall in Great Britain declined by more than a third between 1971 and 1991—road accidents by more than a third, and accidents within the home by a third.[253] If the mining and shipping industries (both declining) and aviation are excluded, deaths in industrial accidents were falling throughout the twentieth century, and fell more than fourfold between 1940/49 and 1990/97. It was government regulation that lay behind the drop in firework injuries requiring hospitalization in 1981 to the second lowest figure ever recorded.[254] Reinforcing breathalyser tests to prevent road accidents were important palliative improvements: in resuscitation and in the emergency treatment of accident victims hitherto viewed as beyond hope. Pedal-cyclists voluntarily followed motor-cyclists in wearing helmets, and seat belts were somewhat belatedly made compulsory, though amidst ongoing controversy,[255] for those sitting in front seats in 1983, and for rear-seat passengers in 1991. The former allegedly reduced fatal or severe injuries by 7,000 a year, and deaths per vehicle on the road fell well below inter-war levels.[256]

Pressure continuously accumulated for more expenditure: from trade unions, interest groups, charities, new professions. Thatcher at the party conference in 1982 wanted to 'make one thing absolutely clear': that 'the National Health Service is safe with us', adding in the following year that it was safe *'only* with

---

[250] See the useful table in Coleman and Salt, *British Population*, 245.

[251] K. Dunnell, 'Population Review (2): Are we Healthier?', *Population Trends*, 82 (Winter 1995), 13. *Social Trends* (1995), 131. [252] i.e. in *Rafiq Mughal v Reuters Ltd* (1993).

[253] *Social Trends* (1995), 133. [254] *TCBST* 303. *T* (16 Apr. 1983), 3 (fireworks).

[255] Professor Coleman referred me to Professor John Adams's website at http://john-adams.co.uk/

[256] *T* (31 Jan. 1986), 10; the reform had been introduced into 23 countries by 1980.

us'.[257] A Conservative government could not afford completely to ignore the middle-class conscience, and was also particularly vulnerable to the middle-class interests that clustered round tax concessions, state expenditure, and public welfare: the farming lobby, the householders clinging to mortgage-interest tax relief, and relatively long-lived middle-class old-age pensioners. Middle-class parents with children in state schools also benefited most from free schooling, given that their children were more likely to stay on into the sixth form, and thus get to university. When Keith Joseph threatened to cut student grants in 1984, Conservative backbenchers, responding to the furious parents of state-subsidized university students, destroyed the plan. Given their relatively heavy demands on pensions, and on relatively expensive medical and educational facilities, the middle classes had hitherto gained more than other classes from public welfare.[258]

Trade unions had a special leverage on health expenditure because, whatever care they might take to avoid disrupting emergency services, there was always the risk that in a structure so complex as a hospital, a strike might kill people.[259] In 1990 Kenneth Clarke said that in dealing with the Health Service as Secretary of State for Health 'you get exposed to the most appalling, vitriolic personal attacks once you come into conflict with any of the interest groups inside it'.[260] Even under a Conservative government the number of local authority social workers in England rose from 10,000 in 1971 to 22,000 in 1974, and the number of home helps from 33,000 to 42,000—all entrenched by new formal qualifications and training courses.[261] Claimants on welfare expenditure were being continuously drummed up by the new and rapidly growing counselling professions, operating through such organizations as the Citizens' Advice Bureaux, the Samaritans, Cruse, and Relate.[262] The short-term and often expert recommendation to spend more on causes obviously good in themselves was morally and politically powerful, and readily generated new welfare pressure groups and professional alignments. Longer-term, less particular, and more balanced policies inevitably made less impact, and could prevail only if politicians were willing to brave unpopularity. The one-time reluctance to claim state benefits had now been eroded at every social level. Though a boom might reduce welfare claims, there was a long-term trend for their becoming permanent once a claim had been lodged: take-up rates rose during each depression and during the subsequent boom did not fall back to their earlier level. Whereas in 1951 only 4 per cent

---

[257] Thatcher, *Conservative Party Conference Speeches*, 84, 90; the emphasis is not supplied in the published version, but was given to this word as broadcast at the time.
[258] Townsend, *Poverty in UK*, 155–8.
[259] See e.g. the bitter disputes of 1973, *T* (10 Mar. 1973), 2 (Derby); (23 Mar. 1973), 1 (York); (13 Apr. 1973), 2 (Leeds).   [260] Interview, *Ind* (25 Feb. 1990), 21.
[261] *T* (21 July 1976), 4.
[262] For more on these see above, pp. 142, 224. For growth figures see *TCBST* 606–8.

of the population were on national assistance, this had doubled by 1971 and had doubled again by the mid-1990s.[263] Peter Townsend set out at the national level to alert the public to the needs of new deprived minorities: fatherless families, the long-term hospitalized, the disabled, and the carers.[264] Bradbury vividly evoked the mini-Townsends operating locally, the Kirks at Watermouth University: 'a familiar pair in the high-rise council flats, going up and down in the obscenity-scrawled Otis lifts, hunting out instances of deprivation to show the welfare people', alerting council officials to 'the fleshed-out statistic, the family that has not had its rights, not had just benefits, not been rehoused; and . . . raising consciousness, raising instructive hell'.[265]

New welfare movements straddled the divide between self-help and state help. New types of disease and disability were diagnosed (autism, for example), whose sufferers banded together in self-defence, accumulating evidence from their own members and pushing doctors and politicians on to the defensive. The many impulses included the victim, the victim's distraught relatives, or relevant professionals. Betty Westgate had a mastectomy in 1968; four years later, repudiating reticence, she set up at her Croydon home with her husband's help the organization which became Breast Cancer Care. When Anthony Nolan contracted a rare bone disease, his mother could find no register of tissue-typed potential donors of bone marrow and in 1974 got the Anthony Nolan Register established; he died in 1979 but she continued the work, and by 2000 the register was among the largest such databases in the world, with more than 300,000 tissue-typed volunteers. When in 1986 the rheumatologist Allen Dixon and the health administrator Dickie Rowe wanted to set up what became the National Osteoporosis Society, Rowe suggested his neighbour Linda Edwards, a housewife and mother working from home. She then knew nothing about osteoporosis but much about public relations, became the Society's Director for sixteen years, and made osteoporosis a household word.[266]

When the Labour MP Jack Ashley suddenly became deaf in 1968 he gained his party leader's sympathy and converted himself into a one-man pressure group for the deaf, seeking to boost their share of research funding. The number of deaf people in England and Wales doubled between 1950 and 1980, and the 'hard of hearing' rose more than threefold. Ashley in his own person epitomized both the need to enhance understanding and the sufferer's capacity to respond constructively to misfortune. The deaf were, he said, 'the Cinderella of the disabled': deafness was 'a very curious disability', especially challenging to the

---

[263] ST (4 Jan. 1998), iv, 9. See also Bill Robinson's interesting 'Soft Heart of our Problem', FT (27 July 1993), 16.   [264] Introduction to his The Social Minority (1973), p. xiii.
[265] M. Bradbury, The History Man (1st publ. 1975, paperback edn. 1985), 3–4.
[266] Westgate obituary, G (4 Jan. 2001), 20. 'Anthony Nolan', ODNB. Edwards obituary, T (20 Dec. 2002), 33.

imagination 'because . . . invisible . . . an unseen individual cage'.[267] Helping to open the cage was British Sign Language. It was at first alleged to hinder the deaf from speaking and lip-reading, but it won acceptance during the 1970s, and from 1980 was regularly seen on television. In 2003 the government recognized it as a language in its own right, with educational expenditure to match; by then it was the preferred means of communication for about 70,000 people in the UK, making it second only to Welsh as a minority language.[268]

Integral to democracy was an equal opportunity that in itself prompted welfare expenditure, especially on education and health. Governments had to combat unpredictable suffering as best they could, and it was difficult openly to ration care even on the basis of cost or age, let alone on other grounds. Democracy also required medical expenditure to correct imbalances in health, which were still distributed unequally between social levels after 1970. Children of unskilled parents were less likely to survive and much more likely to die in accidents than those of professional parents,[269] and in adulthood manual workers of both sexes were much more likely than non-manual to die from all causes. The contrast owed something to industrial accidents, even in the new industries: for example, 167 people died in the Piper Alpha oil-rig disaster on 6 July 1988, eight days after the Department of Energy's safety inspection. There were relevant contrasts, too, in environment, overcrowding, and income, where differentials widened significantly in the 1980s. Added to these were contrasts in diet and lifestyle, much healthier among non-manual workers of both sexes; both male and female non-manual workers were far quicker than manual to give up smoking, for example.[270] Class and regional imbalances often overlapped. When Edwina Currie as a junior health minister tried to wean northerners from their relative enthusiasm for drinking, smoking, and chips, she encountered indignant rebuttal from people who knew they were on weak ground.[271] Regional inequalities in mortality were widening between 1951 and 1991, even holding social class constant, and in 1981 the areas of above-average mortality were in the inner cities, Scotland, and the north of England. Health contrasts were visible: in 1980 people in the south of England were taller than the average, and in almost every age-group people were on average shorter by several inches in households headed by manual rather than non-manual workers.[272]

A democracy could not ignore health imbalances between the sexes. There were strong pressures to curb deaths from breast cancer: better screening and treatment ensured that its five-year survival figures showed steady improvement

[267] *HC Deb.* 5 Dec. 1969, c. 1870. *TCBST* 526.   [268] *G* (19 Mar. 2003), 14.
[269] *DT* (28 Sept. 1981), 8.   [270] *DT* (2 Jan. 1991), 3. *TCBST* 120–1.
[271] *G* (24 Sept. 1986), 1. *T* (6 Oct. 1986), 2.
[272] M. Shaw, D. Dorling, and N. Brimblecombe, 'Changing the Map: Health in Britain 1951–91', *Sociology of Health and Illness* (Sept. 1998), 694–709. Knight, *Heights and Weights*, 8.

between 1971 and 2001. Deaths among women from lung cancer were levelling off between the 1970s and the 1990s, but those from bladder cancer were increasing.[273] There were limits to what democracy could achieve in the health sphere. It could not raise the average height of women by five inches to match that of men,[274] nor was it obvious that insurance companies should treat the sexes equally in their premiums. Most companies charged women less for life cover, given that in 1970 women in England and Wales could expect to live for six years longer than men; men were relatively exposed to lung cancer, for instance, because they smoked more, to traffic accidents because they travelled more, and to suicide perhaps partly because of relative pressure for career success.[275] In 1985 the Equal Opportunities Commission lost its case against higher health premiums for women, given that women took more sick leave than men; 120 million working days were lost due to menstrual problems annually in the 1960s, more than three times as many as from the decade's industrial disputes.[276]

Medical advances did not always increase costs. The Oxford haematologist John O'Brien's important clinical trials discovered, for instance, that low-dose aspirin could ward off heart attacks,[277] and by the early 1990s miniaturized medical instruments, fibre optics, keyhole and laser surgery were making operations less invasive. The number of hospital beds in Great Britain (including those for mental and geriatric patients) fell from 9.6 per thousand population in 1970 to 5.8 in 1990/1, and the average length of hospital stay for acute surgery fell by a third between 1982 and 1992.[278] At times it even seemed that hospital treatment, with all its dangers of hospital-acquired infections, might eventually come to seem a mere 150-year episode in health-care's long history. Better drug therapy, concern at the psychological consequences of isolation, and a humane watchfulness continued the decline in institutional care for the mentally ill. In asylums, a term which by the 1970s had fallen out of use, whistleblowers had begun to expose abuses, as when mentally ill patients were brutally treated at St Augustine's Hospital, Canterbury, in 1976; one MP even detected 'an element of going back to the Middle Ages in some of our mental hospitals'.[279] Nor did the resulting 'care in the community' generate more homicides by the mentally ill: whereas the number of homicide convictions in England and Wales rose fivefold between the late 1950s and the late 1990s, the proportion involving a mentally ill defendant fell from almost half in the mid-1960s to almost a tenth. The foundation of SANE ('Schizophrenia: A National

---

[273] *DT* (27 Sept. 2001), 18. *Ind* (8 Dec. 1995), 5.   [274] Knight, *Heights and Weights*, 7.

[275] T. McKeown and C. R. Lowe, *An Introduction to Social Medicine* (2nd edn. Oxford, 1974), 71.

[276] *T* (16 Aug. 1985), 3. Dalton, *Menstrual Cycle*, 129; cf. *BST* 195–6.

[277] Obituary, *G* (11 Dec. 2002), 22.

[278] V. Berridge, *Health and Society in Britain since 1939* (Cambridge, 1999), 110–11. *DT* (23 June 1994), 4.   [279] Dr Maurice Miller, *HC Deb.* 31 Mar. 1976, c. 1314.

Emergency') in 1986, however, reflected continuing controversy about the new approach.[280]

Still, public expenditure on welfare in the 1960s and 1970s rose both absolutely and proportionately: from 43 per cent of public expenditure in 1951/2 to 47 per cent in 1971/2, to 52 per cent in 1981/2, and to 56 per cent in 1987/8. Even during the 1980s social security's share of total welfare expenditure continued rising, whereas the share of education and health remained fairly steady, and housing's share markedly declined.[281] NHS and welfare costs continued to rise even after Thatcher came to power. Not only was she committed in 1979 to implementing the Clegg Commission's generous public-sector pay award:[282] the recessions of the early and late 1980s also required her to distribute huge sums in unemployment pay and on youth training schemes. This twice sent public spending's share of gross domestic product (falling before 1979) sharply upwards.[283] Total NHS expenditure rose fourfold in real terms between 1950 and 1990, and in the same period its share of gross domestic product rose from 3.7 to 5.2 per cent. The NHS was, wrote Nigel Lawson, 'the closest thing the English have to a religion, with those who practice [sic] in it regarding themselves as a priesthood'.[284] The NHS could not remain static, if only because (as Powell once pointed out) its employees had 'a vested interest in its denigration'.[285]

From 1960 Britain's total expenditure on health fell, declining increasingly below the OECD average in share of national income: in 1982 the UK spent 5.9 per cent of gross national product on health, whereas the USA spent 10.6, France 9.3, West Germany 8.2, Spain 6.3 per cent.[286] The political impact made by rising welfare costs, however, was all the greater in Britain because by European standards so much welfare spending was channelled through central rather than through local government, or through employers and non-governmental bodies. Welfare costs therefore quickly fuelled direct taxation, whose visibility made it readily resented. By the early 1980s the tension between pressure for more expenditure and for lower taxes had become serious. Benn thought this presented capitalism with an insoluble problem: 'democracy gives the poor and the disinherited the political power to demand hospitals and schools which capitalism can't pay for'. Those with a firmer faith in capitalism had now to ask whether the high levels of expenditure on health and welfare gave the taxpayer full value.[287] Thatcher claimed that Labour, with the welfare state created, had nowhere else to go except Marxism, focusing

---

[280] *G* (6 Jan. 1999), 4 (homicides). *T* (4 Sept. 2001), 2–3 (SANE).

[281] Figures for 1959–75 in *T* (22 Nov. 1976), 5. Useful table in Johnson (ed.), *Twentieth-Century Britain*, 361.   [282] See below, pp. 289, 537.

[283] *Econ* (2 Oct. 1993), 39.

[284] Lawson, *View from No. 11*, 613. See also Loudon et al., *General Practice*, 302.

[285] In 1966, quoted in Letwin, *Thatcherism*, 210.   [286] Johnson, 'Welfare State', 308.

[287] Benn, *Diaries 1977–80*, 547 (9 Oct. 1979). For a useful survey of the problems see I. Hargreaves, 'The Rations get Leaner', *FT* (4 Oct. 1982), 14.

on redistributing rather than creating wealth. A free economy was important
not only for advancing liberty and prosperity, she told the party conference in
October 1975, but 'to have more money to help the old and the sick and the
handicapped'.[288]

Organizational reform in the NHS seemed one way of squaring the circle.
Some on the right criticized Thatcher for being so slow to restructure the
welfare system, and felt that her first two governments focused too exclusively
on getting the economy right; they thought the process should have begun in
1983, and not in the late 1980s.[289] Thatcher had priorities even more pressing
in 1979, and was as yet insecure within her party and in the country as a
whole. Reining in welfare expenditure was the most difficult among her tasks,
and the ground had to be thoroughly prepared. She had first to consolidate
her position within her party, fend off centrist challenge, steadily undermine
the left within local authorities and public opinion, and gain time by winning
general elections. She also had to free up economic growth by improving labour
relations and encouraging the entrepreneur; together with privatization, then
only revving up, these were the areas of highest priority even after 1983. Nor
could it be assumed that a welfare equivalent of the 'winter of discontent' in
1978–9 would present her with the electoral opportunity for pursuing policies
that were electorally so hard to sell.

For all the difficulties, Thatcher did at least make a start, but she diverged
in her approach from earlier welfare reformers. For her the first requirement
was hard thinking and abundant fact-gathering under assumptions that had
grown unfamiliar since Beveridge. On gathering information she favoured
combining firm direction from the centre with spontaneous accumulation at
the periphery through the free market—the 'most wonderful computer the
world has ever known', in Powell's words.[290] . Her zeal for cuts in government
expenditure harmonized well with not wanting to accumulate information
that might facilitate further state interference. The Diamond Commission was
an obvious target, and died with her first election victory. Nor had she any
time for incomes-policy intrusiveness or for centrally planning the economy.
The number of government statisticians more than halved between 1979 and
1989/90, and government information was impoverished further when her first
government abolished exchange controls and established enterprise zones.[291]
In 1981 the census dropped several earlier questions: on country of parental
origin, for example, on weekly hours usually worked, and on housing issues,

[288] Interview with Hugo Young, *ST* (27 Feb. 1983), 33. Thatcher, *Collected Speeches*, 34.
[289] N. Ridley, *'My Style of Government': The Thatcher Years* (1st publ. 1991, paperback edn. 1992),
83, cf. 94–5, 257; see also Cockett, *Thinking the Unthinkable*, 309.
[290] Quoted in Letwin, *Thatcherism*, 75.
[291] *IOS* (29 July 1990), business supplement, 11 (statisticians). *FT* (4 May 1988), 10; (23 Oct. 1989),
22. Lawson, *View from No. 11*, 72.

though parliament reversed a proposal to omit a question on number of cars and vans available for household use.[292] During Thatcher's premiership the royal commission virtually fell into disuse; a woman of action had no need of excuses for delay, nor were the statistics collected within a regulated economy necessarily useful in a deregulated context.[293] By the end of the 1980s the statisticians were worried at their diminished number in government, and that statistics were being wrongly employed, especially those concerned with poverty and unemployment. Pressure built up for their centralized collection under a national statistics commission, rather than being separately gathered within the various policy ministries.[294] Here, as so often elsewhere, Thatcher's economic revolution politicized areas hitherto uncontroversial.

Information after 1979 was collected selectively and purposively. The Thatcher governments sought to secure action through mobilizing inform- ation on public welfare in two ways: first, by alerting ratepayers, parents, patients, and other consumers of state services to their interests through col- lecting and publishing information hitherto unknown or withheld. But, second, by gathering facts only as the basis for rapid action along predetermined lines. For her facts and ideas on policy, Thatcher as party leader after 1975 often drew upon partisan activists in free-market think tanks, and after 1979 relied heavily on successful businessmen. A judicious impartiality was not her mood; she knew what she wanted to do, and her inquiries were concerned with means not ends, as with the inquiries of 1983–4 into the social-security system and health service. By June 1982 she had set up the 'Family Policy Group' of ministers to organize detailed study, and in 1984 Fowler, as Secretary of State for Social Services, launched what he called 'the most substantial examination of the social security system since the Beveridge report'. The inquiry into the NHS that Thatcher launched under Roy Griffiths, a miner's son who became managing director of Sainsbury's, broke with the royal commission's consensual tradition; consisting of only four people, it reported within six months. 'If Florence Nightingale were carrying her lamp through the corridors of the National Health Service today', Griffiths pronounced, 'she would almost certainly be searching for the people in charge.' It remained essential to discover the cost of welfare services, and Thatcher by 1988 was alarmed that so little was known.[295]

By January 1988 there was powerful ministerial support for NHS reform, and the proposals being considered by Thatcher's third government in 1987–8 involved simulating the market within the NHS as far as possible.[296] Hitherto

[292] OPCS, Census 1981, *General Report: England and Wales* (1990), 2.
[293] Lawson, *View from No. 11*, 388, cf. 845–6.   [294] *Ind* (9 Oct. 1989), 3. *FT* (27 July 1990), 6.
[295] Fowler, *Ministers Decide*, 208; Griffiths quoted at 195. See also Thatcher, *Downing Street Years*, 611.   [296] Lawson, *View from No. 11*, 614–16. Thatcher, *Downing Street Years*, 616.

the managerial emphasis of administrative reorganization had not done much to improve the NHS, while distancing it even further from local control.[297] Efficiency was best advanced when government worked with the grain of professional tendencies. For example, from 1966 the Family Doctor Charter boosted general-practitioner morale by cultivating expertise and encouraging economies of scale and divisions of labour within the practice. General practitioners clustered into 'primary health care teams', usually with a nurse attached, which caused the one-man practice to fall from nearly half the total in 1952 to a tenth by 1995; by 1990 about half the practices in England and Wales were computerized, some beginning to abandon handwritten notes altogether.[298] By the early 1990s the influx of managers in the NHS was accompanied by several unfamiliar notions. There was, for instance, the idea (soon consolidated in the Citizen's Charter strategy) of the patient as a customer or consumer who was entitled to specified levels of attention; published league tables then made it possible to compare hospitals' performance on specified criteria. Welfare reform turned out to be unfinished Thatcherite business, but Thatcher claimed that her third government was feeling its way 'towards a new ethos for welfare policy' by following three pathways into welfare: encouraging voluntary provision, discouraging dependence on the state, and fostering 'built-in incentives towards decent and responsible behaviour'.[299] Each deserves further discussion.

On the first pathway, much was made of Thatcher's comment in October 1987 to *Woman's Own* that 'there is no such thing as society', despite the fact that she was echoing words that had evoked little fuss when uttered by Keith Joseph in 1975, and by herself ten years later.[300] Behind her outlook lay a fear of diminishing the individual by reifying an impersonal 'society'. Remarks resembling hers came from Aldous Huxley in 1937: ' "Society" is a meaningless abstraction. A man has no direct experience of his relations with "Society"; he has experience only of his relations with limited groups of similar or dissimilar individuals.'[301] Hayek later elaborated Huxley's anti-totalitarian insight in his *Road to Serfdom*. By detaching Thatcher's remark from its context, her critics felt able to imply that she favoured the sort of atomized and universal individualism that dissolved any bonds of mutual obligation.[302] Quite the reverse: Thatcher felt that public welfare had become too impersonal, too prone to foster passive attitudes, too dependent on large bureaucratized and unionized structures. Her critics usually ignored what follows her much-quoted remark:

---

[297] Webster, *Health Services since the War*, ii. 769, 771–2.

[298] Berridge, *Health and Society in Britain*, 77. Loudon *et al.* (eds.), *General Practice*, 60.

[299] Thatcher, *Downing Street Years*, 629.

[300] *Woman's Own* (31 Oct. 1987), 10. See also Joseph, *Reversing the Trend*, 72 (speech at Oxford, 14 Mar. 1975); Campbell, *Thatcher*, ii. 531.

[301] A. Huxley, *Ends and Means* (1937), 197. I owe this reference to Ivon Asquith, formerly of Oxford University Press.

[302] See Kinnock's travesty of her views quoted in M. Westlake, *Kinnock: The Biography* (2001), 471.

'it's our duty to look after ourselves and then, also, to look after our neighbour. People have got the entitlements too much in mind, without the obligations.'[303] Far from ignoring mutual obligation, her aim was that of the Edwardian 'New Liberals': to emphasize the fruitful interaction between state and volunteer, and the need to render aid more personal, more immediate, and more responsive to moral choice. This could best be attained, she thought, through the network of informal structures that binds together civil society: family, neighbourhood, community, and voluntary association. For her, individualism was neither inherently selfish, nor hostile to ideals of community, and she later found her views endorsed in the works of the American theologian and social scientist Michael Novak.[304]

Thatcher recalled that 'by the time I left office my advisers and I were assembling a package of measures to strengthen the traditional family', though without 'the slightest illusion' that its effects could be 'more than marginal'.[305] Voluntarism was undoubtedly popular in home ownership, but elsewhere it had to be campaigned for: by the 1980s it seemed necessary to retreat from the Scandinavian, tax-subsidized, welfare model which Britain had espoused almost despite Beveridge, towards the liberal 'safety net' model widely favoured in other English-speaking countries, and which incorporated extensive private provision.[306] In encouraging volunteers to reinforce the welfare services, governments after 1979 were working with the grain, given that there were more fit pensioners eager to make themselves useful; furthermore, despite women's increasing involvement in paid work there were still in 2001 5.2 million people looking after elderly or ill relatives.[307] Heath had been impressed at how voluntary bodies had coordinated the reception of evacuees from Uganda, and in 1973 placed a cabinet minister in charge of government support for voluntary societies.[308] Under Thatcher, government's integration with voluntary bodies proceeded much further: voluntary bodies, she thought, 'either . . . can do things which the government cannot do, or they can do them better'.[309]

In welfare, education, and health there were spontaneous trends within the community towards self-help which the Thatcher governments might have been expected to back more strongly. Conservative backing was overt on owner-occupation, somewhat more muted on occupational pensions and independent

[303] *Woman's Own* (31 Oct. 1987), 10; cf. her sermon of Ash Wednesday 1981 in H. Young, *One of Us*, 224.
[304] *Daily Mail* (29 Apr. 1988), 6. See also her interview in *STel* (15 Apr. 1990), review section, iii. For Novak, Thatcher, *Downing Street Years*, 627.   [305] Thatcher, *Downing Street Years*, 629–30.
[306] J. Willman, 'Individual Ways to Coin it', *FT* (3 Nov. 1993), 18.   [307] *DT* (14 Feb. 2003), 6.
[308] *T* (14 July 1973), 2.
[309] Speech, 19 Jan. 1986, to the Women's Royal Voluntary Service annual conference: *T* (20 Jan. 1981), 5. For a wider discussion of this area see B. Harrison and J. Webb, 'Volunteers and Voluntarism', *TCBST* 587–619.

schooling, but less lively on adult education and the Open University than might have been expected,[310] and only cautiously encouraging on preventive medicine and medical self-provision. Thatcher astutely masked her enthusiasm for privatizing welfare, though on eye-testing she braved the opticians' 'howls of rage'[311] and removed restrictions on advertising and entering the trade. Whereas some wanted to curb NHS costs by making benefit more discriminating and by charging for some medical services, others were beginning to favour the solution widely adopted in Europe: combining public provision with private insurance. Even after 1979 such an approach was politically perilous in Britain. Hence the outcome: the spontaneous growth of private medical insurance in parallel with state provision, private provision being encouraged by tax incentives and freer movement of doctors between NHS and private practice. Optional private provision was, for Thatcher, a leaven for the lump: she told the party conference in 1982 that it would bring more funds into health-care and prompt health initiatives.[312]

The largest private health insurance organization, the British United Provident Association, founded in 1947, was within a decade covering 684,000 people, rising to 1,500,000 by 1969. Private health provision in Britain rose particularly fast (relatively and absolutely) in the 1970s, in hospitals as well as in residential and nursing-home accommodation.[313] When, as Secretary of State for Health and Social Security in 1974–6, Castle campaigned against paybeds in NHS hospitals, she unintentionally helped to accelerate the growth of private provision; Shirley Williams did likewise with schools when as Secretary of State for Education and Science in 1976–9 she withdrew state funding from direct-grant schools. In many industrial societies from the 1960s to the 1990s, private health-care expenditure per person rose even faster and from a higher base than in Britain;[314] but even in Britain, in both absolute terms and when related to population, the take-up of private medical insurance increased continuously from the 1950s to the 1990s. Aggressive American health-care organizations began moving into the British market, subordinating the small-scale British entrepreneurs or religious institutions hitherto dominating the field; by 1986 they had captured almost a quarter of it.[315] By 1990 in the UK 6.6 million people, eleven times as many as in 1955, were privately insured against health risk.[316] Labour ministers had for some time feared that the press

---

[310] Though Thatcher had rescued it at birth from attack by her Conservative colleagues—see Campbell, Thatcher, i. 229.   [311] Fowler, Ministers Decide, 197.
[312] Thatcher, Collected Speeches, 207. See also J. Higgins, The Business of Medicine: Private Health Care in Britain (Basingstoke and London, 1988), 85–8.
[313] T (1 Dec. 1969), 8 (BUPA). D. G. Green and D. Lucas, 'Private Welfare in the 1980s', in N. Manning and R. Page (eds.), Social Policy Review, 4 (1992), 35.
[314] For comparative figures see Loudon et al., General Practice, 304.
[315] Higgins, Business of Medicine, 1.   [316] Loudon et al., General Practice, 303.

might publicize their own personal involvement with private medicine.[317] By 1979 at least one trade union contemplated incorporating into wage agreements access to private health-care schemes, and from 1981 tax incentives encouraged schemes catering for workers earning less than £8,500 a year. By 1983, however, only 1 per cent of manual workers had private cover, as compared with nearly a quarter of professional workers and employers or managers.[318]

Discouraging dependence on the state, the second of Thatcher's pathways into welfare, placed her at the centre of a battle for ideas and even for vocabulary. Her formidable energies as prime minister did not prevent her from recognizing (and even welcoming) the limits on what democratic governments can achieve, though she also knew how powerfully the skilful politician can mould the tone of public debate. Like Keith Joseph before her, she felt that since the 1940s through 'Labspeak' the British left had been allowed to capture even the vocabulary. She would have shared Hayek's view expressed in 1983: that the word 'social' was 'probably the most confusing and misleading term of our whole political vocabulary'—a weasel word because it often negated the word or phrase ('market economy', 'justice', 'democracy') that it qualified. She saw the verb 'to care' being transferred from a personal emotion to advocating high public expenditure,[319] and in scornfully rejecting the 'caring' culture of the 1960s and 1970s she was dismissing short-term palliatives that might end by making matters worse, and was substituting what she saw as long-term remedies. This is the context of an unguarded remark, surprisingly under-exploited by her critics, uttered in a television studio during the run-up to the general election of June 1987: not realizing she was being recorded, she referred to people who 'just drool and drivel that they care', and immediately apologized for using the phrase.[320]

Thatcher often publicly deplored the culture of dependency in inner-city council housing estates: surveying some of them in Liverpool after the riots in 1981, she noted that 'what was clearly lacking was a sense of pride and personal responsibility'.[321] She was not alone in her concerns: even Crossman as Secretary of State for Social Security had become increasingly worried by 1969 at how social security payments deterred the lower paid from working.[322] In the 1970s and 1980s even the attack on fraudulent claimants or defaulters was politically controversial, carrying the risk of hard cases stirring public

---

[317] Crossman, *Cabinet Diaries*, iii. 750 (7 Dec. 1969), 761–2 (25 Dec. 1969). Dalyell, *Crossman*, 176. Compare the incident involving Healey, *Ind* (10 June 1987), 9.

[318] *G* (5 Sept. 1979), 4. Higgins, *Business of Medicine*, 88, 164.

[319] 'Beware this Weasel Word', *T* (11 Nov. 1983), 12. *DT* (23 Apr. 1979), 16.

[320] Cockerell, *Live from No. 10*, 330–1.

[321] Thatcher, *Downing Street Years*, 145; cf. 671; *DT* (26 June 1987), 1.

[322] Castle, *Diaries 1964–70*, 694–5 (24, 28 July).

emotions. Prosecutions for welfare benefit fraud had doubled between 1970 and 1975, and even a Labour government in 1976 felt obliged to search more energetically for it. Thatcher looked back wistfully at the days when people had been reluctant to claim benefits from the state, whose advertising now encouraged them into dependence.[323] Beveridge had never intended public welfare to discourage voluntarism and self-help. He had not aimed to substitute state help for voluntary help, she noted in June 1983: 'he gave state help, yes, but added to it there must be plenty of scope for voluntary help and personal self-reliance, so that you can have liberty and fraternity'. Stressing in 1988 that 'when you have finished as a taxpayer, you have not finished your duty as a citizen', Thatcher emphasized the charitable component of economic individualism, and claimed that 'the voluntary spirit of personal giving is part of the British character'.[324]

For Orwell, social reform is beset by two perennial questions, differently answered at different times: 'how can you improve human nature until you have changed the system?' and 'what is the use of changing the system before you have improved human nature?' Thatcher sympathized more with the second question than the first. Her policies ultimately required—though, as she often complained,[325] did not always receive—initiatives on morality from the churches. In advancing her third welfare pathway, encouraging 'decent and responsible behaviour', she was the first to recognize how limited was the politician's power to mould citizens' character. Yet she shared Beveridge's view (cited in her memoirs) that organized welfare should neither stifle initiative, nor encourage insured people to 'feel that income for idleness . . . can come from a bottomless purse';[326] it could not be assumed that the high ideals prompting the collectivist advance were shared by its beneficiaries. In 1948 pensioners constituted the overwhelming majority of claimants for supplementary welfare benefit, but in 1981 non-pensioner claimants (most notably the unemployed and one-parent families) outnumbered them; one-parent families drawing supplementary benefit rose more than threefold between 1970 and 1987, and between 1979 and 1988 the total numbers who depended on supplementary benefit almost doubled.[327] Summoning claimants for interview under the Restart programme reduced claims because many did not turn up, and extensive fraud was exposed; the number of withdrawn claims quadrupled between 1984/5 and 1988/9.[328] During the early 1990s some ministers were concerned that state

[323] *T* (22 Sept. 1976), 6. Thatcher, *Downing Street Years*, 6.

[324] ITV interview with Brian Walden, 6 June 1983. Speech on opening a new cardiac wing of Great Ormond Street, London, children's hospital on 27 Apr. 1988, praising it for raising £17 million in donations: *DT* (28 Apr. 1988), 1.

[325] G. Orwell, 'Charles Dickens' (1940), in Orwell's *Complete Works*, ed. P. Davison, xii (1998), 31. For Thatcher see e.g. *Woman's Own* (31 Oct. 1987), 10.   [326] Thatcher, *Path to Power*, 121.

[327] Field, *Losing Out*, 23–5.   [328] *G* (2 Aug. 1989), 4. *DT* (2 Aug. 1989), 4.

payments to unmarried or separated mothers actually had the effect of creating single-parent and unstable families, and the Major governments slowly tiptoed towards the 'workfare' view of unemployment (benefits only in exchange for work) adopted much earlier in the USA.[329]

Preventive medicine was not prominent among Thatcher's welfare priorities, but it potentially drew together all three of her welfare pathways: it was voluntarist in mood, reduced the citizen's dependence on the state (thereby cutting costs), and cultivated willpower. There was a good pedigree in political economy for viewing the state as guardian of national statistics so as to stimulate spontaneous improvement, and few would have contested government's role in curbing accidents, smoking, dental decay, and malnutrition. And yet the 1980s saw no upsurge in the long-term trend. Preventive medicine had been advancing in an unspectacular but effective way for several decades, and this merely persisted. From the 1960s many general practitioners collaborated with local health authorities in newly established health centres,[330] and in 1970 the local authorities were required to set up integrated social-service departments. These boosted the public-health medicine which in the NHS's early years had lost ground to the hospitals, and in addition between 1977 and 1979 the funding of health education more than doubled.[331] With its wide-ranging booklet *Prevention and Health: Everybody's Business* (1976), the Labour government sought to stimulate public interest in preventive medicine, arguing that 'curative medicine may be increasingly subject to the law of diminishing returns'. There was a further upsurge of public interest in 1983, when dietary fibre was encouraged and fat, sugar, and salt intake discouraged, but the preventive dynamic advanced surprisingly slowly in the 1980s.[332]

Richard Doll's epidemiological research on the relationship between smoking and cancer brought preventive medicine to the fore. In 1979, amidst 'good-humoured cheers, boos and whistles', Bill Sirs successfully proposed a ban on smoking at the TUC, and in 1988 the London Underground and (for domestic flights) British Airways introduced smoking bans. It was a triumph for government education in public health that deaths from smoking in Britain, where men in 1970 had the worst death-rate in the world from smoking, had halved by 1998—a decline that correlated directly with the fall in cigarette sales—a sharper fall than in any other country.[333] There were less obtrusive advances after 1951 in preventive medicine through better dental care. Visits to the dentist in the 1950s were not pleasant: decaying teeth were drilled

---

[329] For more on this see below, p. 362.   [330] Webster, *NHS: A Political History*, 131.

[331] Webster, *Health Services since the War*, ii. 304, 310, 770.

[332] DHSS, *Prevention and Health Everybody's Business: A Reassessment of Public and Personal Health* (1976), 6. J. Obelkevich and P. Catterall (eds.), *Understanding Post-War British Society* (1994), 159–60.

[333] *DT* (4 Sept. 1979), 32 (Sirs). *DT* (8 Sept. 1998), 7.

and filled or were removed with the aid of gas. Between the 1960s and the 1990s, however, the proportion of people without natural teeth halved to one fifth.[334] British dentists cannot be directly credited with a development that was international. Besides, although dentists' number per head in the UK more than doubled between 1961 to 1991,[335] the NHS did not have nearly enough, and private provision grew apace. The improvement seems to reflect interaction between the declining consumption of sugar since the 1970s and the advance since the 1950s of fluoridation in drinking water and toothpaste, the latter energetically promoted by toothpaste companies under American influence since first being marketed in Britain in 1958. Within Britain it was a sign of growing professional commitment to fluoridizing drinking water that the British Fluoridation Society had been founded in 1969. When Gallup asked people in the 1960s and early 1970s whether they would support fluoridation, a large majority said they would, but about a fifth said not;[336] tenacious hostility was overcome only slowly, and had to be fought through the courts. The number of children with decayed teeth at all ages fell from almost 60 per cent in 1973 to less than 30 per cent in 1993. After the 1960s the nation's mouths were steadily and unobtrusively losing their amalgam, with the youngest setting the pace. Thirty years later, dentists had much better equipment for tackling the relatively few fillings and extractions now required, but as the British public swapped their false teeth for bridges and crowns, dentists acquired a new interest in gum disease, in better pain control, and (very necessarily in an ageing population) in restorative and educational dentistry.[337]

Diet was a prize arena for preventive medicine. The growth of desk-bound occupations and the emergence in the 1960s of 'diseases of affluence' required government to resume and then continually adjust its health guidance in response to changing medical fashion. The average man in 1980 weighed 11 stone 8 pounds, and the average woman 9 stone 11 pounds, and in that year 6 per cent of the men aged between 16 and 64 who were surveyed were obese, 13 per cent by 1993; equivalent figures for women were 8 per cent and 16 per cent, with a corresponding increase in the numbers overweight.[338] Fear of heart disease was one reason why people began in the 1970s to consume less whole-milk, white bread, eggs, meat, sugar, and butter, and substituted skimmed milk, brown bread, margarine, savoury rice, poultry, and fruit.[339] Then in February 1979 an influential article in the *British Medical Journal* shifted the fashion by

---

[334] M. C. Downer, 'Changing Trends in Dental Caries Experience in Great Britain', *Advances in Dental Research*, 7/1 (19–24 July 1993), 20. Professor Downer of Berkhamsted gave me a valuable interview on 12 Mar. 1996 and provided much other help.   [335] *Social Trends* (1995), 138.

[336] *Gallup International Public Opinion Polls*, i. 690; ii. 841, 1095, 1270.

[337] *Ind* (8 Dec. 1995), 5 (children). *DT* (29 May 1991), 7 (dentists).

[338] Knight, *Heights and Weights*, 19. *Ind* (8 Dec. 1995), 5.

[339] *Econ* (25 May 1985), 30. For rice see *DT* (11 June 1979), 8.

deploying fruit and fibre not only against the insidious advance of obesity, bowel disease, and heart disease, but also against squandering the world's resources.[340] The overall long-term trend was towards more fruit and less sugar, more cereal and less meat, more poultry and less fat (with a marked decline since 1970 in butter and lard); the pace for change was set in the south-east and only slowly moved northwards.[341] By 1991 sales of skimmed and semi-skimmed milk had risen threefold since 1985, and during the 1980s the consumption of fruit juice almost trebled.[342]

After 1990 Major as prime minister, despite his enthusiasm for sport, set a poor dietary example, and medical shockwaves radiated out from the Happy Eater restaurant where on 9 February 1991 he reportedly breakfasted on bacon, egg, and sausage.[343] But by then the layman who lacked any particular medical problem could be forgiven for questioning all medical prescription on diet, and for choosing moderation in all things. There was safety as well as growing convenience in food variety: from the 1960s onwards the types of food available and the ways of cooking it greatly diversified. Refrigerators, freezers, and enterprising retailers ensured that foods once seasonal became continuously available, and larger shops could stock a wider range of foods. Cuisine once narrowly British had first been diversified by French, Italian, and Chinese styles, but by the 1980s was moving on to Mexican, Japanese, and Indo-Chinese. Ecological and humanitarian complemented health influences: combining all three in 1977, an OXFAM pamphlet wanted the affluent society's 'steak house mentality' replaced by the diet of cereals and vegetables that would exploit the world's food resources less wastefully, and by the mid-1980s the butchers, alarmed at falling meat consumption, were discussing how to improve their public image.[344]

There were many non-medical reasons after 1970 for acting on the doctors' recommendation to eat less and exercise more. In the 1960s, slimming books were beginning to move up in the publishing market by comparison with cookery books, and by the 1980s diet books such as Audrey Eyton's *F-Plan Diet* (1982) and Ann Dugan's *Flatten your Stomach* (1988) had major impact. In 1980 30 per cent of the women and 10 per cent of the men surveyed, many in their thirties, claimed to have adopted a slimming diet during the past year.[345] For many younger women, diet was pursued more for reasons of looks than health, which it sometimes even damaged. After 1970 anorexia nervosa was much discussed, and in 1979 the psychiatrist Gerald Russell identified bulimia (its slim-and-binge variant), soon much publicized by Princess Diana's suffering.

---

[340] R. Passmore *et al.*, 'Prescription for a Better British Diet', *British Medical Journal* (24 Feb. 1979), 528–9.   [341] *TCBST* 116. *Social Trends* (1995), 125; (1996), 138.

[342] *DT* (26 Mar. 1991), 4 (milk). *T* (25 Mar. 1992), 2 (fruit juice).   [343] *IOS* (10 Feb. 1991), 1.

[344] *T* (5 July 1977), 2 (OXFAM). *G* (30 Nov. 1984), 1. For more on the vegetarian advance see above, p. 99.   [345] Knight, *Heights and Weights*, 37.

During the 1980s men showed more interest in dieting, concern for health being more prominent among their motives: the 17 per cent of men surveyed who were trying to lose weight in 1980 had risen to 25 per cent by 2004.[346] Eating took place in new locations: health considerations and mothers-at-work destroyed, at least on weekdays, the traditional English cooked breakfast, which succumbed to cereal, fruit juice, and yoghurt. With women working, lunch was much less frequently eaten at home; afternoon tea, once promoted by chains of cake-shops like Lyons and Fullers, went into marked decline, and take-away or instant dinners became common.[347] The evening also saw a pronounced growth in the 1970s of eating out as a recreation pursued by couples in restaurants, and by 1980 the American phrase 'fast food' had become familiar enough in Britain to shed its quotation marks: the 1980s witnessed an invasion of American-influenced fast-food chains attractive to the young—especially Kentucky Fried Chicken, Burger King, and McDonald's. These, together with declining fish stocks, sent fish-and-chips as the traditional British fast food into decline. Perhaps the distinction between 'eating out' and 'eating in' was itself dissolving, for even meals consumed at home had often been bought in prepared form or 'taken away' from restaurants, and from the 1980s the microwave oven made it easy to heat them up. The pre-prepared meal to eat at home, which in the 1950s did not extend far beyond tinned soup and cartons of American cake-mix, had thirty years later greatly extended in range and quality.

The overall trend in alcohol consumption in Britain was upwards, and deaths from cirrhosis of the liver among both sexes in the age-group 15–44 rose markedly in the last quarter of the century, faster in Scotland than in England and Wales, whereas in twelve other European countries the trend was downwards.[348] But changes in eating patterns and locations inevitably influenced drinking patterns. It became easier for restaurants and food shops to supply drink and for pubs to supply food—changes in consumption which by the 1970s brought the UK closer to Europe. The British people were at last moving towards drinking where they were eating—at home and in restaurants—and mergers caused the big brewers in the 1970s to diversify into hotels, food, and leisure. Television and domesticity forced pubs to offer food or other special attractions, and the number of public-house licences declined in relation to liquor licences of other types. Beer was expanding its market with the young, with women, and the middle class, but in the 1960s and 1970s its consumption rose much more slowly than other alcoholic drinks. Wine's consumption increased fastest of all, then cider, then spirits. Heavy beer-drinking was in decline with the decay of heavy industry and with the

[346] *Ind* (5 Nov. 2004), 28.
[347] *FT* (26 June 1984), 10 (tea). Mintel survey quoted *G* (11 May 1994), 9 (takeaways).
[348] *T* (6 Jan. 2006), 16.

mounting distaste for the 'beer belly', an American phrase increasingly used in Britain from the 1970s. With more men and women drinking together, and with growing concern about the relationship between drinking and road accidents, the long-term trend towards weaker types of alcoholic drink was pushed further. It was in the 1960s that Ind Coope's Skol and Guinness's Harp became fashionable, with the beer can gradually ousting the beer bottle; between 1960 and 1980 lager's share of the beer market rose from 1 per cent to 31 per cent. The 3,000 brands of beer in 1966 had shrunk to fewer than 1,500 a decade later.[349] Cans and big brewers were bugbears of the Campaign for Real Ale (CAMRA), which emerged in 1971 and championed traditional mild and bitter. This largely middle-class pressure group built up 30,000 members and even bought its own pubs, forcing the brewing industry at least to modify its centralizing and standardizing strategy in response to consumer demand. In nourishing the demand for traditional beers and in reviving several small breweries in the 1970s, CAMRA demonstrated consumer power as strikingly in its way as the university students' impact in the 1980s on the banks' attitude to student loan schemes or investment in South Africa.[350]

Self-help in health and welfare was especially lively among the disabled after 1970, and involved consciousness-raising as a route to palliation more than prevention. Full participation in the community was claimed as a right, and partly under the influence of American libertarian fashions and of Vietnam war-veterans there was by the 1980s a growing attempt to apply 'non-judgmental' categories to people who were seen as in some way disadvantaged. Ethnic groups could no longer be labelled by skin colour, feminists espoused a new range of gender-neutral terms, homosexuals became 'gays', and people hitherto labelled 'crippled', 'spastic', 'mongols', or (worse) 'incurables', became 'disabled' or 'suffering from Down's syndrome'.[351] Combining rejection of dismissive labelling with encouragements to self-assertion, vocabulary reshaped in this way sometimes, in its humourless loss of proportion, hindered the very causes it aimed to promote. Yet it confronted a serious issue: labels can demoralize and discredit. By the 1980s the term 'spastic', for example, was being used contemptuously as a synonym for 'one who is uncoordinated or incompetent':[352] if only for that reason, it had to go. Likewise with the term 'midget', hitherto familiar but now sometimes used dismissively; in 1971 Baroness Phillips, President of the newly formed Association for Research into Restricted Growth, wanted to ensure that the 2,000 people in this category were included as beneficiaries under the Chronically Sick and Disabled Persons

[349] Gourvish and Wilson, Brewing Industry, 474–7 (mergers); 569 (licences); 452–7 (consumption); 581–4 (beer belly). For lager see 454, 458, 480, 558, and for beer brands 558.
[350] Ibid. 567–8. A. Sampson, The Changing Anatomy of Britain (1982), 310.
[351] 'The Wilder Shores of PC', editorial in Ind (21 July 1992), 16.
[352] Oxford English Dictionary online gives its first citation as 1981 when used in this sense.

Act (1970).[353] People too often confused disability with disease, and disability needed to be demedicalized. Far from advocating segregation into separate educational or medical institutions, campaigners for the disabled wanted them fully integrated. The Education Act (1981), for instance, encouraged handicapped children into normal schools, though at least one prominent advocate later repudiated this policy.[354] 'We are disabled by buildings that are not designed to admit us . . .', wrote Simon Brisenden; 'the disablement lies in the construction of society, not in the physical condition of the individual'. In his view 'we are disabled by a society that is geared to the needs of those who can walk, have perfect sight and hearing, can speak distinctly, and are intellectually dextrous'.[355]

In 1971 private households contained more than three million people with some sort of impairment, two-thirds over 65; nearly a million suffered from what was then by far the greatest single cause of impairment, arthritis. Given the ageing of the population, the disabled category was growing, and an estimate based on a wider definition assigned six million to it, so if family members were included, the disease in some way involved about eighteen million people.[356] Promoting yet another helpful measure in parliament, Alfred Morris, that energetic mid-century champion of the disabled, said that 'I always emphasise, if asked who shall benefit from these provisions, that we are all potentially disabled.'[357] Such an outlook was salutary in so far as it discouraged singling out one among many influences on personality as categorizing the person: hence the renaming in 1990 of the 'Minister for the Disabled' Nicholas Scott as 'Minister for Disabled People'. Yet such sensitivity paradoxically played down the handicap's ongoing significance even after social arrangements had been adjusted. It also downplayed the one characteristic that drew together a group otherwise highly disparate.[358] Statistics on 'the disabled' needed to be refined if those in its numerous subcategories were to be fully integrated. Correctly, from his own point of view, Jack Ashley pointed out that ' "the disabled" do not exist as a homogeneous unit, except in the public mind . . . Some live in total darkness. Some live in total silence. Some cannot speak, and some cannot walk. Indeed, tragically, some cannot even think, they are mentally disabled.'[359]

A newly found self-confidence was the prerequisite for action. Rather than rely solely on 'able' intermediaries like Morris (appointed first Minister for the Disabled in 1974), the disabled needed themselves to mobilize—not least

[353] *HL Deb.* 8 Dec. 1971, cc. 876, 879.   [354] Baroness Warnock, *DT* (9 June 2005), 2.

[355] S. Brisenden, 'Independent Living and the Medical Model of Disability', in T. Shakespeare (ed.), *The Disability Reader: Social Science Perspectives* (1998), 23–4.

[356] A. I. Harris, *Handicapped and Impaired in Great Britain* (1971), 4, 9 (arthritis). J. Ashley, *Acts of Defiance* (1st publ. 1992, paperback edn. 1994), 327.   [357] *HC Deb.* 20 Mar. 1970, c. 911.

[358] As noted in T. Shakespeare, 'Disabled People's Self-Organization: A New Social Movement?', *Disability, Handicap and Society*, 8/3 (1993), 256.   [359] *HC Deb.* 20 Mar. 1970, c. 926.

through a politician such as Ashley, who had every personal reason for showing sympathy. Between them, the Disablement Income Group (launched in 1965) and the all-party Parliamentary Group on Disablement greatly raised public awareness in the late 1960s, deploying helpful overseas precedents for disability pensions. In 1970 the Chronically Sick and Disabled Persons Bill constituted, in Lord Longford's view, 'a fundamental Bill of Rights for the disabled and for the community as a whole'. At last government was coordinating its hitherto fragmented approach. Its arrangements to improve access to buildings eased fuller integration with the community, and the politicians practised what they preached: access to parliament for the disabled greatly improved, and by 1970 wheelchairs were 'a commonplace in the House'.[360] During the early 1970s extended training facilities were introduced to equip the disabled for paid work, building upon the legislation of 1948 and 1964, and improving the job prospects of the disabled. All this was reinforced by the marked progress in producing mechanical and electronic aids to normal living. These efforts to integrate the disabled interacted in complex ways with a further relevant spontaneous development: the growing cult of the body. Such attitudes had earlier encouraged the disabled to hide away, but in the late twentieth century they sought full visibility in competitive sporting events.

In so far as physical self-help fostered exercise and did not prompt self-starvation, it harmonized with much that doctors were recommending. It also harmonized with Thatcher's cost-cutting objectives, though not with her promotion of a 'go-getting' entrepreneurship, for that fostered the striving 'type A personality' which was increasingly alleged to cause heart attacks. Self-help in health and the cult of the body coalesced in British nudism, whose pedigree stemmed from inter-war German and Swiss health-cure movements. By 1953 the forty-one British nudist clubs had 4,000 members, three times as many members by 1974, and twice as many again by 1994.[361] Just when colonial peoples were putting their clothes on, the imperial race was beginning to take them off. In terms of area of flesh exposed, however, commerce and sexuality, more than physical self-help, were the driving forces: profits and pleasure, more than high-mindedness—with the warm overseas beach rather than the chilly hole-and-corner British suburban nudist 'colony' as destination. By European standards British nudism was underdeveloped,[362] and Phil Vallack's *Free Sun: Nude Sea Bathing...in 1979*, by providing a 'good beach guide' to Europe, promoted the practice of nudism if not the theory, and went into several editions. This was a let-down for the nudist movement: the 'holiday-only

---

[360] *HL Deb.* 9 Apr. 1970, c. 241 (Longford). *HC Deb.* 20 Mar. 1970, c. 927.

[361] *British Naturism*, 46 (Nov. 1975), 11; 120 (Summer 1994), 7. See also B. Harrison, 'The Public and the Private in Modern Britain', in P. Burke, B. Harrison, and P. Slack (eds.), *Civil Histories: Essays Presented to Sir Keith Thomas* (Oxford, 2000), 339.

[362] As argued by Alan McCombe in *British Naturism*, 53 (Aug. 1977), 4.

naturist' movement might prosper, but unlike early nudism it was only part-time, and its members often only part-exposed. The grand nudist vision for humankind had faded, for the pioneer nudists had not been mere sunbathers: they sought, not less clothing, but no clothes at all. Besides, as one nudist traditionalist put it, 'big is not necessarily beautiful'.[363]

There was a Victorian pedigree for late twentieth-century self-help in health, whose self-directed rationalistic advocates carried forward something of the Victorian radical's hostility to the doctor-as-priest. They chimed in with the revived wariness of natural science and medicine,[364] and helped to fuel growing scepticism about medical professionalism. Late twentieth-century doctors could not be expected to go on delivering breakthroughs on the scale of the 1940s. Furthermore, new diseases or strains of disease appeared or spread as the world shrank into a global village. The iconoclastic American author Ivan Illich's *Limits to Medicine: Medical Nemesis* (1976) cast doubt on doctors' alleged achievements, argued that the pretensions of 'the medical establishment' threatened health as well as liberty, and claimed that they turned life 'into a pilgrimage through check-ups and clinics back to the ward where it started'; instead he preached the gospel of medical self-help. Ian Kennedy acknowledged Illich among those 'to whom my debt is great' in the preface to his widely discussed Reith lectures of 1980.[365]

Trenchant, irreverent, and quotable, Kennedy's lectures emphasized the doctor's professional self-interest and questioned his scientific and other pretensions. Through categorizing rather than curing, the doctor was allegedly empire-building; through following 'the technological imperative', he had converted the NHS into 'an illness service' which was preoccupied with glamorous cures, big hospitals, and mechanistic rather than environmental and holistic approaches to the body;[366] and in matters of birth and death the doctor was straying well beyond his sphere of competence. In recommending preventive medicine, in urging doctors' need to justify their expenditure to the taxpayer, and in emphasizing medicine's subjective elements, Kennedy's analysis was salutary: 'being ill is not a state, it is a status', he declared, 'to be granted or withheld by those who have the power to do so'.[367] His analysis was also timely for Conservatives newly in power and keen to cut welfare costs. As a lawyer Kennedy was not above empire-building himself, however, recommending the patient-as-consumer to resort more frequently to

[363] John W. Courtney, 'Naturism into the Nineties', *British Naturism*, 100 (Summer 1989), 29.

[364] Harrison, *Seeking a Role*, 366, 448; see also below, p. 398.

[365] I. Illich, *Limits to Medicine: Medical Nemesis. The Expropriation of Health* (1st publ. 1976, paperback edn. 1977), 87. I. Kennedy, *The Unmasking of Medicine* (1981), p. xi.

[366] Kennedy, *Unmasking of Medicine*, 143. *Listener* (20 Nov. 1980), 677; cf. Dr Peter Draper, Director of the Unit for the Study of Health Policy, Guy's Hospital, *T* (3 Sept. 1980), 1.

[367] Kennedy, *Unmasking of Medicine*, 8.

the courts, and some of his remedies were vague and impracticable. Equally irreverent towards professionalism was the assault on Freudian theory and medico-biology conducted by the British psychiatrist Garth Wood in his *Myth of Neurosis* (1983), which saw the term 'neurosis' as diagnostically useless. He saw the therapist with his alleged expertise and allegedly remedial drugs as empire-building, as bamboozling the patient into addictive dependence and dangerous introversion. Self-help through 'moral therapy' would, by contrast, encourage problems to be confronted rather than evaded, and (with friends providing common sense, empathy, and experience) would endow the alleged neurotic with the self-respect that health and happiness require.

Reissued by Penguin as a paperback in 1977, Illich's book adopted a slash-and-burn approach which probably carried little weight in Britain, and Wood probably made less impact there than in America, where psychotherapists wielded more influence. Nonetheless, both authors voiced doubts about professional expertise that were coming to be widely held. These prompted the late twentieth-century trend for doctors to act upon Joseph Fletcher's insight: to keep patients more fully informed and to listen to them more often.[368] The AIDS epidemic highlighted the value of informal and lay self-help groups, at the same time as paramedical services were making themselves indispensable. Given the need for rapid action in emergency cases, it was sensible to bring hospital facilities to the patient rather than the patient to the facilities. In heart-attack cases, for instance, the cardiologist Frank Pantridge had realized in 1965 the good sense of equipping ambulances with defibrillators, and these by the 1990s were carried by all frontline ambulances.[369] The term 'paramedic', to denote people trained to provide specialist emergency care, originated overseas in the 1960s, but by the 1990s had become a familiar term within the UK. Nurses' status and duties were advancing too, both within hospitals and in the general practitioners' new health-centres of the 1960s.

As if all this was not enough, a new point of access for private medicine appeared: revived 'alternative' or 'complementary' medicine. If the acupuncturists, chiropractors, homoeopathists, hypnotherapists, and osteopaths practising in the UK in 1981 were aggregated, they were one-sixth as numerous as general practitioners. To them should be added the herbalists and the rapidly growing pseudo-profession of aromatherapy. Immigrants fuelled complementary medicine's revival: Hindu immigrants guided by their vaids, Muslims by their hakims, were following paths alien to Western medicine, and eighty were practising in the UK by 1981.[370] By the early 1980s complementary medical practitioners were increasing five or six times faster than

---

[368] J. Fletcher, *Morals and Medicine* (1955), 60–1; cf. Loudon *et al.*, *General Practice*, 225.

[369] Obituary, *G* (6 Jan. 2005), 25.

[370] *G* (5 Mar. 1979), 2. S. Fulder, 'Alternative Therapists in Britain', in M. Saks (ed.), *Alternative Medicine in Britain* (Oxford, 1992), 168.

doctors.[371] For the indigenous population, the doctor had never fully ousted the patent medicine and the self-help cure; in 1972 about two-thirds of the adults surveyed had taken a self-prescribed medicine during the previous two weeks.[372] The health store Holland and Barrett was becoming a high-street name, and millions of cod-liver oil, vitamin, garlic, echinacea, evening-primrose-oil, and other pills were disappearing down the throats of a nation that hoped thereby to ward off all manner of ills. Minimally interventionist, holistic in approach, and demanding the patient's active participation, 'alternative' medicine was indeed complementary. Here again Prince Charles diverged from the professions: his speech to the British Medical Association in 1982 prompted sponsored systematic investigation in the area.[373] Despite continuing professional scepticism, the House of Lords, in debating the subject on 11 November 1987, almost unanimously favoured variants of medicine which were moving from 'fringe' to 'alternative' to 'complementary'. The general practitioners' hostility was waning: by 1981 8 per cent of them had joined complementary medicine's professional bodies.[374] Alternative medicine too was now on the familiar road towards the professions' formal association, training, examination, and exclusiveness.

5. OLD AGE REMAPPED

The demographic trends established before 1970 continued thereafter, with more people above retirement age, and with an older age-balance among them, though among ethnic minorities the age-balance was much more youthful.[375] The pensionable rose from 16.2 per cent of Great Britain's total population in 1971 to 18.7 per cent in 1991,[376] and between 1970 and 1990 average UK life expectancy rose from 71.7 to 75.6 years. Others among ten OECD countries, however, were improving even faster. UK men born in 1950–5 could expect to live for 66.7 years, and those born in 1995–2000 for 74.7 years; but between these periods the UK had fallen from fourth place among the ten to seventh; the equivalent figures for women being 71.8 and 79.7, respectively, with a fall from

---

[371] S. J. Fulder and R. E. Munro, 'Complementary Medicine in the United Kingdom: Patients, Practitioners, and Consultations', *Lancet* (7 Sept. 1985), 545. For comparative statistics on its incidence in several Western countries 1985–92 see Webster (ed.), *Caring for Health* (3rd edn.), 229.

[372] V. Berridge and G. Edwards, *Opium and the People: Opiate Use in Nineteenth-Century England* (1981), 238.

[373] Dimbleby, *Prince of Wales*, 306, 309. See also his opening of the Cancer Help Centre at Bristol, *DT* (16 July 1983), 1; and his comments in *T* (17 July 1984), 1.

[374] Fulder, 'Alternative Therapists', 169.

[375] D. Owen 'Size, Structure and Growth of the Ethnic Minority Populations', in Coleman and Salt (eds.), *Ethnicity in the 1991 Census* (1993), i. 115. Haskey, 'Overseas-Born Populations', 23.

[376] A. M. Warnes and R. Ford, *The Changing Distribution of Elderly People: Great Britain, 1981–91* (King's College, London, Dept. of Geography and Age Concern Institute of Gerontology, Occasional Paper, 37), 4.

fifth place to ninth.[377] The UK's overall dependency ratio, rising in the 1950s and 1960s, fell thereafter because the marked fall in youthful dependants more than counteracted the steady rise in aged dependants;[378] the usefulness to demographers of the term 'demographic bonus' to indicate this situation reflects its widespread world incidence. Pensioners were not evenly distributed throughout the UK after 1970: they clustered in Wales and in the south and south-west of England, especially in seaside resorts. In 1991 they made up more than a third of Christchurch local authority's population in Dorset;[379] notably youthful by comparison were London, the statutory new towns, and Northern Ireland.

Old people's growing salience reflected more than longevity and numbers. They were increasingly likely to retire while still able to wield political and commercial influence. Throughout Western Europe, men were withdrawing from the workforce earlier,[380] partly because jobs were not available, partly because the spread of occupational pensions made it easier to retire voluntarily. By the end of the 1980s middle-class unemployment often became statistically invisible, concealed as willingness to take up rather shadowy 'consultancies'. In effect, the average age for retirement had been falling since the 1970s.[381] Some tried repeatedly but failed to get work and were classified as 'discouraged' unemployed; others gave up looking for work, their lowered morale in effect disqualifying them for it, and so joined the 'long-term unemployed' or even 'unemployable' categories. The pace of modern life and the pursuit of modernity was often held to disqualify the old. Peter Walker's local government reform of 1972, for example, pushed out the aldermen: in a modern Britain, direct democracy must be seen to prevail, so out went these older and more experienced councillors whom colleagues had earlier been happy to re-elect for a second three-year term to enhance continuity and capacity in local affairs.

The proportion of the male labour-force over 65 and in work fell from three-quarters in 1881 to only a tenth a century later, partly reflecting diminished agricultural employment, where even in the nineteenth century the workforce had been relatively old.[382] By the early 1980s the earlier retirement age for women, introduced in 1940 to persuade them into war work, seemed increasingly anomalous at a time of equal opportunities, and there was much debate about equalizing the retirement age by raising that of women and lowering that of men.[383] There was not as yet much sign in Britain of a grey

---

[377] Figures from *T* (29 Apr. 1994), 2. Association of the British Pharmaceutical Industry, *Healthcare Handbook 2008* (2008), 45. [378] *TCBST* 75.

[379] Warnes and Ford, *Changing Distribution of Elderly People*, 14.

[380] For comparative figures see *FT* (25 Aug. 1999), 10.

[381] See D. P. Smith's letter in *T* (9 Dec. 1992), 25. F. Williams, 'Have we Already Reached Three Million Jobless?', *T* (26 Nov. 1980), 27.

[382] P. Johnson, 'The Employment and Retirement of Older Men in England and Wales, 1881–1981', *Economic History Review* (Feb. 1994), 108, 116–17, 126. [383] *T* (15 Apr. 1982), 2.

panther movement or of widespread indignation about 'ageism', but Help the
Aged had 113 gift shops by 1977, and its housing association was by then
growing fast; renaming itself the Anchor Housing Association in 1975, it was
accommodating 10,000 tenants by May 1978, and was thereby pioneering the
concept of 'sheltered housing', a phrase which first gained currency in the
mid-1970s.[384] Age Concern, too, was prospering under its Director (1970–87)
David Hobman, a skilful publicist. These were pressure groups organized for,
rather than by, the old. It was the pensioners' persisting political weakness
that enabled the first Thatcher government in 1980 to break the link between
state pensions and average earnings. The state's old-age pensions were tied
thenceforward only to prices or earnings, whichever was the higher, and the
state pension's ratio of average earnings fell markedly thereafter. In his last
budget (1989) Lawson abolished the pensioners' 'earnings rule', which docked
the pensions of those who continued to work during the five years after they
had reached retirement age, but this reform owed nothing to mass pensioner
pressure.[385]

Occupational pensions, complementing the state pension, continued to grow
apace after 1970, covering 19 per cent of pensioners in 1963 and 39 per cent
twenty years later. Final-salary schemes benefited the non-manual employee
because his earnings peaked later and were less likely to decline towards the
end of the working life. The percentage of full-time employees in the 1970s
in occupational pension schemes declined with the descent from professional
to skilled manual to manual worker, from male to female, from full-timer to
part-timer, and from public to private sector.[386] The Labour Party predictably
disliked such schemes, and favoured an earnings-related state pension which
would redistribute funds downwards; by 1969, however, Labour was ready
to operate a partnership between the occupational schemes and a new 'state
earnings-related pension scheme'. Implemented in 1975, the scheme came into
effect in 1978; it aimed to pay from 1998 full earnings-related pensions to
men and women based on earnings during their best thirty years of work, and
thus to obviate paid-up pensioners' need thereafter to claim supplementary
benefit. Within a year, more than ten million people in occupational pension
schemes had contracted out of the state scheme, which the Conservatives almost
abolished in 1985. Their alternative, however—allowing each individual to take
out with an insurance company a pension plan which he felt best met his own
needs—was not popular enough to be politically feasible.[387] Meanwhile, the
number of pensioners depending on supplementary benefit (from 1966 renamed

---

[384] K. Hudson, *Help the Aged: Twenty-One Years of Experiment and Achievement* (1982), 193, 131, 193.
[385] Lawson, *View from No. 11*, 879.
[386] M. R. Miller, 'The Development of Retirement Pensions Policy in Britain from 1945 to 1986:
A Case of State and Occupational Welfare' (University of Kent Ph.D. thesis, 1987), 150–1, 204, 216,
282, 303.   [387] Ibid. 217, 251.

'national assistance') continued to grow: from 1.5 million in 1948 to 4.4 million in 1979 to 8.2 million in 1988.[388]

Longer life after 1970 further subdivided 'the old' as a social category. The number of people in England and Wales aged 80 and above rose steadily after 1911 at the rate of 2–3 per cent a year, and by 1991 3.9 per cent of Great Britain's population came from this age-group.[389] From 1956, reflecting a world-wide trend for industrial societies, the number of centenarians in England and Wales rose at an annual rate of 7 per cent: in 1992 Buckingham Palace sent out 2,738 congratulatory telegrams to centenarians, eight times more than thirty years earlier.[390] The frontier of extreme old age seemed to be advancing: whereas in 1951 only eight people in England and Wales lived beyond 104, by 1981 there were 92.[391] In these circumstances, the idea slowly gained ground that the life-cycle should now subdivide into four phases rather than three: instead of continuously shifting the boundaries of 'middle age' forward, some suggested intruding a 'third age' between middle age and old age. In Britain the reality of the third age had begun to appear in the 1950s, with expectation of life at 65 rising fast from 1951 for women, and more slowly for men; elsewhere in Europe the same trend was observed in the 1960s, but the phrase (never widely used) did not become current until the first of the 'British Universities of the Third Age' was founded at Cambridge in 1981.[392] With longer life and earlier voluntary or obligatory retirement, new opportunities opened up; at the same time, doctors were encouraging the old to live longer by edging them into enhanced intellectual, economic, and even sexual activity. Kinsey may have enjoyed shocking his readers with adolescents' erotic feats, but Masters and Johnson emphasized that octogenarians need not rule themselves out.[393] Longer life, however, did not necessarily mean longer healthy life: by 1971 over 700,000 elderly people in England and Wales were classified as handicapped. At age 65 healthy-life expectancy for men remained almost constant between 1976 and 1992 at about seven years, whereas for women it rose between 1988 and 1992 from nine years to ten.[394]

In the late twentieth century old people were in some respects growing away from the young, and not just because change was now so fast. They were much less likely to occupy the same house as their children: when fit and adequately

[388] Field, *Losing Out*, 23; cf. 126.

[389] A. R. Thatcher, 'Trends in Numbers and Mortality at High Ages in England and Wales', *Population Studies*, 40 (1992), 414. Warnes and Ford, *Changing Distribution of Elderly People*, 4.

[390] R. Thatcher, 'The Demography of Centenarians in England and Wales', *Population Trends* (Summer 1999), 6. For telegrams see *G* (16 July 1993), 26; cf. *DT* (28 Sept. 1981), 8.

[391] See the valuable table in Thatcher, 'Trends in Numbers', 415.

[392] P. Laslett, 'The Emergence of the Third Age', *Ageing and Society*, 7/2 (June 1987), 133, 144.

[393] Robinson, *Modernization of Sex*, 146.

[394] R. M. Moroney, *The Family and the State: Considerations for Social Policy* (1976), 41. *Ind* (8 Dec. 1995), 5.

backed by the social services, they preferred to live alone when they could afford to do so. Because they now lived so long, their bequests tended to arrive well after their children's period of maximum need.[395] From the 1960s, usage of the term 'geriatric' escalated,[396] often pejoratively. Assaults by young people on pensioners, whose black eyes and scarred faces were photographed on the inside pages of the *Daily Telegraph* during the 1980s and after, appalled its readers and others besides, including the Prince of Wales. The decade witnessed a growing tendency to regard the elderly as a 'burden' on society.[397] This was not because they cost appreciably more: social-security payments to pensioners remained at about 11 per cent of government expenditure in the 1970s and 1980s, and though in the 1980s pensioners' share of gross national product was slowly rising, payments to younger age-groups in respect of unemployment and poverty ensured that pensioners' share of total government expenditure on social security (excluding NHS expenditure) fell quite sharply.[398]

Who, then, cared for the old? The family had not yet vacated this scene, least of all among immigrants from South Asia: the two-generation household of married couples was far more prevalent among Asians than among whites or Caribbeans in Britain, and most elderly Asians lived in large and complex households.[399] Among other groups, the old were less likely to live with offspring, who often now pursued careers in a world whose transport changes had dispersed the population widely; daughters-at-home, once such a prop to the old, were now a rarity, and were anyway often in paid work. British welfare policy after 1951 aimed very much to enable the old to stay in their own homes, assisted by chair-lifts and other mechanical aids to independence and by home-based welfare services: home helps, meals on wheels, and the like. In 1981 nearly a third of people aged between 65 and 74 lived alone, and nearly half of those aged 75 and more.[400] The number of meals served at home in Great Britain for elderly and physically disabled people rose from sixteen million in 1971/2 to 37 million in 1991/2. Home helps, responding to the growing numbers in England and Wales who needed their services, doubled between 1970 and 1990 when expressed as full-time equivalents.[401]

Parents too old for the family to cope with their disabilities moved to old people's homes, which in 1985 accommodated 223,000 people.[402] As so often, charities and pressure groups pioneered recognition of needs which the free market subsequently supplied. By the 1980s estate agents, builders, and local

---

[395] Anderson, 'Modern Life Cycle', 76.   [396] As indicated by a COPAC search.

[397] *T* (8 Mar. 1984), 32 (Prince of Wales); and see the protest by Robert Bessell in *T* (6 Aug. 1983), 7.

[398] See the important table in P. Johnson and J. Falkingham, 'Intergenerational Transfers and Public Expenditure on the Elderly in Modern Britain', *Ageing and Society*, 8/2 (June 1988), 141.

[399] Modood and Berthoud (eds.), *Ethnic Minorities in Britain*, 44–6.

[400] Coleman and Salt, *British Population*, 225.

[401] *Social Trends* (1995), 145 (meals). See table 15.4 in *TCBST* 519 (home helps).

[402] Coleman and Salt, *British Population*, 231.

authorities increasingly recognized how saleable were halfway houses between the private home and the public institution—from pensioners' residential compounds to old people's homes containing individual rooms owned by the pensioner. The house-building firm McCarthy & Stone specialized from the mid-1970s in catering for pensioners' housing requirements, and by 2000 had captured 70 per cent of this market.[403] By the 1980s the practice of what was later known as 'equity release' had become widespread: thereby, aged house-owners in a rising housing market boosted their income by mortgaging what were often quite large houses. So keen were the old to remain in their own homes that there was some debate in the 1970s about whether a person should be allowed to die there rather than be pushed into receiving better but institutionalized medical care. 'After all', wrote one Medical Officer of Health, 'voluntarily to elect to die alone . . . is not a crime in this country'.[404]

The hospice movement, whose breakthrough had occurred in the 1960s, faced the fact that doctors, having cured or prevented so many diseases, could increasingly now only postpone and palliate, but could not avoid ultimate failure. Central to the hospice outlook was doctors' growing capacity for managing pain. This encouraged doctors to redirect some of their research enthusiasm towards resuming their earlier role in alleviating symptoms rather than pursuing cures. Among them was John Lloyd, who founded the first specialist centre for pain relief in Britain at Abingdon Hospital in 1972.[405] This shift in research priorities also entailed a shift within hospital power-structures. 'It cannot be stated too emphatically', said Ian Kennedy in 1980, 'that the definition of death is not a scientific, technical matter.'[406] The hospice movement needed no such reminder: there the medical specialist stepped off his pedestal and consulted more overtly with nurses, social workers, chaplains, and even patients. Hospices treated the patient as still, however precariously, a whole person. They gave more influence to women: 'this was very much nurse-led', Cicely Saunders recalled, 'it's nurse-power'. By the early 1960s she was combining organizing, fund-raising, learning, and nursing with accumulating an international network of experts and promoting what had become an international movement. She had simultaneously to ride the two horses of promotion and rebuttal in an area where misrepresentation was all too easy. After 1970 British hospices grew through what she called 'the snowball effect': drawing closer together within the UK, diversifying into home-care and day centres, encouraging pain research, and propagating overseas their special mix of professional and lay involvement. Having begun by hiving off from hospitals, the hospice movement was by the 1980s fertilizing them with its new insights. By the

[403] S. Mesure, 'The Senior Service', *Ind* (20 June 2001), business review, 3.
[404] E. W. Kinsey, letter to *T* (8 Jan. 1973), 13. See also letters in *G* (3 Jan. 1976), 10.
[405] Harrison, *Seeking a Role*, 287–9. Lloyd's obituary, *DT* (19 Oct. 1999), 29.
[406] Kennedy, *Unmasking of Medicine*, 161.

end of the century there were 400 hospice and palliative care units in the British Isles.[407]

For Saunders the hospice's palliative care, by injecting dignity and even opportunity into the dying process, undermined the case for euthanasia. For euthanasia's advocates, however, the hospice's scarce and expensive facilities failed to meet the need of the individual who simply wanted to die. Given the potential conflict of interest between young and old, there was every reason to be cautious about euthanasia. *World Medicine* in 1968 pointed out that medical advance, reinforced by organ transplants, now enabled the old to live on at the expense of the young: 'there is a problem which is caused not by too many births but by too few deaths'. For Archbishop Coggan in 1976, to prolong human life could not be an end in itself: he wanted to end the 'conspiracy of silence' in this area, and while fully aware of Nazi horrors, thought the public should be alert to competing spending priorities within an overstretched NHS.[408] In 1976 opinion polls showed support among all religious denominations except Roman Catholics (evenly divided) for the idea that the doctor should with the patient's consent terminate life 'if a patient is suffering from a distressing and incurable physical illness': 62 per cent of those surveyed agreed, as compared with 55 per cent in 1950. Voluntary euthanasia attracted 50 per cent of those polled in 1969, 72 in 1985, 75 in 1989, and 79 per cent in 1993.[409]

In the 1960s the Voluntary Euthanasia Society was a tiny pressure group, with only a tiny staff, and depended heavily on volunteers. It was recruited largely from educated non-religious members of the professional classes, often from people distressed by the painful death of a friend or relative. It was, however, a world-wide movement, and its British supporters owed much to more lively movements overseas, especially in the Netherlands during the 1980s and in the USA during the 1990s. The hazards of moving in such territory were vividly exposed, however, in 1979 when the Society briefly changed its name to EXIT and became more radical in tone and methods. In 1980 its membership rose from 2,000 to 10,000 while it was gearing itself up to publishing a booklet, *The Guide to Self-Deliverance* (1981), with a preface by Arthur Koestler informing its members on how to kill themselves.[410] The Society was especially keen to prevent bungled suicides; more than 6,000 copies of the booklet sold during its first fifteen months, and several suicides seem to have flowed directly from it.[411] In 1981 the organization Life accused

[407] Author's interview with Saunders on 1 Sept. 1997 (snowball effect). P. C. Jupp and C. Gittings (eds.), *Death in England: An Illustrated History* (Manchester, 1999), 272.

[408] Quotations from *T* (14 Aug. 1968), 2, and from Coggan addressing Royal Society of Medicine, *G* (14 Dec. 1976), 30.

[409] Voluntary Euthanasia Society, *Newsletter*, 3 (Jan. 1979), 1; 49 (Sept. 1993), 3.

[410] Voluntary Euthanasia Society, *Newsletter*, 14 (Jan. 1982), 8 (citing a survey); 11 (Jan. 1981), 2 (EXIT).   [411] *O* (28 Oct. 1979), 1. *G* (31 Oct. 1981), 4. *T* (31 Oct. 1981), 3.

Dr Leonard Arthur, a Derby paediatrician, of trying to murder a Down's syndrome baby; he was acquitted,[412] but when in the same year Nicholas Reed, EXIT's General Secretary, was convicted of assisting suicide and had to resign, the Society backtracked, resumed its former name, and ceased to distribute the *Guide*. Backed by public figures such as the broadcaster Ludovic Kennedy and the actor Dirk Bogarde, however, the Society did not fade entirely from the news, if only because in the new situation created by modern medicine its concerns were so widely shared.

The male suicide rate in the UK rose in the 1970s and 1980s, levelled off in the 1990s, and then declined, whereas the suicide trend for women (much lower than for men) differed: steady in the 1970s, it declined in the 1980s and early 1990s, and then again levelled off. Among men from 15 to 24 the suicide rate was rising (in a world-wide trend) to new peaks in the 1980s, and then levelled off, but it remained three times as common as among women in the same age-group. In other age-groups too, men were much more likely than women to kill themselves, though the contrast was less marked. The number of Samaritan branches and volunteers continued rising during the 1970s but stabilized thereafter, though its verbal contacts with people needing help continued to rise during the 1980s, not stabilizing till the 1990s.[413] Chad Varah thought its 18,500 volunteers as at 1975 created 'oases of humanity in the desert of man's selfishness and indifference'. Taking a pride in the Samaritans' lay participation and amateur status, he envisaged their growing away from reliance on the clergy, and as satisfying a need within the welfare state for altruistic outlets.[414]

The long-term secularizing trend in Britain by no means weakened the need for ceremonial in death. In what had hitherto been one of the most conservative areas of British life, death ceremonial showed signs of diversifying. From the early 1970s there began a trend among bereaved parents for formally commemorating stillbirths and late terminations, and by the late 1980s this had transformed hospital policy throughout Britain. Secularized self-help styles of commemoration were spreading during the 1980s: AIDS funerals from mid-decade were decidedly inventive, and the practice of laying flowers and symbols at the place of death first became manifest on a large scale after ninety-four people died in a crush when Liverpool were playing Nottingham Forest on neutral ground at Sheffield Wednesday's Hillsborough stadium on 15 April 1989; in the subsequent week about a million people visited Liverpool's home stadium, Anfield, to deposit flowers and footballing regalia (Plate 14). Although

---

[412] *O* (8 Nov. 1981), 12.

[413] Chart 7.15 in www.statistics.gov.uk/statbase/ssdataset (suicides). Statistics on Samaritan branches collected from annual reports by Josephine Webb as background material for *TCBST* 608.

[414] C. Varah (ed.), *The Samaritans in the '70s to Befriend the Suicidal and Despairing* (1977), 14, 29, 30, 37, 71.

the demand for humanist funerals was growing by the 1980s, it remained small, with only about 1,300 conducted in 1988.[415] And whether the memorial service, increasingly popular, was overtly humanist or not, it was humanist in effect: its emphasis lay on the earthly career and personality of the departed rather than on their hopes for another world.

Nonetheless, the secularization process was subtly at work even within the religious funeral ceremony, where the growing concern for the psychological health of the bereaved had almost ousted preoccupation with the spiritual health of the departed. Secular and even popular music was increasingly heard at funerals, and there was a less stiff preoccupation with the proprieties. Medical, bureaucratic, and even commercial priorities left less room for anything other than a vague form of religion,[416] and gave much less prominence to the clergyman. The funeral director now possessed the growing expertise that was required. Cremation and the medicalization of death made disposal of the corpse less protracted: by the late 1980s nearly three-quarters of deaths occurred away from home, and of those who died, nearly three-quarters were cremated, one of the highest rates in the world. Partly as a result, there were large economies of scale and many mergers in the late twentieth-century funeral trade. The effect of all these changes was to concentrate the management of death into male hands: the decline of home deaths, as of home births, weakened women's control over these major events. What with amalgamation among the funeral firms and growing geographical mobility among their customers, the funeral had now become less a dignified and prolonged community celebration, more a cursory and even furtive family function.[417]

6. FRIENDSHIP IN FLUX

Many of the changes discussed in this and other chapters had profound implications for the nature and incidence of friendship. Before the 1960s the separation of spheres between the sexes was widespread, though without precluding friendship between spouses. In 1867, in the first British parliamentary speech to recommend votes for women, the distinguished philosopher John Stuart Mill had spoken of the 'silent domestic revolution' already occurring whereby 'women and men are, for the first time in history, really each other's companions'.[418] Yet romantic love by no means necessarily shaped Victorian marriages from the start, let alone later, and friendships from the highest

---

[415] Jupp and Gittings (eds.), *Death in England*, 277. M. J. A. Naylor, 'The Funeral: The Management of Death and its Rituals in a Northern, Industrial City' (University of Leeds Ph.D. thesis, 1989), 367.

[416] Naylor, 'The Funeral', 177. Jupp and Gittings (eds.), *Death in England*, 276.

[417] Naylor, 'The Funeral', 163, 361. P. C. Jupp, *From Dust to Ashes: The Replacement of Burial by Cremation in England 1840–1967* (Congregational Lecture 1990), 27. *T* (13 Feb. 2002), 14.

[418] *HC Deb.* 20 May 1867, c. 821.

social levels downwards frequently took a single-sex direction. With men, such friendships often originated and flourished outside the home through the many semi-private enclaves within public life: in pubs, sports clubs, professional bodies and boardrooms, political parties, single-sex Oxford and Cambridge colleges and public schools, fashionable London clubs, and in parliament itself. There it was assumed that business could and should be mixed with pleasure in an atmosphere of male companionship which generated the intense personal loyalties so prized in British life. Only within this context can many social, intellectual, and political movements be understood, up to and including CND, the Gaitskellites, and the SDP. Women, too, had their single-sex networks, the many semi-public enclaves within private life—held together by correspondence, close family bonds, neighbourhood groups, childcare structures, voluntary and religious bodies, and latterly by feminist organizations. Until early in the twentieth century these networks had been enriched by the cross-class friendships between women that charity and domestic service had made possible.

By the 1960s, however, two major changes had weakened sex-segregated friendship. Smaller families and better homes made friendship within the family more feasible, whether between spouses (married or unmarried) or between parents and children; and diminished pregnancy and easier divorce made the female prostitute and mistress less integral to the late twentieth-century conventional family structure.[419] Mill's domestic revolution had matured, but at the same time women's growing pursuit of careers gradually prised open centres of power hitherto exclusively male, from coeducational schools upwards, aiming to replicate in public life the more relaxed friendship between the sexes that was now feasible in private life. The time and the emotional resources integral to friendship are finite, however: if friendship grows in some directions, it contracts in others. Single-sex bonds between mother and daughter and between female neighbours, once so central to the closeness of slum and suburban life, began to weaken. Slums were fast disappearing, and the suburb was fast becoming a dormitory area for both sexes, its friendships either generated elsewhere (at work) or at home (behind closed doors). It was the intermediate, community-based friendships that suffered.

With increasingly relaxed sexual relations in society as a whole, however, and with sexuality more frequently viewed recreationally, an overt sexual component became more feasible within friendships of any kind. In 1968 *The Times* noted that whereas a generation earlier the unmarried student who had sexual relations felt guilty, 'now it is the student who stays chaste who is more likely to be loaded with the neurotic burden of society's own sexual anxiety'.[420] And with women enjoying more wealth and power, there was growing late

---

[419] Harrison, *Seeking a Role*, 237.   [420] *T* (23 May 1968), 11 (leader).

twentieth-century talk of older women taking younger male partners. The frontier between citizen and prostitute, whether male or female, was in this as in other respects becoming blurred. By the late 1990s London female prostitutes were said to be catering for more than 80,000 men each week, or for one in sixteen men in London aged between 20 and 40, but most female prostitutes now operated from massage parlours, clubs, and saunas, advertising with stickers in telephone booths, rather than soliciting in the streets.[421] Growing acceptance of homosexuality simultaneously simplified and complicated friendships between men. Where there had been a strong sexual component in such friendships, they could now increasingly be seen for what they were; where there had been no such component, heterosexual males now felt it necessary to make this clear. Liberation for some entailed constraint for others.

The range of any one person's friendships broadened with the growing mobility that in an affluent society flowed from such developments as motorways, the tourist industry, paid work for women, and universities aiming for national rather than local recruitment. Friends and relatives were now more dispersed, and neighbours were now relatively ephemeral. The national average for number of friends in 2003 was 33 at any one time, only six of them close, with a total of 396 during a lifetime, but with advancing age their number declined, especially during people's thirties. On passing age 35, one in six of a man's friends lived overseas, and one in ten of a woman's. All the more necessary to friendship, then, was improved electronic communication, and we have seen how telephone calls were escalating after 1970, chased after the mid-1990s by e-mails and text-messages. Online technology was also creating a new category, the 'silent friend', rarely spoken to or seen; in 2003 such friends featured in the lives of one in three UK people in their twenties and thirties, communicating up to four times a day by e-mails and text-messaging.[422] The internet was also creating 'virtual' communities of people with shared opinions or tastes who could not have found one another by any other means. On the other hand, growing informality and changing manners—moulded by American culture, by the business schools, and by the media—were by the 1990s eroding any overt distinction between friends and the rest. A mood of simulated friendship reflected an Americanized grooming of customers by employees who had learnt their manners on special courses.

In this chapter we have seen how the progressive unfolding of the sexual revolution, with all its implications for women's employment and the function of the family, continued apace after 1970, and carried substantial implications

---

[421] *Ind* (26 Sept. 1997), 9.

[422] *T* (28 Nov. 2003), 12. MSN Messenger press release 28 Nov. 2003 at www.microsoft.com/uk/press/content/presscentre/releases/2003/11/pro3170.mspx, consulted 1 Aug. 2006. For telephones see above, p. 76.

for the lives of children. With the boundary between adolescence and adulthood increasingly blurred, and with legal challenges to the parents' authority building up, the young experienced gains as well as losses. Advances in welfare and health-care were formidable for all age-groups, and gave more independence and longevity to the old. Like all the changes discussed in this chapter, they also had implications for evolving patterns of friendship.

All eight motifs have proved relevant in this discussion. Public welfare's internal dynamic advertises the politician's limited room for manœuvre within a pluralist society (the seventh motif), when so much of the dynamic was powered by volunteers, especially by the whistleblowers and the self-organized sick and disabled. On moral and family questions, too—though for different reasons—the politician depended heavily on outside pressures, and usually took care to lag behind the times or keep a low profile. British political institutions retained stability amidst rapid social change (the sixth motif) by doing the same, belatedly encouraging more women into parliament and benefiting from public welfare's stabilizing impact. Here the Second World War's legacy was not at all equivocal (the first motif): it had accelerated both public welfare and women's paid employment, both of which were still growing apace in the 1970s and 1980s. Public welfare did much to render the general public more content than the politicians with the UK economy (the third motif), continuously concerned as politicians had to be about its funding. With planning increasingly introduced at a personal level into birth, parenthood and death, the insecurities which had fuelled religious belief were undermined, and the one-time religious basis for family institutions (one dimension of the fifth motif) was undermined; the counselling professions and funeral directors increasingly encroached on the clergyman's terrain. The time-saving devices which enabled married women to work and required the old to learn from the young, brought the familiar and highly paradoxical speeding up of daily life (the fourth motif). Family change in the 1970s and 1980s to a large extent provided an arena for the contest between traditionalists resisting overseas innovation and progressives receptive to it (the second motif): it mobilized pressure from UK Europeans on UK youth employment, euthanasia, and corporal punishment; from Americans and Scandinavians on UK sexuality, welfare, and feminism. In none of this was there any distinctive world role for the UK (the eighth motif): if anything, an earlier role was lost, given that the British 'welfare state' no longer blazed a world-wide trail; indeed, the UK variant had now become controversial.

CHAPTER 5

Industry and Commerce

In 1970 wartime consensus ideas were very much alive, even under a self-consciously non-interventionist Conservative government. Britain's political and intellectual elite still envisaged promoting economic growth through the wartime route: corporatist cooperation between trade unions, employers' organizations, and an interventionist government. Both Conservative and Labour parties in the 1970s travelled in the same vehicle (corporatist planning), aimed for the same destination (relative as well as absolute material prosperity, without inflation), and diverged only on how best to get there. Yet during the 1970s the difficulties posed by corporatist structures became increasingly apparent, and were illuminated through the attempt by governments of both parties to operate an incomes policy. This crisis was as much political as economic, and is discussed in the first section. The outcome, surprising to many, was a marked shift in the political agenda, whose origin is discussed in the second section. The consequences for the British economy are outlined in the third section, and for the workforce in the fourth. The chapter concludes with a section which briefly discusses the impact of these and other changes on the consumer. The UK therefore saw major changes in its political economy between 1970 and 1990, though all-party acceptance for a rebased party-political consensus took rather longer.

1. CORPORATISM IN CRISIS

Inflation rose continuously in Britain after the war, but by 1970 it was rising much faster than in the USA and OECD countries,[1] accentuating 'the British disease' of bad labour relations, low productivity, and poor-quality goods unreliably delivered. Inflation's reduction (together with curbing unemployment) was a major government priority for the next two decades, yet it was thrice accelerated by government itself. The attempt by Anthony Barber, Heath's Chancellor of the Exchequer, to curb unemployment in the pre-election boom of 1973–4 added to an inflation already worsened by rapidly rising oil prices. At

[1] F. Hirsch and J. H. Goldthorpe (eds.), *The Political Economy of Inflation* (1978), 10–11.

first the Labour government from 1974 dangerously delayed resolute counter-measures, allowing inflation to trigger the threshold agreements built into the Heath government's incomes policy. Then in 1979, after Labour's three years of successful wage restraint, it set up the Standing Commission on Pay Comparability, chaired by Hugh Clegg. During the election campaign of that year the Conservatives promised to act upon its awards, and did so in 1980, though they took care to abolish the Commission soon after-wards, yet inflation with full encouragement from an oil-strengthened pound rose even faster. Its effects were more than narrowly economic. It encour-aged debt and mortgages because over time it painlessly shrank them in real terms; it prompted annual wage reviews whose aim was always upwards, with consequent friction about differentials; it made accounting methods, tax rates, wage bargaining, and returns on saving less transparent; and it fostered an overall strike-prone, fractious mood of economic and even polit-ical uncertainty. The common sense of the individual gave way to collective unreason.

After 1970 there followed two governments with contrasting ways of tackling inflation. Both failed, yet their failures were a necessary preparation for what followed; prudence in the short term and democracy in the longer term both required that the corporatist strategy be tested to destruction. The Heath government (1970–4) at first struck an unfamiliar note by emphasizing the need for self-help: the aim was to rejuvenate wartime corporatism by requiring its participants voluntarily to deliver within a less interventionist climate. Failing firms would not be baled out, but the law would advance further into industrial relations. Wilson seized upon the Conservatives' pre-election policy-forming meeting in January 1970 at Selsdon Park to exaggerate the scale of this change, labelling the allegedly new type of Tory as 'Selsdon man'. In reality, Selsdon Park involved little more than a change of tone: it contrasted only with the more interventionist mood introduced by Macmillan in the late 1950s and carried forward by Wilson after 1964, and would have been familiar enough to observers of Conservative election campaigning in 1950 and 1951. Heath himself was consistently a man for interventionist consensus, Macmillan's right-hand man as chief whip from 1955–9. As cabinet minister, Heath's prime preoccupation had been with getting Britain into the EEC, where corporatist ideas were even more entrenched than in Britain. Among his cabinet colleagues, the dominant figure in 1970 was Iain Macleod, his one-nation Conservative Chancellor of the Exchequer, and Heath's government drew heavily on traditional elite families: Whitelaw, Carrington, and Douglas-Home, later joined by Pym and Gilmour. Even Thatcher and Joseph gave little inkling in cabinet of their subsequent free-market radicalism, as Heath waspishly pointed out in his memoirs. Enoch Powell, the one prominent Conservative whose ideas anticipated what was to come, had in effect excluded himself from direct influence by his views on immigration. After 1970, as before, IEA ideas remained on the political fringe.

So when surprised by the fierce hostility to its trade union legislation in 1971 and by the flying pickets and the militancy of miners and shipyard workers in 1972,[2] the Heath government retreated through a so-called 'u-turn' into an unabashed corporatism which did not seem so very uncongenial, least of all to Heath himself. When Rolls Royce, symbol of British manufacturing prestige, went bankrupt in 1971, Wilson told parliament that 'the whole country will regard this as an extremely grave tragedy',[3] and amidst rising unemployment the state could hardly stand by in such a case. Unemployment reached the symbolic figure of a million in January 1972, and inflation was accelerating dangerously. To any one-nation or paternalist and traditionalist Conservative, a corporatist response seemed at first sight the most democratic, sensible, and humane approach—all the more attractive to Heath because compatible with EEC structures and attitudes. A u-turn would of course be embarrassing, especially given Conservative backbench hostility to it. 'When are you going to introduce your national plan?' one MP asked the Secretary of State for Trade and Industry amid Labour MPs' delight, when in March 1972 the government showed signs of intervening further.[4] Heath was not a man to shirk any painful task if the national interest seemed to require it: his mood was pragmatic and never narrowly partisan. Reasonable men, he thought, should be able to agree at least as readily in 1972 as in 1940. Yet given the concurrent serious crisis in Northern Ireland, people began to ask whether the country was governable.[5] It seemed essential to uphold democracy by placing the formation of policy on a broader and therefore politically more stable foundation. Benn was not alone in thinking that it would be safer to enlist than resist the trade unions' new-found power: 'the old classical economics are no longer relevant to a wholly new political situation', wrote Maudling in September 1972, urging a return to incomes policies.[6]

Renewed interventionism, however, required public support, and Heath was no Lloyd George. Uncomfortable with the media, he was an uninspiring speaker, too shy to nourish a strong national following. It later became clear that he earnestly desired national unity and reconciliation, but trade union leaders so intensely disliked his industrial-relations legislation of 1971 that, however much they might privately respect him, they could not risk being seen publicly to back him. His government's statutory incomes policy launched in November 1972 could win public support from trade union leaders only if they knew it would not alienate their rank and file. The only full-blown incomes policies

[2] For the industrial-relations dimension of this period see above, p. 153.
[3] HC Deb. 4 Feb. 1971, c. 1932.   [4] Cited by David McKie in G (23 Mar. 1972), 1.
[5] e.g. R. Butt, 'Should Heath Go to the Country?', ST (13 Feb. 1972), 12.
[6] 'Maudling Memorandum on Incomes', T (12 Sept. 1972), 12; cf. below, p. 308.

hitherto implemented had been under Labour governments with close trade union links, and even those policies had eventually wilted. Popular at first, their reconciling role only postponed trouble: they tended to accumulate anomalies and pressures that could not ultimately be contained, and the attempt to enforce them threatened the credibility not only of governments, but of the political system itself. Stage I of Heath's policy, from November 1972 to January 1973, involved a freeze; stage II, from February 1973 to October 1973, envisaged a wage norm of £1 a week plus 4 per cent, monitored by a Pay Board and a Price Commission. But it was stage III, from November 1973 to February 1974, which exposed the limits to an incomes policy's reconciling role. Heath might present his strategy as a 'giant step towards social justice',[7] but the fact remained that the crisis involved in enforcing it seemed artificial. It was real enough for one of its key participants: William Armstrong, head of the civil service. His impartiality had suffered from identifying too closely and too publicly with Heath's policies, and his civil service career ended tragically. Chain-smoking at the height of the crisis, he talked 'very wildly' to intimates 'about the whole system collapsing and the world coming to an end', and summoned a meeting of permanent secretaries at which he 'told them all to go home and prepare for Armageddon'; then, 'babbling incoherently', he was led from the room to hospital.[8]

To have any hope of success, Heath needed a strong endorsement for his policy, but at the general election of February 1974 less than a third of the voters backed him, six million voted Liberal partly in the hope of conciliation, and more than eleven million voted Labour partly in the hope that Wilson might manage things better. This was not the most comfortable moment in British history. 'I have been expecting the collapse of capitalism all my life', wrote the historian A. J. P. Taylor late in 1973, worrying about industrial relations and the three-day week: 'now that it comes I am rather annoyed'. Labour, which succeeded the Conservatives in office in March 1974, seemed at first to have no remedy for the problems Heath had confronted except what looked like appeasing irresponsible trade unionists. Whitehall's mood was gloomy, and at a meeting between the CBI and the new prime minister in March, the industrialists gave what Benn described as 'just one long moan'; the CBI, beset by uncertainties, 'sounded absolutely licked'. Lord Rothschild in October, retiring from the heart of British government as Director-General of the cabinet's CPRS, felt 'increasingly fearful about the effects of the growing political hostility between and among our people'.[9] Academics began to write in

---

[7] Speech at Free Trade Hall, Manchester, *G* (21 Feb. 1974), 6.

[8] Donoughue, *Downing Street Diary*, ii. 153 (23 Feb. 1977), reporting Robert Armstrong's account. For other accounts see Hennessy, *Whitehall*, 240–1. Benn, *Diaries 1973–6*, 422 (22 July 1975).

[9] Quotations from A. Sisman, *A. J. P. Taylor: A Biography* (1st publ. 1994, paperback edn. 1995), 369. Benn, *Diaries 1973–6*, 130 (28 Mar. 1974). Rothschild letter to H. Wilson entitled 'Farewell to the Think Tank', quoted in Hennessy, *Whitehall*, 247. For the CPRS see below, pp. 444–5.

their learned journals about the problems of 'overload': of governments being unable to satisfy the electors' high expectations.[10]

Yet almost since losing power in 1970 Wilson had been planning an alternative route to Heath's destination which would give Labour the edge over the Conservatives. The idea of pursuing a corporatist strategy through a 'social contract' between the labour movement's political and trade union wings apparently originated in 1970 with the economist Thomas Balogh's reference to 'a new *"contrat social"*' in a Fabian Society publication, and by spring 1971 Wilson was using the Anglicized terms 'social compact' and 'social contract' interchangeably.[11] Jack Jones, increasingly powerful as TGWU General Secretary, then began private discussions. These produced a breakthrough on 18 February 1972, when he publicly advocated setting up a voluntary conciliation and arbitration agency for resolving industrial disputes; the joint liaison committee between National Executive Committee, Parliamentary Labour Party (PLP), and TUC held its first meeting three days later.[12] The labour movement had much to gain from a compact: Labour politicians wanted to demonstrate that they could run the country better than the Conservatives and so win the next election, and the trade unions wanted a Labour government to jettison Heath's legislation on industrial relations. 'This Government is God's gift to militants and trouble-makers', said Wilson, shortly before the general election of February 1974.[13] Like Heath, Wilson aimed to outmanoeuvre extremists: for example, the Communist miners' leader Mick McGahey, who envisaged the miners' dispute of 1973–4 as leading to class confrontation in which government troops and strikers would fraternize.[14] When confronted by serious disputes within the community, Wilson as a good parliamentarian wanted to get the political process back into its customary reconciling role; he and Heath diverged only on how this was best done.

Edging the trade union leaders rather faster towards a compact than they wanted to go, Wilson during the general election in February claimed that Labour was better than the Conservatives at working with the trade unions: its 'great social contract' between government, industry and the unions could produce 'a dramatic change for the better in industrial relations'.[15] Until well after the election it remained unclear whether it was a 'social compact' or a 'social contract',[16] but Wilson envisaged it as an evolving relationship. He knew

[10] e.g. A. King, 'Overload: Problems of Governing in the 1970s', *Political Studies* (1975), 288–9, 295.
[11] T. Balogh, *Labour and Inflation* (Fabian Tract; Oct. 1970), 44, cf. 54, 60. Wilson, *Final Term*, 43, 253.
[12] J. Jones, 'How to Rebuild Industrial Relations', *NS* (18 Feb. 1972), 202. Benn, *Diaries 1968–72*, 406 (21 Feb. 1972). *G* (29 Mar. 1974), 19.
[13] *T* (4 Jan. 1974), 2.   [14] *T* (28 Jan. 1974), 2.
[15] Speech at Nottingham in *G* (18 Feb. 1974), 7. For hesitations from Scanlon, AUEW General Secretary, see *T* (19 Feb. 1974), 4; *ST* (24 Feb. 1974), 17; *Listener* (28 Feb. 1974), 266.
[16] Castle, *Diaries 1974–6*, 84 (22 Apr. 1974).

well enough that trade union leaders' experience of incomes planning in the 1960s precluded any statutory policy. But he hoped that by deploying as a bait the Labour government's powers to tax and redistribute, he could edge the trade unions towards voluntary wage restraint. Some Conservatives saw this as a sell-out: any party could keep the trade unions on board by merely granting their wishes. It was easier to press for state subsidy than directly to improve competitiveness by catering for the consumer under the ultimate sanction of bankruptcy. Wilson's policy was subtler than that, however, for one appeases only an enemy, whereas Labour saw the trade unions as friends. Besides, in the outcome, the trade unions gained little from the compact.

The Conservatives apparently had no practicable alternative: 'they would like a social contract too', Wilson purred in September. Yet his conciliatory strategy was dangerous, for by the mid-1970s inflation was running at record levels, and close observers were surprised at Wilson's lack of urgency: in June 1974 the well-informed diarist Bernard Donoughue, Wilson's adviser on social policy, thought economic strategy and incomes policy 'not properly in the government machine at all', but fragmented between separate committees and 'simply operating privately in the minds of Healey and Foot'.[17] Wilson later recalled that, rather than rush into an incomes policy that would not stick, 'we had to play for time'. In May 1975 Crosland announced that 'the party's over', and by July the need for a national pay limit had become urgent.[18] The success of voluntary restraint was all too doubtful, but support for it had to be canvassed; failure after giving voluntarism a fair run would prepare the ground for something stronger. Once the 'yes' vote on the EEC referendum on 5 June 1975 had strengthened Wilson against Labour's left, he could promote what became phase I of the Labour governments' three-phase incomes policy: Jack Jones's proposal of a flat-rate increase of £6 a week for which anyone earning less than £8,500 a year was eligible, though not necessarily entitled.

Wilson decided that voluntary restraint on this basis could succeed only if successfully sold to the NUM's annual conference. In drafting his speech, with its emotive references to labour history, and to the need for loyalty to a Labour government 'at a critical hour in the nation's history', he later claimed to have taken unprecedented care, 'dictating, writing, amending, inserting, discarding and drafting again'. 'Well, you did what you came for', McGahey told him on 7 July when he sat down; with Gormley's help, Wilson prevailed. He could then tell the Durham miners at their gala that 'one man's wage increase is

[17] Quotations from *T* (6 Sept. 1974), 4 (Wilson speech at TUC on 5 Sept.). B. Donoughue, *Downing Street Diary*, i (2005), 135 (7 June 1974); cf. 145 (21 June 1974).

[18] Quotations from Wilson, *Final Term*, 113. Crosland's speech at Manchester, May 1975, quoted in K. Jefferys, *Anthony Crosland* (1999), 184.

another man's price increase' and 'could mean another man's ticket to the dole queue'.[19] Backing from Jones and Murray was crucial at this point. Indeed, in an 'electrifying' outburst against the government's critics on the left, replete with ripe language, Jones at Labour's party conference in October revealed how central his role had now become.[20] The public knew it: a Gallup poll in January 1977 showed that 54 per cent ascribed more power to him than to the Prime Minister. In its promotional pamphlet, the government claimed in 1975 that the drive against inflation 'will only work if it has public backing. Your backing'; it hoped that 'further powers' would not be needed since 'a democracy works best when it relies on persuasion and consent'. Thus did Labour's leaders restore the parliamentary influence over the trade union movement which Heath had sacrificed. Asked in 1979 what he would like to be remembered for as Chancellor of the Exchequer, Healey replied: 'for getting the country through the most difficult period since the thirties with its economy and society in goodish order'.[21]

The price paid for this was at first sight high, for what the trade unions brought to the contract proved ephemeral: as so often with incomes policies, this latest variant began to unravel in its second and third years. The Labour government spent far too long during 1974 in trying to coax the trade unions towards voluntary restraint, and in retrospect its attempt to cut inflation through the 'social contract', which involved consultation and mutual concession, seems a mere holding operation. At the time, however, it seemed the most democratic way to prevent unemployment: even a way of upholding parliamentary government and civilization itself. The non-statutory phase I of Labour's incomes policy was promoted by an ambitious publicity campaign, and Wilson made a televised appeal in August 1975 for people to make the coming year 'a year for Britain'.[22] The strategy of taming through persuasion reached its high point in 1976, when Healey publicly offered to trade tax cuts for wage restraint on a scale which would allegedly halve inflation by the end of 1977. When Conservatives complained that a budget's details could not constitutionally be settled through bargaining publicly with a pressure group, both Healey and Heath (now on the Conservative back benches) explained that this was simply to bring into the open procedures long pursued in private.[23] There was more substance, however, in Thatcher's complaint at her party conference in October: that in

[19] Quotations from Wilson, *Final Term*, 116–18. *O* (20 July 1975), 1 (Wilson to miners). Joe Haines, *Glimmers of Twilight*, 108, says that he (Haines) wrote most of the speech, and that Wilson's claims about it were 'fantasy'.

[20] Quotation from Castle, *Diaries 1974–6*, 512 (1 Oct. 1975); see also 435 for a useful summary of events, and 658 (23 Feb. 1976), 662 (25 Feb. 1976). Benn, *Diaries 1973–6*, 444 (1 Oct. 1975), cf. 445 (1 Oct. 1975).

[21] *T*, 4 Jan. 1977, 1 (Gallup). *The Attack on Inflation: A Policy for Survival* (pamphlet Cmnd. 6151 [1975]), 11. Healey, *G* (15 Feb. 1979), 13.   [22] Wilson, *T* (21 Aug. 1975), 1.

[23] Healey, *O* (11 Apr. 1976), 15. Heath, *HC Deb.* 7 July 1976, c. 1412.

consulting trade unions about all aspects of policy the Labour government lent undue influence to a handful of trade union leaders. To them 'I am bound to say . . . "with great respect, that is not your job. It is Parliament's"', Parliament is the only body which represents all the people.'[24] The outcome during the compulsory but not statutory phase II was to impose a 5 per cent limit, with a maximum increase of £4 a week and a minimum of £2.50.

Although Labour's leaders in 1974–6 were skilfully defusing a dangerous political situation, their interventionist approach to improving Britain's relative prosperity was failing. With Italy's Institute for Industrial Reconstruction as its model, the fourth Wilson government revived in 1975 the Industrial Reorganisation Corporation, the merger-promoting, state-funded body which from 1967 to 1971 had sought to render British industry more competitive. Rebranded as the National Enterprise Board, it envisaged 'planning agreements' with private industry sector by sector, shaped with trade union consultation in mind. But the Board's dynamism suffered from being entrusted with 'lame ducks' such as Rolls Royce and British Leyland (nationalized in 1975), and there were more to come. Scotland's craft-based, small-scale shipbuilding methods could not cope with building the huge giant tankers now required, and in 1977, with the employers' full consent, British Shipbuilders was born, the last of Scotland's heavy industries embraced by the state. The UK's share of world manufacturing exports had nonetheless been declining since the 1870s,[25] for all Labour's special preoccupation with manufactures. Whereas in the 1930s the collapse in manufacturing employment had been only partial and segmental, manufacture's decline between 1966 and 1982 occurred across the board: 60 per cent in textiles, 53 per cent in metal manufacture, 43 per cent in mining, 38 per cent in construction, 35 per cent in vehicles, with compensating growth only in services.[26] Manufacturing production from the large firms encouraged by Labour's interventionism could not rival the performance of countries where firms were smaller.[27] In computers, Britain's early lead was lost, and ICL did not prosper: it was taken over by the National Enterprise Board, and after losing nearly half its employees between 1980 and 1985 it was taken over by a multinational concern.[28]

John Jewkes, the free-market economist swimming as usual against the tide, questioned in 1972 whether government investment and rationalization would produce good returns from such projects as Concorde, ICL, and nuclear reactors; if government failed in its primary role of maintaining national security and keeping order, it should perhaps retreat from economic roles where it was

[24] Thatcher, *Party Conference Speeches*, 26 (8 Oct. 1976).
[25] B. R. Mitchell, *Abstract of British Historical Statistics* (Cambridge, 1988), 524.
[26] J. Burnett, *Idle Hands* (1994), 270–1.
[27] T. Kelly, *The British Computer Industry: Crisis and Development* (1987), 110.
[28] Ibid. 76, and see Harrison, *Seeking a Role*, 314–15.

even less expert.[29] Yet Britain's motor-cycle industry illustrates how private enterprise was no wonder cure. In this fast-growing market, manufacturing was shifting from Western Europe to Japan, which by 1975 made a third of all the world's machines. In the face of this, British firms, mostly in the West Midlands, fought between themselves and made bad policy decisions, so that a British production which had more than doubled in the 1950s waned thereafter; by the 1970s Britain had become a major net importer.[30] On the other hand, private enterprise brought off a chance discovery that in the late 1970s promised to make everything come right: North Sea oil. 'For years . . . Government and Opposition had played a macabre game of musical chairs', Wilson recalled, 'in the hope of being in possession of the chair when the oil began to flow in quantity'.[31] Already by May 1974 the word 'bonanza' was being applied to it: 'by golly it is a bonus', Callaghan told Robin Day in 1976.[32] At the Labour Party conference three years later, Callaghan saw this as a prize opportunity for the state planning of new-found wealth: Britain could now 'become the master of events and never again be their slave'. The UK's first offshore oil was landed in 1975, its production equalled total national consumption by 1980, and Britain had become the world's fifth largest oil producer by 1984. Government revenue from the North Sea in 1984/5 was equivalent to a third of all receipts from income tax.[33] Spin-offs were important too: to explore the Forties field in the early 1970s, for example, four steel jackets were required, each twice the height of Big Ben, and each using more steel than the Forth railway bridge had required. These huge engineering feats created jobs not only in ailing shipyards and steelworks, but in underwater engineering, which in 2007 employed 30,000 in the UK, and exported services worldwide.[34]

This was the context for the major economic crisis that erupted late in 1976. In response to the massive increase in oil prices in 1973, both the IMF and the OECD recommended industrial countries to reflate so as to minimize its deflationary impact. For the Labour government such a policy had the added attraction of making it easier to respond to the trade unions' agenda under the 'social contract': more subsidies, more welfare payments, no statutory incomes policy. Unfortunately for Britain, world trade shrank because Italy was the

[29] J. Jewkes, *Government and High Technology: Third Wincott Memorial Lecture* (1972), 6, 12, 24.

[30] B. M. D. Smith, *The History of the British Motorcycle Industry 1945–1975* (University of Birmingham Centre for Urban and Regional Studies, Occasional Paper, 3, Oct. 1981), 10, 12, 13, 35, 37–8.

[31] Wilson, *Final Term*, 16.

[32] Quotations from Lord Strathcona and Mount Royal in *HL Deb*. 8 May 1974, c. 503, and Callaghan in R. Day, . . . *But With Respect: Memorable Television Interviews with Statesmen and Parliamentarians* (1993), 160 (30 Sept. 1976).

[33] *T* (5 Oct. 1977), 6 (Callaghan speech on 4 Oct.). G. C. Band, 'Fifty Years of U.K. Offshore Oil and Gas', *Geographical Journal* (July 1991), 179, 181.

[34] B. Cooper and T. F. Gaskell, *The Adventure of North Sea Oil* (1976), 73. *FT* (5 Dec. 2007), supplement 'Doing Business in the North Sea Region', 2.

only other country to reflate, so Britain's exports and balance of payments suffered; as Healey pointed out, 'it is not possible for a country like Britain to grow alone when the rest of the world is contracting'. Although the British economic situation was worrying throughout 1975–6, the North Sea oil about to come on stream provided some excuse for a delayed response. Healey in September 1974 had claimed that by 1977 the new oil supply would meet half Britain's requirements, at which point 'there will be great confidence in the UK economy. People will be delighted to lend us money.' From autumn 1975, however, the IMF was watching British government expenditure closely, and in March 1976 sterling began to weaken. On 28 September Healey and the Governor of the Bank of England Gordon Richardson were at Heathrow on the point of departing to Manila for the annual IMF conference, but a rapid fall in sterling forced Healey into an embarrassing return to the Treasury. There it was decided to seek the loan from the IMF that was formally requested on the following day: the sum sought was 3.9 billion dollars, the largest sum ever requested. 'For the first and last time in my life', Healey recalled, 'for about twelve hours I was close to demoralisation.'[35]

Thereafter the situation improved, partly because the conditions attached to the IMF loan endorsed the deflationary directions government policy was already taking,[36] and partly because of Callaghan's skill. He had succeeded Wilson as prime minister in April 1976, and cleverly held his cabinet together while it agreed on cuts in government expenditure which would satisfy IMF conditions. Noting later that Treasury forecasts proved unjustifiably pessimistic, Healey argued that 'in a sense, the whole affair was unnecessary'. Certainly the British balance of payments recovered quickly, so that only half the IMF's loan was ever drawn upon. Healey also admitted, though, that 'you can not buck the markets': they may respond to information that is true, but only if the truth is accessible at the key moment. Callaghan's speech on 28 September to the Labour Party conference is often seen as launching the retreat from Keynesianism: 'we used to think that you could spend your way out of a recession and increase employment by cutting taxes and boosting Government spending', but 'that option no longer exists, and . . . insofar as it ever did exist, it only worked on each occasion since the war by injecting a bigger dose of inflation into the economy, followed by a higher level of unemployment as the next step'. Callaghan laid no claim to have launched such a shift in the history of ideas: he claimed only budgetary prudence.[37] It was from necessity, not from conviction, that his government between 1976 and 1979 anticipated much of

---

[35] Quotations from Healey, *Time of my Life*, 393, 429. E. Dell, *A Hard Pounding: Politics and Economic Crisis 1974–1976* (Oxford, 1991), 84.

[36] For Healey's 'letter of intent' to the IMF, 15 Dec. 1976, see K. Burk and A. Cairncross, *'Goodbye, Great Britain': The 1976 IMF Crisis* (New Haven, 1992), 229–36.

[37] Quotations from Healey, *Time of my Life*, 432, 427. Callaghan, *Time and Chance*, 426–7.

the Thatcherite programme: it cut public expenditure through applying 'cash limits' to government departments, sold off BP shares, pursued a medium-term economic strategy, and (from July) published money-supply targets for the first time. While denying that he was a Friedmanite monetarist, Healey took a pride in getting his cabinet colleagues to 'pay more attention to the financial elements in economic policy'. By later standards, Healey's was a weak variant of monetarism: it simply entailed deciding in autumn 1977 to reduce the growth in the money supply by allowing the exchange rate to rise. In retrospect, the labour movement had much yet to learn, given that Labour government policy after the IMF crisis resumed largely where it had left off. In July 1980, when Labour criticized Conservative economic policy, the Chancellor of the Exchequer attacked them as 'funk monetarists', running away from their own policies.[38]

Successful in 1976 at securing continued pay restraint from the TUC, Healey could not repeat the feat in 1977: he offered a 2 per cent cut in basic tax rate in exchange for a third round of pay-restraint, but had eventually to back a non-statutory 10 per cent maximum pay increase under phase III without trade union support. The price trade union leaders paid for participating at national level in framing incomes policies now seemed too great; this was despite a poll showing that 90 per cent of the public in November 1977 backed the government's wage guidelines—for Callaghan, 'one of the most astonishing and remarkable that I have seen in many years'.[39] Although Britain had by the late 1970s shaken off the profound gloom of 1973–6, it was not yet clearly on course: Labour's incomes policy was not restraining unemployment. Memories of the 1930s lay behind the labour movement's many schemes for state-subsidized 'job creation' and training for work proposed in the 1970s and 1980s. But already by the mid-1970s scepticism about such schemes was being voiced, if only because both inflation and the unemployment which inflation was supposed to prevent were by then worsening with each economic cycle. Since 1958 the so-called 'Phillips curve' had suggested that these two evils were inversely related, but the facts no longer seemed to tally; besides, in 1968 the 'curve' had already come under theoretical attack in articles by the economists Milton Friedman and Edmund Phelps.[40] Overseas comparisons sharpened disillusion. In 1979 Sir Nicholas Henderson was acutely aware in his valedictory despatch of how seriously economic problems damaged the UK's international standing. He detected 'lack of professionalism' in British managers, underpaid by international standards and much less likely than in France to spend time in government at the highest levels. There was, he wrote, a relative lack of vision and purpose in British government's management of major capital projects,

---

[38] Healey interview with Kenneth Harris, O (27 Mar. 1977), 25. Howe, HC Deb. 29 July 1980, c. 1414.
[39] As Callaghan emphasized in HC Deb. 10 Nov. 1977, c. 848.   [40] Econ (19 Feb. 1994), 94.

and 'to arrive nowadays at London Airport from a French or German airport is to be made immediately aware that our standards have slipped'.[41]

At this point, two alternative strategies to the government's were on offer. Throughout 1975–6 Benn seems to have expected an all-party coalition on the model of 1931. Casting himself as the Arthur Henderson who would carry Labour's rump into the wilderness and maintain its traditions unsullied, his alternative to the coalition's likely policies included defence cuts, higher taxation of the rich, leaving the EEC, and closer government control over investment and financial institutions.[42] For a party of the left with a Liberal pedigree it was a curiously insular package. It apparently assumed that British import controls would not prompt retaliation, and perhaps even relished the likely offence given to the EEC;[43] nor could it guarantee that British industry thus protected would become more competitive. It owed something to the protectionist ideas then recommended within the Department of Applied Economics at Cambridge under its Director, Wynne Godley. For them, import controls were better than deflation for curbing imports because they would not foster unemployment; instead they would allegedly enable the government to expand the economy faster without producing another balance of payments crisis. The Department's prestige stemmed partly from its skilful publicity, vigorous language, and unorthodox approach to big issues; partly from the relatively congenial non-deflationary remedies it favoured; partly from having accurately predicted the collapse in 1974 of the Barber boom; and partly from an appetite in British public life for gloom, which reached a minor peak in the mid-1970s and a major peak in the early 1990s.[44]

Benn's alternative strategy involved arguing for 'a trade-off of wealth and power', whereby trade union cooperation would be purchased through a taxation and planning structure which redistributed wealth: 'the market economy is incompatible', he claimed, 'with strong trade unions and the ballot box'. This ignored the affinity between trade union and free-market attitudes. It also underestimated the tenacity of the two-party system and of that powerful troika committed to enforcing the government's strategy: Jones (General Secretary of the TGWU), Healey (Chancellor of the Exchequer), and Callaghan. Nor did Benn spell out the fall in living standards involved in his alternative. When in September 1976 the IMF's terms for a stand-by loan reinforced the overall thrust of the government's policy, Healey told the nation on television that the alternative would be 'economic policies so savage that they would lead

---

[41] *Econ* (2 June 1979), 30.

[42] Benn, *Diaries 1973–6*, 302 (16 Jan. 1975), 324 (25 Feb. 1975), 458 (6 Nov. 1975). Castle, *Diaries 1974–6*, 400 (22 May 1975), 585 (5 Dec. 1975).

[43] As Healey argued in the Labour Party conference on 30 Sept. 1976, *T* (1 Oct. 1976), 4.

[44] For useful discussions see *T* (6 June 1978), Europa supplement, p. iv. *G* (26 Feb. 1979), 13; (17 Apr. 1980), 19.

to riots in the streets, an immediate fall in living standards, and unemployment of three million'.[45] Callaghan was much more plausible than Wilson as the nation's consensus-seeking father-figure, and Benn's standing slipped so markedly between 1975 and 1979 within the cabinet that many wondered why he stayed there. But in one respect Benn shared his colleagues' outlook: he failed to see how the government's strategy was slowly rendering politically practicable a Conservative 'alternative strategy' that had been ruled out of court since 1940.

Thatcher's electoral prudence deterred her from airing her alternative to the government's strategy as openly as Benn, but Keith Joseph and the IEA made its essentials clear enough. The state must greatly curb its role in economic management: it must introduce a self-acting restraint on inflation and wage demands by curbing the money supply, and brave short-term rising unemployment in order to secure long-term economic revival. There had been monetary discipline of a sort throughout the Keynesian period. The fixed exchange rate till the early 1970s tied the pound to the dollar, a currency managed by a country whose policies till the Vietnam war were non-inflationary; after the devaluation of 1967, for instance, one condition of international backing for the pound had been that the money supply must be monitored.[46] During the 1970s the money markets became so internationalized that no government could introduce a lax budget without rapidly prompting higher interest rates. A Conservative government with firmer and more explicit monetary targets, however, could at least in theory dispense with incomes policies, freeing trade unionists to resume their customary role, which was not to mould a Labour government's policies across the board, but to safeguard their members' interests in a non-party manner through free collective bargaining.[47] Since the demise of the Prices and Incomes Board, incomes policies had degenerated into mere emergency wage-restraint policies, hastily cobbled up from year to year, without appraising society's overall distribution of wealth. In so far as they were socialist at all, their 'socialism in one class' redistributed wealth only within classes and not between them.[48]

There was clearly common ground between Thatcher and trade unionists hostile to incomes policies, an 'unholy alliance' whose potential was noted by close observers.[49] Yet trade union leaders, beset with traditional Labour

---

[45] Benn, *Diaries 1973–6*, 641 (10 Nov. 1976). Healey, *T* (30 Sept. 1976), 1; cf. Castle, *Diaries 1974–6*, 585 (5 Dec. 1975).

[46] For Benn this was 'the beginning of monetarism' in his *Diaries 1968–72*, 125 (21 Nov. 1968).

[47] Speech to conference of Scottish businessmen in Glasgow, *T* (10 Jan. 1978), 1.

[48] L. Panitch, *Social Democracy and Industrial Militancy: The Labour Party, the Trade Unions and Incomes Policy, 1945–1974* (Cambridge, 1976), 244.

[49] Peter Walker, speech to Worcester constituents on 20 Feb. 1977, *G* (21 Feb. 1977), 20. See also David Steel, speech to 1977 Liberal Party conference, *O* (2 Oct. 1977), 1.

loyalties and a half-digested socialist rhetoric, could not yet publicly embrace the free-market option—though their members were as voters free to desert to the Conservatives, and did so in droves at the general election of 1979. No Labour government after 1970 felt able to confront the trade unions by confessing to aims which had so soured trade union relations under the Wilson government after 1966. A gulf was opening out between the labour movement's industrial and political wings, and despite his close affinities with the trade union movement, Callaghan now diverged from some of its orthodoxies. He told the TUC in September 1977 that under free collective bargaining 'the lion's share goes to the lion'; neither equality nor social justice resulted, only 'free collective chaos', he had told parliament in February, and when he said something similar to the TUC in September he was 'received in somewhat shifty silence'.[50] He told parliament in December that he had 'ceased to worship' free collective bargaining '10 years ago', and in 1979 distinguished clearly between the moral status of the picket seeking to dissuade blacklegs and the secondary picket seeking to persuade workers not involved with the dispute. Besides, he said, 'everyone in this country is entitled to cross a picket line if he disagrees with the arguments that are put to him'; he would cross it himself if he thought it right to do so.[51]

The incomes policy seemed at the time remarkably successful: its first three phases had apparently curbed inflation and wage increases, kept unemployment well below the levels of the early 1980s, and defused the political crisis of 1974. When the Callaghan government in 1978 moved to a phase IV, however—on the basis of a 5 per cent ceiling unilaterally imposed without trade union agreement—it stretched trade union loyalty too far. Neither trade unions nor employers could now be relied upon to back it. There were even hints during phase IV that the government was behaving illegally, with secret cabinet committees aiming to achieve covertly and with inadequate legislative and administrative resources what the Prices and Incomes Board had earlier openly, legally, and for a time effectively proclaimed. When government threatened to exclude Ford Motors from public-sector sales for exceeding its phase IV pay ceiling, the Conservatives acquired the major asset in a parliamentary debate of appearing to defend democracy, liberty, and honest government against an unjust, secretive, and arbitrary interventionism.[52]

[50] Quotations from T (7 Sept. 1977), 4. HC Deb. 22 Feb. 1977, c. 1221. P. Jenkins, G (7 Sept. 1977), 13, discussing Callaghan's speech on 6 Sept.

[51] HC Deb. 1 Dec. 1977, c. 713. HC Deb. 16 Jan. 1979, cc. 1546–7. HC Deb. 23 Jan. 1979, c. 201. Callaghan had intended to qualify his statement by applying it only to secondary picket lines, but neglected to do so—see Donoughue, Downing Street Diary, ii (2008), 431 (23 Jan. 1979).

[52] W. H. Fishbein, Wage Restraint by Consensus: Britain's Search for an Incomes Policy Agreement, 1965–79 (1984), 195. For Conservative comment see e.g. Lawson in HC Deb. 7 Feb. 1978, cc. 1355–61; Prior in HC Deb. 13 Dec. 1978, cc. 694–9; cf. T (6 Jan. 1978), 1–2.

Callaghan himself felt uncomfortable: 'the use of powers without parliamentary authority is weighing on my conscience a little', he told cabinet in December 1978. Incomes policies pushed to the fore the conflict between trade union voluntarism and the socialist sense of community, and Callaghan thought it 'our task to mobilize the general will against the particular interest'.[53] These were not the only problems corporatism presented to the employers, especially the CBI. Not only was it a federation of autonomous structures weaker than the TUC: it did not even have a socialist rhetoric to deter its members from mutual competition. Indeed, its philosophy if anything sanctified competition. The CBI had been restive with Heath's three-day week and trade union legislation,[54] and from 1974 until 1979 it combined an attempt to rival the trade unions in public visibility with internal debate about how far it should champion the free market.[55] Free-market ideas were constrained within the CBI by its inclusion of nationalized industries and large corporations closely interacting with government. After 1974 it was the Institute of Directors that increasingly mobilized employers sympathetic to free-market ideas, together with freelance entrepreneurs.

As for the trade unions, the Chief Secretary to the Treasury claimed that 'the only give and take in the (social) contract was that the Government gave and the unions took'. This was not Len Murray's view.[56] In reality, the trade union movement was internally too divided in the 1960s and 1970s to have much to offer governments: it could not deliver its members into securely backing incomes policies, nor did it have much power collectively to curb strikes. So the trade unions got rather little of what they wanted: they failed to prevent incomes policies, they could not prevent Heath from passing his Industrial Relations Bill in 1971, and their gains from collaborating with the Labour governments of 1974–9 were small. They secured neither economic growth, nor selective import controls, nor planning agreements, nor a wealth tax. In collaborating with the government, they found their loyalties stretched into supporting legislation they disliked and into sacrificing the freedom they relished. Consultation on a wide range of government policy of course enhanced their leaders' status, but at the price of weakening the leaders' hold on the rank and file. Incomes policies pressed the unions into a policing role which exacerbated tensions with their members, and drew the leaders ineluctably towards becoming an arm of government. For this was the unions' logical destination under corporatist

---

[53] Callaghan quoted in Benn, *Diaries 1977–80*, 412 (7 Dec. 1978). Callaghan, *HC Deb.* 8 Nov. 1977, c. 480.

[54] *T* (7 Sept. 1973), 1; (27 Feb. 1974), 1; (24 Apr. 1974), 21. K. Middlemas, *Power, Competition and the State*, ii. *Threats to the Postwar Settlement: Britain, 1961–74* (1990), 386.

[55] See e.g. the internal debate about regional aid, *DT* (20 July 1979), 10.

[56] J. Barnett, *Inside the Treasury* (1982), 49. For Murray see R. Taylor, 'Last Testament of a Troubled Trade Unionist', *O* (2 Sept. 1984), 9.

economic planning, whereas their instincts remained, as always, to defend their members' interests by operating freely within a pluralist context. From the late 1960s pressures to devolve control within the TGWU and AEU were being espoused even by their leaders. In January 1979 trade union restiveness was so serious that Callaghan, while admitting that it was clumsy to legislate on industrial relations, issued a warning: 'there do come times when a nation's patience may run out'.[57]

The drawbacks of trying to operate an incomes policy in the British context were becoming clear. After the miners' strike in 1972 Heath had looked to West Germany as exemplifying 'a more sensible way to settle our differences'. Visiting the German Chancellor Willi Brandt, Heath had been told on leaving about who was assembling for Brandt's next appointment: 'there are sixteen union leaders out there', said Brandt; 'they are the men I run Germany with'.[58] There were no British equivalents: British trade unions were too fragmented, and their traditions too voluntarist, for any such strategy to be feasible, and British fears of inflation were for deep-rooted historical reasons less pronounced than the German. When the trade unions would not cooperate, governments could only appeal over their heads to the general public. But the unfocused and only discontinuously mobilized general interest was no match for the trade unionists' sharply focused and continuous promotion of particular interests. The attempt to enforce incomes policies so precarious gave governments the worst of both worlds: they had to build in a show of enforcement, yet had no teeth. So in order to avoid losing face they had to design their policies to avoid offending the really powerful, which meant successfully confronting only the relatively weak.[59] This entailed sacrificing the incomes policy's major theoretical attraction: fairness.

All these problems culminated in the cluster of strikes of winter 1978–9, later labelled the 'winter of discontent'.[60] Heath's consensual approach to industrial relations after 1972, continued by Labour after 1974, paradoxically turned out to generate confrontations which put the status of elected governments at risk. A system of central planning through liaison with the trade unions, oriented towards 'creating' or 'saving' jobs, inflated the citizen's expectation of what governments could achieve, and when expectations of incomes policies were disappointed the political structure became the scapegoat. The need to police corporatist settlements ultimately drew in the army. By December 1979 its aid had been invoked in at least twenty-three industrial disputes since 1945, seven of them since 1970, and in 1979 more working days were lost in industrial

[57] *HC Deb.* 23 Jan. 1979, c. 202.   [58] Quoted by S. Fay and H. Young, *ST* (22 Feb. 1976), 33.
[59] For a good account of the government's enforcement difficulties see A. Hamilton and W. Keegan, 'Pay Policy Lists into Stage Four', *O* (12 Feb. 1978), 11.
[60] For useful chronology of events see *Contemporary Record* (Autumn 1987), 38–9.

disputes than at any time since 1926.[61] Headlines were readily caught in January and February 1979 by the food shortages resulting from lorry drivers' strikes, by London's piled-up rubbish (Plate 10), and by the impact on hospitals of strikes by public-service workers. Trade union action was transforming Thatcher's image: from shrill and impracticable sectarian, she was becoming guardian of decent consensus values. 'Now we find that the place is practically being run by strikers' committees', she told parliament on 16 January 1979, 'and that they are using such language as "allowing" access to food, "allowing" certain lorries to go through.' In cabinet on 1 February the Prime Minister 'said he was more depressed as a trade-unionist now about the future of this country than he had been for fifty years. He never believed it would come to this.'[62]

In later years the greed and money-mindedness of the Thatcher years were often contrasted unfavourably with what had gone before. This involved a double misunderstanding. Competition for wealth was in full spate before 1979, but was more collective in procedure, whereas the focus after 1979 was on wealth-getting by individuals; the competition for wages before 1979 fostered rivalry between identifiable groups, whereas entrepreneurial competition operated within a relatively impersonal free market. But, secondly, the subsequent stress on free-market greed ignored an important concealed affinity which the theatre director Peter Hall perceived in January 1979: 'the Labour party, financed by the unions, is advocating restraint . . . The Conservative party, financed by big business, is advocating what the unions prefer, free collective bargaining.'[63] This underlying classless free-market alignment was a reality, but before 1979 it had been moderated by incomes policies and masked by a party system still misleadingly oriented round class.[64] Under the Conservative governments of 1951–64 and 1970–4 the free-market affinity had been made quite explicit by some trade unionists, though their political loyalties had remained with Labour. And it was in 1975, under a Labour government, that Hugh Scanlon, the influential President of the AEU from 1967 to 1978, when referring to the miners' recent generous pay settlement, echoed a remark of Frank Cousins, TGWU General Secretary in 1956: 'if there is to be a free-for-all', he said, 'my union wants to be part of the all'.[65] Such remarks

---

[61] C. J. Whelan, 'Military Intervention in Industrial Disputes', *Industrial Law Journal*, 8/4 (Dec. 1979), 222. *BPF* (8th edn.), 400–1: 162,233,000 in 1926; 29,474,000 in 1979.

[62] Thatcher, *HC Deb.* 16 Jan. 1979, c. 1531; cf. *DT* (17 Jan. 1979), 1. Callaghan as reported in Benn, *Diaries 1977–80*, 450 (1 Feb. 1979).

[63] P. Hall, *Peter Hall's Diaries: The Story of a Dramatic Battle*, ed. J.Goodwin (1984), 407 (13 Jan. 1979).

[64] The Liberal leader David Steel, addressing his party conference on 1 Oct. 1977, found little to distinguish Clive Jenkins, with his 'snout jostling at the wage trough', from the free-market Conservatives: *O* (2 Oct. 1977), 1.

[65] Castle, *Diaries 1974–6*, 319 (1 Mar. 1975). See also Harrison, *Seeking a Role*, 454.

encapsulated the trade unions' prime and historic function: directly to promote their members' short-term interest by protecting their wage differentials.

For all their altruistic image, cultivated through pressing governments for welfare measures, the trade unions in their day-to-day activity in the 1970s were no more directly promoting the interest of the community at large than were the employers: both were promoting it only indirectly by jockeying for position within a competitive economy flexible and innovative enough to promote overall prosperity. Paul Johnson, influential as editor (1965–70) of the *New Statesman*, exposed the conflict between trade unionism and socialism in 1975. Throwing off the sycophancy then so widespread among left-wing intellectuals when discussing trade unions, he claimed that these over-mighty subjects accentuated inflation with their escalating wage demands, promoted strikes which caused the weakest to suffer, and fostered a war of all against all in which the best-organized gained most. Wage inflation, he said, 'sets group against group and makes self-interest the guiding principle of life . . . It turns money . . . into the chief preoccupation . . . of every human being'.[66] Greed infused both corporatism and Thatcherism, but in the 1970s Thatcherism gained ground because its variant of greed increasingly seemed compatible with the general interest, and could win widespread support among both employers and employees.

Images from the 'winter of discontent' remained politically potent for decades, with Thatcher and her party assiduously keeping the memory green.[67] Picket-line violence, hospitals denied supplies, the dead unburied—these, Geoffrey Howe recalled in his budget speech of March 1980, 'would have been unthinkable 20 years ago'. 'I can't *bear* Britain in decline' said Thatcher in May 1979, commenting on the preceding 'winter of discontent': 'I just can't. We, who either defeated or rescued half Europe, who kept half Europe *free* when otherwise it would have been in chains, and look at us now.'[68] She owed to the 'winter' her electoral success in 1979 and her ultimate triumph over the trade union movement. The trade unions only slowly learnt to combine their rejection of incomes planning with a more overt acceptance of the free market; the EETPU's two general secretaries Frank Chapple and Eric Hammond acted as outriders in that protracted process. Society 'has to have some discipline', Chapple had argued in the mid-1970s, and 'it is better that that discipline should come in the loose and imperfect manner of the market place in a mixed economy, than the tight and imperfect manner of the state and its police. That state should hold the ring, not get into it.' In 1982 one of the SDP's four founder leaders, William Rodgers, told parliament why he was backing

[66] P. Johnson, 'Brotherhood of National Misery', *NS* (16 May 1975), 652–6.

[67] For an early version on 1 May 1979 see her speech at Bolton, *DT* (2 May 1979), 1.

[68] *HC Deb.* (26 Mar. 1980), c. 1443 (Howe). Thatcher quoted in *Thatcher: The Downing Street Years*, BBC1 television programme, 20 Oct. 1993.

Thatcher's trade union legislation: 'the events of the winter of 1978–9 were absolutely decisive . . . I never believed that trade unionists would prevent people from entering a hospital when they were at risk. I never believed that trade unionists would refuse to bury the dead. But all those things happened.'[69]

2. A FREE-MARKET ALTERNATIVE

In Britain's complex relationship between individualism and collectivism since the 1760s there have been three broad phases. The first, like its successors, has two parts. From the 1760s to the 1820s individualism fought for supremacy with feudal and mercantilist interventionism, and thereafter until the 1880s became an orthodoxy. The second phase ran from the 1880s to the mid-1970s. In its first part from the 1880s to the 1930s collectivists battled with individualists for supremacy; during its second part, from the 1940s to the mid-1970s, collectivism became the orthodoxy. The third cycle began in 1930s and persists. During its first part, from the 1930s until the 1980s, individualism struggled with collectivism for supremacy.[70] In that struggle the years 1975–9 were crucial, for by the mid-1970s some came to see corporatist strategies as creating more trouble than they removed. The resultant intellectual shift transformed the political climate, generating the first serious and frontbench Conservative challenge to collectivism.

Economists had long debated the relationship between money and prices, but by the 1970s the term 'monetarist' was increasingly applied to a group of economists who diverged from the 'Keynesians'. In the 1950s and 1960s British macroeconomic policy-making was dominated by the demand-management ideas that Britain had earlier exported to the world, but in the highly inflationary circumstances of the 1970s monetarist ideas pioneered in the 1960s by the Chicago School of economists struck a chord in Britain through claiming that among social evils Keynes had exaggerated unemployment's importance by comparison with inflation. When in 1971 the dollar was in effect floated, the pound lost another source of stability; in response to pressure on sterling, it was floated in the following year.[71] The authorities could no longer then use the exchange rate to manage the economy and control inflation, and resorted instead to limiting the growth in money supply. Both 'monetarist' and 'Keynesian' schools of economist saw the state as playing an important economic role, but they disagreed on its nature. Monetarists wanted the state to focus on ensuring that the market worked smoothly: it should maintain order and political

[69] F. Chapple, speech in mid-1970s at Newcastle University, quoted in his *Sparks Fly! A Trade Union Life* (1984), 140. Rodgers, *HC Deb.* 8 Feb. 1982, cc. 757–8.

[70] Cockett, *Thinking the Unthinkable*, 6.

[71] For the circumstances of this see Heath, *Course of my Life*, 409–10.

stability, curb monopolies, ease the entrepreneur's task, and free up access to labour, to information, and to new manufacturing and commercial methods. They wanted the state to abandon its two recently acquired roles of promoting growth directly through fiscal and monetary policy and of suppressing inflation through incomes policies. Instead they envisaged inflation being suppressed automatically through restricting monetary growth. Economic growth, freed from undue constraints through the taxation structure or the labour market, would then enable the unemployed to 'price themselves into' jobs; prosperity would then grow spontaneously without inflation. Fewer decisions would then be required from the Whitehall planner, more from within the community at large, and people would recover responsibility for their own fate. Monetarists felt that the differentials in wealth that spontaneously emerged from market forces were less likely than planned differentials to evoke resentment. Government's standing and structure would not then be undermined when it struggled and failed to meet the expectations its interventionism had aroused.

The monetarists' variant of monetarism was very different from the pragmatic variant applied by Healey between 1977 and 1979: for them, an excessive growth in the money supply was the sole cause of inflation, and contracting it would produce only temporary unemployment, facilitating a relatively painless control over inflation. British monetarists took a distinctive view of post-war economic history. Until the 1970s 'most people'[72] had ascribed Britain's historically high post-war levels of employment to skilful central management of the economy through fiscal policy. With inflation relatively low, effective demand had allegedly been maintained by an economy that was growing fast by historical standards, reinforced by public welfare and regional planning which mopped up residual areas of poverty. The Keynesian orthodox view was the more beguiling because its strategy's benefits were immediate and visible, whereas its drawbacks were gradual and concealed. British governments in the run-up to general elections tended to exploit a simplified Keynesianism to justify expanding demand so as to curb unemployment and boost prosperity. Not till the 1970s, when both inflation and unemployment began rising dangerously fast, did doubts grow (especially among monetarists) about this view. Thereafter it was more frequently noticed that in the 1950s and 1960s 'other countries . . . had at least as good luck without following Keynesian policies or even knowing what they are'.[73] Credit for post-war full employment was then retrospectively ascribed to factors beyond governments' control such as changing terms of

[72] R. C. O. Matthews, 'Why has Britain had Full Employment since the War?', *Economic Journal* (Sept. 1968), 555; Matthews was dissenting from the orthodoxy.
[73] H. G. Johnson, 'Keynes and British Economics' (1973), in Johnson's *On Economics and Society* (Chicago and London, 1975), 87–8.

trade, new patterns within the labour market, and the war's differential impact on the efficiency of British and foreign economies.

Ideas are often most vulnerable when they seem safely entrenched: many people's opinions come from what they think that others think, wrote Bagehot, but 'in secret, each has his doubts, which he suppresses, because he fancies that others who have thought more about the matter have no such misgivings; but if a shrewd examiner were to scrutinise each man's mind, they would find much tacit, latent, accumulated doubt in each'.[74] From the early 1970s two influential financial journalists publicized their doubts: Samuel Brittan in the *Financial Times* and Peter Jay in *The Times*, with help from William Rees-Mogg (editor of *The Times*), and vigorously but unobtrusively backed by Sherman in the CPS. This Conservative think tank was founded in the wake of the Conservative defeat at the general election of February 1974, but originated in prior discussions between Sherman and Keith Joseph. These pioneers drew upon right-wing ideas and Conservative backbench grumbles whose intellectual pedigree stretched back to Hayek's *The Road to Serfdom* (1944) and Popper's *The Open Society and its Enemies* (1945). The libertarian and free-enterprise philosophy informing these two influential books was promoted by the ideas that fed into bodies such as Aims of Industry (founded in 1942), the Mont Pelerin Society (founded in 1947), and the IEA (founded in 1955). The latter long remained a politically marginal non-party think tank, but in the 1960s Powell took up its philosophy, courageously and almost alone making himself a parliamentary advocate for free-market ideas.[75] Then in the 1970s the IEA at last moved centre stage, and Ronald Reagan, as Governor of California and later as President, demonstrated that in the American context monetarist sympathies did not preclude electoral success.

The Heath government's 'u-turn' of 1972 drove it into implementing what some Conservatives saw as socialist policies. Indeed, in his remarkable memorandum on incomes of September 1972 Maudling claimed that a new distribution of class power required a new economics: what remained of the free market, with its wide differentials in income, must succumb to the planned economy.[76] On May Day in 1973 a trade unionist described what he thought 'the most ridiculous situation in British industrial history', whereby a Conservative government was implementing socialist restraints on profits and prices while TUC leaders were threatening to strike on behalf of ' "free enterprise" bargaining'.[77] Many of Heath's restive backbenchers agreed, and

[74] W. Bagehot, 'Count your Enemies and Economise your Expenditure' (1862) in Bagehot, *Collected Works*, ed. N. St John-Stevas, viii (1974), 50.

[75] Middlemas, *Power, Competition and the State*, ii. 87 credits 'the first counterblast of new right thinking' to three anonymous letters (possibly by Powell) published in *The Times* during Apr. 1964.

[76] 'Maudling Memorandum on Incomes', *T* (12 Sept. 1972), 12.

[77] J. L. Winterbottom, GMWU shop steward, Pontefract, letter to *T* (4 May 1973), 19.

were hardly reassured when Benn told trade unionists in January 1974 that discussions on pay relativities must open out from discussing differentials between working people into considering the distribution of wealth in society as a whole: 'in the long run', he claimed, 'Mr. Heath cannot win'. This proved true in ways that Benn did not anticipate. When Barber as Chancellor had imitated his predecessor Maudling ten years earlier by launching a 'dash for growth' in 1973, he combined devaluation with cutting taxes and raising government expenditure. Monetarists saw the subsequent inflationary peak as demonstrating the close link between inflation and the money supply, thus fuelling an intellectual shift to the right rather than to the left.[78] In September 1974 Joseph concluded that 'inflation is largely a self-inflicted wound', and deplored governments' simultaneous weakening of the economy and courting of the electorate with their pre-election booms: 'the old saying "not in front of the children" has become "not in front of the electors—at least until after the election"'.[79]

So by 1974 interests and resentments were building up behind the idea of a radical shift in Conservative economic policy. Corporatist policies might benefit property speculators, mortgage holders, and big business (as represented in the CBI), but entrepreneurs, small businessmen, and some trade unionists and sections of the middle classes were becoming restive. High taxation and incomes policies eroded profits and starved investment at the same time as trade union power and state intervention weakened the power to manage. Consumers, the non-unionized, and people on fixed incomes had everything to lose by incomes policies which ultimately failed to curb inflation and simultaneously entrenched producer power. Backbenchers alienated by Heath's aloofness or failure to promote them could now deploy the self-interest of the party and its supporters against him. There seemed no hope for Conservatives, and arguably by then for the country, in a corporatist strategy which, even if successful, required trade union collaboration and thereby gave Labour a built-in advantage. Corporatism had promised to take large areas of the economy out of politics yet achieved the opposite, whereas monetarism promised to free entrepreneurs, consumers, and the Conservative Party from the additional layer of uncertainty stemming from political entanglements. Still more importantly for Conservatives, this new direction had the attraction of requiring no incomes policies, and hence no trade union collaboration.

Beset by this powerful conjuncture between political and economic tendencies, key Conservatives, for all their party's anti-intellectualism, now had to do some hard thinking. Not only must Conservative electoral strategy be

---

[78] Benn, G (28 Jan. 1974), 4. Britton, *Macroeconomic Policy in Britain*, 268, prints a table showing both money supply and inflation, but see ibid. 97–8, 104.

[79] Speech at Preston, 5 Sept. 1974, in Joseph, *Reversing the Trend*, 20, 29.

reassessed: a less pragmatic approach to political economy must now be adopted, for the Party was girding itself for a shift in the public agenda comparable only with Joseph Chamberlain's campaign to replace free trade by tariff reform more than seventy years before.[80] Democratic politicians know, or should know, how limited are the changes that they can produce in society at large, and such perceptions lay at the heart of the Conservative policy revolution in the 1970s. Keith Joseph was central to it, and his place in history rests on his being the first leading Conservative fully to exploit this major political opportunity.

Born into an affluent metropolitan liberal Jewish background, he had displayed a strong social conscience in practical ways even as a boy. With a fine academic and war record, he entered parliament in 1956, made himself an expert on the social services, and during his steady advancement thereafter he accepted the prevailing corporatist orthodoxies. He backed Heath's selection as party leader in 1965, but in the previous year had paid the first of many visits to the IEA, and by 1970 he had established a link with Sherman. From his subsequent conduct as a compassionate Secretary of State for Social Services in Heath's high-spending government, one would hardly have guessed it. 'It was only in April 1974', he wrote, 'that I was converted to Conservatism.'[81] His new gospel was not, in truth, Conservatism at all: it was a radical variant of free-market Liberalism which through individualist twentieth-century Liberal refugees from the left had long been seeping into the Conservative Party. Moral courage—the quality Joseph prized above all others, and which he had earlier reproached himself for lacking—was in no way lacking now. He saw himself as embattled against hostile media and decidedly intolerant academic opinion. A less likely crusader than Joseph could hardly be imagined: unclubbable and self-tormented, he preferred reading to lobbying. He hated being televised, and in interviews did not always appear to advantage because of the almost physical pain that questions evoked: before any answer emerged there were anguished expressions, with a vein noticeably throbbing in his forehead, or else long silences, head in hands. Yet Joseph had important assets. His political innocence, even naivety, was not necessarily a drawback in this exceptional party-political and national situation. Besides, he was something of a phrase-maker, and liked to cut a dash.

Joseph was no original thinker, nor is original thinking the politician's role, but other people's ideas interested him, and he possessed the creative politician's essential quality: knowing when new ideas are needed, what they are, where to find them, and how to project them. More than anyone else, Joseph was the creator of 'Thatcherism' in its domestic rather than overseas dimension, but to have any hope of success it needed recruits from other political parties and from

---

[80] This crucial episode is more fully discussed in Harrison, 'Mrs Thatcher and the Intellectuals', *TCBH* 5/2 (1994), 210–20.　　　　　　　　　　[81] Joseph, *Reversing the Trend*, 4.

no party, and Joseph's contacts were wide. Sherman at the CPS guided him towards broad and voracious reading. Its components became nationally known when, soon after arriving as a minister at the Department of Trade and Industry in May 1979, Joseph presented his civil servants, at their request, with his famous reading list. Its twenty authors included Schumpeter, Tocqueville, and Adam Smith; its recommended publications included many from the IEA and CPS, as well as studies of Labour's failed rescue-attempts for the manufacture of motor-cycles and ships at Meriden and the Upper Clyde, respectively.[82] The new right was now deploying the one-time weapons of the left: the pamphlet and the lecture. Educating the nation through several intellectually demanding and much-publicized speeches, Joseph established a new policy agenda, even generated a new political vocabulary. Words, the politician's stock-in-trade, were central to his achievement, for between 1974 and 1977 he was preoccupied with what he later called 'my mission':[83] speaking at over 150 university and polytechnic campuses. Far from combative by nature, Joseph nonetheless enjoyed these often rowdy encounters. He retained throughout life a youthful inquisitiveness, enjoyed argument, and responded vigorously to hecklers. He honed up his ideas by conducting what was in effect a prolonged nation-wide Socratic tutorial, aiming always to unsettle his critics by claiming his right to ask them a question, and being surprised thereby to discover how weak was the anti-capitalist case.

Joseph wanted his party to vacate the 'middle ground', if defined as a point midway between the existing policies of the Conservative and Labour parties. Such ground was, he thought, continuously shifting, a will-o'-the-wisp which drew pragmatic Conservatives ineluctably into Labour territory. This 'socialist ratchet' must be halted by moving the terms of debate on to safer territory. But with what policies? Joseph aimed for what he called the 'common ground': a consensus that reflected, not a lowest common denominator between existing party views, but a more stable set of new policies that might attract people from all parties and those from none. Central to his new direction was a bold move towards the free market which almost everyone had hitherto thought politically impracticable. Seeking to rescue Keynes from the Keynesians, he emphasized that inter-war unemployment had misled politicians who faced a post-war economic situation very different from that of the 1930s. He thought competitive business values more popular even among trade unionists than the Labour Party allowed: free collective bargaining and free enterprise went together. Beneath this lay a view of human nature, readily misrepresented, that ranked self-interest higher among the incentives to action. Joseph believed that trade unions, for all their socialist pretensions, were driven as much

---

[82] The list is in *NS* (25 May 1979), 738.
[83] Author's tape-recorded interview with Lord Joseph, 7 Aug. 1992.

by self-interest as anyone else, but that socialist policies were converting them from genuinely representative structures into pseudo-altruistic agencies of an increasingly centralized state. For Joseph as earlier for Powell, trade unionists who opposed incomes policies were not being irresponsible: they were performing their traditional and necessary role of defending their members' interests. To monetarism Joseph now brought all the enthusiasm of the recent convert, with too little thought for the complications, though he never saw it as a stand-alone panacea. He thought six 'poisons' were destroying Britain's prosperity: excessive government spending, high direct taxation, egalitarianism, excessive nationalization, a politicized trade union movement, and 'an anti-enterprise culture', which he saw as dominant in the political parties, the universities, and the media. The UK was, he said, the only country in the world with all six: 'we are over-governed, over-spent, over-taxed, over-borrowed and over-manned'.[84]

Conservatives needed to recapture the political vocabulary from the left, and here too Joseph's contribution was important. 'Unemployment', for example, should no longer be an emotive, inflated, and global figure: it should be resolved into its subcategories—frictional, voluntary, fraudulent, regional, short-term, long-term, and so on—a procedure which Keynes would have found entirely acceptable.[85] Thence flowed relatively diverse remedies whose relevance was not at first clear, such as reviving the rented housing sector, new incentives to change jobs, and reformed procedures for welfare payment. The 'customer' and the 'taxpayer' now received a new prominence in public discussion. Using words and phrases that were often unfamiliar, even eccentric, Joseph sometimes arrested attention by inverting accepted values. Welfare payments pauperized; planning produced chaos and stagnation; trade unions did not create employment but destroyed it, and encouraged the relatively inexperienced young to price themselves out of jobs;[86] even Healey as Chancellor of the Exchequer had pronounced lower average wages preferable to unemployment.[87] Joseph thought the British economy unduly politicized, too readily distorted by politicians' short-term vote-catching priorities. Nationalized concerns did not benefit the general public but only the trade union leaders and the interventionist governments which they locked into a partnership of mutual short-term self-interest. In the longer term, nationalized industries demanded subsidies, which in turn pushed up taxes, thereby further weakening the economy's more

[84] See Joseph's discussion on 30 July 1979 with Michael Charlton on Radio 4; cf. his speech of 6 Oct. 1976, *T* (7 Oct. 1976), 4. K. Joseph, *Monetarism is Not Enough: The Stockton Lecture* (1976), 19.

[85] See Joseph's speech of 5 Sept. 1974, *T* (6 Sept. 1974), 14, 16. See also, more generally, W. Eltis, 'The Failure of the Keynesian Conventional Wisdom', *Lloyds Bank Review*, 122 (Oct. 1976).

[86] *T* (30 June 1980), 1 (comments on radio, 29 June 1980); cf. Thatcher's comments during interview on Radio 4's 'The World this Week-End' (4 Jan. 1981).

[87] Speech at Leeds, Jan. 1975, quoted in F. A. Hayek, *Full Employment at Any Price?* (1975), 29.

Fig. 4. Keith Joseph massages the unemployment statistics, *Sun* (5 Aug. 1975).

competitive parts. Each well-intentioned intervention distorted the economy further, drumming up further needs, precedents, and vested interests behind an unending socialistic spiral, and culminating in foredoomed incomes policies, with all their centralized and impracticable intrusiveness.

His critics' crude misrepresentation of one passage in Joseph's Edgbaston speech destroyed him as candidate for the Conservative succession to Heath, but Joseph disclaimed ever being suited to party leadership. Having backed Thatcher, he subsequently enjoyed ready access to and respect from the Party's longest-serving twentieth-century prime minister: 'Joseph articulated ideas, Howe formulated policies, and Mrs Thatcher was the essential conduit from one to the other.' Joseph's ideas made little immediate impact on public opinion, but they gained credibility from the Labour governments' mounting difficulties between 1974 and 1979, and influenced an ever-widening band of significant opinion. 'An admirable anthology from my speeches on this subject in recent years' was Powell's view of Joseph's important speech of 1974 advocating

monetarist solutions for inflation.[88] Powell had indeed often stressed in the
1970s how ineffective were politicians' attempts to shape the economy, and
how curing inflation would require unemployment temporarily to rise.[89] Like
Joseph, Powell assumed that his audiences could follow a close and complex
argument. If Powell had not made the mistake of simultaneously challenging
orthodoxy on two fronts—economic and racial—he might have made more
impact. And if, after dismissal from the shadow cabinet, he had not nurtured
something close to a vendetta against Heath, his motives would have seemed
less mixed. Unlike Powell, Joseph was more obviously selfless, readier to
compromise, and after 1975 much closer to the party leader.

The new right had now to reclaim Keynes from the Keynesians. In 1980
Lawson, the rising young Conservative minister soon to become Chancellor
of the Exchequer, said that the association between Keynesianism and state
intervention had been a purely chance wartime conjuncture: the war which
had taught Germany to fear the state had taught Britain to love it. There
had been severe limits even in the 1940s to British statism, however: in 1984
Thatcher reminded her party conference of half-forgotten passages in the white
paper of 1944 on employment which emphasized the need for productivity,
enterprise, and self-help. Such passages were 'vintage Maynard Keynes', and
were also integral to the policy of her government; Keynes, she said, 'had
a horror of inflation, a fear of too much state control, and a belief in the
market'.[90] Monetarists claimed that in the changed post-war circumstances,
Keynes's recommendations would have been very different from those of the
1930s. After 1945 trade unions had been strong enough to engineer monopoly
even amidst unemployment, and the British economy had become far more
vulnerable to international trade pressures, yet 'Keynesian' interventionism
now seemed to be helping to distract trade unions from their central role:
defending their members' immediate interests. It cramped their freedom to
negotiate with the employers, yet evolved no long-term approach towards a just
wage or redistribution of wealth. This trend in policy, said Thatcher in 1977,
would logically end in trade unions becoming redundant: mere adjuncts of a
state which determined conditions in their area of responsibility regardless of
their members' special needs and circumstances.[91]

Not content with asserting the free market's relative efficiency, Conservatives
in the 1980s contested the alleged moral superiority of socialism by emphasizing the free market's moral underpinning. Thatcher viewed the inflationary
alternative to Howe's counter-inflationary budget of March 1981 as 'the most
immoral path of all': to print money instead would have undermined incentives

[88] Quotations from Young, *One of Us*, 107. Powell, *O* (8 Sept. 1974), 1.

[89] e.g. speech on 27 Sept. 1972 at Shoreham, *T* (28 Sept. 1972), 2; *HC Deb.* 17 Oct. 1973, cc. 244–5.

[90] Thatcher, *Party Conference Speeches*, 101, cf. 104. Lawson, 'The New Conservatism' (1980), quoted
in his *View from No. 11*, 1047–9, cf. 1042.   [91] Interview with Brian Connell, *T* (9 May 1977), 8.

to investment and thrift, substituting a random and unauthorized assault on people's savings and real incomes for the targeted and democratically endorsed remedy involved in raising taxes or cutting expenditure.[92] She and Lawson also repeatedly stressed the moral growth arising from freedom to choose. The free market rewarded employers and employees displaying the 'Victorian virtues' that had been somewhat undervalued during the Keynesian years: punctuality, hard work, efficiency and alertness to the customer's needs. It encouraged the decision voluntarily to benefit family, community, or both simultaneously through setting up a family business. The free market, they thought, was better than the state at reconciling self-interest with the public interest. Hayek had long ago seen the real choice as lying between the free market and the command economy: the good intentions inspiring collectivist initiatives would not necessarily transfer into the institutions entrusted with implementing them.[93]

Support for the new direction built up gradually from the late 1970s, beginning with Thatcher herself. Important here were Joseph, Sherman, and Howe, the British-born economist Brian Griffiths, and the American apostle of monetarism Milton Friedman, who often visited England and was impressed by Thatcher.[94] As a minister in a spending department in 1970–4, she like Joseph had not dissented from the Heath government's main line of economic policy, and her role in creating the CPS was much smaller than Joseph's. There were two aids to her conversion: she knew that new policies were needed and were best sought early on in opposition, and her Grantham upbringing irradiated monetarism with an instant moral and emotional glow. Joseph's new gospel was not easily advanced within the upper regions of the Conservative Party. Indeed, Joseph bypassed the Party's own research department by working through the CPS, ultimately leaving the research department a shadow of its former self. Permeation of the political and intellectual elite was slow and never complete.

University teachers and civil servants, committed to Wilsonian planning, had disliked Heath's brief and timid anticipation of Thatcherism in 1970–1, and rebellion against prevailing orthodoxies came not from 'the great and the good' or from Oxford and Cambridge, but from scattered and sometimes unexpected intellectual centres: Buckingham, Liverpool, St Andrews, York, and the business schools of London and Manchester, as well as from the LSE.[95] The

[92] Speech at the *Guardian* Business Man of the Year Lunch, 11 Mar. 1981. See also her interview with Hugo Young, *ST* (27 Feb. 1983), 34.

[93] N. Lawson, 'A Paean of Praise to Capitalism', *FT* (4 Sept. 1993), weekend supplement, p. xiii. N. Lawson, *The New Britain: The Tide of Ideas from Attlee to Thatcher* (1988), 13. See also F. A. Hayek, *The Road to Serfdom* (1944), 101.

[94] D. Smith, *The Rise and Fall of Monetarism* (Harmondsworth, 1987), 74–5.

[95] S. Brittan, *The Economic Consequences of Democracy* (1977), 28. D. Walker, 'Tories' Academic Allies', *THES* (18 Jan. 1980), 8.

economist Alan Walters's influence with Thatcher lay through unfashionable redbrick and American economics departments before he acquired his chair at the LSE; nor were Patrick Minford at Liverpool and Alan Peacock at York located within the golden Oxbridge/London triangle. The influential Canadian economist Harry Johnson divided his time equally after 1966 between the LSE and Chicago, whose ideas he enthusiastically exported to Britain.[96] He was one of eight prominent monetarists who with about forty Conservative MPs signed a pamphlet protest to Heath against his u-turn of 1972. Key figures in the London Business School slipped from their earlier Keynesian moorings during the 1970s. 'Thatcherism' was, in short, an anti-establishment protest against major national institutions which had allegedly appeased and compromised for too long. Influential articles by the Oxford economists Walter Eltis and Robert Bacon in the *Sunday Times* in 1974–5[97] saw state expenditure as 'crowding out' the private sector by denying it investment and resources, and were among the few exceptions to this provincial free-market provenance.[98] The CPS's first publication, Samuel Brittan's *Second Thoughts on Full Employment Policy* (1975), did much to popularize monetarist ideas, and in 1977 he and Peter Lilley in their full-scale published assault on incomes policies saw themselves as swimming against the tide. Such policies were not inevitable, they insisted, and intellectuals had much less excuse than politicians for assuming that they were: 'events happen because sufficient people decide they should and insufficient people want something else to happen instead'.[99] Then in 1980 Friedman's American television series *Free to Choose* was compressed into six programmes for British television.

Ideologically it would have been highly paradoxical if Conservative free-marketeers had drawn their impetus and ideas from civil servants: this was not the civil servant's constitutional role, especially given that at the key moment in 1974–9 the Conservatives were in opposition. It was the pressure group, especially the 'think tank', that propagated Thatcherism—less through any direct impact on the public than through influencing the politicians, who then acted as megaphones, none more powerfully than Thatcher herself. In the 1950s and 1960s voluntarist pressure groups had clustered on the welfare state's advancing frontier,[100] but after 1970 their location shifted more influentially to the state's retreating frontier, centring upon the Freedom Association (founded as the National Association for Freedom in 1975 and renamed in 1979), the

---

[96] Johnson's 'The Keynesian Revolution and the Monetarist Counterrevolution' (1970) in Johnson, *On Economics and Society*, 91–106, is perhaps the most entertaining as well as the most trenchant presentation of the monetarist case against the Keynesians.

[97] Published as *Britain's Economic Problem: Too Few Producers* (1976).

[98] For more on this see Harrison, 'Mrs Thatcher and the Intellectuals', 214–15.

[99] S. Brittan and P. Lilley, *The Delusion of Incomes Policy* (1977), 234, cf. 232.

[100] Harrison, *Seeking a Role*, 200, 265–8.

Adam Smith Institute (founded in 1977), and above all the CPS, with the long-established IEA bringing up the rear. Not only did right-wing think tanks promote privatization: they privatized policy's formulation. Nor did they vanish after 1979. A radical government needed their resourcefulness, empathy, and commitment—qualities necessarily absent from civil servants professionally bound to neutrality. The think tanks' partial autonomy as advisers was valuable for extending the bounds of the politically possible, especially as they were deniable when inconvenient. They appropriated for the right the campaigning and questioning techniques of the left, and they interacted with the separate groups that were growing up to contest sixties orthodoxies in schools and universities.[101] The public schools were also acquiring a new self-confidence, and were reinforced in the late 1970s when so many direct-grant schools freed themselves from the state.

So the corporatist retreat entailed a contest between two categories of voluntarist structure, the individualist and the statist. Both pursued the moral and organizational power of a much older category that was now resuming something of its one-time influence: the charity, oriented round the volunteer. Statist pressure groups like Shelter and World Poverty Action had been so closely involved in formulating Labour's agenda that Benn in 1971 had wanted the Party to assign them 'consultative status'; their local branches would then (like trade union branches) affiliate to Labour's. Many of them attended Labour Party conference fringe meetings, and affiliation promised to reinvigorate party politics with much of the enthusiasm that had recently been drifting away to single-issue groups.[102] Heath, by contrast, presented himself as champion of the unorganized: 'we as the Conservative Party and as the Conservative Government represent all the people', he insisted in February 1974. 'We are the trade union for the pensioners and children... the disabled and sick... the unemployed and the low-paid.'[103] In advocating a better deal for pensioners[104] Jack Jones was the only prominent trade union leader who campaigned publicly (rather than manoeuvring privately) to assist non-unionized groups as well as his own members. Heath's inability after 1972 to co-opt the trade unions into his reinforced corporatist scheme prepared Conservatives shortly to resume their less statist traditions; the emergence and resurgence of free-market pressure groups after 1974 reflected rejection of Heath's strategy. The think tanks focused on countermining their statist precursors by exposing their 'conspiracies against the public', and by challenging their claims to altruism. It was a sign of the times that in April 1976 the Child Poverty Action Group and the CPS clashed publicly on how prevalent

---

[101] See below, pp. 384–90. [102] *T* (26 Jan. 1971), 12.

[103] A last-minute addition to his Manchester speech of 20 Feb. 1974, *G* (21 Feb. 1974), 6; cf. his broadcast on the miners' strike on 27 Feb. 1972, *T* (28 Feb. 1972), 2.

[104] *T* (1 Aug. 1974), 3; (4 Sept. 1974), 2.

unemployment really was.[105] By enfranchising the consumer, empowering the parent, multiplying the owner-occupier, and diffusing share-ownership, Thatcher hoped to enable the state substantially to withdraw, and her governments encouraged intermediate groups—local authorities, trade unions, business organizations—to respond more alertly to their ratepayers, members, and customers. This was made easier when government abandoned national wage planning, legislated for trade union ballots, required comparative statistics to be published, broke up monopolies, reformed taxation, and promoted competitive tendering.

Both Heath and Thatcher championed the charity and the volunteer, but in rather different ways. Heath had been much impressed when sixty voluntary bodies had recently collaborated to welcome the Uganda refugees, and saw 'the encouragement of voluntary effort' as lying 'at the heart of our Conservative philosophy'.[106] His government from the outset sought ways of coordinating and encouraging voluntary action, a task that in 1973 was for the first time entrusted to a cabinet minister, Lord Windlesham. But his impulse came more from long-standing Conservative philanthropic traditions than from any anticipation of minimal state philosophies. Thatcher's enthusiasm for charity entailed more emphasis on its affinities with individualism. She felt entirely comfortable in 1983 with Beveridge's individualist variant of public welfare, and five years later cited with approval Wesley's dictum: 'gain all you can, save all you can, give all you can'. She denied that the citizen had discharged all obligation after paying taxes.[107] and often praised the municipal improvements which Victorian cities owed to successful businessman-philanthropists.[108] Her governments lent substance to Heath's aspirations by encouraging charity through the tax structure in the budgets of 1980 and 1986. Charity after 1979 showed an adaptability and vitality, especially in media matters, that would have surprised its many inter-war socialist critics, and culminated in massively mobilizing pop singers on behalf of the starving in Somalia. We have seen how resourceful were late twentieth-century medical charities in mobilizing sufferers and sponsoring research.[109] In 1983 about seven million people (almost a fifth of the UK adult population) were involved in full- or part-time charitable work.[110]

---

[105] T (12 Apr. 1976), 2. K. Joseph, *Stranded on the Middle Ground? Reflections on Circumstances and Policies* (1976), 23.

[106] Addressing Buckinghamshire Conservative associations at Aylesbury, T (14 July 1973), 2. See also Windlesham's *Politics in Practice* (1975), chs. 2 and 3.

[107] Thatcher, ITV interview with Brian Walden, 6 June 1983 (Beveridge). Address to Conservative women's conference on 25 May 1988, FT (26 May 1988), 1. Speech at Great Ormond Street Children's Hospital, DT (28 Apr. 1988), 1 (Wesley).

[108] e.g. in her speech of 9 Oct. 1987 in Thatcher, *Party Conference Speeches*, 129.

[109] See above, pp. 254–7, 271–3.

[110] F. Prochaska, *The Voluntary Impulse: Philanthropy in Modern Britain* (1988), 10.

The scale of this shift in policy ensured that a host of changes pressed on Thatcher when taking office, and her busy activism thereafter masked her belief in the firm limits to the politician's power. On the other hand, she and 'us' (her word for her closest associates, initially embattled within the Party, let alone in society as a whole) were well aware how central are words and symbolic gestures to the politician's repertoire. It was Joseph as Secretary of State for Industry who bore the initial brunt of the new government's intellectual and propagandist effort—patiently yet passionately didactic, lucid and often arresting in explicating unwelcome home truths, vivid in his metaphors. The steel strike of 1980 gave him a prize opportunity. The strike was, he said, 'a classic example of several aspects of the British disease', reflecting pressure for higher wages without higher productivity: if the British Steel Corporation had not been state-owned it 'would be bankrupt'. He denied in parliament that he was taking the management's side: 'the very use of the concept of "sides" ' was 'another symptom of the British disease'. The more the taxpayer funded loss-making industries, the less there would be for public services and tax cuts;[111] a steel industry whose output per man-year was half that of the Europeans could neither pay higher wages nor equip governments to raise welfare benefits.[112] In discussing state subsidies to industry Joseph liked pointing out that government has no money of its own: its resources consist solely of 'taxpayers' money', and raising taxes would in itself obstruct job creation. For governments cannot create jobs, he claimed, nor can trade unions preserve them: jobs 'occur'.[113] Subsidizing one industry involves taxing other workers, often low paid, without even rendering the subsidized industry profitable. He had earlier pointed out that government-created jobs were 'Dead Sea fruit', probably destroying as many jobs as they created. Fond of saying that 'there should be a monument to the unknown unemployed, the men who have lost their jobs because of state aid elsewhere', he pointed out that 'you cannot save Peter without sacking Paul, and possibly Paul's mate or assistant as well'.[114] Joseph also claimed that nation-wide wage-agreements, by ignoring productivity in particular places, undermine national prosperity by shielding employees from the consequences of their own wage-claims. 'Regional differences will not be reduced simply by redistributing money from taxpayers . . . ', he argued. 'Nothing will do more for the prosperity of a region than a reputation for effective work, high productivity and co-operation between work force and management.'[115]

Employers and trade unionists under a government so self-limiting were at first alarmed after 1979, and in wage settlements initially experienced a

---

[111] *HC Deb.* 17 Jan. 1980, c. 1886; 14 Jan. 1980, c. 1219. *HC Deb.* 17 Jan. 1980, c. 1893.
[112] Joseph's answers to Brian Walden's questions in ITV's *Weekend World* (20 Jan. 1980).
[113] *T* (25 Aug. 1978), 11.
[114] Quotations from *O* (5 Aug. 1979), 9; (22 July 1979), 21. *T* (2 Sept. 1978), 2. See also *HC Deb.* 14 Jan. 1980, cc. 1208–21.   [115] *HC Deb.* 17 July 1979, c. 1307.

collective agoraphobia. Free at last to resume their prized free collective bargaining, they lacked guidance from any 'going rate' for wages during the coming year. Trade unionists found it disquieting, too, as well as mildly insulting, not to be invited for their customary talks with the Prime Minister; yet with no incomes policy, where was the agenda? Rusty free-market machinery had to be dusted down. As one trade unionist at the TUC told a journalist, 'you're on your bloody own—and it's not nice'.[116] Likewise with the government's response to North Sea oil. As Secretary of State for Energy, Lawson evoked some surprise by refusing even to have such a thing as an 'energy policy', and by preventing Whitehall from interfering with commercial decisions about the pace of extraction; how could the government possibly know how much energy the UK would require in twenty years' time? He was relatively unconcerned that North Sea energy supplies would rapidly run out.[117] The preceding Labour government had envisaged using oil revenues partly for tax cuts, but also for industrial re-equipment and retraining, for conserving and diversifying energy supplies, and for improving social services, but Thatcher wanted 'the lion's share' for tax cuts. These, she argued, would boost profits, then investment, then job-creation. Lawson denied that government could or should select which aspects of British industry should benefit from Britain's oil: that was 'the job of industry and commerce', and it was clear to him even in 1984 that the growth areas 'would not be the same industries that many people attempted to persuade us to subsidise while oil production was building up'.[118] After 1979 people soon stopped discussing the good causes to which government might divert North Sea oil revenues. Instead they were to be channelled, in the form of tax cuts and unemployment benefits, directly to the taxpayer, who would individually have his own good causes to promote, and whose painful transition to new patterns of employment would thereby be eased.

Compatible with this outlook was a growing all-party belief in encouraging small firms. This was partly because large firms had not generated the hoped-for economies of scale, but also because of the newly fashionable idea that 'small is beautiful', because middle-class pressure groups were active, and because encouraging smallness could win votes in the middle ground. Healey in his budget of 1978 had described small businesses as 'a prime source of innovation in British industry', and made tax concessions to encourage them. His successor Howe in his budget speech of 1980 depreciated

---

[116] G. Turner, 'Brothers without a Cause', *STel* (2 Sept. 1979), 19. For the employers see *FT* (22 Aug. 1979), 16 (leader).

[117] Lawson, *View from No. 11*, 163–5, 186. Speech at Cambridge, *FT* (10 Apr. 1984), 1; *View from No. 11*, 195.

[118] See the important confrontation between Callaghan and Thatcher in *HC Deb.* 21 Mar. 1978, cc. 1326–8 on the government white paper 'The Challenge of North Sea Oil'. Lawson, *FT* (10 Apr. 1984), 1.

'the fashion for industrial elephantism',[119] and made it easier for merged firms to fragment.[120] Instead of a few large government projects protecting old jobs, Thatcher wanted thousands of small projects promoting new jobs, for she thought unemployment best curbed by managers and employees responding to tax incentives. The new government encouraged the small firm with deregulation, tax cuts, and promotion of a more flexible labour market.[121] In the early 1980s there was a rapid escalation in management buy-outs,[122] and fragmentation was among privatization's many hoped-for charms.

Thatcher readily reinforced the moralism inherent in the new outlook: indeed for her, the morality came first and the monetarism second. Where the two conflicted, as with owner-occupation's restraints on labour mobility, she opted for the morality. In her free-market world, governments should set standards in personal morality, and could not ultimately stave off punishment for sin: the depression's austerities followed the over-indulgences of boom as ineluctably as night follows day. 'Thatcherism' in her own definition 'stands for sound finance . . . It stands for honest money, not inflation; it stands for living within your means; it stands for incentives . . . It stands for the wider and wider spread of ownership of property, of houses, of shares, of savings. It stands for being strong in defence.' In her new-year message for 1983 she contrasted her government with its precursors: 'we repay our debts. We pay our way in the world. We honour our obligations. We keep our word.'[123] She saw her attacks on inflation, when defending the deflationary budget of 1981 for example, as pursuing the 'moral' course. By not printing more money to fund greater state expenditure she was safeguarding the savings of the thrifty, and throughout she bore the misfortunes of her own thrifty relatives in mind.[124] She once told a journalist that she was 'in politics because of the conflict between good and evil',[125] and in her later years as prime minister she thought it important to swap text for text with her Anglican and Methodist critics; in 1988 she even addressed the General Assembly of the Church of Scotland on a religious topic.[126]

---

[119] Healey, *HC Deb.* 11 Apr. 1978, c. 1188. Howe, *HC Deb.* 26 Mar. 1980, c. 1484.

[120] For government schemes to encourage small firms as at May 1983 see T. Dickson, 'We're All Small Firms Ministers Now', *FT* (3 May 1983), small businesses supplement, p. ii.

[121] Thatcher, *HC Deb.* 28 Mar. 1979, c. 465, and see D. Macintyre, 'Freeing Firms from Red Tape', *T* (3 Jan. 1986), 2.

[122] For a useful discussion see M. Dickson, 'Finance Aplenty to Back Deals', *FT* (8 Dec. 1986), venture capital supplement, p. vi.

[123] Day, . . . *But With Respect*, 233 (8 June 1987). *DT* (31 Dec. 1982), 30; cf. her Georgetown speech, *T* (28 Feb. 1981), 1.

[124] *T* (12 Mar. 1981), 2. *ST* (27 Feb. 1983), 34 (interview with Hugo Young).

[125] Young, *One of Us*, 352.

[126] e.g. interview with Bruce Anderson, *STel* (28 June 1987), 23; comments on Jimmy Young show, *Ind* (6 June 1987), 1; speech to Conservative women's conference, *FT* (26 May 1988), 1. For an attack

For both symbolic and practical reasons, one of the new government's first tasks was to rein back inflation, and here Howe was centre-stage. 'Nothing, in the long run', he said, 'could contribute more to the disintegration of society and the destruction of any sense of national unity than continuing inflation.' So during the government's first six months, he and a small group of advisers which included Lawson devised a 'medium term financial strategy'. It aimed to boost the economy by cutting government expenditure, taxation, and the money supply, and therefore inflation. A combination of libertarian and entrepreneurial theory, populist instinct, and electoral calculation had made tax cutting a continuous theme in British politics from the 1970s onwards; for taxpayers inflation was, after all, an escalator into higher tax brackets unless deliberately adjusted. 'The twin policies of over-man and over-tax', said Joseph in 1977, 'are suicidal for the standard of living and social services of this country.' The Thatcher governments saw cutting tax levels, cutting unemployment, and boosting the resources for welfare as interlinked. Tax cuts were, for Thatcher, 'the incentive to create the wealth which pays for higher benefits',[127] and Joseph had for some time denied that inequality generated poverty: citing Scandinavia, West Germany, and the Netherlands, he pointed out that 'many of our neighbouring countries . . . have . . . more prosperity . . . Yet they have much greater inequalities of earned income.'[128] The green paper which accompanied Lawson's first budget in 1984 sounded the trump: 'spending decisions taken issue by issue have steadily raised the burden of total spending without regard to what taxpayers will tolerate or to the consequences for incentives and growth. This process cannot be allowed to continue indefinitely.'[129]

If encouraging enterprise was the central objective, upward redistribution seemed necessary. In reducing the top rate of income tax from 83 per cent to the European average of 60 per cent, Howe in his first budget speech emphasized that Britain had to compete with other countries not only in selling goods and services but 'in attracting and retaining the talent required to run our industry efficiently and profitably', thereby increasing employment. It was hoped that tax cuts would prompt a 'virtuous circle': that the resultant faster growth would in turn generate more revenue, so that taxes could fall further. It was thought that a lower tax rate could ultimately generate more revenue than a higher. Lawson implied in his budget speech of 1988—labelled by Thatcher 'the epitaph for socialism'[130]—that he had reached that happy destination. In cutting the higher

from the President of the Methodist conference, see *Ind* (25 June 1988), 1. For her General Assembly text see *G* (23 May 1988), 38.

[127] Howe, *HC Deb.* 26 Mar. 1980, c. 1443. Thatcher speech to Conservative women's conference on 25 May 1988, *FT* (26 May 1988), 1.

[128] *HC Deb.* 8 Nov. 1977, c. 510; 21 Jan. 1974, c. 1223.   [129] *FT* (14 Mar. 1984), 24.

[130] Howe, *HC Deb.* 12 June 1979, c. 259. Lawson speech at Buxton, 19 Mar. 1988, *Ind* (21 Mar. 1988), 5.

rate of income tax from 60 per cent to 40 per cent, he pointed out that the top 5 per cent of taxpayers were now paying as much again in real terms as in 1978/9, when they had been taxed at 83 per cent. Between those years the top rate of inheritance tax had also fallen, from 75 per cent to 40 per cent, and the basic rate of income tax from 33 per cent to 25 per cent; in 1988 Lawson set as a target a basic rate for income tax of 20 per cent. In all this Lawson knew as well as Howe in 1979 what was happening in other countries, and cited as precedents cuts in the higher tax rate already made in several European and English-speaking countries. There were outraged cries from Labour MPs, yet by May 1990 their leader was proposing to raise the higher rate no higher than 50 per cent,[131] and the Party later retreated even from that.

The trend towards tax cuts and the move from direct to indirect taxation had been launched by Healey after 1976. His budgets had moved away from direct to indirect taxation[132] partly for administrative reasons: direct taxes were increasingly difficult to collect when employment was dispersing into smaller firms and self-employment. At the same time the service sector was growing, and indirect taxes were more easily collected by the ever-larger retail units. From the 1970s purchase and petrol taxes delivered markedly more revenue, as did VAT. The latter, a remodelled purchase tax imported from Europe in 1973, turned every trader into a tax collector, and counterbalanced the dwindling revenue from other indirect taxes such as those on tobacco and beer.[133] Unlike its precursors, VAT was levied on services as well as goods, and was paid at each link in the distributive chain. It entailed a huge administrative and retailing revolution, and much error and evasion were at first the outcome.[134] Another way to bypass income tax, with its unpopular directness, was to step up national insurance payments, which after the 1950s waxed in their share of total taxation while income tax and death duties waned. By 1979 VAT was sufficiently established for Howe in his first budget to make the bold but well-prepared move of raising its rate from 8 to 15 per cent. For a year or so after taking office, the Conservatives publicized a 'tax and prices index' (TPI); its aim was to highlight taxation's overall impact on prices, thereby counteracting the cost of living index's emphasis on indirect taxation. Dismissed by Len Murray as the 'try and pretend' or 'take your pick' index, it took no account of the 'social wage', and was too obviously partisan ever to catch on.[135]

Within the community as a whole, hostility to paying taxes was often collectively irrational, given the growing twentieth-century importance of transfer payments: that is, the state's transfer of spending power between

---

[131] Lawson, *View from No. 11*, 815, 817, 819, cf. Kinnock, *O* (27 May 1990), 3.
[132] See e.g. his budget speech, *HC Deb.* 29 Mar. 1977, c. 271.
[133] For a useful table on the changing incidence of taxes see *Econ* (17 Sept. 1983), 20.
[134] For a good discussion of this see B. Hale, 'Not So Many Happy Returns for VAT', *T* (2 Apr. 1976), 19.   [135] *FT* (15 Aug. 1979), 6. *G* (6 Sept. 1979), 4.

individuals. Between 1955/9 and 1974 such payments rose from a seventh to nearly a quarter of gross domestic product, largely reflecting the claims of the old on state pensions, and the claims of the poor and the unemployed on subsidies and social-security payments.[136] The community's shared interest and the individual's personal interest were not identical, however, and the high marginal rates of tax in Britain spawned numerous avoidance devices; the unending trench warfare between tax collector and tax adviser was fought ever more ingeniously. By the 1960s 'fringe benefits' were increasingly prominent among the business executive's rewards: company cars, chauffeurs, pensions, free health-checks, free meals.[137] G. S. A. Wheatcroft's *The Taxation of Gifts and Settlements* (1953) was in effect the first book on tax planning, and three years later he founded the *British Tax Review*; by 1972 tax law was being taught in thirty-two of the forty-one institutions offering law degrees.[138] The phrase 'tax haven' had come into use by the early 1970s to describe facilities available in the Channel Isles and the Isle of Man. It was when criticizing payments made in the Cayman Islands to directors of the Lonrho Group, to avoid complying with his incomes policy, that Heath had coined his famous phrase about 'the unpleasant and unacceptable face of capitalism'.[139]

Tax avoidance was not closely correlated with wealth: it was the very wealthy and the very poorest (often retired single people) who were least likely to participate in the black economy.[140] In 1986 a third of people receiving unemployment pay said they had worked for cash in hand, and in 1994 the poorest fifth of the population funded about a third of their spending from income unknown to the authorities.[141] This statistically invisible army of moonlighting window-cleaners, gardeners, cleaning ladies, hairdressers, home decorators, and small-scale entrepreneurs—reinforced by the woman-at-work and the husband on his allotment—were helping to stabilize households during years of unusually disruptive economic transition. In 1979 Sir William Pile, Chairman of the Board of Inland Revenue, thought that undeclared income could amount to as much as 7.5 per cent of the gross national product.[142] The demand for £10 and £20 notes (convenient for large unrecorded transactions) was by the late 1970s rising almost three times as fast as for smaller denominations. Marks & Spencer discovered in 1979 that shops in areas where unemployment was high did not sell noticeably fewer goods than elsewhere, and a survey of 1985 showed that 750,000 people in Britain (3 per cent of the

[136] T. Congdon, 'Mounting Public Expenditure and the Role of Transfer Payments', *T* (16 Feb. 1976), 16.   [137] Sampson, *Changing Anatomy of Britain*, 337.
[138] See J. F. Avery Jones's memoir in *ODNB*.   [139] *HC Deb*. 15 May 1973, c. 1243.
[140] *FT* (10 June 1995), 4.   [141] *FT* (8 Aug. 1986), 6; (10 June 1995), 4.
[142] *G* (28 Mar. 1979), 17. Even those who put the figure much lower at between 2.0 and 3.5% agreed that the black economy had been growing since the mid-1970s, *T* (17 Sept. 1980), 16.

employed workforce) held down more than one job.[143] So rapidly did the 'black economy' seem to be growing that by then it received almost as much comment as spivs and under-the-counter deals in the late 1940s.

The 'shadow economy' also deserves mention. In these years escalating but domesticated mechanization hid from the authorities activities which had earlier been highly visible because then communal. Rising affluence and cheaper tools and home-based machinery enabled people to outwit the taxman entirely legally by doing for themselves what others had been paid to do: they could now wash their clothes, decorate their homes, drive their own cars, serve themselves with petrol, deliver their own shopping, and so on. Less legal, and difficult to police, was the 'alternative economy' of unofficial work, which young inner-city West Indians often preferred to what jobcentres offered.[144] The prevalence of such devices may help to explain why the general public in these years were so much less gloomy than their political leaders about the economy, and also why rising unemployment did not provoke more indignation.[145] Conservative tax reforms in the 1980s did not of course eliminate tax evasion, and there was much talk thereafter of its new directions: through car-boot sales, for example, and even through substituting barter for currency. From running at about 8 per cent of gross domestic product in 1984, the black economy accounted for about 12 per cent in 1996.[146] Nonetheless, without the tax reforms of the 1980s that figure might have been higher still.

During 1980 British industry experienced a serious squeeze stemming from the unexpected conjuncture of four separate developments which collectively damaged British manufacture and raised unemployment to a dangerous extent: tight monetary control, the inflationary impact of the government's commitment to meet the Clegg pay awards and of Howe's marked shift towards indirect taxation, the consequent high interest rates, and the strengthening pound at a time when world oil prices were rising fast and Britain was becoming a major oil producer. The government decided in March 1981 to meet depression by combining relaxed monetary control with a deflationary remedy. In a protest organized from Cambridge by Robert Neild and Frank Hahn, 364 economists (a quarter of economics teachers in British universities, including 76 professors) then wrote to *The Times*. They saw no theoretical or empirical basis for the idea that deflating demand would bring inflation permanently under control and thereby cause output and employment to recover; on the contrary, it would deepen the depression and erode Britain's industrial base. The time had come 'to reject monetarist policies' and seek alternatives. Four years earlier Hahn had publicly warned fellow economists not to discredit their discipline by

---

[143] *FT* (9 Apr. 1979), 16 (notes). *G* (28 Mar. 1979), 17 (Marks). *FT* (18 Oct. 1985), 7 (survey).
[144] *T* (11 Aug. 1980), 2.
[145] As suggested by Victor Keegan in *G* (28 Mar. 1979), 17. See also above, pp. 179–82.
[146] *FT* (26 May 1997), 6.

pronouncing on complex matters such as the effects of EEC membership,[147] but this seemed a technical question on which economists could usefully express a view. The government ignored their warning, and because the trough of the depression had already passed, the economists' fears were not realized. Their protest remained controversial, but its short-term effect was to distance the government still further from university opinion, as well as to lower the prestige of economics as a discipline. In 1992 Lawson was even prepared to argue that the strong pound had been salutary: 'some degree of shock treatment was needed, and the exchange rate provided it'.[148]

Critics of government policy in the early 1980s alighted enthusiastically on the expansionary policy Reagan pursued in the USA; its high central bank rate attracted funds from other countries, unemployment fell well below British levels, and taxes were cut. American economic policy was one area where the Reagan/Thatcher accord was less than close, and where Reagan ignored Thatcher's lectures. 'I rejoice at what Reagan is doing' said Macmillan in his maiden speech in the House of Lords in 1984: 'he has broken all the rules, and all the economists are furious'.[149] Lawson disagreed completely, ascribing the American success to a culture contrast: American entrepreneurs were vigorous, he said, and in a relatively flexible labour market shrewd American trade unionists priced themselves into work, if necessary by moving about the country. It would anyway have been doubly difficult for Thatcher to expand the British economy in the American fashion, given Britain's relative propensity to import and her larger budget deficit in 1979. Events in 1981 had distanced Thatcher still further from her economist critics, and in March 1987 she ignored the recommendation by four former chief economic advisers that her government should change course and curb unemployment through a budget for jobs;[150] she went on to win the general election three months later.

The Thatcher governments were less successful than they had hoped in reducing government's share of national expenditure. The need to honour existing commitments, rising unemployment in the early 1980s,[151] and restraints on government borrowing caused taxation's initial incidence actually to increase. The difficulty of reining back expenditure was vividly revealed on 13 July 1982 when the government's majority sank to eight, the lowest to date; at that point eighteen Conservative MPs voted to restore the 5 per cent cut in unemployment

[147] For the list see *G* (30 Mar. 1981), 1–2. Hahn, *T* (18 June 1977), 15.

[148] For controversy see e.g. *FT* (2 July 1990), 13; (5 July 1990), 23. Lawson, *View from No. 11*, 63.

[149] Macmillan, *HL Deb.* 13 Nov. 1984, c. 239; cf. Gilmour, *Dancing with Dogma*, 53–4. See also M. Smith, 'Britain and the United States: Beyond the "Special Relationship"', in P. Byrd (ed.), *British Foreign Policy under Thatcher* (Deddington and New York, 1988), 26.

[150] Lawson, Mais lecture, *FT* (19 June 1984), 10; Lawson, *View from No. 11*, 431–2. W. Eltis, 'Why Thatcher Cannot Follow Reagan's Lead', *T* (31 Oct. 1984), 16. See also letter in *FT* (16 Mar. 1987), 23, signed by Sir Fred Atkinson, Sir Alec Cairncross, Sir Bryan Hopkin, and Sir Donald MacDougall.

[151] See above, p. 248; below, pp. 358–63, 537.

benefit imposed in 1980. Government expenditure's share of gross domestic product stood at 43 per cent in 1977/8, but rising unemployment had helped it to reach 47 per cent in 1983/4; by 1988/9 it had fallen to 39 per cent, but by 1993/4 it was up again to 44 per cent.[152] Howe's initial 'medium term financial strategy' had aimed to transcend the short term with a timetable for curbing the money supply at a politically practicable pace over a longer period. The Treasury was ill-prepared for such a scheme, lacked sympathy with it, and thought it would soon be abandoned; this led Lawson later to wish that the Conservatives had done more work on monetary policy before 1979. Ministers soon found that effective control entailed more than merely exerting financial discipline from conviction rather than (as under Labour) from IMF compulsion; it required exact ways of measuring the money supply to guide practicable policy.[153]

The narrowly monetarist doctrine of controlling monetary aggregates was not easily reconciled with liberalizing the financial markets: the rapid improvement in international communications during the 1980s created a world trade in currency which decoupled the pattern of overseas currency transactions from the pattern of overseas trade. There was also by then a widening tension between the instincts and traditions of the nation-state and pressures from an increasingly internationalized economy.[154] Furthermore, lighter regulation of the British economy generated fewer statistics about its working. Two consequences flowed: the currency markets fluctuated far less predictably; and governments, in deregulating the banks, denied themselves their chosen guideline on how manage the economy—that is, the money supply reliably measured. Difficult technical questions presented themselves: should the measure of money supply be Mo (coin and notes) or the widening definitions M1 (coin, notes, and current accounts), M2 (coin, notes, current accounts, and other more liquid assets), M3 (coin, notes, and all sterling bank deposits), or something wider still? Whatever the measure selected, and the measures did not all move in the same direction, the government did not come even near to meeting its targets[155]—so much so, that Sir Ian Gilmour could plausibly tell Conservatives by October 1981 that monetarism was 'the uncontrollable in pursuit of the indefinable'. The economist C. A. E. Goodhart identified a further difficulty: 'any observed statistical regularity will tend to collapse once pressure is placed upon it for control purposes';[156] that is, whatever is publicly defined as money for the purposes of monetary control will be replaced by substitutes aiming to evade that control. It was a problem in social science whose application extended far beyond monetarist economics.

---

[152] *T* (14 July 1982), 1; (1 Dec. 1994), 12.   [153] Lawson, *View from No. 11*, 17, 26.

[154] On which see D. Held, *Democracy and the New International Order* (Institute for Public Policy Research, 1993).   [155] See the table in Lawson, *View from No. 11*, 1079.

[156] Gilmour, address to a Conservative Party fringe meeting at Blackpool on 14 Oct. 1981), *G* (15 Oct. 1981), 7. C. A. E. Goodhart, *Monetary Theory and Practice: The UK Experience* (1984), 96.

Already by March 1982 Heath felt able to announce that 'monetarism is dead and the alien doctrines of Friedman and Hayek remain only to be buried'. Macmillan in November 1984 quizzically likened the monetarist and Keynesian schools to the rival remedies peddled in the Victorian nursery: 'feed a cold' was the prescription of the nanny who 'was a neo-Keynesian', whereas 'starve a cold' emanated from the nanny who 'was a monetarist'. Lawson as Chancellor after 1983 gradually abandoned the idea of controlling inflation through aiming at fixed money-supply targets. In October 1985 he announced that his main weapons against inflation would now be to restrain government spending and manipulate the exchange rate, and in his budget of 1987 he announced the end of such targets altogether. His thinking while Chancellor 'developed', as he put it, and he began to put more faith in international economic cooperation as a way to curb inflation and unemployment.[157] He retained the monetarist enthusiasm for technical rules which would free decision-makers from being tempted to cultivate short-term popularity through manipulating the economy, but he gradually transferred his faith to 'shadowing' (that is, tying the pound to) a currency controlled by strongly anti-inflationary policy: the deutschmark.

The logical consequence of such a policy, applied from March 1987, was for Britain to join the ERM, for which Lawson was by then privately campaigning. Yet paradoxically when pursuing that logical consequence, the Major government in 1992 found itself even more seriously beset by events beyond its control. Perhaps the most serious government information failure of the decade occurred in 1986–9, when the series on the gross domestic product did not forewarn the Treasury how strong was domestic demand and how serious was the threat of inflation. When inflation began to escalate, Thatcher wished aloud that she had not agreed to abandon 'the plan' (the Medium Term Financial Strategy), and later even claimed not to know of Lawson's decision to shadow the deutschmark.[158] John Major, Lawson's successor (1989–90) took an entirely pragmatic view of the ERM, which seemed the best way to stabilize the currency and curb inflation. The practicalities drove both him and Thatcher towards joining the ERM on 5 October 1990 in a move that was welcomed by almost everyone who mattered, from the CBI to the Labour Party, and from the *Daily Telegraph* to the *Guardian*.

The Keynesians remained more influential and resourceful in Britain than in America in the 1980s, but in that decade mutual concession broke down any simple polarity between them and the monetarists. Compelled to concede the difficulty of controlling the economy through so imprecise a benchmark as the quantity of money, the monetarists fell back on indirect control through

---

[157] *HC Deb.* 15 Mar. 1982, c. 37 (Heath). *HL Deb.* 13 Nov. 1984, c. 238 (Macmillan). Lawson, *View from No. 11*, 422, 1023, 1025.

[158] Interview with Simon Jenkins, *T* (19 Nov. 1990), 14. Thatcher, *Downing Street Years*, 699, 701.

the interest rate. They and the neo-Keynesian school of economists had always been more closely aligned than was widely thought. In a highly complex situation, whose uncertainties included much ignorance about the money supply's operation, both sought a simple and even automatic solution to economic problems.[159] Both, when the policies seemed to fail, blamed extraneous factors, claiming that their policies had not been applied in the right way or in the right circumstances. Adam Smith pointed out that like other types of believer, the economist 'who is waiting around for the perfect practical application of his ideas will have to wait a long time'.[160] In retrospect we can see that while Keynesians moved towards accepting an inflation target, monetarists accepted that governments must cut interest rates during recession, and became less prone to view the economy as self-correcting.

3. THE ENTREPRENEUR RETURNS

British politicians between 1945 and 1979 hardly displayed a Victorian enthusiasm for the entrepreneur. Labour was too closely tied to the trade unions, too 'labourist' in mood and support, for its leaders' defence of the entrepreneur to sound more than plaintive. 'I do wish so many of the comrades would stop equating profits with incest or lechery', the Minister of Labour Ray Gunter told supporters in 1967, emphasizing that profits facilitated investment and therefore created jobs. Callaghan preached the same message to the Labour Party conference in that year: 'I do not rejoice when profits are low . . . Profit is the only measure we have of the efficiency of a firm's management.'[161] Conservative leaders, still hugging the corporatist middle ground, usually thought votes were best husbanded through leaving the entrepreneur's defence to others. The Chairman of British Leyland, for example, complained in 1974 that 'the urge for security, social service careers or other non-physically productive activities seems to have replaced the entrepreneurial instincts of previous generations'. *The Times*, surveying the Queen's first quarter-century on the throne in 1976, thought Britain 'a country that resents being poor, but is not prepared to make the effort to be rich'. For the Duke of Edinburgh, whose remarks made something of a stir in the following year, the balance had been got 'slightly wrong' because a society 'over-concerned with failure' seemed too keen to blame the better off for the fact that some people were poor.[162]

[159] Andrew Graham, interview with Anthony Seldon in *Contemporary British History* (Spring 1996), 154, 164.   [160] Smith, *Rise and Fall of Monetarism*, 162.
[161] Gunter, speech to the Scottish Council of Labour, Glasgow: *ST* (20 Aug. 1967), 1. Callaghan, *T* (4 Oct. 1967), 10 (on 3 Oct. 1967).
[162] Lord Stokes, presidential address on student career-choice to Manchester University Institute of Science and Technology, *G* (22 Jan. 1974), 17. 'Twenty-Five Years On', *T* (31 Dec. 1976), 15 (leader). For the Duke, *Director* (Jan. 1977), 33.

There was in fact ample enterprise in Britain before 1979, but much of it occurred outside working hours: discovering how to avoid paying taxes or get the most from public welfare, or devising new types of recreation and improvements for the home. We have already described landowners' ingenuity in husbanding their wealth, middle-class aptitude for capitalizing on public welfare and house-purchase (though not for buying shares), and trade union assiduity in developing an informal power structure within the workplace, sometimes in collusion with their employers.[163] Sociologists found that Luton's affluent workers of the early 1960s were prone to self-help, not through seeking promotion at work, but through dreaming of setting up their own businesses.[164] During the 1980s many seem to have realized their dreams, for during that decade the self-employed were over-represented at both lower and upper ends of the income range, and their number nearly doubled; by 1990 they accounted for one in eight working people. By international standards their share of non-agricultural civilian employment had by then become high.[165]

Heath's tone had sometimes anticipated Thatcher's: in February 1974, for example, he pointed out that 'if you want to see the acceptable face of capital-ism' you should 'go out to an oil rig in the North Sea'.[166] Energy production advanced there in successive waves, first with the Netherlands boom in North Sea gas in the 1960s, then with the oil rush of the 1970s and early 1980s, then with the UK and Norwegian gas finds of the late 1980s and 1990s. Heath's government did not push his entrepreneurial insight fully home, whereas Thatcher in 1975 struck a more robust note, dismissing Labour complaints about overseas companies reaping the oil profits, and braving Labour jeers by emphasizing that this was an achievement of private enterprise.[167] 'The North Sea', she told her party conference in 1977, was 'not a Socialist sea and its oil is not Socialist oil. It was found by private enterprise; it was drilled by private enterprise; and it is being brought ashore by private enterprise.' Benn's response was very different. He was impressed in 1973, after a three-day visit, by the scale of the North Sea oil installations, but this 'absolutely convinced me of the need for public enterprise to come in' so as to protect the future from the international companies. He was impressed two years later, as Secretary of

---

[163] For upper and middle classes see Harrison, *Seeking a Role*, 162–4, 185–8, 264, 319, and see also above, pp. 88–9, 133–4, 150, 255, and below, pp. 393, 414–15. For the working class see *Seeking a Role*, 211–12, 308, and above, pp. 156–7, 169.

[164] J. H. Goldthorpe *et al.*, *The Affluent Worker*, i. *Industrial Attitudes and Behaviour* (Cambridge, 1968), 131–2.

[165] *FT* (19 Sept. 1994), 8 (self-employed), and see the useful comparative table in R. Barrell (ed.), *The UK Labour Market: Comparative Aspects and Institutional Developments* (Cambridge, 1994), 31.

[166] *G* (19 Feb. 1974), 6.

[167] e.g. *HC Deb.* 21 Mar. 1978, c. 1326. For the jeers see *T* (22 Mar. 1978), 10.

State for Energy, by the 'complete science fiction world' on the rigs,[168] but like his colleagues he wanted North Sea revenue deployed by the state to modernize British industry.[169]

In 1976 *The Times*, in its retrospective view, claimed that 'the creative elements in society need more scope, less restraint', not only through tax reform and restored differentials, but through displaying 'greater respect for achievement', and rather less preoccupation with 'social provision'. It claimed that 'no government can fashion a public mood, but a government which now moves in that direction will find an answering sentiment in the public'. Thatcher, as the first British Conservative leader to combine origins outside the elite with a free-market and meritocratic scepticism towards it, was well equipped to meet the need. Her opportunity lay in the fact that enterprise within corporatism entailed neglecting the interests of several groups whom a reoriented Conservative Party might hope to capture: people on fixed incomes, old-age pensioners, and other groups ill-equipped to organize themselves in self-defence. Her initial difficulty lay in the fact that corporatist enterprise hindered enterprise of the most crucial kind: the resourceful entrepreneurship in manufacturing and commerce necessary for funding other desired objectives. Her task involved less inculcating enterprise of the desired type than releasing the full and spontaneous power of a quality inherent in human nature but diverted by corporatism into unprofitable channels. For her the free market required the entrepreneur as dynamo, and throughout her career she rebutted cynicism, pessimism, and negative attitudes, for within her sphere she was herself entrepreneurial in outlook. Schumpeter defined entrepreneurship as venturing beyond routine expectations, braving resistance to change, and 'getting things done';[170] it was a quality she relished, and it pervaded the small embattled group with whose aid she captured her party.

Such an outlook distanced her from the CBI, which was nervous about her free-market approach and her dismissive view of the trade unions. 'Employers were always advising me to be tough except in their own industry', she recalled.[171] From employers' organizations as from trade unions, she wanted more effective and politically less partisan representation of their rank and file, together with an overriding concern for the customer. In 1980 when an overvalued pound was hampering exports, the CBI's Director-General Sir Terence Beckett publicly urged the need to defend business against government policy in a 'bare-knuckled fight', but he seems to have been

---

[168] Thatcher, *Party Conference Speeches*, 30. Benn, *Diaries 1973–6*, 72 (20 Oct. 1973); 419 (16 July 1975).

[169] See his speech at the Party conference on 5 Oct. 1978, *T* (6 Oct. 1978), 6; cf. Callaghan on 2 July 1977, *T* (4 July 1977), 2; and his (4 Oct.) party conference speech (5 Oct. 1977), 6.

[170] *T* (31 Dec. 1976), 15 (leader). J. A. Schumpeter, *Capitalism, Socialism and Democracy* (1st publ. 1943, 5th edn. 1976), 132. [171] Thatcher, *Downing Street Years*, 356.

knocked out in his subsequent meeting with Thatcher because nothing more of the 'fight' was heard. Thatcher thought the CBI suffered from over-representing large firms, manufacturing, and even nationalized industries with an interest in state subsidy.[172] Employers' organizations, though less distracting than corporatist structures to the businessman, diverted his energies; British Leyland, as one of the first moves in its recovery programme, withdrew from the Engineering Employers' Federation so as to avoid being entangled in strikes which originated outside the company.[173] More congenial to Thatcher was the resolutely free-market Institute of Directors, which represented individuals rather than firms. Even more to her taste were selected individual entrepreneurs. Whereas Arnold Weinstock, Managing Director of GEC, was out of favour for opposing privatization and seeking to protect the manufacturing sector, Lords King, Hanson, and Palumbo were often seen in her company.[174]

British management's 'lack of professionalism', its low pay, and its lack of talented recruits by comparison with France and Germany were themes Henderson discussed in his valedictory despatch of 1979.[175] All this soon began to change. Managers were freed immediately from the distractions of incomes policies, and gradually from the continual need to ward off industrial disputes or firefight once they broke out. They could now demand the worldwide going rate for the job, backed by a government which made controlling inflation its first priority, lowered taxes, and lent the labour market a new flexibility. Managers could focus on their prime task: seeking out and satisfying the customer. Thatcher's ideal was the shirt-sleeved, 'go-getting' (her phrase), and accessible manager: he ate in the works canteen, and through hard work, enterprise, and imagination developed and promoted a product which satisfied home and overseas customers. Her ideal was by no means always realized. The more technical aspects of management—marketing, stock-control, accounting, planning and restructuring the workforce—were widely taught in the Americanized business schools of the 1980s, but the theoretical bias of business studies did not always bring practical benefits. The long-term trend since the 1930s for moving accountants into British industry's top posts did not cease in 1979: the proportion employed there rose from 49 per cent in 1951 to 64 per cent in 1991, by which year they supplied a fifth of company chairmen and managing directors, and more than a fifth of all directors. By contrast, Thatcher on a visit to Japan was impressed with how often it was the engineer who held the top post: 'a clue to Japanese industrial success', she thought.[176]

[172] For a good general discussion of the CBI's situation see H. Duffy, 'An Awkward Inheritance', *FT* (22 Oct. 1986), 28.   [173] *FT* (30 May 1984), 12.
[174] Ridley, '*My Style of Government*', 44–5.   [175] *Econ* (2 June 1979), 30.
[176] Thatcher, *Downing Street Years*, 496. See also D. Matthews, M. Anderson, and J. R. Edwards, 'The Rise of the Professional Accountant in British Management', *Economic History Review* (Aug. 1997), 410–11.

1. (*left*) Sir Freddie Laker, airline entrepreneur 1 January 1980. *See p. 19.*

2. (*below*) Counting the votes in the EEC referendum 1975. *See pp. 28, 47.*

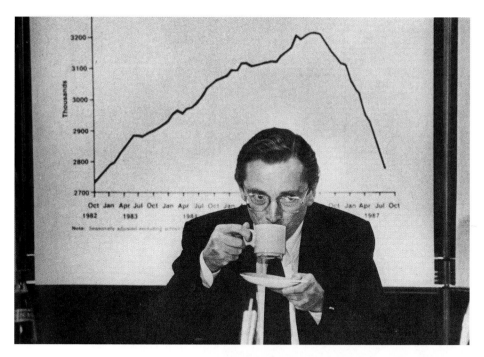

15. Norman Fowler, Secretary of State for Employment: press conference at the Employment Department in 1987, showing unemployment falling. *See p. 360.*

16. Lord Scarman during his inquiry of 1981 into the Brixton riots. *See p. 472.*

More welcome to the government was the decline in the 'personnel manager', rendered less necessary by improved industrial relations. As for the 'responsible' employer, he began to seem as antique as the 'responsible' trade unionist: each could now focus on his primary purpose. The Toxteth riots[177] produced a brief resurgence under Heseltine of enthusiasm for 'responsible' employers who would corporately concern themselves directly with the social problems in their community, but for Thatcher the employer's prime responsibility lay in creating and managing well-run firms which generated profits and local employment through efficiently providing a service. Only then, through voluntary donations and personal service outside working hours, could employers be expected as individuals to substitute altruism for ill-considered personal expenditure. Where a locality seemed in special need, the employer received direct help from 'enterprise zones'. The idea originated in 1977 with Peter Hall, a professor of geography, and by February 1981 eleven such zones had been designated.[178] Cutting regulation, reducing rates, and bypassing obstacles presented by Labour-dominated local authorities, the zones were test-beds for free-market ideas, and were supplemented after 1981 by urban development corporations. Beginning with Merseyside and London's docklands, the corporations arrived in two further waves: five in 1987 and four more in 1988/9. Zones and corporations both aimed at a twofold catalysis: to use government money only to stimulate private investment, so that businesses would voluntarily move in; and to provide a focus for growth that would permeate surrounding areas. By the late 1990s with the aid of private investment their achievements included a transformed London docklands and Cardiff Bay, the huge land reclamation involved in Liverpool's Albert Dock project, and a Tyneside waterfront reinvented as a cultural centre.

Thatcher's cultural revolution did not easily gain even a foothold, and many thought it would be ephemeral. Sherman was struck by Machiavelli's remark in *The Prince* that 'there is nothing more difficult to take in hand, more perilous to conduct, or more uncertain in its success, than to take the lead in the introduction of a new order of things' because the innovator has for enemies 'all those who have done well under the old conditions, and lukewarm defenders in those who may do well under the new'. The same quotation was framed on the wall of the unit formed in 1979 by Derek Rayner to induce efficiency in the civil service.[179] Thatcher confessed in 1988 that she 'used to have a nightmare for the first six years in office that, when I had got the finances right, when I got the law right, the deregulation etc,

---

[177] See below, 526, 529–30.
[178] For their launching see A. Moreton, 'Enterprise Zones', *FT* (24 Aug. 1981), 15.
[179] Machiavelli, *The Prince* (Everyman edn. 1908), 29–30, cited in Sherman's interview with the author, 19 Mar. 1992; see also Hennessy, *Whitehall*, 595.

that the British sense of enterprise and initiative would have been killed by socialism'.[180] Effective entrepreneurs had been familiar enough in Britain before 1939, and were by no means absent afterwards, and during the 1980s some of those who had departed to English-speaking countries resumed prominence in Britain, with all the advantage of being relatively distant from British class attitudes. Several made key contributions to Thatcher's achievement.

The first was Michael Edwardes, already mentioned. Educated in South Africa, he was no intimate of Thatcher, and strongly criticized her government in the early 1980s for high interest rates and an overvalued pound.[181] His five-year term at British Leyland nonetheless foreshadowed a changing national mood. On first arriving there in 1977 he was surprised that its accountants did not know which vehicle made a profit and which a loss.[182] The incentives behind his restructuring and his drastic cuts in the workforce were mounting unemployment, the fear of bankruptcy in the face of mounting international competition, and the highly provisional backing received after 1979 from a sceptical Conservative government. He left the company with rising productivity, though declining market share, and only the prospects of collaboration with the Japanese firm Honda offered real hope. Rechristened the Rover Group, British Leyland was by the late 1980s beginning to move up-market and make a profit.[183] In 1988 a government subsidy helped British Aerospace at last to relieve the state of what free-market Conservatives had long seen as an incubus.

Lawson in 1984 saw the UK as reimporting from the United States 'what made Britain great': the 'enterprise culture' which Britain had once exported there. In 1987 Timothy Waterstone, who lost his job in the early 1980s, recalled his visit to the labour exchange as 'the most horrific experience of my life', and he told himself 'I'd reached rock bottom, and could only go up'. New York bookshops had impressed him as attractive and accessible, and he borrowed money to import the same concept to Britain, eventually creating the bookshop chain bearing his name.[184] Others, like John Hoskyns, the computer millionaire who became one of Thatcher's key advisers, were shocked at the contrast between American prosperity and British decline, and were determined to do something about it. Still more central to Thatcher's battle with the trade unions was the Scottish-born workaholic Ian MacGregor,

---

[180] Interview with Brian Walden, *ST* (8 May 1988), C2.

[181] *T* (13 Sept. 1980), 17; (11 Nov. 1980), 18. See also above, pp. 156–8.

[182] P. Whitehead, *The Writing on the Wall* (1985), 264.

[183] For a good survey see K. Gooding, 'The Legacy Left by Sir Michael', *FT* (18 Sept. 1982), 14, and the motor industry survey in *FT* (20 Oct. 1988), 3.

[184] Lawson, *G* (11 Oct. 1984), 19. T. Waterstone, 'My First Million', *O* (1 Nov. 1987), colour supplement, 15.

who made his name in the USA, helped Edwardes to secure British Leyland's recovery, and then consecutively reorganized British Steel and British Coal along business lines, with fewer committees, greater emphasis on profits, and stronger and more devolved leadership. Slimming down the coal industry's workforce was even more protracted, and the decline in its output even more drastic. The Canadian Graham Day showed a special zest for sitting on hot seats, and as Chairman of British Shipbuilders from 1983 to 1986 won Thatcher's admiration. From there he went to the Rover Group in 1986–8, and then became Director of British Aerospace. In 1987 he told an interviewer that 'I often say to people, I never lie and I never bluff. A couple of people tried that on me here. Quite senior people. They don't work here any more.'[185]

The miniature cultural revolution within these state-owned concerns helped to fuel Thatcher's larger transformation, as did a cluster of Jews and second-generation immigrants, some of whom also crowded into Thatcher cabinets.[186] Jews' role in advertising was crucial. After a mini-boom in the early 1970s, British advertising plunged in 1974 but rapidly recovered until the late 1980s, growing faster in that decade than in any other during the century; of total expenditure in the 1980s, the press accounted for 58 per cent, television for 28 per cent, and posters for 11 per cent.[187] It was an American business-school author who in 1983 helped inspire the Jewish immigrant from Iraq, Maurice Saatchi. In a powerful partnership with his brother Charles, Saatchi & Saatchi's aggressive and imaginative methods enabled it to surpass less vigorous competitors, float on the Stock Exchange, buy up rivals, and globalize. During the early 1980s several other British advertising agencies equipped themselves to buy larger American firms by floating on the Stock Exchange.[188] The decade also saw major growth in directory advertising, the Post Office having appropriated the American 'Yellow Pages' concept; by 1990 a tenth of total press advertising expenditure went in this direction and nearly a quarter of all classified advertising. By 1988 in the world's hierarchy, Britain was behind only the USA and Spain for share of gross national product taken up by advertising at market prices, and with Finland was well ahead of the rest.[189]

The advertisers' skills were integral to the decade's most substantial boost to the entrepreneur: privatization. In 1980 nationalized industries employed a far larger share of the British workforce than in the USA and Canada,

[185] H. Duffy, 'The Harsh Light of Day', *FT* (16 Feb. 1987), 16.   [186] See above, p. 198.

[187] *Advertising Statistics Yearbook* (1995), 25–8; (1990), 14.

[188] I. Fallon, *The Brothers: The Rise and Rise of Saatchi and Saatchi* (1988), 201. D. West, 'Multinational Competition in the British Advertising Agency Business, 1936–1987', *Business History Review* (Autumn 1988), 484–5, 499–501.

[189] *Advertising Statistics Yearbook* (1995), 146 (Yellow Pages); (1990), 172.

about the same as in Germany, but a far smaller share than in France, Austria, Italy, and Sweden.[190] The dynamic behind nationalization had been gradually winding down since 1951: indeed, a winding-down was built into the entire nationalization process from the start. First, the legislation which nationalized an industry delimited the areas where it could operate, freeing the private sector to cater for growth areas. Second, the trade unions' relatively entrenched influence and the statutory restrictions on overseas ventures made nationalized concerns relatively inflexible. Third, the centralized and often monopolistic pattern adopted for nationalization made management if anything more remote from employees and customers: 'the state is naturally centralist, the market naturally pluralist'. Wry smiles must surely have greeted Morrison's expectation as late as 1964 that nationalized industries would be 'more consumer-conscious than similar undertakings not publicly owned', and his claim that 'the visitor from the public corporation is never so happy as when he is helping that customer out of his or her troubles'.[191] Fourth, to the extent that nationalized industries experienced political control, they experienced one more layer of uncertainty than private concerns. The Atomic Energy Authority had to cope with Benn at the Ministry of Technology, for example: he himself knew in 1966 that 'my big problem is that I am so ignorant of industry'. To the extent that they were subsidized, the nationalized industries' political influence introduced inefficiency into the economy as a whole, especially when governments were tempted to throw good money after bad. For the Conservative Party's policy group on nationalized industry in 1968, nationalization seemed 'a built-in system of misallocation of capital in our economy'.[192]

Even Labour voters in the 1960s and 1970s gradually lost enthusiasm for nationalization,[193] though in the early 1970s the Party still planned to extend it. One among several sources of friction between Tony Benn and Jack Jones was Jones's recognition that nationalization was unpopular: 'we were not a socialist party and it was too late to convert us into one', he told Benn in 1973.[194] A Labour government at this time could hardly be expected to privatize. Donoughue wanted council-house sales encouraged, and won Wilson's support, but the reform could not overcome hostility within the cabinet and civil

[190] See the useful table in L. Hannah, 'The Economic Consequences of the State Ownership of Industry, 1945–1990', in Floud and McCloskey (eds.), *Cambridge Economic History of Britain*, iii (2nd edn.), 169.
[191] Quotations from John Kay, *FT* (8 May 2003), 21. H. Morrison, *Government and Parliament: A Survey from the Inside* (3rd edn. 1964), 275, 279.
[192] Benn, *Diaries 1963–7*, 474 (15 Sept. 1966). S. Ball and A. Seldon (eds.), *The Heath Government 1970–74: A Reappraisal* (1996), 144.
[193] I. Crewe in H. R. Penniman (ed.), *Britain at the Polls, 1979: A Study of the General Election* (Washington, DC, and London, 1981), 298–300. Harrison, *Seeking a Role*, 307–8, 445, 452.
[194] Benn, *Diaries 1973–6*, 46 (12 June 1973); cf. 183 (24 June 1974).

service.[195] Corporatist attitudes and centrist strategies had for decades muted Conservative hostility to nationalization. This was despite Powell's pronouncing in 1968 that denationalization would be administratively and financially easy, and despite the Party's policy group on nationalized industry in that year recommending extensive sales of nationalized concerns.[196] For the time being, this was only a backbench cause, nourished by the right-wing pressure group Aims of Industry, with 4,000 subscribing members (mostly middle-sized companies) by January 1974.[197] Even in 1979 denationalization under Thatcher was by no means assured. Nicholas Ridley had seen as early as the 1940s, when working in a Tyneside shipyard, how public corporations 'were dominated by their workforce, not their customers', but the Party did little work on the subject when in opposition after 1974, even with Thatcher as leader. Privatization's low profile at this stage reflects the Conservative fear that it would be unpopular.[198]

Conservatives also feared that 'denationalization' sounded negative, a reversion to the past, as Powell and the policy group had earlier pointed out.[199] As early as 1970 David Howell imported an American remedy: 'privatization'. The word seemed ugly at the time; he was somewhat apologetic about it, and Thatcher at first refused to use it, yet the word was useful, and familiarity soon made it seem inoffensive.[200] Privatization aimed to achieve far more than denationalization: it sought new patterns of ownership, embraced activities not hitherto in the private sector, and aimed to change attitudes to business and to share-owning. The Party's forward move on this occurred in 1976–7, but its manifesto in 1979 did not include the word, though it proposed to sell off the National Freight Corporation, to encourage new bus operators, and to 'sell back to private ownership' the recently nationalized aerospace and shipbuilding concerns.[201] The privatizing process seems in retrospect far smoother, and was both more extensive and more successful, than at first seemed likely.[202] John Redwood, the young Conservative who in the early 1980s helped pioneer the process, later thought that an unnecessarily complex method of privatizing was chosen.[203] Quite apart from employees' inertia and trade union hostility, a Labour or Labour-dominated government always seemed a possibility in the

[195] B. Donoughue, *Prime Minister: The Conduct of Policy under Harold Wilson and James Callaghan* (1987), 106, 108; cf. his comments to Bryan Magee in Radio 3's programme 'What's the Big Idea?' on 20 Nov. 1991.

[196] Powell speech at Watford, *T* (13 Sept. 1968), 1. Ball and Seldon (eds.), *Heath Government*, 144.

[197] *G* (7 Jan. 1974), 14, provides an informative survey.

[198] Ridley, *'My Style of Government'*, 3. Lawson, *View from No. 11*, 199.

[199] *T* (13 Sept. 1968), 1 (Powell). Ball and Seldon (eds.), *Heath Government*, 144 (policy-group report, Nov. 1969). [200] Author's collection: Rt. Hon. David Howell to author, 16 Jan. 1996.

[201] Dale (ed.), *Conservative Manifestos*, 272. See also O. Letwin, *Privatising the World: A Study of International Privatisation in Theory and Practice* (1988), 10.

[202] For a highly sceptical comment at so late a date see A. Kaletsky, 'Popularity and Privatisation', *FT* (13 Feb. 1986), 29. [203] Redwood, *Popular Capitalism*, 72.

1980s, and shares had to be sold in a market which feared renationalization—a market whose resources should at no stage be overstretched. The industries concerned often had commitments (to pensions, reprocessing, compensation, or nature conservation, for example) which would deter private investors, and some were unprofitable. In preparing for the transition, state concerns were encouraged to behave like businesses, and as the caged birds learnt to fly, efficiency was fostered and new talent and even profits were attracted before privatization occurred. British Steel, for example, had last made a profit in 1974/5, and the late 1970s saw substantial closures and preparation of the recovery plan which led to the strike of 1980. Profits soon reappeared, and the turnaround in productivity, even more remarkable than the car industry's, occurred within the nationalized concern, beginning before MacGregor became Chairman in 1980, though it was boosted later by impending privatization (in 1988). It became one of the world's two lowest-cost producers,[204] though only through cutting its workforce by four-fifths after 1974, and with all the disruption entailed in transferring steel production from Scotland to south Wales.

The privatizing process was gradually learnt. There were serious problems of share allocation as between overseas and British investors, between employees and others, and between rich and poor British investors. It was difficult to price the issues so as to attract enough investors but without giving them what would seem an unfair short-term return, especially as the nature of the nationalized industries' accounts made pricing difficult. Some candidates for privatization were decidedly unprofitable. During the 1980s these difficulties were eased as the financial markets opened up, as successful precedents were established, and as the nationalized concerns became more profitable during the privatizing process.[205] In his amusing, widely quoted, and somewhat mischievous maiden speech in the House of Lords, Macmillan likened privatization to selling off the family silver. Some critics feared that the silver had been sold off too cheaply, to judge from the profits rapidly made by the purchasers. To this the privatizers replied that such hindsighted judgements were easily made, and that a quick but cheap sale benefited the community more than a delayed sale for a larger sum. Ridley thought in retrospect that 'it pays infinitely better to sell them cheap, or even give them away' rather than fuss unduly about pricing.[206] Macmillan's objection was wider: he opposed the very idea of selling off the state's capital assets. Yet to his critics his analogy was misleading: the citizen's control over his silver had been, to say the least, indirect; much of it was expensive to maintain and to that extent was well

[204] I. Rodger, 'The Mixed Legacy of a Septuagenarian Enigma', FT (29 Mar. 1983), 24. T (9 July 1986), 21. Hannah 'State Ownership of Industry', 183.
[205] For some figures see FT (25 Mar. 1987), 12.   [206] e.g. Ridley, 'My Style of Government', 64.

lost to government; nor was it 'lost' to the community, for the privatized concern would become more productive, generate profits, and therefore boost tax revenue.[207]

The most formidable obstacle, however, was public opinion, almost invariably hostile (as measured by opinion polls) to any particular privatization proposal. There was opposition, too, from interested parties. Weinstock, for instance, in strongly opposing BT's privatization, suspected (wrongly) that the sale would fail and (rightly) that its success would weaken GEC's bargaining position within the telecommunications industry. In May 1982 Wandsworth witnessed friction between two rubbish-collection groups: the younger, largely black, and hitherto largely unemployed private contract men employed by the Conservative council were pitched against the older and largely white official dustmen who were striking against privatization and were shortly due for dismissal.[208] Thatcher could outmanœuvre opponents only through mobilizing or creating rival interests: employees tempted by the terms of share offers and by generous redundancy payments, managers hoping for a buy-out, and advertisers skilled in attracting the private investor.[209] If the British political system had required governments to win short-term public endorsement for all their measures, and if a simple-majority electoral system had not been in place, privatization would probably never have occurred: the requisite political coalitions could not have been assembled. The two-party system, however, normally gave a government tenure for four years, so Thatcher's policies were safe if the next election could be won—as occurred in 1983, 1987, and 1992.

Privatization's ultimate drivers were threefold. First, economic: the need to enhance efficiency through competition, to cut government borrowing (especially as selling off government assets turned out to be far easier than cutting government spending), to encourage entrepreneurship and create smaller economic units, and to reduce government subsidies and clarify management objectives. Second, constitutional: the need, which pervaded the Party's manifesto in 1979, to protect political stability by shielding government from exaggerated expectations. If the free market's extended operation could ensure that costs automatically informed the discussion of how to satisfy demand, a major source of pressure on the political system could be diverted, government's 'overload' could be lightened, and ministers could focus more firmly on essentials; to which should be added the libertarian argument for breaking nationalization's dangerous yoking of economic to political power. Third, party-political: privatization would weaken both

---

[207] See e.g. J. Redwood, 'Golden Chance, Not Silver Sold', *T* (14 Nov. 1985), 14, and letter from Iain Sproat, 15.   [208] Young, *One of Us*, 362 (Weinstock). *T* (26 May 1982), 26 (Wandsworth).
[209] For examples see Letwin, *Privatising the World*, 111–15.

the large public-sector unions and socialism. Privatization had the additional attraction for the right of lending it the participatory clothes of the
left: employees would acquire a stake in their companies by a capitalist
rather than co-operative or socialist route. Conservatives wanted to diffuse
better understanding of the economic system, and Howe in his second
budget made it easier for employees to own shares in the firm where they
worked.[210]

The privatizing dynamic built up slowly. In his first budget Howe announced
a phased sell-off of government holdings in British Petroleum. In 1981 more than
half British Aerospace and nearly half Cable and Wireless were sold, followed in
1982 by the radiochemicals group Amersham International and by the National
Freight Company (on a management buyout). In 1983 half Associated British
Ports were privatized, but it was in 1984 that the real breakthrough occurred,
with the privatization of British Telecom (BT). When the Post Office became
a public corporation in 1969 it had been separated from direct political control;
then in 1981 its telecommunications dimension was separated from the rest
into the British Telecom Corporation and was exposed to competition. It
was then decided to sell BT as a single unit, as this would enable Britain to
compete powerfully in world telecommunications markets. The new investment
opportunity was energetically publicized so as to boost the capital available.
Enlisting ordinary savers, BT employees, and overseas investors, the share
offer was abundantly oversubscribed: more than 93 per cent of BT employees
took up the offer of free shares, 84 per cent boosted their holding through
buying specially discounted shares, and the general public applied for five
times more shares than were allocated to them. More than 90 per cent of the
Union of Communication Workers' 130,000 members were among the new
shareholders, 80 per cent of them choosing also to buy discounted shares.
The Union's General Secretary Alan Tuffin could hardly refrain in 1987 from
urging the TUC to rethink its hostility to share-ownership schemes, or from
pointing out that Labour's renationalization proposals would not be feasible, let
alone popular. Still, it was only against opposition from a significant minority
of delegates that the TUC then passed a motion 'recognising the need' to take
account of the growth in individual and worker share-ownership schemes; a
motion condemning the government's privatization programme could then be
passed unanimously.[211] Trade union hostility to further privatization schemes
continued into the 1990s. Nonetheless, according to the Minister of Information
Technology, BT's employees had 'voted with their chequebooks', and had
delivered 'a massive gesture of defiance to the Labour party'.[212]

---

[210] Letwin, *Privatising the World*, 48. Howe, *HC Deb.* 26 Mar. 1980, c. 1481.
[211] K. Newman, *The Selling of British Telecom* (1986), 145, 166. *FT* (10 Sept. 1987), 11.
[212] Geoffrey Pattie, *HC Deb.* 3 Dec. 1984, c. 20.

BT was the largest company ever floated on any stock market, and attracted 2.3 million shareholders; many were buying shares for the first time, encouraged by the government's having weighted the allocation towards the small investor. Until then, only 3 per cent of the UK population owned shares, as compared with 20 per cent in the USA.[213] The privatizing momentum was now unstoppable, and a much larger share of British Gas was sold off two years later at a well-judged price and raised an even larger sum. Towards the end of the decade, sales of utilities, very complex to mount, were regularly producing what would in 1979 have seemed huge sums for the government,[214] leaving only coal and railways among the Attlee governments' great nationalizing achievements to be unravelled. Suitable arrangements for regulation after sell-off had to be organized, and serious and unexpected problems emerged, sometimes only after a long interval. Several privatized concerns were natural monopolies, which even Ridley hesitated to privatize intact. He was won over to the idea by two arguments: that only privatization would secure the capital investment that these industries needed; and that further efficiency could be obtained through regulations that would require, among other things, an annually specified price level below the prevailing rate of inflation.[215] For some privatized concerns—BT and British Gas, for example—continued monopoly seemed desirable within the UK for at least two reasons: first, because it would hardly be efficient to duplicate such extensive supply networks; but, second, there was no monopoly outside the UK, and in that jungle only big beasts could compete. The state could if necessary help to break up the domestic monopoly later if rival concerns did not emerge; besides, for free-marketeers, faster privatization was preferable to slower, and privatized monopoly preferable to state-owned.[216]

'They had created a nation of home owners', Lawson told the party conference in 1985. 'Now they were in the process of creating a nation of share owners.' In his budget of 1986 he introduced his 'personal equity plan' to encourage share-owning;[217] at the same time compulsory competitive tendering (introduced in 1980) for building and road works was speeding up privatization of local authority services. By March 1986 Thatcher had embraced as her own the term 'popular capitalism' to describe privatization's diffusion of property, shares, and small businesses.[218] In value, the largest privatization by far was the sale of a million council houses between 1979 and 1988.[219] In his budget speech of March 1987 Lawson noted that 'the creation of a genuine popular capitalism'

---

[213] *Econ* (19 Oct. 1985), 42–3.
[214] For a useful table of privatizations by share offer, 1981–91 see Lawson, *View from No. 11*, 241.
[215] Ridley, *'My Style of Government'*, 62.
[216] See e.g. Lawson, *View from No. 11*, 239. Thatcher, *Downing Street Years*, 681.
[217] *T* (10 Oct. 1985), 4. *HC Deb.* 18 Mar. 1986, c. 178.   [218] J. Campbell, *Thatcher*, ii. 231.
[219] L. Hannah, 'State Ownership of Industry', 172; cf. the useful table in Lawson, *View from No. 11*, 241.

was 'a central theme and purpose' of the government's policies: 63 per cent of households were now owner-occupiers, 2.5 million more than in 1979, and a fifth of the adult population now owned shares, roughly three times as many as in 1979. The scale of the change had not been planned from the outset, and its party-political potential emerged only incidentally with the offers' success, but the Conservative manifesto in 1987 saw it all as 'a profound and progressive social transformation',[220] well worth exploiting by well-targeted mail-shots at the general election.

After 1970 the entrepreneur was making strides in the banking world, too, but not because of any close links with manufacturing. In August 1974 Len Murray thought Stock Exchange gloom out of touch: 'I should like to see these people go out and see a factory working and see how irrelevant a small parcel of shares changing hands on the Stock Exchange is to industrial life.'[221] He was not alone in his doubts, given the conflict between Thatcher's personal habits and a culture of money-making for its own sake. She lived frugally, shunned debt, disliked bank cards, and was thrifty on behalf of the state too, voluntarily forfeiting from the outset a quarter of her prime-ministerial salary. Hence her psychological distance from the city and the Stock Exchange: wealth should be earned by making or selling real goods and services, she thought, not by speculating.[222] Here was a rare instance of affinity with the trade unions: from their shared and somewhat moralistic provincial perspective, the City seemed in some sense parasitic on the economy, and unduly distant from the 'real' world of manufacture. Furthermore, it was the professions, not the trade unions, who were operating the restrictive practices in the square mile, and Thatcher opposed such practices anywhere. For Conservatives there was no future in capitalizing manufacture through the sort of politicized investment agency that Labour tried to operate in the 1970s: they wanted reforms which would encourage manufacturers to make profits which in turn would attract investors spontaneously. In trying to encourage small businesses early in the 1980s, the government complained that the banks were not sufficiently helpful, and this helped to push them into providing 'venture capital', though still not on an American scale.[223] In addition, the Stock Exchange in 1980 set up its 'unlisted securities market' for companies with less of a proven track record, over three years as opposed to five. It did well, and drew into the main market several companies once they had got established. There was less public interest, though, in the 'third market', set up in 1987 to cater for even smaller and more speculative concerns.[224]

---

[220] HC Deb. 17 Mar. 1987, cc. 823–4. Dale (ed.), *Conservative Manifestos*, 320.
[221] *T* (22 Aug. 1974), 1.   [222] Campbell, *Thatcher*, ii. 248–50.
[223] T. Dickson, 'Venture Capital', *FT* (28 Nov. 1984), survey, p. i.
[224] R. C. Michie, *The City of London* (London and Basingstoke, 1992), 143.

The finance sector doubled its share of UK output between 1979 and 2005, when it contributed some 8.6 per cent of UK output.[225] The fall by nearly two million in manufacturing employment between 1979 and 1988 was matched by growth almost equally divided between finance/business services, and public/professional/miscellaneous services.[226] Even pawnbroking revived, from about 50 firms in the early 1970s to 850 by 2006;[227] the Consumer Credit Act (1974) had simultaneously removed old restrictions and provided new safeguards, and the sharp economic fluctuations of the 1980s generated custom. The banks had now begun to advertise financial 'products' purchasable as though in a supermarket, and numerous savings options appeared. Share-dealing was more widely discussed, and advice on how to avoid paying tax became much more accessible. All these changes increased the need for financial guidance, ever more prominent in the media. By the 1980s the newspapers' 'business supplements' of the 1960s were being complemented by 'personal' or 'family finance' supplements, which catered for people seeking mortgages and wondering where to put their savings. At the same time the *Economist* and *Financial Times* were rapidly evolving from investors' specialist organs into mainstream publications.

Entrepreneurship in banking was most evident in international finance: 'the square mile of the City has become like an offshore island in the heart of the nation', wrote Sampson in 1982.[228] Globalization produced huge changes. British banks in the City were ill-equipped to profit by the new growth-sector in international securities, and the need for reform exposed a further contradiction within Thatcherism: it combined free-market attitudes with recognizing the need in the financial area to supplant the old informal self-regulation by state employees wielding statutory powers. The Financial Services Act (1986) entrusted a Securities and Investments Board with administering a licensing system throughout much of the financial services industry. Still, the 'big bang' on 17 October 1986 made Stock Exchange procedures and fees more flexible, opened out its membership, brought in more capital, and made its outlook more international; by 1990 more than a third of its member-firms were owned abroad.[229] Mergers, longer hours, computerization, and wider recruitment changed the City's culture, and the long-standing distinction between retail and investment banking gradually dissolved: henceforth 'the austere stone-and-marble high street exterior had a louche casino in the back room'.[230] By the mid-1980s about 2,000 young investment bankers, stockbrokers, and

[225] ONS website, National Income Blue Book, table 2.3. I am grateful to the late Andrew Glyn for this reference, and for valuable help on this point.
[226] C. Feinstein and R. Matthews, 'The Growth of Output and Productivity in the UK: The 1980s as a Phase of the Post-War Period', *National Institute Economic Review*, 133 (Aug. 1990), 83.
[227] *G* (20 Oct. 2006), ii. 12.   [228] Sampson, *Changing Anatomy of Britain*, 263.
[229] Michie, *City of London*, 143.   [230] *O* (22 Feb. 2009), 28 (leader).

commodity brokers were earning £100,000 a year, and were advancing their careers by continually moving between firms. As 'yuppies', they were getting themselves much discussed,[231] and even inspired a popular television series, *Capital City*, launched in 1989. Given that the telephone was still dominant in the early 1980s, these changes were not driven by the new computerized technology, but they prompted huge investment in it.

The scandals involving the entrepreneurs Robert Maxwell (the publishing tycoon found drowned in November 1991 at the height of his financial difficulties) and Peter Clowes (imprisoned in 1992 after the collapse of his investment company, Barlow Clowes) showed how rogues could still bamboozle key City figures and outmanœuvre or bully the auditors. There was pressure on space, too, and the City's international preoccupations, together with the high rents flowing from them, pushed much domestic financial business elsewhere within the UK—a shift eased by rapidly improving communications. It was no longer necessary to work from London to get ample information, and by 1981 the City of London accommodated only a fifth of UK employees working in financial institutions. Insurance companies and building societies, many of which had originated outside London, found they could now combine the cost advantages of their provincial base with technical advantages once available only in London.[232] Through the SEAQ (Stock Exchange Automated Quotations) system launched in October 1986, stockbrokers outside London could participate in the domestic securities market on virtually equal terms with City-based firms.[233] Edinburgh in fund management, Bristol in insurance, Birmingham in corporate banking, and Leeds in building societies and insurance all made strides during the 1980s. Leeds in the 1980s also gained from the economic shift within the UK from west to east, its financial employment growing six times as fast as its non-financial.[234] Manchester, too, by 1990 was gaining in self-confidence as a self-sufficient regional financial capital.[235] London's dominance as a financial centre was eroded not only by national decentralizing trends, but also by provincial centralizing trends: nourished by local prosperity, Leeds for example was becoming the financial centre for northern England at the expense of Newcastle and Sheffield, just as Birmingham was gaining over Nottingham and Leicester.[236]

[231] D. Kynaston, *The City of London*, iv. *A Club No More 1945–2000* (2001), 714.

[232] M. Moran, 'Finance Capital and Pressure-Group Politics in Britain', *British Journal of Political Science*, 11 (1981), 400.

[233] A. Leyshon and N. Thrift, 'South Goes North? The Rise of the British Provincial Financial Centre', in J. Lewis and A. Townsend (eds.), *The North–South Divide: Regional Change in Britain in the 1980s* (1989), 115. See also 'Leeds: Streets Paved with Brass', *Econ* (29 Aug. 1998), 27.

[234] 'Pinstripe City', *Econ* (28 Mar. 1993), 23. *FT* (29 July 1987) survey 'Yorkshire and Humberside', p. i.

[235] See I. H. Fazey, 'Half Mile Bubbles Over', *FT* (20 Feb. 1995) survey on 'Manchester'.

[236] Leyshon and Thrift, 'South Goes North?', 115, 133, 154. *FT* (20 June 1995), 14, 16.

Day-to-day domestic banking was changing fast. Between 1976 and 1983 the share of the adult population in Britain with a current bank account rose from 45 per cent to 62 per cent, and employees paid through a bank account rose from 39 per cent to 56 per cent.[237] From the late 1960s there were extensive mergers between banks, and much rationalization of their branch structures;[238] the close relationship between bank manager and customer could not survive such changes. The banks had begun to resemble shops in their opening hours, and with 24-hour telebanking (launched in 1989 by the Midland Bank through First Direct) and access through cashpoints, the concept of the 'bank holiday' was becoming a misnomer.[239] Automated teller machines almost doubled between 1985 and 1990 to more than 13,000, increasingly located separately from bank branches, and often in shopping centres. By March 1985 one British adult in three possessed a credit card;[240] as for the debit card, Barclays in 1987 were again the pioneers. A new 'privatized Keynesiansim' had come into being: the individual, rather than the state, was taking on debt to stimulate the economy.[241] The 1980s saw the final dissolution of any clear distinction between banks, savings banks, and building societies, given that the Building Societies Act (1986) allowed building societies to diversify beyond the savings and mortgage markets into banking services. Banks were providing mortgages and building societies were becoming banks. The Trustee Savings Bank and Abbey National Building Society were floated on the Stock Exchange in 1986 and 1989, respectively, and were hugely oversubscribed. The number of building societies fell throughout the twentieth century, and very sharply between 1970 and 1990—years in which building society borrowers almost doubled, branches rose threefold, and depositors sevenfold. As for friendly societies, their members had made up 14 per cent of the entire population in 1950, but only 5 per cent in 1990.[242]

Major changes occurred in insurance. As with pension funds, its share of total equity owned was still rising: from 12 per cent in 1969 to 20 per cent in 1990. The unassuming Ronald Artus, the Prudential's chief investment manager, controlled one of Britain's largest share portfolios between 1975 and 1990, and no large takeover deal could succeed without his approval: 'he was little known outside the Square Mile', wrote his obituarist, 'but commanded very high

[237] Brown, *Banking in Britain*, 19. See also CPRS, *Cashless Pay: Alternatives to Cash in Payment of Wages* (1981), 5–7.
[238] R. Pringle, *A Guide to Banking in Britain* (1973), 27–8, 33, 52, 55, 57, provides detail.
[239] As argued by Brian Capon, spokesman of British Bankers Association, *ST* (25 Aug. 1996), s. v, p. 5.
[240] K. Watson, 'The Financial Services Sector since 1945', in Floud and Johnson (eds.), *Cambridge Economic History of Modern Britain*, iii. 179–80. *FT* (28 Mar. 1985), 9.
[241] C. Crouch. 'What will Follow the Demise of Privatized Keynesianism?', *Political Quarterly* (Oct.–Dec. 2008), 481.
[242] Building Societies Association, *Building Societies Yearbook 1992–3*, 301–2. TCBST, 605.

respect within it'.[243] Rapidly rising in the insurance world was Peter Wood, founder in 1985 of Direct Line, the first insurance firm to focus on selling direct by telephone. Beginning with motor insurance, he soon diversified, and by greatly reducing costs he could cut charges to customers; by 1990 he had captured an eighth of the UK motor insurance market.[244] Computer databases, cheaper telephone charges, and credit cards interacted to import from the USA the 'call centre', a phrase which became familiar in the 1990s; it was the centralized administrative facility which supplanted the local branch and the sales representative. The contrast between 1970 and 1990 in the distribution of assets among UK financial institutions captures the continued growth in pension funds (up from 10 per cent of the total to 16 per cent), but masks the major changes within the building society and insurance worlds, down from 15 and 21 per cent in 1970 to 12 and 15 per cent, respectively, in 1990. This was partly because the earlier clear separation between insurance firms, building societies, and banks had changed so radically: transfers between categories help to explain why the banks' share rose from 46 per cent of the total in 1970 to 54 per cent in 1990.[245]

With the entrepreneur's revival came the collectivist trade unionist's decline. Prominent trade union leaders had become accustomed to continuous dialogue with government, and argued that democracy involved more than voting every five years. They claimed that if governments refused to consult them, they would have 'nowhere else to go but the streets'.[246] When they found the government unsympathetic, they fought back, and the outcome remained in doubt until the miners' defeat in 1985. As early as 1980, however, there were signs of change: in that year Mostyn ('Moss') Evans, General Secretary of the TGWU, was puzzled that his rank and file were so hostile to militancy.[247] The new climate was accentuated by a mid-decade shift in leading trade union personnel. Departing were Murray of the TUC, McGahey of the NUM, Evans of the TGWU, Buckton of the Associated Society of Locomotive Engineers and Firemen, Sirs of the ISTC, and Chapple of the EETPU. The TGWU was among the last to reflect the changed mood: as late as 1988 its refusal to make a single-union agreement with Ford's denied Dundee, an area of high unemployment, the chance of 1,500 local jobs—presenting Thatcher with a propaganda weapon which she readily deployed within Scotland.[248] Also

[243] Central Statistical Office, *Share Ownership*, 8. *T* (26 July 1999), 23 (Artus).

[244] O. Westall, 'Invisible, Visible and "Direct" Hands: An Institutional Interpretation of Organisational Structure and Change in British General Insurance', *Business History* (Oct. 1997), 57.

[245] Calculated from table 7.1 in Floud and Johnson (eds.), *Cambridge Economic History of Modern Britain*, iii. 171.

[246] *T* (5 May 1980), 2 (Murray to Wales TUC annual conference, 2 May 1980); cf. Murray, *DT* (5 May 1979), 1, and Basnett, *ST* (12 Dec. 1982), 1.

[247] S. Milligan, 'What has Happened to Bevin's Pride and Joy?', *T* (16 Sept. 1980), 12.

[248] *T* (18 Mar. 1988), 1. *DT* (14 May 1988), 2. *T* (31 Mar. 1988), 2.

fuelling the new trade union mood were high unemployment and the rewards for accepting voluntary redundancy; more important as an influence, as time went on, were the good industrial relations cultivated in Japanese-run British car factories.[249] Slowly the trade union moderates, on the defensive for almost two decades, began to resurface.

4. THE WORKFORCE DIVERSIFIES

'The British go on feasting' said German newspapers in 1976, commenting on the extended Christmas holiday then spreading within Britain;[250] casual commentators often then ascribed Britain's relative economic decline to the British workforce's relative laziness. The statistics to back such a claim are inevitably lacking in an economy whose service sector was growing so fast, especially at a time of rapid computerization. The British economy was then all too readily monitored through the rear-view mirror, with an undue focus on manufacturing and better-documented types of traditional economic activity. After 1970, as before, the new jobs were politically less salient than the lost jobs.

Were the British more reluctant than other nations to take up paid work? Not significantly so. The UK workforce's share of the population aged between 15 and 64 in the first three of the four periods 1960–73, 1974–9, 1980–9, and 1990–4 was higher than the combined six-country average for the UK, USA, Japan, France, Italy, and Canada.[251] In all four periods the UK male labour-force's share of the male population between 15 and 64 remained above the average among the six, though that share was steadily declining.[252] The full-time-equivalent workforce for most of the 1980s drew on a smaller proportion of Great Britain's population than in 1951, 21.7 million in 1951 and 20.5 million in 1983, but by 1990 the workforce had risen to just under 23 million.[253] Were British women keen to take paid work? We have already seen how they were increasingly attracted to part-time work,[254] which made up 12 per cent of British women's employment in 1951 and 43 per cent in the early 1990s.[255] This did not reflect female full-timers choosing to work part-time; rather, it denoted married women's decision to move out of the home so as to take paid work. Part-time working rose sixfold in Britain between 1951 and 1996, increasing its share of the workforce almost as fast in the 1980s as in the 1950s; by the early 1990s more than a quarter of the British workforce were part-timers. Whereas in 1951 part-timers (working for thirty hours a week or less) accounted for only 4 per cent of the workforce, by the late 1980s they accounted for about a fifth,

---

[249] See above, pp. 12, 296, and below, p. 356. [250] *T* (30 Dec. 1976), 1–2.
[251] OECD, *Historical Statistics 1960–1994* (Paris, 1996), 44. [252] Ibid. 41.
[253] Hakim, 'Myth of Rising Female Employment', 103.
[254] Harrison, *Seeking a Role*, 253–4, 327; see also above, pp. 227–8.
[255] P. Bassett, 'Price of Workplace Flexibility may be Rising Job Insecurity', *T* (11 June 1996), 31.

and four out of five part-timers were women. By then part-timers were most numerous (in descending order) in retailing, education, hotels and catering, and health services.[256]

The relative enthusiasm of British married women of all ages for taking paid work meant that Britain's overall participation rate in work did not change very much between 1911 and 1981, averaging at 62 per cent, and in the 1980s Britain's gross domestic product per head of population, though far behind the USA, was not far behind France, Germany, and Italy. In 1988 British men worked for an average of 45.1 hours a week, well above the European average (42.5); only Irish, Portuguese, and Spanish men worked for longer.[257] In manufacturing, although average annual hours worked per person fell steadily in the UK (as in Japan) from 1951 to 1999, Germany's hours were falling still faster, so that by 1995 British hours were longer than German, though shorter than the USA's and Japan's. In a survey of 1989 25 per cent of the men and 21 per cent of the women sampled worked for more hours than contracted, as did 15 per cent of women part-timers.[258]

When it came to gross domestic product per worker, however, Britain compared far less well.[259] The British problem lay not in hours worked, but in productivity per hour. In the Thatcher governments' better years, the UK raised productivity faster than its EEC rivals, though without catching them up. If the UK could only raise its productivity by a quarter while retaining its present working hours, wrote one expert in 1991, 'it would overtake all the other EU countries, with a similar rise in living standards'.[260] Productivity could now gain more from quality than quantity of hours worked, as well as from investment in plant, especially in the era of automation and computerization. In the heavily unionized minerals, engineering, chemicals, and electronics industries during the 1980s, enhanced productivity owed much to better technology and working methods.[261] The desire for pay at overtime rates had for decades prolonged the hours worked in Britain,[262] but the TUC in 1978 launched a drive to restrict overtime working to twenty hours a month, and the TGWU's General Secretary urged a cut in working hours to thirty-five a week so as to curb unemployment.[263] When in autumn 1979 the engineering workers, after a ten-week strike, broke the forty-hour-week barrier, breached by office

[256] P. Bassett, 'Price of Workplace Flexibility may be Rising Job Insecurity', 31. *T* (31 Aug. 1987), 5.

[257] *BST* 168. D. Kavanagh and A. Seldon (eds.), *The Thatcher Effect* (Oxford, 1989), 19. C. Marsh, *Hours of Work of Women and Men in Britain* (1991), 81–2.

[258] S. Broadberry, 'The Performance of Manufacturing', in Floud and Johnson (eds.), *Cambridge Economic History of Modern Britain*, iii. 64. Marsh, *Hours of Work*, 37.

[259] See the table in Kavanagh and Seldon (eds.), *Thatcher Effect*, 19.

[260] Christopher Johnson, 'The British Way of Working: High Employment But Low Productivity', *Ind* (5 Dec. 1997), 26.

[261] *Econ* (6 Apr. 1996), 30.   [262] Harrison, *Seeking a Role*, 45, 327.

[263] TUC, *T* (22 July 1978), 2. Moss Evans (2 Oct. 1978 at Labour Party conference), *T* (3 Oct. 1978), 6.

workers a decade earlier, it seemed a major change. With their new standard week of thirty-nine hours and their fifth week of annual holiday, they seemed to be setting the pace for workers throughout Europe. For many, however, this was simply a disguised pay increase, since the engineers had no intention of working for fewer hours.[264] In 1981, with unemployment rising fast, 18 per cent of employees were still working overtime, 7 per cent for more than ten overtime hours a week; indeed, overtime hours worked, after falling in 1980–1, rose concurrently with the rising unemployment rate, and went on rising till the end of the decade, even though from 1986 the unemployment rate was falling.[265]

Was the British workforce relatively inflexible? Cross-cultural data and clear criteria for measurement are both lacking. Suffice it to say that the British workforce was becoming much more flexible after 1970, not just in complementing full-time work with part-time, but on working times more generally. Changing work-time patterns are best discussed consecutively within the day, the week, the year, and the lifetime. The experimental repositioning in the 1960s of daylight hours[266] was dropped, and the twice-yearly one-hour transition into and out of 'British summer time' resumed. The arguments for a year-long 'summer time', which included the commercial benefits of synchronizing with the EEC, were so strong, however, that the pressure to reintroduce the change persisted; many people would have been happy to lose an average of twenty-four minutes' daylight in the morning if they gained fifty-five minutes of daylight in the evening.[267] Concern for the safety of children going to school in winter still hindered change, however, though if schools had been less conservative about their timetables, the obstacle could have been overcome. When in 1985 the comprehensive Tideway School in Newhaven introduced the 'continental' school day, beginning at 8 a.m. and ending soon after lunch, the innovation was unusual enough to get into the national newspapers; it was still working well nineteen years later, yet remained unusual.[268]

Nonetheless, working hours within the day were diversifying, and the municipal clock was diminishingly central to the community's life. Timekeeping was in a double sense becoming privatized, with help from the growing private ownership of cheaper and more convenient watches and radios;[269] indeed, in the early 1980s many firms ceased giving watches, clocks, or other presents to

---

[264] *G* (5 Oct. 1979), 1. *FT* (5 Oct. 1979), 11. For the outcome see *T* (3 Jan. 1984), 2.
[265] Marsh, *Hours of Work*, 61, and see the interesting graph in Barrell (ed.), *UK Labour Market*, 45.
[266] Harrison, *Seeking a Role*, 326–7.
[267] J. Gershuny and M. Hillman, 'Shedding Light on the Clock', *New Society* (25 Mar. 1988), 20–2.
[268] *T* (25 Sept. 1985), 3; author's collection: Adrian Money, headteacher, to author, 19 Apr. 2004.
[269] See the interesting leading article in *Ind* (30 Dec. 1994), 13; cf. (4 Jan. 1995), 13 (letter from Gideon Berman).

long-serving employees on departure.[270] Diversity in working hours was also encouraged by traffic problems. The need to moderate rush-hour pressures caused many firms to introduce 'flexitime', which blurred the edges of the nine-to-five day at its start and finish. About 200,000 workers were already on flexitime by 1975, and by 1994 these included about 10 per cent of male and 15 per cent of female full-time employees.[271] New technologies made traditional curbs on working hours difficult to police, if only because workplaces were now becoming smaller, more scattered, more fragmented, and more diverse—nor was British government after 1979 eager to police such curbs. Flexibility in working hours was also encouraged by the trend for household tasks to be shared between the sexes, and by the diminished need in computerized service-occupations for all employees to be in the same premises at the same time. By 1989 only a minority (57 per cent of full-time women workers, 41 per cent of full-time male workers, and 8 per cent of part-time women workers) worked for the alleged standard working day: that is, starting between 8 a.m. and 10 a.m. and finishing between 4 p.m. and 6 p.m.[272]

Flexibility in daily work-times also owed something to the trend towards working at or from home: by 1981, 658,000 people were involved, 2.8 per cent of the workforce if the category omits construction, transport, and workers in family services.[273] Women contributed nearly three-quarters of home workers.[274] Trade unions disliked the trend, fearing (correctly) that it would erode their membership and (incorrectly) that it would correlate with low pay.[275] Home-based working included people from different social levels performing a wide range of occupations, with home-based manufacturing diminishing and home-based service activities increasing. Home-based workers were educationally above average, and a fifth were in the top tenth income bracket, though women usually took the lower-paid occupations.[276] To describe this growing category, the word 'teleworker' arrived from the USA in the late 1980s. A complex of electronic changes involving word-processors, FAX machines, conference networking, and improved telephone services by then made it easier to transfer information efficiently without needing to transfer people. There were even signs that the British workforce might be turning full circle, and reverting to the dispersed, rurally located, and family-based workforce which had existed before the industrial revolution changed everything.

[270] T (1 July 1981), 18.   [271] Econ (1 Feb. 1975), 72. Social Trends (1995), 71.
[272] Marsh, Hours of Work, 35.
[273] C. Hakim, Home-Based Work in Britain (Dept. of Employment Research Paper, 60; 1987), 20. But see the estimate of only one employee in a hundred teleworking as at 1995, according to FT (15 June 1995), supplement on 'Telecommunications in Business', p. xi.
[274] Hakim, Home-Based Work, 43.   [275] Ibid. 243.
[276] Ibid. 27, 240, 242. See also Marsh, Hours of Work, 41.

Weekly work-time patterns changed after 1970 in response to four other changes: the continued decline in manufacturing, the growth in the service sector, the advance in women's paid work, and accelerating secularization. With manufacture's decline, two well-established sources of flexibility in weekly work-time diminished: shiftwork for full-timers, and absenteeism. Shiftwork is defined as 'a pattern of hours which changes over regularly over a fixed period of time',[277] and had long been prevalent among full-time male workers in large firms operating expensive machinery. There were now fewer such firms, though the removal under feminist pressure of restraints on shiftworking for women made more full-timers eligible for shiftwork. Women had traditionally been less prone to it than men, particularly for night shifts, but their pressure for equal pay made these conventions less defensible.[278] By 1989 shiftworkers made up 13 per cent of the people sampled. These included 19 per cent of the total male workers sampled, clustering among manual workers, especially in manufacturing, transport, and communications; the women (7 per cent of the total women sampled) clustered within retailing, hotel work, and catering.[279] We have already seen, though, that shiftworking was gaining ground in a new form, not among full-timers, but among part-timers (many of them women working in the service sector), each taking a quota of shifts.[280] Absenteeism from work, a long-standing and voluntary source of diversity in work-time, was also declining. Its incidence varied markedly: much lower among the employees of Japanese companies in Britain, lower among private employees than among public, lower outside the north and Northern Ireland where unemployment was also high, lower in small firms than in large, lower in light industry than in heavy, lower among white-collar than among manual workers, lower before the weekend than after. Of the first six of these seven areas, those where absenteeism was lower were advancing within the British economy after the 1970s, whereas those where absenteeism was higher were declining.[281]

The service sector's growth was associated with an affluence which boosted employment in recreation and welfare, catering for needs that were continuous rather than readily confined to a nine-hour working day. Saturday working as a regular component of the working week had been under attack since the mid-Victorian period, and for many workers the idea of regularly working on Saturday morning had faded away after 1970, so that thereafter the weekend consisted of two complete days. No sooner had this come about, than weekend work re-entered by the backdoor, drawing heavily upon female and teenage part-timers; this was because in dual-career households the weekend was often becoming the sole opportunity for shared shopping and leisure activities, and

---

[277] Marsh, *Hours of Work*, 59.

[278] e.g. at Ford Motors, *G* (13 Feb. 1969), 1. The Equal Opportunities Commission pressed for equality here, *DT* (28 Mar. 1979), 2.   [279] Marsh, *Hours of Work*, 59.

[280] See above, p. 228.   [281] *T* (16 Oct. 1985), 4. *DT* (11 Mar. 1993), 9.

with the advent of Americanized hypermarkets in the 1980s shopping became a car-borne, family-based adventure. In spring 1994, 6 per cent of all UK employees worked at nights, 12 per cent on Sundays, 16 per cent on shifts, and 25 per cent on Saturdays.[282] Many thought it time to abandon altogether the concept of the 'weekend', with its special rates of pay and restricted opening hours.[283]

Saturday's materialism competed with Sunday's spirituality, not just for time but in values: the aisles so full in Saturday's food cathedrals were increasingly empty in Sunday's churches: the family that shopped together stayed together. Likewise with the year as a whole: weekly retail sales in December were nearly a third higher than the annual average, in a society whose commercialized Christmas was diminishingly Christian.[284] Secularization weakened the arguments for Sunday's remaining special: furthermore, in so far as religious commitment persisted, Britain's religious public was diminishingly Christian, which made it less obvious that Sunday should be the special day. Two pressure groups had in somewhat incongruous alliance long resisted paid Sunday work: the sabbatarians and the Union of Shop, Distributive and Allied Workers (USDAW). Behind each lay two powerful restrictive influences: the Labour Party, protecting producer against consumer; and the churches protecting their waning Sunday congregations. Sunday reform's parliamentary supporters and opponents came from all parties, and the issue split the Conservatives between free-marketeers and traditionalist paternalists.[285] Despite this legislative logjam, the law was falling into disrespect, and between 1975 and 1984 the proportion of the employed population who worked regularly or occasionally on Sundays rose from 34 to 42 per cent.[286] Terence Conran of Habitat knew well enough that many couples could shop only on Sundays; from the 1970s he backed Open Shop, a campaign to let retailers trade on Sunday, deliberately broke the law, and was fined. Scotland had been left out of the Shops Act (1950), and because Sunday opening was legal there, its popularity with tourists and gardeners by the 1980s could set the pace for the UK,[287] where Sunday was now the day for gardening and do-it-yourself.[288] The well-organized rearguard campaign to 'Keep Sunday Special', launched with public-relations advice in 1986, warded off change for a time, but opinion polls revealed two-to-one support for reform,[289] and the law was increasingly flouted.[290]

---

[282] *Social Trends* (1995), 72. See also Marsh, *Hours of Work*, 43.

[283] A. Sandles, 'The Obsolete Weekend', *FT* (19 Feb. 1982), 19. M. Jacques, 'Labour and the Sabbath', *T* (26 Dec. 1990), 8.   [284] *Social Trends* (1995), 106.

[285] e.g. in the Sunday Entertainment Bill's second reading on 28 Feb. 1969, *G* (1 Mar. 1969), 1, and in Ray Whitney's attempt to amend the Shops Act (1950), *FT* (5 Feb. 1983), 1.

[286] *FT* (13 Nov. 1985), 10.   [287] *HL Deb.* 9 Feb. 1982, c. 114.

[288] BBC, *Daily Life in the 1980s*, ii. 232–7.

[289] A. Raphael, 'Sunday, Bloody Sunday', *O* (12 Feb. 1989), 6. See also 'Almighty Defeat', *Econ* (19 Apr. 1986), 25.   [290] *FT* (2 Dec. 1991), 16.

Work-time patterns during the year reflected the rigidity in the school-year, still divided into three terms; there were short holidays at Christmas and Easter and a longer holiday from July to September. In their annual holiday allowance, British workers were far from lazy by European standards. National agreements covering full-time manual workers show a continuous advance in British holiday entitlement between 1951 and 1991: the two-week norm in the 1950s crept up to three weeks in the 1960s, to four weeks in the 1970s and to five weeks in the 1980s.[291] In 1970, however, the British had fewer public holidays than in many other European countries, and EEC membership helped to generate more. The number of 'bank holidays' was extended, and in 1978 they were designated for the first Monday in May in England, Wales, and Northern Ireland, and for the last Monday in May in Scotland. Less formal in its growth was the Christmas holiday's extension through to New Year's Day; this change occurred gradually during the 1970s and 1980s in response to employers' and employees' decisions. The trend was well under way by 1972, when absenteeism on New Year's Day was so widespread that many felt it should become a public holiday, as elsewhere in the EEC; this first occurred in 1974.[292] Lack of orders during the recession carried the trend further in 1980, and ten years later the trend had become so universal that the shortage of leisure services during the Christmas break had come to seem irksome and even irrational.[293]

As for the working lifetime, there too flexibility was advancing in the 1970s and 1980s. The industrial revolution had eroded the craftsman's notion of a job for life, with its associated apprenticeship. Automation by the 1960s carried this change further by encouraging the idea of changing jobs frequently during the working life.[294] Computerization by the 1980s carried such notions deep into the middle classes, simultaneously advancing the case for wider educational curricula and for moderating the long-standing contrast between the sexes in career patterns. In the 1960s employment agencies proliferated in response to growing job mobility, especially among office staff; there were at least 3,000 by 1966, soon prompting the state's employment exchanges to spruce themselves up with self-selection and card-indexed 'job shop' makeovers.[295]

Working methods, too, were becoming more flexible. Japanese companies in Britain during the 1980s reversed the rapid decline in British car manufacture which had begun in the 1960s, and by the late 1990s production levels close to the country's one-time peak manufacturing volume were being regained after a massive intervening decline, though the British were less good at making

[291] *TCBST* 631–2. See also *T* (1 July 1981), 18.
[292] 'How Many Days of Christmas?', *T* (27 Dec. 1972), 7 (leading article). *T* (2 Jan. 1973), 1; cf. (30 Dec. 1976), 1.   [293] *T* (23 Dec. 1980), 1. Jacques, 'Labour and the Sabbath', 8.
[294] See e.g. Sir L. Bagrit, *The Age of Automation: The BBC Reith Lectures 1964* (1965), 36.
[295] *HL Deb.* 16 Feb. 1973, c. 1691. For exchanges see *T* (29 Dec. 1969), 2; (26 May 1970), 21.

commercial vehicles. Regional newspapers set the pace in curbing restraints on printing technology;[296] computer typesetting brought major productivity gains in the 1980s, and from 1 May 1982 *The Times* no longer emerged from hot-metal composition. In modern times the UK has seen five successive, bunched, and therefore eventually transformative waves of economic innovation: the industrial revolution, the steel-and-railway-based revolution, the chemical/electrical revolution, and the mass consumer-goods revolution involving electronics and cars.[297] Last of all came the computer revolution: computers simultaneously presented the service sector with an opportunity and a threat. They required from each employee greater skill and flexibility, and greatly enhanced their productivity. The word-processor swept through Britain's offices in the 1980s, and contracted the clerical workforce more slowly than many had predicted, though after 1989 the staff employed by the leading banks began to dwindle fast. In the professions, as with clerical occupations, the computer's initial impact was to improve services, with databanks making more information readily available and reducing routine tasks: already by 1969 one examination board was using 'an electronic machine' to mark its physics papers.[298] In 1987 Thatcher, always quick to identify with economic growth-points, laid the foundation stone of the Canary Wharf project for redeveloping London's dockland as an office area, and in 1988 drove in the first pile. Standardized legal documents, spreadsheet accounting systems, and computerized diagnosis were bound in the long term to expose the middle classes to the insecure employment that working people had long experienced. They also accentuated the need to improve the training and calibre of the workforce's new recruits.

By the end of 1983 one in ten British homes had a computer, and by March 1984 Britain had more per head than any other country.[299] With ample government encouragement, the cheap computers of Clive Sinclair and Alan Sugar complemented the achievement by penetrating the domestic market. Britain led Europe in liberalizing its telecommunications market, and its governments subsidized computers' incursion into every school. School inspectors in 1985 recommended the use of calculators, thereby removing much misery by consigning long division and log tables into oblivion: they now required only the simplest sums worked out on paper.[300] By the 1970s computers were quietly transferring manual records on to magnetic tape, greatly easing stock control and management of payrolls and accounts; they later moved into

---

[296] Broadberry, 'Performance of Manufacturing', 67 (cars). *Econ* (7 Apr. 1984), 23 (newspapers).

[297] P. Hall, 'The Geography of the Fifth Kondratieff', in P. Hall and A. Markusen (eds.), *Silicon Landscapes* (1985), 1–19.   [298] *DT* (17 Sept. 1969), 22.

[299] J. Crisp, 'Love Affair with Home Computers', *FT* (28 Mar. 1984), supplement on 'Electronics in Europe', p. vi; cf. J. Gray, 'Micromania Sweeps through Britain', *FT* (11 Apr. 1983), supplement on 'Computers in Business', p. xv.   [300] *G* (25 Apr. 1985), 3.

such areas as production control, passenger reservations, and holiday bookings. The cartoons of the time often captured the serious problems of adjustment involved: flexible data were necessarily fragile. Computers gradually delivered huge overall efficiency gains, however, making accessible a wealth of information hitherto concealed. They now experienced the spontaneous integration and standardization that had created a nineteenth-century British railway system out of hitherto autonomous company lines. As a result, to take only one example, when the settlement of stock exchange business was centralized, and when in the late 1960s and early 1970s all UK and Irish Republic stock exchanges were integrated into a single organization, their employees emerged blinking from their one-time exclusive clubs into an international market-place.

The computer revolution re-shaped regional employment patterns. Of the five waves of economic innovation,[301] the first two had brought relative benefit to the north and west, the last three benefited the south and east. The fifth (computer) wave was geographically more dispersed than the first four because silicon chips are almost weightless; as with the biochemical industries, also prospering, its major components were employees' skills and brains, and these needed to be tempted. Service-sector employees required pleasant environments[302]—in government (often defence-related) research establishments, for example, or in university towns. Oxford was linked to the M4 motorway's 'silicon valley' corridor from London and Newbury to Bristol; Cambridge joined East Anglia's mounting prosperity to London via the M11; and Edinburgh linked itself to the 'silicon glen' in Fife.[303] There was a marked overall shift in the economic balance from west to east. Leeds gained over Manchester as a financial centre, Humberside and Felixstowe over Merseyside as seaports. Within Scotland, at the same time as heavy industry was declining in the west, North Sea oil and closer EEC links fostered growth in the east. So in the UK as a whole, reinforcement was provided for the east–west alignment that had earlier been superimposed upon the even older divide in Scotland between Highlands and Lowlands, and in England between north and south. This sent south Wales and the north-west into relative economic decline, and accentuated growth in eastern Scotland, East Anglia, and the south-east.

Governments from Thatcher's to Blair's contested simplistic notions of any uniform economic divide between north and south. In 1988 Thatcher attacked southern stereotypes of the north, and drew attention to the renewed self-confidence of the north-east and the Midlands and to the continuing inner-city problems in the south, especially in London.[304] While the Home Counties

[301] See above, p. 354.
[302] For a useful discussion see P. Marsh, 'The Lure of the Silicon Glen', *FT* (12 Nov. 1986), 24.
[303] For good discussions see Kelly, *British Computer Industry*, 72, 128, 174, 195. *Econ* (30 Jan. 1982), 78–9.   [304] Interview with Press Association, *Ind* (5 Jan. 1988), 2.

were the locality with the largest share of higher-rate taxpayers in 1993–4, the localities with the lowest were by no means always in the north: they included Tyne and Wear, South Yorkshire, and Durham but also Somerset, Cornwall, Leicestershire, Devon, and the West Midlands, with the Isle of Wight lowest of all. In all regions the economy was diversifying: in 1921 Northern Ireland, Wales, East Anglia, and the north-east of England were the four least diversified regions; by 1971 Wales and north-east England had broken out of that category, and by then Scotland and (as in 1921) the north-west and south-west were the most diversified.[305] Regional economic diversity owed much to the Japanese firms encouraged by government aid into development areas, most notably in south Wales, the Scottish Lowlands, and north-east England.[306] Coal and steel had now lost their one-time Welsh salience to new high-tech industries: 'we have reached the end of an era of industrial decay and decline', said Nicholas Edwards, Welsh Secretary, in May 1987. By the mid-1990s regional contrasts in levels of prosperity were still moderating in Britain, and were far less marked than in France, Italy, Spain, and Germany, where they were sometimes still growing.[307]

Nonetheless, British people were reluctant to move from declining to growing areas, and were often unintentionally hindered in doing so by corporatist welfare and planning structures. There was anyway little incentive in the 1970s to forsake friends, relatives, and neighbours for all the drawbacks of living among strangers. Housing arrangements did not help: the privately rented sector was small, council housing was often scarce in areas of growth, and pronounced regional house-price differentials deterred the owner-occupier from moving into high-cost housing locations. The Heath government continued the policy launched in the 1930s of designating development areas, which under its Industry Act (1972) covered nearly half the working population. The Act divided the entire UK into five zones, classifying as development areas Northern Ireland, Scotland, much of northern England, almost all Wales, Cornwall, and parts of Devon; 'intermediate' was the classification for the swathe of territory surrounding the prosperous south-east, where alone further growth was discouraged. In the early 1980s the trade unions and Labour local authorities, relatively powerful in the declining areas, tried with strikes and locally funded welfare schemes to insulate them against economic change, and still more against Thatcherism. Their high rates and unreliable workforce deterred new industries. Liverpool's image suffered further in the mid-1980s from the controversial local government role of the Marxist splinter-group 'Militant

[305] *FT* (9 Feb. 1996), 6. C. M. Law, *British Regional Development since World War I* (Newton Abbot, 1980), 72.

[306] J. H. Dunning, *Japanese Participation in British Industry* (1986), 25. *FT* (18 July 1996), supplement on 'Inward Investment', p. iv.   [307] *FT* (11 May 1987), 12 (Edwards); see also (22 Dec. 1997), 14.

Tendency', and from events at the Heysel stadium on 29 May 1985.[308] The depressed areas seemed sucked into a downward vortex, and the local authority funding problems of the 1920s seemed to be returning: central government curbs on inflationary local authority expenditure deterred the depressed localities from trying to raise themselves by their own bootstraps. One aim of the poll tax was to discourage local authority expenditure through exposing it to the self-interest of informed electors, so that restraint could henceforth stem from local endorsement, not from central coercion.

Government's instincts on regional economic policy after 1979 were to extend the self-improvement ideal from the individual to the entire economy: high hopes were placed in the spontaneously rejuvenating impact made by Schumpeter's waves of 'creative destruction'.[309] Whereas Labour governments' regional employment policies had aimed directly to benefit Labour's supporters in the north and west, the Thatcher governments' retreat from intervention aimed at a less direct but (as it thought) more effective approach: to free the economy of the south and east spontaneously to diffuse its prosperity more widely. So on coming to office in 1979 as Secretary of State for Industry, Keith Joseph almost halved the area assigned development status, and made government aid increasingly selective.[310] Selectivity operated at another level, too, for governments after 1979 abandoned incomes policies and tried to end the notion of a nominal nation-wide equality in pay; the latter in practice privileged employees in the declining areas (given their lower living costs) over the growing. There was ample evidence that many vacancies remained unfilled even in the 1980s when unemployment was at its height; the largest number of long-term unemployed lived in the south-east, where most vacancies were also to be found.[311] Prominent Conservatives like Tebbit, Secretary of State for Employment, wanted the unemployed to cure their own problems, and he was applauded at the Conservative Party conference in 1981 for urging them to follow his father's example in the 1930s and get on their bicycles.[312] Two years later, much publicity attended his claim that among the three million unemployed there was nobody to paint his garden gates in Berkhamsted; the resulting demonstrations outside his home forced the Tebbits to spend 'some unhappy weekends in our London flat'.[313]

The 1970s were the decade when the USA's pejorative term 'workaholic' reached Britain, with much debate about work and its distribution. There was

---

[308] See above, p. 20.
[309] Schumpeter, *Capitalism, Socialism and Democracy*, 83. See also Joseph, *Stranded on the Middle Ground?*, 64.
[310] *FT* (11 Jan. 1984), 13.   [311] *FT* (11 Oct. 1985), 12; cf. Lord Young, *G* (25 Feb. 1985), 13.
[312] *T* (16 Oct. 1981), 4 (Tebbit to the Conservative Party conference on 15 Oct.); cf. Thatcher to the annual conference of the Conservative Party in Wales on 19 July 1980, *T* (21 July 1980), 2; *T* (7 Oct. 1985), 2 (Jeffrey Archer).   [313] Tebbit, *Upwardly Mobile*, 199.

mounting concern about the divide between those with too much work and too little; the former were increasingly urged for family and medical reasons to reduce work pressures. This was difficult for the growing numbers in the service sector. With both partners usually in paid work, help at home was scarce and expensive, whereas work demands were escalating: more travel, more complexities, information flowing faster, deadlines and regulations tighter, and no fixed hours. On the other hand, in the 1970s and early 1980s growing numbers lacked any paid work at all. Voluntary leisure might still bring status, but involuntary leisure did not. Several new ideas about the relation between work and leisure gained ground: ideas for work-sharing, for 'sabbatical leave for all' during the working life,[314] and for retraining to change jobs more than once during a working lifetime. Prior, soon to be Secretary of State for Employment, speculated in March 1979 on whether a 'move away from the Protestant work ethic' might make it easier to share productivity's rewards more fairly.[315] This was also the language of Benn and of many trade union leaders, seeking to replace 'destructive idleness' by 'positive leisure'. Jack Jones in April 1976 recommended an immediate cut in the male retirement age by between one and two years, aiming ultimately to equalize the retirement age for both sexes.[316]

Laziness is a subjective category, and few would apply the word to involuntary unemployment, a major source of inefficiency in the British economy after 1970. The unemployment of the 1980s has already been discussed in its social-class and political dimension;[317] it must now be set in its overall economic context. Unemployment was rising in corporatism's latest phase: when shown as a percentage of total UK employees, the unemployed in official figures averaged at less than 2 per cent between 1945 and the late 1960s, but thenceforward there was a rising trend, with ever higher peaks in 1972 and 1977.[318] Between 1950 and 1966 the numbers employed and the numbers available for employment had risen in parallel, but thereafter the government's continued pursuit of 'Keynesian' policies did not prevent the two from diverging, for the job market contracted sharply at the same time as the numbers available for work continued to rise quite fast—by half a million men and a third of a million women between 1981 and 1988.[319] 'Keynes is dead', Powell declared on 26 November 1971—a phrase which Sherman pressed upon Keith Joseph in 1974. In discussing economic subjects, politicians began to display a new

---

[314] e.g. by Catherine Goyder in her Fabian pamphlet, *T* (15 Dec. 1977), 4.

[315] *G* (22 Mar. 1979), 3 (addressing a conference on micro-electronics).

[316] David Basnett, General Secretary of the General and Municipal Workers and Chairman of Congress at the TUC in Brighton, *T* (5 Sept. 1978), 3; cf. Benn, *HC Deb.* 29 Oct. 1980, c. 515. For Jones see *T* (19 Apr. 1976), 2.

[317] See above, pp. 179–83.   [318] *BST* 174.

[319] Coleman and Salt, *British Population*, 367. See also S. Broadberry's illuminating graph in Floud and McCloskey (eds.), *Economic History of Britain since 1700*, iii (2nd edn.), 196.

humility, with less confrontation.[320] In the early 1980s unemployment at 3.2 million had reached levels comparable with those of the 1930s, and the Thatcher government seemed even to be encouraging it. A massive process of demanning in the mid-1980s shifted unproductive workers from the employer's payroll on to the taxpayer's. This occurred on a huge scale in the newly privatized industries, especially among manual labourers. Central and local government employees, too, were decanted on to the labour market in their hundreds of thousands from deliberate government policy after 1979. In addition these were years of massive labour turnover, and to all these types of regional and frictional unemployment was added the massive cyclical unemployment that resulted from the depression after 1980.

Whereas until the late 1960s full employment had seemed the norm and the inter-war years an aberration, the picture as viewed from the 1980s looked very different. In the first two of the four periods 1960–73, 1974–9, 1980–9, and 1990–4 the unemployed made up a smaller share of the total UK labour force than the six-country averaged total for the USA, Japan, France, Italy, Canada, and the UK, but their share in the third period was much higher and in the fourth period marginally so.[321] The percentage of the UK workforce who were unemployed was larger from 1973 to 1986 than in the EEC, though the discrepancy was not great, and in the late 1980s the British percentage fell substantially below the EEC's. Even at its peak in 1986 Britain's level of unemployment, at 11.6 per cent, was lower than in Italy (14.3 per cent), Belgium (16.5 per cent), and Spain (21.5 per cent).[322] Unemployment's fall after 1982 was much sharper, however, in the United States, and was consistently far lower in Norway, Sweden, and Japan.[323] There was now much talk about 'hysteresis': about the idea that once unemployment's level rises it will not revert to its earlier level. The new (raised) level comes to seem 'natural', the trade unions defend the employed against competition from the unemployed, and the psychological effects of exclusion render the unemployed unemployable.[324] We have already seen how unemployment for many men by the 1980s merged ineluctably into early retirement, and how they were less inclined to undertake paid work beyond retiring age.[325]

Yet later developments belied the 'hysteresis' theory. More helpful was the unravelling of 'unemployment' as an over-generalized category. Unemployment statistics reflected less objective facts than administrative categories: 1,365,775

---

[320] Powell quoted in D. Wood, 'How the House Grew Humble', *T* (29 Nov. 1971), 13. For Sherman see his obituary in *T* (29 Aug. 2006), 45.   [321] OECD, *Historical Statistics 1960–1994*, 45.

[322] Dept. of Employment figures in Coleman and Salt, *British Population*, 365. See also D. Goodhart, 'Europe isn't Working', *FT* (17 Dec. 1992), 18.

[323] See S. Brittan's useful tables in Kavanagh and Seldon (eds.), *Thatcher Effect*, 23, and S. Broadberry's in Floud and McCloskey (eds.), *Economic History of Britain since 1700*, iii (2nd edn.), 201 (OECD figures).   [324] Britton, *Macroeconomic Policy in Britain*, 113–14.

[325] See above, pp. 181, 277. See also Harrison, *Seeking a Role*, 35, 284.

people said they were unemployed during the week before the census of 1971, for example, yet the Department of Employment's figures showed only 773,800 then registered as unemployed.[326] The genuinely unemployed had to be distinguished from the unemployed registered for benefit. Cultural change enlarged the latter category because inhibitions against registering were waning: by the 1970s, for example, many university students were registering during their vacations. In the 1980s, as in the 1930s, men were far more likely than women to declare themselves unemployed. Nonetheless, a widely discussed survey in 1984 by the Department of Employment found 250,000 men and 620,000 women who were looking for work but without claiming benefit. Furthermore, the claimants included many not entitled: 560,000 men and 380,000 women (nearly a third of those who claimed) were in work or not looking for it.[327] Estimates in 1986 showed that the 3.2 million then defined as unemployed because registered for benefit included four very different subgroups: 17 per cent were in the 'poverty trap'—the term was first widely used in the early 1970s and referred to those poor enough to be made worse off by a pay rise which would deny them a fair share of state benefits. In addition, 13 per cent, mostly older people, had in effect retired on the dole; 12 per cent for health reasons saw themselves as unemployable, and 8 per cent felt they could afford not to seek work.[328] It was important, too, to bring the under-employed into the discussion: many Conservatives saw the allegedly rising unemployment of the early 1980s as having brought the hitherto under-employed out into the open. All this would have confirmed Keith Joseph in his long-held view (echoing Keynes, as he realized[329]) that to lump people together indiscriminately as 'unemployed' was to hinder the search for effective remedies: he saw sociological, statistical, and economic, but also party-political justifications for refining the term through subdividing it.

Never before the early 1980s had politicians focused so narrowly, so anxiously, and for so long from month to month upon the statistical trend relating to a single problem (Plate 15). All but one of the twenty-four changes made between 1979 and 1988 in how to calculate the unemployment figures had the effect of reducing the total,[330] and Labour politicians were understandably sceptical. Labour protests had been vigorous enough in 1972 when Heath's government removed the 'temporarily unemployed' category from the published monthly statistics of unemployment,[331] and such protests continued throughout the

[326] G (17 Nov. 1972), 1.   [327] Employment Gazette (Oct. 1985), 394.
[328] FT (8 Aug. 1986), 6.
[329] Speech of 5 Sept. 1974, T (6 Sept. 1974), 14; cf. his letter in ST (10 Aug. 1975), 42.)
[330] The changes are conveniently listed in G (15 Mar. 1989), 21.
[331] Heath, HC Deb. 21 Nov. 1972, c. 1083. T (22 Nov. 1972), 6, cites Labour MPs' comment: 'twister! Chiseller. He wriggles like a sardine.' See also Heath's correction to his remark at HC Deb. 22 Nov. 1972, cc. 1300–1.

changes made during the 1980s. By November 1983 critics on the left felt that the official total of 3,094,000 should really be 4,437,000, whereas critics on the right would have cut the total to 1,668,000 by removing from it the frictional, unemployable, illegal, and voluntary unemployed.[332] The government made its changes in statistical procedure with remarkably little public discussion or explanation, and there were also distortions in how it publicly interpreted the statistics.[333] By the end of the decade, statisticians were growing increasingly worried about the integrity of government statistics in other spheres, too.

Beneath all the controversy about unemployment was a cumulating long-term trend that persisted into the twenty-first century: the state's growing involvement in promoting industrial training to achieve (among other things) a better relative national economic performance. Wage differentials were widening in the 1980s partly because for highly educated workers the demand rose faster than the supply, whereas for unskilled workers the reverse was the case. The aim was to encourage more of the unskilled into the highly educated category. Commenting upon Hayek's *Road to Serfdom*, Keynes noted that Hayek conceded the need to draw a line somewhere between state intervention and the free market, but complained that Hayek did not specify the line's location.[334] Deeply influenced by Hayek though they were, the Thatcher governments defined the state's educational responsibilities very widely. Intentionally or unintentionally they were accelerating the long-term process whereby paid work became less salient within the individual's lifetime: more young people were now extending their education and training, and more older people were retiring early.

Between 1979 and 1987 the total helped by employment schemes rose from 344,000 to 810,000.[335] Thatcher entrusted David Young with tackling the unemployment problem in 1984–7, and selected his 'action for jobs' programme for special praise in her memoirs. Self-made, with extensive business experience and a flair for publicity (including self-publicity), Young was the son of a Lithuanian immigrant, and moved in north London Jewish circles. He had not been alone among Thatcher's close following in wondering during the gloomy situation of 1974 whether to emigrate. An outsider to both the establishment and politics, he brought an energetic resourcefulness into an area of policy then crucial to the government's image, and soon entered the cabinet. 'Other people come to me with their problems', Thatcher allegedly said, 'David Young comes to me with his achievements.'[336] In his budget of 1985 Lawson introduced a

---

[332] *ST* (6 Nov. 1983), 62.

[333] e.g. in the choice of base-year for claims about improvement. See Gilmour, *Dancing with Dogma*, 72–3.

[334] *FT* (14 Feb. 1994), 19. See also R. Skidelsky, *John Maynard Keynes*, iii. *Fighting for Britain: 1937–1946* (2000), 285.   [335] Britton, *Macroeconomic Policy in Britain*, 255.

[336] Quoted in *ST* (16 Sept. 1984), 10. See also Thatcher, *Downing Street Years*, 421.

clutch of employment-creating measures, and the Party's manifesto of 1987 claimed credit for the jobclubs and enterprise allowance scheme that had by then been set up.[337] By mid-decade, government attitudes to job-creation were beginning to shift. The MSC came under criticism from both right and left. For the left, it was a palliative: one of many structures designed to defuse public concern by demonstrating that 'something was being done', yet without tackling fundamentals. The right saw it as perpetuating the notion that the state, rather than entrepreneurs, could 'create' jobs. Government's further advance into industrial training had begun, after all, in 1964 in a corporatist climate and had prompted employer complaint.[338] The MSC was, said Alan Clark in 1984, 'a completely Socialist concept. Nanny State, with just a hint of Orwell', and Lawson thought that 'the employer, rather than the taxpayer, should pay for training', as in Germany.[339]

As the unemployment tide began to ebb in mid-decade, the government grew bolder in challenging prevailing attitudes to the unemployed. Even in 1981 it had cut unemployment benefits in real terms, braving fierce opposition from Heath for doing so.[340] By 1983 benefits for the unemployed in Britain were running at a lower percentage of average earnings than in any other leading West European country, and had been falling sharply during the previous decade.[341] In government circles it was still widely thought that the unemployed were 'pricing themselves out of' work, and Tebbit was pushed only reluctantly into paying 'the rate for the job' to those long-term adult unemployed whom the Community Programme aimed to help with part-time work, often in the public sector.[342] Thatcher and Lawson would have liked to go further and introduce an American 'workfare' scheme, paying unemployment benefit only in return for work, but cabinet colleagues would not back the idea.[343] 'Workfare' was a transatlantic term of the 1960s denoting what was in the UK a revived Beveridgean strategy of requiring recipients of unemployment benefit either to work or go on a training programme, and by mid-decade ministers were drawing attention approvingly to Beveridge's more coercive side.[344] In the USA 'workfare' lost its inverted commas in the 1970s, but in the UK retained them for much longer. The government's Restart programme of 1986 involved interviewing the long-term unemployed, with the effect either of helping them into training places or jobs or of removing them from the register.[345] This cut official unemployment levels conveniently in time for the general election of

[337] Dale (ed.), *Conservative Manifestos*, 328.   [338] *Econ* (19 Apr. 1975), 76–7.

[339] A. Clark, *Diaries*, 89 (24 July 1984). Lawson, *View from No. 11*, 439.

[340] *HC Deb.* 8 Dec. 1981, c. 742.   [341] United Nations survey quoted in *T* (24 Oct. 1983), 4.

[342] Tebbit, *Upwardly Mobile*, 191.

[343] Lawson, *View from No. 11*, 434. For a useful list of cuts in unemployment benefit 1979–88 see Barrell (ed.), *UK Labour Market*, 75–8.

[344] e.g. in D. Young, 'Less Money, More Incentives', *T* (5 Dec. 1984), 12; cf. leader (6 Dec. 1984), 17.

[345] C. Huhne, 'Why Jobless Total will Fall Before Thatcher Goes to Polls', *G* (30 Oct. 1986), 29.

1987. Unemployment benefit in Great Britain remained static in real terms between 1979 and 1987, but fell appreciably in relation to average earnings.[346]

In sum, it is clear that after 1970 by most criteria, including international comparison, many more British teenagers and adults, male and female, were ready to seek paid work when given the chance. Furthermore, the workforce was growing more flexible on working practices and on time and place of work; it was becoming readier to change jobs, though for structural reasons peculiar to the UK it was reluctant to move out of depressed areas; its industrial relations were improving markedly; its working hours were longer and its holidays fewer than in many European countries. If its levels of unemployment were higher than elsewhere, the idleness was usually involuntary; and if its productivity per head was lower than elsewhere, this seems more to reflect outdated equipment than personal idleness. Allegations of laziness cannot help to explain Britain's relative economic decline, from which anyway after the 1970s it slowly recovered. Nor does any of this mention the importance of hard work outside the workplace. Work done at home easily eludes the official economic statistics, yet nobody would claim that most women part-timers were idle when they got home. As for the 901,000 men who by the early 1990s were in part-time work,[347] many would have preferred full-time jobs if available. Indeed, the growing male tendency to share in household tasks, the prevalence of 'moonlighting', and of labour-intensive home improvements suggest that even these men were decidedly busy.[348]

5. FREE-MARKET CONSUMERISM

Mass consumerism proceeded apace after 1970, as before. It rested on pride in the home, which was becoming much more than a mere launching pad for work and recreation taken elsewhere; for many, the home was becoming the centre of recreation and the very purpose of work. After 1945 the proportion of consumers' expenditure assigned to housing rose steadily, reaching its highest twentieth-century level in 1984. The share of personal wealth taken up by consumer durables, like that of the home itself, doubled between 1957 and 1984. The long-term twentieth-century trend was also for a rise in the share of UK consumers' expenditure assigned to cars and consumer durables: from 6 per cent in 1950 to 17 per cent in 1984;[349] housing absorbed a rising share of household expenditure, whereas a declining share went on food, tobacco, and clothing.[350] Indeed, the more affluent the individual and the society, the smaller

---

[346] See the useful table in Britton, *Macroeconomic Policy in Britain*, 257.

[347] Bassett, 'Workplace Flexibility', 31.

[348] For moonlighting see above, pp. 324–5. For do-it-yourself see above, pp. 89, 234, 325, 352, and below, p. 367. For shared household tasks see above, pp. 229, 234, 285.   [349] *BST* 150, 156.

[350] See the useful table in Obelkevich and Catterall (eds.), *Understanding Post-War British Society*, 144.

the proportion of household expenditure on food, whose share in Britain fell from 30 per cent in 1930 to 25 per cent in 1950 to 20 per cent in 1970 to 12 per cent in 1990.[351]

Demand was insatiable: soon after one item had been acquired, a new model or a new want superseded it in self-generating escalation. Smaller families meant more space, and the refrigerator (owned by 60 per cent of households in 1969 and rising to over 90 per cent by 1978) greatly improved the home's storage capacity. Then, in the 1970s, came the deep-freeze: only 9 per cent of households had them in 1973, but 40 per cent by 1978. By 1970 peas in the pod had become scarce because four-fifths had already been bought up for canning or freezing.[352] Perishable foods bought in bulk could now be stored at home as well as in the shop. Next came the microwave oven; in 1984 the number owned doubled within one year, and could be found in a tenth of British households; the British market for them was by then the third largest in the world, surpassed only by the USA and Japan. Video-recorder sales, too, were booming—present in a fifth of British homes by 1983. Alone among consumer goods, the dishwasher failed to take off in Britain, located in only 5 per cent of British homes by 1983.[353] The one consumer durable to decline after 1970 was the black-and-white television, though only because colour television was ousting it. Apologizing in 1975 for having to raise VAT on so many items, Healey confessed that 'very few classes of goods are now generally accepted to be luxuries'.[354]

Central heating was one among many new wants: 5 per cent of homes had it in 1960, 84 per cent in 1991; it ensured that dust and cinders filled far less of the family's dustbin in the 1980s than in the 1960s, let alone between the wars.[355] Then came double-glazing, whose salesman supplanted the used-car salesman in popular demonology as the archetypal man on the make; no longer was it necessary in the home to hurry through draughts and cold from one heated location to another. By 1991 saturation point for telephones (in 88 per cent of homes), deep- or fridge-freezers (83 per cent), and washing machines (87 per cent) had almost been reached; and video recorders (68 per cent), microwaves (55 per cent), and tumble dryers (48 per cent) were racing to catch up.[356] In access to consumer goods, Britain was well up with other industrial countries: during the 1970s the UK was eighth in the international league for telephones within the home, and at fifth position on owning televisions was significantly

[351] Calculated from *TCBST* 342–3.
[352] C. Johnson, 'The Durable Revolution', *Lloyds Bank Economic Bulletin*, 15 (Mar. 1980), 2. *T* (5 May 1978), supplement on 'Grocery Retailing', p. i. *T* (16 Feb. 1970), supplement on 'Food in Britain', p. iii (peas).
[353] *FT* (18 Oct. 1984), 5; (11 July 1984), 3 (video recorders). For dishwashers, *T* (11 July 1984), 3. See also the correspondence in *T* (25 Oct. 1971), 13 launched by Patricia Heren.
[354] *HC Deb.* 15 Apr. 1975, c. 303 (budget speech).   [355] *TCBST* 479–80. *FT* (5 Aug. 1987), 6.
[356] *Social Trends* (1995), 105.

outclassed only by the USA and Canada. This was partly because the lowest income groups in Britain were (at 80 per cent) keen to own television sets, though (at 25 per cent) much less keen on telephones.[357] There was also an age-lag, given that older generations did not share youth's yearning for the latest consumer fashion.[358]

Continuity in purchasing trends was not matched by continuity in government policy towards the consumer, which went through three post-war phases. In the first, it was hoped that nationalization and the co-op movement would serve the consumer by enhancing efficiency and a sense of public service.[359] From the late 1950s a slowly evolving second phase saw all concerns (whether nationalized or not) monitored by organized consumers. The Consumer Association continued to grow: its magazine *Which?* had 625,000 subscribers in 1982,[360] and in the 1980s shoppers armed themselves with it, just as diners-out wielded their *Good Food Guide*. As so often, voluntary action paved the way for the state, especially as the attempt to control incomes under both Labour and (after 1972) Conservative governments entailed a simultaneous attempt to regulate prices. Howe from 1972 to 1974 was 'Minister for Trade and Consumer Affairs', and in 1975 the last Wilson government made grants to local authorities which established consumer advice centres. Though the 1960s saw the consumer at least partially enfranchised against the retailer, corporatist structures could not adequately protect consumers against producers, and the Labour Party with its trade union bond was vulnerable, as Castle realized, to producer capture. In 1965 Powell was already foreshadowing the advent of a third phase: the return to the market. 'Everyone who goes into a shop and chooses one article instead of another', he said, 'is casting a vote in the economic ballot box. . . . In this great and continuous general election of the free economy . . . we are all voting all the time.'[361]

Conservative MPs cheered in July 1970 when Robert Carr declared competition 'the most effective means of safeguarding the consumer', rather than the Prices and Incomes Board, disbanded in the previous month.[362] The frontier between consumer-policy phases two and three was blurred, however, not just by Heath's 'u-turn' in 1972, but by Labour's last corporatist foray from 1974 to 1979. The Secretary of State for Prices and Consumer Protection in those years was not entirely abolished thereafter, though the Price Commission disappeared in 1979: a Minister for Consumer Affairs lingered on from 1979 to 1983. Nonetheless, after 1979 when the third phase was revving up, Thatcher's

---

[357] Johnson, 'Durable Revolution', 3. Rubinstein, *Capitalism, Culture, and Decline*, 42.
[358] W. D. Rubinstein, *Wealth and Inequality in Britain* (1986), 85, 100.
[359] Cf. above, p. 336.   [360] *FT* (11 Oct. 1982), 8.
[361] Powell quoted in J. Wood (ed.), *A Nation Not Afraid: The Thinking of Enoch Powell* (1965), 27. See also *G* (31 Dec. 1975), 7. Castle, *Diaries 1974–6*, 309 (11 Feb. 1975).
[362] *HC Deb.* 23 July 1970, c. 769, cf. *T* (24 July 1970), 6.

governments set out to deploy the free market so as to enfranchise consumer against producer. There were drawbacks. To begin with, many consumers were also producers, and would not necessarily gain from the stiff competition between firms that consumer enfranchisement fostered. Besides, not all consumers had the time or energy required to participate fully in rational and informed choice. There remained an important role for the state, given that unfettered choice was otiose if between identical items labelled differently, and potentially dangerous if between contrasting items labelled identically.

Whereas the co-op movement's collectivist approach to quality provision had helped to fuel the late Victorian socialist pioneers, the new multiples' managerial and entrepreneurial skills fuelled Thatcherism a century later. The co-ops' market share fell steadily from 1955 to 1990, and in the same period their shops dwindled from 30,000 to 5,000: their pioneering role in retailing had now passed to others. 'Do we really want to nationalize Marks and Spencers to make it as efficient as the Co-op?', Healey ironically asked Labour Party enthusiasts for state control in 1973.[363] Thatcher often shopped in Marks & Spencer, and when the Brighton bomb on 12 October 1984 denied clothes to some of those present at the Conservative Party conference, it was to Marks & Spencer's local branch that they resorted, getting its clothing department to open early (Plate 7). Sir Derek Rayner, a director of the firm, worked on Ministry of Defence procurement in 1971–2, and in 1979 he became Thatcher's unpaid part-time aide (1980–2) in curbing government waste. If he could 'teach the Civil Service to manage itself as well as he manages Marks and Spencer's', she said in the following year, 'I should be very pleased'. When reform of the NHS management structure was being contemplated in 1983, it was to Roy Griffiths, Chief Executive of Sainsbury's, that Norman Fowler resorted as Secretary of State for the Social Services.[364] The Sainsbury family made notable donations to national art collections, David Sainsbury gave the SDP key financial backing, and leading retailers became well-known national personalities.

Thatcher's supermarket enthusiasms were in two respects surprising: she disliked largeness in any institution, and supermarkets were the death of the urban general store whence she had come. The small shop could neither offer a range so wide nor prices so low, and could survive only by offering a distinctive benefit such as longer opening-hours, personal service, or convenient location. The many family shops run by East African Asian immigrants often rose to the occasion, and their entrepreneurial flair competed as damagingly with inner-city traditionalist shopkeepers as did Japanese imports with traditionalist

---

[363] Quoted in M. Hatfield, *The House the Left Built: Inside Labour Policy-Making 1970–75* (1978), 197. See also L. Sparks, 'Consumer Co-operation in the UK 1945–93', in J. Benson and G. Shaw (eds.), *The Retailing Industry*, iii (1999), 151–3.

[364] *HC Deb.* 13 May 1980, c. 1057. See also Thatcher, *Downing Street Years*, 382; Fowler, *Ministers Decide*, 195.

manufacturers. The early supermarkets were located near other shops in the city centre, if only because the car could still reach them, and because most customers then used public transport or walked; but supermarkets gradually grew larger, offered huge price cuts, and migrated to the suburbs. Free competition by no means here precluded powerful planning; they were triumphs of organization, through coordinating the presence in one place of goods in abundance and variety, often perishable, and through forecasting or creating and responding to the customer's broadening tastes. Then came the 'superstore', defined as offering 25,000 square feet of self-service sales area, a wide range of food or non-food, and ample parking space; by 1981 the UK boasted about 300.[365] The term 'hypermarket' was sometimes used as a synonym for superstore, but others reserved it for shops whose sales area occupied 50,000 square feet or more.[366] Early in supermarket history, planning permission became crucial to success, and in the 1980s superstores gained much from diminished regulation. A specialized kind of superstore gained much, too, in the late 1980s, from depression: the discount grocery store. Pioneered by Kwiksave, it was joined by such names as Morrisons and Pricerite. Their discounts reflected centralized buying, close computerized stock-control, a bleakly utilitarian out-of-town warehouse locale, and a sharp focus on quickly turning over a limited range of goods.[367] The distinction between shop and warehouse was becoming blurred, given that the 'retail warehouse' was likely to be found nearby, especially in the south-east of England—selling furniture, carpets, electrical goods, and do-it-yourself materials direct to the public.[368]

Supermarkets were by no means the small local retailer's sole difficulty. He was also hit by Heath's enthusiastic abolition of resale price maintenance in 1964, the need from 1973 to administer VAT, mounting shoplifting and inner-city disorder, diminishing facilities for parking and delivery, and (in the many areas of declining industry after 1970) declining custom. Standards were rising in shop interiors, display, health, and hygiene; the hard floorboards gave way to carpets, and goods were moved beyond the counter towards the customer, with the multiple stores setting the pace. Stiff after-hours competition also came from the diversified sales at petrol stations, from the car-boot sale, and from the charity shop—all novel developments flourishing in the 1980s. There was some room left, especially in the larger cities, for the specialist shop—the delicatessen, the dress shop, the dealer in health and ethnic foods, and the

---

[365] *T* (22 June 1981), 17.

[366] K. Davies and L. Sparks, 'The Development of Superstore Retailing in Great Britain 1960–1986: Results from a New Database', in Benson and Shaw (eds.), *Retailing Industry*, iii. 230, cf. 89.

[367] L. Sparks, 'Spatial-Structural Relationships in Retail Corporate Growth: A Case-Study of Kwik Save Group PLC', in Benson and Shaw (eds.), *Retailing Industry*, iii. 247, 256; cf. 101, 103.

[368] A. Gibbs, 'The Retail Warehouse: A Hybrid Form of Development', in Benson and Shaw (eds.), *Retailing Industry*, iii. 191–2, 202.

antique dealer—but between 1960 and 1990 the number of grocery outlets in the UK fell by two-thirds,[369] and there was diminishing scope for the greengrocer, the butcher, the fishmonger, and the ironmonger.

Far from feeling deprived by the shop assistant's retreat, many customers felt liberated, with choice unconstrained, wide avenues of free selection spreading out, opening hours greatly extended, and half-day mid-week closing ended. Yet the multiple-retailer revolution brought at least three drawbacks. First, shops in towns were increasingly standardized. Dolcis, Boots, W. H. Smith, Marks & Spencer, Sainsbury, Mothercare, Pronuptia, and the like ousted the local firms which had earlier diversified the community. Second, in the mass retailing concern, few could guide, let alone know, the customer. The old regime before the 1960s had suited the old better than the young. Much had then been delivered to the home—not just by postmen, newsagents, and milkmen, but by butchers, grocers, greengrocers, and even fishmongers. Retailing had offered all the attractions of smallness and intimacy, and a manageable quantity of items could then be bought from the local shops. The suburban middle-class housewife who walked out mid-morning with her shopping basket or travelled on the bus encountered friends doing the same, as well as friends behind the counter in the shops she regularly patronized. It was a constricting life for women, and the supermarket responded to women's widening opportunities, but it banished the smells and the sights of the weighings up, the hand packaging, and the personal contact. Recreation re-entered shopping in new guises, though: the drive to reach the supermarket, the snacks in its restaurant, and the excitements of manipulating the trolley down the aisles and selecting from a huge range of attractively packaged goods. This more hygienic and all-embracing world could meet the needs of the entire family, with recreation for the children, parking and fuel for the car, bank tellers offering cash.

The changing world of the mail-order firm exemplifies the retreat from intimacy. Up to the 1960s friendship lay at its heart, and its share of non-food retail sales by value rose from 5.7 per cent in 1964 to 9.2 per cent in 1979. In the new and increasingly computerized world of late twentieth-century retailing, however, no such intimacy could survive. In the 1970s there were still about four million mail-order agents,[370] but slum-clearance had already begun to break up the tight working-class communities where they flourished, and the agents were slowly edged out. The postal strike of 1970 alerted the firms to motorways as the basis for an independent delivery network, growing phone ownership in the early 1980s substituted phone- for mail-ordering, and from the 1990s the

---

[369] *FT* (1 July 1991), 30.
[370] R. Coopey, S. O'Connell, and D. Porter, *Mail Order Retailing in Britain: A Business and Social History* (Oxford, 2005), 53, 56. See also *Seeking a Role*, 25, 332.

internet made credit-worthiness and other information instantly available.[371] Mail-order firms grew larger: Great Universal Stores had 40 per cent of total mail-order sales by value in 1981, Littlewoods 30 per cent, and Freemans 13 per cent.[372] From size and anonymity came supermarketry's third drawback: the simulated and formulaic friendliness which replaced the shop's one-time genuine intimacy. Here as elsewhere from the late 1980s the programmed and Americanized informality of 'nicespeak', inculcated by management gurus like Tom Peters and propagated in commercial training centres, swept the country.[373] Its otiose 'Enjoy your meal', 'Have a nice day', and 'How may I help?' were uttered in a tone of instant familiarity, reinforced by vapid 'mission statements' and 'visions'. Unlike Orwell's 'Newspeak', 'nicespeak' could not be countered by plain English because it lacked any clear meaning to controvert. A quiet and private irony was perhaps the only defence against it, together with the knowledge that if silly fashions come, they also go.

This chapter has shown how the Second World War's impact on industry and commerce persisted throughout the 1970s and 1980s, but differently as between the two decades. In the 1970s its legacy's interventionist aspect predominated: in the 1980s, its libertarian aspect. A combination of perceived national relative economic decline, party-political interest, and the problems of operating corporatist structures in a voluntarist climate enhanced the attractions of Thatcher's new move in 1979. The 1980s saw Conservatives occupying territory where the politician can exert most influence: in changing the climate of public debate, with a free-market outcome which involved huge changes in the composition and conduct of the workforce. As for the consumer revolution, its already rapid pace was if anything accelerated by these changes, encouraged the general public to feel more optimistic than the politicians about the economy, and generated a direct confrontation between materialistic and religious values. Yet materialistic accumulation was decidedly selective in promoting the 'Victorian values' favoured by Thatcher—values which were perhaps ultimately necessary to her success.

The first, seventh, third, and fifth, respectively, of our eight motifs have therefore already surfaced, but so also have the remaining four. The strongly accumulative culture fostered in both decades, for all its ever-cheaper labour-saving devices, paradoxically tightened time pressures (the fourth motif), especially within the dual-career family, nor did the computer necessarily reduce the pressures at work. And while Thatcher might from conviction oppose significant change in British political institutions, the ferment involved in the return to the free market led many to see attractions in constitutional reform as a safeguard against any such prime minister ever appearing again.

[371] Coopey et al., Mail Order Retailing, 55, 67, 183, 192–3, 198, 236.   [372] Ibid. 66, 68.
[373] D. Cameron's 'The Tyranny of Nicespeak', NS (5 Nov. 2001), 25–7, is essential reading.

Partly for this reason the sixth motif (political stability amidst social change) was less relevant for the 1990s than before. Free-market ideas might at first sight have been expected to challenge the UK's hermetic tendencies (the second motif), and they certainly consolidated the Anglo-American connection. Yet given the interventionist traditions within EEC and Commonwealth, and given Thatcher's impatience with both, Britain's free-market commitment at first made difficulties for the UK in both arenas. In the longer term, however, free-market ideas harmonized with globalizing trends, and Thatcher temporarily gave the UK a new world role (the eighth motif) as exemplar of successful privatization. In a bravura performance, she did not hesitate to link this with the defence of liberty and democracy, and preached her gospel on both sides of the iron curtain.

CHAPTER 6

Intellect and Culture

An affluent society can afford increasingly lavish cultural and recreational provision, but this chapter's first section shows how in Britain this helped to accelerate the decline in religious observance from the 1960s: the new facilities generated competing priorities and values. The schools system, discussed in the chapter's second section, continued to expand, but without realizing the high hopes of the post-war generation, or of the progressive reformers who created the comprehensive school ideal in the 1950s. These schools therefore became central to party-political controversy after 1970, whereas the independent schools not only survived but flourished. The same picture of rapid growth combined with doubts and controversy beset the subject of the third section: universities. Nor did the extraordinary growth and diversification of culture and recreation, the fourth section's theme, receive a universal welcome. Hence the need in the chapter's concluding section to consider the widely discussed fears of 'dumbing down'.

I. RELIGIONS OLD AND NEW

On 7 December 1978 Callaghan tried to rally Labour MPs at a party meeting to fend off a crucial parliamentary defeat on the government's pay policy. 'As he got up to leave for the chamber he sang us a hymn—I think it was "We'll meet again with the Lord". It was completely unaffected and not embarrassing.' Bernard Donoughue was a close observer of the prime minister, and his diary records that Callaghan 'sings hymns at times of stress and crisis'.[1] On this occasion Callaghan prevailed, and the conduct of this one-time Baptist Sunday-school teacher exemplifies Christianity's protracted influence within a secularizing society, for secularization proceeded apace after 1970. Among Western industrial nations in the 1980s Britain ranked low in any list for the proportion of the population attending religious services, high in the proportion saying they had 'no religion'. In their share of the UK population, those claiming to be Christians fell from 80 per cent in 1950 to 64 per cent

[1] Donoughue, *Downning Street Diary*, ii. 399 (7 Dec. 1978).

in 2000, and members of Christian congregations fell from 24 per cent to 13 per cent.[2] By every measure (number of churches, number of parish clergy, church attendance, Easter Day communicants, number of church marriages, membership as a proportion of the adult population) the Church of England was in decline after 1970. In 1985 there were only half as many parish clergy as in 1900. Religious marriages as a share of the total in England and Wales fell from 70 per cent in 1960 to 53 per cent in 1980.[3] Still worse was the plight of other leading British Protestant denominations: between 1970 and 2000, Methodist members were down by 43 per cent, Presbyterian by 40 per cent, Baptist by 18 per cent. Between 1950 and 2000 the number of church buildings and congregations fell from eleven to eight per 10,000 population, and members per church fell even faster: from 169 to 122.[4]

Absence from religious institutions does not in itself denote loss of faith. Growing domestication and specialization were denuding secular communal institutions too: pubs, cinemas, and railway stations, for example. By the early 1970s the Ordnance Survey was already grappling with the logical and other problems posed by needing to display disused railway stations as well as disused churches. Mutual aid associations, youth organizations, political parties, and (after 1979) trade unions, too, were losing members.[5] Freemasons in England and Wales halved between 1950 and 2000, and in 2002 Britain's 450,000 freemasons were on average aged almost 60.[6] Yet there was ample evidence of continuing supernatural belief: while those surveyed who said they did not believe in God almost tripled between the 1960s and the 1990s, and those who rejected an after-life almost doubled, more than two-thirds still said they believed in God, and well over a third in life after death. The distinction between attendance and belief prompted claims that the British people were, as in many European Protestant countries, 'believing without belonging'.[7] The beliefs were not necessarily Christian: almost a third of those surveyed in 1989 said they believed in ghosts, twice as many as in a comparable survey in 1973; a seventh (almost four times as many as in 1973) claimed to have seen one, and more had come to believe in horoscopes, black magic, flying saucers, thought transference between the living, and communication with the dead.[8] The Post Office's provision of a horoscope telephone service in the Birmingham area in 1972 prompted protest in the House of Lords that the government was spending millions 'on public education to spread knowledge and truth' while

---

[2] *T* (16 Nov. 1989), 7. *TCBST* 652–5.   [3] *BST* 527, 538. *TCBST* 663.
[4] *TCBST* 655, 669. See also table 3 in Davie, ' "An Ordinary God" ', 401.
[5] See W. A. Seymour's interesting letter in *T* (3 Jan. 1973), 13. B. Knight and P. Stokes, *The Deficit in Civil Society in the United Kingdom* (Foundation for Civil Society, Working Paper, 1; Birmingham, 1996), 10, 12, 13, 18.   [6] *Econ* (2 Mar. 2002), 36.
[7] *TCBST* 663. Davie, ' "An Ordinary God" ', 413.
[8] Gallup poll of nearly 1,000 people, representing a cross-section of society, *STel* (24 Dec. 1989), 4.

allowing 'a service to increase gullibility and foster superstition'; Gallup polls soon afterwards revealed that about a quarter of those surveyed said they believed in horoscopes.[9] John Beloff, at Edinburgh University from 1962, built up Britain's only laboratory of parapsychology, and it was there that Robert Morris became Britain's first professor; when Morris died in 2004 the UK had ten departments in the subject.[10] So the decline in institutionalized religion did not necessarily signify the advance of reason, but in so far as non-Christian supernatural beliefs persisted, they were so vague and unstructured as to lack institutional focus; their status rose no higher than that of pipe dream or attention-seeking whim.

In growing numbers, secularized pilgrims visited the more notable Christian buildings, primarily for recreational and aesthetic reasons. Their noise and numbers complemented on the ground[11] the intellectually secularizing impact that the incursion of 'comparative religion' made within university theology departments. If churches remained important centres for music in the 1980s, this was now less because the music was religious in nature, more because churches could accommodate an organ, an orchestra, a choir, and a large audience in an aesthetic setting. The churches made two logical responses to their buildings' changed role. First, they began charging for entry, for why should a dwindling number of worshippers maintain the crumbling fabric of the fine buildings whose role had so greatly changed? By August 1973 Salisbury Cathedral, eager to preserve its spire, was charging non-pastoral visitors for entry.[12] But, second, the churches could revert to the early churches' informal and weekday worship,[13] informality being at least as feasible at home as in church. The house church movement began unobtrusively in Halton, Leeds, in 1952. Enthusiastically evangelical in mood, it was loosely structured—united more by magazines, preachers, and conventions than by buildings. From its small base it was by the 1980s among the fastest-growing religious groups, and its informality spread from its buildings to its liturgy, merging the worlds of religion and secular recreation. Its membership rose thirteenfold between 1980 and 2000. Even in religious buildings, formal ceremonial was waning: by 2000, kneeling in Anglican and Catholic churches was in such decline, partly because ageing congregations lacked the aptitude, that a campaign was launched to revive it.[14] In conduct, as in belief, the Christian and the secular were becoming less distinct.

---

[9] Lord Conesford, *HL Deb.* 23 Mar. 1972, c. 939. *Gallup International Public Opinion Polls*, ii. 1283 (Oct. 1973), 1418 (June 1975), 1418.

[10] *Scotsman*, 14 Sept. 2004, 33 (obituary of Morris). *T* (16 June 2006), 68 (obituary of Beloff).

[11] See the complaints of Edward Knapp-Fisher, Archdeacon of Westminster Abbey, in *T* (1 Sept. 1980), 17.   [12] *G* (2 Aug. 1973), 1.

[13] As Archbishop Carey recommended in 1994, *T* (26 May 1994), 1.

[14] *TCBST* 655. *STel* (24 Dec. 2000), 6 (kneeling).

After 1970 two very different Christian responses to decline seemed promising: the other-worldly priorities involved in the churches' traditional preoccupation with personal conduct, and the this-worldly priorities involved in crusading on current issues. A firm limit to the first had earlier been set by growing secular expertise on moral issues,[15] and by the undignified confrontations resulting from such public crusades such as the 'Festival of Light' in 1971: processing traditionalists in morality merely provoked progressives into counter-demonstrations.[16] Besides, on moral issues, church hierarchies risked moving dangerously ahead of their congregations, especially given changing theological attitudes. Christians were now saying less about sin and redemption: indeed, in the 1990s it was Conservative politicians, not clergymen, who created a stir by branding rioters as 'wicked', and by emphasizing the 'choice: good or evil' that lay behind the spread of crime.[17] Changes in the hymn-book reflected the prolonged trend towards subordinating other-worldly to this-worldly concerns, with love for others ousting preoccupation with sin and therefore with salvation. Faith was increasingly seen as resulting from an act of will, and intellectually powerful defences of it were less frequently offered. Bishop Jenkins of Durham outraged Conservatives with his political views, and compounded this sin by urging the laity to dilute traditional Christian doctrine. He explained how theology had itself become secularized: by 1988 the virgin birth and the empty tomb had been questioned, and by 1993 hellfire was going the same way. In 2007 34 per cent believed in both hell and heaven, though only 1 per cent in hell without heaven.[18] Few theologians rejected Jenkins's ideas, but some wondered whether he was prudent to publicize them.

The lay public was slowly moving in the same direction. Survey evidence from 1989 showed that while belief in the devil, heaven, hell, and God had not significantly changed since 1968, disbelief in all these had grown quite markedly, thereby eroding the 'don't knows'; far fewer, too, were convinced after 1957 that Jesus was son of God. A survey of Catholic opinion in England and Wales in 1978 revealed marked divergence from the hierarchy on moral issues: a quarter did not believe in hell, and a seventh doubted the existence of heaven, life after death, and the devil. The declining Catholic birth-rate also demonstrated the limits to the hierarchy's impact on conduct. Furthermore, secular change reacted back on doctrine and liturgy.[19] Women's presence in the Church of England's General Synod House of Laity rose from a fifth to more

---

[15] Harrison, *Seeking a Role*, 343.   [16] Ibid. 519.

[17] See Tebbit's comments at the Conservative Party conference, *T* (8 Oct. 1985), 1; Waddington on the poll-tax riots, *G* (3 Apr. 1990), 4; J. Patten, 'There is a Choice: Good or Evil', *Spec.* (18 Apr. 1992), 9–10.

[18] *T* (4 Apr. 1988), 5. For hellfire see *Ind* (15 Dec. 1993), 3. *G* (15 Dec. 1993), 3. Representative telephone quota sample of 1,005 adults in Britain aged 16 and above, *T* (31 Oct. 2007), 9.

[19] *STel* (24 Dec. 1989), 4. *G* (29 Jan. 1980), 4. For birth-rate, see *BST* 97.

Fig. 5. *Times* (25 Sept. 1971).

than half between 1970 and 1990: it was inevitable not only that women would be ordained, as first occurred in 1994, but that the male God of power should acquire more of women's relatively humane outlook.[20] Likewise homosexual liberation encouraged recurrent notions, at first angrily rebutted, that Jesus had been a homosexual. Seeking in 1967 to explain why Jesus was celibate, Hugh Montefiore (subsequently Bishop of Birmingham) claimed that the homosexual explanation 'is one which we must not ignore'.[21] In such a difficult situation, the

---

[20] Davie, *Religion in Britain*, 119–20, 169.

[21] O. Chadwick, *Michael Ramsey: A Life* (Oxford, 1990), 140. D. Fernbach, 'Ten Years of Gay Liberation', *Politics and Power* (1980), 180. H. Montefiore, *Taking our Past into our Future* (1st publ. 1978, paperback edn.), 88.

Church of England, inclusive by instinct and tradition, benefited considerably from having as its leader Robert Runcie (Archbishop of Canterbury from 1980 to 1991), a man divided within himself by conservative instincts and liberal sympathies. Difficult to pin down on the ordination of women and homosexuals, he was once described as 'sitting on the fence with both ears to the ground'.[22]

In his radical and influential *The Sea of Faith* (1984) the Cambridge theologian Don Cupitt went so far as to abandon God 'as an objectively existing superperson'. In place of the theological concepts which now failed to carry conviction, he recommended a 'religion . . . wholly of this world, wholly human, wholly our own responsibility'; Christianity, he thought, should now be preoccupied with political activism and moral crusading.[23] This, the second political option for Christians, crystallized during the 1980s in the opposition to Thatcher, and drew heavily on the continuing alliance in Britain between church and state. The Church of England remained established, and its two archbishops and twenty-four of its bishops sat as of right in the House of Lords throughout the twentieth century. Although when Chief Rabbi Jakobovits became a peer in 1988 there were demands that a Catholic bishop should go there too,[24] the demands came to nothing, and there was no vigorous demand for disestablishment. This was partly because the Church of England retained the nominal allegiance of many non-churchgoers—accounting for well over half the UK's prison inmates in the 1970s and 1980s, for example. It was also by far the largest allegiance claimed within England, just as the Presbyterians predominated in Scotland and the Roman Catholics in the Irish Republic.[25] Anglican bishops, even when educated at independent schools and at Oxford or Cambridge,[26] saw themselves as representing their entire diocese. This, together with their background, bestowed the confidence and standing needed for prominence in public life. Bishop David Jenkins felt as much obligation in the 1980s to speak up for striking Durham miners as did Bishop David Sheppard for deprived Liverpudlians. The clergy were politically more radical than their congregations, and Conservative MPs often rebuked them for pronouncing too readily on public questions, too rarely on personal conduct.[27]

The Archbishop of Canterbury's commission on urban priority areas, *Faith in the City* (1985) highlighted the political option for Christians. Self-help was less prominent among its remedies for deep-rooted social problems than the statist benevolence that many of its witnesses favoured. It criticized inner-city

---

[22] Bishop of Leicester, quoted in George Austin's unsympathetic article in *O* (8 Sept. 1996), 25.
[23] W. Hopkinson, 'Changes in the Emphases of Evangelical Belief 1970–1980: Evidence from New Hymnody', *Churchman*, 95/2 (1981), 130–3. P. Badham (ed.), *Religion, State, and Society in Modern Britain* (Lewiston, 1989), 24–5. D. Cupitt, *The Sea of Faith: Christianity in Change* (1984), 270, 273.
[24] *STel* (3 Jan. 1988), 1.
[25] *BST* 553. See the useful table in R. Rose, *Governing without Consensus: An Irish Perspective* (1971), 61.   [26] S. Faulks, 'What Makes a Modern Bishop?', *STel* (8 July 1984), 11.
[27] See the survey results in *T* (10 Dec. 1984), 4; and see e.g. John Stokes in *T* (24 July 1981), 9.

churches and the training their clergy received, yet showed a touching faith in what these Anglican structures could achieve through ecumenical attitudes, through rationally deploying scarce religious resources, and through stirring the social conscience of busy middle-class suburban commuters. Yet the amateur's involvement in public questions within a society that valued expertise risked dividing congregations and neglecting the churches' own speciality: otherworldly concerns. Archbishop Runcie later recalled saying, in his enthronement sermon of 1980, that 'clergy, when it comes to social care, are amateur, anecdotal and generalised; whereas in social work people are professional, succinct and specific'. Likewise George Carey confessed, after retiring as Archbishop of Canterbury, that 'archbishops . . . are not expert in assessing the practical effects of different political or economic options'; government criticisms of the report had, he thought, been 'at least partly justified'.[28] Besides, such political ventures propagated a diluted faith hardly distinguishable from that of an unbeliever such as Kinnock, who claimed in 1991 that his faith 'is a social faith and the motive is to do everything I can to secure the advancement of humanity'; the political option risked secularizing 'religion' into merely 'doing good'.[29] The need to unite behind reform conveniently blurred Christians' potentially divisive theological and liturgical concerns, but also had the effect of obscuring what distinguished them from their (numerous) irreligious fellow campaigners. Of the many abortion-law-reform activists of the mid-1960s who had been brought up as Christians, for instance, three-quarters had lost their faith.[30] So the Conservatives who urged religious leaders to focus on promoting individual morality carried some weight with serious Anglican commentators like Edward Norman and Eric Mascall.[31]

Organized irreligion contributed almost nothing to the decline in UK organized religion. Whereas in the 1950s some expected a humanist alternative to advance as Christianity retired, twenty years later this seemed far less likely. The twentieth century did not match the resourcefulness and serious-minded efforts of the non-Christian Victorians—Owenites, phrenologists, positivists, theosophists, spiritualists, secularists—who devised alternatives to orthodox Christianity. Now that religion's artificial defences had so greatly weakened, the British Humanist Association showed few signs of growth: from the 1960s to the 1990s its (mainly English) membership hovered between two and three thousand.[32] The most serious threat to reason after 1970 came not from

---

[28] Quotations from H. Carpenter, *Robert Runcie: The Reluctant Archbishop* (1st publ. 1996, paperback edn. 1997), 164; *T* (15 Nov. 1996), 8.

[29] *DT* (30 July 1991), 3 (Kinnock). E. R. Norman, 'A Christmas Message No One Really Wants to Hear', *DT* (21 Dec. 1991), 16.   [30] K. Hindell and M. Simms, *Abortion Law Reformed* (1971), 120.

[31] For a fuller list see A. Hastings, *A History of English Christianity 1920–1985* (1986), 651.

[32] I am most grateful to its Executive Director, Hanne Stinson, for a valuable run of statistics provided on 15 Dec. 2005.

organized but from informal religion. Self-service was advancing not only in the shops, but in the supermarket of religious faiths. At just the moment when nonconformity entered rapid decline, its logical consequence—the individual's self-determined designer-faith, shaped to suit personal need—became increasingly feasible and acceptable. In the House of Lords debate of 18 January 1979 on unidentified flying objects, both reason (embodied in a determinedly rationalistic Lord Trefgarne) and guided unreason (embodied in an anxious Bishop of Norwich, Maurice Wood) were at one in their defensive mood when confronted by this newest of self-chosen faiths. Trefgarne was convinced that such sightings could usually be explained 'by logical scientific theory', and that the rest would become so 'if our knowledge were more advanced or if we had more information about the sightings'. As for the Bishop, he insisted that Christ has 'literally a galactic significance' and that 'all the far corners of the creative world, right out further than we can ever see or even know by radio, are within the plan of the Creator'; he feared the 'climate of credulity' and 'ersatz spirituality' developed in UFO groups, which drew their members 'into a sub-Christian, and . . . sometimes a non-Christian cult', obscuring 'basic Christian truths'.[33]

So-called 'new age' beliefs were gaining ground. Their adherents created their own mix of beliefs and practices from a wide range of ideas, often drawn from non-Christian cultures. Eclectic and mystical in belief, amorphous in structure and ideas, 'new age' enthusiasts owed much to the irruption in the 1960s of 'alternative' influences from oriental religions; they also fed upon the widening scepticism about natural science and its effects which from the 1950s fuelled green, animal liberation, fringe-medical, and anti-nuclear movements. They were by the 1980s advancing in the most affluent parts of the country, especially in south-eastern England, though they were tempted to migrate into remoter parts (Wales, the Lake District, and northern Scotland) where they felt they could more effectively commune with natural forces.[34] During the 1960s, when religion's share of books published in Britain was declining, titles on occultism doubled their proportion of religious titles, and till 1990 continued slowly to rise;[35] there were enough adherents to ensure that late twentieth-century bookshops created special shelves for 'new age' items. Closely associated was the movement for free festivals. The Glastonbury festival originated in 1970 as a free and counter-cultural event, somewhat mystical in tone, and usually annual; it attracted 10,000 in 1971, rising to 75,000 by the early 1990s.[36] The annual Stonehenge free festival was staged during the summer solstice from 1974, a focus for the 'new traveller' culture; ten years later it was attracting

[33] *HL Deb.* 18 Jan. 1979, cc. 1253 (Trefgarne), 1270–2 (Wood).

[34] S. Bruce, *Religion in Modern Britain* (Oxford, 1995), 114.   [35] *TCBST* 667.

[36] M. Clarke, *The Politics of Pop Festivals* (1982), 36, 81. www.netcomuk.co.uk/~drbob/glasto/ whatisglastonbury.html, consulted 6 Apr. 2005.

70,000 people. There was much concern in the 1980s about drugs, squatters, and public order, however, not to mention the security of Stonehenge, and in 1985 the police forcibly dispersed the festival. The Public Order Act (1986) temporarily ended the British free festival movement, though the authorities could not prevent the many illegal rave parties that sprang up during the 1980s in increasingly remote locations.[37] Like all religions, the 'new age' groups sought to make sense of the inexplicable, and flourished partly because so few people realized the likelihood of coincidence: people were surprised in 1995 when told, for instance, that in a random gathering of only twenty-three people, probability theory gave them a 50-50 chance that two would share the same birthday.[38] But 'new age' also owed much to the long-lasting influence of the sixties outlook: an open-minded eagerness for self-expression, novelty, and freedom, and a youthful impatience with formal and hierarchical structures.

Among the more articulated, building-based religious groupings in Britain after 1970, significant growth occurred only among those associated in some way with ethnic or regional loyalty; British membership of the Greek Orthodox Church grew threefold between 1950 and 2000, for instance. In 1985 membership of Christian churches in its share of the adult population was lowest in England, twice as high in Wales, almost three times as high in Scotland, and nearly seven times as high in Northern Ireland.[39] Of all the major churches in England and Wales, the Catholic Church had long welcomed immigrants, and had gained greatly from Irish migration to the UK. In the early 1980s a seventh of UK Catholics claimed pre-Reformation English origins, a tenth were English converts, a seventh second-generation Irish immigrants, a seventh immigrants from outside the British Isles (with Italy and Poland contributing most), and a tenth second-generation immigrants from outside the British Isles; the remaining third were from mixed backgrounds, but most with an Irish ancestry. Catholics also benefited from Britain's growing European connection; like Scottish Presbyterians and many English nonconformists, their European links were stronger than those of the English national church. So UK Roman Catholic membership fell more slowly than other large Christian groupings; indeed, during the 1970s Catholic members overtook Anglican in their share of the UK's adult population.[40] Huge crowds greeted Pope John Paul II at several places in spring 1982 during the only papal visit ever made to Britain; a huge meeting in Glasgow's Bellahouston Park attracted nearly half the Catholics in Scotland. In these years Roman Catholicism was after a long interval drawn back to the centre of British life, with Basil Hume presiding

---

[37] See www.efestivals.co.uk/festivals/stonehenge/2001/historyopinion.shtml, and http://news.bbc.co.uk/1/hi/entertainment/music/3662921.stm, both consulted 6 Apr. 2005.

[38] R. Matthews and S. Blackmore, 'Why are Coincidences so Impressive?', *Perceptual and Motor Skills*, 2 (June 1995), 1121–2.   [39] *TCBST* 655. Davie, ' "An Ordinary God" ', 399.

[40] Badham (ed.), *Religion, State, and Society*, 86. *TCBST* 655.

as a saintly and popular Cardinal Archbishop of Westminster from 1976 till his death in 1999. The trend owed something to the waning contrasts between the Catholic and Protestant churches. Intellectually and in other ways the late twentieth-century Catholic laity were gaining ground over the priesthood, whose numbers (together with those of Catholic nuns) were falling fast from the 1960s. Catholic membership fell by a third between 1970 and 2000—though Anglican, Presbyterian, and Methodist members declined even more. After the 1960s conversions and Catholic marriages fell away markedly, and attendance at mass became less regular.[41] Diminished UK hostility to Roman Catholicism owed more to growing religious indifference than to more positive sentiments.

Religion meant even more to 'New Commonwealth' immigrants than to their Irish, Italian, and Polish predecessors. Immigrants from the Caribbean, Africa, and South Asia were far more likely to say that religion mattered in their lives, to profess religious allegiance, and to attend religious services. So the Pentecostal Church, rare among Christian groupings in growing at all, grew faster than any other: more than fivefold between 1950 and 2000.[42] When Letty, the Malvern-born white middle-aged lady in Barbara Pym's *Quartet in Autumn* (1977), timidly asks her black hymn-singing fellow-tenants to make less noise as 'some of us find it rather disturbing', her landlord Mr.Olatunde replies that 'Christianity *is* disturbing'. Muslims were fervent enough in 1992 to succeed where Christians had failed, and to ensure that Jesus, for them a prophet, was removed as a rubber puppet from the television show *Spitting Image*.[43] Minarets had by then begun to diversify British urban skylines, and redundant nonconformist chapels were finding new religious uses. Already by the 1970s, for example, the Carey Memorial Hall in Leicester, commemorating the Baptist cobbler who from 1792 did more than anyone to establish Christian missionary work in India, had become a Sikh temple. The relativism in religion that had flourished on the frontiers of nineteenth-century Britain's empire now penetrated to the heart of the mother country; with the presence in late twentieth-century Britain of so many strongly held religious beliefs, relativist attitudes to religion inevitably spread among both Christians and (in the second generation and beyond) among non-Christians. The schools were in the front line, and had to cultivate an ecumenical mood with a reach far wider than anything envisaged by the Christian theorists of reunion, and with greater practical success. The alternative was too dangerous to contemplate. When the Ayatollah Khomeini's *fatwa* against Salman Rushdie for his *Satanic Verses* (1988) found support among British Muslims, the Education Secretary claimed

[41] *T* (2 Apr. 2005), 7 (Pope). *TCBST* 655. D. Sewell, *Catholics: Britain's Largest Minority* (2001), 149, 152.

[42] Modood and Berthoud (eds.), *Ethnic Minorities in Britain*, 356: Policy Studies Institute survey conducted in 1994 by questionnaire and sample. *TCBST* 655.

[43] B. Pym, *Quartet in Autumn* (1977), 65. *STel* (18 Oct. 1992), 1 ('Spitting Image')..

in 1989 that 'those who wish to make their home in Britain . . . cannot deny to others the very freedoms which drew them to this country in the first place'.[44]

Christianity's revival in Britain was often predicted but never occurred. The results of Archbishop Coggan's 'call to the nation' in October 1975 disappointed him.[45] Christian decline was in many ways liberating, but there were associated losses. Successor structures, often state-run and relatively impersonal, were less able to offer what the churches had provided: sympathetic counselling and a sense of belonging; recurrent reassuring, colourful ceremonial; and opportunities within small institutions for self-expression and self-realization. Still less could they bring the sense of security that springs from inner conviction: from a system of beliefs that claims to explain events otherwise apparently random and beyond human control.

2. CLASSROOM COUNTER-REVOLUTION

At first sight, British schools changed little between 1970 and 1990. The school year still had three terms with three long intervening breaks, the school week still usually had five days, and the school day still began at about nine and ended at about four. Children still normally began school when aged 5 and had to stay there full-time until the official leaving age. School attendance was, however, gradually extending at both ends. More and more children under 5 went to school full- or part-time: a fifth of 3- and 4-year-olds in 1970 and over half in 1992/3, with corresponding growth in the numbers cared for in registered playgroups or by child-minders. The number of children aged between 2 and 4 in UK schools doubled between 1976 and 1996.[46] At the top end of the school, 1973 saw the latest in the century's several extensions to the school-leaving age when the minimum was raised from 15 to 16. More teenagers were staying on voluntarily after that, and sixth-form colleges were created to encourage the trend. By the 1980s, however, indiscipline, truancy, and a higher priority for vocational training blunted enthusiasm for further raising the leaving-age, and even prompted calls for back-tracking.

Public expenditure on state education rose appreciably in real terms during the 1960s and 1970s, stabilized in the 1980s and then resumed rising in the 1990s; in its share of gross domestic product and of public expenditure, it rose until the mid-1970s and fell slowly thereafter. Pupil–teacher ratios in English state primary schools improved continuously after the early 1950s, a trend which (with help from demographic change) accelerated in the 1960s and

[44] K. Baker, G (2 Mar. 1989), 20.

[45] C. Longley, 'Why Archbishop's Call to the Nation Fell on Stony Ground', T (4 Jan. 1977), 12.

[46] Social Trends (1996), 71–2. Central Statistical Office, Annual Abstract of Statistics, 123 (1987), 90. Office for National Statistics, Annual Abstract of Statistics, 141 (2005), 68.

1970s; in English state secondary schools, improvement began only in the 1960s and was slower.[47] Schoolteachers in state schools increased by more than a fifth in the 1970s but fell by nearly a tenth between 1980/1 and 1994/5, whereas other West European countries cut less drastically, and so gained ground over the UK in pupil–teacher ratios.[48] Nonetheless, in English primary schools there had been one teacher for 31 pupils in 1951, rising to one for only 22 in 1990; equivalent figures for English secondary schools were 21 and 15. From such improvements major educational progress might have been predicted, but smaller classes do not alone explain the marked improvement in examination performance in the 1970s and 1980s:[49] the raised school-leaving age and changes in the examination structure also contributed much. In 1988 the Certificate of Secondary Education merged with O levels to form the single 'General Certificate of Secondary Education' (GCSE). By extending a continuous ladder of measured school achievement over a wider ability-range, incentives were maximized, and so with each generation throughout the century the proportion with no qualifications fell, while the proportion with O and A levels or their equivalents rose.[50]

The 1980s, however, highlighted two major worries. First, the boys seemed to be under-achieving: fewer girls than boys left with no qualifications, and the qualified girls raced ever further ahead of the qualified boys. Second, some feared that the improved examination results for both sexes reflected only reduced expectations, with pupils selecting easier subjects and being examined through easier methods (modules, coursework, and the like). These doubts were only the latest voiced by the growing number who questioned the inter-war liberal teaching methods that had been so influential until the 1970s. Already by 1970 British schools were witnessing a retreat from the progressives' wartime and post-war hopes. The independent schools survived intact, and were if anything more isolated from state schools than before. The technical schools had been in decline almost from the start: their 70,000 pupils of 1950 had dwindled to only 2,500 by 1985.[51] Numerically, the comprehensive school made great mid-century strides: whereas in Great Britain the secondary modern and grammar schools' share of state-sector pupils plunged in the 1970s, the comprehensive school was endorsed by governments of both parties and accounted for 86 per cent of all state pupils in England by 1990/1. Its supremacy was still greater in Wales and Scotland, whereas in Northern Ireland

[47] Paul Hamlyn Foundation, *Learning to Succeed: A Radical Look at Education Today* (1993), 369. *TCBST* 206.

[48] S. Szreter, 'British Economic Decline and Human Resources', in P. Clarke and C. Trebilcock (eds.), *Understanding Decline: Perceptions and Realities of British Economic Performance. Essays Presented to Barry Supple* (Cambridge, 1997), 98–9.

[49] For statistics see Dept. of Education and Science, *Education Statistics for the United Kingdom* (1992), pp. ix, 21.   [50] *TCBST* 209.

[51] Ibid. 210–12. Johnson (ed.), *Twentieth-Century Britain*, 378 (technical schools).

the selective schools remained far stronger than elsewhere.[52] However, many felt that the comprehensive school, as an inclusive neighbourhood school, merely reflected the tone of the surrounding community, whereas the meritocratic grammar school could offer a ladder out of it: it was organized to cater better for the really able child, whereas the comprehensive school never captured its mood of intellectual achievement, even when it 'streamed' its pupils by aptitude.

A frontal challenge to educational orthodoxy on both teaching structure and methods came from the five *Black Papers* on education—booklets of essays contributed by authors, several well-known, and all disillusioned with prevailing educational trends. The first four (published in 1969–70 and in 1975) were edited by Brian Cox and A. E. Dyson, the fifth (1977) by Cox and Rhodes Boyson. There was no necessary connection between comprehensive education and liberal approaches to discipline, but the case of Risinghill (opened in 1960 and closed amidst controversy in 1965) illustrates how the two often coincided. 'Children are not naturally good', the fourth *Black Paper* pronounced in 1975: 'they need firm, tactful discipline from parents and teachers with clear standards. Too much freedom for children breeds selfishness, vandalism and personal unhappiness.'[53] In teaching methods the *Black Papers* wanted discipline and instruction to oust the fashion for spontaneity and self-discovery: the state should revert to the grammar-school tradition of promoting equal opportunity, as against Labour's pursuit of equality through education-as-social-engineering, and parents should have more influence. The *Black Papers'* co-editors had founded the literary journal *Critical Quarterly* in 1959; neither was combative by temperament, neither could be labelled, even after 1969, as right-wing, and both had a grammar-school background. Dyson was a pioneer of homosexual law reform and a university lecturer in English. Cox, Professor of English Literature at Manchester University, had emerged from the sort of Methodist, leftish, and self-improving, working-class provincial background that helped to fuel Thatcherism. Of similarly competitive, nonconformist, but hitherto Labour-voting, respectable working-class background was the future Conservative minister Rhodes Boyson, headmaster of Highbury Grove (comprehensive) School until elected Conservative MP in 1974; as opposition spokesman on education from 1976 to 1979, he brought these ideas to the political forefront. This small group was shocked to encounter the fierce hostility mounted against them by the well-born, independent-school-educated exponents of the prevailing educational orthodoxies: Crosland, Brian Simon, and Shirley Williams.

---

[52] *TCBST* 199.
[53] The first of the ten 'black paper basics', which were published in the fourth black paper: *Black Paper 1975: The Fight for Education* (1975), 1.

The *Black Papers* captured a mood that spontaneously welled up from below. Cox tried to channel it into national politics on a non-party basis through the National Council for Educational Standards, founded in 1972. His observation of student unrest at Berkeley and teaching methods in the state school attended by his own children had led him to break with educational orthodoxies. 'We had broken a taboo', he later recalled, 'by asserting the commonsense proposition that some people are cleverer than others'—or as Kingsley Amis put it in 1960, in the context of educational expansion, 'more will mean worse'.[54] The parental complaints about liberal teaching attitudes came from all quarters: from inner-city blacks[55] but also from suburban middle-class whites. Employers were beginning to complain that young employees were innumerate and illiterate,[56] and the free-and-easy teaching methods at William Tyndale junior school in Islington hit the headlines in the mid-1970s. By then the Conservatives in Greater Manchester's Tameside local authority were embattled against Labour's policy of substituting comprehensive schools for the locality's five grammar schools. The 'troubles' in universities and polytechnics led some teachers there too to question educational trends, and turned some university staff politically rightwards; early among them was Caroline Cox (no relative), co-author in 1975 of *The Rape of Reason*, which recounted student unrest at North London Polytechnic, where she taught. With little short-term hope of capturing education's professional organizations and trade unions, the challenge to educational orthodoxies eventually fuelled a right-wing network of interlocking pressure groups and pamphleteers which interacted with the Conservative Party's CPS, and (viewed retrospectively) prepared the ground for the Education Reform Act of 1988.[57]

Educational worries were not confined to the right. International comparisons of numbers continuing into the sixth form[58] and university disconcerted those who knew that Britain must live off its wits, nor did school syllabuses seem adequately to encourage science and technology. Such comparisons fuelled pressure for educational reform well beyond 1990. Despite playing so prominent a role in creating comprehensive schools in the 1950s and 1960s, the middle classes in the 1970s were steadily opting out of them. It was, said Boyson, 'one of the most deplorable, selfish betrayals in British social

---

[54] A. Hopkins, 'Meet the Man in Black', *ST* (27 Mar. 1977), 37. Amis, 'Lone Voices', *Encounter* (July 1960), 8–9.
[55] See e.g. Scarman, *Brixton Disorders*, 26, 166, and cf. Bernie Grant on his children's inner-city London school experience, *Ind* (25 Jan. 1996), 2.
[56] M. Wilkinson, *Lessons from Europe: A Comparison of British and West European Schooling* (1977), 4; cf. the Prince of Wales's complaints about his employees, *T* (29 June 1989), 1.
[57] For a good discussion see P. Wilby and S. Midgley, 'As the New Right Wields its Power', *Ind* (23 July 1987), 11.
[58] As the Public Schools Commission pointed out in 1970, see J. S. Maclure (ed.), *Educational Documents: England and Wales. 1816 to the Present Day* (3rd edn. 1973), 344–5.

history'. Public discussion began with the so-called 'great debate' on education which Callaghan launched with his speech in Oxford on 18 October 1976. Anticipating many subsequent reforms, he argued for a core curriculum of basic knowledge, and for better ways of monitoring standards (especially on literacy and numeracy) and allocating educational expenditure; he did not think teachers the sole experts on such matters.[59] Eight one-day regional conferences followed, each attended by about 200 parents, educationists, and industrialists; though unable to agree on the core curriculum's content, they broadened significant educational discussion beyond the interested parties.[60] When in the same year the government withdrew funding from direct-grant schools, it achieved the reverse of its objective: Manchester Grammar School declared itself independent, and by 1988 the former direct-grant schools contributed more than 70 of the Headmasters' Conference (HMC)'s 228 independent schools. The Conservatives were already from the mid-1970s planning to bypass Labour's strategy by evolving an 'assisted places scheme' which would admit poor but promising children to selective education at independent schools.[61]

Callaghan's government could not push educational reform fully home because soon beset by major troubles on several other fronts, and Thatcher's initial priority concerned economic management and the trade unions, not education. But with schools as with local government, the need to cut government expenditure eventually prompted in the 1980s more fundamental probings of policy; these involved mobilizing parents and central government against the teachers' unions and local authorities. The government began in 1979 by ceasing to comprehensivize grammar schools, and when Keith Joseph became Secretary of State for Education in 1981 he brought to a relatively low-status cabinet post all the creative capacity for thinking the unthinkable that he had earlier brought to his party's strategy and economic policy. On arrival he circulated only one item to his civil servants, the CPS booklet *Lessons from Europe* by the educational journalist Max Wilkinson; it outlined many of the new directions British educational policy soon took. By the 1980s international comparisons had convinced many diverse but influential people that the entire educational system in Britain had been unduly moulded by the humanistic and even anti-vocational traditions of grammar schools, independent schools, Oxford, and Cambridge. Attention focused on the many obstacles to British educational and vocational opportunity: on the many low-achievers in British

---

[59] Boyson to the conference of the Council for the Preservation of Educational Standards at Cambridge on 2 Jan. 1972, *T* (3 Jan. 1972), 3. Callaghan, *T* (19 Oct. 1976), 1.

[60] T. Devlin, 'At Last Education is Coming Out of the Classroom and into Society', *T* (11 Apr. 1977), 6. D. Tytler, 'Lord Callaghan's Curriculum', *T* (14 Oct. 1991), 26.

[61] G. Walford, *Privatization and Privilege in Education* (1990), 6. J. Rae, *The Public School Revolution: Britain's Independent Schools. 1964–1979* (1981), 178.

schools, on the educational system's undervaluing of practical and vocational skills, on the early specialization which closed off too many options, and on the pupils' relative eagerness to leave school at 16.

Wilkinson favoured shifting the curricular balance from theoretical towards practical or vocational studies, thereby narrowing the gap between the parents' desire to equip their children for work and the teachers' desire to develop 'creative, personal and moral qualities'. For so cerebral a politician, Joseph's concern for the non-academic child was surprising but salutary. Central to his concerns was the 'sink' class 5K in Nigel Williams's play *Class Enemy*: 'I think, frankly, that you'd be better off in the streets don't you?', the master tells them.[62] Joseph was working with the grain, given that the MSC in its concern about rising unemployment in the late 1970s had become increasingly preoccupied with education for work. The Departments of Employment and Education were moving closer together: the pilot schemes of the Technical and Vocational Education Initiative (TVEI) began in 1983, and gave local authorities financial incentives to foster vocational studies for teenagers in their schools. The scheme expanded so fast that by 1987 every school could apply to join. The National Council for Vocational Qualifications, set up in 1986, established a system of national vocational qualifications (NVQs) which, through simplifying and rationalizing existing arrangements, made them more popular. By 1994 the 500 NVQs covered 150 occupations, representing 80 per cent of all jobs.[63]

Joseph's educational initiatives identified a new 'common ground' where challenging old orthodoxies could win new recruits for Conservatism. All this required an enhanced influence in national education for central government which was familiar enough in Europe but absent in Britain. Joseph's questioning approach pushed education politically to the fore. The exhausting work entailed and the furious hostility he evoked from the teachers' unions led him to retire in 1986. Yet this innovative minister was John the Baptist for his successor, Kenneth Baker, for whose Education Reform Act (1988) Joseph had prepared the ground. The Act eroded local authority power from two directions: through introducing the national curriculum and devolving financial management to school governors. Wielding populism and publicity as its weapons, the government undermined sixties ideas at the Department of Education and Science, together with the close influence there of the local authorities and teachers' unions. Education's consumers gained over its producers in the pattern of simultaneous centralization and devolution so often replicated among Thatcher government reforms. It was the intermediate bodies—interest groups and local authorities—that lost influence, and in 1988 the Inner London

---

[62] Wilkinson, *Lessons from Europe*, 10. Williams, *Class Enemy*, 39.
[63] www.qca.org.uk/610_1807.html, consulted 18 Dec. 2005.

Education Authority was disbanded. Information on educational attainment now became available in unprecedented abundance. The results were not so very surprising: schools in the relatively affluent outer suburbs did best, truancy and performance were at their worst in the inner cities.[64] The league tables were often blunt instruments crudely deployed, but this was an argument for refining them, not for secrecy: parental and national decisions could now become more soundly based.

One reforming route which some Conservatives had favoured since the early 1960s was not taken: the enfranchisement of the parent as educational consumer. In his independent-minded *Education and the State* (1965), which went into two further editions, Edwin West showed how extensively Victorian parents had funded voluntary schools before the state intervened to 'fill the gaps' after 1870. Interpreting education history from what was then an entirely unfamiliar and unfashionable perspective, West argued that mid-Victorian parents had been better informed on their children's needs, and better qualified to get those needs met, than the self-consciously professional teachers and administrators who later took control. An entirely voluntary system after 1870 could, he argued, have been cheaper, more efficient, and better for economic growth. He wanted the educational market restored through equipping parents with educational vouchers for use in any state or independent school. The IEA took up the cause, but unsuccessfully, partly because the Thatcher governments had more urgent business, partly because there was insufficient public pressure to push through an inevitably complex and controversial reform, partly because Joseph as Secretary of State for Education failed to back it;[65] on this issue the politicians lacked the leverage to outmanœuvre unsympathetic civil servants and professional interests.

Nonetheless, educational enterprise kept breaking through all the obstacles, colonizing the worlds of nursery school, crammer, language school, and secretarial college. Integral to the classroom counter-revolution of the 1970s and 1980s was the independent schools' revived self-confidence. From 1970 to 1987 their share of full-time primary- and secondary-school children in England and Wales remained steady at about half a million (6 per cent of the whole), thus arresting decades of decline. They gained much from the state school's difficulties, most notably from allegations about its falling standards and from much-publicized disputes between government and the schoolteachers' unions.[66] At the prep-school level, the year 1981 saw a marriage between the Incorporated Association of Preparatory Schools (IAPS), hitherto representing

[64] *FT* (19 Nov. 1992), 9. *DT* (17 Nov. 1993), 1.

[65] See West's 'Parents' Choice in Education' in the IEA's *Rebirth of Britain: A Symposium of Essays by Eighteen Writers* (1964), 170–85. For West's obituary see *DT* (16 Oct. 2001), 25. Denham and Garnett, *Joseph*, 369–73, 421.   [66] e.g. in 1985–6, *FT* (30 Apr. 1986), 9. *T* (29 Apr. 1987), 3.

only boys' and coeducational schools, and the Association of Headmistresses of Preparatory Schools (founded in 1929), which endowed the union with its 120 schools, bringing the IAPS total to 548. With an average of one teacher to 11.6 pupils, the Association's thirteen districts by 1990 covered the whole of the UK and the Irish Republic. Each school had on average fewer than 200 pupils, about a fifth of them full boarders. The preparatory departments of the independent boys' secondary schools were larger. About 8 per cent of their pupils were under 10, whereas 22 per cent was the equivalent figure for the schools represented by the Girls' Schools Association, then the female equivalent of the HMC, with a pedigree going back to 1874.[67]

Among the growing number of children who after 1951 stayed on at both state and independent schools beyond 16 (the school-leaving age from 1973), the independent-school share was much larger, and between 1970 and 1987 rose from 11 per cent to 19 per cent.[68] Shedding much of their philistinism and anti-intellectualism, the independent schools were becoming meritocratic parent-driven engines: pupils were now expected to pass the examinations that had become the gateways to career success. The pursuit of vocationally relevant merit entailed other significant changes. The close study of classical texts which had once brought glory to independent-school sixth forms went into decline, while earlier discouragements to the natural sciences were eroded. Many companies had contributed to the Industrial Fund for this purpose, and by 1980 over half the boys from independent schools attending university were studying science, engineering, or medicine.[69] Although there was a striking decline from the 1960s to the 1980s in the proportion of independent-school teaching staff drawn from Oxford and Cambridge, the schools' advantage in pupil–teacher ratio was considerable: in UK state secondary schools there were 18 pupils per teacher in 1970/1, 15 in 1990/1; in independent schools, there were 14 and 11, respectively.[70] The independent schools' sixth forms between 1961 and 1981 were leaping ahead in A-level success: in 1961 3 per cent of state-school pupils left with three or more A-levels, 7 per cent in 1981; the equivalent figures for independent and direct-grant schools were 20 and 45 per cent. Educational inequality increasingly stemmed less from differential access to a sixth form than from differential examination performance when there. In 1987 universities drew about a quarter of their first-degree students from independent schools, while Oxford and Cambridge drew about half.[71]

---

[67] *Independent Schools Yearbook 1990* (1990), 562. Walford, *Privatization and Privilege*, 9–10.
[68] Walford, *Privatization and Privilege*, 16–17.
[69] Sanderson in Johnson (ed.), *Twentieth Century Britain*, 386.
[70] G. Walford, *Life in Public Schools* (1986), 88. *Social Trends* (1996), 72.
[71] A. H. Halsey *et al.*, 'The Political Arithmetic of Public Schools', in G. Walford (ed.), *British Public Schools: Policy and Practice* (1984), 26. Walford, *Privatization and Privilege*, 1.

'We find public school boys settle in far more quickly than your average prisoner', a prison officer told Jeffrey Archer, imprisoned at Belmarsh high-security prison in 2001.[72] The officer did not realize that boys' independent schools had by then become much less intimidating. In their quest for merit and funds they had begun admitting girls, much to the alarm of the independent girls' schools, who feared losing their best talent. It is not feminism, but the combination of rising demand and willing supply that explains the change, which worked with the grain of parents' and pupils' wishes. Havelock Ellis had long ago seen coeducation as discouraging homosexuality, and in their social life teenagers of both sexes were by the 1960s mixing much more freely. Such influences also enhanced the slow long-term decline in boarders' share of independent-school pupils in England between the 1940s and the 1990s: down from 131,000 in 1975/6 to 94,000 in 1992/3.[73] In 1975 there were about seventy girls' boarding schools, about five of them closing each year. The number of girls in IAPS schools (hitherto single-sex male) rose more than threefold between 1971 and 1978, and among secondary schools Marlborough set the pace for mixed boarding schools when it admitted fifteen female pupils in 1968.[74] Between 1974 and 1984 girls' share of HMC pupils rose from 3 per cent to 12 per cent, and by the mid-1980s more than half these schools admitted girls, either throughout the school or within the sixth form. HMC schools, whether mixed or single-sex, were also appointing more women teachers, especially to posts in art and music: fifteen times as many in 1984 as in 1966. The independent schools' combination of good housekeeping and responsiveness to spontaneous demand also explains their growing overseas intake, 5 per cent of the total by 1977. Another windfall was political in origin: cuts in funding during the 1980s led Local Education Authorities (LEAs) to close many of their boarding schools. Their pupils had included many children whose boarding-school education was funded by the government allowance to service personnel, whether stationed at home or abroad; so nearly 6,000 children transferred to independent schools between 1982 and 1988.[75]

Labour's failed grappling with the independent schools in 1964–70 discouraged further attempts in the 1970s, if only because the public were not aroused on the issue. Asked by Gallup in 1967, 1968, and 1973 whether they approved of independent schools or wanted them abolished, the samples in all three years approved of such schools by large majorities, and when asked in 1968 whether

---

[72] J. Archer, *A Prison Diary by FF8282* (2002), 65.

[73] H. Ellis, *Studies in the Psychology of Sex*, ii. *Sexual Inversion* (1st publ. 1897, 2nd edn. Philadelphia, 1908), 194. *Social Trends* (1995), 50.

[74] R. Lambert, *The Chance of a Lifetime? A Study of Boys' and Coeducational Boarding Schools in England and Wales* (1975), 290. Rae, *Public School Revolution*, 150. For Marlborough see *T* (10 Sept. 1968), 3.

[75] Walford, *Life in Public Schools*, 142, 166–7, 181 (women). *T* (2 Oct. 1978), 3 (overseas intake). Walford, *Privatization and Privilege*, 75–6 (service personnel).

they would like to see entry to them eased for poorer children, 70 per cent said yes.[76] Nonetheless, apprehension about the next Labour government's policy prompted the establishment in 1972 of the Independent Schools Information Service (ISIS), a lobbying organization, and from 1973 the independent schools as a collectivity replaced their misleading prefix 'public' by the more accurate and seductive 'independent'.[77] Amalgamation and cooperation were very much the independent schools' mood after the 1960s, when the prep schools mobilized themselves. By 1990 ISIS represented four-fifths of independent-school pupils, though only about half of their schools, the remainder being mostly small and for the very young. In its manifestos of 1974 Labour promised to remove charitable status from independent schools 'as a first step towards our long-term aim of phasing out fee paying in schools',[78] but the independent schools' vitality no doubt helped to bury the commitment. ISIS cultivated media contacts, and two public schools became the subject of BBC documentary programmes: Westminster (1979), attracting twelve million viewers, and Radley (1980).

In 1980 the 'assisted places scheme' was introduced, designed to bridge the divide between state and independent sectors by subsidizing for independent-school places the children of parents unable to pay the fees. Subsidy was paid on a sliding scale according to parental income. In its first year (1982) 4,700 benefited under the scheme, and more than six times as many in 1990.[79] Of the 430,000 children at independent schools surveyed in 1987, the fees of almost a fifth were in some way subsidized, including the 25,000 then being assisted by the scheme;[80] the largest number of subsidized pupils in ISIS schools received their subsidy from the school—nearly 40,000 of them in 1982, rising to 57,000 in 1988. For the general election of 1983 ISIS set up more than a hundred action committees in constituencies throughout the country, and at the general election of 1987 it published a full-page advertisement headed 'warning: in 8 days you could lose the freedom to choose your child's education'.[81] After the Conservatives' third consecutive election victory the independent schools thought their charitable status for the time being secure: social engineering through state education had fallen out of fashion.

---

[76] *Gallup International Public Opinion Polls*, ii. 918, 1006, 1270; for admission of poor children, see 1006.

[77] Sampson, *Changing Anatomy of Britain*, 121. The phrase 'public school' was abandoned altogether by the Headmasters' Conference in 1985, according to *T* (25 Sept. 1985), 2, as conveying 'unwelcome and undeserved overtones of social exclusivity'.

[78] Walford, *Privatization and Privilege*, 10–12. Dale (ed.), *Labour Manifestos*, 205 (Oct. 1974). Also ibid. 190 (Feb. 1974).

[79] My discussion of the Assisted Places Scheme benefits from generous help given in August 2006 by Mr Sam Freedman, Head of Research, Independent Schools Council.

[80] *T* (29 Apr. 1987), 3. For the scheme's origins see Letwin, *Thatcherism*, 240–1.

[81] Walford, *Privatization and Privilege*, 75. *T* (26 May 1986), 1 (1983 election). *T* (3 June 1987), 11.

3. UNIVERSITY GROWING PAINS

After 1970 demand within the British educational system continued to push up spontaneously from below: larger sixth forms and a later school-leaving age meant more university applicants. Unlike the decades before and after, the 1970s and 1980s saw no burst of new universities, but existing universities grew considerably. University student numbers under 21 in Great Britain rose from an eighth of their age-group in 1970/1 to a fifth in 1990/1. The student body's composition was changing. Of first-degree students in UK universities 13 per cent were part-time in 1970/1, 20 per cent in the universities of Great Britain in 1990/1, and in the same period the women's share of the full-timers in higher education went up from 40 to 46 per cent; their advance into full-time higher education was one of Britain's untrumpeted post-war educational success stories, and in both years they were more likely than men to be full-timers. About two-fifths of the full-timers in both years went to universities, the rest to other institutions of higher education.[82] On the ground, universities grew like airports—by accretion in response to short-term and often unexpected developments. However distinguished the individual buildings, the university area tended to grow shapelessly, and universities on their fringes accumulated student accommodation which all too often blighted the locality: for their occupants the fate of the global environment mattered more than the state of the front lawn.

Older people were entering university in ever larger numbers, and in 1990 there were for the first time more mature students than 18-year-olds. The Open University catered especially for mature students, and by 1980 had registered 61,000 students for its first-degree courses. Already by 1973 its part-time students outnumbered London University's full-time students, and by 1991 it was attracting nearly two-thirds of all the UK's part-time university students.[83] In its first four years, applicants' chosen options split roughly equally between arts, social science, and maths/science/technology.[84] During its first twenty years the housewives' contribution to the University's applicants rose slowly from a tenth to a sixth, teachers and lecturers fell from a third to a twentieth, the arts and professions consistently contributed about an eighth, 'technical personnel' consistently about a tenth.[85] In its early years the University's applicants were high in their share of population in south-eastern England and Northern Ireland, and low everywhere else; the typical applicant was 'a man, in his thirties, in a white-collar job; although he is now apparently middle-class,

---

[82] *TCBST* 228–30.
[83] *T* (19 Aug. 1992), 14 (1990). W. A. C. Stewart, *Higher Education in Postwar Britain* (1989), 283 (1980). Tunstall (ed.), *Open University Opens* (1973), p. ix. For 1991 see DES, *Education Statistics for the United Kingdom 1991* (1992), p. viii. [84] Tunstall (ed.), *Open University Opens*, 49.
[85] Registrar's statistics kindly provided to the author in 1999.

his parents were probably working-class and he himself may well still call himself working-class'.[86] The regular application of the phrase 'university of the air' to the Open University in its early years was misleading: central to the student's effort was home-based study under a tutor's guidance. The demands on a student's family were considerable: without family support 'it is hopeless', said its Chancellor, Gerald Gardiner, himself a student, in 1974.[87] Because its study was home-based, the University gave the disabled a new opportunity, and raised the status of study in the area. Its first course on 'disability', however, launched in 1975, allegedly catering 'for the shoe-bound, aurally conversant and visually informed student with ability', was criticized by the disabled themselves, and had to be reshaped in 1980–2. Given that home-based students required relatively few staff and minimal investment in accommodation or teaching facilities, unit costs were far lower than in other universities.[88]

Students were diversifying in yet another significant way. The growing number of first-degree students pushed up the demand for postgraduate degrees; the number awarded almost quadrupled in the 1960s, and though such a rate of increase could not continue, there were still nine times as many postgraduates in 1980/1 as forty years earlier. Their number rose by more than a sixth between 1970/1 and 1990/1, an increase which almost exactly matched the growing number of women postgraduates, whose share of the total rose from 25 to 42 per cent.[89] To manage this vast bulk of teaching and research, British full-time university staff quadrupled during the 1960s and 1970s, and by the late 1980s Britain's university teachers outnumbered the university students before 1914. British universities were getting larger: fourteen by 1981/2 catered for more than 6,000 students, whereas between the wars none had been so big.[90] These clusters of brain-workers boosted their localities' economic, political, and cultural vitality. Their growing cultural prominence was ironically acknowledged with the university novel's notable late twentieth-century revival as a literary form, as well as with the launch in 1971 of a new weekly, the *Times Higher Education Supplement*. In staffing alone, UK higher education employed 317,700 people full-time by the mid-1990s, nearly half of them teaching and researching.[91]

Why, then, was gloom the university mood? Amis's 'more will mean worse' outlook had not vanished even from university circles. There were structural

[86] Naomi McIntosh, Head of the Survey Research Dept., quoted in Tunstall (ed.), *Open University Opens*, 54; cf. 48.   [87] *HL Deb.* 23 May 1974, c. 1617.

[88] V. Finkelstein, 'Emancipating Disability Studies', in Shakespeare (ed.), *Disability Reader*, 39. For figures, see Gardiner, *HL Deb.* 23 May 1974, c. 1618.

[89] R. Simpson, *How the Ph.D. Came to Britain: A Century of Struggle for Postgraduate Education* (Guildford, 1983), 165. *TCBST* 228–9.

[90] *BST* 282–3. *Higher Education in Postwar Britain*, 275.

[91] For a useful breakdown see table 3.1 in National Committee of Inquiry into Higher Education, *Higher Education in the Learning Society: Main Report* (1997), 29.

reasons why university examination results lent credibility to such ideas. Readier access to educational statistics led each university to compare the proportion of 'good' degrees awarded between its academic subjects, as well as to compare such proportions with those of other universities. Now increasingly viewed as a single system, UK universities tended when classifying degrees awarded to think comparatively and in terms of proportions, rather than of absolutes—and this for the best of reasons: from concern for fairness to their pupils. So what Americans called 'grade creep' gradually occurred. Expansion was accompanied by cuts in government funding, and eventually by early moves towards replacing student grants by student loans. There were also many problems of adjustment. Staff recruitment on the scale of the 1960s had somewhat lowered the profession's standard of entry, and later denied posts to much younger and often abler talent; traditional career-patterns, customary pecking orders, pay relativities, and established practices were vulnerable, and there were growing doubts in both political parties about university expansion. The Wilson governments had scarcely advertised the virtues of intellectuals in government or the practical value of the social sciences, and in the 1960s the relationship between universities and a prosperous economy was shown to be at best indirect. Labour's dream of drawing working-class children into universities was disappointed. More university students did come from working-class origins, but in the universities, as so often elsewhere, it was the middle classes who gained most from public funding. Hence the effectiveness in 1986 of student pressure on Barclays Bank to sell off its South African interests: no bank could let rivals poach potentially high-earning customers.[92]

Conservatives, too, were disappointed. This was partly because of student radicals' damage to the universities' image. Between the late 1960s and late 1980s the British student seemed to the ordinary taxpayer amply leisured, to judge from the almost continuous student protests on behalf of impossible causes—all the more provocative because spiced by such frequent moralistic bitings of the hand that fed. The angry style of student politics was imported from abroad, and only ever reflected the ephemeral views of a small minority. Students' political influence was hampered still further by recurrent in-fighting, but the minority was highly visible, if only because often so unconventionally dressed. Late-night parties in Norwich, 'principled' thefts of Marxist texts from Oxford bookshops, riots at Cambridge, shoutings down of opponents at many a political meeting—such episodes deterred private fund-raising and made it easier for politicians to withhold public funds. One dimension of the Conservative reaction in the 1970s was memorably captured in Malcolm Bradbury's novel *The History Man* (1975), with its sinister image of Kirk, the

---

[92] See table 7.16 in *BST* 293. M. Linton, 'The Issue that Got the Bank on the Run', *G* (25 Nov. 1986), 25.

left-wing university teacher who wields his power to destroy the careers of pupils who disagree.

Given all this, and given the persistence of high unemployment, ministers' priorities in the 1980s understandably shifted from the educational needs of the clever child to those of the school-leaver with no hope of entering university, but also to the need for closer interaction between educational institutions, industry, and commerce. It also became increasingly clear in the 1980s that British higher education was by international standards relatively expensive. Almost by accident during the 1950s the Oxbridge residential model had been extended to the entire British university system, with central government grants to match, whereas British universities had earlier been largely local in their inspiration, funding, and recruitment. Although universities in Scotland and Northern Ireland recruited a high proportion of their students locally between 1977 and 1983, in southern England only a fifth of those opting for higher education chose their local university, so that English students predominated in Welsh universities, and the overall tendency to seek higher education well away from home was increasing.[93] Universities were in effect now gathering their talent nationally rather than locally.

By the 1980s taxpayers in Britain as elsewhere wanted to combine lower taxes with better university facilities and access. Hence the quest for flexibility: the attack on the dominance of the single-subject degree, and on the many obstacles to moving between layers of higher education and between universities. Even before the 'student revolt' of the late 1960s, politicians felt a growing need to monitor mounting taxpayer subsidies to universities, and their autonomy was slowly and unobtrusively undermined. The new free-market style of Conservative had two further motives in the 1980s for scrutinizing university finances closely: a desire to cut government spending overall, and a distaste for the 'anti-enterprise climate' prevailing within an educational system allegedly 'divorced from industrial understanding'.[94] Hence the gradual move to substitute student loans for Britain's unique system of means-tested state grants. The reform was at first strongly and successfully resisted by the NUS as well as by Conservative backbenchers responding in 1984 to middle-class parental pressure.[95] But gradually the 1980s saw the counter-argument winning through: that the present system required the less privileged to subsidize the more—and on a growing scale, given the growing intake. A loans-based strategy, which in 1980 had seemed politically impracticable, was by the early 1990s moving up the politician's agenda. In addition, universities were encouraged to follow the American university model and diversify their funding, attracting more from

---

[93] Coleman and Salt, *British Population*, 409. See also the useful table 3.2 in A. H. Birch, *Political Integration and Disintegration in the British Isles* (1977), 37. See also Harrison, *Seeking a Role*, 360.

[94] Keith Joseph, speech at Conservative Party conference on 6 Oct. 1976, *T* (7 Oct. 1976), 4.

[95] *HC Deb.* 4 Dec. 1984, written answers cc. 90–2; 5 Dec. 1984, cc. 360–81. *T* (5 Dec. 1984), 4.

alumni, from industrial sponsorship, and from closer links with the nearby community. In Bradbury's novella *Cuts* (1987) the Vice-Chancellor, recently knighted at Thatcher's behest, encourages 'sponsored tutorials' in which lecturers discuss the poems of Catullus or mathematical equations 'wearing teeshirts and little caps that said on them "Boots" or "Babycham" ' '.[96]

All this shaped university teachers' political alignment. The academic professionalism that seemed to demand state-funded salaries, together with expensive libraries and equipment, from the 1940s converted university teachers in effect into government employees, and this was the section of the middle class most prone from the 1960s to align with Labour. Universities profited from the state's advance after 1945 but suffered from its retreat after 1979. Parliamentary grants contributed 73 per cent to the income of Great Britain's universities in 1969/70, falling quite sharply to 38 per cent in 1990/1, with a counterbalancing rise in income from fees and research grants, but little advance in donations and endowments.[97] Boosting the last of these was on Thatcher's uncompleted agenda. She had opened the privately funded University College of Buckingham in 1976, and subsequently ensured that it became eligible for LEA mandatory grants; a royal charter granted in 1983 enabled it to award its own degrees and restyle itself the University of Buckingham, the sole British university founded between 1970 and 1991. Universities adjusted only slowly to the new political situation, and in 1985 Oxford University, self-styled champion of its less affluent sister universities, rejected Thatcher for an honorary degree.[98] On the other hand, the cuts provoked much rethinking of traditional university practices—so much so, that the chairman of the Committee of Vice-Chancellors and Principals told a press conference that the past six years' cuts had provided academic life with 'an enormous kick up the pants'.[99]

There were significant changes and sex contrasts in the balance of subjects studied at first-degree level. In 1950/1, 37 per cent of men at British universities had studied for arts degrees, which then included the social sciences; the latter's rapid growth in the 1960s marked a shift within the arts category, whose overall hold on men remained the same in UK universities in 1981/2. Between these years the male take-up of pure-science degrees moved up only slowly, from 21 to 26 per cent, technology rose fast from 16 to 24 per cent, and medicine fell from 21 to 11 per cent. The universities' massive expansion did not boost the natural sciences as much as had been hoped, let alone the applied sciences most directly relevant to industry. The mounting number of women in universities accentuated the problem, given that the separation of spheres influenced their choice of university subject. Women were far keener on arts degrees (again

[96] M. Bradbury, *Cuts* (1987), 40.   [97] *TCBST* 246–7.
[98] On which see Harrison, 'Mrs Thatcher and the Intellectuals', *TCBH* 5/2 (1994), 238–44.
[99] *STel* (21 June 1987), 6.

including social science), but as with men there was little change over time: such courses attracted 63 per cent of women at British universities in 1950/1 and 62 per cent in 1981/2; likewise pure science moved only modestly upwards from 17 per cent to 19 per cent. The sex contrasts lay in medicine, whose share for women fell less sharply than for men (from 17 per cent to 12 per cent) and in technology, where women's advance was minimal (from 1 per cent to 4 per cent); technological subjects remained a male province throughout the period.[100] Not till the late 1970s did a combination of stick and carrot begin to push enrolment towards the natural sciences, and even towards the applied sciences.[101]

In comparison with nine other leading industrial nations in 1973, UK government expenditure on research and development, expressed as a share of gross domestic product, was strong. The UK's proportion of such funding devoted to big technology (most notably defence, nuclear energy, civil aviation, and advanced electronics) was higher in 1975 than for any other country except the USA; yet to the ten countries' total industry-funded research and development, the UK in 1967 and 1975 contributed only 10 and 7 per cent, respectively—less than West Germany and Japan, and far less than the USA's 50 and 43 per cent.[102] Huge British government investment went on the aircraft industry, whose collaboration with the French on Concorde was a commercial failure. The UK's substantial investment of the 1950s in nuclear power contributed little to exports, and relatively little British research went on applied industrial technology, yet it was in engineering, vehicles, and chemicals that Britain's rivals were growing fastest.[103]

The pressure within universities during the 1980s at least to complement the theoretical with the practical, the 'pure' with the 'applied', became strong indeed. It was a climate which, for example, enabled Robert Pennington with his key publications to turn company law 'into a mainstream scholarly subject' as Professor of Commercial Law at Birmingham from 1968 to 1994.[104] But vocational pressures were felt most strongly in natural science. The applied sciences contributed just over a quarter of the UK's postgraduates in the 1960s and 1970s, a smaller proportion than between the wars, and there was much discussion in the 1960s and 1970s about the relatively low status of engineering in Britain. It culminated in the Finniston report of 1980: engineering was often viewed as a subordinate branch of natural science, the report complained, 'rather than as a culture and activity in its own right'.[105] Engineers, less

---

[100] *TCBST* 236–7.   [101] See e.g. Rhodes Boyson in *DT* (22 Aug. 1979), 1.

[102] P. Gummett, *Scientists in Whitehall* (Manchester, 1980), 58.

[103] T. Kelly, *The British Computer Industry* (1987), 105–6. M. W. Kirby, 'The Economic Record since 1945', in T. Gourvish and A. O'Day (eds.), *Britain since 1945* (1991), 22–3.

[104] Obituary in *T* (14 Mar. 2008), 78.

[105] Simpson, *How the Ph.D. Came to Britain*, 166. M. Finniston (Chairman), *Engineering our Future* (1980), 41, cf. 25.

prominent than other professional groups in top management, especially by international standards, were less likely to become role models for the young. Whereas in several European countries engineers were trained in specialist institutions with more prestige than universities, in Britain they were taught in universities with a theoretical emphasis. Seen from this perspective, the absorption of the Colleges of Advanced Technology into the British university system in the 1960s did not necessarily advance technology's role in British manufacturing.[106] On the other hand, North Sea gas and oil exploration and development had huge implications for research in engineering, metallurgy, hydraulics, meteorology, oceanography, geology, and physiology. The near-universal acceptance from the 1960s of 'continental drift' plate tectonics ideas, pioneered by Alfred Wegener in 1912 but subsequently controversial, occurred in Britain, a year or two before the USA.[107] Graythorp 1, the first oil production platform completed (with American expertise) for the UK's northern North Sea oil province, stood in 420 feet of water with a superstructure rising 100 feet above the sea; built in a Teesside former ship repair yard, it was then the largest structure of its kind ever built anywhere in the world.[108]

To be preoccupied with notching up national scores and 'firsts' would be childish, and would also misrepresent the mood of modern science. Sir Richard Woolley's preoccupation, for example, was consistent: to discover how the laws of physics determine the working of the universe. His distinguished career was conducted in four countries: his first degrees came from Cape Town and Cambridge, his doctoral research was in California, and he held posts as Director (1939–55) of Mount Stromlo observatory in Australia, eleventh Astronomer Royal (1956–71) in Britain, and Director (1971–6) of the new South African Astronomical Observatory. Scientific breakthroughs occurred through ranging between subjects as well as between continents. Physics and chemistry might be declining after 1970 as distinct areas of study, but they were unobtrusively growing through combining with adjacent subjects into such new specialisms as biophysics, biomathematics, biotechnology, and biochemistry. In so collaborative and capital-intensive an enterprise as natural science, too much energy should not go into unravelling who was the first to discover what and when. 'DNA was still a mystery, up for grabs,' the American James D. Watson recalled of the early 1950s, 'and no one was sure who would get it'.[109] He and his older English colleague Francis Crick, brilliant in scientific dialogue, sparked off one another in Cambridge, and in April 1953 published in *Nature*

---

[106] *Engineering our Future*, 36, 90.
[107] E. Bullard in F. A. Donath *et al.*, *Annual Review of Earth and Planetary Sciences*, 3 (1975), 19, a reference I owe to my colleague Dr Andrew Fowler.
[108] B. Cooper and T. Gaskell, *The Adventure of North Sea Oil* (1976), 152–4.
[109] J. D. Watson, *The Double Helix: A Personal Account of the Discovery of the Structure of DNA* (1968), 4.

the key paper which proposed DNA's double-helix structure, subsequently of the greatest diagnostic and forensic importance. The second major British breakthrough in biotechnology also occurred in Cambridge, and in 1975 was also first announced in *Nature*: the hybridoma technique evolved by the immunologists George Kohler (born in Germany) and Cesar Milstein (born in Argentina) for producing monoclonal antibodies.

Here lay the basis of major late twentieth-century commercial ventures. Little scientific research after 1970 was funded by private individuals, and of total UK expenditure in 1975 on research and development, 52 per cent came from government, 41 per cent from industry, and only 7 per cent from elsewhere. Of this research, 62 per cent was carried out by industry, 26 per cent in government institutions, 8 per cent in universities and places of further education, and only 3 per cent elsewhere.[110] University interaction with industry was tightening. In 1971 Trinity College Cambridge launched Britain's first 'science park' north of the city. The science park was an American concept, but soon caught on, and during the 1980s science parks sprang up at several other universities: Warwick (1982), Aston (1983), Manchester (1984), Keele (1987), and Oxford (1989). They thrived on the rapid late twentieth-century recombinations of natural-science 'subjects', particularly in the biological sciences and computing. Computer firms were likely to spring up near any university because of local demand, because the locality could supply skilled staff, and because they were often 'spun off' from university-based research.

In parallel with these major developments, the humanitarian and environ-mentalist critique of the natural sciences mounted. When in 1990 animal-rights extremists planted three bombs, one of them at Bristol University under the car of a researcher into pain relief, a counter-move was mounted by Andrew Blake. Struck at age 14 by Friedrich's ataxia, he had been shocked by the bomb and was surprised that no organization existed to mobilize patients in support of vivisec-tion for medical research. He founded the pressure group SIMR (Seriously Ill for Medical Research) in the following year; it had 800 members or supporters by 2002, the year he died; his outlook had bucked the trend. Environmentalist pressure threatened nuclear physics. Tony Benn, visiting the huge nuclear reprocessing complex at Windscale as Energy Minister in 1978, was 'struck, on the one hand, by the skill and scientific knowledge of the people who run it and, on the other, by the exceptional vulnerability of such a complicated system'.[111] Its vulnerability was soon revealed: the public debate in 1977–8 on the proposal to make Windscale a centre for nuclear reprocessing uncovered much hostility; nor was it long before man-made disasters vividly advertised the hazards.[112]

---

[110] Gummett, *Scientists in Whitehall*, 55.

[111] Obituaries of Blake in *Ind* (29 May 2002), 18; *DT* (22 June 2002), 25. Benn, *Diaries 1977–80*, 310 (9 June 1978).   [112] See Harrison *Seeking a Role*, 313.

Yet the natural sciences' reach was now so wide that one area of science could claim to solve the problems created in another: scientific expertise was now required even to conserve humanitarian and environmental values. There was much activity on the frontier between the social and natural sciences. Ethology was much in vogue in the 1960s, and broke through to popular consciousness with such books as Konrad Lorenz's *On Aggression* (1966), Robert Ardrey's *The Territorial Imperative* (1966), Desmond Morris's *The Naked Ape* (1967), and Anthony Storr's *Human Aggression* (1968). The science of nutrition in its impact on diet and smoking was rearranging social anthropology, statistics, and physiology into new combinations. The state of the social sciences, which disappointed many high hopes of the 1960s, illustrates the multi-layered fragmentation that was now accelerating. With the natural scientists establishing the model to follow, there was first the fragmentation within academic life between areas of scholarly study, each with its esoteric specialist vocabulary, its admired exemplars, and its special concerns. But there was also fragmentation at a higher level, between intellectual life as a whole and other sections of the national elite:[113] political, economic, religious, even recreational. Sport's growing professionalism was eroding the universities' once powerful status in team games, for example. The growing professionalism of university teachers in the social sciences and humanities led them to seek approval primarily from colleagues rather than from society at large, pursuing as they did value freedom and professional integrity. Sociologists' growing professionalism, for example, seemed to require rejection of their subject's earlier empirical mood and practical purpose in the UK,[114] and political scientists distanced themselves from practical politics by focusing upon political theory and abstruse (preferably statistical) approaches to empirical inquiry.

Economists forsook the book for the journal article, and practical relevance for arcane abstraction. Theory and sophisticated numeracy, not empiricism and practical utility, were becoming their route to status. No longer for them the 'big issues' tackled by economists in the tradition of J. S. Mill, Marshall, Keynes, and Meade. Forced into developing ever more complex models, the economist had the limits to his usefulness exposed during the elaborate cost-benefit analyses[115] designed to select sites for London airports. One component of the retreat from corporatism was the economists' inability to deliver on their promises; economic forecasting suffered from too many variables and from data insufficiently precise. Healey as Chancellor from 1974 to 1979 was not at all hostile to planning, but claimed in his budget speech of 1974 that managing demand from economic statistics was as unreliable as predicting election results

---

[113] For more on this see Harrison, *Seeking a Role*, 19, 54, 193, 197, 371; also above, p. 140, and below, pp. 426, 429, 448.

[114] For more on this see Harrison, *Seeking a Role* 177, 497, 502 and below pp. 522–3.

[115] See above, p. 75.

from opinion polls. In his budget speech four years later he wondered aloud about the allegedly scientific status of economics, given that it dealt in variables so imponderable, and used statistics so unreliable; furthermore, it centred on the conduct of human beings, 'the most unpredictable of all creatures'.[116] In 1979 Lawson pressed Howe to abolish the Treasury models of the economy, and instead to follow the Americans in drawing upon the alternative models available outside government; he later wished he had pursued the matter when Chancellor himself.[117] Economists' status suffered further in the 1980s when their objectivity seemed suspect. The public disputes between Keynesians and monetarists revealed them as subject to fashion, and as not at all resembling technicians operating a machine. We have seen how their expansionary advice was rejected in 1981; Lawson later noted that seven years of steady economic growth had followed the rejection,[118] yet experience after 1981 had also undermined any idea of a precise relationship between aggregate demand and money supply.

Conservatives were particularly unhappy about sociology, whose professional irreverence had never matched their mood. When Nigel Eastmond was discovered on 9 July 1981 in Westminster Palace armed with a knife, he had just taken an A-level examination in sociology, and told police: 'I decided anarchy was the only way. I decided I had to do something myself so I decided to go and kill Mrs Thatcher.' The prosecution at his trial claimed that his actions reflected what he had been reading.[119] Sociology had been associated with the corporatist attitudes the Thatcher governments repudiated, and in 1982 Keith Joseph as Secretary of State for Education removed the word 'science' from the title of the Social Science Research Council: it became the Economic and Social Research Council. To compound sociology's difficulties, the general public were beginning to suffer from 'clipboard fatigue', so response-rates to survey questionnaires were falling.[120] As for political studies, a growing professionalism distanced the politicians from the universities as both parties reached out for wider support elsewhere. Labour's intellectuals from the 1970s to the 1990s were carried along in their party's search for a more demotic image;[121] Thatcher, too, lent her party a more populist flavour. We have seen how little 'Thatcherism' and its think tanks owed to the elite universities,[122] and few intellectuals after 1979 were as eager to advertise their new Conservative stance as Amis had been in 1970; Pinter subsequently felt ashamed of the Conservative vote that, in common with Peter Hall, he had cast in 1979.[123]

[116] HC Deb. 26 Mar. 1974, cc. 289–90; 11 Apr. 1978, c. 1189.
[117] Lawson, View from No. 11, 49, 51.
[118] HC Deb. 17 Mar. 1987, c. 818, and see above, pp. 325–6.
[119] T (13 Jan. 1982), 1.   [120] Ind (16 Mar. 2000), 1.
[121] For more on this see Harrison, Seeking a Role, 523; and above, pp. 140, 145–6, and below, p. 492.
[122] See above, pp. 315–16.
[123] Spec (20 June 1970), 812 (Amis). G (4 Sept. 1999), review section, 7 (Pinter). See also above, p. 144.

Douglas Hurd recalled how his civil servants dissuaded him as Home Secretary from quoting Housman when speaking on capital punishment because, with no shared cultural ground, such quotations would make no impact.[124] For this, students of the arts and humanities were themselves partly to blame, given that after 1970 they too displayed a 'professional' tendency to talk only to each other. In philosophy, a 'professional' distancing of the public from its subject matter had begun in the 1930s and 1940s when the growth of analytical philosophy marked a final break with the idealist tradition—though after 1970 the British approach to philosophy, while remaining influential, could not hope to retain its earlier world-wide impact. The last place to expect unnecessary technical jargon was the university department of English, and yet there too a popular following was eroded after 1970, partly under French influence. Salutary, however, was their move from preoccupation with a limited 'canon' of great writers to analysing the cultural impact made by the new media, by feminism, and by popular fiction. The New Left and the campaign for 'cultural studies' had for some time been pushing the broader literary agenda pioneered by Orwell, Raymond Williams, and Hoggart in new and fruitful directions. With classical studies, decline brought scholarly and other gains. Given curricular pressures, there were opportunity costs involved in perpetuating Latin and Greek as mainline subjects in schools and universities, and their decline emancipated classical scholarship from being weighed down by reluctant conscripts. The smaller numbers who braved all subsequent discouragements to classical study were now willing volunteers. Their teachers, with a diminished linguistic emphasis, were alert to new approaches from Marxism, literary criticism, and social anthropology, as well as eager to digest the archaeologists' ample discoveries. Agility at prose and verse composition and unseen translation, once at the heart of British elite classical education, gave way to the enthusiasts' less technical but broader study of literature, history, and culture in the classical world.

History opened out towards a wider public with help from A. J. P. Taylor, the History Workshop movement, industrial archaeology (with its array of volunteers), the 'heritage' industry (with abundant custom from tourists and leisured pensioners), and the vogue for 'oral', family, and 'contemporary' history. The last of these was much boosted by the Institute of Contemporary British History, launched in 1986; it soon became a forum where scholars, media people, and politicians could fruitfully cooperate. Although a vigorous rearguard action in defence of 'high political' history was launched from Cambridge, and although political biography retained widespread appeal, constitutional and diplomatic history went into decline, whereas the history of the 'common

---

[124] D. Hurd, typescript (kindly provided by Lord Hurd) of his speech on 14 Apr. 1994 to the Royal Society of Literature, 5.

people'—social, labour, and economic history—continued to prosper. The media set out to meet the public demand which humanities departments in universities were coy about supplying. Television serials of major fictional works broadened the readership for English literature's 'canon'.[125] Towards the end of the century, television did for history what it had earlier done for archaeology: it helped to satisfy a mass thirst for knowledge that professional historians would not or could not satisfy. Unexpected audiences suddenly emerged for historical programmes of a wide-ranging and well-presented visual kind. Yet one scholar can perhaps stand for the many in the humanities who after 1970 shunned the distractions of publicity or fashion, and who gave decades of commitment to an important subject. Late in the 1930s the Cambridge biochemist Joseph Needham became interested in Chinese culture through his graduate student (much later his wife), Lu Gwei-Djen. In 1950 he planned a seven-volume study of *Science and Civilization in China*. Four of its volumes had been published by 1971, and thereafter it grew into a huge multi-authored collaborative project backed by a growing research collection; in 1987 this was housed in its own library within a research institute devoted to the subject. It was a university achievement as substantial, original, and significant as any other that the twentieth century witnessed.

Research had never been confined to universities, where the early nineteenth-century German notion of the university as research institute gained ground only slowly. Not until the 1960s did it do serious battle with the primacy of undergraduate teaching in Oxford and Cambridge. After the Second World War research was taking place not only in universities but in industrial firms, public and private research institutes, government departments, consultancies, charities, think tanks, royal commissions, survey organizations, campaigning groups, and the media—not to mention the volunteer writers, bird watchers, botanists, amateur archaeologists, and family, oral and local historians who contributed so much. They attracted less attention than was their due[126] partly because so diverse and weakly structured, but partly because university-based professionalism entailed devaluing the amateur who had once enjoyed such status in the UK.[127] Yet the informal sanctions on the 'amateur' from his peers to get things right were often at least as strong as the formal sanctions upon a university researcher. Indeed, it was because the constraints on creativity were in some respects weaker outside universities than in, that many subjects subsequently respectable were pioneered (or at least suggested or funded) from elsewhere: African history, astrophysics, oral history, business studies, the

---

[125] See below, p. 431.

[126] R. Finnegan (ed.), *Participating in the Knowledge Society: Researchers Beyond the University Walls* (Basingstoke, 2005) at last began to do them justice; see esp. 2 (Finnegan) and 246 (F. Webster), and Finnegan's 'Should We Notice Researchers Outside the University?', *British Academy Review*, 10 (2007), 58–9.   [127] Finnegan (ed.), *Knowledge Society*, 6 (Finnegan), 248 (F. Webster).

history of childhood, women's studies, and even—far back in the past—natural science itself.[128]

4. CULTURAL AFFLUENCE

Leisure time and activity continued to extend and diversify so fast in Britain after 1970 that recreation increasingly shaped priorities and values. We have already seen how travel had itself become a recreation after 1970,[129] but rapid technological change added ever more recreations even to the lives of those who stayed at home. Recreation and culture responded after 1970 to at least five major influences: electronic innovation, internationalism, commercialism, professionalism, and humanitarianism. The first offered unprecedented recreational opportunity. The BBC's sample survey of family timetables for those aged 4 and above in summer 1983 shows that on weekdays 72 per cent of the sample were at home in the evenings; at no point during Sunday were fewer than 61 per cent at home, and on Sundays as well as weekdays three-quarters of the sample were still awake at 10 p.m.[130] The media absorbed much home-based leisure at the expense of those old rivals, church and pub. Drinking was increasingly likely to occur within the woman's empire: the home. Off-licence sales grew fast, and of the beer drunk between the 1960s and the 1990s, the share drunk at home rose from 2 per cent to more than 20 per cent.[131] The pub could counter-attack only feebly by encouraging more female custom and by providing facilities the home had not yet acquired. There were social-class and regional contrasts, given that the pace of late twentieth-century family change was not uniform. The BBC survey shows, for instance, that on average in Britain the professional and higher classes got up later, took their evening meal later, and went to bed later than the semi-skilled and unskilled workers; and also that the evening meal grew later as one travelled south.[132]

Among the home-based media, the national press remained important, especially on Sundays, and became increasingly recreational in tone overall. 'The magic ingredients' for success, wrote Larry Lamb, influential editor of the *Sun* (1969–71, 1975–81), were never to talk down to the reader, and 'always remember that . . . it is no longer a newspaper's duty solely to inform': it must simultaneously 'aim to stimulate, educate, coax, coerce, cajole—shock when necessary—but, above all, to entertain'.[133] By comparison with television in 1970, the London-based national press was a stagnant world, with declining

---

[128] Finnegan, 'Should We Notice Researchers?', 59–60.   [129] See above, pp. 17–20, 68–9, 73–4.
[130] BBC, *Daily Life in the 1980s*, ii. 229–30, 343–5.   [131] *FT* (3 Aug. 1993), 17.
[132] BBC, *Daily Life in the 1980s*, ii. 379–81, 409–29.
[133] L. Lamb, *Sunrise: The Remarkable Rise and Rise of the Best-Selling Soaraway 'Sun'* (London and Basingstoke, 1989), 237–8.

circulations and more newspaper deaths than births. By then there were ten London-based national morning papers, two London evening papers, and seven Sundays. The eleven national morning dailies sold a daily average of 16.6 million in 1958, whereas the nine that survived in 1978 sold only 14.3 million.[134] Between 1971 and 1989 provincial papers, too, were in decline: Sundays by 5 per cent, mornings by 17 per cent, evenings by 25 per cent, and purchased weeklies by 38 per cent, partly because in the 1980s provincial freesheet circulation more than doubled.[135] The freesheet, produced by a relatively small and sometimes non-union workforce, devoted only a fifth of its space to editorial material. Delivered free to homes in many parts of the country, its circulation rose almost sixfold between the early 1970s and early 1980s, its advertising revenue twenty-seven-fold.[136] Its success, based entirely on advertising revenue, illustrates how important such income now was to newspapers. By the early 1970s no national daily paper could survive without attracting either the middle class or a high proportion of the working class, with its associated advertising revenue. In 1981–9 advertising expenditure going into all provincial weeklies more than doubled, but this figure incorporated quadrupled expenditure on freesheet advertising.[137] Among purchased papers, the colour supplements made advertising particularly important for the Sunday 'quality' papers; there, after rapid growth since the 1960s, it contributed 77 per cent of total revenue in the 1980s. For the quality dailies, however, advertising was by then less important: 63 per cent of total revenue, as compared with 47 per cent for the popular Sundays, and 29 per cent for the popular dailies.[138] Shortage of advertising was central to the demise of the weekly *New Society*. Launched in 1962 on a welfarist wave, it had depended heavily on publishing classified advertising for welfare posts. When these dried up during local authority cuts in the early 1980s, with the *Guardian* and *Community Care* competing for what remained, the paper admitted defeat, and in 1988 merged with the *New Statesman*. The London evening papers, too, were declining—their circulation falling by two-thirds between 1958 and 1978;[139] after the *Evening News* closed in 1980, only the *Evening Standard* remained.

The national dailies jockeyed continuously for position. The 'quality' papers' share of total newspaper sales rose fast during the 1960s to 15 per cent, but then stabilized in the 1970s with over six million well-educated readers, more than

[134] See the useful table in J. Cunningham, 'National Daily Newspapers and their Circulations in the UK, 1908–1978', *Journal of Advertising History* (Feb. 1981), 17.

[135] H. Henry, *Key Regional Newspaper Trends: An Analysis of Circulations and Revenues during the Past Decade* (Henley-on-Thames, 1990), 5, 21.

[136] *FT* (30 Nov. 1983), 10; cf. the figures in *T* (16 Sept. 1982), supplement on advertising, p. vi.

[137] A. Smith (ed.), *The British Press since the War* (Newton Abbot, 1974), 16, 18, 42. Henry, *Key Regional Newspaper Trends*, 57.   [138] *Advertising Statistics Yearbook 1995*, 202.

[139] P. Barker in 'Painting the Portrait of "The Other Britain": *New Society* 1962–88', *Contemporary Record* (Summer 1991), 49, 57–8. Cunningham, 'National Daily Newspapers and their Circulations', 17.

half of them drawn from London and the south-east.[140] Between 1958 and 1978 the share of the *Sun* (formerly *Daily Herald*) moved up to 28 per cent, and the *Mirror* to 27 per cent, whereas the *Daily Express* fell to 17 per cent; the *Daily Mail* (with help from amalgamations) had risen to 14 per cent, and the *Telegraph* to 10 per cent. No other 'quality' paper exceeded *The Times*'s 2 per cent.[141] In 1969 *The Times*'s proprietor noted the contrast between press editorials and press managers: whereas the former frequently urged trade union reform in general, the latter resisted their own industry's restrictive practices only feebly. He feared that the newspaper world was too fragmented for this ever to change: 'the policy has always been to profit by each other's difficulties'.[142] Times Newspapers' expensive eleven-month dispute in 1978-9 with the trade unions, whose disruptions to production and resistance to new technology it was trying ineffectually to curb, closed *The Times, Sunday Times,* and the three *Times* weekly supplements. The outcome was hardly a triumph for either side: the *Guardian* stole a lasting advantage over *The Times*, and in the absence of the *Times Literary Supplement*, the *London Review of Books* got launched in 1979. The *Sunday Times* soon recovered, and both manning levels and access to new technology improved greatly, but a strike by *Times* journalists in August 1980 gave the Thomson management the sought-for opportunity to sell the paper. Rupert Murdoch bought it in February 1981 amidst fears of his likely impact on the quality press. Hitherto *The Times*'s letters page had been the place where the elite conversed. Just under half the letters in 1978 came from London, and the rest came largely from the home counties. A twelfth of the total came from MPs or peers, and men contributed nine times as many letters as women.[143] In *The Times* of the 1980s, however, only shorter and more entertaining letters got published and its supplements grew frothier, its leaders less weighty.

We have seen how during the 1980s the balance of power between employers and the print unions suddenly changed.[144] Many now hoped that the new technology would generate an array of new papers. Several new provincial papers and ten nationals were indeed launched, but technology's main beneficiaries were the established national papers, which rapidly digested this new bonus without halting their long-term decline in circulation. Among the new national papers only the *Independent* (launched in 1986), with the *Independent on Sunday* (launched in 1990), precariously survived. The newspapers' content did change, however, with a general search for the journalistic centre ground. From being 'responsible' and serious, identifying instinctively with government, the 'qualities' acquired something of the *Mirror*'s irreverence and scepticism, while

---

[140] C. Sparks, 'The Readership of the British Quality Press', *Media Culture and Society* (Oct. 1987), 429—'quality' being defined as *Financial Times, Daily Telegraph, Times,* and *Guardian*.

[141] Cunningham, 'National Daily Newspapers and their Circulations', 17.

[142] Roy Thomson, quoted in Castle, *Diaries 1964-70*, 725 (4 Nov. 1969).

[143] R. J. E. Taylor's letter in *T* (14 Nov. 1979), 13.   [144] See above, pp. 168-70.

the popular tabloids began taking themselves more seriously. Meanwhile David English, USA-influenced anti-socialist editor of the *Daily Mail* (1971–92), converted his paper into a tabloid which could straddle the centre ground. Journalists, diminishingly anonymous, developed the art of entertaining—of embellishing the facts with humour, comment, and colour—rather than merely recording them. The late twentieth century saw the rise of the newspaper political columnist, whose views were eagerly awaited. Hugo Young's high-priestly tones resounded regularly through the late twentieth-century *Guardian*, but by then (as he himself admitted) he was only one among numerous latter-day Cassandras, whereas in the 1960s each paper had boasted only one.[145] Direct reporting of parliamentary debates gave way to shorter and sometimes even facetious commentary. In the 1980s the printed equivalent of the 'sound bite' (a term imported from the USA) catered for shorter attention-spans, and television's visual priorities were replicated. Comic strips invaded the *Guardian* and filled a *Sunday Times* supplement, and by the late 1980s the scholarly and somewhat earnest treatment of pop music, pioneered by the underground counter-cultural press of the 1960s, resurfaced in the national quality dailies; in their quest for younger readers they deployed deeply ruminative articles on the thoughts and skills of footballers and pop singers.

The only significant counter-trend to this cultural decline was the sudden realization in the national press during 1986 that readers could be seduced by the obituary as an art form. The new style of fuller and more rounded obituaries was pioneered by the *Daily Telegraph* and *Independent*, and then spread to *The Times* and *Guardian*. The early 1990s saw obituaries of unprecedented range and depth, each paper developing its own specialities, from the *Guardian* with its mavericks and reformers to the *Telegraph* with its servicemen and aristocrats. By 1990 only the *Financial Times* could compare in seriousness and depth of coverage with British national daily newspapers as at 1914. The weeklies and monthlies, with their volatile and usually declining circulations, were particularly vulnerable, undermined by the Saturday and Sunday papers' growing role as weekly magazines. Thatcherism owed more to the *Sun* than to the *Spectator*, and death overtook *New Society* (1988), *Encounter* (1990), and the *Listener* (1991). The *New Statesman* precariously survived, but its one-time central role in British cultural life had long passed, and the *Economist* could flourish only because increasingly international in emphasis. A growing internationalism helped the weekly *Nature*, too, to buck the declining trend. With John Maddox, physicist son of a Welsh furnaceman, as editor (1966–73, 1980–95) it not only became the world's best outlet for scientific news, but trained key journalists in a new category: the science columnist who interpreted science research to the general public lucidly and interestingly.[146] The journalists' salary improved in the 1980s with their growing visibility, yet paradoxically journalism became an increasingly prized destination for clever university graduates at just the time when the press was well launched on cultural decline.

The electronic advances which nourished recreational affluence saw each superseding or sometimes rejuvenating its precursor.[147] Politicians' desire after 1970 for more pluralism in broadcasting worked with the grain of technological change. In the increasingly multi-layered media world after 1970, radio skilfully renewed itself: reception improved greatly as VHF channels gradually covered the country; broadcasting hours almost doubled between 1962/3 and 1973/4; and from 1967 local radio burst upon the scene. Offshore pirate radio stations, of which ten were operating at their peak, forced the issue in 1964–7; though killed off in 1967 by legislation excluding their advertisers, commercial radio had demonstrated its potential for profitability, and in 1972 local commercial radio stations were authorized. Radio Leicester, launched on 8 November 1967, was the first of eight BBC local stations, and between 1973 and 1976 these were joined by nineteen commercial local stations. The latter expanded further after 1979, and by the end of 1982 60 per cent of the population could receive them,[148] 95 per cent by the end of 1990; commercial radio had by then forced the BBC's share of total listening below 60 per cent. Four or more radio sets were owned by a sixth of listeners in 1980, and by nearly a half in 1990.[149] Together with the record-player, radio retained its great advantage over television: it did not monopolize attention, but could accompany driving, housework, and many other activities. Radio was not now oppressively educational. Under the competition from commercial radio, Reith's educational objectives for the BBC were abandoned, and in 1970 radio channels were restructured in such a way as simultaneously to cater on different channels for contrasting tastes. News was no longer seen as a finite body of facts to be objectively chosen and calmly purveyed; it became an inexhaustible treasury continuously raided for stimulation. 'News has a right to be boring and dull on occasion', wrote the seasoned broadcaster Alvar Lidell, espousing a lost cause in 1979;[150] by then the occasional claim in the BBC's earliest days that 'there is no news today' seemed merely quaint. News had become entertainment, there was growing eagerness for instant comment on current events; with 'news-desks' and eye-catching 'virtual' studios, the very process of gathering and reporting news became part of the drama.

[146] Maddox obituary, *Econ* (25 Apr. 2009), 87–8.
[147] *Annan Report on Future of Broadcasting*, 11, 12, 82, 88.
[148] dspace.dial.pipex.com/town/pipexdsl/r/arar93/mds975/Content/radmem.html, consulted 27 Dec. 2005, a valuable website.
[149] A. Feist and J. Eckstein (eds.), *Cultural Trends: Issue 9. 1991* (1991), 43, 45, 46.
[150] *Listener* (3 May 1979), 620.

Television's impact grew partly because it was becoming ever more accessible, and between 1967 and 1979 viewing rose from an average of sixteen to twenty hours a week. In summer 1972 a higher proportion (52 per cent) of British working-class than middle-class families had a colour TV. By 1981 commercial television could reach 97 per cent of homes in the country, and three-quarters of these received it in colour.[151] A fifth of homes by then owned more than one television set, and video cassette recorders (then in only 2 per cent of homes) were about to take off.[152] Television helped to revive some rival pastimes, most notably cookery, gardening, and reading. As with so many successful television programmes, Delia Smith's cookery courses also appeared as best-selling books. It was in the 1980s that books on conservatories began to escalate, beneficiaries of many televised gardening programmes. Best-selling books emerged from Bronowski's *Ascent of Man* (1973), from the animal programmes of the fictional vet James Herriot in the 1970s, and in the 1980s from David Attenborough's natural history programmes. The loquacious Magnus Pyke, enthusiastically waving his arms while lengthily answering questions in the 1970s, was for the general public the archetypal eccentric scientist. Large sums could be raised for charity through television: on 3 October 1980, for example, the first British telethon was so successful that during the next twelve years four more followed, and £66 million was raised for welfare causes.[153]

Television's presence within the home inevitably made it controversial, not least as a subject of academic study; Marshall McLuhan, Professor of English at Toronto, made much impact in the 1960s, especially with his *The Medium is the Message* (1967). By the early 1980s there were a dozen first-degree courses in media studies, 107 by 1997. British adults watched television for two and a quarter hours a day between 1960 and 1983,[154] and cinemas could compete with home-based entertainment only through offering several programmes not available at home for different types of audience simultaneously in several smaller auditoria.[155] As with any important recreational innovation, commentators dwelt moralistically on what the new media had destroyed rather than joyfully on what they were creating. Media-based recreation was passive and enervating, they said. Yet if the art of conversation was the regretted casualty, its decline had begun long before, together with the arts of debating and letter-writing. The change stemmed more from a diminished respect

---

[151] C. Johnson, 'The Durable Revolution', *Lloyd's Bank Economic Bulletin*, 15 (Mar. 1980), 2–3. A. Briggs, *The History of Broadcasting in the United Kingdom*, v. *Competition* (Oxford, 1995), 848. B. Henry (ed.), *British Television Advertising: The First Thirty Years* (1986), 209.

[152] Henry (ed.), *British Television Advertising*, 210.

[153] P. Bonner, *Independent Television in Britain*, v. *ITV and IBA, 1981–92: The Old Relationship Changes* (London and Basingstoke, 1998), 138–9.

[154] Bonner, *Old Relationship Changes*, p. xi. S. Bowden and A. Offer, 'Household Appliances and the Use of Time', *Economic History Review*, 47 (1994), 736–7.

[155] For a useful discussion see P. Waymark, 'Cinema: Back in Twos and Threes', *T* (19 Dec. 1970), 10.

for leisured wit than from media changes. Likewise with letter-writing: in 1985 women wrote twice as many personal letters as men,[156] but paid work was eroding even their leisure, with the telephone as a ready alternative. Television's critics were especially concerned about children, who on average in 1975 watched twenty-four hours' television a week, much of it designed for adults.[157] School performance may sometimes have suffered when screen-reared children were confronted by a paper-based syllabus, but television was by no means the sole visual medium moulding children's outlook: in 1974, for instance, nearly all children between 5 and 15 read at least one comic each week, with higher circulation for the *Beano* and *Dandy* than for *The Times* and *Guardian*.[158] It was not long before the computer game transferred to the home many of the amusement arcade's excitements without their tawdry accompaniments,[159] and these often required skills from the young which astonished their elders—skills highly relevant, furthermore, in the labour market. Home-based television in one respect united the nation: through bringing the sexes together in their recreation. However, the abundance of media and channels (BBC2 arrived in 1964, Channel 4 in 1982) eroded the unifying impact which had once stemmed from large numbers simultaneously watching the same programmes. Besides, the video shop had arrived in the high street, and by 1983 nineteen million people were watching videos each week—a higher proportion on an average night than went to the pub. The video cassette recorder diversified recreation still further by bringing to film what the tape recorder had earlier brought to sound: it widened choice by making viewing times flexible. Book issues per head of the UK population from public libraries were falling in the 1980s, but audio-visual issues were rising, though from a low base.[160]

Television enhanced recreational affluence through funding and diversifying sport. About half the British population watched the televised broadcast of the World Cup on 25 June 1978, producing a big surge in the demand for power at half time.[161] For ITV, as for the footballers themselves,[162] sporting broadcasts, with their predominantly male viewers, were a huge source of revenue. At the Conservatives' youth rally during the general election of 1983, superstar sportsmen mingled with famous comedians and politicians in Wembley conference centre,[163] and by the early 1990s more than 200 football 'fanzines' (a term current in the USA by the 1940s to denote magazines for fans) whipped up enthusiasm among their annual readership of a

---

[156] *T* (30 Aug. 1985), 3.
[157] Children between 5 and 14, *Annan Report on Future of Broadcasting*, 349. For exposure to violence, ibid. 247, 249, 254. [158] *T* (16 Dec. 1974), 3.
[159] See the aspersions cast upon it in Rowntree and Lavers, *English Life and Leisure*, 141.
[160] *T* (10 June 1983), 4 (videos). *Social Trends* (1996), 221 (books). [161] *T* (26 June 1978), 4.
[162] On their perspective see Harrison, *Seeking a Role*, 389, 391. [163] *G* (6 June 1983), 1, 21.

million.[164] Employees in sport almost doubled between 1970 and 1986,[165] partly because sporting affluence was cumulative: the new or newly popular sports did not oust the old. Given the growing levels of urban noise, noiseless sports such as ski-ing, hang-gliding, ballooning, wind-surfing, and sailing acquired a new recreational appeal, as did rural sports. Transport trends may have sent the working horse further into his long decline, but the racehorse prospered, and Lamont in his budget speech of 1993 saw racing as 'an important industry, and a vital part of our national life'.[166] In its readership and aims *The Field* of 1990, much glossier than forty years before, had not changed: field sports remained central, and to judge from the expensive items advertised, affluence accompanied them. Membership of the British Horse Society almost doubled in each of the four decades from the 1950s to the 1980s, and by 2007 had reached 67,000.[167]

The media helped to reinforce internationalism as the second major influence on cultural and recreational change in Britain after 1970. Sporting internationalism was powerful enough in the UK to ensure that Thatcher did not go unchallenged in 1980 when urging a boycott of the Olympic Games in Moscow.[168] Of more continuous importance were the recreational precedents set for Britain by countries overseas, especially the USA. For example, the rich humanitarian hotelier and restaurateur Robin Howard funded the migration to Britain of American contemporary dance, and Robert Cohan, born and trained in the USA, made 'The Place' in London the headquarters of contemporary dance in Britain; as the London Contemporary Dance Theatre, it assisted the great expansion in the UK numbers working in dance. In 1977 the American fashion for skateboarding so captured Britain that within the year two million skateboards had been sold, with a National Skateboarding Association established,[169] and it is from New York's marathon that the pedigree of London's stems.[170] The 'race against time' on 25 May 1986 was a genuinely international sporting event in which about 200,000 people ran a six-mile course in Hyde Park to raise money for famine victims in Africa; an estimated twenty million people participated world-wide in similar events, watched on television by more than 1.5 billion people.[171]

Cultural influences on Britain after 1970 were less cosmopolitan than might have been expected, especially given the EEC's importance for Britain after 1973, and the rapid growth of tourism in Europe. In a leading article on the day after the Commons vote to enter the EEC, *The Times* felt that history must henceforth be taught in the schools rather differently: 'students should

---

[164] J. Williams and S. Wagg (eds.), *British Football and Social Change: Getting into Europe* (Leicester, 1991), 180–1.   [165] *T* (17 Dec. 1986), 36.
[166] *HC Deb.* 16 Mar. 1993, c. 191.
[167] Statistics kindly provided in May 2008 by the British Horse Society.   [168] See above, p. 51.
[169] *T* (7 Jan. 1978), 13.   [170] See below, pp. 424–5.   [171] *T* (26 May 1986), 1.

be taught a European history, related to the history of the whole world, rather than the narrowly British history which is still too common . . . schools will, when the settlement is final, have to educate for a European future'.[172] This did not happen quickly. Quite apart from the introversion encouraged by the decline of empire, it was perhaps inevitable that such overseas influences as there were should come from English-speaking countries—most notably from Ireland, the USA, and other one-time colonies, especially India.[173] The thrillers and spy stories so much in mid-century vogue, especially Ian Fleming's James Bond stories and John Le Carré's complex portrayals of cold-war espionage in all its seediness, provided a fictional arena for exercising traditional British male virtues which now lacked any colonial outlet. Some of the most successful in the genre—Frederick Forsyth's *The Day of the Jackal* (1971), for example, or Jack Higgins's *The Eagle has Landed* (1975)—blurred the frontier between journalism and fiction, included much factual material, and gained immensely from being memorably filmed.

It was the USA that most powerfully influenced British publishing after 1970. The rapid post-war expansion in British publishers' output could hardly be maintained thereafter, yet growth continued fast enough: 79 per cent for total titles and 42 per cent for reprints and new editions between 1970 and 1987.[174] This expansion occurred in a rapidly changing context, for the 1960s saw an end to the genuinely creative gentlemanly regime where authors knew their publishers, even in a big concern like Penguin. The small publishing firm, with small print-runs, diverse products, and a relative unconcern with management and marketing, could not survive invasion from the huge American publishing machines, and the 1970s and 1980s saw an almost complete turnover among the leading publishing personalities. The combination of rapid inflation, bad labour relations, falling library demand, and rising oil and paper costs compelled extensive mergers and rationalizations. From 1974 British publishers were subjected to a literary equivalent, American in origin, of the 'top of the pops': the best-seller list. There was a growing practice of manufacturing best-sellers according to a formula, especially when aimed at television. The former academic Henry Babbacombe, in Bradbury's *Cuts*, discovers that 'writing for television was teamwork', and that in the production team 'everyone else was there to change everything else that everyone else did'.[175] With the private lending libraries vanished, the second-hand book trade in decline, university libraries cutting back, and the paperback fully established, everything depended by the 1990s on what barcoded paperbacks the publishers could tempt readers

---

[172] *T* (29 Oct. 1971), 15.   [173] See above, pp. 47–8.

[174] Calculated from statistics in *Mumby's Publishing and Bookselling in the Twentieth Century* (6th edn. 1982), 220, supplemented by figures in Publishers Association, *Quarterly Statistical Bulletin* (Mar. 1988), 19.   [175] Bradbury, *Cuts*, 76, 78.

to buy from closely stock-controlled airport lounges, railway stations, and book supermarkets such as W. H. Smith.

Yet the supermarket publisher did not entirely oust the small but literate and well-connected delicatessen publisher and bookseller who knew his market, could back hunches, and cater for significant minorities. So the monoliths did not take over completely: there were continuous contractions and expansions in the UK publishing world throughout the 1970s and 1980s. Furthermore, publishing costs fell markedly from the 1980s, and this too helped the small publisher. Library purchasing of books continued to grow up to the mid-1970s, but went into marked decline thereafter till the universities started expanding from the late 1980s. But reticence was no longer possible for the author: media-boosted publicity was important for sales, and authors had to participte in poetry readings, literary 'events', book festivals, chat programmes, and book signings. The age of book-prize ballyhoo had arrived, with the Booker Prize (for a British author of a fictional work published in Britain within a named period) first awarded in 1968. From Cheltenham in 1949 to Hay-on-Wye from 1988 the literary festival, too, had arrived: amateur at first, but increasingly hard-nosed and commercialized.[176]

The advance of commercialism over state funding was the third major cultural influence of the 1970s and 1980s, and was an innovation. Britain's early integration into a unitary state ensured that it did not experience the dispersed governmental funding that grew out of the small-scale autocratic but cultivated aristocratic regimes of pre-democratic Italy, France, and central Europe, and UK central government's pronounced move towards funding the arts was well under way in the late 1940s.[177] Of the total public expenditure on the arts (museums, performing and creative arts, films and crafts) in Great Britain in 1981/2, three-fifths came from central government, and only two-fifths from local authorities—with crafts more likely to be funded locally, the performing and creative arts nationally. By 1971 the arts were 'a major industry in their own right', influential on people's decision about where to live and work, and employing 132,000 people as musicians, painters, authors, actors and creative artists.[178] After its long gestation, the National Theatre at last opened in 1976, and by 1990 there had been a huge expansion in the Royal Shakespeare Company, in state-subsidized theatres, and in national companies and performances.

In one small but significant respect, state funding even extended after 1970. The British were by world standards keen to borrow but reluctant to buy books,[179] so with their lost royalties British authors were in effect subsidizing

---

[176] D. J. Taylor in *G* (25 May 2002), Saturday review, 3.   [177] Harrison, *Seeking a Role*, 55–6.
[178] House of Commons Education, Science and Arts Committee, *Eighth Report, Session 1981–2: Public and Private Funding of the Arts*, i. *Report* (1982), pp. xxxiii, xxxvii, cxxxiii.
[179] For interesting comparative statistics see *Econ* (27 Dec. 1975), 15; *HC Deb.* 10 Nov. 1978, c. 1374.

the public-library system. Authors, as participants in this ultimate of cottage industries, were highly dispersed individualists and loners with no formal training and with 'nothing in common but a label that they may not choose to wear'.[180] Launched in 1959, the campaign for a Public Lending Right (PLR) battled against many obstacles: it was difficult to agree upon a single practicable loan-based rather than purchase-based scheme, backbench Conservative free-marketeers disliked public subsidy and wanted the consumer-borrower to pay, authors were difficult to mobilize behind the scheme, and librarians feared for the free-library concept and for their revenue. But Scandinavian precedents helped, and by the late 1960s the Labour government's ear had been bent. During the early 1970s computers made loan-based schemes practicable, and in 1976 the Labour government introduced a Bill which got through parliament in 1979. The first PLR payments were made in 1984. The government's arts budget paid funds annually to authors on the basis of their books' estimated loans, and the measure incorporated a redistributive element whereby some revenue from much-borrowed authors was transferred to the less fortunate.

Yet PLR's advent bucked the overall trend after 1970, which in the arts as elsewhere lay away from reliance on the state and towards more diversified arts funding on the American model. The trend reflected the growing demand for arts provision in a more affluent and educated society, the fear that public funding could not adequately meet the demand, the recognition that the fine arts needed to sell themselves more vigorously, and the growing awareness of their hold on talented employees and their contribution to tourism—arguments all reinforced by an overall political shift towards the free market. The arts lobby was tightly organized and articulate, and governments did not wish to seem philistine, but arts funding was high enough among the Heath government's priorities for it to invest political capital in championing admission charges for the small number of national museums and art galleries that were free. There were inter-war precedents for such charges, but they roused the art world's anti-commercial hackles and the highly articulate section of the middle class that was wedded to state funding. Roy Strong, then the notably successful Director of the National Portrait Gallery (1967–73), autobiographically recalled the 'once impoverished grammar-school boy who owed everything to free access';[181] this adult-education theme was often harped upon in parliamentary debates by the charges' opponents, concerned as they were to defend the free entry which made a convert of the experimental and casual visitor sheltering from the rain or the repeat visitor who at last saw the light. And might not museum charges be the thin end of a wedge that would be driven into public libraries and parks? There were illogicalities and inconsistencies on both sides of the

[180] R. Findlater (pseud. for K. B. F. Bain), *The Book Writers: Who are They?* (1966), 6.
[181] Strong, *Diaries*, 53.

debate, but the charges were introduced. Only briefly, though, because the Labour government scrapped them in March 1974, at which point the Tate Gallery ran up celebratory balloons on its flagstaff.[182] Attendances had declined while charges were in place, and the experiment's apparent failure helps to explain why library loans remained free. The Adam Smith Institute was in the mid-1980s well aware, however, that these one-time self-improving institutions had been diverted to middle-class recreational purposes; why should they be subsidized at the expense of commercial provision, it asked, and why should recreational reading be thus favoured rather than (say) football or films?[183]

Thatcher was ever seeking ways of undermining the socialist enemy, and in drawing commerce and the arts together her governments went further than Heath's. Already during the late 1970s the mood was changing on both the funding and the display fronts, partly because Strong had himself demonstrated how galleries and museums might attract visitors through a more outgoing approach and a more imaginative display. Television, improved art publishing, and colour supplements were publicizing what was on offer, and were raising standards of presentation. The great national repositories were increasingly expected to combine their traditional role of promoting fine-arts scholarship with nourishing and funding a mass recreational demand. As Director of the Victoria and Albert Museum (1974–87), Strong found himself beset by acidulous scholars, recalcitrant trade unionists, and the unexpected need to display fund-raising skills, for not only were expectations rising: government funding was falling. Government grants to the Arts Council had almost doubled in real terms during the 1950s, rose more than threefold in the 1960s, and more than doubled in the 1970s.[184] Even then they were running at a level much lower per head of population than in Sweden, Holland, and West Germany,[185] yet in the 1980s Arts Council funding ceased to rise in real terms.[186] No wonder Strong by the mid-1980s had begun to speak the language he had repudiated in the early 1970s. It was, he said, 'a turning-point' when on 1 April 1984 the National Maritime Museum introduced an admissions charge. In 1985, the year the Victoria and Albert Museum introduced voluntary donations, Strong was beginning to liken museum visitors to consumers whose needs must be taken fully into account. If they are required to pay, he argued, they will expect good amenities and high standards: 'if people pay for something they expect

---

[182] *T* (30 Mar. 1974), 2.

[183] Adam Smith Institute, *Ex Libris* (1986), 2, 10, 32, 37, 42–3. The booklet was written by Douglas C. Mason.   [184] Calculated from *Public and Private Funding of the Arts*, ii (1982), 308.

[185] R. Stevenson, *The Oxford English Literary History*, xii. *1960–2000: The Last of England?* (Oxford, 2004), 389.

[186] See the figures in A. Beck, 'Thatcherism and the Arts Council', *Parliamentary Affairs* (July 1989), 366.

value'.[187] Commercial sponsorship of the arts was the only other resort: in 1984 Strong noted that 'virtually no major exhibition can now be staged without a sponsor'. It might even be necessary to end the huge increase in museum staff, to allow art works to leave the country, and to disperse existing stock—for 'what is the point of keeping on acquiring things, when what you've got is presented or maintained badly?' The aim should not now be to add to public collections, but to get more art into private hands, and to increase the number of collectors.[188]

This revolution went further after Strong departed. The business sponsorship incentive scheme, set up in 1984, led the arts to depend rather less heavily on government. The controversial appointment in 1988 of Elizabeth Esteve-Coll as Director opened up the Victoria and Albert Museum still further. If both Strong and Thatcher had not resigned, Strong might later have shifted his view still further, given that the reform of arts funding was yet another item on Thatcher's long unfinished agenda. The populist case against state funding of the arts had long been a backbench cause supported in such locations as the *Daily Express*, and in the 1980s the free-market think tanks were limbering up to spread free-market ideas into new territory. An Adam Smith Institute pamphlet interpreted taxpayer grants to the arts as requiring the lower paid once more to subsidize the higher-paid. For Amis in 1981, subsidies emancipated the artist from any need to find purchasers, viewers, or listeners.[189] He attacked modernism as 'a great fraud', which could prosper only when funded by a 'socialist quango'; market forces would, by contrast, empower a general public 'usually right' on such matters. Here he was at one with Larkin, who attacked the 'irresponsibility' of most modern art.[190] The private collector could move quickly, using his own money to fund shifts in taste without cost to the public, and knowing full well that he must live with his purchases. Striking instances of the enthusiasm and innovation encouraged by enlightened private patronage come from the world of opera, not only from the Christie family at inter-war Glyndebourne, but in 1989 when Leonard Ingrams opened up his own house at Garsington for a repertoire that in the 1990s blazed many trails.[191] It was partly approval of unsubsidized opera that led Thatcher to visit Glyndebourne on several occasions,[192] but other priorities precluded any full-blown Thatcherite challenge to the idea of public funding for the arts.

Two painters illustrate how an unsubsidized self-taught artist could attract a mass following quite independently of connoisseur and self-described expert:

[187] Quotations from Strong, *Diaries*, 356–7; *FT* (26 Apr. 1984), 27. See also Strong's 'Towards a More Consumer-Oriented V&A' (typescript of speech on 3 Oct. 1985), 2, 6, kindly made available to me by Sir Roy.
[188] Quotations from Strong, *Diaries*, 357; Strong, 'Museums: Two Contributions Towards the Debate' (xerox copy, 1985), 3, cf. 6, 8, 9. I owe this copy, too, to Sir Roy.
[189] D. C. Mason, *Expounding the Arts* (Adam Smith Institute, 1987), 28. *T* (3 Aug. 1981), 11 (Amis).
[190] H. Ritchie, *Success Stories: Literature and the Media in England, 1950–1959* (1988), 93.
[191] Obituary, *DT* (4 Aug. 2005), 27.   [192] Campbell, *Thatcher*, ii. 413.

the Scottish painter Jack Vettriano and the Plymouth-based Beryl Cook. The critics had little time for Vettriano's romantic and nude themes, of which his 'Singing Butler' was the most famous, yet by 2004 he had sold more than three million poster reproductions and earned £500,000 a year from royalties. Emphasizing the importance of craftsmanship in a rare interview of 2004, he claimed that if the national galleries were really catering for the British people with the taxpayer's money, 'they would buy my work. . . . But they don't'.[193] With Cook, as with Vettriano, commercial success began with a hobby. Shy but observant, she saw herself as a 'maker of pictures', not as an artist.[194] Yet her poignant 'folk baroque' themes, developed as a release from anxiety while running Plymouth guest-houses, were popular enough by 1976 for an exhibition of them to be held in Plymouth when she was nearly 50, and fame soon descended.

Little public subsidy was required after 1970 for that vibrant area of British culture: pop music.[195] For most groups the sheer excitement of mutual entertainment enhanced by teenage hormones was the starting point, and was seldom absent later. 'We know that money is important', Mick Jagger confessed, 'but we're in this business principally because we enjoy it, because we get pleasure out of it. Cut off the money and you'll still find us playing this kind of music.'[196] Seeking the necessary skills through self-help, they ceaselessly combined and recombined in ephemeral groups and networks, and honed their expertise through closely studying records made by their role models.[197] The record industry was already highly commercialized in the 1950s, and rock musicians thereafter, whatever their personal values and public image, were in practice highly competitive, individualistic, and classless. Yet wealth and a respectability of sorts, not to mention advancing age, were always at risk of eroding the spontaneity and warmth that joined teenage performers to their audiences; new talent continuously welled up from below in a world where careers were vulnerable to rapid shifts in fashion, and to the inevitable redundancy stemming from lost youth. Furthermore, by the 1980s counter-cultural and even secretive tendencies within dance music were nourished by wariness of the police and by new inexpensive modes of production; anonymous performance and decentralized 'white label' production seemed more compatible with creativity than selling out to the big companies.[198]

[193] O (11 Jan. 2004), 3.   [194] Obituary, G (29 May 2008), 36.
[195] Here, as in my Seeking a Role, I gratefully acknowledge help patiently and generously provided by Dr Andrew Callingham and by my former pupil Mel Johnson.
[196] Miles, Mick Jagger in his own Words (1982), 125–7.
[197] All this is brilliantly captured in Ruth Finnegan's The Hidden Musicians: Music-Making in an English Town (Cambridge, 1989).
[198] D. Hesmondhalgh, 'The British Dance Music Industry: A Case Study of Independent Cultural Production', British Journal of Sociology (June 1998), 236–40.

Like their contemporaries at Saturday afternoon football, pop groups were engaged in a predominantly male escape from domesticity and female control, but unlike the sporting spectators they were carving out a future. Women were far less prominent in the groups than among their fans, mobilized as they were by their magazines, clubs, and record shops. Magazines such as *Rolling Stone*, *Melody Maker*, and *New Musical Express* drew together 'something which, strictly speaking, has no business to exist, a pop intelligentsia': they provided cohesion and cultivated expertise in a youthful community whose code language and loud sounds distanced the adults.[199] Disc jockeys on radio became famous, both Tony Blackburn and John Peel having launched themselves in the UK through pirate radio in the mid-1960s. A pop group, once drawn into a relationship with a recording company, experienced many pressures: disputes within the group over possible new musical and stylistic directions, for example, and argument about how much commercial guidance to accept. Because musical entrepreneurs saw themselves as more than mere administrators, and could make expensive equipment and technical expertise available—the group could well lose control of its music and become distanced from its fans. After the 1960s, rebellion against convention was often an important component, and in the punk groups of the 1970s there was an almost deliberate repudiation of respectability, flaunted with bizarre Mohican hairstyles. The small meeting-places, often pubs, where punk performers gathered ensured that band and fans drew even closer together against a hostile world, or against a world they wanted to offend. Yet self-help was important there at a new level, extending from musical technique to commercial self-promotion. Performances were self-recorded on tape and self-distributed under independent labels after performances and with help from fan-based magazines.[200] 'New wave' music annexed punk's vigour and volume and, with added technical sophistication and capital investment, drew it into the mainstream.

UK sales by value in real terms of records in all formats reached a plateau in the early 1970s, and did not resume their earlier rise till the late 1980s. But with changes in the fashionable format, the number of units sold escalated in an ongoing undulation of risings and fallings. By the 1960s the 33.3 r.p.m. 'long-playing record' and the 45 r.p.m. extended-play 'single' discs reigned supreme, having pushed the 78 r.p.m. disc into outer darkness; the number of singles units sold reached its peak in the late 1970s, and then went into slow long-term decline.[201] The tape cassette, introduced into the USA in 1965, had captured

[199] K. Hudson, *A Dictionary of Teenage Revolution and its Aftermath* (London and Basingstoke, 1983), p. xix.

[200] For a useful discussion see C. Cutler, 'Progressive Rock in the U.K.', in his *File under Popular: Theoretical and Critical Writings on Music* (1985), 192. I owe this reference to Dr Callingham.

[201] M. Hung and E. G. Morencos (eds.), *World Record Sales 1969–1990: A Statistical History of the World Recording Industry* (1990), 58. This source collects invaluable statistics.

less than 5 per cent of the UK market by 1971,[202] but between 1973 and 1978 sales of blank cassette tapes rose tenfold by value; this reflected an enthusiasm for home-taping which sent the number of long-playing records sold, after its peak in the mid-1970s, into gradual decline throughout the 1980s—a decline accentuated by the rapid growth from mid-decade in compact discs.[203] The UK was an important market, buying far fewer recorded units than the USA whatever the format, but usually in the same league as France, Japan, and West Germany, and well ahead of other industrial countries. In 1975–9 the UK absorbed 13 per cent of world-wide singles units sold, 9 per cent of long-playing records sold, and 6 per cent of tapes; equivalent figures for 1985–8 were 18, 11, and 9 per cent.[204] The cassette and later the CD were more portable, and so could eventually be enjoyed while in motion with radio cassette and personal stereos. Throughout this ongoing electronic revolution, the range of music available greatly extended, together with the range of performances for any one musical item, at a steadily falling real cost. By the 1980s even street buskers were performing to accompaniment from a battery-operated cassette recorder.

The combinations and recombinations driving forward UK music-making groups were replicated in music-recording companies, but by the late 1980s UK music production and consumption were dominated by an Anglo-American-Japanese triad of large multinational firms.[205] Pop music events became larger and more tightly organized. The USA's Woodstock festival, which attracted more than half a million people in August 1969, set the precedent for large UK gatherings, including Fiery Creations' huge and profitable Isle of Wight festival soon afterwards. Smaller but free pop festivals, often with an environmentalist or mystical component, were in vogue from the early 1970s, with what became the Glastonbury Festival prominent among them. Such events often deeply influenced those present, and many fans named their children after revered pop stars. The politicians, alert to these changes, knew that politics as itself a recreation had long been in decline. Amidst so many new types of entertainment, they had to secure their position by harnessing them. The festival movement was not commercial in origin, but the rise of 'The Mean Fiddler', organizers of entertainment, shows how commerce could fruitfully advance movements partly philanthropic and even political in impulse, safeguarding their finances and preventing disorder. Originating in the eponymous Harlesden club opened by Vince Power in 1982, the firm branched out into several entertainment concerns in London, and eventually promoted events overseas. The annual

[202] L. G. Wood, 'The Growth and Development of the Recording Industry', *Gramophone* (Nov. 1971), 801.

[203] *FT* (22 Sept. 1979), 16. Hung and Morencos (eds.), *World Record Sales*, 58, 72–3, 74–5.

[204] Calculated from ibid. 72–3.

[205] K. Negus, 'The Discovery and Development of Recording Artists in the Popular Music Industry' (Dept. of Social Science, Southbank Polytechnic, London, Ph.D. thesis 1991), 45.

three-day Reading festival originated in a jazz and blues festival first held in 1961 which moved to Reading in 1971; it did not really take off, though, till the late 1980s, when The Mean Fiddler were asked to organize the entire event, and from 1999 it grew to incorporate a sister site at Leeds; in 2002 The Mean Fiddler also assumed operational control of the three-day Glastonbury festival.[206] In the previous year the Stonehenge festival revived, after its setback in the 1980s. About 15,000 people watched the sun rise to the accompaniment of singing, dancing, drumming, and chanting; two years later it attracted more than 30,000 people.[207]

Expenditure on sports-related goods and services was big business: £4.37 billion in 1985, of which more than a quarter was absorbed by gambling (mainly on horse-racing), a sixth by sports clothing, a seventh by sports goods and equipment, and an eighth by sports participation.[208] Team games for working men which mobilized the municipal pride and community loyalties of industrial and provincial cities seemed much more compatible with socialist values than with the commercialized sport which emerged after 1970, where highly paid sportsmen were bought and sold in a national and even international talent market. Televised sport could attract so many viewers that advertisers soon seized the opportunity, and commercial sponsorship injected funds into the game. In the 1960s cricket secured media-based sponsorship, orienting the first-class game towards the Gillette Cup. Important innovations included one-day county cricket, international one-day cricket between Test countries (from 1966), and Sunday cricket (from 1969). Without television, professional cricket could hardly have survived.

Electronic innovation, internationalism, and commercialism all enhanced the fourth major cultural shift in these years: towards professionalism. Recalling many years later his four-minute-mile triumph of 1954, Roger Bannister noted the absence then of any notion of continuous training: 'our concept then was simply of ups and downs—you shouldn't peak too soon; you shouldn't be stale . . . you would build up to the event . . . we had really no idea how much the body could stand'.[209] Television was hardly likely to favour amateurism in its pejorative sense, and sponsorship was hardly compatible with it. Besides, few could now fund the expense and time that sporting prowess now required; and with growing professionalism came waning capacity for any individual to shine in more than one sport. With cricket as with football, meritocracy

[206] Websites www.readingmuseum.org.uk/collections/festival/history.htm, www.reading-festival.org.uk/readingfestivalhistory.asp, www.netcomuk.co.uk/~drbob/glasto/whatisglastonbury.html, and www.leedsfestival.co.uk/displayPage.asp?ArticleID=359&URLID=50, all consulted on 6 Apr. 2005.

[207] http://news.bbc.co.uk/1/hi/entertainment/music/3662921.stm, consulted 6 Apr. 2005.

[208] Henley Centre for Forecasting, *The Economic Impact and Importance of Sport in the United Kingdom: A Study Prepared for the Sports Council* (1985), 99.

[209] E. Whitley, *The Graduates* (1986), 124.

advanced when players were freed to move more frequently between teams. This they were encouraged to do after organizing themselves in the 1960s to get better pay; with the hierarchy of clubs becoming increasingly meritocratic, sporting worlds became markets for talent and transfers more frequent. Such meritocratic transfers within a meritocratic hierarchy of clubs had the effect of shifting funds from the top clubs in exchange for talent drawn from the rest; the players' incomes rose almost threefold in real terms in Football League clubs between 1973/4 and 1993/4.[210] Forewarned by George Best's grim precedent,[211] superstar footballers took financial advice and learned to handle publicity, but on the field there was much more playing to the gallery, and much less of the modesty and scrupulous respect for the rules hitherto thought central to British sport. It had become financially important to win, so it became important not just to play well, but to know how to get round the rules: pain, genuine or feigned, became a counter in the game, and if only for that reason the earlier link between sportsmanship, fair play, and courage became less direct. The referee's lot was becoming less happy, and sometimes even dangerous.

The specialization that accompanied professionalism in sport did not apply to the fine arts where (as in scholarship) progress often entailed straddling frontiers. Computerized lighting and scenery changes, laser lights, and ever more complex combinations of film, tape, and technology transformed opportunity in the theatre. Authors were no longer reluctant to write plays for television, which could both greatly enlarge their audiences and (with the development in the 1980s of video-recording) lend their creations permanence. Sculpture, painting, and weaving became interchangeable, static artistic objects began to move and emit light and sound, and the rock musician (whose key figures owed much to art schools) readily invaded the world of fashion. As fashion designers, Vivienne Westwood and Jasper Conran owed much to punk, and the designers who worked on record sleeves could as readily work on shop design and on clothing. Lifestyles as well as clothes were matters of fashion, and the two interacted: impacts were made, and attitudes were struck.[212]

The fine arts might flourish on imagination and the desire to shock, but they also needed the professionalism developed by powerful engines of painstaking scholarship. The gramophone record's inexorable growth rested upon major advances in musicology, just as the visual arts required refinement in the history of costume, theatre, and the film. Scholarly expertise in the fine arts had hitherto clustered round museums, libraries, and galleries, and had played little

---

[210] S. Dobson and J. Goddard, 'Performance, Revenue, and Cross Subsidization in the Football League, 1927–1994', *Economic History Review* (Nov. 1998), 774–5.

[211] Harrison, *Seeking a Role*, 391.

[212] For a useful discussion see J. Street, 'Youth Culture and the Emergence of Popular Music', in Gourvish and O'Day (eds.), *Britain since 1945*, 311, 317, 318.

part in university syllabuses. Sir Francis Watson's thirty-seven years at the Wallace Collection, for example, set new standards in studying and cataloguing furniture, but such secluded careers were becoming less feasible: a self-conscious professionalism now overtook the expanding areas of librarianship and 'museology'. Looking back on his succession to John Pope-Hennessy in 1974 as Director of the Victoria and Albert Museum, Roy Strong saw him as 'a member of a dying species, the aesthete museum director', wielding great national influence through his scholarship and personal connections, and feared by his subordinates as 'his fish-like eyes loomed behind thick rimless spectacles'. A decade later Strong predicted 'the end of the age of the scholar-director and the scholar-curator and the advent of administrators'.[213] Up to 1960 London University's Courtauld Institute had been alone in providing a first-degree university course in art history, but thenceforward the upper-class amateur, the connoisseur, and the museum curator interacted more closely with the universities. The interdisciplinary academic mood from the 1960s onwards fostered more such courses in art history,[214] and these helped to compensate for the distractions from academic research that by the 1980s had built up within museums, galleries, and libraries. Even instruction on 'creative writing' was available after 1970, when the University of East Anglia launched—with Ian McEwan as sole pupil—what became a distinguished course. It was a mark of the fine arts' growing professionalism and influence that by the early 1980s schemes were afoot (very much with Strong's approval) for an institution (as yet unrealized) which would do for the fine arts what the Royal Society did for the natural sciences; there was, he complained, 'no equivalent in the Arts', as it had 'no united professional voice'.[215]

A fifth influence on recreation and culture after 1970, fully compatible with the rest, was of longer standing: humanitarianism, in the broad sense that combined the attack on violence and cruelty with an enhanced valuation of human health. In a trend which modestly countervailed the overall trend towards recreational diversity, the Victorians had tamed the less humane sports through rule-making and legislation, and had seen organized games as a route to social harmony—as diversions from disorder and even from war. Prize-fighting and sporting cruelty to animals came under an early ban, and by the 1950s medical opinion was turning against boxing. The analogy with cock-fighting and bear-baiting had been made explicit by boxing's leading political opponent, the veteran Labour MP Edith Summerskill; she noted that the Victorian humanitarians had been as much concerned with degraded spectators as with injured combatants, and televised boxing now seemed to enhance the degradation. Gallup polls revealed that a large majority of those surveyed in

[213] Strong, *Diaries*, 116–17; 'Museums: Two Contributions', 9.
[214] Cornforth, *Country Houses of England* (1998), 70, 72.   [215] Strong, *Diaries*, 294 (18 Nov. 1981).

the 1960s and 1970s opposed banning boxing,[216] but the sport was dropped, initially from state schools. It then ebbed away from the independent schools: from Eton in 1976, from Winchester in 1985, and from Clifton, the sport's last public-school redoubt, in the same term—autumn 1987—that women were admitted.[217] For similar reasons independent schools during the 1990s advanced soccer over rugby football, though also relevant here was the pupils' growing taste for soccer, by then losing its lower-class image. Opinion was also already building up for the attack on foxhunting: Gallup polls of 1958, 1972, and 1975 favoured curbs by a two-to-one majority.[218] Even anglers, a twelfth of the population in 1979,[219] began to feel vulnerable, though their humbler social status protected them under a Labour government, whereas in 1983 the Party had come out for the first time with a commitment to abolish hunting and coursing.

Yet unless legislation goes with the grain of the relevant opinion groups, physical violence curbed at one point tends to re-emerge at another. Violent activity banned decades earlier could unpredictably reappear if it lacked endorsement from relevant opinion groups. In February 1981, for example, the police had to break up a crowd of 600 gypsies who had flocked into Cambridge to watch an illegal and betting-ridden bare-knuckle contest attended by people in expensive cars; similar contests were going on elsewhere.[220] Football, too, saw the recurrent re-emergence of the violence which its improved nineteenth-century organization had aimed to prevent. The 'skinheads' of the 1960s exposed football spectators to the tribal masculine loyalties of a working-class gangland culture; their unpolitical racism and chauvinism reflected a violent but traditionalist localism. When travelling outside their territory, they set out to 'take' the 'end' terraces which the home team's younger and more excitable supporters viewed as their own. Barriers and pens were erected to contain the hooligans, rendering it paradoxically more dangerous to watch football matches after 1970. Because the authorities did not at first see that this required heavier levels of policing, fences and walls accentuated the worst late twentieth-century football disasters at Heysel and Hillsborough (Plate 14).[221] Already by the late 1960s football violence had become serious

[216] *HL Deb.* 10 May 1962, cc. 349, 353. *Gallup International Public Opinion Polls,* ii. 869 (June 1966), 1215 (Dec. 1972), 1433 (Aug. 1975).

[217] For this information I am most grateful to Mr Tom Gover, who taught at Clifton for forty-one years.

[218] *Ind* (3 Oct. 1999), 5 (soccer). For hunting see *Gallup International Public Opinion Polls,* i. 457 (Mar. 1958); ii. 1215 (Dec. 1972); 1433 (Aug. 1975).

[219] J. Paxman, *Friends in High Places: Who Runs Britain?* (1st publ. 1990, paperback edn. 1991), 338. For anglers, *T* (1 Oct. 1980), 5.   [220] *T* (2 Feb. 1981), 4.

[221] J. Bale, *Sport, Space and the City* (1993), 50. See also above, pp. 235, 356–7. For a good discussion of football hooliganism see J. Williams, 'Having an Away Day: English Football Spectators and the Hooligan Debate', in Williams and Wagg (eds.), *British Football and Social Change,* 165–9.

enough for the Home Office to show concern,[222] and in the 1980s it won Thatcher's sustained attention. Hooliganism from British fans became serious in 1974 at Rotterdam, and between then and the Heysel tragedy in 1985 their hooliganism in almost all major European football-playing countries seriously damaged Britain's overseas reputation, and forced the UK police eventually to set up their National Football Intelligence Unit. Chauvinism was not the root cause of such violence, as was later revealed by its cure, and British sport remained inexorably locked into competitive international networks at several levels—Commonwealth, European, and world-wide—with profound consequences for British styles of performance and funding arrangements.

At the root of the violence was the failure of commercialized sport in the 1980s fully to exploit its opportunities. Many football and cricket clubs capitalized only slowly on spectators' enthusiasm, and failed fully to milk their grounds and their image for funds. In many football clubs, accounting methods were lax, and supporters were rarely consulted. While the glass-fronted boardrooms might be well appointed, spectators' overcrowded terraces had not moved with the times: seating was inadequate, lavatories were primitive, litter abounded, and near the seedy grounds 'fans eat their hamburgers or chips standing outside in all weathers' amidst 'a prevailing stench of stewed onions'.[223] Football stadia on cramped grounds needed replacing and were often dangerous: fifty-six people died when Bradford City Football Club's Valley Parade main stand caught fire on 11 May 1985. Hooliganism threatened to deter commercial sponsors. Television caused annual attendance at football matches to fall from the early 1950s, and by 1971/2 it had almost halved since its peak of 41,250,000 in the 1948/9 season,[224] so football hooliganism merely accentuated an existing problem. During the 1980s the remedy was found: purpose-built all-seat stadia, with closer closed-circuit television (CCTV) surveillance to identify troublemakers; regulation under the compulsory licensing of football grounds, first introduced in 1975, was simultaneously enhanced. The whole family could then return, and in the late 1980s both attendance and gate revenue began to rise:[225] here commercialism and good order went together.

Television's impact was not unreservedly humane. The culture of violence, more American than British in origin, percolated into television and videos after mid-century. Even BBC television succumbed to American films because they could be imported cheaply once their huge American audience had been satiated. Mary Whitehouse's was among the earliest organized rejoinders to the

---

[222] *T* (27 Sept. 1969), 2.

[223] *The Hillsborough Stadium Disaster 15 April 1989: Inquiry by the Rt.Hon. Lord Justice [Peter] Taylor: Final Report* (Cm. 962; 1990), 6.

[224] C. Critcher, 'Football since the War', in J. Clarke, C. Critcher, and R. Johnson, *Working-Class Culture: Studies in History and Theory* (1979), 168–9.

[225] Dobson and Goddard, 'Performance, Revenue, and Cross Subsidization', 767, 772.

mounting power and occasional self-righteousness of media people. She saw herself as embattled against an entrenched liberal establishment, and sought to rouse public opinion against it with her populist emphasis on the conflict between humane values and the media defence of artistic creativity against censorship. For her it was 'plain common sense' to argue that 'if you constantly portray violence as normal on the screen you will help to create a violent society'.[226] For progressives she was at first a figure of fun, but her concerns were felt in circles well beyond her customary following, and included even some film directors—as exemplified in the response to two films: the British low-budget *Peeping Tom* (1960),[227] and the American *Clockwork Orange* (1971, based on Anthony Burgess's short story). The latter's memorably violent scenes prompted imitations in real life that led its director Stanley Kubrick in 1973 to ban its performance except in France and the USA. Many thought this surreal film with its psychedelic imagery even more dangerous than *Peeping Tom* because by foreshadowing urban anarchy from utterly amoral teenagers it seemed to glamourize what must at all costs be averted.[228]

In the ever-growing cult of the human body, however, humanitarianism coincided with influences electronic, international, commercial, and professional. In the 1980s the long-standing affinity between sport and physical health was strengthening. The late twentieth-century quest for health and beauty saw a new burst of what the Victorians called 'physical puritanism', with exercise bicycles invading spare rooms, slimfoods filling larders, swimming pools colonizing gardens. These trends fused with tourism and sixties-style informality to ensure that in the 1980s sportswear (often adorned with brand-names such as Adidas and Nike) was worn as often off the sports field as on. In hotter and culturally less formal climates, a small number of casual easily packed clothes boosted the track suit and the zoot-suit; people began wearing them when going about their ordinary business, and young people lavished funds on the trainers whose status-value prompted widespread theft. For young adults the vogue became denim, trainers, and designer stubble—a fashion which owed much to tennis heroes. Self-help in health was now big business: health farms and clubs soon lost their cranky image.[229] The machine rooms in high-tech gymnasia shrank 'beer bellies' into 'washboard stomachs', street joggers breathed in fresh air simultaneously with carbon monoxide, and in what was in some ways a culmination of individualism, the self-improvers of the body tested themselves in machine rooms against their self-imposed targets.

The London marathon saw the culmination of these trends. After participating in New York's marathon of 1979, the first of the city marathons, the British athlete Chris Brasher was inspired to introduce it to London. Sponsorship from

---

[226] *STel* (12 Mar. 1989), 13.   [227] Harrison, *Seeking a Role*, 397.   [228] *G* (5 Feb. 1993), 2.
[229] A. Sandles, 'Fitness and Fat, Fat Profits', *FT* (23 July 1984), 10.

Gillette got over the initial financial difficulties, and on 29 March 1981 the first such event took place, attracting 7,700 participants, whereas only 4,000 had been hoped for; by the early 1990s the London marathon was attracting 30,000 participants, with a further 20,000 turned away.[230] The marathon had now been given to the people, but the growing commercialization of the 1980s enabled it to retain the two other components of success: participation by professionals, and the media attention flowing from it.[231] Behind the late twentieth-century British sporting boom lay a growing army of aids and helpers. An estimate of 1985 identified 376,000 in the UK if people administering and reporting sport and manufacturing sportswear and equipment were included. It was a larger total than were by then employed in agriculture, forestry, and fishing.[232]

5. DUMBING DOWN?

Late twentieth-century educational and cultural trends were controversial. The previous subsection's heading 'cultural affluence' captures the abundant cultural opportunity then opening up, together with associated major advances in the scholarly study of culture in its more vocational dimensions: in musicology, art and architectural history, theatre and media studies. Yet some would label the overall trend 'cultural impoverishment', or even 'dumbing down'. The latter inter-war American phrase, not prevalent in Britain till the 1990s, illustrates the cross-cultural nature of the alleged problem. Mme Furtseva, USSR Minister of Culture, at the conference of the United Nations Educational, Scientific and Cultural Organization (UNESCO) on culture in 1970, saw it as a problem for the USSR too. Attacking media dissemination 'of so-called commercial art which runs counter to the principles of humanism and helps foster the cult of war, violence and racialism, pornography and brutality', she declared that 'we must not let the pseudo-heroes of ersatz culture replace for our young contemporaries the eternal beauty of art'. Viscount Eccles, Conservative minister with responsibility for the arts, showed some sympathy, claiming that 'we have little time to lose because, before long, the mass media may have blanketed whole populations either with the trivialities of the consumer society or with political propaganda'. *The Times* in a leading article responded by recommending a 'counter-attack' on the environment's cultural as well as physical pollution.[233]

In the second and third sections of this chapter we have also seen how fears of 'dumbing down' were present in schools and universities too. In Britain such

---

[230] *T* (30 Mar. 1981), 1. For obituaries of Brasher, *G* (1 Mar. 2003), 24; *Ind* (1 Mar. 2003), 24; *DT* (1 Mar. 2003), 29. For provincial marathons in 1981 see *G* (29 June 1981), 2; *T* (24 Aug. 1981), 1.

[231] There is a good discussion of this in J. Bryant, *The London Marathon* (2005), 110–12.

[232] Henley Centre for Forecasting, *Economic Impact and Importance of Sport*, 98.

[233] Eccles, *T* (1 Sept. 1970), 4; (3 Sept. 1970), 9 (leading article).

worries were not new. Already in 1869 Matthew Arnold was complaining about
the lack of objective literary and cultural standards, and in 1887 he saw W. T.
Stead's 'new journalism' as 'feather-brained' like the democracy it served.[234]
The 'yellow press', as championed by the novelist George Gissing's enthusiastic
Whelpdale, aimed at 'the quarter-educated' new generation being turned out by
state schools 'who can just read, but are incapable of sustained attention . . . their
attention can't sustain itself beyond two inches. Even chat is too solid for them:
they want chit-chat.'[235] A crusade to uphold standards was launched by the
Leavises from inter-war Cambridge,[236] and in 1944 the Cambridge historian
G. M. Trevelyan questioned the outcome of mass education: 'whether in the
twentieth or twenty-first centuries the lower forms of literature and journalism
will completely devour the higher has yet to be seen', he intoned. The spread of
literacy, he said, had created a new problem: literature and journalism 'now cater
for millions of half-educated and quarter-educated people, whose forebears, not
being able to read at all, were not the patrons of newspapers or of books'.[237] For
Trevelyan, as for the Leavises, the universities must become defensive redoubts
whose 'endowed priesthood' would uphold the cultural standards 'otherwise
disappearing with the disappearance of all forms of aristocratic tradition'.[238]

Pessimistic intellectuals seeking a remedy were weakened by a divisive
professionalism that encouraged groups of specialists to talk only to each other.
In 1932 the historian G. M. Young was already voicing alarm at how academic
professionalism and democracy had fragmented the Victorian clerisy; it must
quickly be restored, he claimed, 'if our civilization . . . is to survive the deluge
of picture-thinking and mass-suggestion bearing down on us from East and
West and always welling up in our midst'. Four years later, when discussing the
increasing specialization of the 1880s, he complained that 'through the gateway
of the Competitive Examination we go out into the Waste Land of Experts,
each knowing so much about so little that he can neither be contradicted
nor is worth contradicting'.[239] Young was far-sighted, given the British elite's
fragmentation after 1951, intellectually and in other ways. Yet in 1945 it was
still widely believed that democracy could be reconciled with high culture. The
Leavises and the adult educationists nurtured in the Army Bureau of Current
Affairs (ABCA) laced their leftish contempt for London's literary potentates
with high hopes of democratized access to education and leisure. If *Scrutiny*

---

[234] 'Culture and Anarchy', in M. Arnold, *Complete Prose Works*, ed. R. H. Super (Ann Arbor, 1965),
v. 147–8. 'Up to Easter' (May 1887), ibid. (1977), xi. 202.
[235] G. Gissing, *New Grub Street* (1st publ. 1891, paperback edn. Oxford, 1993), 460. I owe this
reference to my friend Mark Griffiths.   [236] Harrison, *Seeking a Role*, 54, 55.
[237] G. M. Trevelyan, *English Social History* (1st publ. 1944, Reprint Society edn. 1948), 588.
[238] Quotations from Trevelyan in 1954 and 1955, respectively, in D. Cannadine, *G. M. Trevelyan: A
Life in History* (1992), 233, 236.
[239] 'Victorian History', in *Selected Modern English Essays: Second Series* (1932), 276–7. G. M. Young,
Victorian England: Portrait of an Age (1936), 160.

ceased publication in 1953, this was partly because it seemed no longer needed, so wide had the Leavises' influence become. Optimism within organizations like ABCA and the WEA owed much to the nineteenth-century ideal of the self-improving artisan. Optimists hoped that compulsory state schooling would now buttress his self-driven and often solitary strivings, but the Victorian improving artisan's energy and articulateness gave a misleading impression of his numbers and impact.[240] The optimists did not always see how fragile were the foundations on which they hoped to build.

During the 1950s the pessimist case slowly cumulated. Commentators like Hoggart began to worry about the impact of commercialism on popular culture, and about the 'knowing, permissive treason of the clerks': the educated people who thought it fashionable to go along with falling standards.[241] Penguin Books in its commercialism of the 1960s sacrificed the firm's distinctive educational ideals, and by then the traditions of working-class self-education were waning, with WEA and national press assuming increasingly recreational roles. If 'quality' papers were losing circulation more slowly than the rest, it was claimed, that was only because their quest for larger sales sent them down-market.[242] There were worries, too, about the indirect effects of the commercialized media. In 1955/6 ITV almost from its beginnings thought survival required a larger audience,[243] and in the 1960s its following was much stronger lower down in society than higher up.[244] American television demonstrated how, quite apart from programme content, the periodic intrusion of advertisements shortened the attention span and trivialized the overall mood. From the 1960s commercialism ineluctably permeated radio as well,[245] throwing the BBC by the 1970s on to the defensive. Its one-time central place in British life, consolidated by the Second World War, was now doubly undermined: first by the accelerating erosion of its monopoly but, second, by its divergence from Reith's educational ideals and its descent despite its licence-fee subsidy into competing with ITV and chasing audience ratings.

Add to all this the growing concern about the media mood; even the 'quality' newspapers became intellectually less demanding and more visual after the 1950s.[246] Films, wrote Leavis in 1930, 'involve surrender, under conditions of hypnotic receptivity, to the cheapest emotional appeals', and radio 'tends to make active recreation, especially active use of the mind, more difficult'.[247] Similar comments were made in the 1950s about television; it became the

---

[240] See above, p. 175.
[241] e.g. Richard Hoggart, 'Speaking to Each Other', in N. Mackenzie (ed.), *Conviction* (1958), 130–1.
[242] See above, pp. 403–6.
[243] B. Sendall, *Independent Television in Britain*, i. *Origin and Foundation, 1946–62* (London and Basingstoke, 1982), 328–9. [244] *TBS* 557 (figures for 1960–1 and 1968).
[245] Above, pp. 407, 417. [246] Harrison, *Seeking a Role*, 392–3 and above, pp. 405–6.
[247] F. R. Leavis, *Mass Civilisation and Minority Culture* (Cambridge, 1930), 9–10.

moralists' predictable target, accused of enervating viewers. Politicians in the 1960s had difficulty in projecting their message—less because of deliberate bias, more because the mass media seemed increasingly to demand slick and often merely visual impact. Tony Benn, though himself instinctively populist, complained in 1968 that news was telescoped, fragmented, oversimplified, spiced up, and trivialized;[248] immediacy and impact were now of the essence. For similar reasons news readers by 1979 seemed too intrusive for their seasoned exemplar, Alvar Lidell: 'news has a right to be boring and dull on occasion', he wrote. 'The thing that must be ruthlessly avoided is *synthetic* excitement.'[249] Viewers and listeners were not alone in allegedly being corrupted. In 1987 Bradbury's *Cuts* redirected to media people the satirical portrayal of amoral, extravagant lifestyles that he had earlier applied to universities; in the insincere and meretricious media world the academic-turned-scriptwriter is taken up, taken over, exploited, soiled, and ultimately discarded.

The moral component of the pessimist case, blaming both teachers and taught, shaped pessimist analyses of school performance. Articulateness, orally and on paper, was allegedly declining, and if more young people were attaining higher examination grades, that reflected slipping standards or easier subjects studied, not genuine improvement. Pessimists thought that the quest for equal opportunity had introduced methods of examining designed to give everyone prizes: the new approaches to calibrating and publicly presenting performance reflected a well-intentioned but ultimately harmful and even patronizing reluctance to identify failure. If more young people were staying on longer at school, and if the universities absorbed an ever larger share of the age-group, the pessimists saw the newcomers as doomed ineluctably to lower the sixth-form and university standards prescribed in more exclusive times. Some even feared that pseudo-scientific justifications were eroding the moral dimension in intellectual achievement: bad spellers and poor readers were protected against accusations of low intelligence by downgrading such skills, or by branding them as culture-bound, or even as clinically identifiable hindrances to the emergence of innate intelligence. In 2005 the complaint was still heard, for instance, that the relatively new and allegedly scientific concept of 'dyslexia', applied to children with reading and spelling difficulties, involved neither clear diagnosis nor predictable remedy.[250]

Late twentieth-century cultural pessimism is in no way invalidated by the fact that its pedigree stretches so far back, and some pessimist fears had force. There was, for example, a gradual twentieth-century shift towards informality in language and accent which was not always scrupulous about nuance and

---

[248] Harrison, *Seeking a Role*, 468–9.   [249] Letter in *Listener* (3 May 1979), 620.
[250] J. Elliott, 'Dyslexia Myths and the Feel-Bad Factor', *Times Educational Supplement* (2 Sept. 2005), 18.

felicitous phrasing. We have seen how after the 1960s some sections of the middle class lacked the courage of their convictions, and allowed fashion to press them into populism—their inverted snobbery leading them to adopt language, manners, and accents not their own.[251] Still less justifiable was a middle-class progressive move from the 1960s towards repudiating 'elitism', given that the pursuit of excellence is integral to sporting achievement and the professional ethic, let alone to intellectual and cultural activity of any kind. Nonetheless, Soviet concern in 1970 about declining cultural standards should have rung alarm bells, for dumbing-down grumbles often reflect competing (though not always explicit) interests: of old versus young, of declining versus rising classes, of statists versus free-marketeers, of politicians versus the media, of the arts and humanities versus the natural and social sciences, of roundheads versus cavaliers.

The rejoinder to pessimist fears is inevitably complex and nuanced, and the four major components of their case must first be distinguished: their objections to specialization, media trivialization, secularization, and commercialism. In all four dimensions the pessimists' backward-looking yearnings were unconstructive and led nowhere. On intellectual fragmentation, G. M. Young nowhere clarifies his alternative. The advance of research, which inevitably entails specialization, has produced undeniable benefits which neither can nor should be disinvented, pseudo-science's deliberate obfuscation must of course be rejected. The pessimists would more fruitfully have focused upon how to minimize the associated drawbacks—for example, through encouraging Sir George Thomson's competent intermediaries, informed interpreters, and sophisticated popularizers.[252] As for school curricula, those who condemned the decline of 'hard' subjects like the classics or modern languages did not allow for the opportunity cost involved in retaining them, given that the advance of knowledge pushed into school curricula ever more subjects and skills with legitimate claims on the child's time. The young even sometimes found themselves teaching such skills to elders who found them decidedly 'hard'.

Media trivialization grew out of irreversible technological change. Its downside was clear enough. Just as the Victorian railway generated the railway novel, with its hasty reading and cruder emotions, so a late twentieth-century British abundance of distractions and rapid-fire exchanges of phoning, e-mailing, and texting magnified the casual informality that had already begun for other reasons. Informality owed much to a faster pace of life and to new electronic ways of communicating which the young were the first to embrace. The old might half jealously depreciate them, but it was neither possible nor desirable to disinvent the laptop and the mobile telephone. Television programmes were

[251] On which see Harrison, *Seeking a Role*, 495, 496, 523, and see above, pp. 145–6, and below, p. 492.
[252] Harrison, *Seeking a Role*, 365.

driven forward by competition for audiences within a market, and it was at the market, not at the medium, that pessimist complaints should have been directed. As ITV's first Director-General pointed out in 1960, popular television must reflect popular taste and, if 'people of superior mental constitution' cannot realize this, 'it is not really television with which they are dissatisfied. It is with people.'[253] The broadened recreational market created by widening affluence and mass education presented opportunities which the media could not afford to neglect. The logic of the pessimist position would have been for the BBC to resume both its monopoly and its high-minded purpose. In 1977 the Annan committee edged towards that position, arguing that the BBC's 'main objective' should not be to attract half the viewers, but 'to provide interesting and entertaining programmes which will amuse and enrich the experience of large numbers of people'. Because the challenge was never taken up, Thatcher was left sceptical of the BBC's case for a compulsory licence fee: 'the public broadcasters', she later wrote, 'were claiming the rights of poetry but providing us with pushpin'.[254] Her logic pointed to a BBC which used mass funding to benefit the minority, but the pessimists never explained how politicians could decide what precisely would 'enrich the experience of large numbers of people', or how they could promote it and still get elected.

Fears of 'dumbing down' presented dilemmas both to the right and the left. From the viewpoint of the left, if ever there was a case for socialism, in the sense of interventionist paternalism, it was here, with the added incentive provided by distaste for commercialism's contribution to the down-market move: here the customer was arguably not always right. Yet the left shied away from a strategy that might lose working-class votes and seemed to favour elitist censorship. A more comfortable option for the left was a populist anti-elitism, often paradoxically espoused by progressives in the fine arts who were unconcerned about the exclusive directions in which their prized modernism was taking them. The right, too, was torn. At the back of the pessimist mind lay a half-conscious yearning for the old and the educated to provide guidance from above, confident enough to pronounce upon what was good. Yet this was to yearn for a less secularized, less commercialized, and more hierarchical society with all the illusionary security and stability that curbs on free choice provide. The sixties had nourished a society of personal choice in belief, conduct, and lifestyle that left the authorities only utilitarian justifications for civilized and cultivated behaviour, and these were not always forthcoming. Furthermore, Conservatives' moral collectivism, traditionalism, and residual taste for hierarchy conflicted with the

[253] Sir Robert Fraser, address to Manchester Luncheon Club, 17 May 1960, quoted in Sendall, *ITV*, i. 317.

[254] *Annan Report on Future of Broadcasting*, 94; see also 450, 453–5, 457–8. Thatcher, *Downing Street Years*, 635.

populist free-market commercialism now capturing their Party. The pessimist on the right had few defences against a market-driven shaping of desires that tended always towards the lowest common denominator. An 'amateur' literary culture inevitably lost ground in a democratizing and specializing society: leisure no longer now coincided with cultivation, nor could national cultural boundaries now be securely policed, as the internationalism of radio's history demonstrated. Many pessimist complaints reflected distaste for the consequences of wider access to facilities—newspapers, cultural opportunity, schools and universities—hitherto confined to the few. At the very least, a choice was involved between a high and narrowly based culture in an hierarchical society or a lower but more broadly based culture in a democratic one.

Much in this and earlier chapters shows recreational development in a more optimistic light, for technological change brought major intellectual benefits. Access to the fine arts extended after 1951, though for many this did not happen fast enough. And though the calibre of comment on political and intellectual life declined markedly from the 1980s, even in 'quality' newspapers, their coverage of art, music, design, and business improved substantially. Television transformed knowledge of the political and electoral process,[255] its natural-history films enriched popular understanding of nature, and it greatly advanced historical awareness and literary range.[256] Serializing a classic on television greatly boosted the book's sales, and the public library service issued almost twice as many books in 1971 as in 1953, though some of this growth admittedly reflected custom transferred from the moribund subscription libraries. Locations featured in popular films spurred viewers enthusiastically to visit: Lyme Park after the BBC's *Pride and Prejudice* (1995), for example.[257] And we have seen how after the 1940s the mass media, far from encouraging passivity among young people, nourished musical creativity.[258] Nor was informality in itself regrettable, so long as compatible with creativity and precision, clarity and conciseness. Minorities could organize themselves into majorities if they cared enough, free as they were to communicate in new ways, and to devise new ways of testing merit; nor was there anything inevitable about the deference to 'ratings' shown by tax-subsidized media. What affluence and the twentieth-century media undeniably achieved was an unprecedented freedom of recreational choice. Any associated problems could be tackled through the self-correcting mechanisms of the UK's free, affluent, and meritocratic multi-layered society.

This chapter has shown how institutionalized religion in the 1970s and 1980s was in danger of being crowded out by abundant secularized cultural

[255] Harrison, *Seeking a Role*, 467; and see below, p. 510.
[256] Harrison, *Seeking a Role*, 398; see also above, p. 440.
[257] *BPF* (8th edn.), 367. *G* (16 June 1999), 12 (Lyme Park).
[258] See Harrison, *Seeking a Role*, 379, and above, pp. 416–17, 420–1.

and recreational opportunity. Within the schools and universities there were growing vocational and utilitarian pressures, reinforced by advancing state control. From culture and recreation, however, the British state had conventionally remained distant, and in this sphere the late twentieth-century trend lay more towards commercialism and private funding. Schools, universities, and sport all felt the impact of a fragmenting professionalism in these years, with curricular dilemmas, diminished contact with the public, and downgraded amateurism as, respectively, the outcomes. With university studies, as with advances in culture and the arts, however, progress often emerged from rearranging professionalism into new and more specialist combinations.

Six of the eight motifs have featured in this chapter. Voluntarist curbs on the politician's power (the seventh motif) were especially important, given the UK's traditional wariness of political interference in education and recreation, and on the issue of educational vouchers the politician's impotence without a supportive public opinion was in the 1980s all too evident. International influences (the second) were so central to scientific achievement, recreational opportunity, and sporting prowess that the UK's receptive prevailed over its hermetic tendencies, though the limits to the EEC's cultural impact on the UK were notable. Religious structures were threatened (the fifth) in the 1970s and 1980s not just by recreation's competition for people's time, energy, and values, but also by significant challenges to the humane standards that Christians had nourished in Britain since the evangelical revival—challenges issuing from football terraces and the media. Burgeoning recreation doubly distanced the politicians: it accentuated the decline of politics-as-recreation, and weakened the impact of the politicians' worries about the economy (the third motif). Time-saving devices (the fourth) directly fuelled recreational growth to the extent that so much recreation now entailed precise timing and moving fast. Yet the crowding in of new recreations in itself constituted a new source of time-pressure on the spectator, and the strength of commitment demanded by sporting professionalism pushed out the relatively leisured amateur. As for the UK's world roles (the eighth motif), in a sphere where so much depended on national wealth and size of population, the UK could no longer retain such world-wide leadership in intellectual and sporting spheres as it had once enjoyed.

CHAPTER 7

Politics and Government

British political institutions from 1951 to 1970 were the vehicle of a two-party system that jointly and continuously carried forward the Second World War's domestic agenda. In the 1970s and 1980s that agenda came increasingly into question, and after much sharp argument between and within the parties, together with a brief and failed attempt to break out of the two-party system altogether, the political system gradually adjusted to a new, and eventually to a large extent shared, agenda.[1] By 1990 British political institutions had outwardly changed rather little since 1970. Such reform as occurred was gradual and stemmed more from unplanned social and technological change than from deliberate intent, let alone from legislation; change when deliberate reflected short-term governmental need or party interest, not sustained and objective reflection. Political structures that can so readily weather such a major shift in policy are flexible indeed. During the 1970s and 1980s the customary courtesies between government and opposition were never completely abandoned. Heath and Wilson, Callaghan and Thatcher, Thatcher and Foot or Kinnock probably disliked one another, but bipartisan policy—on Northern Ireland, for example—could survive even at the height of party antagonism. On 20 February 1981, in a chance railway encounter, Benn and Joseph, from the opposite political extremes, could hold a sustained lively conversation about British politics all the way from Bristol to London in an empty first-class compartment. According to Benn, 'it was great fun. I said, "At least we can agree on this, Keith, that the last thirty-five years have been a disaster!" . . . we got on famously!'[2]

By 1970, however, respect for British political institutions—the faith that had pervaded Morrison's *Government and Parliament*, for instance[3]—began to seem complacent and even arrogant. This shift originated partly in a sequence of events which showed politicians in a poor light, and was cumulative in its impact: Suez in 1956, the Profumo affair in 1963, the Poulson corruption

---

[1] For a fuller discussion see B. Harrison, 'The Rise, Fall and Rise of Political Consensus in Britain since 1940', *History* (Apr. 1999), 301–24.   [2] Benn, *Diaries 1980–90*, 93 (20 Feb. 1981).
[3] Harrison, *Seeking a Role*, 403.

scandal in 1972, and (in the USA) abused executive power in the Watergate scandal of 1972–5. In the Profumo affair—which offered all the excitement of a government minister brought down by a scandal that combined sex, spies, and country houses—media probing shook many illusions about public life. The journalist Bernard Levin thought it a 'traumatic moment', revealing public men as not so very different from private men: 'from that moment we may date Britain's start on the road back to full national health, which is to say full national self-recognition'.[4] Britain now began looking to France and Sweden for ideas on governmental structure, to the USA for how best to monitor the executive and uphold liberty, and to West Germany, the Netherlands, Ireland, or Israel for ideas on electoral reform. EEC membership carried this further, slowly edging Britain away on constitutional matters from kindred political systems in USA and Commonwealth. By the late 1960s, however, enthusiasm for rejuvenating Britain's major institutions—civil service, local government, universities, parliament—had begun to wane.

From the mid-1970s there re-emerged a differently motivated enthusiasm for constitutional reform, owing less to any rationalistic and progressive urge to modernize than to a growing partisan conviction that British institutions were unfair and even dangerous. The Liberal Party had special reasons for disliking a simple-majority system whose high electoral threshold denied them governmental experience by requiring them to grow substantially before they could reap seats in proportion to votes won. With the media and the public at large, however, dissatisfaction with the British political system moved closer in the 1970s and 1980s towards distaste. Disillusionment is built into a simple-majority two-party system within a pluralistic society. The Second World War had the effect of temporarily terminating inter-war attacks on the British political system,[5] but thereafter the successive disillusionment with governments of both parties could resume. Elements of both parties successively exaggerate how much can be achieved by gaining office, but overall disillusionment is kept within bounds because an alternative government is always waiting in the wings, and government's eventual failures stir renewed hopes in its rival—in an unending sequence.

Labour voters were disillusioned with the first two Wilson governments, in which they had invested such high hopes in 1964; there are parallels between the British response to Wilson's departure in 1970 and the Australian response to Gough Whitlam's in 1975. Distaste focused as much upon style as on policy, and did not come only from the anti-parliamentary left. Jenkins, for example, sought in 1972 to counter a cynicism about politics that he thought 'already widespread': he thought politics more than 'a mere game of "ins"

[4] B. Levin, *The Pendulum Years. Britain and the Sixties* (1970), 88.
[5] Harrison, *Seeking a Role*, 53, 59, 61, 69, 403, 425, 533, 543.

and "outs", linked to House of Commons tricks and manoeuvres'.[6] As for Conservative backbenchers, the Heath government's u-turn of 1972 seemed deeply disappointing, and led some to favour structural reform packages which included electoral reform, coalition government, and devolution as safeguards against a seemingly inevitable socialism. Experience of Labour governments in 1974–9, however, convinced others in the Party—most notably Joseph and Thatcher—that a new policy direction was required. The far left drew a very different conclusion: that existing policies should be pushed further, with help from the labour movement's extra-parliamentary traditions. Thatcher believed, correctly, that she could win without coalition or electoral reform, and constitutional reform died for a decade. Then in 1990 Thatcher's ouster prompted furious faction-fighting within the Conservative Party at what some saw as a Thatcherite revolution unexpectedly arrested by traitors from within. Within the Labour Party, a yearning to oust Thatcher accumulated pressure in the 1980s for remodelling the Party, in the hope of winning power and so enacting constitutional reforms to prevent any more Thatchers from emerging. There was, however, a quite separate impulse to constitutional reform. In 1951 ignorance of British government's workings had been bliss, whereas by the 1970s familiarity bred relative disrespect. The intervening period saw cabinet ministers' diaries published which uncompromisingly, and some thought dangerously, exposed unsavoury realities of life at the top: Crossman's (published in 1975–81), Castle's (1980–4), and Benn's (1987–2007). With the media less reverential and better informed, complaints about British political institutions reached a climacteric in the mid-1990s.[7]

This chapter does not aim to narrate British political history between 1970 and 1990, though a cursory approach to that appears earlier in this book,[8] and the raw material for a more detailed narrative appears in the chronology of events below. The aim here is successively to outline and analyse change in the political structure's leading components between 1970 and 1990, beginning in this chapter's first section with the executive (monarchy, cabinet, prime minister), and in the second with the two houses of parliament. Discussion then turns, in the third section, to the administrative structure: civil service, devolution, regional and local government. This prompts, in the fourth section, discussion of the tension between enforcement through the judicial and penal system on the one hand, and libertarian attitudes and structures on the other; the judicial system, police, and prisons then come into view. In sections 5 and 6 trends within the Conservative and Labour parties, respectively, are considered in detail. A concluding section focuses on one of the most important yet

[6] *O* (12 Mar. 1972), 2.
[7] For more complaints, see Harrison, *Transformation of British Politics*, 340–1, 346.
[8] See above, pp. xvii–xviii.

intangible late twentieth-century changes in British politics: the transformed interaction between privacy and publicity.

1. A CONTROVERSIAL EXECUTIVE

Whereas adaptation and transition are the themes pervading the monarchy's social role in the 1970s and 1980s,[9] the themes pervading its political role involve continuity and stability. During the 1960s commentators became less reverential. The rejection of the syrupy sycophancy that had afflicted the British monarchy in the 1950s was welcome, together with the more balanced and informative approach to modern monarchy that such rejection encouraged—in Robert Lacey's *Majesty* (1977), for example. By the end of the 1960s, however, the cartoonist Gerald Scarfe's sharp tone was reminiscent of the Regency period. The Sex Pistols' performance, 'God Save the Queen', a sneering attack on British ideals and institutions, was released to coincide with the Jubilee celebrations in June 1977, and had sold 200,000 copies by the end of Jubilee week.[10] At first sight more threatening to monarchy than this childish publicity stunt was the somewhat mocking tone that became fashionable in the 1980s among journalists, whether on right or left, consolidated by the caricature of the royal family that featured on *Spitting Image* in the 1990s. Much of this apparent disrespect more closely resembled tweaking a nose unlikely to be put out of joint. Few failed to acknowledge the Queen's sheer professionalism in performing for so long a most difficult role—a professionalism facilitated by what *The Times* on her fiftieth birthday saw as 'the best justification of the hereditary principle': a lifetime 'spent in one cause'.[11]

Nowhere did the Queen accumulate experience more valuable to British governments than in her knowledge of the Commonwealth. She was probably more preoccupied with it than were her British subjects, though her attempt to brand a coup in Fiji as illegal in 1987 proved ineffectual.[12] Yet prime ministers, most notably Thatcher at the Lusaka CHOGM in 1979, profited considerably from the Queen's diplomatic skills and influence with Commonwealth heads of state.[13] Less frequently acknowledged was her physical courage. As an essentially symbolic figure, she was particularly vulnerable in an age when some saw publicity as an end in itself, and when terrorists aimed high. In 1979 her father's cousin, Earl Mountbatten, was blown up by a booby-trap bomb in Ireland, yet his assassination, far from undermining the monarchy's ceremonial role, provided an occasion for a state funeral which memorably emphasized it. Two years later, six blank shots were fired at the Queen during the trooping

---

[9] See above, pp. 125–31.   [10] Hewison, *Culture and Consensus*, 199.
[11] *T* (21 Apr. 1976), 17 (editorial).
[12] See E. Powell in *T* (2 Oct. 1987), 16; leader in *Ind* (3 Oct. 1987), 12.
[13] Young, *One of Us*, 491; cf. Longford, *Elizabeth R*, 247, 352.

of the colour by a teenager who sought publicity comparable to that of John Lennon's assassin in 1980 and President Reagan's would-be assassin in 1981.[14] Elaborate precautions were taken against terrorists at the royal wedding in July 1981, with sniffer dogs in the Cathedral overnight, helicopters surveying the processional route, sewers searched beneath it, marksmen located at key vantage points, 400 detectives distributed among the sightseers, and two armed police sergeants disguised as footmen riding with the royal coaches.[15] Here, as much as anywhere, history must conjure up what did not happen: among the precautions taken by Bart's Hospital near the Cathedral was getting in supplies of blood to match that of the royal family. When in 1994 the Prince of Wales experienced what at first looked like an assassination attempt, his sister thought such incidents 'a permanent possibility . . . We just have to live with it.'[16]

The Queen's role in choosing the prime minister had not completely disappeared after 1970: indeed, it was enhanced by the fluid parliamentary situation created by a weakened two-party system. This made the refusal of a dissolution to a prime minister more likely as long as somebody else might win the necessary majority within the existing parliament.[17] As events turned out, the Queen maintained good relations with Conservative and Labour party leaders whose temperaments contrasted markedly. She did not fail even when required to interact for more than a decade with a prime minister whose pretensions, for all the depth of her curtseys, were themselves almost regal, and whose abrasive policies at home and in the Commonwealth the royal family probably disliked.[18] The paternalist mandarin 'wets', against whom Thatcher struggled in the 1980s, deeply permeated the royal family. Thatcher was not left unaware of the Queen's anger in October 1983 when she learnt only from television news that the Americans had invaded the Commonwealth island of Grenada to defend their citizens against its Marxist regime.[19] But such friction as occurred reached the public only through rumour. In an age when her father's self-discipline and sense of duty were out of fashion, the Queen amply displayed both—nowhere more than in the reticence her strict political neutrality required. Late twentieth-century British republicanism therefore took only theoretical directions. The company the Queen chose to keep might be too limited, her manner might be too shy and formal for media sparkle, and her infectious sense of humour might rarely emerge in public—yet she

---

[14] S. Tendler, 'The Teenager who Wanted Fame', *T* (15 Sept. 1981), 30.
[15] *T* (28 July 1981), 3. See also *T* (30 July 1981), 1, 4 (souvenir number); *G* (30 July 1981), 26.
[16] *T* (28 July 1981), 3; (30 July 1981), 4. *G* (30 July 1981), 26. For Princess Anne see *T* (27 Jan. 1994), 3.
[17] As Robert Armstrong and Lord Crowther-Hunt advised Wilson in Mar. 1974, *DT* (29 Oct. 2005), 14.   [18] It was a close-run thing, though; see *DT* (4 Mar. 1987), 17.
[19] *T* (23 Nov. 1990), 5.

was almost universally respected. She might not win the intense affection lavished upon her mother, and in her later years she and her family were exposed to merciless publicity and mounting criticism. Yet somehow she seemed never to lose her dignity and good humour, never betrayed a secret, and never shed the family trait of common sense and moderation. Moving cautiously—sometimes perhaps too cautiously—with the times, she infused with a new usefulness and flexibility the British monarchy to which she dedicated her life.

The cabinet did not evolve in linear fashion after 1970. The prime minister's personality and circumstances were the main factors moulding its mood and function, and the institution's continued flexibility emerges clearly from the contrasting uses to which it was put. The humane patriotism of the decent, courageous, idealistic, and hard-working politician who became prime minister in 1970 had been forged in resistance to Hitler both before and during the Second World War. Heath's wartime experience evoked in him not a self-indulgent nostalgic chauvinism but an unsentimental, determined, and forward-looking internationalism. Many-sided in his talents, he could on leaving university have succeeded in at least three careers: musical, administrative, and political. He rightly rejected the first, but mistakenly sacrificed the second for the third. He had passed equal first in the civil service examination of 1946, and served for a year as a civil servant in 1946–7. His industrious and well-organized but almost apolitical outlook helps to explain his unusually close affinity as prime minister with Sir William Armstrong, head of the civil service from 1968 to 1974. In moving towards corporatist policies, Heath encouraged Armstrong to be more visible than was customary for civil servants, and (as Armstrong himself admitted) even induced him in high-level negotiations 'to say something which was not normal for a civil servant'.[20] The qualities of this authoritative bachelor prime minister were bound to evoke respect from cabinet colleagues. Always serious and aloof, he was laconic in the chair, but efficient and well able to delegate. Heath enjoyed being prime minister, but deployed his musical and sailing interests to preserve the balance and proportion that successful leadership requires, and refrained from Wilson's fussy activism and publicity stunts.

Instinctively a man of government, Heath did not shirk difficult decisions, many of which were needed during the peculiarly difficult period when he was prime minister. With his government seriously damaged at the outset by the premature death of Iain Macleod, Heath was loyally backed by Alec Douglas-Home, his predecessor as Conservative prime minister. Partly as a result, this was a united, leak-free, and even friendly cabinet, despite capsizings of policy amidst a sea of troubles. Heath did little to advertise his virtues: his shyness made him too brusque for the conciliatory arts of party leadership,

---

[20] *T* (27 Mar. 1974), 6.

or for the presentational aspects of government so important in a media age. He was a pedestrian speaker, and it is characteristic that of the two memorable phrases attributed to him, one he never said, and the other he apparently said only by mistake.[21] Edward Heath was the Robert Peel of his day, a lonely and socially awkward man well able to attract loyalty from close associates, but expecting too much from the backbenchers whom he did so little to cultivate. When he accompanied a high-handed executive style with failure in all but his main objective, getting Britain into the EEC, his backbenchers grew surreptitiously—and, after he lost office, openly—critical. Nourishing their grievances in the House of Commons smoking room which he so rarely visited, they prematurely destroyed him. Thatcher's subsequent triumphs rested upon and required his earlier gallant failure, but so painful was that failure that Heath ruled himself out from claiming any credit for her achievements. When, in the 1980s, she was riding high, he lurked in the shadows awaiting her fall, which came much later than he had hoped. He relished it when it came, but by then he was too old and too unpopular with his party to benefit by it. Throughout it all he remained loyal to what he saw as his Party's traditions, and offered a firm, consistent, and sometimes justified resistance to intrusive and often cheap and trivial comment from the media people whom he could never bring himself to conciliate. Even in his later years, flickers of shy and wry humour could still sometimes light up a personality whose bitterness against his successor became his hallmark. It was both a psychological puzzle and a personal tragedy that the talented and genial Oxford undergraduate so popular in the late 1930s with his Balliol College contemporaries could end his days as an inconsiderate and contrary old curmudgeon.

The mood within Wilson's cabinet in 1974–6 differed from both Heath's and from Wilson's earlier cabinets. Wilson had by now evolved from his party's Macmillan into the nation's Baldwin, apparently pursuing the quiet life, and taking care to smoke in public the pipe which in private gave way to a cigar. He took pride in presiding over a Labour Party which he had at last fashioned into a party of government,[22] and now saw himself as the seasoned impresario, coordinating a cabinet rich and diverse in talent. He brought his ministers forward more readily, and delegated more willingly to them and to cabinet committees. Outsiders thought him more relaxed, yet privately he was nervous, especially about facing parliamentary questions, and was drinking too much brandy. He remained suspicious of colleagues, and could still in private conversation with Castle describe a reshuffle in June 1975 as 'pure poetry';[23]

[21] Campbell, *Edward Heath*, 528.
[22] See his speech at the Labour Party conference on 20 Sept. 1975, *T* (1 Oct. 1975), 5.
[23] Castle, *Diaries 1974–6*, 413 (10 June 1975).

prime-ministerial intrigue and deviousness had not gone away.[24] Accessible
and totally unpompous, Wilson relished relaxed and bantering political gossip
with his cronies late into the night, and close observers were astonished at how
much prime-ministerial time was eaten up by squabbles among his associates
in 10 Downing Street.[25] He remained preoccupied with politics almost to
the exclusion of any other interests, and was obsessive about the press and
cabinet leaks; this was partly because newspapers gave him, in his insulated
and politically preoccupied personal life, his one link with the outside world.
To the very end of his premiership he was trying to manipulate the press,
'leaking himself and blaming others'.[26] Since 1970 party unity had been Wilson's
overriding aim, and we have seen how his astute handling of the EEC issue
held the Party precariously together in opposition, at the price of some loss
of dignity for himself.[27] He sought also to draw the Party's parliamentary and
trade union wings more closely together. This was the role of the foursome
presiding over the central policy questions in Wilson's last government and in
Callaghan's which followed. The foursome were the prime minister, Michael
Foot, Denis Healey, and the TGWU General Secretary Jack Jones—a single-
party coalition far more stable than the inter-party 'national' coalition that
others at the time favoured. Also crucially stabilizing was the relationship
between Wilson and Callaghan, now closer and less tense. Some had thought
Wilson intended to be an Attlee and stay on long enough to prevent his ageing
rival from succeeding him, but Callaghan's ambition to lead the Party had died
in 1970,[28] and thenceforward his relationship with Wilson, uncomplicated by
rivalry, ripened into mutual respect.

Wilson's resignation on 16 March 1976 surprised the public, though it had
frequently been pre-announced to intimates. It was a response to realized
ambition for himself and his party, and to personal exhaustion: if he had
won the general election of 1970 he would probably have retired earlier. He
may also have felt that his powers were waning, for his performance now
varied markedly—from 'his best, which is superb, and his worst, which is
tatty'.[29] He may also have seen how limited must be the term for a style
of party leadership centring on tactics rather than on policy. As he once
privately told Haines, 'Joe, the trouble is that when old problems recur, I
reach for the old solutions. I've nothing to offer any more.'[30] Yet tactics were
not to be despised: it was a major achievement to convert Labour into a
party of government, thereby equipping it to make its final bold, sustained,

---

[24] See e.g. the extraordinary episode in Benn, *Diaries 1973–6*, 137 (10 Apr. 1974).
[25] e.g. Donoughue, *Downing Street Diary*, i (2005), 58, 97 (10 Apr. 74).
[26] Ibid. i. 720 (5 Apr. 1976).   [27] See above, pp. 27–9.
[28] Callaghan's interview with Kenneth Harris in *O* (3 Dec. 1978), 29.
[29] Donoughue, *Downing Street Diary*, i (2005), 128 (24 May 1974).
[30] Haines, *Glimmers of Twilight*, 110, cf. 116.

and in the medium term necessary attempt to operate a corporatist economy. Besides, the importance of timing and tactics were clear enough to those who witnessed the political and social disarray in which Heath's truculent honesty had left the country in 1974. Wilson recognized the distinction between conciliation and appeasement, displayed a shrewd understanding of British social and political structures, and did more than most to ensure their survival through very difficult times. There may have been long-term strategic failures in these years, but Wilson's qualities, like Callaghan's, were crucially important at a major moment of transition—from the old bipartisan consensus round wartime interventionism within the nation-state, to the new bipartisan consensus round free-market institutions within the EEC. To Donoughue, who worked so closely with him in 1974–6, Wilson seemed 'basically a nice kind man', now past his prime, and carrying 'too much heavy luggage from the past'. His departure from 10 Downing Street on 5 April 1976 seemed poignant: without a backward glance, 'he just walked out, slightly stooped, brushing back his grey hair, a plump little man in a crumpled suit'.[31]

The cabinet's mood changed again under Callaghan from 1976 to 1979. His premiership was launched to an almost audible sigh of relief at his candour, his fearless and blunt statement of home truths, and his willingness to discuss big issues in full cabinet. Tensions relaxed because he had achieved more than the height of his ambition, and enjoyed being prime minister. The kitchen cabinet and the intrigue disappeared, there were fewer gimmicks or reshuffles and no obsessions about the media. Callaghan's influence like Wilson's stemmed partly from his considerable hold over parliament, but his appeal was wider. 'And I never even went to university', he said, when told that he had won the Labour leadership—the first British prime minister so placed since Ramsay MacDonald. Jenkins could not recall from memory or from history anyone in politics who 'combined such a powerful political personality with so little intelligence',[32] but this was indeed a narrow and arrogant definition of intelligence, and still more of political intelligence. Besides, Callaghan's unacademic background brought him two major advantages: a close affinity with the trade union movement's tough pragmatic mood and a remarkable rapport with the general public. Instinctively conservative and, despite his Welsh power-base, decidedly English, Callaghan conveyed an almost Dickensian bonhomie. Yet he could be tough and even ruthless, and with his physically impressive presence he made a persuasive and skilful speaker. The son of a naval petty officer, he took pride in being invited by the Queen to the naval review at Spithead,

---

[31] Donoughue, *Downing Street Diary*, i. 721 (5 Apr. 1976).
[32] Quotations in Pimlott, *Wilson*, 685, and Jenkins, as reported by Crossman, in *Cabinet Diaries*, iii. 627 (5 Sept. 1969).

yet the same man could break out (rather tunelessly and with no loss of dignity) into a music-hall song at the TUC to the delegates' 'loud cheers of "more" '.[33] In his own person he epitomized the Labour Party's long-standing role as vehicle for the full political recognition and integration of organized labour. His avuncular manner and populist common sense usefully prolonged Wilson's defusing of the national mood after Heath's conflicts with the miners. Callaghan knew that the country could be governed only through engineering consensus, which for him meant working closely with the trade unions; when in the 'winter of discontent' they failed him, he had no other recourse, and hard choices could no longer be shirked. He knew his party through and through, but he was not equipped or inclined to open it out to new ideas and influences. Nonetheless, Callaghan was his Party's greatest asset at the general election of 1979, as well as the preferred choice as prime minister of one in eight Conservative and two-thirds of Liberal voters.[34] If Callaghan's party had been equally popular, Thatcher would have been a mere footnote in the history books.

There now followed one of the most remarkable episodes in British cabinet history. Thatcher was the first woman prime minister, and showed no feminist scruple in exploiting the fact. Not only did she sometimes surprise male colleagues by attacking them more sharply than they expected from a woman; she reinforced intimidation by encouraging courtship. What was extraordinary about her handling of the cabinet was less her sex than her attitude to her role. Before taking office she announced that she 'couldn't waste time having any internal arguments',[35] and she never even attempted to act as cautious and conciliatory chairman. The judicious summing-up was not for her: in any discussion she made her views so forcibly clear at the start as to deter the counter-arguments which she would have relished. With an almost Gaullist sense of mission about the need to rescue her country, she did not see the cabinet as a sounding-board for opinion, for her mind was already made up. If defeated there, she would embarrass, out-trump, and sometimes betray and humiliate cabinet colleagues by publicly seeking support from admirers in the parliamentary party or in the country at large. On her own admission, public disagreement with cabinet colleagues was an occasional but useful device for pushing 'reluctant colleagues further than they would otherwise have gone'. Her cabinet, like Wilson's, was leaky, and again the prime minister was often the leaker, but her leaks were often overt, not surreptitious. 'I am the rebel head of an establishment Government', she told a reception in Downing Street in 1980, kicking off her shoes and standing on a chair to give an impromptu speech.[36] She wanted action, and if in 1980 the Yorkshire police were making no

[33] *T* (6 Sept. 1978), 1, 4. See also Callaghan, *Time and Chance*, 461.   [34] *FT* (2 May 1979), 22.
[35] *O* (6 May 1979), 9 (to K. Harris on 6 May 1979).
[36] Thatcher, *Downing Street Years*, 579. N. St John-Stevas, *The Two Cities* (1984), 83, at a reception in aid of the Covent Garden Appeal Fund on 24 June 1980.

headway in catching the 'Yorkshire Ripper', she would go to Leeds to manage the investigation herself; only with great difficulty did Whitelaw as Home Secretary restrain her.[37] Peter Sutcliffe was arrested and convicted in the following year for murdering thirteen women since 1975 and for attempting to murder seven more.

In her first two years as prime minister, Thatcher's situation was precarious, and on Rhodesia and Vietnamese immigrants Carrington her Foreign Secretary steered her into uncongenial compromise. She could get her radical economic policy through only by appointing 'dries' to the leading economic posts, by ensuring that policy was formed only in the cabinet's 'E' committee, and by showing a Wilsonian reluctance to discuss big issues in full cabinet.[38] After the memorable disagreements on economic policy in the cabinet on 23 July 1981, however, she realized that she could prevail only through a reshuffle, implemented in September. Thereafter she worked closely with her loyal Press Secretary Bernard Ingham, and cabinet ministers out of favour were at risk of being publicly undermined and then dismissed. The persistence of Wilsonian manipulation at the heart of her government became manifest during the Westland affair of 1986, when Heseltine resigned.[39] Symbolic of Thatcher's continuing sense of vulnerability within her cabinet even after winning two successive general elections was the fact that she could allow a dispute between two of her ministers (Michael Heseltine and Leon Brittan) on a relatively minor issue to become so public and prolonged, and to end by losing both.[40] When in October 1989 she lost Lawson, her Chancellor of the Exchequer in a rather similar way, and when in November 1990 she also lost Howe, her Deputy Prime Minister, after a semi-public dispute with him about the government's increasingly anti-European tone—the last two ingredients of her political demise were in place. Her extraordinary style of cabinet leadership prevailed against all the odds between 1979 and 1981, and thereafter produced a major shift in national policy, yet ended by destroying its creator. The tragedy was Greek in its symmetry and inevitability. But the office she held survived in all its flexibility. Her successor John Major's visit to the 'Happy Eater' restaurant near Doncaster in 1991 was symbolic of a very different and less grandiose style. He had been travelling through snow to the Young Conservatives' conference at Scarborough; the 19-year-old waiter Gavin Ward reported that 'a black Daimler rolled up and a man came in and said, "You might think I am off my trolley, but I've got the Prime Minister here. Is it all right if we come in?" . . . I was very surprised. I didn't speak to him, but he asked for some brown sauce.'[41]

---

[37] Young, *One of Us*, 237.   [38] Ibid. 149–50.   [39] See below, pp. 447, 449.
[40] As argued in Fowler, *Ministers Decide*, 234–5.
[41] *DT* (10 Feb. 1991), 1. Sir John Major, in interview with the author on 5 Mar. 2008, informs me that the brown sauce was ordered by one of his protection officers. I am most grateful to Sir John for allowing me to cite this interview.

The cabinet after 1970 was as flexible an instrument as before, without significant long-term institutional change. Its membership remained at just over twenty, with more than thirty ministers outside it, and nearly fifty junior ministers; but the number of paid government posts, having risen for much of the century, stabilized at just over a hundred between 1970 and 1990. Their efforts were coordinated by the Cabinet Secretary, who presided over the Cabinet Office's mounting numbers: 565 in 1970 and 1,484 twenty years later.[42] The long-term clustering of subcommittees round the cabinet had by 1970 freed it to focus on ratifying and coordinating decisions taken lower down. This structure persisted after 1970, at first because driven forward by ongoing interventionist fashion, but after 1979 by Thatcher's energy in reversing that fashion. Moderating the pressure, however, was Thatcher's preference for informal ways of doing business, in one-to-one meetings with her ministers or in ad hoc committees. This meant that both cabinet and cabinet committees needed to meet less often; by 1987 the cabinet was meeting less than once a week, and almost half as frequently as under Attlee and Churchill.[43] Policy in another area, the EEC, had important implications for the prime minister's relations with colleagues, and especially with the Foreign Secretary. Britain's membership enhanced the long-term trend whereby prime ministers conducted foreign policy directly rather than through the Foreign Secretary. Overseas meetings held not too far away were now numerous and useful for acquiring direct knowledge of European personalities and policies. Among the most important was the European Council, which closeted together the elected heads of state twice or thrice a year. Here was yet another opportunity for prime ministers to escape from domestic difficulties and perform on an international stage, though such meetings were not to Thatcher's taste. For John Major in the 1990s the currency of such meetings had become 'debased in proportion to their alarming proliferation', major distractions from the prime minister's many other duties.[44]

The growing quantity and complexity of legislation, the pressures of public opinion, and increasing participation within the political parties led prime ministers after 1970 to seek ways of ensuring amidst day-to-day events that manifesto commitments were kept and the larger picture periodically highlighted. Hence Heath's creation in 1971 of the CPRS, a team of clever young administrators, businessmen, and academics of whom fifteen had been assembled by 1973. Seconded to the CPRS for an average of two years, they aimed to help the cabinet as a whole periodically to assess where it was going, though its role later shrank into acting as a sort of trouble-shooter or roving

---

[42] *BPF* (8th edn.), 71, 310.
[43] On this see Harrison, *Transformation of British Politics*, 287.
[44] J. Major, *The Autobiography* (1999), 516.

royal commission on problems that the cabinet found pressing but taxing. From 1974 to 1979 it was reinforced by the Social Policy Unit, which coordinated social policy by drawing together the Labour government's special advisers from the relevant ministries, and was responsible directly to the prime minister. It was from this more partisan body that Thatcher's relatively small No. 10 Downing Street policy unit descended, though she used it more directly than her predecessors as a prime-ministerial instrument. The CPRS only precariously survived Thatcher's advent, and after some embarrassing leaks from it she abolished it in 1983. Here, as elsewhere, she was a conservative on constitutional matters.

The cabinet's flexibility was strikingly revealed on 21 January 1975, when on the EEC issue Wilson 'announced a fundamental change in our constitutional convention as casually as if he had been offering us a cup of tea':[45] a public agreement within the cabinet to differ for just over four months about continued EEC membership until the referendum settled the matter. In general, however, the cabinet conventions of ministerial and collective responsibility were upheld during the 1970s and 1980s—though precariously, given the diminished secrecy for cabinet subcommittees, the publishing of diaries by Labour cabinet ministers, and Thatcher's public disagreements with her ministers. There were no published diaries from Conservative cabinet ministers after 1979, but several informative autobiographies published in the 1980s shed further light on how government worked. Countervailing this increasing openness, however, was politicians' growing insulation from the public by the need to ward off the IRA—one source of the alleged 'presidentialism' of party leaders at the general election of 1979: they tended to arrive unannounced, surrounded by policemen, reporters, and cameramen, to address only selected audiences.[46]

2. PARLIAMENT IN DECLINE?

In almost every generation parliament is allegedly in decline, and yet it survives. At least two considerations complicate assessments of its status: it consists of two assemblies; and it provides both the executive and its critics; so its overall status will not necessarily suffer from any shift between its executive and critical roles. Between 1970 and 1990 it proved as difficult as at any period in modern British history to sustain parliament as the place for resolving conflicts of interest. In restraining trade union power, conflict between the Labour and Conservative parties centred on whether parliament's control would be better preserved through confronting or conciliating the extra-parliamentary power. The attempt to run both simultaneously was bound

---

[45] Castle, *Diaries 1974–6*, 287 (21 Jan. 1975).   [46] *Econ* (28 Apr. 1979), 21.

to fail, as Heath demonstrated between 1970 and 1974 when, after his 'u-turn' in 1972, he sought to combine much-resented curbs on trade union power with an ambitious incomes policy requiring trade union collaboration. At the general election of February 1974 he reluctantly raised the cry of electors versus a well-organized sectional interest, given that some miners' leaders were publicly trying to use their strike power to bring down a Conservative government.[47] His electoral defeat seemed ominous for parliament's supremacy, but we have seen how Labour's leaders sought to uphold it through pursuing a more collaborative route.[48] Wilson coasted along to an adequate majority at the general election in October 1974, but with little help from the CPGB's industrial organizer Bert Ramelson: any idea proposed by the Communists early in the year, said Ramelson, had become Labour Party policy by the autumn.[49]

Thatcher as Conservative leader from 1975 saw herself as parliament's champion when opposing trade union backstairs influence over Labour's policies, especially when Healey in 1976 offered in his budget speech to bargain tax reduction for wage restraint.[50] *The Times* saw this as a 'constitutional innovation', as 'the first conditional Budget in British history . . . the first Budget to depend for its main element on the will of an outside body'.[51] Still, Labour's leaders in these years—Wilson, Callaghan, and Foot—were influential in the House of Commons, were fond of it, and were scarcely justified targets for such a line of attack. The Conservatives themselves were not above reproach: there was, for instance, 'wild disorder' on 27 May 1976 when by one vote the Labour government overcame a Conservative technical objection to nationalizing aircraft and shipbuilding, with Heseltine seizing the Mace and blows exchanged behind the bar of the House.[52] Thatcher's free-market alternative to incomes policies, pursued resolutely after 1979, threatened again to inflame Labour's extra-parliamentary wing, and in the month after her victory Callaghan and Gormley felt the need to warn trade unionists against using direct action to remove an elected government.[53] Much of Foot's energy as Labour leader between 1980 and 1983 went into guiding towards parliament extra-parliamentary protest against unemployment and Thatcherism. He was simultaneously containing Benn's attempt to strengthen conference and constituency-party power over Labour MPs,[54] another continuing threat to parliament at this time. Like Thatcher, Foot was conservative on constitutional matters, and the danger passed.

[47] See Heath's televised broadcast in *T* (8 Feb. 1974), 1. See also above, pp. 154–5, 292–8.
[48] Above, pp. 155–6, 290–1.   [49] Obituary, *DT* (14 Apr. 1994), 21.
[50] *HC Deb*. 6 Apr. 1976, c. 285. Thatcher, *Party Conference Speeches*, 26 (8 Oct. 1976).
[51] 'A Budget on Approval', *T* (7 Apr. 1976), 15 (editorial).   [52] *T* (28 May 1976), 1.
[53] *DT* (15 June 1979), 1 (Gormley). *FT* (18 June 1979), 1 (Callaghan).
[54] On these issues see esp. his interview in *G* (13 Nov. 1980), 15; and his attack on Benn in *O* (10 Jan. 1982), 13.

The contribution made to parliament's defence by Labour politicians who seceded to form the SDP in the 1980s was somewhat equivocal. While in their party's structure they took care to uphold the MP's status, their secession weakened the labour movement's respect for MPs and for the European connection. At the end of the 1980s Thatcher left parliament much stronger in relation to outside interests than when she became leader, and she was sometimes herself made very conscious of its power: 'you know, Alan, they may get rid of me for this', she told her economic adviser Alan Walters just before Howe's deflationary budget speech of 1981. 'I may not be prime minister by six o'clock tonight' she told one associate before leaving 10 Downing Street for the House, to defend herself on the Westland issue on 27 January 1986.[55] On both occasions she survived, but her control over parliament was far from complete. It rejected her candidate for Speaker (Pym) in favour of Weatherill in 1983; three of her five leaders of the House after 1979 (Stevas, Pym, and Biffen) were 'wets', and the only 'dry' was Howe. It was Howe's resignation speech from the back benches on 18 November 1990, together with Conservative backbenchers' accumulated fears and resentments, which destroyed her.

Parliament was threatened from a second quarter: the EEC. Quite apart from the entry legislation's unexpected brevity, which in effect bypassed parliament, Labour feared that the (relatively well paid) European parliament at Strasburg might become a rival. EEC membership also risked enhancing executive power generally: its effect, said Benn in 1978, 'has been to produce a radical transfer of power from the British Parliament to the British Government, from the British Government to Europe, and from Ministers to officials'.[56] Given the relatively statist traditions of so many European governments, this was indeed a danger, and the defence of parliament's sovereignty was prominent in the Eurosceptic case. On the other hand the EEC paradoxically provided the occasion for Labour to threaten parliament from a different direction, through the referendum it introduced in 1975 to settle its own internal split and resolve the issue of entry (Plate 2).[57] Its success attracted Thatcher to the referendum as a device for enabling a Conservative government to overcome trade union resistance;[58] this did not ultimately prove necessary, but she periodically threatened on other issues to 'let the people speak' through this route. As events turned out, the referendum became a rather useful device for entrenching constitutional change—on devolution, the settlement in Northern Ireland, and issues arising from EEC membership.[59]

More insidious as a threat to parliament, because creeping up gradually from within, was its weakened capacity to criticize the executive. As long

---

[55] Quoted in Young, *One of Us*, 215, 454.   [56] Benn, *Diaries 1977–80*, 40 (28 Nov. 1978).
[57] See above, pp. 27–9.   [58] Thatcher, *Party Conference Speeches*, 35 (14 Oct. 1977).
[59] See V. Bogdanor's excellent 'Britain: the Political Constitution', in V. Bogdanor (ed.), *Constitutions in Democratic Politics* (Aldershot, 1988), 67.

as parliament remained the final career aspiration for many people—trade unionists, knights of the shire, prosperous businessmen—government office offered few temptations. For many such backbenchers, it was sufficient simply to have arrived in parliament as itself a mark of success. In representing their constituents they did not need databases and personal aides: their long experience and their extensive social networks sufficed. Needing little from government and carrying weight as individuals, they could sometimes be formidable as critics. Until the 1970s there had been a substantial minority of non-careerists even in the cabinet, but thereafter the reduced salience of upper-class social and political obligation and a growing specialization of roles made career politicians dominant in the cabinet, and ensured that most backbenchers arrived in the House to make a career there rather than rest securely upon careers already made. The black jacket and striped trousers of the 'amateur' Conservative politician were vanishing,[60] and ambitious trade unionists preferred careers outside parliament. The worlds of politics, scholarship, religion, and the professions were diverging, so that parliament, hitherto the major national forum for wide-ranging non-specialist public debate, was now less frequently fertilized by the publications, subordinate assemblies, and informal conversations of educated people. Like the *Times* correspondence columns, it suffered from the fragmentation of the UK's elite.

The future seemed to lie with the full-time 'professional' politician—professionalism consisting in spending much time at Westminster, cultivating expertise on parliament's subject matter, and yearning for government office. Less in request was the confirmed backbencher who mixed more widely within the community, perhaps pursuing another occupation in parallel, and whose expertise lay in sounding out opinion and in bringing wide experience and common sense to bear on a broad range of issues. From 1970 to 1990 the proportion of MPs in paid government posts remained at the historically high level reached in 1970: one sixth.[61] Meritocratic tendencies chimed in with political careerism to alter the House of Commons's composition. Working-class representation declined in favour of 'communicators' (teachers, journalists, authors), and women's representation grew from its plateau of under thirty to new heights: forty-one in 1987, sixty in 1992. In 1987 the first Asian MP since 1929 was elected, together with the first Afro-Caribbean MPs. By 1992 there were six non-white MPs, one of them Conservative. The House also offered an arena where handicapped people could advertise their competence for the most demanding of jobs. Jack Ashley did not allow his deafness to preclude his

---

[60] A. King, 'The Rise of the Career Politician in Britain—and its Consequences', *British Journal of Political Science* (1981), 270. J. Ramsden, *The Winds of Change: Macmillan to Heath, 1957–1975* (1996), 399.   [61] *BPF* (8th edn.), 71.

becoming a well-known backbencher from 1966 to 1992, and David Blunkett without fuss did for the twentieth century what Henry Fawcett had done for the nineteenth: courageously demonstrated a blind person's capacity to hold down a frontbench government post.

A career-ladder was needed for ambitious MPs who for whatever reason did not hold government posts. Although the Congressional model was less influential after 1970, the all-party committee still seemed a useful focus for criticizing the executive, especially to Conservatives concerned after 1974 about the Labour government's growing pretensions. In 1979, after Callaghan had lost office but before Thatcher realized how inconvenient to government they would be, twelve specialist all-party committees were established, each shadowing a government department, and each developing cumulative expertise in an area of policy. Created by a Conservative government, they became natural centres of Labour and 'wet' Conservative resistance to Thatcher's economic policies, and made much trouble for her first government, given its small majority. The committees provided enough dramatic and televisable confrontations to weaken attendance at the House's floor debates except on major occasions.

Throughout the 1980s the new committees pushed at their frontiers. In 1980 the Head of the Home Civil Service published a battery of limitations on what types of committee question civil servants could answer,[62] and the Westland affair in 1986 illustrated how readily ministers and civil servants could collaborate to conceal government's inner workings from parliament. Leon Brittan (Trade and Industry Secretary), backed by Thatcher, diverged from Michael Heseltine (Defence Secretary) on how far government should intervene in aid of Westland, Britain's ailing and last remaining helicopter manufacturer. Heseltine resigned in protest against the prime minister's way of running the cabinet, and in the course of damage limitation Thatcher and Brittan appear to have used civil servants to leak confidential information against Heseltine. When parliament's defence committee sought more details, the government banned key witnesses from appearing, blocked access to some documents, and limited what witnesses could be allowed to say. Brittan put on a bravura display of blocking tactics when appearing before the defence committee,[63] and covered up for the prime minister, though he was eventually forced himself to resign. Such governmental reticence did not reflect secretiveness, but concerns that seemed more important than openness: for ministerial accountability to parliament, for the considered and unconstrained framing of government policy, for preserving the relatively recent convention of anonymity among the senior members of what was still seen as a non-partisan civil service, and ultimately for the directness of the government's relationship with the electorate. Given

[62] T (22 May 1980), 1.   [63] G (31 Jan. 1986), 4.

that relationship, the committees could not ultimately coerce the government on policy or even force it to answer questions, but they could at least embarrass governments by exposing their lack of candour.

The all-party committee was not MPs' sole compensation for lack of office: they had many other sources of influence. Most were informal, but the more formal sources were very evident after 1970. The backbencher's ultimate sanction lay in voting against the government in the division lobbies. Earlier chapters have shown how direct could be their impact on policy when governments' majorities were small (as between February and October 1974 and in the later stages of the Callaghan government), on non-party issues such as Sunday trading and hanging, and when parties were internally divided (most notably on EEC membership). Single-party committees had not lost their teeth. It was the 1922 committee of Conservative MPs that forced Carrington's resignation as Foreign Secretary in 1982, and two years later humiliated Joseph as Education Secretary. In one respect Conservative backbenchers after 1965 had more power than Labour, for they elected their leader, and up to 1997 exercised the power four times: in choosing Heath in 1965, Thatcher in 1975 and Major in 1990, and in confirming Major as prime minister in 1995.

After 1970 as before, MPs were wary of the media, which seemed to rival parliament as forum for public debate. In 1994 Benn noted that whereas the media had once come to parliament, MPs now went to the media: to give their interviews, they took the six-minute walk to 'this huge television and radio headquarters at 4 Millbank', whose numerous employees never came to the House, and merely watched its debates on a screen.[64] MPs frequently rejected the radio broadcasting of parliament until they at last succumbed in 1978. Television's irruption into the party conferences in the 1950s had made parliament's reticence increasingly anomalous, and helped to weaken MPs in relation to the party machines. Radio broadcasting advertised the confrontational mood of the House of Commons, and had the effect of making Speaker Thomas nationally known and much respected. He so obviously rose above party bickering that he came to embody decency and common sense; as Thatcher put it, on his retirement in 1983, 'you have become a legend in your lifetime'. The broadcasts fuelled the anti-partisan feeling which the Liberals and the early SDP exploited. Referring in 1979 to the radio broadcasts, the Liberal leader David Steel declared that 'most sensible people are fed up with yah-boo politics'.[65] By contrast, the broadcasts revealed the House of Lords as refreshingly non-partisan, well-informed and dignified, and less fractiously

---

[64] T. Benn, *Free at Last! Diaries 1991–2001*, ed. R. Winstone (1st publ. 2002, paperback edn. 2003), 291 (12 Dec. 1994).

[65] Thatcher, *HC Deb.* 12 May 1983, c. 920. Steel at Louth, 17 Apr. 1979, *G* (18 Apr. 1979), 4.

emotional. The second chamber's standing further advanced after 1985 when its debates were first televised, prompting the House of Commons to do the same from November 1989—though only under quite stringent restrictions on what and how the cameras could film.

The House of Lords enhanced its reputation in other respects after 1970. It was becoming more meritocratic in two ways. From 1964 the creation of hereditary honours ended almost completely, while at the same time the number of life peers steadily grew; whereas in 1950 the hereditary peers contributed 96 per cent of the whole, by 1990 they contributed only 66 per cent.[66] The attendance of both groups was rising, but in the mid-1980s life peers' attendance began to overtake that of hereditary peers. The second chamber was in some ways more representative than the lower house. In David Pitt, who became a peer in 1975, it acquired a black member earlier than the lower house, whose proportion of women members it also surpassed until 1992. And although recruitment through heredity specially hindered women, even that sometimes made the House more representative—through introducing younger members, for example, and through diluting what might otherwise have been an unduly political or even meritocratic membership. When a Liberal in 1968 suggested that the House be selected by lottery, Viscount Monckton rejoined that 'we have that in the Peers' bedrooms already'.[67] Peers of all types brought the House valuable expertise not always available in the lower house: on rural and university questions, for example, on old age and disablement, diplomacy and the civil service; a sixth of the House in 1981 was drawn from the civil and diplomatic services.[68]

The second chamber also accumulated expertise through its increasingly professional committee work from the early 1970s, and more frequently felt able to amend government legislation—making almost three times as many amendments in 1987/90 as in 1970/3. The long-term decline in the Conservatives' hold over recruitment to the House helped to ensure that Conservative governments faced a growing number of defeats there: more than twice as many in 1987/90 as in 1970/3.[69] During Thatcher's premiership the defeats owed something also to Conservative dissidence, given that the more paternalist type of Conservative was relatively influential in the House, together with crossbench bishops; the second chamber inflicted more than 150 defeats on her governments. On the other hand its improved committee structure and revising function made the Lords increasingly useful to a lower house overpressed with legislation. Sitting days in the House of Lords rose

---

[66] P. Norton (ed.), *Parliament in the 1980s* (1985), 104. Mrs Mary Bloor (Information Office, House of Lords) to author, 2 Feb. 1994.

[67] P. Norton, *Does Parliament Matter?* (Hemel Hempstead, 1993), 142 (Pitt). *HL Deb.* 19 Nov. 1968, c. 822 (Monckton).   [68] Norton (ed.), *Parliament in the 1980s*, 105.

[69] Bogdanor (ed.), *British Constitution in Twentieth Century*, 212–13, 216, 224, 233.

by a quarter in 1972–91 by comparison with 1951–68, and the average length of sitting rose by two-fifths.[70] For three reasons the second chamber was not comprehensively reformed in the 1970s and 1980s: the House of Commons feared that to make the Lords more democratic would be to rear up a rival to itself; it feared any option that might enhance front-bench patronage powers; and it recognized that through piecemeal reform the existing second chamber had made itself rather useful. If in these years the Lords became more representative and more effective in scrutinizing legislation, these were gains for parliament as a whole.

3. A REVOLUTION IN GOVERNMENT

How did the rise and fall of corporatism[71] affect British central government? In the 1960s the fashion for economies of scale had harmonized well with the continuing belief in 'big government'. Interventionist politicians, merged businesses, and amalgamated trade unions aimed to manage ever larger areas of British life. With a Labour Party in the 1970s still firmly committed to planning and to redistributing wealth through the tax and welfare systems, and with Heath's government reluctantly dragged along in its wake, statist ambitions extended still further. Between 1974 and 1979 the Diamond Commission was preparing the statistical foundations for redistributing wealth. Policies designed to enable government to control incomes and prices seemed to be moving government in the same centralizing direction, but depended heavily on public cooperation, especially in their voluntary phase of 1975.[72] Government therefore found itself sucked into moulding opinion through energetically advertising, leafleting, and exhorting in ministerial speeches. At the same time the Treasury through the relatively new discipline of econometrics was planning and predicting. Indeed, by 1978 the Central Statistical Office's Director thought the government's statistics so up-to-date that policy-makers might mistakenly tweak their fine-tuned policies too often.[73] Whereas between 1953 and 1967 the civil service's administrative class from permanent secretary to principal shrank by a tenth, between 1968 and 1980 it grew by 64 per cent. By 1980 the UK in relation to its size and wealth had three times as many central government administrators as international comparisons would lead one to expect.[74]

On how to control this huge machine, the parties diverged even before 1979, let alone afterwards. Conservatives tended to argue that a determined minister

---

[70] Norton, *Does Parliament Matter?*, 27. Grantham and Hodgson in Norton (ed.), *Parliament in the 1980s*, 115. R. Walters in Bogdanor (ed.), *Constitutions in Democratic Politics*, 199–200.

[71] For the rise, see Harrison, *Seeking a Role*, 41–7, 301–6; for the fall, see above, pp. 288–347.

[72] For a good account of the government's Counter Inflation Publicity Unit see *T* (30 Dec. 1975), 13.

[73] Sir C. Moser in *T* (7 June 1978), 2.

[74] R. Rose 'The Political Status of Higher Civil Servants in Britain', in E. N. Suleiman (ed.), *Bureaucrats and Policy Making: A Comparative Overview* (New York, 1984), 163. *FT* (13 Jan. 1984), 17.

should not need partisan assistants in order to get his way, whereas conspiracy theories were more prevalent in the Labour Party, which felt socially more distant from civil servants, and especially from the Treasury. So after 1964 Wilson sought reinforcement on economic matters by enlisting the economists Nicholas Kaldor and Thomas Balogh; by June 1974 he had appointed thirty-eight ministerial advisers to all but four cabinet ministers[75]—aggregating some of them, as we have seen, in the newly created Social Policy Unit. There were signs well before 1979, however, that the interventionist trend could not continue. The retreat from nationalization had begun early in the 1950s, and during the 1970s industrial mergers and enlarged local authorities interacting with large 'super-ministries' at the centre did less for economic growth than had been hoped, if only because they entrenched big business and trade union restrictionism and undermined the small entrepreneur. Nor did such large entities enhance democracy: entrenching producer against consumer, they distanced the power-structure still further from the citizen. So the aggregation of ministries ceased after 1970, and Armstrong's breakdown in 1974 symbolized diminished aspirations for the state well before 1979; his successor as head of the civil service, Sir Douglas Allen, kept a lower profile and rarely visited the prime minister. The integration of ministries went into reverse when the Department of Trade and Industry split three ways in 1974, when Transport was hived off from Environment in 1976, and when Health and Social Security became separate ministries in 1988.

'The nation-state has now become too small for the big problems of life', wrote the American sociologist Daniel Bell, 'and too big for the small problems'.[76] Shifting power upwards to international structures was not a Conservative instinct; more congenial to them was devolving power to subordinate institutions within the nation-state. We have already seen how the retreat from 'big government' interacted with economists' changing attitudes and with the Conservatives' political plight to render a policy revolution feasible after 1979.[77] In 1974 Hayek had questioned the value of the information underpinning planning decisions. He thought that no individual's knowledge could match the collective knowledge of the free market: 'I prefer true but imperfect knowledge . . . to a pretence of exact knowledge that is likely to be false.' Healey admitted in 1979 that for all the interventionists' efforts to improve the government's economic forecasting, the results were 'immensely unreliable'.[78] Lawson, looking back on his chancellorship, claimed that with less prediction and better knowledge about the recent past, policy would improve, if only

[75] D. Wood, 'The Ministers' Men Invade Whitehall', *T* (10 June 1974), 15.
[76] D. Bell, 'Previewing Planet Earth in 2013', *Washington Post* (3 Jan. 1988), B3.
[77] See above, pp. 306–29.
[78] Hayek, Nobel Memorial Lecture in his *Full Employment at Any Price?* (1975), 36. Healey, interview with F. Cairncross, *G* (15 Feb. 1979), 13.

because 'the past is at least in principle knowable'.[79] Ideas of this kind were contained in the reading-list Joseph presented to his civil servants at the Department of Trade and Industry on taking office in 1979.[80] The growing opinion among Conservatives by then was that, if taxes were cut, if government absorbed less of the nation's talent, and if economic were separated from political power, inflation would fall and enterprise would revive. Such theoretical considerations were reinforced by party interest, for interventionism fitted more awkwardly with Conservative instincts and structures than with Labour's socialist traditions and trade union links. It was also increasingly unpopular with electors, who world-wide were now demanding better services at lower cost.

Thatcher's governments attacked the problem from several directions. Thatcher wanted not only to slim down the government machine, but to fragment it. So public-sector jobs were pruned through privatization, and through local and central authority 'contracting out' and 'competitive tendering'. The privatization of political advice entailed less influence for civil servants, more for independent think tanks and seconded businessmen like Sir Derek Rayner. There were businessmen too in Thatcher's policy unit at 10 Downing Street, initially run by Sir John Hoskyns the computer millionaire, and in the right-wing think tanks she consulted. Cuts were particularly energetic under Heseltine at the Department of the Environment, where civil service numbers fell by more than a quarter in three years.[81] The Management Information System for Ministers (MINIS) that Heseltine created in 1980 at the Department, later generalized throughout Whitehall, aimed to decentralize management within the Department's directorates, to clarify and cost the responsibilities of each, and to cut red tape and establish machinery which would equip him closely and continuously to monitor progress.

Behind all this lay restored influence for the Treasury. Its stock had been rising since Wilson lost office in 1970, and the Labour governments of 1974–9 made no attempt to moderate its influence through reviving the Department of Economic Affairs. The Thatcher government aimed from the start to scale down the cost and scope of the civil service, and in 1981 the Treasury recovered overall control of it from the Civil Service Department, which was abolished. Thatcher preserved some autonomy even from the Treasury, whose views were not always hers. Control ultimately rested with the small group of 'dry' ministers reinforced by her policy unit and by Sir Alan Walters, her personal adviser on economic matters from 1981 to 1983 and again in 1989. She was

---

[79] Lawson, *View from No. 11*, 807, cf. 845–6.   [80] See above, p. 311.
[81] M. Heseltine, *Life in the Jungle: My Autobiography* (2000), 192. For a useful discussion of MINIS see G. K. Fry, *The Changing Civil Service* (1985), 147–50.

even keener to acquire autonomy from the Foreign Office, and appointed Sir Anthony Parsons as her personal adviser on foreign policy from 1982 to 1983, then Charles Powell (who drafted her Bruges speech of 1988) from 1984 to 1990. In foreign policy as in some other matters, Thatcher liked to formulate policy through seminars; in September 1983 one of these first alerted her to Gorbachev's importance as the man she could 'do business with'.[82]

Her attitude to the civil service was, to say the least, wary. Early in her premiership she rode out into Whitehall like Queen Elizabeth I on a royal progress, and made an explosive impact—humiliating ministers in the presence of their civil servants, civil servants in the presence of their subordinates, while getting to know the leading personalities. She regularly scrawled irreverent comments on civil servants' documents like a teacher correcting a pupil's essay, and reserved a special aversion for civil servants who used what she called 'Eurospeak'. When she thought they were talking nonsense she did not hesitate to write 'gobbledey-gook' on their scripts. During her first nine years as prime minister, civil service numbers fell by more than a fifth, and between 1979 and 1993 more than a million public-sector jobs were transferred to the private sector.[83] Rationalization and privatization ensured that industrial civil servants were the hardest hit: their share of the total fell from 41 per cent in 1950 to 12 per cent in 1990; by 1986 only 96,000 remained, though in that year more than a quarter of all employed people were still working as public employees. Of those in government work in 1986, a third were employed in central government (in the armed services, NHS, or civil service), nearly a half in local government, and nearly a fifth in nationalized concerns.[84] By the 1970s some government departments had become virtually colonized by special interests—so much so, that one observant half-insider thought 'corporate pluralism' or 'pluralist corporatism' an appropriate phrase.[85] The power of the teachers' unions and local authorities in the Department of Education and Science has already been discussed,[86] and there were similar situations in the Home Office (colonized by the police), the DHSS (by the doctors), the Department of the Environment (by the local authorities and building societies), and the Ministry of Agriculture, Fisheries and Food (by the National Farmers' Union).[87] In such cases, civil service power could best be scaled down by policy or structural changes which decoupled the interest from the ministry, or which mobilized or empowered alternative outlets for opinion.

---

[82] For the seminar, A. H. Brown, 'The Leader of the Prologue', *TLS* (30 Aug. 1991), 5. The remark was made on 17 Dec. 1984 on BBC television after his visit—Campbell, *Thatcher*, ii. 286, 830.

[83] C. Thain and M. Wright, *The Treasury and Whitehall: The Planning and Control of Public Expenditure, 1976–93* (Oxford, 1996), 381. R. Mottram, 'Developments in the Public Sector' (unpubl. typescript address to the Joint University Council, 7 Sept. 1993), n.p.

[84] G. Drewry and T. Butcher, *The Civil Service Today* (2nd edn. 1988), 56, 59.

[85] Donoughue, *Downing Street Diary*, ii. 331 (23 May 1978).   [86] See above, p. 386.

[87] Ibid. ii. 330 (23 May 1978).

A television programme surprisingly popular in the 1980s, and not only in Britain, was *Yes, Minister*. It portrayed the wily and power-hungry Permanent Secretary Sir Humphrey Appleby as manipulating and outmanœuvring his vain, populist, and somewhat vacuously ambitious minister Jim Hacker. There was two-way interaction between the programmes and real life. Herself an enthusiast for these programmes, Thatcher wrote a script for and performed in the broadcast on 20 January 1984. Civil servants, too, watched the programmes, feeding ideas into them, and getting ideas from them. Yet the civil service's entire history in the 1980s exposes the programmes as fantasy, for Jim Hacker's triumph was complete: every shrinkage in the civil service testified to the politician's supremacy. This had been Thatcher's intention from the outset, and the programme's creator Anthony Jay received preliminary advice from the head of her policy unit Sir John Hoskyns; when presented with the jointly authored book of the series, Hoskyns found it inscribed 'from two of your allies'.[88] Sir Humphrey's apparent resistance to his political master reflected little more than an entirely reasonable concern to uphold equity between citizens, and to render the politicians' measures practicable, given that it was the civil service which had to implement them.

In expenditure the winners among government departments were those involved in law and order, and in public welfare, with large rises in real terms and in share of GDP; trade and industry and housing were the big losers, whereas the share of transport, education, agriculture, employment, and defence did not appreciably change.[89] On local government expenditure, these years also witnessed the unexpected and ill-planned assault which grew out of central government's attempt to curb inflation. Rate-capping and cuts in central government grants were accompanied by attempts to shift power either upwards to central government through enterprise zones, development corporations, a national curriculum, and opted-out schools directly under the Secretary of State—or downwards to the community at large through empowering parents, hospital trustees, housing trusts, schoolteachers, and house-owners. The metropolitan county councils were abolished, though the 'wets' remained influential within the few areas where substantial region-al planning persisted: in Northern Ireland (Prior's enclave from 1981 to 1984), Wales (Walker's fiefdom from 1987), and the Scottish Development Agency.

The serious civil service resistance to Thatcher's cuts came not from the Humphrey Applebys, but through leaks and strikes by his subordinates. Leaks of confidential documents during the 1980s reinforced the Thatcher governments'

---

[88] J. Hoskyns, *Just in Time: Inside the Thatcher Revolution* (2000), 150. The book was J. Lynn and A. Jay, *The Complete Yes Minister. The Diaries of a Cabinet Minister* (1984).
[89] Thain and Wright, *Treasury and Whitehall*, 445–7.

fears that hostile pressure groups had colonized the civil service areas concerned with defence and public welfare. Labour politicians even deployed some of these leaked documents during the general election campaign of 1983.[90] There were two climacterics: in 1984, when Clive Ponting was exposed as having fed information to an MP about the sinking of the *Belgrano*; and in 1987, when the British spy Peter Wright ignored his secrecy oath and published his secret-service revelations in his book *Spycatcher* in Australia. The government's world-wide attempt from 1985 to prevent the book's publication and circulation, and its persistence in trying to achieve this in Britain after the book had been published, verged on the obsessive, and was certainly counterproductive, if only because the publicity helped to make Wright a multi-millionaire.[91] On 2 August Tony Benn, defending 'our inherent, inalienable and ancient democratic rights', read extracts from the book to a crowd of several hundred at Speaker's Corner in Hyde Park, daring the media to report him.[92] The episode illustrates how contagious open government had become world-wide, and how no one country could easily resist it. Because Britain came late to the world-wide trend for visibility in intelligence services, and to the opening up of public documents, Thatcher had found herself outflanked. The leaks perhaps represent a half-conscious and irresponsible acknowledgement that Britain needed to catch up on the open-government front. A coalition of pressure groups seeking open government was set up in 1984, backed by the Liberal, Labour, and SDP leaders, though not by Thatcher.[93] The Chairman of the *Washington Post* claimed in 1974 that Britain's secrecy laws would have hindered her paper from exposing a scandal like Watergate, but she conceded that within the British political system any such scandal would have been less likely to occur.[94]

Governments in the 1970s and 1980s were also obstructed by damaging strikes organized by civil service unions. Inspecting computerization at Newcastle in 1968, Crossman had already noticed that all but one of the civil servants there were below the administrative grade. The one-hour strike on 10 January 1973, which brought out British Museum employees for the first time in the Museum's history,[95] illustrated how seriously inflation, and the incomes policies designed to curb it, had by then undermined the public-service ethic. By 1979 some unions were conserving their resources during strikes by calling out only key personnel in strategic locations such as tax computers and defence installations. During the 1980s strikes impinged even more directly on aspects

---

[90] D. E. Butler and D. Kavanagh, *The British General Election of 1983* (1984), 97–8. *FT* (30 Aug. 1983), 1.
[91] For valuable background see R. J. Aldrich, 'Policing the Past: Official History, Secrecy and British Intelligence since 1945', *English Historical Review* (Sept. 2004), 922–53.   [92] *T* (3 Aug. 1987), 2.
[93] *T* (6 Jan. 1984), 4.   [94] Granada Guildhall Lecture, *G* (28 Mar. 1974), 8.
[95] *Cabinet Diaries*, iii. 169 (2 Aug. 1968). *T* (11 Jan. 1973), 1, 4.

of government policy. By 1980 the Department of Social Security had within the government service become the largest and most experienced user of information technology,[96] at once a source of strength and weakness. The twenty-one-week civil service strike in support of a pay claim in 1981 hit the recipients of pensions and family allowances and severely cut government revenue: while some of the Department's civil servants were by then on strike, others were helping the government devise ways of countering strikes.[97] The NHS workers' strike in 1982 caused 147,000 operations to be cancelled, and the strike among 380 computer staff at Longbenton in Newcastle, where the Militant Tendency was influential, lasted for thirty-six weeks from May 1984, again delaying pension payments.[98] Tactics of this kind, said Shirley Williams, 'take a poke at the employer and end up giving a black eye to the public', and may well have backfired.[99] This is the context within which to comprehend a government step in 1983 so seemingly drastic as banning trade union membership at GCHQ in Cheltenham. The civil service unions admitted that their success depended 'upon the extent to which . . . defence readiness is hampered', and to American alarm this had prevented GCHQ from operating properly in 1979–81, thereby endangering collaboration on intelligence.[100]

Such events reinforced the Thatcher governments' desire to shrink, decentralize, and fragment the civil service. A decentralizing dynamic was already in place when the Fulton Committee in 1968 recommended 'accountable management' and 'hiving off' some departmental functions. Semi-autonomous managerial 'agencies' began to appear under the Heath government, most notably those associated with the MSC. The Thatcher governments, always seeking opportunities to privatize, were especially keen to promote enterprise within the government machine, and all this harmonized well with Heseltine's MINIS structures. The dynamic speeded up when Thatcher's efficiency unit published its 'Next Steps' inquiry in 1988, claiming that the drawbacks of a unified civil service outweighed its advantages. Flexible structures, diversified pay patterns, managerial accountability, enhanced interaction with the private sector, initiatives from below, better value for taxpayers—these now became the government's covert or overt aims. An agency could cross the line into the private sector where practicable, and clients would be treated like customers where possible. The emerging structure would be shrunk at

---

[96] H. Margetts 'The Computerization of Social Security: The Way Forward or a Step Backwards?', *Public Administration* (Autumn 1991), 326.

[97] Young, *One of Us*, 227. Drewry and Butcher, *Civil Service Today*, 118, 120, 124.

[98] For a good summary of events see *FT* (21 Jan. 1985), 8.

[99] Williams addressing Fabian Society meeting at Blackpool TUC, *DT* (6 Sept. 1979), 10. For two backfires see H. Arbuthnot's letter in *T* (1 Feb. 1971), 11, and Paul Johnson in *NS* (16 May 1975), 654.

[100] *HC Deb.* 27 Feb. 1984, c. 28. See also Howe, *Conflict of Loyalty*, 340. Sir Brian Tovey (GCHQ Director 1978–83) quoted in *DT* (16 May 1997), 13.

the metropolitan policy-forming centre but expanded at the policy-executing provincial periphery. By the end of 1991 nearly half of all civil servants were working in one of fifty-seven agencies, with more to come.[101] Though launched with little public discussion, this was the most substantial revolution within the civil service since the 1850s.

Thatcher combined her economic policy's libertarian and devolutionary aspects with a fierce political unionism, and in the latter she resembled Wilson and Callaghan in her own generation, and Kinnock and Major in the next. Both Conservative and Labour leaders shared memories of the UK's collective achievement in the Second World War, and for both parties patriotism and the union seemed interlinked. The nationalism Conservatives favoured was the nationalism of the UK and of the Ulster Unionists with whom they were closely aligned. For socialists the union brought the additional attractions of removing threats to class unity and of giving the widest possible geographical scope to planning, welfare structures, and egalitarian objectives. The unionism of both parties seemed at first sight to fit the facts, given the UK's growing economic and social integration. Diversification in the Scottish economy, together with the UK's regional economic policy, ensured Scotland's late twentieth-century convergence with the UK economy in such areas as unemployment levels, earnings, and industrial relations. Furthermore, between 1951 and 2001 there was an 84 per cent growth in what had become Scotland's largest migrant minority by far: the English-born.[102] Postal communications in 1979 did not suggest that Wales and Scotland were relatively shut off from the rest of the UK: there was little difference between Wales, Scotland, and most English regions when it came to the proportion of first-class post leaving the region. The regions least prone to commune only with themselves were Outer London (31 per cent) and the south-east (39 per cent), but most regions sent about half their post within their region, and only Northern Ireland (with 71 per cent sent within the region) stood out as being postally more introverted than the rest.[103]

The mid-twentieth-century growth of Welsh and Scottish nationalism seems puzzling also because central government was so responsive to the distinctive needs of the UK's nations. The 'Barnett formula' was established in the late 1970s by Joel Barnett, then Labour's Chief Secretary to the Treasury, by his own account 'on the back of an envelope',[104] to ensure a distribution of

[101] *Econ* (21 Dec. 1991), 28.

[102] L. Hunter, 'The Scottish Labour Market', in R. Saville (ed.), *The Economic Development of Modern Scotland 1950–1980* (Edinburgh, 1985), 181. M. Watson, 'Using the Third Statistical Account of Scotland to Expose a Major Gap in Scottish Historiography', *Contemporary British History* (Spring 2004), 104.

[103] Post Office Users National Council, *Report on the Delivery Performance and Potential of the Post Office's Mail Services* (Report 17; Jan. 1979), 34 (annex 1). [104] *DT* (16 Oct. 2008), 6.

public spending that reflected contrasts in economic prosperity and catered for regional variations in social need: by the mid-1990s Scotland had two-thirds more hospital beds per patient than England, hospital waiting-lists a fifth shorter, and a pupil–teacher ratio 14 per cent lower.[105] Of the 607 Acts passed in the 1970s, only 49 per cent applied throughout the UK, whereas 22 per cent were uniform only within Great Britain, and the remaining 29 per cent applied only within England and Wales combined, or separately within Scotland, Northern Ireland, or Wales.[106] And while Northern Ireland was under-represented at Westminster in relation to its population, Wales and Scotland were over-represented there. In its share of UK population, Wales for most of the century had stabilized at about 5 per cent, whereas Scotland's share had been slowly falling: 10.1 per cent in 1951, 9.4 per cent in 1971, 8.8 per cent in 1991; allocation strictly according to population in October 1974 would have reduced Scottish MPs from 71 to 57, Welsh from 36 to 31.[107]

There are several ways of resolving the puzzle of nationalist growth. Closer contact does not necessarily promote harmony: for example, English unoccupied holiday homes and threats to Welsh and Scottish culture were not welcome.[108] By the mid-1970s North Sea oil's discovery enabled Scottish nationalism to retain its romantic idealism without seeming to threaten Scottish living standards. Joining the EEC made the idea of directly representing Scotland at Brussels more attractive. And the protest vote, since the 1950s an important component of the nationalist vote, was growing ever larger and fiercer. By the mid-1970s disillusion with the Wilson governments had been compounded by the Heath government's major setbacks. With joint achievement in war and empire receding in the memory, and with pride in a shared political system and in relative economic prosperity rapidly waning, the UK seemed less of a going concern, and many Scots thought they could do better on their own. By the 1970s the constituency Labour parties long dominant in much of Scotland were not always dynamic or outward-looking, and some were corrupt. Labour's leaders, acting from expediency rather than conviction,[109] had to press the Labour Party in Scotland to head off the nationalist threat by compromising with devolution. Even this did not prevent some Scottish Labour enthusiasts for devolution from seceding in 1976 into a new Scottish Labour Party.

Wales differed from Scotland in many respects. There was no Welsh equivalent of Scottish oil, and with its Welsh routes running from east to west, the UK motorway system drew Wales still closer to England, prising

[105] *FT* (28 Apr. 1997), 15.

[106] R. Rose, *Understanding the United Kingdom: The Territorial Dimension in Government* (1982), 131.

[107] Central Statistical Office, *Annual Abstract of Statistics*, 132 (1996), 16. Hansard Society Commission on Electoral Reform, *Report, June 1976* (1976), 7, cf. 17.   [108] See e.g. *T* (6 July 1970), 2.

[109] For the cabinet's mood on devolution see Castle, *Diaries 1974–6*, 173 (5 Sept. 1974).

north and south Wales still further apart. Given that Wales was relatively accessible to England, and given that by 1990 almost a quarter of Wales was designated as either a national park or an area of outstanding natural beauty,[110] the English tourist invasion was more intrusive in Wales than in Scotland, and injected into Welsh nationalism a much stronger defensive cultural component. Despite the importance of education in Welsh culture, or perhaps because of it, Welsh school-leavers were far more prone than Scottish to attend English universities.[111] Concern for the Welsh language's survival was especially strong, and during the 1970s Welsh road-signs gradually became bilingual. Here even a Conservative government was quick to make concessions: in 1980 the violence of the Welsh language's defenders was not allowed to divert the first Thatcher government from accepting the idea of a separate Welsh television channel, and it was introduced in 1982.[112] The Scottish National Liberation Army claimed responsibility for several letter bombs sent to British ministers in 1983, but the political option was always viable enough in Scotland to deny such tactics widespread nationalist support; besides, it was a major priority for Whitehall and Westminster to ensure that Wales and Scotland did not become another Ireland.

So by the 1970s Scottish and Welsh nationalisms were for different reasons advancing, especially after October 1974 when the Labour government's parliamentary majority was so small. In neither nation was there any organized counteractive unionist force to compare with Ulster Unionism. From 1951 up to and including 1970, Labour came near to capturing half the votes cast in Scotland at general elections, and usually won at least forty seats. The Conservative share of the Scottish vote and seats began to tumble in the 1960s, whereas the Scottish National Party (SNP) share of the vote was rising fast, with nearly a third in October 1974 and eleven MPs.[113] Rather less impressively, the vote for Plaid Cymru was rising too, with 11 per cent of the Welsh votes cast in October 1974 and three seats won. There were strands within both Labour and Conservative parties which in the right circumstances could have conciliated and defused Scottish and Welsh nationalist sentiment. Quite apart from both parties' desire to steal a march on opponents by aligning with growing areas of opinion, the Conservatives disliked the class preoccupations and centralized planning of Labour-style unionism, while Labour had from its early days been strong in south Wales and the Scottish Lowlands. Callaghan's Labour government felt bound to head off the threat, and devolution measures for Wales and Scotland were enacted in 1978, but were nullified when in the subsequent referenda the 'yes' votes failed by large margins to reach the required

---

[110] Dept. of Environment, *This Common Inheritance* (1990), 238.
[111] A. H. Birch, *Political Integration and Disintegration in the British Isles* (1977), 36–7.
[112] *T* (18 Sept. 1980), 1, 15.
[113] See the useful table in R. Parry, *Scottish Political Facts* (Edinburgh, 1988), 3.

40 per cent threshold. Labour's real sentiments were probably best expressed by Kinnock, then a young backbencher for whom UK unity was best promoted 'by exposing and destroying those who for petty political ends and antediluvian national purposes would seek to profiteer out of the economic resentment of the people'.[114] The referenda results were a major setback for Welsh and Scottish nationalism: at the general election of 1979 both parties registered a marked decline in votes won and in votes cast per opposed candidate, and a further decline in 1983. In 1987, however, the SNP began to recover on both counts, and in 1992 both nationalist parties recovered markedly.

When confronted by nationalism, long-standing Conservative suspicions of central government could have been marshalled behind a pre-emptive strategy: after all, Heath recalled, 'as a party, we believe in freedom'. Hence his tentative moves in the late 1960s towards devolution. Aspects of free-market Conservatism, too, could have chimed in with nationalism: there was a devolutionary aspect to Thatcher's privatization programme, not to mention the affinities between her Methodism and Scottish Presbyterianism. 'The Scots invented Thatcherism long before I was thought of', she told Scottish Conservatives in 1988.[115] Yet the Conservatives had long been losing Scottish support. In the 1880s Unionist hostility to Gladstone's home-rule proposals for Ireland had masked the Conservatives' long-standing weakness in Scotland by aligning it with disaffected Liberals. A century later, the Irish question was no longer being posed in its old form, and the old vendetta between Protestants and Catholics in urban Scotland had lost its bite. At the general elections of 1983 and 1987, therefore, the Scottish Conservatives plumbed new depths in terms of seats won and share of the votes cast; the latter fell from a third in February 1974 to only a quarter in 1992.[116]

In this as in so many areas, Thatcher was unblushing in her forthright rejection of earlier conciliatory moves. She was far more frontally unionist in her sympathies than Heath, and after 1975 slowly edged her Party away from devolution, leaving a dissenting Heath 'appalled by the total lack of intellectual backing' for the Party's evolving anti-devolutionary position.[117] After 1979 her secretaries of state for Scotland merely irritated the Scots by complaining publicly about the need to revive Scotland's lost entrepreneurial values.[118] Scottish Presbyterian hearts were not adequately seduced by Thatcher's Methodist values, nor were Scottish entrepreneurs enthused by privatization's decentralizing potential. Conservatives in the 1980s somehow failed to benefit from the many growth-points in Scotland's economy: oil rigs, 'silicon glen', finance, tourism,

---

[114] *HC Deb.* 15 Nov. 1977, c. 475.
[115] Heath, *Course of my Life*, 566. Thatcher, *DT* (14 May 1988), 2.
[116] See the useful table in Seldon and Ball (eds.), *Conservative Century*, 676.
[117] Heath, *Course of my Life*, 567.
[118] e.g. Rifkind, *Ind* (23 Dec. 1987), 4, cf. Lawson, *T* (24 Nov. 1987), 2.

and service industries, all owing much to enhanced foreign investment. Scottish headlines were grabbed instead by shipyards shutting, mines declining, and in 1990 by the long-postponed closure of Scotland's last remaining steel plant at Ravenscraig. In the outcome, Thatcher's pronounced Englishness and her resolute assertion of central government power in non-economic matters evoked a Scottish hostility fierce enough to reinvigorate Scottish nationalism. Her relationship with Wales was rather less abrasive, and she allowed her secretaries of state for Wales to preserve what was in effect an interventionist fiefdom within her free-market empire,[119] with more local political impact than the Scottish Development Agency wielded in Scotland, yet this could not prevent Welsh Conservatives from trailing far behind Labour.

Devolution, then, was designed to head off nationalism from independence. It was toyed with and dropped by the Conservatives, was backed by Labour from opportunism, and by the Liberals and Liberal Democrats from conviction; the Liberals were even able to capitalize on the Scottish nationalists' alleged neglect of Orkney and Shetland.[120] Labour could in the short term have benefited electorally in Wales and Scotland from Thatcher's unblushing pursuit of the free market. Its revival of the class loyalties within Scotland which had earlier nourished Labour might also have weakened nationalism with a useful diversion. Yet such a strategy offered little in the longer term, especially as by the 1980s devolution was spreading within Europe. Switzerland's government had long been decentralized into cantons, the German lander operated within a federal structure after 1945, the governments of the twenty-two French regions were chosen by direct election from 1986, and Spain after Franco held itself together through responding to growing pressure for regional autonomy. So in the 1990s Labour in Wales and Scotland made terms with the nationalism it could not resist. Within England, by contrast, devolutionary pressures were weak, and the pressures for regionalism came from above rather than from below. At least since the 1930s governments had been transferring local responsibility for welfare, transport, and the utilities upwards—initially to the county and the county borough, and later to central government, which often then found it convenient to devolve administering such policy-areas to regional level. Pressure for regionalism from below was stifled, however, by London's dominance, and by British provincial cities' weak political and cultural identity. Central government's growing power over local authorities in the 1950s and 1960s helps to explain why turnout was relatively low at local elections; there, national political considerations increasingly shaped voting.[121]

---

[119] For Edwards see *FT* (11 May 1987), 12. For Walker, *O* (12 Feb. 1989), 13; *ST* (16 Apr. 1989), B3.
[120] See Grimond's speech in *HC Deb.* 19 Jan. 1977, cc. 355–62.
[121] For a useful table showing this, see H. V. Wiseman (ed.), *Local Government in England 1958–69* (1970), 14.

The history of English local government in the 1970s and 1980s involved three successive and contrasting attempts at reinvigoration, all under Conservative governments. In the first attempt, in the early 1970s, the growing integration of trade and communications made it seem sensible to revive local participation by enlarging the units of government, especially in the big cities. Hence the major local government reform enacted in 1972, in retrospect one of the century's least popular measures. Expert opinion, as marshalled by the Maud Commission (1966–9), strongly backed the idea for expanding local government units to match the enlarged local administrative units that central government now increasingly required. This seemed all the more necessary because British local government boundaries still reflected a somewhat antique clarity of distinction between town and country. The concept of the 'conurbation' or 'city region' was central to the proposals of the Commission, which thought it 'obvious that town and country must be planned together'.[122] If a larger, all-purpose, single-tiered local authority could henceforth manage most local services, central government need interfere less, and voters in local elections would become better informed. So the Commission recommended sixty-one new local government areas outside London, each covering both town and country; fifty-eight of these would be single-tiered, but in Birmingham, Liverpool, and Manchester local government would be divided between a metropolitan authority and metropolitan district authorities.

Peter Walker, the minister responsible, accepted the broad thrust of these proposals, but compromised with tradition and local opinion by retaining as many of the old boundaries as seemed feasible. In England and Wales he abolished county boroughs, and opted for two-tiered authorities: county councils reduced from fifty-eight to forty-seven, subdivided into 333 district councils or boroughs; and seven metropolitan county councils, including London, with their sixty-nine metropolitan district councils. 'My guiding principle', he later recalled, 'was to see that every function was as close to the people as possible.'[123] Walker's outlook reflected the contemporary assumption that size made for efficiency, so the reform was not at first unpopular. Indeed, the trend towards larger units in local administration persisted with the transfer in 1974 of local authority health services to a reorganized NHS, and with the transfer of water, sewerage, and land drainage to new government-appointed regional water authorities. Yet Walker's reform eventually seemed an unsatisfactory compromise—expensive, disrupting, and unpopular. Its rationalization of boundaries did not go far enough for the planners, but went too far for the layman. The latter did not welcome new administrative

[122] Lord Redcliffe-Maud (Chairman), *Royal Commission on Local Government in England 1966–1969,* i. *Report* (Cmd. 4040), 26. [123] P. Walker, *Staying Power* (1991), 78.

areas such as Avon, Cleveland, and Humberside because still in thrall to familiar but now-discarded names like Westmorland, Huntingdonshire, and Rutland.

The Thatcher governments, though irreverent towards much of Heath's legacy, did not set out to overturn Walker's reform. Freedom and diversity for local authorities might accord fully with Conservative instincts and traditions, and with Thatcher's free-market objectives, but in the 1980s cuts in staffing and expenditure seemed the first priority. In his first budget speech Howe noted that since 1974 local authority staffing had risen by more than 200,000, a growth-rate that could not possibly persist,[124] and the drift into a second phase of Conservative local government reform originated with the need to curb inflation. Thatcher's governments found themselves imposing ever more stringent curbs on local authority expenditure, especially on high-spending Labour-controlled metropolitan authorities. Thence they stumbled—pragmatically, piecemeal, and by accident—into structural reforms far more substantial than Walker's, rendering local government politically more salient and controversial than at any time since the early 1920s. Throughout the early 1980s the Thatcher governments fought a complex running battle with local authorities, which when Labour-dominated sometimes even tried to run miniature Keynesian enclaves of their own; when they overspent, central government cut their grants. Then when the authorities responded by raising rates, central government from 1984 encroached further by 'capping' such rises. Other ways of curbing local authority spending-power lay through devolving it to autonomous bodies such as housing associations or through transferring it to centrally administered schools, or to the individual citizen in his capacity as consumer, ratepayer, parent, patient, or householder.

Among Labour's local government leaders of the 1980s, the most provocative was Ken Livingstone, the lab technician who became leader of the Greater London Council (GLC) in 1981, and who at the local level provided the right-wing popular press with what Tony Benn provided at the national level: a bogey who could exemplify the hazards, and even the absurdities, of socialism. Embracing from his Maida Vale bedsit a battery of left-wing causes from lesbianism to Sinn Fein, this young, politically dedicated, persistently cheerful populist seemed a permanent affront to Thatcher's Victorian values, especially when GLC slogans were flaunted on the façade of County Hall across the river from parliament. It was unusual indeed in the UK, though not in Europe or the USA, for local government to provide a basis for national achievement; here Livingstone was the equivalent in the 1980s of Joseph Chamberlain in Birmingham in the 1870s or of Herbert Morrison in the 1930s.[125] He was

---

[124] *HC Deb.* 26 Mar. 1980, c. 1454.   [125] Bogdanor, *New British Constitution*, 242.

in the 1980s London's tactically adroit and weightier equivalent of 'Degsy', Liverpool's flamboyant, sharp-suited young adventurer Derek Hatton, Deputy Leader of its city council from 1979. Conservatives delightedly fomented the 'loony left' image ascribed to left-wing local authorities.[126] The Conservatives, too, had lively personalities. At the national level the fluently plausible and ruthless local government minister (1984–5) Kenneth Baker was more than a match for Livingstone, and Conservative-run councils like those at Bradford, Wandsworth, and Westminster gave Conservative entrepreneurs platforms for bravura performances in local privatization and rate-cutting. The most colourful was Westminster's Shirley Porter, multi-millionairess daughter of Jack Cohen, the barrow boy who had founded the supermarket chain Tesco. As terrifying to her subordinates as was Thatcher to her colleagues, this controversial but practical woman-of-action, subsequently discredited, dressed more vividly than the prime minister she admired and led the Council from 1983 to 1991, including 'cleaning up London' among her recreations listed in *Who's Who*.

The Thatcher government's hasty decision to abolish the GLC and Walker's other six metropolitan county councils exemplifies the unplanned origins of the Party's second-phase local government reform. The Bill got through the House of Lords in 1984 only narrowly and amidst much fierce controversy. For Heath it had been inspired by 'sheer bile against an authority which at the time, did not happen to be Conservative', leaving no overall structure to tackle the problems of a great world city.[127] The GLC's responsibilities were henceforth dispersed among numerous bodies, including its constituent boroughs, reflecting the city's earlier history as a collection of distinct subordinate communities. County Hall, Ralph Knott's fine riverside monument to Edwardian civic culture, was sold in 1993 to a Japanese firm for development as a hotel, and its associated buildings were converted into flats. County Hall's decline and fall was a forcible reminder of parliament's sovereignty within the British political system, and of the dangers involved in lightly tweaking parliament's nose; but it also demonstrated the limited impact of ill-prepared non-consensual legislation, for in 2000 the GLC reappeared in a new format as the Greater London Authority, with Livingstone soon ensconced as London's mayor in the purpose-built City Hall that it occupied from 2002.

It was during the second phase of Conservative local government reform that the full implications of free-market ideas for local government's role became apparent. The first and largest privatization—of local authority housing—immediately scaled down local government responsibilities. Council housing had incurred some discredit not just because of high-rise horrors, but

---

[126] For Tebbit's list of local authorities with 'crazy campaigns' see *G* (13 Dec. 1986), 2.
[127] *HC Deb.* 27 Mar. 1991, c. 986.

because of the Poulson bankruptcy case. Corruption in building council houses had sent Labour's city boss in Newcastle, T. Dan Smith, to prison in 1974 for seven years. The disgraced architect John Poulson, imprisoned for five years, had paid £334,000 to various people between 1962 and 1970, over half of it to Smith.[128] Thatcher's government immediately set about superseding the local authority's housing responsibilities by extending the tenant's right to buy or to opt for a new landlord. By mid-decade the government was groping towards a new view of local government's role: central government was now to set the financial and policy framework, while local authorities were to facilitate and regulate services provided (in or out of house) increasingly on a commercial basis to ratepayers who were now viewed as customers.

Legislation from 1980 sent more and more local authority services out to tender, though in-house labour forces were free to compete. Competitive tendering was required in building and road-works from 1980, in the NHS from 1983, in buses from 1985, and in school meals, cleaning, maintenance, and refuse collection from 1988. Some Conservative-controlled local authorities had begun much earlier: by May 1982 in Wandsworth, a council held by the Conservatives from 1978, a private contractor was employing teams of relatively young and black recently unemployed dustmen who for £125 per week were ready to brave the official dustmen's picketing and sabotage. By 1985 staff numbers in Wandsworth had fallen by a third.[129] 'Inside every fat and bloated local authority', wrote that enthusiast for competitive tendering Nicholas Ridley in 1988, 'there is a slim one struggling to get out'.[130] By 1989 competitive tendering had not pushed much work outside the councils' workforce, but its impact on manning levels and work practices had been substantial.[131] Between 1979 and 1995 full-time local-government employees in England and Wales fell from 2.5 to 2.1 million, with manual staff declining much faster (by 31 per cent) than non-manual (3 per cent). After 1979 the long-term rise in central government grants' share of local authority income was arrested, the long-term decline in the rates' contribution was reversed, and drastic cuts in local authority capital expenditure helped to ensure that between 1978/9 and 1988/9 loans' share almost halved.[132]

These remarkable changes coincided with the Thatcher governments' growing determination not to allow initial public hostility to prevent what they saw as necessary reforms. The polls had not at first shown public enthusiasm

---

[128] For obituaries, *T* (4 Feb. 1993), 19 (Poulson); (28 July 1993), 17 (Smith).
[129] *T* (26 May 1982), 26. N. Ridley, *The Local Right: Enabling Not Providing* (1988), 27.
[130] Ridley, *Local Right*, 26.
[131] *Econ* (2 Dec. 1989), 34. *FT* (11 Mar. 1991), supplement on 'Contracted Business Services', p. ii.
[132] *FT* (13 Dec. 1995), 6. G. C. Baugh, 'Government Grants in Aid of the Rates in England and Wales, 1889–1990', *Historical Research* (1992), esp. 233–7.

for such free-market policies as privatization, trade union reform, and an end to incomes policies—yet once enacted, these changes had been accepted.[133] 'A sensible Government does what it believes to be right', wrote Lawson, 'explains why it is doing it, and stands to be judged by the results'.[134] The third phase of Conservative local government reform flowed naturally from the second, but unlike the first two it was too cavalier about public opinion. Some of the blame rests with Thatcher, who was increasingly using the cabinet as sounding-board for only her own views. The community charge (popularly labelled the 'poll tax') aimed to tackle local government's problems at root. The twentieth-century advance of central government subsidy had gradually undermined the directness of the local voter's interest in the local authority's policies: by the late 1970s domestic rates funded less than a fifth of local government's total spending.[135] Partly for this reason, turnout at local elections declined, making it easier for high-spending local politicians to capture the local authority, especially as central government subsidy masked their extravagance. Further undermining the directness of the voter's interest was the fact that the rating valuation of residential property was based on a notional rental value whose periodic reassessments were sometimes postponed through political expediency; besides, such valuations were increasingly artificial, given the long-term shrinkage in the rented sector's share of the housing market. Abolition of the business vote in 1969 (except in the City of London) denied local businesses any direct say in rate-fixing, though rates could profoundly affect their prosperity. Rates had the further drawback that they were assessed on a property rather than on people, so were not based on ability to pay.

What, then, could be done? As a replacement for the rates, local sales and incomes taxes seemed administratively too cumbrous and commercially too disruptive, whereas there was an attractive simplicity about imposing on all resident adults a flat-rate tax with partial rebates for those on low incomes. To tax the individual rather than the property would broaden the tax base, and because all would pay something, all would have an interest in curbing the spendthrift local authority. A Victorian vitality might then return to local government, with a higher turnout punishing high-spending local politicians: socialists could thus be automatically curbed without need for central government interference. The business rate would be set at a uniform level nation-wide, with its proceeds distributed to all authorities on a per capita basis. For Thatcher the poll tax had the 'inestimable benefit' of being a 'transparent' system providing everyone with a 'ready reckoner',[136] and seemed a stout buttress for the Victorian virtues.

---

[133] D. E. Butler et al., Failure in British Government: The Politics of the Poll Tax (Oxford, 1994), 57, 126, 217.   [134] Lawson, View from No. 11, 1036; cf. 201.
[135] R. Jackman in M. Loughlin, M. Gelfand, and K. Young (eds.), Half a Century of Municipal Decline 1935–1985 (1985), 157.   [136] Thatcher, Downing Street Years, 653, cf. 645.

There would henceforth be no representation without taxation, and 'a whole class of people' would be 'dragged back into the ranks of responsible society and asked to become not just dependants but citizens'.[137] Healthy influences would then counterbalance what Ridley called 'the poisonous power-base on which extremism thrives':[138] the groups with an interest in campaigning for higher rates which they did not pay. The poll tax's advocates felt a special concern for the widow who lived alone in a house: her rates were partly set by local government voters who directly paid no rates at all. Thatcher was pushed into action by the response to the Scottish rating revaluation in 1985. She had long wanted to reform the rating system, and was also seeking ways of arresting the Conservative decline in Scotland; the storm among well-to-do Scottish Conservatives seemed to provide a useful opportunity. Acquiescent civil servants, ambitious politicians, and pressure from the party conference drove the reform forward.

Given the intelligence and ingenuity of the poll tax's inventors, and the ample research and discussion preceding its introduction, its defects seem in retrospect surprisingly obvious. A tax on people was far more complex and intrusive than a tax on property. To impose dramatic and regressive changes in liability during a decade when the rates' share of local authority revenue had been rising fast—without phasing in the reform over a long period, and without countervailing compensation—inevitably aroused resentment. All the more so when the tax turned out to be much heavier than predicted. To go ahead with a reform which the country had never widely demanded involved a prodigal expenditure of the Party's political capital, already on the ebb. In the outcome, the tax (introduced in 1990) seemed unfair and was unenforceable. London's anti-poll-tax rioters in 1990 appeared to carry weight only because they advertised a problem already well known to local government officials, backbenchers, and electors. Indeed, Labour had refrained from advertising the problem earlier partly because Kinnock wanted to distance the Party from its less obviously respectable but vigorously anti-poll-tax hangers-on, branded as 'toytown revolutionaries'.[139] As for Thatcher, for all the merits of her proposed reform she paid dearly for its major mishandling of opinion. It fuelled the shift in backbench Conservative opinion that within months had driven her from office.

4. LIBERTY COMES AND GOES

Between 1970 and 1990 British politicians and civil servants responded as energetically as ever to initiatives generated within the community. Despite

---

[137] Ibid. 661, cf. 658–9.
[138] Quoted in M. Trend, 'When the Poll Tax had Pals', *DT* (26 Mar. 1990), 17.
[139] *HC Deb.* 8 Mar. 1990, c. 999.

declining electoral turnout and party membership, people were if anything more eager to join pressure groups, and the American phrase 'think tank' was domesticated in Britain during the 1970s as it reached new levels of influence. Liberty's dimensions had never been probed so penetratingly, and public concern about civil liberties had never been more lively. As for civil society more generally, women's growing involvement in paid work weakened their volunteering, just as faster transport weakened commitment to locality, but there were at least three countervailing factors: the growing numbers and longevity of the retired; the continuously emerging groups of the newly self-aware (medical, international, ethnic, philanthropic, humanitarian, libertarian); and the electronic revolution's new facilities for the self-organized. The growing 'tertiary' pressure groups and voluntary bodies might often require less sustained commitment or mutual contact than the declining 'secondary' religious and political structures,[140] but they readily invoked help from government and the professions. Social growth-points of this kind, like economic growth-points, are slow to affect opinion, let alone official statistics, but their long-term importance is considerable.

There were relevant changes, too, within that bulwark of British pluralism, the legal system. Lord Hailsham, a former Lord Chancellor, thought it healthy in 1975 that the British legal profession was 'extraordinarily small', yet it was already growing: between 1960 and 2002 the number of barristers rose sixfold, excluding Scotland, and by 2003 there was one lawyer to 480 in the population.[141] It was from the 1960s that judicial review of executive actions revived,[142] and the same decade saw much concern about class bias in recruiting for high judicial posts and about the limited access of the poor to legal protection. The profession was opening out. A built-in structure for drafting law reform measures, the Law Commission, was established for England and Wales in 1965, and worked judiciously to promote reform in selected areas by collaborating with government departments and avoiding giving unnecessary offence to ministers.[143] In the 1970s American neighbourhood law-centres—with their longer opening hours, more suitable locations, more relevant expertise, and more overtly educational purpose—provided models for similar ventures in the UK. By 1974 London had ten, with plans for more in other cities.[144] By 2000 the legal system had become less closely tied to upholding property rights, and within the legal profession there was

---

[140] R. D. Putnam's *Bowling Alone: The Collapse and Revival of American Community* (New York, 2000), 52, distinguishes a 'tertiary association' from a 'secondary' with the claim that in a tertiary association 'the only act of membership consists in writing a check for dues or perhaps occasionally reading a newsletter'.   [141] Sampson, *Who Runs This Place?*, 178, 182–3.

[142] A. King, *The British Constitution* (Oxford, 2008), 123–4.

[143] S. Cretney, *Law, Law Reform and the Family* (Oxford, 1998), 21, 23, 26.

[144] *HL Deb.* 15 May 1974, c. 1051.

'less evidence of the progression from one monastic order to another: prep school to public school to Oxbridge and on to the Temple'. The parliamentary draughtsmen offered stiff resistance in the early 1970s to introducing 'plain English' into government legislation,[145] but during the 1980s pressure built up for demystifying the law in several ways. Its esoteric language—with its archaic forms, Latinisms, and formulaic phrasing—was now being challenged, and American precedents ensured that the cameras now active in parliament began to hover on the courtroom's threshold. As for wigs and gowns, more people now felt that these 'priestly garments' unduly distanced the judges 'from ordinary men and women'.[146]

European and American precedents for the formalized defence of civil liberties through written constitutions, charters, and bills of rights[147] had long encountered the British objection that parliament in a majoritarian political system is liberty's best defence. In a culture with a presumption in favour of liberty, codifying its defence might even prove counterproductive by circumscribing its scope, while perhaps also politicizing the judiciary. The law's entanglement in enforcing industrial relations legislation between 1971 and 1974, for example, through John Donaldson's presidency of the National Industrial Relations Court, had politicized and subsequently held back his career. In the 1960s, however, the more institutionalized approach to liberty's defence gained ground, and already by 1973 Sir Robert Mark was beginning to feel the strain. In his Dimbleby lecture of that year he complained about the fragmented approach to the criminal: 'politicians make the laws, police enforce them, lawyers run the trials, and the prison or probation services deal with convicted offenders. None of these groups is obliged to give much thought to the problems of the others or to consider the working of the system as a whole.' He deplored the suspicion of the police and the procedural ingenuity displayed by 'a minority of criminal lawyers' who 'do very well from the proceeds of crime', and in 1978 saw recent reforms in criminal procedure as almost always 'favourable to the wrongdoer'.[148] By 1981, however, the Police Federation felt it had more to gain than lose from the improved complaints procedure which they had hitherto opposed, and the Police Complaints Authority was set up in 1984.[149]

During the 1980s Lord Scarman epitomized libertarian concern. A cautious but unpompous son of an insurance broker, he pioneered a more accessible style for the judiciary, while approaching his inquiry into the Brixton riots of 1981 from the broadest contextual perspective; some colleagues were alarmed to see a judge chatting to parents while holding their babies and casually visiting local

---

[145] Quotation from Louis Blom-Cooper, *FT* (23 Mar. 1992), 34. For 'plain English', Howe, *Conflict of Loyalty*, 60. [146] D. Pannick, *Judges* (Oxford, 1987), pp. v, 10, 143, 148, 151, 191.
[147] Harrison, *Seeking a Role*, 270, 431–2.
[148] R. Mark, *In the Office of Constable* (1978), 150–5. *T* (18 Oct. 1978), 1. [149] *O* (8 Nov. 1981), 1.

clubs (Plate 16). He was by then among the most influential advocates of a Bill of Rights, arguing that 'we must legislate now not for the homogeneous society we have known for centuries but for a plural society', given that the common law had 'never succeeded in tackling the problem of the alien . . . the woman and . . . religious minorities'.[150] In gaining self-consciousness at this time, all three groups cut across class boundaries, and in this they resembled the homosexuals identified many years earlier by 'D. W. Cory' as likely to 'broaden the base for freedom of thought and communication'.[151]

By the end of the 1970s liberty in the economic sphere was moving to the forefront of discussion. The tendency of British law to defend the individual against the collectivity was also to the fore: the trade union member who refused to strike, for example, or the non-member denied work by the closed shop. As Master of the Rolls, Lord Denning in 1979 even pronounced the large trade union to be the greatest threat to the rule of law, and cited Lord Acton on all power tending to corrupt.[152] During the UK's corporatist apogee in the 1960s and 1970s, however, the trade unions pursued a two-dimensional approach: they combined their zeal for 'free collective bargaining' and desire to ward off the law from industrial relations with the concept of 'positive' liberty: that is, with the idea that the individual's freedom could be effectively defended only through collective trade union action in the industrial sphere and through collective state provision through public welfare. Such a perspective sidelined any conflict of interest between producer and consumer, and in so far as the consumer was thought to need defending, the mid-century remedy seemed to lie in government regulation of the manufacturer and retailer through a designated minister, reinforced by consumer crusaders modelled on the American Ralph Nader; the Liberal publicist Des Wilson was to the fore during these years. After 1979 the priorities shifted again. The free market, rather than the state, was increasingly seen as the consumer's best defence,[153] though Thatcher's outlook left a large role for the state as auditor, monitor, and regulator of the utilities and services which the private sector now increasingly provided. The cost of such structures—ombudsmen, OFWATs, OFCOMs, OFSTEDs, and the like—rose much faster than total government spending between 1976 and 1995.[154]

Terrorism raised civil liberties issues at several levels. For its victims it curtailed liberty in the most conclusive manner, and resisting terrorism seemed to justify enhanced state power. The Birmingham pub bombing on 21 November 1974 killed 21 and badly injured another 184; it was held to justify passing in a mere forty-two hours the Prevention of Terrorism (Temporary Provisions) Bill. Extended thereafter, it was replaced by a new Act in 1976 whose annual renewal

---

[150] HL Deb. 29 Nov. 1978, cc. 1345–6.   [151] Cory, Homosexual Outlook, 235; see also 152.
[152] DT (21 Apr. 1979), 1.   [153] See above, pp. 365–6.   [154] FT (25 Sept. 1997), 22.

became almost ritualistic. Between 1977 and 1986, 4,000 were held under the Acts outside Northern Ireland and between 1977 and 1989 over 8,000 within Northern Ireland.[155] Computers empowered the individual against the state by enhancing his resources for gathering and conveying information and forming autonomous groups, but they also made it easier for the state to monitor him.[156] By 1976 the Bomb Intelligence Unit at Lisburn was computerizing its huge data bank on the nationalist population, and forcing the IRA to adopt a cellular structure.[157] Terrorism provided yet more excuses for tapping telephones and intercepting mail.[158] Security considerations increasingly distanced leading politicians from the public: Downing Street became a gated and ramped fortress, and the bomb designed to destroy the cabinet at the Grand Hotel in Brighton in 1984 (Plate 7) terminated the party conferences' hitherto easy association between leaders and led. Thatcher was not at all reluctant to deploy the full force of the law to defend state secrets; prosecutions under the Official Secrets Acts escalated in the early 1980s.

Here was fuel for campaigning groups of the late 1980s such as Charter 88: to them, Thatcher's pursuit of liberty in its economic and even anti-terrorist dimensions seemed so authoritarian in tone and method as to require a more directly political approach to liberty's defence. Furthermore, IRA terrorism eventually exposed serious defects in the British judicial system, as well as flaws in methods of enforcing the law. After internment without trial had been introduced in Northern Ireland on 9 August 1971, the European Court of Human Rights in 1978 condemned the British army's use of five techniques: wallstanding, hooding, continuous noise, and deprivation of food and sleep. Still more serious was the injustice committed in the courts in 1975, when three groups had been falsely accused of involvement in the IRA bombings of 1974. The 'Birmingham Six' were sentenced to life imprisonment for the Birmingham pub bombings. The 'Maguire Seven' (six from the Maguire family and a family friend), accused of running a bomb-making factory for the IRA, were sentenced for up to fourteen years' imprisonment. The 'Guildford Four' (who included Gerry Conlon, and also received long prison terms) were accused of a pub bombing in Guildford which killed five and injured 65; two of them were also convicted for a pub bombing at Woolwich which killed two.[159] IRA terrorists publicly admitted responsibility for the Guildford and Woolwich bombings as early as 1977, yet it was only after long campaigns and several appeals that

[155] K. D. Ewing and C. A. Gearty, *Freedom under Thatcher: Civil Liberties in Modern Britain* (Oxford, 1990), 214, 225–6.

[156] See e.g. the fears expressed in D. Campbell and S. Connor, 'The Monster that Just Grows', *NS* (5 Mar. 1982), 6–8.　　　　　　　　　　　[157] R. Faligot, *Britain's Military Strategy in Ireland* (1983), 99.

[158] For figures see *T* (1 Apr. 1980), 4.

[159] For vivid accounts of the nightmarish situation into which two of the alleged 'Guildford Four' found themselves drawn after arrest, see Gerry Conlon's *Proved Innocent* (1990) and Paul Hill's *Stolen Years: Before and after Guildford* (1990).

the Guildford Four were released in 1989, and the Birmingham Six and the Maguire six (one of whom, Giuseppe Conlon, had by then died in prison, still protesting his innocence) in 1991. It turned out that confessions had been extracted through shameful methods, backed by false forensic 'evidence'. All this was damaging for Lord Chief Justice Lane, who had been so dismissive of the Birmingham Six appeal; he retired early in 1992. The context for such police methods was the immense pressure on them to find the culprits—a pressure whose power became perhaps most evident when the police took so long to find the 'Yorkshire Ripper', especially after the media had widely publicized an anonymous and somewhat sinister but hoax tape from a person claiming to be the perpetrator.[160] Context explains but does not excuse, and in 2005 the prime minister publicly declared himself 'very sorry' that the Maguire and Conlon families, whom he then met privately at Westminster, had experienced such 'injustice', such an 'ordeal'.[161]

This episode had a still wider impact. Murder statistics bore no relation to trends for any other serious crime, and after hanging's abolition they increased more slowly than other crimes, suggesting that hanging was a deterrent no more effective than life imprisonment.[162] For the murderer, the passions and mental disorders involved were far more immediate and pressing than thoughts about hypothetical state penalties; the Law Commission's plans of 2005 for subdividing the murder category to reflect degrees of culpability were long overdue for introducing nuance. The exposure in the late 1980s of the miscarriages of injustice in 1975 destroyed any serious case for restoring hanging: as the judge in the Guildford Four case had pointed out, if their alleged crime had occurred only a decade earlier, the unjustly convicted bombers would have been hanged: 'what a monstrous addition' the nine or ten people involved in these cases would have been, said Jenkins in the debate of 1987, 'to the already unacceptable level of people falsely or doubtfully convicted in capital cases'.[163] Quite apart from considerations of humanity and justice, even lawful execution would carry the drawback of creating martyrs. Yet in the thirty-four years up to 1990 the continuing support for hanging prompted seventeen parliamentary debates on capital punishment, and when a Gallup sample of December 1974 was asked whether hanging should return for terrorists and bombers, 75 per cent said yes and only 15 per cent no, with 10 per cent undecided.[164] During the debate of 1987, Heath deplored the retreat since the

---

[160] The police handling of the case is discussed in *T* (23 May 1981), 5; the hoaxer turned out to be John Humble, prosecuted in 2005. [161] *Ind* (10 Feb. 2005), 4–5.

[162] T. Morris and L. Blom-Cooper, *Murder in England and Wales since 1957* (1979), 3–6.

[163] Heath, *HC Deb.* 1 Apr. 1987, c. 1138. Jenkins, *HC Deb.* 1 Apr. 1987, c. 1145. See also Conlon, *Proved Innocent*, 132.

[164] For a chronology see *T* (18 Dec. 1990), 7. See also *Gallup International Public Opinion Polls*, ii. 1380.

1950s from Butler's research-oriented preoccupation with 'the psychology of crime, the social reasons for it and the means of dealing with it'.

Crime statistics, however defective, are 'social facts' to which politicians must respond. In Britain after the 1950s people directly concerned with crime were far less resourceful than their Victorian predecessors, and were less perceptive than their contemporaries in several industrialized societies. For example, instead of beginning with the fact that crime stems overwhelmingly from males under 30 who seek opportunities for adventure and yearn to demonstrate their masculinity, enforcement agencies stumbled with all too little reflection from one temporary punitive expedient to another, so that prison numbers rose in parallel with rising crime. Looking back in 1993 at the twenty Home Secretaries who had come and gone since he had arrived in Britain in 1936, the distinguished criminologist Leon Radzinowicz found it difficult to specify two among them who could compare in dedication and reforming outlook to the nineteenth century's Sir Robert Peel and Lord John Russell. His subject had grown apace in the interval, and yet he thought criminologists too reticent on matters of public concern, too reluctant to spring to their own defence when attacked.[165] The gulf between theory and practice was partly to blame: among leading policemen perhaps only Sir Robert Mark on police/public relations, and John Alderson (Chief Constable of Devon and Cornwall from 1973 to 1982) on community policing showed any real imagination. At the same time the criminologists were too prone to engage in high-flown theory and vocabulary: Mark recommended more research on police matters, but complained with some reason that university research in the area had 'little to do with reality and the practical problems confronting the police'.[166]

Police strength in England and Wales rose by more than a third between 1970 and 1990, and relations with the public were moulded by at least four further tendencies. First, the police were no more exempt than any other mid-century occupation from privatizing and specializing trends. During the 1970s employees in private security firms outnumbered the Regular Army, and even government departments were extensively supplementing the police by employing such firms to protect their property and personnel; in 1978 there were 20,000 security personnel in Securicor alone, and 4,000 in Group Four.[167] In this respect, order-keeping in Britain was in effect slowly and unobtrusively returning to its eighteenth-century origins in private policing. The trend was reinforced from the 1980s by the growth of 'neighbourhood watch' schemes on American precedents. The first was established in

---

[165] L. Radzinowicz, 'Reflections on the State of Criminology', *British Journal of Criminology* (Spring 1994), 101, 103.

[166] Address at National Police College, Bramshill, in R. Mark, *Policing a Perplexed Society* (1977), 120.

[167] *G* (7 June 1978), 13. Statistics from H. Draper, *Private Police* (Harmondsworth, 1978), 23.

Mollington, Cheshire, in July 1982, and three months later the Commissioner of Metropolitan Police backed the idea; by 1990 there were 81,000 such schemes.[168]

A second tendency was the rising proportion of policewomen. Growth had been fast enough (though from a low base) since 1950, but between 1970 and 1990 it accelerated from 3.9 per cent of total police numbers to 11.5 per cent.[169] More police did not necessarily mean more on the beat because the third policing change—far more paperwork—escalated. This cultural shift had its drawbacks, but it helped to generate a wealth of new statistics on crime, though in 2000 their pronounced and continuing local variations reflected inconsistent compilation.[170] The figures were enhanced by the growing numbers involved in criminological research, whether inside or outside the Home Office. The latter's British Crime Survey, conducted at irregular intervals from 1982 and annually from 2001/2, at last shed light on unreported crime. The fourth tendency was towards technical sophistication. The police had 1,450 personal radios at the end of 1965; by autumn 1974 they had 26,500, with twice as many radios in police cars. The national file of stolen vehicles became much more accessible when transferred to the police national computer, and was usable from April 1974.[171] Other resources were added to it, including the national fingerprint collection two years later, and in 1984 Scotland Yard installed its first automatic fingerprint recognition system. By 1990 the unending contest between authority and its critics had begun to turn in on itself when computerized research was increasingly needed for detecting computer crime. The police move off the beat and into panda cars[172] from the late 1960s, and their policy from the late 1980s of patrolling in London only in pairs,[173] distanced them further from the public. Though police numbers were at record levels, the public seemed to see less of them.

The police wisely resisted pressures for centralized control and all the depersonalization involved in using sophisticated armour and weaponry. Their public image needed all the more care because there was growing distrust of authority in any form: in 1992 the Chief Inspector of Constabulary felt that 'in this more doubting age, the service may never again return to the post-war position of being a national institution'.[174] Police corruption cases were infecting white adults with the same wariness about the police that ethnic minorities and the young already displayed. Growing police corruption was to some extent illusory: memoirs of the 1930s, when police prestige was at its height, reveal much covert bending of the rules, and this the subsequent

[168] T. Bennett, *Evaluating Neighbourhood Watch* (Aldershot, 1990), 11, 14. L. Johnston, *The Rebirth of Private Policing* (1992), 146.　　　[169] *Annual Abstract of Statistics: 1976*, 92; *1996*, 86.
[170] *Ind* (14 July 2000), 9.　　　[171] *HL Deb.* 31 Oct. 1974, cc. 168–9. *T* (1 Nov. 1974), 9.
[172] Harrison, *Seeking a Role*, 434.　　　[173] *DT* (17 Mar. 2009), 1.
[174] Sir John Woodcock's annual report, quoted in *G* (18 June 1992), 1.

erosion of deference and secrecy merely uncovered.[175] Mark later admitted that the Criminal Investigation Department was by the late 1960s 'the most routinely corrupt organization in London'. In 1969 *The Times*, lacking faith in Scotland Yard's capacity to police itself, published damaging revelations without first consulting the police. This corruption was rooted out only with extreme difficulty,[176] and during Mark's period of office more than 400 of his subordinates chose to resign rather than face disciplinary charges;[177] the Obscene Publications Squad was disbanded when revealed as deeply implicated in corrupt relations with retailers of pornography.[178] The problem was self-reinforcing because the police, hindered by the restrictions endorsed by a wary public, were tempted to bend the rules. As one chief constable later admitted: 'everyone knew it happened like that: judges, magistrates, the whole criminal justice system had a sort of conspiracy... If you didn't do it that way, you couldn't actually convict guilty people.' When such practices ended, detection rates fell.[179]

All this undid years of favourable publicity through *Dixon of Dock Green*. Public disaffection was, however, selective. On violent crime, especially terrorism, the public were supportive, and they were keener than MPs on the death penalty for murder.[180] The capture of four IRA gunmen in the Balcombe Street siege in 1975 was widely praised, and the funeral of Blackpool's police chief, Superintendent Gerald Richardson, shot by a gunman in 1971, was attended by 100,000 mourners and provoked much anxious correspondence in the press. 'The great silent majority who are on the side of law and order', said the Roman Catholic Bishop of Lancaster, 'must stand up and be counted'.[181] No policeman was more alert to the need for public cooperation than Mark. The police, he thought, had everything to gain from explaining themselves to the public: 'trust begets trust'. In September 1972, early in his time as Commissioner, he summoned a conference of press and media editors and promised less reticence; in his Dimbleby lecture he rejected the 'curious, old-fashioned belief that there is something vaguely improper in a policeman talking about the law, the courts and lawyers'.[182] The BBC television programme *Crimewatch*, launched in 1984 and inviting its regular viewers (soon between nine and thirteen million) to respond to its reconstructed crime scenes, exemplified the value of the relationship Mark sought to establish.[183]

---

[175] R. Reiner, 'Fin de Siècle Blues: The Police Face the Millennium', *Political Quarterly* (Jan.–Mar. 1992), 48.   [176] M. Leapman, *Treacherous Estate* (1992), 49, provides a good account.
[177] *T* (15 Apr. 1981), 3.   [178] *T* (23 Dec. 1976), 1.
[179] Charles Pollard, Chief Constable of Thames Valley, among other remarkable admissions made in *T* (5 Apr. 1993), 7.   [180] e.g. in 1983 according to polls discussed in *O* (17 July 1983), 7.
[181] *T* (27 Aug. 1971), 1.   [182] Mark, *Policing a Perplexed Society*, 7 (preface), 72.
[183] P. Schlesinger and H. Tumber, 'Fighting the War Against Crime: Television, Police, and Audience', *British Journal of Criminology* (Winter 1993), 19.

Mark's successor, Sir David McNee, had the imagination in 1979 to commission an objective survey of police and people in London from the Policy Studies Institute, published in four volumes. The empirical and qualitative approach adopted in the second and fourth of its four volumes reflected the fruitful interaction of participant observation with sociological insight, and provides a rare portrait of the police in their day-to-day operation and outlook.[184] Authoritarian and even military in structure, the Metropolitan Police were governed by precise rules and procedures whose scale seemed to outsiders 'Byzantine' and 'simply amazing'.[185] Huge quantities of statistical and other information were routinely accumulated, but little use was made of this for constructively appraising staff or for helping them to improve their clear-up rate. An over-centralized emphasis on short-term formalities rather than overall objectives discouraged initiatives from below and consultation between ranks on strategy. By rewarding those who played safe rather than showing a talent for police work, the system weakened morale. All this discouraged direct contact with the public, and failed adequately to illuminate what was actually happening in the community.

At the lower levels of policing a huge inertia was the outcome, with a deep scepticism about change in any form, and observers were surprised at how little direct supervision the higher ranks exercised over day-to-day policing.[186] The system could be made to work only through developing an informal culture which got round the rules. Impatient with mere 'figures', this male-dominated culture was, as we have seen, deeply permeated in its conversation by racism,[187] but also by the glamour of violence, with its associated contempt for the effeminate homosexual stereotype. Through hard drinking, toughness could be demonstrated, colleagues' loyalties and temperaments tested, and criminals and informants contacted.[188] Ordinary policing combined long periods of boredom with much-relished bursts of excitement involving car chases and an arrest, during which it was important psychologically not to lose the upper hand, and above all not to lose face:[189] 'just as glaziers hope for broken windows, so police officers . . . look forward to news of a punch up, a burglary or a rape'.[190] In such a context, the incidence of crime in London was less an objective reality than the outcome of a subtle interaction between public expectations and police response.

The late twentieth century failed both to combat crime and to rehabilitate the criminal. By the mid-1970s prisons had not caught up with rising living standards; overcrowding, undue segregation from family and community, inadequate

---

[184] D. J. Smith et al., Police and People in London (4 vols. 1983), a study which informs the paragraph that follows.   [185] Smith and Gray, Police in Action, 48.

[186] Ibid. 274, 283, 303.   [187] See above, pp. 202–4.

[188] Smith and Gray, Police in Action, 81–5.

[189] Ibid. 51–2; cf. 66–7 and D. J. Smith, Police and People in London, iii. A Survey of Police Officers (1983), 47.   [190] Smith and Gray, Police in Action, 31; see also 90–1, 97.

and degrading labour, and poor sanitation made them counterproductively unsavoury places, continuously prone to unrest.[191] Their alleged curative power was belied by the high reconviction rates; in 1986 these were (within two years) 63 per cent for male young offenders, 42 per cent for male adult offenders, and 34 per cent for female offenders.[192] Between 1970 and 1990 the average daily convicted prison population in England and Wales rose by 38 per cent, and the number of prisoners per thousand population from 0.53 to 0.69.[193] The prison service after 1970, running to stay in the same place, exemplified 'producer capture'. By the end of the 1980s many Conservatives saw the Prison Officers' Association as a nest of restrictive practices, the last of the trade union dinosaurs and ripe for privatization. The very serious riots at Strangeways in 1990[194] advanced the privatization cause, and Britain's first privately managed remand prison opened in 1992. On taking early retirement as Governor of Wormwood Scrubs in 1982, John McCarthy recommended a state convict system only for really dangerous offenders; all other offenders should, he thought, go to local prisons, which would then be used as only a last resort because ratepayers would have every incentive to reduce prisoner numbers. He condemned the prison service as 'a faceless bureaucracy which had long ago lost faith in what it might achieve'.[195]

The BBC serial *Porridge* (1974–7), with Ronnie Barker in the lead role, gave a view of prison life which, though sanitized, was authentic enough to attract viewers as enthusiastic inside prison as outside. Because prisoners from the 1950s were now more literate and less deferential, they wrote about their experience more often—with, as usual, middle-class prisoners (alleged terrorists, homosexuals, conscientious objectors) in the lead. The Home Office was now opening prisons to visitors of many kinds, and both parliamentary committees and the Prison Commissioners in their annual reports became increasingly outspoken. Condemning the degrading 'slopping out' process, whereby prisoners emptied used chamber pots every morning, the Chief Inspector of Prisons pointed out in 1984 that 'the stench of urine and excrement pervades the prison', with many prisoners preferring the option of hurling excrement packages from cell windows. Lord Woolf, reporting in the wake of the Strangeways disturbances of 1990, pronounced slopping out—abandoned in many European countries—'a blot on our prison system'.[196] The humanely avuncular Judge Stephen Tumim, Chief Inspector of Prisons for England and Wales from 1987 to 1995, carried prison publicity to a climax. Accessible to prisoners, unafraid to ask rather basic questions, adept with the media, and

[191] See e.g. leader in *T* (30 Dec. 1976), 11.
[192] Lord Woolf and S. Tumim, *Prison Disturbances April 1990: Report of an Inquiry* (Cm 1456; 1991), 242–3. [193] *Annual Abstract of Statistics 1976*, 7, 99; *1996*, 16, 92.
[194] *FT* (8 Aug. 1992), 7; Baker, *Turbulent Years*, 456. [195] *G* (31 Dec. 1982), 15.
[196] Sir James Hennessy, quoted in *G* (13 Apr. 1996), 11. Woolf and Tumim, *Prison Disturbances*, 277.

on good terms with Douglas Hurd, the Home Secretary who had appointed him, Tumim shed floods of light into one of the murkiest areas of British life, and helped to ensure that in English prisons 'slopping out' ceased in 1996. 'The great majority of prisoners', wrote Tumim, 'are not murderers, rapists or desperate villains. They are ignorant young men under 30 who have failed at school or been failed by school, and have no strong family or community links with anybody of sense. They are in urgent need of education in every way.'[197]

5. CONSERVATIVES TRANSFORMED

At first sight British political parties changed remarkably little after 1970. With names unaltered, the Conservative and Labour parties in 1990 remained dominant within what was still an adversarial political structure resting upon a simple-majority electoral system which penalized the Liberals (renamed Liberal Democrats after 1989) as a regionally dispersed third party; the nationalist parties, because regionally concentrated, did not suffer likewise. The Green Party (founded in 1972 as the People Party, and rechristened the Ecology Party soon afterwards until 1985) gained no firm regional base, and despite contesting 133 constituencies in the general election of 1987, it never matched even the Liberal Democrats' nation-wide strength. It fell back after 1989 when the economic downturn focused minds on more immediate issues, and when environmentalists disagreed about whether to be a pressure group or a party. Debate within the Labour and Conservative parties, by contrast, continued to focus on which party could most effectively generate wealth—a materialist orthodoxy all the stronger for remaining uncontested beneath the surface of two-party competition. As for the SDP, its challenge to adversarial party politics was frontal but eventually failed.[198]

Yet by 1990 almost everything about British party politics had changed: policy, structure, and image. In both policy and image, Labour in the 1970s and 1980s slowly began loosening its ties to working-class structures and prepared for its eventual retreat in the 1990s from state-managed socialism. The Conservatives were simultaneously shedding their socially hierarchical image while fully embracing the free-market policies favoured by their earlier individualist Liberal recruits. The Conservative transformation began well before Thatcher became leader. As a lower-middle-class meritocrat, Heath exemplified the philosophy he stood for: modernization. His party had always won extensive support at every social level, but had hitherto assumed an aristocratic and deferential veneer. No longer so: Heath in 1970 did not overtly repudiate his party's earlier image, yet he launched his government with the

---

[197] Quoted in obituary, *T* (10 Dec. 2003), 39.   [198] See below, pp. 496–501.

somewhat abrasive self-help tone later associated with Thatcher. His humbler origins were clear from his accent, and his approach to both foreign policy and governmental structures was radical. True, 'Selsdon man' had always been a fiction, and did not reflect his consensual inclinations; but he had not at first intended entirely to slip back into the Wilson governments' statist mould. His government's initially abrasive tone soon gave way, however, to a more consensual 'one nation' rhetoric; with the u-turn of 1972 the left resumed setting the political agenda,[199] spreading defeatism among many Conservatives. The left, armed with their special vocabulary—'caring', 'compassionate', and 'committed' to their 'social' panaceas—seemed even to have captured the English language.[200]

The Conservative response to the Heath government's setbacks was to dispense with him, but not with his modernizing aims. One politician, Enoch Powell, had been firm and consistent in his free-market attitudes since the mid-1960s, a man whose expulsion from the shadow cabinet in 1968 Thatcher had opposed, and later viewed as 'a tragedy'.[201] Seldom has a populist emerged from so improbable a quarter. Powell had once been a professor of Greek and had published several works on history, religion, and the classics. Much of his impact stemmed from a mesmeric speaking style, compelling in its high-pitched and emphatic tone. His speeches' highly coloured and almost apocalyptic language attracted attention with their biblical and classical resonances, even if his audiences did not always recognize them. Pursuing his lonely independent course, Powell was sustained by a belief in his star; his grim and austere manner matched his role as Cassandra, predicting almost ineluctable disaster. The hunched shoulders, the Midland accent, the piercing eyes, and the beetling brows guaranteed publicity for a fine communicator whose austerely logical arguments required his audiences to choose between stark options and seize last chances. The fierce emotions surging beneath the logical exterior were scarcely concealed: the people had but to open their eyes and they would see.

For one man to capture the public for at least a decade, with no media or party machine behind him, was something of a bravura performance. Powell's career abounds in multi-layered paradox. The dedicated Englishman, who almost alone among leading politicians preached patriotism of the old-fashioned kind, was himself profoundly un-English in his intellectualism and contempt for illogical compromise; the committed parliamentarian found himself out of tune with most MPs; the austere rationalist found himself widely suspected of Fascist tendencies by those intellectually too lazy to grasp his language and purposes; and the enthusiast for power was self-excluded from ever enjoying it to the full. Powell's career was wrecked by breaking so vigorously in 1968 with immigration

---

[199] See above, pp. 290–1, 308, 316. [200] DT (23 Apr. 1979), 16.
[201] Thatcher, Path to Power, 147.

orthodoxies, and he went on to break with other orthodoxies too: on the EEC, incomes policies, feminism, Northern Ireland, the Commonwealth, and foreign policy. Not content with all this, the orator who so forcibly outlined the overall directions the nation should take offered surprisingly few practical suggestions on implementation; and the man of principle could sometimes seem calculating and even malicious in his zest for diverging from his leader and eventually from his party. Some might see as far-sighted imagination what others branded as poor judgement, but none could conceal Powell's occasional lapses from tact and even from courtesy. From a career point of view, Powell's major mistake was one of timing. If he had contained his rebellion until the end of Heath's government, he could have played Disraeli to Heath's Peel, rallying principled backwoods backbenchers against the centre's pragmatic and aloof administrative competence. As it was, he lost all remaining credit by urging Conservatives to vote Labour at the general election of February 1974, and then unexpectedly found a bolt-hole as an Ulster Unionist MP. Thatcher, who shared so many of his views and instincts, could not, for all his qualities, offer him office, though he had been earlier in the field even than Joseph in pioneering what later became her new free-market orthodoxy. Like Thatcher, and like Joseph who channelled many of his ideas towards Thatcher, Powell saw himself as battling against something close to a media conspiracy. Perhaps there was some satisfaction to be derived after 1974 from seeing so many of his ideas adopted by the party that he had forsaken.

Between 1974 and 1979, during an extraordinary episode in Conservative Party history, the customary relationship between pressure group and party was reversed. The interest groups were now on the left, whereas the cause groups aiming to subvert them were on the right, and the Party prepared itself for a crusade that appropriated the fervour and techniques of the left. Wielding the pamphlet and the lecture, Joseph harnessed the prevailing concerns about the nation's moral and economic decline behind a movement which challenged the dominant orthodoxy. Instead of bidding for the centre ground, he and Thatcher had the long-term aim and effect of shifting the entire centre ground rightwards. In the mid-1970s the Conservative Party was still historically conscious enough to have learnt from its splits in 1846 and 1903–5, and Joseph and Thatcher took care not to criticize Heath in personal terms. Nonetheless, when asked after a year as leader what she had changed, Thatcher coolly replied: 'I have changed everything.'[202] A crucial lubricant at this point was William Whitelaw, for as Heath's loyal lieutenant and as a country gentleman with a good war record, he was a traditional type of paternalist Conservative, much respected in the Party. Without him, Thatcher would probably not have held her own within the shadow cabinet or have prevailed after 1979 over her many

---

[202] Cosgrave, *Thatcher*, 197 (12 Mar. 1976).

'wet' critics in the cabinet; she would then have been unable to bring off the transition from the somewhat mandarin 'one nation' style of Conservatism to its free-market and populist successor. Her style of leadership ruffled many feathers, and Whitelaw was the very necessary conciliator, counterweight, and sheet-anchor.[203]

Thatcherism was about tone as well as about content. She had no time for the mid-1970s defensive constitutional reform package—devolution together with proportional representation—which some Conservatives hoped would restrain socialist governments. Backed by several centrist Conservatives, industrialists, and intellectuals in 1976, the package involved acquiescing too readily for her taste in Labour's retention of the centre ground:[204] she thought the Party could win on its own. Conservatism was acquiring a new self-confidence and evangelical vigour, reflecting her claim to be a 'conviction politician': 'the Old Testament prophets didn't say "Brothers, I want a consensus". They said: "This is my faith, this is what I passionately believe. If you believe it too, then come with me".'[205] Confident in her lower-middle-class entrepreneurial enthusiasm, she felt none of the guilt in the presence of Labour that infected Conservatives higher up. The country's plight was urgent, the remedy was clear, and apologies were otiose. In policy terms, too, Thatcherism involved a formidable combination of right and left: a Churchillian, even Gaullist, patriotism abroad yoked to a libertarian and free-market domestic programme whose pedigree was Liberal. The Party's give-and-take attitude towards Labour suddenly disappeared: socialism was to be rooted out through incessantly probing its vulnerable points. Her anti-socialist crusade owed much to the knowing contempt for the left that was felt by those who had only recently left its fold, for Thatcher always extended a special welcome to converts from the left. In concurrent assaults on trade unions, left-wing local authorities, state-run industries, and council housing, the enemy was ruthlessly pursued.

Thatcherism geared in with long-term social trends which she accelerated through encouraging home-ownership. Conservatives since the mid-Victorian period had benefited from the middle-class advance through the professions and the suburbs. Each redrawing of constituency boundaries in response to demographic change brought benefits, whereas the manual working-class voters, employed in large and often state-run concerns and living in council-rented accommodation, were dwindling. From the outset as Conservative leader, Thatcher unblushingly championed what she saw as 'middle class values'.[206] This may have accorded with Heath's private views, but her combative rhetoric

[203] See the excellent leader on his retirement in *G* (11 Jan. 1988), 12.
[204] For the list see *T* (23 June 1976), 4.   [205] Speech at Cardiff, *G* (17 Apr. 1979), 30.
[206] Thatcher, *Path to Power*, 274. For more on this see above, pp. 142, 147.

was not his. Throughout 1974 his had been a class-reconciling theme, with appeals to 'the common beliefs and loyalties we all of the nation share'.[207] It was not at all clear in 1975 where Thatcher was to find her escape-route from Heath's strategy of retaining mass support while simultaneously aiming to modernize the economy. Her leadership was at first decidedly insecure, and many then thought an all-party coalition inevitable. When in 1979 Labour's corporatist alternative fell apart, however, Thatcher could build upon Heath's experience and consolidate her hold over the growing social forces in the country: uniting to people on fixed incomes the self-employed, the small entrepreneurs, and the socially mobile in middle and working class. The Party's appeal to such groups had already attracted such significant recruits as Norman Tebbit and John Major. As a 15-year-old from the North London lower middle class, Tebbit had been a rather unusual Young Conservative in the Enfield of the late 1940s, but after 1975 what Brian Walden (then hostile) called 'the carnivorous section of the lower middle class' at last came into its own. 'Patronising and offensive' was the image Lambeth's Labour Party hierarchy acquired in the eyes of the young Major, seeking to move up in British society. Impatient with 'all that talk about "our people" as if we were their serfs', he felt that the Conservatives did not 'box people in', and at the earliest possible date, on his sixteenth birthday, he joined them.[208] At Thatcher's three general election victories, nearly a third of trade unionists voted Conservative,[209] and at the general election of 1992 the Conservatives won more votes than at any previous general election, whereas Labour had reached its peak as far back as 1951. While Heath resorted to class-reconciling rhetoric, Thatcher gambled on substituting the reality of unashamed and expanding class identity and interest. Thatcher's background was not so very dissimilar to Heath's: provincial, lower-middle-class, and meritocratic, with Oxford offering the way out. Given that when serving in his cabinet she had not obviously dissented from his programme, he felt understandably miffed at being ousted by her, and still more at being excluded from her shadow cabinet and cabinet. Matters were made worse in 1979 because for him the post she offered (British ambassador at Washington) was that of a mere 'postman', well beneath his dignity.[210]

In launching free-market ideas on the British public, the general election of 1979 turned out to be a critical election, comparable to those of 1886, 1931, and 1945: it transformed the British political agenda, together with the overall shape of party relations. Callaghan's Labour government might have anticipated some aspects of Conservative policy after 1979—cash limits,

---

[207] T (19 Jan. 1974), 1.
[208] T (17 Apr. 1971), 22 (Walden). Interviews with Major, STel (8 Oct. 1989), 4; O (2 Dec. 1990), 50. See also FT (28 Nov. 1990), 6.   [209] FT (10 Oct. 1988), 10.
[210] Campbell, Edward Heath, 715.

control of the money supply, cuts in public expenditure, restraints on local government expenditure, even privatization—but Labour's stance had owed less to conviction than to economic pressures endorsed by the IMF. These policies reflected a mere temporary concession in an emergency, whereas for Thatcher they reflected a conviction that was permanent and cumulative. Unlike Heath, however, she did not launch her premiership combatively, but consensually. The Conservative manifesto gave no hint of the subsequent policy revolution, and only later did she emerge in her true individualist colours. Hers was more an attitude than a fixed set of ideas, and her policies gradually evolved in response to experience; enterprise zones and precise monetary targets were prominent earlier, privatization gained momentum in the middle period, reform of education, public welfare, and local government came towards the end. There were also contradictions within Thatcherism, and failures to think through what was involved. Its meritocratic thrust clashed with its modest revival of hereditary honours. In cultivating 'Victorian values', it found no way to revive the religious impulse to personal austerity and altruism that had earlier been integral to those values. Two aspects of Thatcher might have been expected to lead her towards devolution: her preference for small face-to-face structures, and her pragmatism, which might (with Gladstone) have seen devolution as a way to strengthen the union, but she took quite the opposite direction. Likewise with local authorities: her belief in the minimal state, in itself so integral to self-help, did not lead her to encourage local autonomy—though perhaps if she had secured the poll tax, thereby enhancing the local authorities' zeal for economy, she might have acted otherwise.

Had Labour won in 1979, the Conservative Party would have taken a very different direction: perhaps with Thatcher supplanted by a middle-of-the road Conservative such as Pym, who might later have coasted to power on a coalitionist electoral-reform and devolutionary ticket.[211] In downgrading 'wet' colleagues like Gilmour, Soames, and St John-Stevas after 1981, Thatcher sought to bring her party's leadership closer to its rank and file. 'The trouble is', said Pym, 'we've got a corporal at the top, not a cavalry officer'; her rejoinder is implicit in her comment to Ingham after their joint triumph at a hostile press conference: 'the thing about you and me, Bernard, is that neither of us are *smooth* people'.[212] The decline of Pym, who left office in 1983, was the obverse of the rise of Tebbit, unashamed of his lower-middle-class origins and instinctively sharing Thatcher's outlook. Viewed over the longer term, the overtly consensus values espoused by the paternalist ex-serviceman and the Tory squire had captured the Conservative Party

[211] As D. E. Butler predicted to Benn on 26 Mar. 1979 in Benn, *Diaries 1977–80*, 476 (26 Mar. 1979).
[212] Quoted in Young, *One of Us*, 331, 166.

only briefly, between 1940 and 1965; this daughter of a provincial Methodist shopkeeper was inciting it to resume its prolonged ingestion of middle-class and nonconformist Liberal-individualist values. The Conservative u-turn in policy after 1979—which Labour, the trade unions, and even the 'wets' predicted as Thatcher's equivalent of Heath's in 1972—never happened. Rather the reverse: the SDP's split from Labour in 1981 presented Thatcher with the precious bonus thereafter of a divided opposition and 'wets' still further weakened within her own party, as one of them ruefully acknowledged.[213] She was therefore free to edge her party rightwards. The 'wets' were in one respect the Conservative equivalents of Labour's Social Democrats, but with the crucial difference that they did not desert their party. At no stage did Heath even consider joining the SDP;[214] only Christopher Brocklebank-Fowler (MP for Norfolk North-West) did that. Nonetheless, the former colleagues whom Thatcher had handbagged—Biffen, Gilmour, Heseltine, Howe, Lawson, Prior, Pym, St John-Stevas—gradually and ominously accumulated on the Conservative back benches.

When in difficulties Thatcher could always appeal against her critics within cabinet or parliament to the party in the country, with which she instinctively identified. Since the 1950s the party leaders had been growing more prominent in the party conference, and after 1965 Heath went further, making a point of attending throughout. After 1975 Thatcher went further still. The adulatory mood of her first party conference as prime minister, with 'Hello Maggie' played on the organ at her advent,[215] was repeated throughout the 1980s, and contrasted markedly with the party in-fighting which Labour Party conferences advertised. The much-discussed 'Dear Bill' letters in *Private Eye*—purportedly from Thatcher's gin-totting, golfing husband Denis to his friend Bill Deedes—humorously reinforced the party link by highlighting a popular personality even further to the right than his wife. The letters reached London stage and television audiences in the form of *Anyone for Denis?* (1981), though on seeing it his wife's constricted sense of humour was stretched almost to its limit. Behind the scenes there was shrewd Americanized organization and marketing in a party entirely at home with the latest commercial and advertising practice. Cecil Parkinson as Party Chairman was using a computer as early as 1982 to experiment with direct-mailing techniques, and at the general election in the following year half a million letters went to people identified as potential Conservative supporters in sixty marginal constituencies.[216] In 1986/7 letters went to more than a million shareholders in British Telecom, easily located from its share register, in a fund-raising campaign that more than paid for

[213] Gilmour, *Dancing with Dogma*, 43.   [214] Campbell, *Edward Heath*, 726–7.
[215] *FT* (13 Oct. 1979), 6.
[216] Butler and Kavanagh, *British General Election of 1983*, 33–4. *T* (25 May 1983), 4.

itself. For Tebbit it was 'the most successful direct mail campaign in British politics'.[217]

Thatcher's hold on her party stemmed from her personal qualities. Like Harold Wilson a grammar-school product, with all the facts and figures at her fingertips when speaking in parliament, she diverged from him in her didactic manner: 'when she talks to you on the telly', said a Huddersfield woman in 1979 during the election campaign, 'you feel about five years old'.[218] She won the leadership in 1975 through prowess in parliamentary debate, for in close exchanges on the Finance Bill she was well able to get the measure of Healey as Chancellor of the Exchequer. As leader of the opposition she took time to get into her stride, and Callaghan sometimes worsted her. But she had a good memory for faces and personal details, enjoyed informal encounters, and avoided Heath's mistake of remaining aloof from Conservative backbenchers. In the early 1980s her loyal and industrious personal private secretary Ian Gow briefed her fully as prime minister on parliamentary opinion, and at a more elevated level Whitelaw was crucial in helping her to hold the parliamentary party together. She always did her homework and usually passed her examinations, preparing for the twice-weekly question-time as assiduously in her tenth year as in her first, though she recalled that beforehand 'I was like jelly inside'.[219] Like Powell she thought parliament should ventilate people's worries, however unfashionable—on race and industrial relations, for example. 'The foundation of my political belief', she said in 1987, 'is my conviction that the overwhelming majority of the people of this country are sensible, decent and honourable',[220] and she toyed with the idea of getting through to them by applying referenda to issues other than Europe and devolution.

Yet it was because Thatcher was no mere populist that she achieved so much, for she had no fear of challenging orthodoxies when necessary, and the polls showed that before the Falklands venture she had as prime minister a lower average satisfaction rating than any since the war.[221] Right-wing think tanks often helped her to skirmish ahead of public opinion: they tested opinion without committing her, so that her decisions could rest on an informed guess at their likely reception. She thought most people would come round to her view, and on privatization, tax cuts, industrial relations reform, and the repudiation of incomes policies, they eventually did—though with the poll tax she pursued the strategy once too often. The art of persuasion is partly a matter of strategy and tactics: in outwitting Scargill (himself skilful with the media)

---

[217] Tebbit, *Upwardly Mobile*, 247. *FT* (27 Jan. 1987), 21. [218] *STel* (29 Apr. 1979), 17.
[219] *DT* (12 June 1995), 15. See also H. Young, *One of Us*, 428.
[220] Interview with Bruce Anderson, *STel* (28 June 1987), 23.
[221] A. King (ed.), *The British Prime Minister* (1st publ. 1969, 2nd edn. 1985), 113; cf. D. Kavanagh, *Thatcherism and British Politics: The End of Consensus?* (1st publ. 1987, 2nd edn. 1990), 269.

during the miners' strike of 1984–5 she ruthlessly marshalled a combination of forethought, patience, persistence, cautious day-to-day watchfulness, and sheer cunning, for this was a battle she had to win. In handling extra-parliamentary opinion Thatcher often appealed over the heads of intermediaries directly to those whom they allegedly represented: from cabinet to party, from churchmen to congregations, from trade union leaders to rank and file, from local authorities to ratepayers, from the professions to their clients, from pressure groups (on race, education, industrial relations) to public opinion.

She was no natural orator, either in content or delivery, but unlike Heath she had histrionic potential. She knew the loyalty value of symbolic acts at key moments: her cool response to the Brighton bombing on the following morning, for example, was spontaneous. Her famous 'walk in the wilderness' at Stockton on 16 September 1987 (Plate 5) may have been a publicity stunt, but the same cannot be said of her silent tribute on the windswept Northolt airport six months later, when she bowed her head before the coffins of two Royal Signals corporals who had been beaten, stripped, and shot in Belfast after being caught up in an IRA funeral procession.[222] Furthermore, she was prepared to learn. If the public career-woman seemed unfeminine, then she would be filmed shopping, cooking, or displaying her favourite clothes. Not for her the feminist assumption that woman's personal advancement entails unconcern with personal appearance. From the mid-1970s she applied herself dutifully to a rigorous course in cosmetic self-improvement, and with the media in mind, teeth were adjusted, clothing and hairstyle were transformed, and the voice was softened and lowered.[223] If women when speaking loudly sounded shrill, she would harness the tape-recorder to secure a somewhat breathy huskiness—for some, a remedy worse than the disease. Yet if advancing her early career required elocution, and her later career de-elocution, she did not shirk the necessary u-turn. Advancing her policies came first, and trivialities would not hold her back. New technological aids were embraced. President Reagan's use of a transparent teleprompter screen or 'sincerity machine' to supplement his teleprompter enabled him to seem more sincere because he could read while seeming to look more directly at his audience, as when addressing parliament in 1982; she appropriated the device with considerable effect when addressing Congress in 1985. The media expert Gordon Reece completely won Thatcher's confidence and persuaded her to relax before the cameras: he was 'a Godsend'.[224]

[222] T (24 Mar. 1988), 1, 24.

[223] A. Raphael and G. Wansell, 'The Selling of Maggie', O (22 Apr. 1979), 9. 'Image Maker to the PM', O (12 June 1983), 7.

[224] Thatcher, Downing Street Years, 468–9. Cockerell, Live from No. 10, 36, 54. M. Atkinson, Our Masters' Voices: The Language and Body Language of Politics (1984), 66. For Reece see Thatcher, Path to Power, 294.

Thatcher took huge trouble with her party conference speeches: ideas were collected from all directions, then in the weekend beforehand they were laid out on the table in the Great Parlour at Chequers, and link passages were written. Phrase-making, purple passages, and jokes (which sometimes had to be explained to her) were then invited from the playwright Ronald Millar, source of the lines from St Francis which she uttered on first entering 10 Downing Street, and of the motto from Abraham Lincoln which she treasured in her handbag: 'you cannot enrich the poor by impoverishing the rich. You cannot strengthen the weak by weakening the strong.' It was to Millar, too, that she owed the Old Testament prophets and consensus, and 'the lady's not for turning'.[225] By no means the first prime minister to seek such help, she was unusually receptive to it. Then the efforts produced by her team of aides went into her mincing machine and were still being churned up well into the night before the speech was due for delivery.[226]

How could Conservative backbenchers have ousted this formidable woman in November 1990? Seldom has so great a downfall been so public and so predictable. Not guilty was her disgruntled predecessor. Heath detested her leadership's style and substance, and he gave her none of the loyalty he had received from Douglas-Home. But so counterproductive had Heath's hostility become by the late 1980s that even his disciples began to back away. Thatcher's downfall in 1990 is the UK's equivalent of Nixon's downfall in 1973, for both episodes show the political systems of those two great democratic nations operating differently but in textbook fashion to monitor the executive. Thatcher's problems began in the cabinet, where the initial abundance of critics led her to adopt an embattled style that became a counterproductive habit. As early as autumn 1980 the components of her political demise were moving into place: she was already abusing Howe, whose dogged manner she found irritating, in front of officials. By June 1981 Lawson was urging on Howe the gains to monetary discipline that would accrue from joining the European Monetary System.[227] When in 1985 Lawson and Howe agreed on the need to join the ERM, but failed to persuade Thatcher, the scene was set for the disagreements which ultimately extruded both from the cabinet. With Heseltine's departure over the Westland affair in 1986, too much disgruntled talent was lining up on the Conservative back benches. In failing to recruit and chair the cabinet so as to make it an effective sounding-board for opinion, Thatcher created two difficulties for herself. First, she alienated or distanced significant opinion, especially in her own party, for her chosen colleagues tried to anticipate the wishes of so forceful a prime minister, telling her only what she wanted to hear. But, second, her governments grew too lightly committed

[225] Obituary, T (17 Apr. 1998), 12, 23. J. Ranelagh, Thatcher's People (1992), 24.
[226] Thatcher, Downing Street Years, 302, 567.   [227] Lawson, View from No. 11, 85, 111.

to questionable legislation, insufficiently tested in the cabinet forum, and so became liable to sudden and impulsive lurches of policy. This was dangerous by 1990, when Conservative backbenchers were growing worried about hostility to the poll tax, the latest among her governments' 'banana skins'—following on from earlier mistakes such as the overhasty proposals for football identity cards and means-testing student grants. With a general election looming, Thatcher was beginning to seem a liability.

So by 1990 cabinet, parliament, and the electorate all helped to build up the threat to Thatcher, whose long premiership and earlier successful resistance to significant orthodoxies blinded her to the danger, and led her later to ascribe her downfall to conspiratorial betrayal and disloyalty. Europe was the trigger for her political demise. She seemed at last to have pushed socialism on to the defensive within Britain, yet here it was springing back from a European direction, apparently with help from the Foreign Office (whose influence she had long deplored) and from her party's Europhiles. In forcibly resisting the diversion, she pushed them to their limit. It was a European issue that alienated Heseltine, her leading challenger in 1990. It was a former diplomat, worried by Thatcher's distaste for the EEC, who as a backbencher first challenged her as Conservative leader: Sir Anthony Meyer in 1989.[228] When Howe resigned on 1 November 1990, again on the European issue, parliament moved centre-stage. Twice at this juncture it strikingly demonstrated its ultimate power, together with its capacity for theatre: first when Howe made his damaging resignation speech from the back benches on 13 November, and then on 21 November when it became clear that Thatcher lacked enough support from Conservative MPs to carry on. Her resignation publicized next day provoked strong and conflicting emotions in the general public when they learnt of it. Her dignified, courageous, moving, and sometimes even amusing speech during the confidence debate that afternoon rounded off her premiership in such style as to provide the House of Commons with one of its great twentieth-century occasions.

'Mrs Thatcher fell this morning', wrote Lees-Milne in his diary on 22 November. 'The great and glorious woman has resigned.'[229] Her distress at losing power in the midst of a full agenda was painfully apparent. Her achievement will long remain controversial, and here we are concerned only with its political dimension.[230] Her view of government's capacity and role was very limited: it was there to maintain sound finance, national defence, and the rule of law; to curb monopoly, to maintain 'a . . . fundamental framework' of civil law, to enlarge opportunity, and to maintain 'fundamental social services'. She could not as a politician 'offer people salvation', for she thought that

---

[228] Sir A. Meyer, 'Why I am Challenging Thatcher', *T* (30 Nov. 1989), 14.

[229] J. Lees-Milne, *Ceaseless Turmoil: Diaries, 1988–1992*, ed. M. Bloch (2004), 198 (22 Nov. 1990).

[230] For its economic dimension see below, pp. 534–40.

counterproductive strategy of Tony Benn. Entering the cabinet young, Benn was articulate, talented, energetic, committed, charming, amusing, and with endearing eccentricities. Looking back, he saw himself as then 'just a career politician' with corporatist but not socialist views.[239] Had he remained in his party's parliamentary mainstream after 1970, retaining his EEC commitment and defending the Wilson governments in which he had served, he might well have beaten Healey and Jenkins, and certainly Kinnock, to Labour's leadership. In 1974–9, however, Benn tried to have his cake and eat it: to remain in what soon became centrist Labour cabinets as a scarcely disguised 'semi-detached' member, often near dismissal or resignation, while serving posterity with his diary. In Wilson's words he 'immatured with age', and became a political Peter Pan. How so?

When Callaghan expressed to Benn his worries about trade union power in January 1974, Benn replied that the City of London ran the Conservative government, yet nobody worried about that: 'it is a question of whose side you are on. It's a gut issue.'[240] Aligning himself with the left's increasingly vociferous direct-action extra-parliamentary forces, Benn thought he detected the onset of Bagehot's late Victorian nightmare: a working class promoting its interests through single-mindedly exploiting party conflict.[241] He assumed that trade union leaders were more in tune with social-class trends, and more representative of their members, than they really were. Among Labour leaders, he alone could have condemned as 'a most disgraceful statement' Callaghan's remark in parliament that people were not morally or legally obliged to refrain from crossing a picket line.[242] Benn perceived a radical opportunity that, as we have seen, was not really there.[243] Doubly contrasting with Bagehot, 'Citizen Benn' over-romanticized the working man, yet knew established institutions from the inside, so insiders saw him after 1970, and still more after 1979, as a class traitor. The British labour movement has recruited two variants on the art of class betrayal: the allegedly unhelpful and self-promoting 'MacDonald variant' (the working-class supporter who allegedly sells out), and the potentially helpful and self-denying 'Cripps variant' (the member of the elite who in social-class terms sells himself short). Benn was in the latter camp.

Early in his career Benn encountered the sort of criticism that (in British politics, at least) greets any dissident: 'Tony is a very able chap', said Gaitskell in 1958, 'but he has no judgement'.[244] Benn's trait grew out of his lively political imagination, reinforced by loyalty to his family and to its nonconformist traditions, by his principled independence, and by his alertness to labour history. His challenge to what he liked to call 'the establishment'

---

[239] Benn, *Diaries 1973–6*, 692 (26 Dec. 1976).   [240] Ibid. 96 (21 Jan. 1974).
[241] Ibid. 619 (5 Oct. 1976); 641 (10 Nov. 1976).
[242] *DT* (17 Jan. 1979), 5; Benn, *Diaries 1977–80*, 446 (23 Jan. 1979), cf. 450 (1 Feb. 1979).
[243] Above, pp. 141, 144–5, 148–9, 172.   [244] Benn, *Diaries 1940–62*, 281 (19 June 1958).

owed much to the sceptical reception that in 1960–3 had greeted his idea of renouncing his peerage; success could apparently come only through mounting a public campaign which, as he recalled, 'taught me many lessons'.[245] A genuine democrat and idealist, Benn wanted socialism realized through public discussion rather than through the cynical mobilization of self-interest, but his youthful yet lifelong energy and idealism led him unduly to credit the electors with such qualities. 'What you don't seem to realise, Tony', said Callaghan—discussing his proposal to call Labour's mid-term manifesto 'Change in the Modern Britain'—'is that our people have had quite enough change already'.[246]

For as long as he seemed a threat, Benn experienced one of the most virulently hostile press campaigns endured by any twentieth-century British politician. When, decades later, the *Sun* rang for a comment, 'all of a sudden my heart froze and it reminded me of the awful period when the press were after me all the time'.[247] Yet Benn retained his dignity throughout. With Labour's defeat in 1979, his moment seemed to have arrived, and for two or three years he was almost ubiquitous in marches, meetings, and demonstrations, with a bevy of disciples. The unapologetic but mellow, tolerant, and attractive figure who emerges from his later diaries differs markedly from the fiercely principled people's tribune who in the early 1980s stridently played to the conference gallery. The contrast between Benn and Joseph is instructive: both aimed to reshape public opinion, but whereas Joseph was consciously and courageously going against the grain of prevailing attitudes, ranging far outside his party, Benn chose only to tell narrower and sympathetic audiences what they wanted to hear. Contemporaries often viewed what turned out to be a self-sabotaged career in terms of personal ambition, but for Benn his career was a side-issue, and because established institutions had no hold over him, he was invulnerable.

Not so his party. If Thatcher had crumbled soon after 1979 without generating an inter-party emergency coalition, Benn might have been the man of the hour. He would eventually have been forced into a general election, however, and there lay his ultimate weakness, for even with Foot in charge, Labour's electoral performance in 1983 was disastrous. Benn was more to blame than anyone for that outcome, for never have such considerable talents been deployed so energetically to damage their practitioner's professed aims so seriously. When the innocently idealistic yet seriously destructive Gregers Werle in Ibsen's *Wild Duck* asks Mrs Ekdal 'you do believe I meant it all for the best, Mrs Ekdal?', Labour Party leaders from Wilson to Blair might

---

[245] Benn, *Diaries 1973–6*, 420 (epilogue).
[246] *G* (6 June 1970), 9. This exchange perhaps occurred during the meeting discussed in Benn's *Diaries 1968–72*, 103 (27 Sept. 1968).   [247] Benn, *Diaries 1991–2001*, 322 (11 June 1995).

well have echoed her reply: 'yes, I dare say you did. But may God forgive you, all the same.'[248] Thatcher, far from crumbling, unexpectedly survived, and indeed profited from a Labour Party cast in Benn's mould. He knew well enough how unpopular he was within a PLP far better attuned to public opinion than he: by November 1980 he felt 'such an outcast' that he found it 'hard to face going into the House. I don't go there unless I have to.' After 1970 he had seriously under-estimated the need even for a radical minister to show himself loyal to present and former colleagues, as well as to win support from MPs and (when in office) from the prime minister. 'National policy is the sole responsibility of government and parliament', Thatcher told her party conference, to applause, in October 1979;[249] Benn forgot that Labour's leaders thought the same.

Disappointment with the Labour governments of 1974–9 caused the labour movement once more to dust down its extra-parliamentary and even law-breaking traditions, with a growing emphasis in the early 1980s on demonstrations and processions.[250] There was even an attempt to substitute works-canteen meetings for party-branch meetings, but in April 1979 the 20,000 Vauxhall car workers at Luton and Dunstable voted to ban them on the ground that lunchtime political speeches would spoil their digestion.[251] The cabinet ministers of 1974–9 felt decidedly on the defensive. Few political reputations have sunk so fast and so completely as Wilson's after 1976, and even Callaghan was embattled after 1979 against attempts within the Party to undermine the PLP. At the same time, the trade unions' strength within the party organization was growing, and was entrenching 'producer socialism' still more deeply; in the reformed procedure for choosing the party leader adopted in 1981 they formed 40 per cent of the electoral college by comparison with the 30 per cent assigned to the PLP, and (in aggregate) to the constituency parties. Wilson in November 1980 despised the 'tomfoolery' involved in thus downgrading the PLP, and he was not alone among Labour loyalists in deploring the clenched fists now raised by young conference delegates while the Red Flag was being sung.[252] Since 1970 the Party's branches had so shrunk that sectarian left-wingers such as the Militant Tendency could easily capture them, and to outsiders the term 'activist' almost became a pejorative term. Pressure built up to proscribe some organizations from affiliating to the Party, but when the general secretaries of the railwaymen and steelworkers tried to get this

---

[248] H. Ibsen, *The Wild Duck* (Oxford World's Classics edn., publ. with *An Enemy of the People* and *Rosmersholm*, 1999), 197.

[249] Benn, *Diaries 1980–90*, 44 (5 Nov. 1970). Thatcher, speech of 12 Oct. 1979, as broadcast on BBC television.

[250] See e.g. Peter Tatchell's article in *G* (8 Dec. 1981), 4 and letters in *G* (11 Jan. 1982), 7, and *T* (14 Jan. 1982), 11. 32 prospective parliamentary candidates seem to have agreed, *T* (23 Feb. 1982), 2.

[251] *DT* (21 Apr. 1979), 1.   [252] *T* (17 Nov. 1980), 1.

discussed at the Labour conference in 1981 they were hissed, and provoked more anger by pointing out that their membership equalled the total voting strength of the constituency parties, which tended to oppose proscription. At last in 1982 it was reluctantly decided to set up a register of non-affiliated organizations[253] which the Tendency must apply to join if it wished to retain influence. All this in-fighting gave Labour a fractious and (to its idealists) an incongruous image.

Benn's extra-parliamentary alignment was too fervent even for Michael Foot, elected Callaghan's successor as Party leader in 1980. Much loved within the labour movement, Foot was a quirky but cultivated and inspiring orator, an instinctive democrat and a dedicated parliamentarian with prolonged backbench service on Labour's left. Many predicted for him a lifetime in opposition, and were surprised when he agreed to become Secretary of State for Employment in Wilson's third government. This had been very much against his inclinations, and he found the compromises of government decidedly painful. But he valuably served both his party and his country by supplying crucially important backing for a consensual approach at a time of dangerous political instability. It was not his fault that Labour went on in 1980 to commit a gross act of self-indulgence in preferring him to Healey as its leader, but something much more substantial in parliament than windy oratory was required to force Thatcher on to the back foot. In the debate on unemployment of 24 June 1981, for instance, Foot was exposed as having nothing whatever to say on a central area of policy beyond party point-scoring, jokes, and vague exhortation to 'Government planning and deliberate action by the Government'.[254] He was also disarmingly unconcerned about Labour's image, and notoriously appeared at the Cenotaph on Remembrance Day in a duffel coat.[255] As leader he never established any firm direction or organizational grip on the Party, nor was he at all the man to broaden its search for support. Despite the radical image conveyed at so many fiery meetings, he was too nice and too unworldly to compel the Party into unity and eventual victory. Healey, ruthless and tough by contrast, would never have pleaded (as did Foot) with critics on the left: they would have been sent packing. Foot prudently resigned after Labour's defeat in 1983 in favour of a younger man, Neil Kinnock.

Callaghan evoked fury within the Party after its lost election by telling its conference that its extra-parliamentary emphasis after 1979 had 'lost millions of votes';[256] Kinnock now had to win them back. Bennite extra-parliamentary strategy had contributed in 1981 towards sending into the political wilderness, via the SDP, much-needed talent and governmental experience. The

---

[253] *DT* (28 Sept. 1981), 10 (1981 conference). For the report recommending a register see *G* (9 June 1982), 3.   [254] *HC Deb.* 24 June 1981, c. 324, and the damning comment in *G* (25 June 1981), 2.
[255] i.e. on 8 Nov: see the letters in *T* (11 Nov. 1981), 11.   [256] *T* (6 Oct. 1983), 1.

split should have been no surprise, if only because through Jenkins and Rodgers its public pedigree went at least as far back as the group of embattled Gaitskellites who had triumphed over unilateralism in 1961, and its private pedigree went back further still.[257] By the early 1970s *The Times* was campaigning for a centre party,[258] and the claim was becoming more frequent that the two-party system, with its class-preoccupied and class-funded parties, inflamed employer/employee relations. The SDP pedigree also drew in the Labour Party minority which with Jenkins helped Heath in 1970–5 to ease the UK into the EEC. Jenkins while campaigning in 1975 for a 'yes' referendum outcome felt he had more in common with 'Europeans' in other parties than with many in his own party.[259] With Jenkins returning in 1981 from his four years as President of the European Commission, and with Thatcher and Benn driving their respective parties to the extremes, the time seemed ripe to launch a conciliatory party of the centre that would draw its funds from individual members rather than from either side of the industrial divide. Several significant individual secessions from Labour—Reginald Prentice, Christopher Mayhew, George Brown—occurred during the 1970s, but this collective secession was much more important, and in the highly fluid political situation of the early 1980s its threat to realign the parties was serious.[260]

The new party originated in private conversations between Jenkins and the Liberal leader David Steel. Many of the hundred people assembled in the Council for Social Democracy at the outset were distinguished, and many were refugees from further left: prominent academics like Fred Dainton and Alan Bullock; well-known economists like Alec Cairncross, Frank Hahn, and James Meade; public figures such as George Brown, Anthony Sampson, Michael Young, and Dick Taverne; and the trade unionist Frank Chapple, though he never became a full member.[261] The thoughtful, well-intentioned, and self-consciously progressive middle classes were on the march, conversing politely with one another in numerous SDP conferences. Healey thought many of them 'self-confessed virgins', reluctant to make the clear choices that government requires: the new party was undemocratic because it dreamt of 'a society administered by men of competence and goodwill in which politics is banished—a sort of irreversible Butskellism based on rejecting both career politicians and bureaucrats'.[262] Certainly the SDP brought many newcomers into politics. Hostile to the trade unions, overwhelmingly enthusiastic for incomes policies and continued membership of the EEC,

---

[257] See B. Harrison, 'Oxford and the Labour Movement', *TCBH* 2/3 (1991), 260–4.
[258] See e.g. *T* (30 Sept. 1972), 15.   [259] Jenkins, *Life at the Centre*, 424.
[260] R. Butt presented these interestingly in his 'SDP: A Game of Political Consequences', *T* (23 July 1981), 14.   [261] *FT* (5 Feb. 1981), 12.
[262] D. Healey, 'Consensus and the SDP', *New Socialist*, 2 (Nov./Dec. 1981), 27.

the new party drew its early members disproportionately from southern England and from Labour rather than Conservative voters.[263] It depended heavily upon suburban people drawn from the growing 'service class' imbued with a public-service ethic, and employed in such spheres as teaching, communicating, and public welfare. They were upwardly mobile meritocrats, disproportionately drawn from cathedral, university, and high-tech communities.[264] Seceding from Labour freed them to be themselves, politically progressive and with no obligation to assume proletarian airs—attracted by a party which yearned for corporatist policies to succeed—a party which, in Ralf Dahrendorf's unkindly penetrating phrase, 'promised them a better yesterday'.[265]

The 'gang of four'[266] who founded the SDP (Jenkins, Owen, Rodgers, and Williams) knew that Foot as party leader would allow the left to render Labour unelectable, and within their first year they recruited twenty-five Labour MPs. In the leadership contest some allegedly backed Foot and not Healey (then ahead on the first round) in order to inflict maximum damage on the party they had decided to leave.[267] Hostility to Labour's alleged totalitarian tendency fuelled defection: reading W. S. Allen's *The Nazi Seizure of Power* (1965) helped to edge Williams into secession, and when Rodgers decided to secede he was reading Crick's biography of Orwell.[268] In mid-1982 the SDP reached its peak membership of 65,000, as compared with nearly three times as many Liberal members and more than four times as many individual members of the Labour Party.[269] Benn frequently derided centrists in the 1970s and 1980s as creatures of the media,[270] but the media respond only to anticipated demand. The party-political situation was now highly fluid. On precedent, the seceders were likely to end up as Conservatives, unless Thatcher's then-precarious venture failed, for Labour was unlikely to reform itself quickly enough to win them back. If the impending election produced a hung parliament, the seceders might (against all precedent) use their new bargaining position to force their terms on Labour. Or they might bargain their way towards a reformed electoral system that would render their centre-party role permanent and periodically governmental, though it was not clear how the reform could ever

---

[263] Survey results in *T* (30 Nov. 1981), 10. *T* (22 May 1981), 2; (3 Sept. 1983), 8.

[264] I. Crewe and A. King, *SDP: The Birth, Life and Death of the Social Democratic Party* (Oxford, 1995), 246–7, 273–4, 281, 293.

[265] Quoted in H. Stephenson, *Claret and Chips: The Rise of the SDP* (1982), 173. In 2006 Lord Dahrendorf told me that he could not recall the context for his remark, but see P. Hennessy, *Having it So Good: Britain in the Fifties* (2006), p. xvii.

[266] The reference was to the trial of Madame Mao in China, and the phrase had already been applied to the team of Conservative MPs who helped Thatcher to exploit parliamentary questions in 1974–9. Tebbit, *Upwardly Mobile*, 147.   [267] e.g. Neville Sandelson, *STel* (14 Jan. 1996), 5.

[268] Crewe and King, *SDP* 82–3, 119.   [269] *FT* (9 Jan. 1984), 1.

[270] For examples, see *T* (7 Oct. 1972), 4; (23 Sept. 1981), 4; Benn, *Diaries 1968–72*, 457 (6 Oct. 1972); *Diaries 1973–6*, 19 (22 Apr. 1973).

tempt either of the two dominant parties.[271] The most likely outcome within the simple-majority system was what actually happened: a divided opposition vote which shoed in Thatcher for her second term, forcing Labour eventually to reform itself along SDP lines, though rather more slowly than if the SDP's leaders had remained within the Labour Party to help out.

Why did the SDP dream eventually fade? Partly because it succeeded far better inside parliament than out. It might attract some inner-city Catholic traditionalist Labour refugees from Labour's left, but many of those were already gentrifying.[272] The SDP's difficulty at this level was that although it saw itself as defending the less organized types of working people who had much to gain from incomes policies and from curbing trade union power, no such programme could attract the most self-confident and articulate among working people: the trade union leaders. Owen's ideas of combining trade union structural reform with 'social partnership' and industrial democracy[273] could not tempt even Chapple and Hammond away from Labour. The first trade union general secretary thus seduced was John Lyons in 1985, but he refused to make an issue of his move.[274] The SDP suffered too, at the start, from tactical disagreements. Jenkins favoured a centrist and Liberal destination not initially favoured by the other three. This disagreement was never resolved. Should the SDP seek to supersede Labour? Or should it seek only to compete with it? Even after the SDP had failed to supplant Labour there was an important tactical debate between those who thought (with Jenkins) that it would be best to merge with the Liberals and those who thought (with Owen) that the two parties in alliance, each appealing to distinct constituencies, would win more support. There was understandable friction, too, between Liberals and SDP: at national level because of the SDP's relatively governmental outlook, and at constituency-branch level because relatively well-entrenched Liberals were reluctant to ease the path of SDP candidates.

Behind these disagreements lay conflicts of personality. Friction between Jenkins and Owen began well before the SDP was created.[275] It would have been less damaging if Williams had contested (and perhaps won) the Warrington by-election of 1981, for she might then have become SDP leader, capable of holding her two colleagues together.[276] As it was, Jenkins, standing in her place, put up a good fight, and by standing at Hillhead in March 1982 and winning, he in effect made himself leader. But by then he had lost youthful vigour, and

[271] Though Sir Ian Gilmour recommended it, *T* (13 Nov. 1982), 2.
[272] C. Longley, 'Glittering Prize of the Catholic Vote', *T* (30 Nov. 1981), 12.
[273] *FT* (15 Jan. 1982), 7.
[274] In his union journal Chapple warned his EETPU members not to leave Labour, *G* (27 Feb. 1981), 3. Lyons, *FT* (7 Jan. 1986), 10.   [275] J. Campbell, *Roy Jenkins: A Biography* (1983), 208.
[276] She and Owen subsequently regretted that she did not stand, in Radio 3's programme 'The Gang that Fell Apart', 11 Sept. 1991.

Fig. 6. Garland, *Independent* (20 May 1987) shows the leading election contenders at the election in that year.

in parliament as leader of a small party with governmental pretensions, he was easily discomfited by irreverent Labour and Conservative backbenchers;[277] his somewhat grandiloquent style was going out of fashion both there and in the media. The SDP's lost momentum at the general election of 1983 was a serious setback, and in its aftermath Jenkins (ineffective on television, tired, with health deteriorating, and feeling too old as leader of a young party) conceded the SDP leadership to Owen. The difficulties of operating a joint leadership within the SDP/Liberal alliance, however, persisted. By 1984 the SDP's subscription income and membership were falling, and the Party depended increasingly on wealthy donors.[278] With no integrating leader, Liberals and SDP began to diverge, and the Liberals at their party conference of 1986 voted against the independent British nuclear deterrent that the SDP wished to retain. In 1987 the friction between Owen and Steel could hardly be concealed, though Labour and the SDP/Liberal alliance were still competing for second place.

With only five Social Democrats in parliament thereafter, the SDP was poised for ignominious demise, for with its sectarian in-fighting it now resembled

---

[277] H. Young, 'Can Roy Jenkins Recover?', *ST* (20 Feb. 1983), 13.   [278] *FT* (8 Aug. 1984), 28.

Labour in the 1970s. Of the 58,509 SDP members balloted in 1987 on whether to merge with the Liberals, over three-quarters voted, and of them 43 per cent favoured closer links with the Liberals short of merger and 57 per cent favoured negotiations on merger. In a ballot of both parties on merger in 1988, an eighth of the Liberals who voted opposed merger, as did over a third of the SDP members.[279] Instead of accepting the majority vote, Owen then chose to prolong the SDP's independent life, leaving his former colleagues to call themselves 'Social and Liberal Democrats'. In the following May, however, he had to admit that with only 11,000 members the SDP could campaign at elections only selectively. In October a further ballot within the Social and Liberal Democrats produced a two-to-one majority for the shorthand title 'Liberal Democrat',[280] and Owen's wind-up of the SDP in 1990 was the end of a sorry tale. Shortly before the general election of 1992 Owen announced his support for Major as prime minister.

The SDP's twelve self-prescribed tasks of March 1981 included 'breaking the mould' of the party polarity which allegedly generated class conflict and violent lurches of policy. In this failed objective the SDP offered nothing that distinguished it from the Liberals, for it broadly accepted the corporatist aspirations of the 1960s and 1970s without explaining how they could be made to work better. Thatcher did not anticipate radical initiatives from those who consciously pursued the centre ground: 'we were the mould-breakers', she said, 'they the mould'.[281] Having retreated continuously from its initial aim of supplanting the Labour Party, the SDP's last resort in the 1990s was to claim credit for Blair's reformed Labour Party,[282] which the SDP's former leaders generously endorsed.[283] In truth, the SDP's secession had if anything slowed down Labour's efforts to make itself electable. By behaving in a simple-majority system as though its desired proportional representation system had already arrived, the SDP rendered still more difficult the plight of those Labour moderates who did not secede, while simultaneously easing Thatcher's task. As she herself argued in 1985, 'they ought to have stayed in and done the infighting and made the extreme left split off. They have not. They took the easy way: they split off.'[284] 1980–3 was a replay of 1886, 1916–18, and 1931 in enabling the Conservatives to profit from their opponents' divisions; but because (unusually) the secessionists from the left did not formally ally with the Conservatives, they did not even receive the consolation prize of being able to moderate Conservative policies.

[279] *DT* (7 Aug. 1987), 28. *T* (3 Mar. 1988), 1.   [280] *ST* (14 May 1989), 1. *T* (17 Oct. 1989), 10.
[281] *T* (27 Mar. 1981), 2. Thatcher, *Downing Street Years*, 265.
[282] e.g. P. Toynbee, 'We Lost, But Son of SDP Will Win', *Ind* (21 June 1995), 21.
[283] *T* (23 July 1994), 15 (Jenkins). *G* (4 Aug. 1994), 1 (Rodgers).
[284] Interview in *FT* (14 Nov. 1985), 28; cf. Thatcher, *Downing Street Years*, 265.

The plight of Labour's moderates under Foot's leadership had indeed been dire. Scargill welcomed the SDP's formation as 'a siphon to take out of our party those elements that were poisoning it',[285] but in a simple-majority system this was a recipe for permanent opposition, and he was at least consistent (ironically, together with the SDP) in also recommending electoral reform. Crosland in the early 1970s urged Labour not to become minority-minded, weighed down by purely middle-class causes—not to become 'the party of women's lib or pot on the national health'. Instead he thought it should focus on the bread-and-butter issues with mass appeal: middle-class environmentalism could not be championed at the expense of working-class jobs.[286] Nonetheless, the Party under Foot almost shrank into a pressure group. Benn in 1979 had even welcomed the tendency: feminist, environmentalist, and ethnic-minority affiliation would, he thought, 'enormously strengthen the Party'.[287] The general election of 1983 was a contest about which political grouping should take second place to the Conservatives: Labour or the alliance between Liberals and Social Democrats.

The SDP's secession did not, as Jenkins claimed, drag Labour 'from the wilder shores of lunacy': it was, for Healey, 'a disastrous error'[288] which by severely weakening Labour's moderates gave Thatcher 'two election victories which she would not otherwise have won'.[289] Labour's recovery had begun before the secession, and the operation of the two-party system would anyway have accelerated recovery in the run-up to the general election of 1983. Political parties do not readily lie down and die, and an election in prospect keeps them on their toes: it highlights practicalities and concern for the public mood, and with their direct access to constituency opinion MPs (especially in marginal seats) readily scale down activists' wishful thinking. Thatcher's resolute Conservatism was a continuous reminder that only a united Labour Party could remove her. For her part, she enthusiastically advertised such Labour extremism as survived—another incentive for Labour to moderate or mask it. In 1983 the Conservatives published full-page advertisements juxtaposing eleven points that Labour's manifesto shared with the Communists under the heading 'Like your manifesto, comrade',[290] and gave Labour its largest order for its manifesto (1,000 copies).[291]

Benn's disloyalty to former colleagues and his distance from parliament spiced Labour's slow move to the centre after 1979 with all the drama of

---

[285] *T* (10 Dec. 1981), 2; cf. Benn's reaction to George Brown's resignation from the Labour Party in 1976, Benn, *Diaries 1973–6*, 525 (2 Mar. 1976).

[286] *NS* (17 Nov. 1972), 709; cf. (8 Jan. 1971), 40, and *ST* (4 Apr. 1971), 16.

[287] Benn, *Diaries 1977–80*, 595 (16 May 1980); cf. 508 (23 May 1979).

[288] *Ind* (23 Sept. 2002), 13 (Jenkins). *Ind* (6 Jan. 2003), 1 (Healey).   [289] *STel* (14 Jan. 1996), 5.

[290] *T* (26 May 1983), 9. For more capitalizing on Labour's manifesto see 18 May 1983, 8; cf. *FT* (28 May 1983), 7.   [291] C. Parkinson, *Right at the Centre: An Autobiography* (1992), 229.

personal animosity. Seasoned Labour leaders like Foot, Shore, Callaghan, and Healey were well able to stand up for their views. Hostility to Benn helped to cement the unity of Foot's shadow cabinet from 1980 onwards, and in November 1981 its composition shifted markedly to the right. Long-established skills on Labour's right at outmanœuvring its left by no means ceased with the SDP's departure, as the energetic career of the tough and astute Labour loyalist MP John Golding testifies. Combining contempt for the timidity of the SDP seceders with irreverence towards the intellectual left, this self-styled 'aggressive moderate' was unobtrusively influential in the Party's recovery up to 1983.[292] The SDP split eased the process, continuous throughout the Party's history, whereby the left moves steadily rightwards within it. Among the so-called 'soft left' was Kinnock, who in 1981 had braved the accusation 'Judas' when rather publicly deserting Benn during the closely contested deputy-leadership contest. 'Responsible' opposition centring on parliament was already Kinnock's strategy, and though he lacked Foot's literary cultivation, the two men were friends and had much in common. Theirs was the traditionalist labour-left world of the Welsh mining valleys, where oratory stirred the emotions. Amidst the pressures of the 1980s, however, Kinnock moved on from his past more adroitly than Foot.

An inexperienced young leader of a fractious and demoralized party lacked freedom of action and even of speech: 'I had to bite my lip a lot', he recalled.[293] In 1983 he did not publicly back the TUC's General Secretary in opposing the printers' union when it defied the law in the Warrington newspaper dispute,[294] and the miners' strike of 1984–5 occurred too early in Kinnock's leadership for him to risk what would look like a betrayal. 'They ducked it', was Thatcher's comment on how Labour had responded to this 'real test of leadership', especially as Kinnock had admitted in 1983 that Scargill was 'destroying the coal industry single-handed'. Kinnock later regretted not having stressed more firmly the need to ballot the miners on the strike—a failure which he thought had delivered 'a huge victory' to Thatcher.[295] But as so often, a Thatcher triumph eased Kinnock's campaign for moderation within his own party. In 1984–5 he showed his mettle as leader by using his most powerful weapon: oratory. Though a tortured syntax weakened his off-the-cuff comment, he was capable of high-flown rhetoric which at crucial moments could stir emotions and precisely hit its target. He prepared meticulously for important speeches, sometimes too much so, but with his brave speech at the party conference in

---

[292] G (28 Sept. 1982), 17. Obituary, G (22 Jan. 1999), 22.
[293] Contribution to BBC2's programme The Lost Leader (5 Dec. 1992).
[294] See the hostile editorial in ST (18 Dec. 1983), 16.
[295] Thatcher to the national Young Conservatives conference on 9 Feb. 1985, O (16 Feb. 1985), 1. See also O (11 Nov. 1984), 5. Kinnock, contribution to BBC2's programme The Lost Leader. See also G (9 July 1993), 8.

1984 he was on his best form: 'when I turned the television set off', David Owen recalled, 'I knew perfectly well that he was on his way'.[296]

Kinnock's most courageous moment occurred a year later, on 1 October 1985, when at the party conference he memorably attacked Hatton and Liverpool's councillors in the Militant Tendency. The Tendency was admittedly a much easier target than the NUM, but at this stage in his leadership Kinnock needed an arena in which publicly to display his courage, his determination, his hold over his party, and what in the late twentieth century could still be achieved through oratory. 'It is a great thing', he recalled, 'especially in the world of politics where so frequently you have to wrap things up in conditions and reservations and maybes—to simply be able to get up and *say* it as you feel it. I enjoyed doing that.'[297] He was booed during his speech but, he said, 'the voice of the people, not the people in here, the people with real needs is louder than all the boos that can be assembled'.[298] It was his equivalent of Gaitskell's 'fight, fight, and fight again' speech, lending Kinnock a national identity; it was thought worth incorporating into the Party's media coverage during the general election two years later. Healey thought the speech 'of historic importance', and likely to shift the Party's image and power balance decisively. The episode was not lost on the young future leader roused to his feet by Kinnock's rhetoric, Tony Blair, who saw it as the moment 'when our journey to Government began'.[299] Kinnock was a thoroughly decent man, with ample compassion for suffering and capable of a fierce anger at injustice. But he also possessed the very necessary toughness and even ruthlessness that Foot lacked. Kinnock's impatience at self-indulgent posturing on Labour's left—at fruitless political game-playing, and at self-regarding preoccupation with principle—elicited from him some scorching speeches in the mid-1980s, and he repeatedly relished trouncing his critics, amidst shouts of hostility at Party meetings. There still remained bogeys enough within the labour movement for the Conservatives to capitalize upon at the general election of 1987,[300] but Labour was now firmly heading in what were later revealed as Blairite destinations.

Kinnock was far less effective in parliament, where he confronted a particularly formidable opponent. Like Foot he lacked the numeracy, the precise recall, and the detailed grasp that alone could shake Thatcher. His speech in the Westland debate, for instance, failed to identify the crucially damaging detail, and so threw away a prize opportunity for weakening her permanently. Week after week she outgunned him in parliamentary questions: for

[296] In Radio 3 programme 'The Gang that Fell Apart', 25 Sept. 1991.
[297] Contribution to BBC2's *The Lost Leader* (televised interview with David Dimbleby, 5 Dec. 1992).
[298] *G* (2 Oct. 1985), 6.
[299] *T* (2 Oct. 1985), 1 (Healey). Blair's party conference speech on 30 Sept. 2003, *T* (1 Oct. 2003), 9.
[300] See the two-page advertisement in *STel* (31 May 1987), 10–11, printing photographs of nineteen Labour candidates together with the extremist remarks for which they had been responsible.

Benn in December 1989 he 'yaps like a little dog at Thatcher's heels and she kicks him aside'.[301] Thatcher's second and third election victories ensured that the momentum behind Labour's self-reform long outlasted the SDP's demise. It was Thatcher who destroyed Benn, Hatton, Scargill, and (for the time being) Livingstone; she who undermined the 'loony left' through rate-capping and abolishing the metropolitan county councils; she who instituted the drive towards privatization and trade union reform. Reform of the Labour Party had long been on her hidden agenda,[302] and it was among her most substantial achievements. There was a certain personal symmetry in this, for in the year when she had been rejected as Conservative candidate for Orpington, John Strachey claimed as Labour's 'greatest single achievement' during the past quarter century 'the transformation of the British Conservative Party'.[303]

To all this Kinnock had to respond, but if only because he was gradually and publicly unlearning his own past the process was slow, painful, pragmatic, and somewhat uninspiring. Kinnock was not a man of ideas, but he knew the importance for the Party of the public-relations skills which Foot had so sorely neglected, and from 1986 he instituted many of the structural and presentational changes later identified with 'New Labour'. Peter Mandelson was appointed Labour's Director of Campaigns and Communications in 1985, and at the Party's conference in 1986—the most tightly organized such event for more than twenty years—the Party's red rose symbol was in place. By 1990 Labour spokesmen were wearing executive suits and ties, and Labour women had shed their boiler suits for power dressing, with Kinnock in firm control. Resentment at the pace of change by 1988 prompted an outburst from TGWU General Secretary Ron Todd at a Tribune rally against men in sharp suits with clipboards and filofaxes.[304] Significant organizational changes were occurring too. By 1986 Labour was using direct-mail techniques to get its literature to trade unionists and to those who subscribed to sympathetic periodicals.[305] By 1987 leading trade unionists were at last coming round to the direct democracy which the SDP and Kinnock had backed much earlier: 'one member one vote' throughout the Party.[306] In 1987, when presenting Labour with his report on its seriously declining strength, Philip Gould was already well acquainted with the 'focus group', whereby small-group discussion enabled researchers to discover 'qualitative' opinion. The following year saw the first dent in trade union power

[301] Benn, *Diaries 1980–90*, 556 (25 Dec. 1988). On Westland, see H. Young, 'How Mr Kinnock Saved the Day—for Her', *G* (28 Jan. 1986), 21.

[302] Not entirely hidden; see her final campaign press conference on 8 June 1983, *G* (9 June 1983), 3.

[303] Strachey's preface to A. A. Rogow, *The Labour Government and British Industry 1945–51* (Oxford 1955), p. x.   [304] *Ind* (6 Oct. 1990), 5. Todd, *G* (6 Oct. 1988), 19.

[305] *FT* (27 Jan. 1987), 21.

[306] See the comments of Jordan and Todd at the Labour Party conference, *G* (29 Sept. 1987), 5.

over the Party when the trade union vote in choosing candidates was limited to 40 per cent. When in 1989 Labour ceased to support the pre-entry closed shop, which the government was about to ban, Blair told his constituency party that the closed shop was incompatible with Labour's respect for the individual, as well as conflicting with EU law; he ensured that his remarks were made available to the press.[307]

No doubt it was his supportive wife and happy family life that nerved Kinnock to endure the necessary but endlessly wearing battles with colleagues, some of them former political allies. He was staunchly backed by John Smith, one of the handful of colleagues who had held cabinet office in the 1970s, and holder of several important shadow portfolios thereafter. Yet even after removing or concealing many of Labour's unattractive features, Kinnock still in 1992 could not raise its share of the total vote beyond 34 per cent. His was an impossible task for a young and inexperienced leader, and he lacked the calm temper, the presence, the intellect, the experience, and the wide perspective that made for statesmanship. Volatile in mood, he was labelled 'Labour's battling boyo',[308] a reference to his short fuse and his taste even for physical combat. After he resigned as leader in 1992 his complex combination of courage and self-doubt prompted self-reproach for apparent failure. Wrongly, if only because winning office is not the party leader's sole important task. Kinnock's faults lay all on the surface, but he grasped opposition's opportunities to ensure that, more than anyone since Gaitskell, he rendered his party electable at a time when its core support was in rapid decline. The task required both courage and adaptability, together with a patience that did not come naturally. Kinnock prepared the ground for his successors' more overt triumphs, and to them he showed (despite private doubts) a public loyalty not displayed after 1975 to their leader by his Conservative equivalents. More than any other individual in his Party, it was Kinnock who ensured Labour's victory in 1997.

7. PRIVACY AND PUBLICITY

In 1956 a distinguished American sociologist found British political life 'strikingly quiet and confined. Modern publicity is hemmed about by a generally well-respected privacy'.[309] Yet by then the situation had already been changing for some time. Five years earlier the Duke of Windsor dated privacy's disappearance—'one of the most inconvenient developments since the days of my boyhood'—well back into the past. In those days the likenesses of public figures had seldom appeared in the press, and there was no television, whereas already

---

[307] *Ind* (14 May 1994), 16.   [308] Headline of leader in *Ind* (3 Apr. 1991), 20.
[309] E. A. Shils, *The Torment of Secrecy: The Background and Consequences of American Security Policies* (1956), 48.

by 1948 difficulties crowded round a reticent politician like Harold Nicolson. His political career suffered from his publicly criticizing the arts of election campaigning: 'the wave of the hand and arm . . .', he wrote, 'is irksome to a shy person', who loathes 'flinging friendliness like confetti in the air, selling cheap what is most dear'. Privacy was invaded further by television, and later by computerized databases and cameras with their increasingly intrusive lenses: 'where ever you are', the Prince of Wales complained in 1994, 'there's somebody hiding behind something, somewhere, and with these immense cameras now, with these huge lenses and magnification'.[310]

It is a mentality, not a technique, which invades privacy: late twentieth-century Britain increasingly upheld privacy for the citizen while increasingly denying it to public figures. After 1970 the latter faced intrusion from diminished formality, from the pursuit of 'open government' and sexual frankness, and from the publication of 'leaks' and diaries revealing conversations whose privacy had hitherto been respected. Anonymous reviews and newspaper articles, and letters signed only by pseudonyms and initials, had long been in decline, and in 1974 the serious reviewer even in the *Times Literary Supplement* lost anonymity;[311] henceforth only the *Economist* protected its reviewers from being thus diverted from their main purpose. Media presenters, too, lost their anonymity: ITN in 1955 imported from the USA the idea of named 'newscasters', and the BBC soon followed.[312] By 1970 radio announcers and news-readers were becoming personalities in their own right. To their predecessors, broadcasters like William Hardcastle seemed in their distinctive mannerisms distracting and even improper.[313] Kenneth Williams in 1971 thought 'announcers trading quips and esoteric asides to each other' were 'invalidating their own comment'.[314]

Privacy's retreat removed much hypocrisy and ignorance from public life, but greatly complicated it. Negotiations in public seldom succeed, least of all on matters affecting national status or the money markets, and it was becoming difficult to retain privacy for key moments of decision. Secularization entailed an earth-bound preoccupation with self-image, self-promotion, even notoriety; with no world to come, this world became the sole arena. Hence the growing press interest during the 1980s in the obituary, the secularized world's equivalent of the last judgment. The 'vocation' or 'calling' succumbed before the

[310] H. Nicolson in *Spec* (19 Mar. 1948), repr. in H. Nicolson, *Diaries and Letters, 1945–1962*, ed. N. Nicolson (1968), 134; cf. N. Nicolson's introduction, 18. Prince of Wales, *G* (30 June 1994), 3, reporting ITV documentary on 29 June.

[311] *TLS* (7 June 1974), 610; (12 July 1974), 748. See also Harrison, *Seeking a Role*, 371, 393.

[312] Cockerell, *Live from No. 10*, 42.

[313] See Alvar Lidell's complaints in his 'Newsweeding', *Listener* (5 Apr. 1979), 478, and subsequent correspondence.

[314] As Kenneth Williams noted in the *Listener* (23 Dec. 1971), quoted in his *Diaries*, 412 n. 28 (13 Nov. 1971).

career and the image. The professional ethic, unobtrusively pursuing objectivity and a long-term relationship, gave ground to an unabashed commercialism and to the short-term contract. The books of records so prominent in a secular and meritocratic world commemorated many people for whom setting any record was better than none. The 17-year-old Marcus Sarjeant, who fired blank shots at the Queen in 1981, felt no animosity towards her, and even forewarned her: on capture he said 'I wanted to be somebody. I wanted to be famous.'[315] The phrase 'serial killer' and 'serial killing' seems to emerge from American contexts in the 1980s, and the reality had become more common in the UK and USA by the end of the century.[316] The cult of worldly success (or notoriety) brought the danger, on failure, of enhanced self-reproach, or could even prompt a counter-active culture of failure. 'Self-sabotage', a feature of sixties counter-culture, remained a dimension of the pop-music and drug scene thereafter. This was not idealistic self-sacrifice in a quest for early admission to paradise: it was the ultimate teenage rebellion, reflecting the sense of futility induced by the high expectations and profound complexities of life in Western industrial society.

Changing child-naming practices reflected the growing cult of celebrity. The shift was from a society with a limited stock of names, many of them handed down within the family from one generation to the next, to a society with a free market in an expanded stock of names, some imported, some invented, and many reflecting shifts in fashion.[317] Whether in naming young children or in singing to them, parents responded to media fashions, and the nursery rhyme slowly gave way to pop songs and television theme tunes.[318] 'Darren' was an American name that leapt from nothing to seventh most popular UK name for children in 1971, reflecting the impact made in the UK during the 1960s by the American television series *Bewitched*.[319] The royal family, by comparison, seems to have had little impact. 'George' had never been a popular name for twentieth-century boys, nor did Elizabeth II's accession prevent the continued decline in the popularity of 'Elizabeth'. Prince Charles's advent did not arrest the long-term decline of 'Charles' from 38th position in 1954 to 44th forty years later, and Princess Anne could not prevent her name from slipping from 10th in 1954 to 60th in 1974, and thereafter out of the top 100 altogether.[320] In a secularizing society, religion can hardly explain the presence among the top ten in 1994 of the biblical names Daniel, Joshua, Luke, and Samuel, none of

---

[315] Tendler, 'Teenager who Wanted Fame', 30.   [316] *T* (3 May 1996), 9.

[317] For statistics see S. Wilson, *The Means of Naming: A Social and Cultural History of Personal Naming in Western Europe* (1998), 326; see also 328.

[318] *FT* (7 Jan. 2003), 4 discussing top names for 2002. *T* (9 July 2007), 5.

[319] L. A. Dunkling, *First Names First* (1977), 177.

[320] Ibid. 186–95. E. Merry, *First Names: The Definitive Guide to Popular Names in England and Wales 1944–1994* (1995), 12–27.

them in 1954's top ten for boys; as with the presence in 1994 of the non-biblical Amy, Emily, Emma, and Jessica among the top ten for girls (all absent in 1954)—a change of fashion was responsible. Only with Muhammad's steady progress from 87th among boys' names to second place in 2006 (if variant spellings are merged) was the UK impact of (non-Christian) religion felt in naming practices.[321] Amidst such eye-catching diversity, the prominence of once-popular names could hardly persist: among boys' names, John, long in decline, fell from first place in 1944 to 39th by 1994, David from second to 24th, and Michael from third to 12th.[322]

Politicians, less in the public eye before the 1960s, had felt little need to sell themselves, and the attempt of the Conservative politician, Sir Laming Worthington-Evans, to build himself up as a popular figure in the 1920s had been counterproductive. By 1979, however, Callaghan's insistence, early in the general election campaign, that 'I will not be packaged like cornflakes' showed what was by then an imprudent reticence by comparison with his rival.[323] Elections were now a marketing exercise, and though little could be done with Heath, much was done with Thatcher.[324] In 1979 afternoon walkabouts for the party leaders were staged with the local and national evening news broadcasts in view, and major speeches were timed to catch the late evening news bulletins.[325] The media and the opinion polls spiralled in their growing interactive impact. The 1970s began badly for the polls when they failed to capture the late swing to the Conservatives at the general election of 1970, prompting a page of delighted letters in *The Times* on 23 June. The pollsters then framed a code of conduct, and did likewise after the general election of February 1974, whose Conservative vote they had exaggerated; in October they exaggerated Labour's vote by an even larger margin. Yet the polls aimed at far more than predicting electoral outcomes; the parties valued pollsters for helping to determine that outcome. At the February election Labour for the first time during an election campaign sponsored daily polls tracking the salience of issues; both parties in both elections of that year ran private polls similar in scale and design, so pollsters helped to mould day-to-day strategy decisions. The general election of 1983 was the first in which all three national parties systematically used private polls, and by 1987 stockbrokers sought in vain to buy pollsters' advance knowledge on the latest statistics.[326]

By then computer technology, already employed at party headquarters in 1983, was beginning to affect the parties' local campaigning, where there was

[321] Merry, *First Names*, 23. *T* (6 June 2007), 8.   [322] Merry, *First Names*, 38–42.
[323] *FT* (2 May 1979), 22. For a useful general discussion of Americanized publicity in British elections at this time see *FT* (15 Mar. 1979), 21.   [324] See above, p. 488.
[325] Butler and Kavanagh, *British General Election of 1979*, 319.
[326] D. E. Butler and D. Kavanagh, *The British General Election of Oct. 1974* (1975), 197–200. Butler and Kavanagh, *British General Election of 1983*, 145. *FT* (6 July 19870, weekend supplement, p. i.

interaction between electoral registers, canvassing cards, and direct-mailing, especially in marginal seats. In 1992 all this went very much further and was reinforced by the fax machine,[327] with Conservatives particularly eager to learn from the latest American practice. During the 1980s computer technology began to mould even wider aspects of politics. It did not impinge on parliament differently from other institutions, but its implications were greater because manipulating information and coordinating groups were integral to parliament's function. Computerization advanced gradually and pragmatically during the 1980s,[328] and its implications for the most efficient use of the Westminster site and for the MP's links with party, civil service, and constituents were in the long term formidable. Although these changes were not imminent in 1990, we have seen how computers had for some years in the trade union world been enhancing communication between leaders and led.[329]

How did these major changes affect democratic participation? On the one hand the new media seemed likely to advance the reasoned understanding of the political process. Reinforced by open government, advancing psephology, and the spread of opinion polls, they ensured that politicians were better informed. By 1964 television during the general election was conveying political information to many who would not have got it from newspapers.[330] The burgeoning mass media substituted a national political community for the declining local political community. Psephology so improved electors' knowledge of elections that tactical voting—feasible in a smaller, locally oriented, and well-informed nineteenth-century electorate—re-emerged in the 1980s as a force in national party politics. Aided by weakening party loyalty and the growth of new parties, it was widely discussed at the general elections of 1992 and 1997.[331] At general elections there was no sign of long-term decline in turnout. The figure of 82.5 per cent in 1951 had been exceptional, the highest since 1906; in the eleven elections thereafter up to and including 1992, turnout averaged at 75.8 per cent. The share of the samples polled who cared which party won rose from two-thirds in the 1960s to three-quarters in the 1980s.[332]

Yet politicians sounded a warning note, and often criticized competitors in their special area of expertise: that is, in gauging public opinion and deciding how to respond. The polls could not supersede their profession. Wilson pointed

[327] Butler and Kavanagh, *British General Election of 1987*, 213–14. D. E. Butler, 'Hi-Tech Replaces Rap of the Knocker', *FT* (31 Mar. 1992), 10.
[328] On this, as on other occasions, I have been most grateful to Dr C. Pond of the House of Commons Public Information Office for generous help.
[329] See above, pp. 167–8.   [330] J. D. Halloran, *The Effects of Television* (1970), 80–1.
[331] D. E. Butler and D. Kavanagh, *The British General Election of 1992* (Basingstoke and London, 1992), 280, 336–7. D. E. Butler and D. Kavanagh, *The British General Election of 1997* (Basingstoke and London, 1997), 309–13.
[332] I. Crewe, A. Fox, and N. Day, *The British Electorate 1963–1992: A Compendium of Data from the British Election Studies* (Cambridge, 1995), 166.

out in 1971 that polling evidence was moulded by the questions asked, and was concerned with a single issue, whereas politicians must simultaneously balance opinion in several areas and also gauge its intensity. Politicians knew how volatile opinion could be, especially in the face of unexpected events, and to these they had to react.[333] Kenneth Clarke, resisting pressure to improve a pay offer to ambulance men during a dispute in 1989, was sceptical about public opinion surveyed on the matter: 'the depth of public knowledge about what they earn, what they are being offered and what they want is nil, absolutely nil. You cannot settle pay negotiations in a health service of a million people by going out and holding opinion polls.'[334] In some respects a participatory democracy seemed, after 1970, to be receding. Television helped to politicize the least politicized. The turnout figures after 1951 in national elections may not have declined, but local election turnout was much lower, and political opinions were acquired more passively. The new media did not necessarily encourage active involvement in the political process: their advance coincided with an almost complete collapse of support for constituency public meetings, and some of the most important episodes at party conferences now occurred in the television studio rather than on the floor of the hall.[335] Party membership was declining: by 1997 the main parties had only two members for every hundred electors, the lowest since the war. Crossman in a gloomy mood referred in 1968 to the 'mass-indifference and mass-alienation' that had disappointed his hopes for political participation, and detected 'a greater gap between government and people than . . . in the time of Disraeli and Gladstone'.[336] We have seen how press reporting of parliamentary debates had long been in decline;[337] the media survive only by responding to their market, and only a tenth of a Gallup poll sample in 1983 saw politics as very important in their everyday lives; for a fifth, politics were not at all important.[338]

So after the 1960s there may be a political analogue of the cultural 'dumbing down' already discussed.[339] Thenceforward the speeded-up and fragmented approach to reporting that the electronic media thought appropriate gradually pervaded the printed page, and even the 'quality' newspapers declined as organs of political reporting. The pursuit of publicity and notoriety slowly had the effect of downgrading the inevitably humdrum processes of democratic government. The franchise, broadened from the 1830s to the 1960s with so much self-sacrifice and effort, was by 1987 so little valued among a sixth of the inner cities' adult population that they did not even bother to register,[340] and by

---

[333] O (14 Mar. 1971), 29.   [334] FT (14 Dec. 1989), 9.
[335] STel (22 Apr. 1979), 4. O (17 Oct. 1982), 7.
[336] Cabinet Diaries, ii. 780 (14 Apr. 1968). See also T (23 Apr. 1997), 12. See also T (6 June 1997), 15.
[337] See above, p. 406.   [338] T (18 May 1983), 2.   [339] See above, pp. 425–31.
[340] T (26 Aug. 1987), 1.

1992 the unregistered had doubled to about a million, partly because non-voting seemed preferable to paying the poll tax.[341] In the 1990s it was humbling indeed to see on television voters in East European and underdeveloped countries patiently standing for hours in long queues to cast newly won votes that in Britain were now valued so lightly.

In this chapter we have seen that in the 1970s and 1980s, as before, British political institutions were changing in reality though not in appearance, for the impact of technological and social innovation could not be warded off, least of all by those parts of the structure whose role was overtly to respond to public pressures. Even the more formal structures—monarchy, prime minister, and cabinet—responded flexibly to changes of personnel and pressures of opinion, just as parliament responded flexibly to the growing pressures of legislation and specialization. This institutional stability was the more impressive given the substantial shift in policy agenda that occurred in 1979. Whereas in the 1970s central and local government struggled to make a success of corporatism, in the 1980s they had to adjust to its rapid winding down. Flexibility was also the response of the two major political parties, both of which accommodated the new policies; even the Labour Party survived a serious split in the early 1980s, and later came to terms with the new situation, and the Conservatives did not allow the Thatcher phenomenon to split them at all. The growing pressures from publicity and infringements of privacy, however, made the task of politician and civil servant much more complex, and in many ways less attractive.

Here, then, is the fourth motif: the paradoxical impact of time-saving devices. Faster communication and instant information increased the strain, especially from pressures of opinion. Thatcher's impact exemplified the seventh motif: the capacity of an energetic and self-confident politician to shift opinion if working with the voluntarist grain, but the poll-tax episode exemplified its failure when lacking a supportive public opinion. As for the second motif, the tension between the UK's hermetic and receptive tendencies, the USA's continued centrality remains evident, despite the UK's EEC membership. Both political parties looked to the instruments of American democracy: the Conservatives sought libertarian inspiration and opinion-moulding devices, Labour sought ideas on how best to ward off an overweening executive. For by 1990 even the externals of the UK's political system were coming under challenge from the left, though its search for ideas on constitutional reform was by no means confined to the USA. The internal contradictions of Thatcherism highlight the fifth motif, for an outlook so preoccupied with economic growth needed a substitute for the austerely Christian structures that had helped to

---

[341] I. Crewe, 'Voting and the Electorate', in P. Dunleavy et al., Developments in British Politics, iv (Basingstoke and London, 1993), 109.

drive it forward in Victorian times, and failed to find it. Two more motifs have been central to this chapter: the sixth, the juxtaposition of a changing political reality with apparently unchanging institutions; and the seventh, the gradual waning of the UK's self-prescribed role as the world's political exemplar.

CHAPTER 8

Retrospect and Prospect

The threads must now be drawn together, first by surveying what has so far been discussed, and then by seeking overall patterns: setbacks for socialism during the 1970s in the first section, then in the second section the high hopes held out for the free market together with the weakness of its critics, whether violent or reflective. An assessment of free-market outcomes follows in the third section, whereas in the fourth section changing attitudes to the future are considered. The final section rounds off by looking again at changes in the UK's world role. In party-political and overall policy terms, the pattern seems clear enough. Remington, in H. G. Wells's *New Machiavelli* (1911), did not see nineteenth-century Britain in terms of continuous progress, but as a sequence of fresh starts, each leaving its debris behind.[1] The same can be said of Britain after 1951. The UK's thermometer of hopes and fears fluctuated from the 1940s throughout the rest of the century. Such fluctuations bore some relation to the parties' alternation in power, though the fit was inexact because big transitions sometimes occurred between elections. There were also regional variegations within this overall pattern. Northern Ireland's 'troubles' occurred on a separate plane, and restiveness in Scotland and Wales often now transferred its hopes to nationalism and away from the UK's two main parties.

Labour's programme in 1945 sketched out what were then seen as only the first steps towards creating a socialist society, yet already by 1950 a 'consolidating' strategy had been adopted: high hopes for a 'New Jerusalem' had begun to fade. Then came the comforting illusion in the early 1950s of a 'New Elizabethan age', with its exaggerated hopes of the Commonwealth as vehicle for British interests. The Suez crisis in 1956 killed off these hopes, and from the late 1950s hopes slowly shifted towards the EEC as a potential source of faster economic growth, and even as the vehicle for the UK's revived world status.[2] Britain's first rejected application to the EEC in 1963 transferred hopes to Harold Wilson's Labour Party, and the young future Labour activist

---

[1] H. G. Wells, *The New Machiavelli* (1st publ. 1911, paperback edn. 1966), 39.
[2] Harrison, *Seeking a Role*, 114–21.

Ken Livingstone felt a 'trembling of excitement' when Wilson won in the general election in 1964. He was soon disillusioned: Labour's radical belief in institutional reform faded, and Wilson's uninspiringly tactical and pragmatic style became ever more evident. Radicals like E. P. Thompson came away from Wilson's published account of his governments (1971) with 'an enhanced contempt for parliamentarians'.[3] Many idealists had lost their faith in him much earlier, and opted instead for an apolitical pursuit of personal fulfilment. To quote a student slogan of the late 1960s: 'tomorrow has been cancelled owing to lack of interest'.[4] These disappointments helped the Conservatives to win the general election of 1970. Revived hopes then centred upon the UK's new allegiance to the EEC, but support for it suffered from its timing. The UK did not join the EEC in the 1950s or 1960s when EEC growth-rates were high, but in the 1970s when they were declining; yet more disillusion was the outcome. During the 1970s, instead of the low British growth-rate levelling up to the European, the European growth-rate levelled down towards the British.[5]

Pessimism then pervaded the entire corporatist agenda that had been pursued since 1940. The failure in 1974 of Heath's central strategy prompted the deepest gloom, for Labour took over with no apparent alternative. 'To my mind it is only a question of time before we are a sort of sub-Ireland, or Italy', wrote Philip Larkin in June, 'with the population scratching a living by sucking up to tourists and the Queen doing two performances a day of Trooping the Colour for coach loads of Middle-Westerners and Russian Moujiks. God, what an end to a great country.' When the Labour government applied for a loan from the IMF two years later, Benn privately likened the establishment's mood to 'the Vichy spirit of complete capitulation and defeatism'.[6] With the initial success of Labour's incomes policy, and with high hopes of North Sea oil, the climate briefly improved in the late 1970s until the collapse of Labour's attempt to plan incomes during the 'winter of discontent' in 1978–9. The corporatist seam then seemed finally to have been worked out.

At that point Thatcher's new variant of Conservatism offered hope to some, especially after the Falklands victory in 1982. By then the country was more polarized on domestic policy than at any time since the 1930s, but on the Conservative side high hopes were maintained of Thatcher's new direction until the depression late in the 1980s. Yet these hopes remained high enough after Thatcher's political demise for her party to win again at the general election of 1992 and continue thereafter on the same course. But gloom then

---

[3] G (28 Apr. 1984), 17 (Livingstone). *New Society* (29 July 1971), 200 (Thompson).
[4] Slogan chalked on the Broad Street wall of Balliol College, Oxford, observed by the author in the late 1960s.   [5] Sanders, *Losing an Empire*, 145.
[6] Larkin to Colin Gunner, 19 June, in his *Letters*, ed. Thwaite, 510, cf. 663. Benn, *Diaries 1973–6*, 595 (15 July 1976).

soon reached a new low, with departure from the ERM and serious Conservative faction-fighting, as well as fierce questionings on the left of the entire British political system. In the mid-1990s Blair's leadership lifted spirits on the left, and he launched his government in 1997 with 'New Labour' incorporating what was seen as the best of Thatcherism without its defects. Gloom once more descended with the Iraq war in 2003, and with the cumulating corrosion stemming from the rivalry between Blair and Brown. Beneath these minor oscillations there lay a single major undulation which bore no simple relationship to political party, and whose long-term outcome remains unclear. This undulation entailed the rise from the 1940s to the 1960s of corporatist approaches to economic management, the struggle till 1979 to make them work better, followed by their quite sudden collapse in the late 1970s. With 1979 as a 'critical' election marking off the UK's corporatist from its free-market phase, a new direction was taken, at first precariously, and throughout the 1980s controversially, until in the 1990s it moved slowly towards something approaching all-party consensus.

The UK's apprehensive public mood about the economy after 1951 is in some ways puzzling, and we have frequently highlighted its contrast with the unprecedented growth in private living standards. On growth-rate in both gross domestic product and gross domestic product per head, Britain's economic performance from 1951 to 1973 compared well with any period since 1856. Total and average incomes grew faster after 1945 at precisely the time when complaints about the UK's decline were at their most anguished. Comparison with Germany and Japan might indicate relative decline, but Crosland thought that if British living standards were likely to double in twenty-five years it was hardly worth worrying if other countries were doing still better: 'there is no point in being vain in these matters'.[7] Why such grumbles, then, when the British people were at last emerging into daylight from what Keynes had called 'the tunnel of economic necessity'?[8] The explanation lies partly in the growing salience during and soon after the Second World War of international statistical comparisons on economic performance; comparative statistics on productivity particularly attracted politicians seeking scapegoats and opportunities for exhortation.[9] These figures fed into the national debate about social-class relations during the 1950s, and fuelled the Labour Party's slow recovery from its setbacks during that decade. Corporatism and the Labour Party's weak variant of socialism were not identical but were intertwined in their fate.

---

[7] C. A. R. Crosland, *The Future of Socialism* (1956), 383. See also B. Supple, 'British Economic Decline since 1945', in Floud and McCloskey (eds.), *Economic History of Britain*, iii (2nd edn.), 320–2.

[8] 'Economic Possibilities for our Grandchildren' (1930) in his *Essays in Persuasion* (1931), 372.

[9] See the important discussion in J. Tomlinson, *The Politics of Decline: Understanding Post-War Britain* (Harlow, 2000), 13–21.

I. SOCIALIST SETBACK

It was in the Labour Party's interest from 1951 to harness corporatist ideas and link them with concern about national economic decline and with worries about manufactures' shrinking share in the UK economy. It could then advertise its special aptitude for tackling the problem through planning and through its trade union links, and at the same time maximize its appeal beyond the working class by stressing its modernizing and meritocratic agenda. Behind that agenda C. P. Snow's 'two cultures' debate marshalled the interests of pure and applied natural science.[10] During the 1960s, however, this new alignment ran into trouble. Incomes policies were central to Labour's handling of inflation and industrial strife, and could be presented as socialist, but were shown from the mid-1960s to infringe the trade unions' libertarian and free-market instincts.[11] There was a second problem: the early Labour Party's outlook had been strongly evangelical, seeking to change opinion rather than merely reflect it. This required not just sympathetic voters but committed and active citizens, yet by the 1970s the Party's leaders were reining in socialist policies because these were allegedly unpopular with voters. Taxation lay near the heart of the difficulty here. In the Party's early days, only the relatively affluent paid income tax, and Labour's support then came largely from the tax-exempt, who with a wider franchise seemed likely soon to form an electoral majority: hence the assumption that higher direct taxation would become electorally viable. The combination of inflation and mounting affluence, however, sharply increased the proportion of the electorate drawn into paying income tax: 25.3 million by 1975/6.[12] Public hostility to higher taxes soon hampered Labour Chancellors of the Exchequer, and globalization introduced a further difficulty: socialists had long thought expertise essential in business and government, but as the market for experts became increasingly international, high taxation risked denying the UK access to it. In 1967 Callaghan was already upsetting an egalitarian Castle by arguing in cabinet that profits and the incentives for managers were too low.[13]

Within the Labour cabinets of 1974–9 such arguments seemed still more powerful. Healey claimed on 22 May 1975 that public expenditure's share of gross national product was too high. Confiscating the income of the rich would achieve little for the poor, he said, in an argument frequently voiced later in the decade. If it was as simple as that, Castle mused, 'we had all better become Tories'. When in the following month Jenkins pronounced it 'absurd' that public expenditure had now reached 58 per cent of gross national product, she

[10] Ibid. 24.   [11] See *Seeking a Role*, 454, 458.
[12] Inland Revenue statistics at www.inlandrevenue.gov.uk/stats/tax_receipts/g_t04_1.htm consulted 12 June 2002.   [13] Castle, *Diaries 1964–70*, 240 (10 Apr. 1967).

asked herself what would then be the justification for a Labour government.[14] By January 1976 Jenkins was publicly questioning whether freedom could survive within a society whose public expenditure absorbed more than 60 per cent of gross domestic product. 'We are here close to one of the frontiers of social democracy', he said, stressing the need to balance liberty against social justice.[15] Healey had been saying something rather similar in cabinet a few months before.[16] Castle, alarmed at the implications for socialism, thought Labour should evangelize by emphasizing the real gains that higher taxation would bring, at least to some, in the form of the 'social wage'.[17] By 1977, however, electoral calculation with IMF endorsement had brought Callaghan close to the Conservative policy of reducing both public expenditure and direct taxation, and he accused Castle of being 'elitist' when in March 1978 she advocated raising government expenditure rather than cutting taxation. 'That's not what they are saying in the working men's clubs', he rejoined: the Party could not insulate itself from public opinion.[18] Added to all this was the difficulty, already discussed,[19] of harnessing trade unionists with free-market instincts to incomes policies that could be presented as socialist. So by the 1970s even the UK's weak variant of socialism, faith in central government economic interventionism, entered upon a decline that far transcended the reaction against urban planning.[20]

Yet socialism, however defined, had only ever been one strand within the Labour Party, and its retreat did not preclude the Party's effective pursuit of its two other linked historic roles: ensuring full working-class representation within the political system, and thereby enhancing its stability. Because the UK emerged in 1990 in reasonably good order, it would be facile to assume inevitability about the UK's gradual and relatively non-violent passage through four decades of massive immigration, economic dislocation, home-grown terrorism, and declining national status. Labour's ongoing achievement here deserves emphasis. There had been race riots in Notting Hill in 1958 and the Grosvenor Square riot ten years later, but these sprang from specific grievances, and did not threaten generalized disorder. From the 1960s, however, the fear and even the reality of violent racial conflict pervaded many British cities,[21] and was defused largely through Labour's double contribution: attracting the support and hopes of the ethnic minorities themselves, and drawing organized labour towards accepting them, together with mounting the welfare policies designed to help them integrate.

---

[14] *Diaries 1974–6*, 398 (22 May 1975); 427 (20 June 1975), cf. 670 (4 Mar. 1976); 463 (14 July 1975, in note to Harold Lever in cabinet).   [15] Jenkins quoted in *T* (16 Feb. 1976), 13.
[16] Castle, *Diaries 1974–6*, 398 (22 May 1975); see also 427 (20 June 1975), 670 (4 Mar. 1976), and Healey, *Time of my Life*, 402.
[17] Castle, *Diaries 1974–6*, 319 (1 Mar. 1975), cf. 326 (2 Mar. 1975), 428 (20 June 1975) and her speech at Scarborough, *ST* (2 Mar. 1975), 6.   [18] *G* (14 Mar. 1978), 6.
[19] See above, pp. 299–303.   [20] See above, p. 336.
[21] See Harrison, *Seeking a Role*, 222, 231, 540, and above, pp. 202–4.

Other dimensions of violence were more difficult to tackle. Until the 1960s there had been no recent well-developed or continuous UK tradition of stunt violence,[22] which still then seemed to resemble the earthquakes and tornados that occurred only in faraway countries of which we knew little. To Labour's chief whip the Angry Brigade's bomb at the house of the Secretary of State for Employment on 12 January 1971 seemed 'so despicable and so un-British as to leave most of us speechless'.[23] All this soon changed, and here the stabilizing achievement must be credited to both political parties. Now that international air travel was so cheap and easy, and international media reporting so greatly advanced, stunt violence drew ineluctably closer. Indeed, increased air travel by the 1960s presented terrorists with a new weapon: hijacking. In the late 1960s international action against it was required; thereafter, airport passengers had to acclimatize themselves to all the delays and inconvenience associated with prevention. Incidents in January 1972 and March 1973 illustrated how vulnerable public figures had become: in the first, ink was thrown at the prime minister in Brussels and hit the target; in the second, Princess Anne narrowly escaped kidnap in the Mall.[24] Events in May 1980 and April 1984 showed how easily violent disputes overseas could spill over into London: in the first, the SAS ended the seizure of the Iranian embassy in Kensington by terrorists seeking autonomy for Southern Iran; in the second, shots fired from the Libyan embassy killed Yvonne Fletcher while she was policing a peaceful demonstration in St James's Square. We have seen how, both in Northern Ireland and internationally, British politicians kept violence of this type down to tolerable levels through their combination of personal courage, tactical shrewdness, and patience.

To all this the 1970s and 1980s added another potential source of violence, inspired by economic grievance. Given rising unemployment and fierce inter-party controversy on how to tackle it, public order was at risk in several urban areas. Politicians from all parties feared that in contrast to the 1930s a better educated and more assertive population would not tolerate rising unemployment,[25] and such fears were reinforced in the 1980s by a new concern about social indiscipline from an unemployed 'underclass'. Until the 1970s the street riot had long seemed safely anchored in the novels of Charles Dickens: it now unexpectedly reappeared in British cities. As at 1984, of the nine states of emergency called since 1945, five had been introduced by the Heath government,[26] but it seemed diminishingly feasible to rely on smaller, overstretched, and more specialist armed forces to maintain essential services in

---

[22] For the distinction between 'stunt' and 'mass' violence, see above, pp. 102–3, 120.

[23] Mellish on 17 Jan., quoted in *T* (18 Jan. 1971), 2. For the Angry Brigade see Harrison, *Seeking a Role*, 503–4.

[24] *T* (27 Jan. 1972), 16 (Heath). For Princess Anne see *T* (21 Mar. 1974), 15 (leader).

[25] See e.g. Leo Abse, *T* (1 Aug. 1980), 1.   [26] *G* (16 July 1984), 19.

a society that was itself increasingly fragmented into specialisms. Government had been powerless, for instance, when confronted by a strike among managers in the power stations, as Labour governments discovered in 1950[27] and again in 1974 during the Ulster Workers Council strike.[28] In dealing in 1972 with the miners' threat, Heath was reluctant to deploy unarmed troops against Scargill's pickets, and instead considered appealing for civilian volunteers to make the necessary strategic moves of coal supplies, though volunteers were not ultimately required.[29] When with further troubles in 1973–4 the electors failed to back him in confronting the miners, there was much defeatism at the highest social levels, and Lees-Milne's diary was alive with concern.[30] More importantly, gloom pervaded Westminster and Whitehall, especially when appeasement of the unions seemed the sole strategy of the Labour governments which followed Heath's. As the seasoned journalist Peter Jenkins put it, in June 1974, 'when Sir Douglas Allen, head of the Treasury, imagines walking to work one morning to find the tanks drawn up on Horseguards Parade nobody is quite sure that he is joking. Nobody knows what to do, few any longer pretend to know what to do. There is no contingency plan for when the "social contract" is broken.'[31]

By summer 1974 David Stirling, creator of the Special Air Service Regiment in the Second World War, was among several groups of retired army officers seeking to identify potential volunteers for maintaining order and essential services if parliamentary government broke down. In September the prominent Conservative MP Geoffrey Rippon even recommended creating a 'citizen's voluntary reserve for home defence and duties in aid of the civil power'.[32] And yet at this dangerous moment the non-violent centre prevailed over the extremes on both right and left. Part explanations include the factionalism that so crippled the British far left;[33] the discredit flowing from the impact of the USSR and of Hitler on the image of both extremes; and the long-standing completeness of the British army's integration into the UK's political, local, and social-class structures.[34] Much more important, however, in defusing the situation Heath left behind him in 1974 was the hold exerted by both major parties in a two-party system over potential sources of dissidence, reinforced by their leaders' skill in handling opinion, timing shifts in policy, and managing significant extra-parliamentary contacts. The arts of judicious reticence and timely concession, and the playing upon traditional loyalties, now came into

---

[27] H. Gaitskell, *Diary*, ed. P. M. Williams (1983), 159 (27 Jan. 1950).
[28] *G* (16 July 1984), 19; cf. P. Hennessy, 'Power Stations Too Complex for Soldiers to Control', *T* (15 Nov. 1979), 6. See also above, p. 153.   [29] *G* (1 Jan. 2003), 7.
[30] See Lord Rothschild's 'Farewell to the Think Tank', quoted in P. Hennessy, *Whitehall*, 247, and Benn's *Diaries 1973–6*, 595 (15 July 1976). Lees-Milne, *Ancient as the Hills*, 128 (6 Feb. 1974), 130 (10 Feb. 1974), 131 (17 Feb. 1974).   [31] *G* (21 June 1974), 14.
[32] Rippon, speech at Whitehaven on 7 Sept, *O* (8 Sept. 1974), 1. See also *T* (29 July 1974), 2.
[33] For a good discussion see *G* (26 Apr. 1975), 11.
[34] *Econ* (20 Aug. 1977), 11. H. Strachan, *The Politics of the British Army* (Oxford, 1997), 197.

their own. There was no need for the all-party crisis coalition that some were demanding, for the reach of the two major parties (coalitions in themselves) was much wider than any multi-party coalition. In the latest and most skilful example of Labour's stabilizing role, its leaders in the mid-1970s geared organized labour behind parliamentary structures, thereby marginalizing rivals on the left.

Labour's leaders after 1970 argued that the Heath government's difficulties with public order did not reflect any sudden recalcitrance among British citizens, but provocation from a government with an abrasive tone and aggressive policies.[35] Labour leaders were eager for office in 1974 more for tactical than policy reasons. Like the Whigs in 1830, keen to supplant Wellington's reactionary government at a dangerous moment in the parliamentary reform crisis, Labour in 1970–4 thought it outclassed its rivals as guardian of public order. Conservatives in 1970–4 stressed that inflation tore society apart, claimed that undemocratic structures and intimidation masked the moderate views of rank-and-file trade unionists, and saw Labour as doing its irresponsible best in opposition to validate its own prophecy that Heath's strategy was doomed. Labour countered by deploying its hold over trade union loyalties and by blaming the Conservatives' simplistic and clumsy legislation for undermining the unions in their stabilizing role. The Party's two non-socialist historic roles—promoting enhanced participation in tandem with social stability—now came powerfully into play.

Labour's strategy abounded in risks, but already in March 1976 Wilson in his retirement statement could plausibly claim credit for rendering Britain governable again; Peter Jenkins thought he had 'come closer than any other politician in his time to an instinctive understanding of the British people'.[36] There was more to Labour's strategy than mere appeasement: patience, political skill, insight, toughness, and courage were required, most notably from Healey, Wilson's Chancellor of the Exchequer. Together with Callaghan, Wilson's successor as prime minister, Healey marshalled sufficient consensus behind the deflationary package that the IMF endorsed in 1976 in return for its loan—and behind the policy of incomes restraint which followed it—to fend off trouble for at least two years.[37] In April 1979 Callaghan was still claiming for the Labour government credit for the 'miracle' involved in saving the country from its 'ungovernable' plight five years before.[38] Labour's manifesto of 1979 reminded electors that 'our inheritance was a Britain in crisis', now defused through 'co-operation in place of

---

[35] See e.g. Wilson, *T* (29 Feb. 1972), 2; Callaghan, *HC Deb.* 1 Dec. 1972, cc. 804–6; Shore at Dorking, *T* (7 Aug. 1972), 2.   [36] *Evening Standard* (16 Mar. 1976), 4. Jenkins, *NS* (12 Mar. 1976), 311.
[37] For more on this see above, pp. 297–301.
[38] At a press conference, *G* (19 Apr. 1979), 4; cf. his similar comment in *HC Deb.* 3 Aug. 1978, c. 932, to 'Labour cheers and Conservative protests', according to *T* (4 Aug. 1978), 10.

confrontation' and 'a new partnership' between the Labour government and 'working people'.[39]

In the preceding 'winter of discontent', however, the trade unions had destroyed their own order-keeping achievement of 1974–6: 'even with the passage of time I find it painful to write about some of the excesses that took place', Callaghan recalled nearly a decade later.[40] Socialism had originated in the crusade against scarcity, and assumed that human competitiveness originated likewise.[41] The trade unions' scramble for advantage during 1978–9, however, was only the most striking illustration to date that affluence had not eliminated this human trait, and even that scarcity was a subjective concept. Political commentators had begun to promote the idea that Britain was becoming ungovernable in the sense that government was 'overloaded'. More was expected of all governments, yet they were denied the power that would enable them to deliver. It was concluded that 'the difficulty lies not in the problem-solvers but in the nature of the problems', and there were gloomy doubts about whether a remedy existed, given that 'it is almost impossible in a competitive democracy to make the political non-political or prevent the potentially political from becoming actually so'. The demand for income, medical treatment, homes and leisure was insatiable, and trying to satisfy it through statist mechanisms prompted so many invidious decisions that (in an imperfect world) allocation through the free market now acquired new attractions. 'There was a deathly calm in No. 10', an insider recalled of January 1979: 'a sort of quiet despair . . . ministers were clearly demoralised . . . their sense of collective and individual depression was overwhelming'.[42] It was now the Conservative Party's turn to seek stability through taking a new and bold direction.

2. FREE-MARKET ASPIRATIONS

As socialism waned, free-market ideas waxed, with Thatcher's critics revealed as surprisingly ineffectual.[43] The role of economists in the socialist and free-market schools diverged: whereas socialist economists saw themselves as providing governments with continuous and expert guidance, free-market economists scaled down their profession's pretensions and sought to distance it from government. Economists' reputation had not been enhanced when revealed as divided and often also misguided on major issues: on how to procure economic growth nationally or internationally, and on how the EEC would affect the

---

[39] Dale (ed.), *Labour Manifestos*, 220.   [40] *Time and Chance*, 537.

[41] See e.g. Orwell's 'As I Please' (21 July 1944), in his *Complete Works*, xvi (1998), 294.

[42] A. King (ed.), *Why is Britain Becoming Harder to Govern?* (1976), 17, 29. Donoughue, *Prime Minister*, 176.   [43] As discussed above, p. 311, and below, pp. 531–2.

British economy. In the early 1980s they disagreed publicly on how to cut unemployment. Doubts were also cast on sociology's claims. Initially an aid to the planner, it was by the 1960s becoming his critic, and the planner's aspirations were being scaled down from hope for the future to respect for the past. The planner's elaborate models and statistics were increasingly thought to distance him from the wants of ordinary people: 'whenever one hears a planner complaining that the public do not understand his meaning', wrote David Eversley in a sustained and scathing attack, 'he is really talking about the shortcomings of his own style, not the public's stupidity'.[44] As a demographer who became Chief Planner (Strategy) for the Greater London Council, Eversley had himself migrated from planning's theoretical to its practical dimension.

We have seen how during the mid-1970s influential Conservatives had once more begun to see the free market's information as superior in many respects to the state's: it seemed increasingly plausible that, if large areas of the economy were depoliticized, the market could help to reduce governmental 'overload'.[45] Central planning might from the 1960s seem in trouble at the surface of events, but one significant and unobtrusive non-party group had been probing more deeply since 1947: the Mont Pelerin Society. Dismayed from the outset at the trend of the time, and firmly libertarian in values and voluntarist in mood, the Society repudiated determinism and insisted that the end never justified the means. In its free exchange of ideas at wide-ranging seminars unreported by the media, it did not seek direct influence over governments, which it distrusted, but instead sought in the longer term to mould the intellectual climate within which governments operated. Central European in origin, with no fixed abode, the Society attracted growing support in the USA; by 1995 it had held twenty-eight self-financed general meetings in twelve countries, and had accumulated 450 self-selected members. In its meetings it 'provided a haven to which the liberal could regularly retreat for comfort and for intellectual renewal'.[46] Bringing businessmen and scholars together on an international basis, it exerted an influence in Britain that can be judged from the distinction of its members, who included Hayek (its first President), Karl Popper, Lionel Robbins, Arthur Seldon, Ralph Harris, Antony Fisher, and several Nobel-prizewinning economists. By the mid-1970s its ideas were becoming better known in Britain, and still more so after 1979, when Labour presented Thatcher with a prize target. Branding socialism as seeking to place every citizen within government's grip,[47] she did not neglect her opportunity.

She had first to tackle her critics within her own Party, and though in power-political terms the task was formidable, intellectually it was not too

---

[44] D. Eversley, *The Planner in Society: The Changing Role of a Profession* (1973), 207.
[45] See above, pp. 292, 339.
[46] Quotation from R. M. Hartwell, *A History of the Mont Pelerin Society* (Indianapolis, 1995), 203; see also 64.   [47] e.g. in an interview in *FT* (14 Nov. 1985), 28.

difficult. For centrist Conservatives contented themselves with appealing to vague 'one nation' traditions and hankering after the corporatist policies which had generated the Party's major setbacks of 1973–4. Heath had consistently deplored the unemployment of the 1930s and had tried to distance his Party from it, but it is difficult to see how in 1981 he could plausibly have hoped to restore exchange control and insulate the European economies from world economic trends, or how he could combine massive expenditure on training and capital investment with cutting interest rates. In 1985 his alternative again involved the familiar combination of increased government spending, reflation, and regional development policy.[48] Still less convincing was the somewhat languid pragmatism of Conservative critics such as Gilmour[49] and Pym.[50] As for Walker, his exhortations to pragmatism and backward-looking remedies offered little practical assistance.[51] His coded warnings about current social problems were easily made, but not very convincing from someone who, like Benn in the Labour governments of 1974–9, seemed content to remain in the cabinet whose main line of policy he criticized. Lawson was impatient with the high moral tone which the 'wets' tended to assume: there was nothing moral about the inflation their policies would generate: 'what we are being offered is little more than cold feet dressed up as high principle'.[52] Furthermore, the much-publicized Christian criticism of Conservative welfare policy in the 1980s carried little weight with Conservatives because its tone was so secular, so similar to what the Labour and Social Democratic parties were saying.[53] Thatcher turned the flank on her critics by emphasizing how central was the act of choice to the moral growth whose importance church leaders seemingly neglected.[54]

While Labour was containing threats to the system in the short term, Conservatives now saw themselves as simultaneously pursuing party interest and deeper-rooted, longer-term solutions. Healey's indignant response in 1979 to Howe's first budget, with its reliance on monetary policy to curb wages, was to predict 'a winter of discontent which will dwarf, in its disastrous effects on the economy and on society, anything we have known in this country in the past'; two years later he again predicted disorder, claiming that Thatcher had 'become recruiting sergeant for revolution in our country'.[55] Conservative ministers knew well enough how difficult it would be, given prevailing attitudes,

[48] Heath speech at Manchester, *T* (7 Oct. 1981), 1. *HC Deb.* 25 Mar. 1985, cc. 51–7.

[49] e.g. Gilmour's policies similar to Heath's put forward at a fringe meeting at the Conservative Party conference, *T* (15 Oct. 1981), 7.   [50] e.g. Pym's speech at Oxford, *T* (1 Dec. 1983), 14.

[51] e.g. *T* (23 June 1981), 1 (speech in New York); (21 Nov. 1984), 2 (Macmillan lecture). *G* (3 May 1985), 11 (Macleod lecture).   [52] Lawson, *View from No. 11*, 137.

[53] See Richard Jones's attack, *Ind* (25 June 1988), 1 and Revd David Mason's comment in his letter to *T* (1 July 1988), 15.   [54] *Ind* (6 June 1987), 1. See also above, pp. 263, 314–15, 374, 376.

[55] *HC Deb.* 13 June 1979, c. 467, and remarks at Labour Party conference, *DT* (29 Sept. 1981), 10; cf. Benn, *DT* (7 Nov. 1979), 12.

to pursue deflationary policies in the midst of rising unemployment. In May 1980 John Biffen, Chief Secretary to the Treasury, told supporters that 'over the next year or so we will go through a period when it will be a protracted winter of discontent' during which 'we shall need to look to all the friends we have got'. Yet of even greater concern to Conservative leaders than the short-term unrest prompted by deflation was the long-running and socially corrosive unrest that inflation provoked. In Howe's words (during his budget speech of 1980, citing the 'winter of discontent' in 1979), inflation 'sets worker against worker, employer against employee, and sometimes even Government against their own employees'.[56]

The riots of the 1980s did not aim at revolution: the peak of Marxist fashion was already passing on the left, and there was little in the claims that the riots had been provoked by agitators, whether inside or outside the communities affected. The riots' random purposelessness did not reflect any assault on the central symbols of capitalism, but aimed at local and small targets such as the police with whom vendettas were waged, and the small shopkeepers whose premises were looted. 'Capitalism had destroyed the social order in inner cities, much as Marx said in the Communist Manifesto', declared Liverpool's Professor of Politics F. F. Ridley in 1981, 'but . . . no real class identity has emerged'.[57] Organizations like Militant Tendency, the Socialist Workers' Party, or the Young Socialists had little rapport with the rioters.[58] In some ways, however, the riots of the early 1980s seemed more ominous than their precursors: they were, according to *The Times*, 'a severe blow to British self-esteem', an offence against British pride in 'the orderliness of our way of life'.[59] Once the riots had begun, television's vivid reporting encouraged 'copycat' riots elsewhere. The riots could readily be linked to the policies of a government whose image seemed unfeeling and whose strategy and tactics seemed inflammatory. Thatcher's response to the Toxteth riots of 1981 was insensitive. She gave few signs of rising to the occasion with reassurance at the national level, and the brevity of her visit to Liverpool also aroused local resentment; Ridley likened her to Marie Antoinette.[60] Her alleged private comment on seeing the first pictures of the Toxteth riots and looting—'oh, those poor shopkeepers!'[61]—seemed to epitomize her narrowness of view. The riots happened in the decayed parts of the inner city; and seemed to symbolize, and at least in the short term to accentuate, its problems. They drew together two separate violent strands: on the one hand the violence that had resulted

---

[56] Biffen to Conservative women's conference, *T* (22 May 1980), 1. Howe, *HC Deb.* 26 Mar. 1980, c. 1443.

[57] F. F. Ridley, 'Will It Take an Away Match To Waken Downing Street?', *G* (13 July 1981), 7.

[58] *STel* (12 July 1981), 3, 40.   [59] Leader 'Where are we Going?', *T* (13 July 1981), 11.

[60] Young and Sloman, *Thatcher Phenomenon*, 86. Ridley, *G* (13 July 1981), 7.

[61] Young, *One of Us*, 239.

since the late 1950s from white racism, insensitive policing, and ethnic-minority resentments;[62] and on the other hand the much older tradition of confrontation between the authorities and deprived urban populations.

The decade's first riot occurred in the St Paul's district of Bristol on 2 April 1980, but the most serious took place during the following year. In Brixton, London, on 10–12 April trouble centred upon antagonism between blacks and the police. On 3 July in Southall, an inner suburb of London, riots resulted from white attacks on Asians, but most serious of all were the riots in Toxteth on 5–6 July, emerging from an inflammatory mix of racial feeling, hostility to the police, and inner-city decay. There followed 'copycat' riots in many other cities,[63] including further riots in Toxteth at the end of the month during which a police van ran over and killed David Moore, a 22-year-old crippled white man on the night before the royal wedding. In summer 1981 the Thatcher regime was not yet well-entrenched, the recession showed no signs of lifting, and recorded unemployment had reached levels unprecedented since the 1930s. At some moments during the riots, all political options seemed open, and Thatcher admitted on 10 July that 'the last ten days have been the most worrying in my term of office'.[64] For the Home Secretary William Whitelaw, that decidedly English and instinctively 'one nation' mainstay of the Thatcher regime, the Toxteth riots were really alarming. He later recalled returning during the riots to his official residence at Dorneywood '*desperately* depressed'. Then, sitting out with his wife in the summer evening and looking out at the fields, he reassured himself with the thought that 'the *real* England, the *real* Britain is the sort of place we're looking at now'. He knew how central to restraining violence was a sensitive political response, and he was deliberately conciliatory: 'the great thing in life' was, he thought, to give people 'a chance to return to normal', and then 'give people a chance to feel that their grievances are at least being looked at'.[65]

The first priority, however, was to restore order, given that the riots made a bad local situation worse, for Toxteth was 'the sort of area where it is hard to tell the riot damage from the urban decay'.[66] Whitelaw as Home Secretary had to lower the barriers between local police forces and divert manpower to where the need was greatest in what turned out to be a trial run for containing flying pickets during the miners' strike four years later. CS gas had been developed by the British in the 1950s to control public disorder, and by 1971 it was familiar enough in Northern Ireland, though not used in Great Britain until the Toxteth riots on 5–6 July.[67] Whitelaw told Conservative MPs that he would if necessary make army camps temporarily available to hold convicted rioters, and

[62] See above, pp. 202–4, 206.
[63] For a lucid summary of these events see *Econ* (3 Apr. 1982), 36–7.
[64] Broadcast on 10 Jan., see *DT* (14 July 1981), 1.
[65] Comments in BBC2 television programme, 26 Apr. 1989.
[66] Charles Laurence, *ST* (12 July 1981), 3; cf. F. F. Ridley in *G* (13 July 1981), 7.
[67] *T* (7 July 1981), 5.

would authorize the use of water cannon if the police wished, though he would not adopt tactics employed by French riot police;[68] on the following day, six senior police officers visited Northern Ireland to seek police advice on how to contain street riots.[69] Some policemen feared that such methods would alienate local opinion, and the Metropolitan Police Commissioner in 1982 thought that using water cannon against rioters would offend the British tradition of policing by consent.[70] The leading spokesman of traditional British attitudes to policing was John Alderson, who claimed that the use of 'de-humanising equipment' would ultimately inflict worse injuries on the police. Instead he promoted the ideal of 'community policing', whereby the police and local authorities would collaborate closely through community police councils, with more emphasis on preventing crime. Alderson refused to train his own officers in Devon and Cornwall to fire plastic bullets and CS gas, and rejected offers of supplies.[71] Nonetheless, the decade's overall trend was for the police, when confronted by hostile tactics not hitherto witnessed in Britain, to diverge from the traditional British view (unusual in Europe) that the police should remain unarmed. The police felt they had to prepare for the worst. On 27 March 1984 striking Yorkshire miners imitated French lorry drivers' tactics and disrupted the motorway in South Yorkshire by driving 150 cars in convoy down the southbound carriageway at five miles an hour.[72] In the Brixton and Tottenham riots of autumn 1985, PC Keith Blakelock was murdered, and the police were fired upon; 348 of the 386 recorded as injured were police officers. This led the police to consider using long truncheons, plastic bullets, CS gas, and armoured vehicles in summer 1986,[73] though these were not ultimately required.

The riots of 1990 against the poll tax happened nearer than any of the others to the heart of government. In Trafalgar Square on 31 March 1990 a mistaken set of governmental decisions evoked a riot that was far more political in cause and consequence than its precursors. Kinnock had carefully distanced Labour from the organizers of violent opposition to the tax, and the All-Britain Anti Poll Tax Federation's organizers had cooperated with the police, but when about 3,000 demonstrators in a crowd of 40,000 broke away, injuries for 331 police and 86 others were the outcome.[74] The Home Secretary David Waddington branded the rioters as 'savage and barbaric', claiming that he could 'identify quite easily the cause of the violence in this case—sheer wickedness'; in her memoirs Thatcher echoed this analysis when she blamed the 'wickedness' of 'a group of trouble-makers'.[75] Such moralistic explanations are superficial because unable to explain why 'wickedness', presumably ever present in human

[68] *HC Deb.* 14 July 1981, 1.   [69] *T* (15 July 1981), 1.
[70] Sir David McNee, *T* (24 June 1982), 3.   [71] *G* (3 Sept. 1981), 4. *T* (9 Sept. 1981), 1.
[72] *T* (28 Mar. 1984), 36.   [73] For a good discussion see *G* (3 July 1986), 4.
[74] *Ind* (2 Apr. 1990), 1.
[75] Waddington, *HC Deb.* 2 Apr. 1990, cc. 894, 898. Thatcher, *Downing Street Years*, 661.

nature, should back violence at one moment rather than another. This was a diagnosis as simplistic as the Federation's claim to have killed the tax. In truth it was repealed only because many Conservative politicians already viewed it as an electoral liability, given that it was widely seen as unfair and unworkable. 'Chris', a spokesman for Class War in the aftermath of the riots, referred to 'a proud 200-year tradition of violence in this country', adding that 'obviously we totally support attacks on the police and destroying symbols of wealth'.[76] This ignored the fact that violence had often held back the good causes it sought to advance.

The trigger for a riot may often be trivial, but when small causes have large consequences, explanations more penetrating are required. Of the 4,000 people arrested during the riots of July and August 1981, two-thirds were under 21, and almost as many had criminal records. All but 8 per cent were male, about half were unemployed, and one-third were black.[77] Statistics like these could fuel several modes of analysis. When confronted by a riot, the Conservative instinct was to combine moralistic diagnoses with force, whereas Labour's was to combine environmentalist diagnoses with welfare. Explanations cast in terms of deprivation carried some conviction, but some of the deprivation itself sprang from earlier well-intentioned government benevolence. For *The Times* in 1981, the large tenement blocks erected by local authorities since the war had now become refuges for the rioter, and had eroded community self-policing.[78] Long afterwards Thatcher recalled the unkempt appearance of the housing estates whence came the young rioters: 'what was clearly lacking was a sense of pride and personal responsibility'. She infuriated Labour MPs by questioning any close correlation between poverty and rioting, pointing out that 'there are many poor societies that are scrupulously honourable in everything they do and would not sink to some of the things that we have seen in Merseyside in recent days'.[79] In 1985 she thought the solution 'must ultimately lie in a strengthening of our traditional sources of discipline and authority—the family, the Church, the school, responsible community and civic leadership and support for the police'. In interpreting the riots, Tebbit was 'unashamed' at the party conference in believing 'that there is such a thing as wickedness', unfashionable as that may have been 'ever since the permissive society was launched upon us'.[80]

Thatcher's critics turned instinctively to deprivation as the riots' cause. 'If you have half a million young people hanging around on the streets all day', said Heath, 'you will have a massive increase in juvenile crime. Of course you will get racial tension when you have young blacks with less chance of getting jobs.'[81]

---

[76] *Ind* (2 Apr. 1990), 1.   [77] *T* (14 Oct. 1982), 2.   [78] *T* (21 July 1981), 15.

[79] Thatcher, *Downing Street Years*, 145. HC Deb. 9 July 1981, c. 575.

[80] Thatcher, *HC Deb.* 6 Nov. 1985, c. 25. Tebbit, speech at Conservative Party conference on 7 Oct. 1985, *T* (8 Oct. 1985), 1.

[81] *T* (2 July 1981), 1; cf. P. Walker's Droitwich speech, *G* (4 Nov. 1974), 6.

The chairman of Merseyside Council police committee, Margaret Simey, created a stir by saying in July 1981 that she 'would regard people as apathetic if they didn't riot' in Liverpool's present conditions;[82] nobody supposed that this aged social scientist was doing anything more than displaying public spirit. The Anglican Bishop and Catholic Archbishop of Liverpool, rare among the professions for still residing in the inner city, became spokesmen for the less articulate.[83] Clergymen, they said, saw 'the social segregation of major cities into huge one-class zones as a prime destructive force'. The bishops rejected Thatcher's view that young people should seek work outside the depressed areas: this would empty Liverpool's inner-city area still further.[84] Labour's leader Michael Foot described Liverpool, where he saw twenty-two sites on which work had stopped since 1979, as 'a monument to Thatcherism';[85] he blamed the riots also on rising unemployment among young people, and favoured channelling more government money towards the inner cities.[86]

Despite its initial hard-line, free-market image, the government in responding to the riots straddled the moralistic and environmentalist positions. The MSC was funded to push state power into new territory with what became the Youth Training Scheme,[87] and Heseltine as Secretary of State for the Environment became in effect minister for Merseyside. On 4 August 1981 he took twenty-nine leading local businessmen on a famous bus trip round Liverpool's depressed areas.[88] Energetic, accessible, resourceful, with a keen eye to publicity, he and his team at the very least conveyed an impression of concern, and visited Liverpool weekly during the following year. He sought to push Merseyside into self-help at every level, and to channel government money only behind initiatives taken and largely funded locally. A year later he saw his bus trip as 'a watershed in our approach to the problems of inner cities'.[89] The riots also helped to raise the Prince of Wales's profile by extending the role of the Prince's Trust, which had been founded in 1976 to help disadvantaged young people. They were the origin of 'Business in the Community', of which the Prince became President; it aimed to alert businessmen to their communities' social problems, and stimulate their sense of social responsibility.[90]

Given the pace of politics and the range of problems hitting government, not to mention Heseltine's move to the Ministry of Defence in 1983, Liverpool's

---

[82] *T* (29 July 1981), 28.
[83] *T* (30 July 1980), 15; (12 Dec. 1990), 5. See also Michael Gottlieb's letter, *IOS* (9 Sept. 1990), 19.
[84] *T* (30 July 1980), 15.   [85] *T* (12 Aug. 1981), 1.
[86] Speech to NUR conference, St Andrews, *T* (7 July 1981), 1; cf. Hattersley *HC Deb.* 6 July 1981, cc. 22–3.
[87] D. Walker, 'Youth Training: The Influence of Geoffrey Holland', *Contemporary Record* (Summer 1988), 15.   [88] *G* (5 Aug. 1981), 2; (6 Aug. 1981), 13.
[89] *FT* (18 Aug. 1982), 13.
[90] *STel* (24 Dec. 1989), 4 (Prince of Wales). R. Cowe, 'More than Just an Enterprise Agency', *G* (9 July 1992), 17.

profile could not remain so high for long; three years later, the local pace had decidedly slowed.[91] Government policy's overall and long-term thrust involved encouraging local and spontaneous initiatives, as became fully apparent from its response (or lack of it) to the report of the Archbishop of Canterbury's commission on urban priority areas, *Faith in the City* (1985). Far from remaining on the defensive, the government accused church leaders of allowing their political and social preoccupations to divert them from their primary task: ethical guidance to the individual. Even Lord Scarman, highly critical of government policy, had pointed out in 1981 that the state funds poured into the inner city between 1950 and 1980 had produced little apparent effect, and blamed lack of coordination between government's different levels.[92] Prominent members of the government in 1985 feared that even coordinated state funding might be counterproductive: 'injudicious public expenditure has often become a cause of the problem rather than being a solution', because self-help and self-respect might be discouraged, and inner-city dependence on socialist municipal authorities increased.[93] All Heseltine's efforts could not brighten Liverpool's tarnished image with potential investors: 'it had to be Liverpool' said the *Economist* in 1989, noting that during the national dock strike Liverpool's dockers stayed out longest. Very different was the response during the 1980s of another Atlantic seaport, Glasgow, whose receptiveness to new industries and whose pragmatic Labour local authority transformed its image.[94] With a quarter of its population of working age unemployed during the 1980s Liverpool's population fell faster than anywhere in Britain except the Western Isles—by 36 per cent between the early 1960s and late 1980s.[95] Visiting Liverpool early in 1987, Lord Snowdon 'was appalled by the disintegration, the deserted streets, the empty and decaying terraces, the smashed churches, the hooligans'; it was, he thought, 'hauntingly awful'.[96]

Yet Labour's riposte to the Conservatives' overall strategy after 1979 was surprisingly feeble. In the 1980s as in the 1930s, splits on the left had entrenched a Conservative government in power. Thatcher's widely scattered critics offered little more than a better yesterday, but with very little idea of how to avoid past mistakes. In so far as the Liberals and Social Democrats offered anything distinctive, it was constitutional change involving electoral

[91] *G* (13 Apr. 1984), 15.   [92] Scarman, *Brixton Disorders*, 158.

[93] K. Baker, Secretary of State for the Environment, *HC Deb.* 11 Dec. 1985, c. 938; cf. Tebbit at St James's Piccadilly, *T* (10 Apr. 1986), 2.

[94] J. Buxton, 'A Modern Tale of Two Cities', *FT* (15 June 1991), 8. P. Hetherington, 'Consensus Reverses Urban Decay', *G* (3 Feb. 1986), 2.

[95] 'Believing in Yesterday', *Econ* (12 Aug. 1989), 25. See also 'Merseyside', supplement to *FT* (19 Oct. 1989); and cf. the incentive to investment offered by the full-page advertisement headed 'Liverpool is Down to a Handful of Strikers', *FT* (14 June 1995), 13.

[96] As reported by J. Lees-Milne, *Beneath a Waning Moon: Diaries, 1985–7*, ed. M. Bloch (2003), 162 (17 Feb. 1987).

reform and devolution—electorally opportunistic, and of dubious economic relevance. The Liberal leader David Steel's plan for economic recovery in January 1981 envisaged creating jobs through a programme of building and renovation directed at permanently improving energy conservation, together with industrial partnership, a long-term incomes policy, expanded youth training, investment in infrastructure, and smaller businesses. These policies were either already being pursued by the Conservatives, or had shown themselves to be unworkable. Nowhere did Steel show how difficulties could be overcome; still less did he show how his compendium of desirable objectives could be combined with three other dimensions of his strategy: lower interest rates, a lowered exchange rate, and international cooperation. With a critic like this, Thatcher could continue to exploit trade union militancy and her predecessors' inflationary policies, emphasizing that 'today's unemployed are the victims of yesterday's mistakes'.[97]

In resisting 'Thatcherism' after 1979 Labour's rejoinder revealed how serious was socialism's current plight. For two or three years Callaghan and Healey still hankered after a Scandinavian-style incomes policy, but offered no clear route towards it, and no way out of its drawbacks in the British context.[98] Labour was now involved in simultaneously embracing an incomes policy and denying that it had one, covering its nakedness with phrases like 'national economic assessment' and 'planned collective bargaining'.[99] Foot's alternative to Thatcherism in 1981 added only insularity to the defects of Heath's: more government spending, a lowered exchange rate, import controls, and subsidized jobs in the depressed areas. Later in the year Powell justifiably attacked such policies as 'an insult to the intelligence of the House' because they had been tried 'not once, but half a dozen times'.[100] Peter Shore's alternative was more sustained and reflective than Foot's, but at least as backward-looking and if anything even more insular. Government spending on welfare, and public investment in the infrastructure and regional employment policies, were in themselves attractive prospects, but they were partly self-cancelling if accompanied (as he recommended) by simultaneous substantial devaluation (which would raise prices) and incomes policies (aimed at lowering them). As for reviving exchange control and imposing import controls, this would have involved bucking the internationalizing trend in world markets.[101] As the decade progressed, Labour said less and less about incomes policies, not because it had pragmatically acquiesced in the trade unions' hostility to them,

---

[97] Speech at Conservative Party conference, 8 Oct. 1982, *Party Conference Speeches*, 82.

[98] Callaghan, *T* (31 Mar. 1980), 2; (1 Oct. 1982), 4 (Healey, 30 Sept. 1982, at Labour Party conference).　　　　　　　　　　　　　　　　　[99] *T* (1 Oct. 1982), 44; (19 May 1983), 1.

[100] *HC Deb.* 5 Feb. 1981, cc. 423–32 (Foot); 28 Oct. 1981, cc. 889–90 (Powell).

[101] His policies are put forward in his H. G. Wells memorial lecture, *T* (23 Sept. 1980), 2, and in *HC Deb.* 11 Mar. 1981, cc. 909–19; 28 Jan. 1982, cc. 1010–23. See also Riddell in *FT* (24 Nov. 1982), 12.

but because it was unobtrusively nerving itself to make terms with the free market.

The extra-parliamentary labour movement was even more reluctant to make painful choices. The more statist welfare pressure groups offered surprisingly little resistance to the new mood of the 1980s, and most of the new thinking on social policy was by then occurring in the think tanks of the right. After Labour's defeat in 1979 Benn chose to promote from the back benches the alternative strategy he had earlier recommended from inside the cabinet. In its concerns for the rights of women and minorities, for freedom of information, constitutional reform, and democratizing British institutions its pedigree was Liberal, with some hope of uniting a 'rainbow coalition' of interests behind Labour. But in its protectionism, its desire to restore exchange control, and its hostility to the EEC, it was Tory protectionist, though with no hope by then of attracting Conservative politicians.[102] Its pedigree was Labour, however, in that its protectionism was seen as temporary 'cover' behind which socialist/corporatist policies for rebuilding British industry could be implemented, in collaboration with the trade unions whose rights would be restored.[103] It was a wide-ranging programme, and far more than the mere vehicle for personal ambition that many supposed. It was suspect, though, because it played to Benn's gallery, telling his audiences what they wanted to hear without alerting them to its drawbacks.

Unlike the politicians, the trade unionists with their 'alternative strategy' did not need to cover the entire spectrum of policy, nor even to render their policy package internally consistent. They focused on reflationary cures for unemployment, and recurrent among their refrains from the mid-1970s was the need to cut the labour supply through reducing working hours and shortening the working life.[104] They also wanted state-sponsored and state-subsidized training courses for the young unemployed,[105] and frequently advocated government expenditure on good causes: housebuilding, welfare, infrastructure, transport, communications, and conservation.[106] But their support for a statutory minimum wage risked exposing the conflict between their wage and employment policies. It also exposed another familiar tension: between on the one hand the need in any one union to respect its members' concern to preserve differentials, and on the other hand to advance the trade unions' collective policy for the nation as a whole.[107] Trade union leaders in the early 1980s tried once more to mediate between government and the discontent pushing up from below that

---

[102] See Benn's programme as candidate for the deputy leadership in *T* (3 Apr. 1981), 2; cf. *HC Deb.* 28 Jan. 1982, cc. 1033–8.   [103] Benn's comments on ITV to Brian Walden, 10 Feb. 1980.
[104] See e.g. J. Jones in *T* (19 Apr. 1976), 2. Basnett in *G* (19 Apr. 1978), 2.   [105] *T* (8 Aug. 1980), 1.
[106] *T* (21 Aug. 1981), 1, reporting the TUC's economic blueprint, *The Reconstruction of Britain*.
[107] See the leaders, 'Nonsense of a Minimum Wage', *FT* (5 Sept. 1986), 24, and 'Bogus Prospectus', *T* (5 Sept. 1986), 15.

they were trying to contain. But for Thatcher they were themselves part of the problem, and in May 1981 she refused to meet the delegation from the People's March for Jobs: 'action of this kind contributes nothing to the real task that faces us, that of improving our industrial performance so as to create more jobs on a permanent basis'.[108]

Many in the early 1980s expected a massive influx into extremist and even revolutionary groupings on the left,[109] headed off by a u-turn in government policy either by Thatcher herself, or by a coalition government formed in the wake of her resignation. Neither occurred, for in a subtle interaction with the Labour leadership, Thatcher was silently reforming both her own party and Labour, which was beginning to distance itself from pressure groups that were an electoral liability. In 1990 Kinnock warned the trade unions that they could expect no favours from a Labour government, and some prominent trade unionists backed him in doing so.[110] So the 'alternative strategy' was not even confronted, let alone implemented: it simply faded away. By November 1984 a Labour policy document could confess that 'the problem we now face is one of a general acceptance that mass unemployment is inevitable; the time for anger passed by three years ago'. The document warned that the public had become sceptical of the Party's promises on jobs: 'we should not promise too much, too soon'.[111] By September 1987 the TUC was pushing Labour to abandon its threat compulsorily to renationalize privatized companies. British Telecom's privatization had shocked the labour movement: 'the plain fact . . . is that, despite our opposition to the sale of public assets, they have continued', said Tuffin, 'and, yes, they have been popular'.[112]

Labour's retreat from statist socialism during the 1980s was cautious and slow, and tactical rather than ideological in impulse, but it was continuous from 1983 and cumulatively substantial. The retreat was eased by the fact that the term 'socialist' had in Labour's rhetoric become a sort of talisman, evoking applause at Labour gatherings so long as it was left vague. After Jenkins had left the Party he admitted publicly that he had not used the word socialist 'for . . . a substantial number of years past, because I regard it as more obfuscating than clarifying'.[113] With the collapse of the USSR, Labour's shift could accelerate, for the Soviet collapse discredited centralized state planning. Non-statist options for the British left, unwisely discarded decades before, could now be revived. The UK's socialist tradition had its libertarian, devolutionary, meritocratic, participatory, and populist aspects, and among Labour's more constructive ways of looking backwards was now to set about revisiting them, while at the

---

[108] G (20 May 1981), 4.
[109] For a well-informed insight into them see P. Keel, 'The Vicarious Road to Revolution', G (11 Feb. 1980), 13.   [110] Kinnock, Ind (5 Sept. 1990), 8; cf. John Edmonds, FT (6 Nov. 1989), 11.
[111] G (30 Nov. 1984), 4.   [112] FT (10 Sept. 1987), 11.
[113] Interview with T. Coleman, G (24 Nov. 1981), 15.

same time pondering new strategic possibilities. So closely were the Labour and Liberal traditions converging by the early 1990s, that some could now plausibly see Labour's secession from the Liberals in 1917–18 as a major mistake. The components of 'New Labour' were gradually moving into position.

3. THATCHERISM AUDITED

In Britain after 1979, then, it was 'Thatcherism' that prompted optimism in some, especially after it proved electorally viable and produced some economic successes. So striking a policy shift inevitably aroused controversy, ran into difficulties, and after a decade remained incomplete. We have seen that 'Thatcherism' was a package with internal inconsistencies, and changed over time.[114] Any overall audit must record failures as well as successes. Thatcher exploited her opportunity to the full and with panache, identifying herself personally in the 1980s with the employers' new-found freedom, energizing her own party while demoralizing its opponents. She thought the state should step back so as to enlist behind economic growth what she saw as the spontaneous harmony of enterprise, self-interest, and the public interest. This would simultaneously safeguard democracy, she thought, by warding off from the political system all the dangers stemming from inflated and therefore ultimately disappointed hopes of what it could deliver. Here she succeeded: we have seen how quickly and unexpectedly trade union power declined, incomes policies vanished, and capital movements were liberated.[115] Nobody in 1979 could have predicted the scale of the privatization implemented by 1990, the new salience in public discussion for entrepreneurship and business values, the decline in strikes to late Victorian levels, or the long-term success by the mid-1990s in getting inflation down to the 1950s levels without resort to incomes policies. In the privatized industries, productivity improved greatly both before and after their transition, and faster than in manufacturing or in the economy as a whole.[116] Privatization succeeded sufficiently in Britain to inspire much imitation elsewhere, and facilitating it became itself a new type of British export.

How effectively did British business use its new-found freedom? The turn-round on profitability was clear. Since the early 1960s there had been a steady fall in the UK return on capital, for which Joseph and Thatcher blamed restrictive practices, with consequent poor performance, inadequate profits, and therefore insufficient investment; corporate profitability rose fast in the 1980s, however, to levels at mid-decade not seen since the early 1960s.[117] For annual growth-rate in British gross domestic product, the 1980s did better

[114] Above, pp. 87, 343, 485.   [115] See above, pp. 320, 343–7.
[116] See M. Wolf in *FT* (5 Oct. 1992), 4.
[117] *HC Deb.* 5 Feb. 1981, cc. 415–23. Kavanagh and Seldon (eds.), *Thatcher Effect*, 13–14.

than the 1970s, though worse than the 1950s and 1960s. By comparison with ten leading industrial nations in 1979–88, however, Britain bucked its earlier downward trend, and was one of only four nations (the others were Japan, the USA, and Sweden) to improve its performance on 1973–9. British manufacturing productivity improved markedly in the 1980s—among ten leading industrial nations, faster than in the other four where this occurred.[118] Here Britain was catching up with France, Germany, and the USA, and grew substantially faster even than between 1960 and 1973.[119] For annual percentage growth in manufacturing output per man-hour, Britain between 1979 and 1994 rose from near the bottom of the league of leading world economies to the top,[120] but not till 1988 did British manufacturing output surpass its previous peak of 1974; by 2003 Britain's manufacturing sector produced about the same as in 1973, and with only half the workforce.[121] The 1980s also saw an arrest to the long-term decline in Britain's world ranking for gross domestic product per person,[122] and Britain's growth in productivity per head and in total output improved markedly in 1979–88 by comparison with 1973–9, though less impressively when compared with 1964–73.[123] Among industrial societies, none could register such a marked turn-round in business-sector productivity by comparison with 1973–9, and six registered a decline.[124] In the early 1980s, however, much of UK productivity's improvement came simply from the less efficient firms shedding labour; the taxpayer had henceforth to support the unemployed, thus driving up the public expenditure which the government wanted to restrain—a strategy likened at the time to 'putting up the batting average of a cricket team by only playing the best eight batsmen'.[125] It was arguably better, though, to have the unemployment out in the open than concealed, and productivity continued to improve throughout the decade.

Milton Friedman criticized the first Thatcher government for being slow to curb public spending,[126] but this was before the scale of the government's privatization schemes became apparent, and before its persistence in cutting civil service numbers over more than a decade could be known. As for rising welfare expenditure, it was not till Thatcher's third term that she was able to focus on it, but the average annual rise in real expenditure on NHS goods and services during her governments was smaller than that of any previous administration, and half that for any administration since 1960[127]—though strenuous efforts were made in the 1980s through restructuring to get better health value for

---

[118] Feinstein and Matthews, 'Growth of Output', 79, 87–8.   [119] M. Wolf in *FT* (5 Oct. 1992), 4.
[120] See statistics in *T* (20 Dec. 1995), 16.   [121] *FT* (22 Sept. 2003), 2.
[122] *Econ* (8 June 1996), 28–9. *FT* (12 June 1996), supplement 'Britain: The Rogue Piece in Europe's Jigsaw', p. ii.   [123] S. Brittan presents figures in Kavanagh and Seldon (eds.), *Thatcher Effect*, 12.
[124] Feinstein and Matthews, 'Growth of Output', 87. See also N. Crafts's statistics in *G* (15 Oct. 1990), 12.   [125] A. Glyn in *FT* (10 Feb. 1982), 19.
[126] See e.g. *T* (17 Feb. 1982), 13. *O* (26 Sept. 1982), 24. See also *T* (16 June 1986), 17.
[127] C. Webster in Kavanagh and Seldon (eds.), *Thatcher Effect*, 171.

money expended. Under the Thatcher governments the overall tax burden fell slightly, whereas in most other countries it was either much higher to begin with, or rose markedly.[128] The Conservatives also shifted taxation's balance from direct to indirect, tilting incentives in favour of saving.[129] Their aim was more to raise the absolute level of income received at the bottom of society than to tackle 'relative' poverty,[130] and in deliberately widening income differentials they abandoned the all-party redistributive agenda pursued since 1945, with startling effect.[131] The philosophy of incentives inspiring these changes was controversial: for most people a cut in income-tax rates was unlikely significantly to prompt greater effort and enterprise, even where the individual could control his work patterns: the incentive was inevitably a year or so away, its quantity difficult to predict, and its share of total income small. Some even claimed that the income released would merely foster a taste for more leisure,[132] and comparative research revealed little correlation in the 1970s between the growth in a nation's gross domestic product and the proportion of it abstracted for tax.[133] Nor was there firm evidence even in 1979, let alone later, to support the idea that those lower down would gain more in absolute terms from the 'trickle-down effect' of there being more disposable income higher up.[134]

Nonetheless, to those who lived through it, the change in the tone of public debate after the mid-1970s seemed at least as striking as its change in content, and that was above all Thatcher's achievement, for it is the context of economic activity, its framework of public discussion, that politicians are uniquely qualified to influence. The 1980s were years of remarkable economic progress, Lamont recalled in his budget speech of 1991, 'but even more striking was the change in attitudes. The crucial importance of the market is now widely accepted both in this country, and even more widely accepted in the House'; this was Thatcher's 'lasting legacy and achievement'.[135] Thatcher was of course working with the trend of the times, and some 'Thatcherite' trends began well before 1979. For example, the strategy endorsed by the IMF in 1976 helped to ensure that government spending fell in real terms by 11 per cent between 1974/5 and 1977/8, whereas unemployment helped to ensure that government spending rose by 10 per cent between 1978/9 and 1984/5; furthermore, government expenditure's share of gross domestic product fell sharply from 1976 to 1978, yet rose again sharply between 1979

---

[128] A. Glyn, unpublished typescript on 'Taxing and Spending' (Oxford, 1995), 3, 8.

[129] *Econ* (2 Oct. 1993), 39.

[130] See e.g. Patrick Jenkin's attack on Peter Townsend in *STel* (2 Dec. 1979), 4; cf. P. Worsthorne in *STel* (28 Oct. 1979), 16.

[131] For a good discussion see J. Hills, *Inequality and the State* (Oxford, 2004), 20–1, 262–3.

[132] The Treasury commissioned what Lawson called C. V. Brown's 'particularly unimpressive' research, reported in *G* (15 Dec. 1986), 1. The report's conclusions and cost infuriated him, *View from No. 11*, 692.   [133] Christopher Johnson's research, quoted in *FT* (11 Oct. 1982), 7.

[134] Archbishop Worlock quoted in *DT* (16 Apr. 1988), 2.   [135] *HC Deb.* 19 Mar. 1991, c. 172.

and 1982.[136] There was 'Thatcherism', too, in other countries, implemented by governments of very different colour, though Britain's example did much to advance it.

Some in the mid-1980s credited the Thatcher governments with bringing off an economic miracle, but such talk was overblown, for there was much that Thatcher did not achieve. She aimed at nothing less than a cultural revolution, and in seeking to bring it about her busy activism paradoxically enhanced central government's role. In attacking socialism she was led into a centralizing assault on its areas of strength: in schools, universities, local government, health, and welfare. On public expenditure the Thatcher governments achieved far less than they had hoped, and did not prevent it from rising in real terms, if only because income support and training for the unemployed during two recessions were expensive. However, they did modestly curb public spending's share of gross domestic product—42 per cent in 1979, 40 per cent in 1997[137]—and they quite sharply accentuated the long-term fall in the annual growth-rate of government's real expenditure: 3.2 per cent in the 1970s, but down to 1.1 per cent in the 1980s.[138] Public employment's share of total employment rose throughout the twentieth century to 21 per cent in 1980, but fell thereafter to 15 per cent in 1994—well below the average (18 per cent) for seventeen industrial societies in that year—freeing labour and resources for private concerns.[139]

Though aided by a party and parliamentary system which allowed strong government, Thatcher had to operate within what was in practice a pluralist political culture, nor could she at any stage focus exclusively on the economy. Rhodesia, Northern Ireland, the EEC, and the Falklands distracted her, as did the need for the extended term of office that her radical aims required. Wilson was centrally concerned in the 1960s and 1970s to reconcile planning with democracy,[140] yet so thoroughly had the planners done their job by the 1980s that Thatcher's problem was to reintroduce the free market while winning elections. Central to her prime-ministerial story was the tension between overall strategy and shorter-term tactics: without winning general elections, her radical strategy would have come to nought, yet a shorter-term payoff would have been tactically helpful. Hence compromise, even sometimes in the economic dimension. She gave priority, for instance, to home-ownership over the mobility of labour that her economic aims required; in 1979 she honoured the Clegg pay settlement, even though it cut clean across her principles, because to advocate its rejection might have endangered her election victory in that year; nor did her free-market beliefs embrace the Edwardian Liberal ideal of freely admitting immigrants.

[136] Thain and Wright, *Treasury and Whitehall*, 430, 436.   [137] *T* (11 Apr. 1997), 29.

[138] Thain and Wright, *Treasury and Whitehall*, 491.

[139] V. Tanzi and L. Schuknecht, *Public Spending in the Twentieth Century: A Global Perspective* (Cambridge, 2000), 26.   [140] Harrison, *Seeking a Role*, 455.

It was easier for Conservative governments of the 1980s than for Labour in the 1960s and 1970s to allow the market to operate freely not only within economic sectors, but between them. Because trade union links and constituency pressures were less powerful in her party, Thatcher's governments could acquiesce in the labour market's ongoing shift to services from manufacturing, whose overall economic role was in relative decline. Nonetheless, Conservative remedies for unemployment took effect only slowly. Unemployment had been a serious problem throughout Western Europe since the 1960s, but we have seen that in the early 1980s UK government policy unintentionally exacerbated it, so that later in the decade it was by international standards running at a high level.[141] The idea that unemployment would curb wages and price people into work was looking implausible by 1985 because employers did not strenuously resist wage demands; instead they and their employees colluded against admitting newcomers.[142] Nor did the retreat from incomes policies, from regional economic policies, and from economic interventionism generally, achieve any rapid result. It did not ensure that wage-rates responded quickly to diverse regional conditions, thus pricing the unemployed back into work. On the contrary, trade union policy, the shortage of rented accommodation, and employers' readiness to cut pay-rolls rather than pay-rates[143] perpetuated the contrast between the economic plight of those in and out of work: the middle-aged and the old held a growing proportion of the jobs at the expense of the young.[144] Not till mid-decade did unemployment peak and then start to fall. So middle-class discomfort at the juxtaposition of affluence and poverty, a major component of late Victorian middle-class socialism, re-emerged in the 1980s: public welfare had become less adept at concealing unpleasant sights from middle-class eyes. By the end of the 1980s government cuts in welfare benefits for the young brought homeless young people on to the streets of London and other big cities to beg and even doss down—sights which British people since the 1940s had come to associate only with New York or Third World countries.

Also limited was Thatcher's success at changing public attitudes to the economy. Conservatives in mid-decade welcomed privatization's widened share-owning and (in their election manifesto of 1987) the resulting educational benefits: it was, they said, 'the first stage of a profound and progressive social transformation—popular capitalism'.[145] Privatization certainly created many small shareholders, yet by the end of the 1980s the typical private shareholder was male, married, middle-aged, relatively affluent, and living in the south-east of England, and the number of shareholders in any income group was positively correlated with income; although almost half men in the

[141] *Econ* (2 Oct. 1993), 37. See also above, pp. 325, 359, 525.
[142] *T* (2 Oct. 1985), 19. *G* (3 Feb. 1986), 12 (leader).   [143] Lawson, *View from No. 11*, 431–2.
[144] As discussed above, pp. 176, 248–9.   [145] Dale (ed.), *Conservative Manifestos*, 320.

professions held shares, only 9 per cent of unskilled manual men also did so, though a third of shareholders were manual workers.[146] The public had of course clamoured to buy shares in privatized industries at bargain prices, but there remained many cultural and other barriers against any deeper move into share-owning,[147] and many new shareholders quite rapidly took their profits and departed. By 1986, for example, the number of shareholders in Amersham International, privatized in 1982, had declined by nine-tenths; in Jaguar, privatized in 1984, by two-thirds.[148] The British people were not averse to a flutter, but as individuals the Stock Exchange was not for them. British Telecom was launched as Thatcher's privatizing flagship in November 1984, with 39 per cent of its shares owned by private individuals, but they rapidly departed, and already by June 1985 accounted for only 29 per cent.[149] Each privatization saw the same pattern: the initial surge of new individual shareholders fell back, to be revived only by further privatizations elsewhere. Much more important in the longer term than the growth in individual share-owning in the 1980s was the politically less salient but steadier growth, which had begun well before 1979, in the individual's indirect share-owning through insurance schemes and pension funds.[150] By the end of 1971 about half of all employees had joined occupational pension schemes, and in the 1970s and early 1980s the trend was away from direct towards indirect investment.[151] Privatization did not arrest this long-term shareholding trend: while the pension funds' share was rising, the share of individuals was falling: from 54 per cent of total equity in 1963 to 38 per cent in 1975 to only 20 per cent in 1990.[152]

Opinion-poll evidence allegedly showed in 1988 that 'after nine years of Thatcherism the public remained wedded to the collectivist, welfare ethic of social democracy',[153] nor did the universities cease to fuel what Joseph had called the 'anti-enterprise culture'.[154] The components of Thatcher's package did not of course have to be accepted entire: it is not at all clear, for instance, that in her attitudes to crime and punishment,[155] to the EEC, and to international relations generally she had consistently promoted the interests of her party, and still less clear that in these areas she had promoted the interests of her country.[156] Yet the unobtrusive and even sometimes advertised ingestion of so many of Thatcher's

[146] General Household Survey quoted in *Ind* (13 Dec. 1989), 5. *FT* (16 Dec. 1989), weekend supplement, p. iii. [147] *O* (18 Jan. 1987), 30. *FT* (16 Dec. 1989), weekend supplement, p. iii.
[148] See the tables in *O* (26 Oct. 1986), 39; *T* (11 Sept. 1987), 14.
[149] K. Newman, *The Selling of British Telecom* (1986), 169.
[150] See Harrison, *Seeking a Role*, 318. [151] *T* (31 July 1974), 4. *FT* (15 Nov. 1983), 44.
[152] Central Statistical Office, *Share Ownership*, 8. See also *FT* (2 Dec. 1994), 9.
[153] I. Crewe, 'Values: The Crusade that Failed', in Kavanagh and Seldon (eds.), *Thatcher Effect*, 243; however, in this area more than most, responses were likely to be heavily influenced by the question's wording, especially when respondents had to choose one of only two pre-defined positions. See also leader in *T* (3 May 1985), 15.
[154] See Harrison, 'Mrs Thatcher and the Intellectuals', *TCBH* 5/2 (1994), 206–45.
[155] See above, pp. 185–6. [156] See above, pp. 21, 23, 30–3, 44–5, 54, 410.

policies by Liberals and Labour after 1990 testifies to her rivals' belief in their election-winning potential, and her strategy's impact can fairly be assessed only in the long term and in comparison with what might have happened if Labour had won general elections in or after 1979. Whereas before 1979 Labour and Conservative had competed on who could best manage a corporatist economy, they were now free to compete on who could best promote, harness, and humanely manage a free-market economy. Thatcher's governments had reversed the socialist ratchet, had prepared the ground for a slow and long-term shift in attitudes and conduct, and had arrested any approach to absolute economic decline. They had championed a smaller direct economic role for the state, had curbed trade union powers, and had emancipated the entrepreneur. It was for this achievement, and for her energetic promotion of it, that—unusually among British political leaders—Thatcher became an 'ism'. Many years later, some blamed her reforms for the banking problems of the early twenty-first century. This is to make a twofold mistake: her sights were inevitably directed at the problems of the 1970s rather than at those of a future that she could not fairly have been expected to foresee, and, as we have seen,[157] the financial world was prone to generate a speculative mood which she had always found alien.

When the screens informed the stock market on 22 November 1990 that Thatcher was withdrawing from the campaign for the Conservative leadership, the FTSE 100 index rose within minutes by 24.5 points.[158] Did her rejection by the party to which she had given so much, and by businessmen whose circumstances she had transformed, indicate disillusion with 'Thatcherism'? Did it indicate yet another shattered hope to set beside the UK's earlier twentieth-century disappointments: with the high hopes of socialism, and later with the Commonwealth ideal and the EEC? Thatcher was certainly hated by large sections of the British public, but in 1990 her opponents in her party and in the City aimed more to preserve her achievement than reject it. They felt that for all her virtues she had lost her touch, and perhaps even her judgement, and that she had become an electoral liability: arguably her legacy would best be preserved under another Conservative leader. Even so, the devotion she stirred in some within her party remained so fervent thereafter as seriously to divide and damage it during the 1990s. Her loss of power caused her much personal anguish, even bitterness, yet on reflection her political demise should not have surprised her. 'When all is said and done', she had said two years before, 'a politician's role is a humble one'.[159] This was no false modesty on her part: it encapsulated the philosophy that pervaded all that she achieved.

---

[157] See above, p. 342.

[158] K. Fleet, 'Not a Churlish City Gesture, Just a Farewell to Uncertainty', *T* (24 Nov. 1990), 37.

[159] Address on 21 May 1988 to the General Assembly of the Church of Scotland, *G* (23 May 1988), 38; cf. Thatcher, *Downing Street Years*, 486.

4. DYSTOPIA IN PROSPECT?

Twentieth-century Britain became as eager to peer into an earthly future as the Victorians into the after-life. The word 'new' had been the catchword of the 1890s—with the New Woman, the New Drama, the New Realism, and the New Hedonism—and the Edwardians followed with the New Age, the New Spirit, the New Humour and the New Fiction.[160] Rejection of the past was integral to the repudiation of Victorianism in the 1920s, and was at its most doctrinaire in the architects' inter-war promotion of the 'modern style' as the only style suited to twentieth-century living. The legal and constitutional approach to political institutions, never challenged by the Attlee governments, enshrined respect for the past, but by the 1950s it was giving way to the behavioural approach, and by the 1960s constitutional reformers showed little reverence towards old structures and conventions. Nevil Johnson, analyst of constitutions, complained in 1976 about 'the atrophy of any language in which we can talk of constitutional issues, of rules, or of the principles of public law'; the outcome was, he thought, 'a kind of constitutional wasteland'.[161] Whereas in the 1940s a pride was still taken in the long history and adaptability of British political institutions, by the 1960s constitutional 'modernization' had come to seem desirable almost for its own sake. Peering into the future was integral to planning, then still very much in fashion, and this increased the pressure for population census results to be processed more quickly, and for a census every five years. Arguing in 1975 for a census to be held in 1976, David Owen said that otherwise 'they would be working as far ahead as 1983 or so . . . on information dating back to 1971'.[162] When so many decisions were being taken with implications so far ahead, the present increasingly reached out towards the future. The Liberal Party, preoccupied in 1969 with competing demands on the countryside and with technology's threat to freedom, even wanted to set up an 'institute of the future' to resolve such dilemmas.[163] Politicians were in danger of forgetting the dictum of J. S. Mill (himself no reactionary) that 'those who never look backwards, seldom look far forwards'.[164]

Meritocracy was built into these modernizing enthusiasms. The aristocrat's authority rests on the past, and conservation is his instinct; the meritocrat, by contrast, powered by hopes for the future, makes his own way, brushing the past aside. The USA's prominence in the 1950s and 1960s as a political as well as cultural influence in Britain harmonized well with this mood, and President

---

[160] P. Grosskurth, *Havelock Ellis: A Biography* (1980), 128. L. Tickner, *The Spectacle of Women: Imagery of the Suffrage Campaign 1907–1914* (1987), 183.

[161] N. Johnson, *In Search of the Constitution: Reflections on State and Sociology in Britain* (Oxford, 1977), 29, 35.   [162] *HC Deb.* 25 Mar. 1975, c. 409.

[163] *T* (27 Aug. 1969), 3.

[164] 'On the Definition of Political Economy' (1836) in his *Collected Works*, iv. *Essays on Economics and Society*, ed. J. M. Robson (1967), 333.

Kennedy's youthful image strongly influenced Wilson's political style between 1962 and 1964—informal, innovative, accessible to the media, and alert to the importance of image.[165] For a meritocratic Labour Party, modernization was a central theme in the run-up to the general election of 1964. The mood resumed under Blair from the mid-1990s,[166] and shaped his hopes for a Lib–Lab alliance. In December 1997 Ashdown as Liberal leader told Gordon Brown that there were 'primarily, three elements' to Lib–Lab collaboration: '. . . modernization of our constitution; modernization of our education and welfare system; and modernization of our approach to Europe'.[167] The modernization theme came naturally, perhaps, to parties of the left, but the Conservatives did not lag far behind: in March 1963 Macmillan in his diary detected 'quite an attractive policy' in showing the public that 'modernization was not simply a slogan', but 'provided a positive context for a controversial policy'.[168] The promotion of Heath and Wilson in their forties to party leadership opened up political careers to a much younger generation.

The post-war pursuit of the up to date extended far beyond politics. By 1957 Hoggart was expressing alarm at the impact made on popular culture by the Americanized, demotic, hedonistic, trivialized 'candy-floss world' of popular magazines; with little thought for the past or the future, they lived in an eternal present where the aim must above all be to avoid seeming dull or behind the times.[169] The cult of youth was closely linked to the growing cult of health and beauty, where the young were supreme. Their world was continuously changing, pervaded by evanescent commercialized fashions in clothes and music, driven forward by new inventions, new models, new media. Urged on by commercial competition, BBC news programmes in the 1950s lost all inhibition about being up-to-the-minute, and became longer and more frequent. Dating from 28 October 1957 was the radio programme 'Today', whose presenters became well-known national personalities; then in 1965 came 'The World at One' and in 1967 'The World This Weekend'. Given that the electronic media were more efficient at conveying the latest news, we have seen how the newspapers gravitated more to commentary, analysis, and prediction.[170] News-gatherers colluded with speakers to exploit the press release and the pre-announcement, so that the media crowded out happenings that had occurred with happenings predicted. Political parties had little to gain from seeming to mull over the past, or even from giving due attention to the achievement

---

[165] Foot, *Politics of Harold Wilson*, 15, 16, 18, 200, 207.

[166] Campbell, *Edward Heath*, 163. A. Seldon (ed.), *The Blair Effect: The Blair Government 1997–2001* (2001), 120, 122.　　　　[167] P. Ashdown, *The Ashdown Diaries*, ii. *1997–1999* (2001), 134.

[168] In this month the Beeching report was published. Quoted in Loft, *Government, Railways and Modernization of Britain*, 90 (20 Mar. 63).

[169] See his *The Uses of Literacy: Aspects of Working Class Life with Special Reference to Publications and Entertainments* (1957), chs. 6–8.　　　　[170] See above, p. 406.

involved in safeguarding the present. Concern with the future was their stock in trade, each now hoped to sell its 'vision' of a better Britain to the voters, and each pursued an image for being more vibrant than its rival in doing so.

Yet the future when peered into seemed increasingly grim. As one well-informed commentator put it, the British people have been seen as 'a people marching backwards into the future, for whom change always means change for the worse'.[171] At least three reasons for this were not confined to the UK. The discontented are at any one time more likely to advertise their pain than the contented their happiness, so 'distress evidence' is relatively salient in the historical record. Secondly, distress interests the media more than happiness. 'The News is relentlessly depressing', Kenneth Williams told his diary on 1 November 1983. 'Cheerful items are either ignored or given sceptical delivery and the accent is forever on some alleged wrong.' Furthermore, given the media's growing global coverage, reports were available from locations whose distress had hitherto been concealed: 'if I see another emaciated famine victim', wrote Williams a year later, after a news item about Ethiopia, 'I think I'll throw up'.[172] Thirdly, there was the doomsday environmental scenario, a late twentieth-century secularized version of the Almighty's visitation upon a sinful people. Whereas in the nineteenth-century story man is the explorer who courageously pushes forward civilization's frontiers, in the twentieth-century story man is the intruder who clumsily destroys nature's bounty. Nineteenth-century fears of the stationary state and of coal supplies running out gave way to twentieth-century fears for a society changing so fast as to risk spiralling out of control, with ecological damage rapidly escalating to a point of no return.

To these factors were added, for Western industrial societies, all the problems of affluence. These made for discontent at two levels. First, affluence depreciated the coinage of pain. The British upper lip was not alone in becoming less stiff, and the term 'misery' was now applied to experiencing anything from late trains to bad weather.[173] Central heating and electric blankets made younger generations intolerant of the cold rooms and draughts which their elders had viewed as unavoidable. But, second, affluence brought new problems: traffic jams, environmental pollution, and 'diseases of affluence'. Disappointed expectations seemed all the more disquieting to individuals in affluent societies because their increasingly materialist outlook fostered the desire to plan their lives. Better diet and control over disease had extended longevity and made its quality less variable; the spread of pensions, personal and public welfare insurance, and women's paid work stabilized family incomes; and birth control (with abortion as the fall-back position) had extended women's control over

---

[171] Paxman, *The English*, 18.

[172] K. C. Williams, *The Kenneth Williams Diaries*, ed. Russell Davies (1st publ. 1993, paperback edn. 1994), 705 (26 Oct. 1984); see also 684 (1 Nov. 1983).

[173] As Jeremy Paxman complained in *T* (16 Feb. 2001), s. ii, 7.

fertility. The iconic intellectual Bertrand Russell was prominent in the debate about nuclear weapons,[174] and questioned the intellectual benefits of ever faster travel, emphasizing that 'it is not by bustle that men become enlightened'.[175] He admitted to a decline in his initial Victorian rationalistic optimism, and there was something grimly determined about his insistence at the end of his life that 'I remain completely incapable of agreeing with those who accept fatalistically the view that man is born to trouble.'[176]

There was room for debate, though, at a more fundamental level. When in 1989 the Archbishop of Canterbury questioned whether there was any automatic link between the creation of wealth and the happy society,[177] he was tapping into an old tradition, for even many Victorians had questioned the link between material and moral progress. The Archbishop's concern was with the misdistribution of wealth, but other pessimists would have highlighted the social scientist's failure to curb rising crime, or the natural scientist's failure to deliver undiluted benefits. The practical benefits of scientific inventions large and small—non-stick saucepans in 1955, pocket calculators in 1972, keyhole surgery in 1982, and the laptop computer in 1986, for example—could hardly be denied,[178] but since the Second World War there had been growing doubts about the longer term implications of scientific advance.[179] 'This debate was about the end of the world and about how one might best delay it', the Archbishop of York told the Church of England General Synod in its debate of 1983 on nuclear weapons;[180] it was a familiar subject for Christians, he said, but until the atomic bomb's invention it had been discussed in a mood of hope rather than fear.

Some reasons for gloom were special to the UK, and twentieth-century British fiction had for some time been anticipating the mood. Its view of the future was ceasing to involve supernatural consolation and was havering instead between earthly utopia and nightmare. H. G. Wells's writings exemplified indecision between the two: there was ample gloom in his science fiction, but he was utopian in his Fabian writings, where man unites science with planning to make the future better than the past. It was E. M. Forster in *The Machine Stops* (1909) who produced the first twentieth-century dystopia, and the two world wars' destructiveness and collectivist assault upon liberal values consolidated in twentieth-century fiction the idea of the future as nightmare. Huxley's *Brave New World* (1934) vividly brought out the malign potential in natural science, and he was later surprised at how quickly some of its predictions came

---

[174] Harrison, *Seeking a Role*, 449–50.
[175] 'Why Man should Keep away from the Moon', *T* (15 July 1969), 9.
[176] B. Russell, postscript to his *Autobiography*, iii. *1944–67* (1969), 220.
[177] *ST* (1 Oct. 1989), A4.   [178] For a longer list see *G* (17 July 2002), 8.
[179] Harrison, *Seeking a Role*, 71, 134, 278, 366, 448, 540; see also above, pp. 274, 378, 398.
[180] *T* (11 Feb. 1983), 5.

true.[181] Sales admittedly demanded that the flesh should be made to creep, but gloomy books will not sell unless their gloom bears some relation to perceived reality. Orwell's *1984* (1949) portrayed a future that was bleak indeed, though in forewarning readers against totalitarian trends it aimed to ward them off. It was not designed as an attack on socialism, but the publisher Fredric Warburg, on seeing the manuscript in 1948, thought it 'worth a cool million votes to the Conservative Party'.[182] Its televised version in 1954 made a great impact, as did the schoolmaster William Golding's *Lord of the Flies* (1954), which adapted R. M. Ballantyne's optimistic *Coral Island* (1858) so as to portray a self-destroying adult world in microcosm. When asked what had inspired it, Golding replied '1. Five years war service. 2. Finding out, afterwards, what the Nazis did. 3. Ten years teaching small boys.'[183] It was pessimism about science and modern life that lent science-fiction films their special excitement in the 1950s and 1960s.[184]

Sharpening the UK's pessimism were relative economic decline and a lost empire, together with the routine operation of the two-party simple-majority system. By providing recurrent hope for the future, the system helped to keep a wide span of opinion within the bounds of practical politics. Seduced by ongoing faith in eventual electoral victory followed by governmental success, one section of opinion is drawn into the political process, but in its ultimate disappointment gives way to the rising hopes of opinion elsewhere, and so on in unending sequence. Many such alternations occurred after 1945—not just in short-term electoral overturns of parties in power, but in the long-term undulation from corporatism to the free market. Earlier hopes were inevitably denied, and new hopes were not yet secure. Pollsters asking British people whether next year would be better than this revealed more pessimism in 1983–7 than in 1957–61.[185] Yet the gloom should be set in proportion, and Callaghan was good at that. In a strategy meeting at Chequers in November 1974 he was very worried about Britain's economic crisis and about the UK's related decline in world status, yet international comparison led to second thoughts: 'sometimes when I go to bed at night', he said, 'I think that if I were a young man I would emigrate. But when I wake up in the morning, I ask myself whether there is any place else I would prefer to go.'[186] For all the complaints, many people remained eager to settle in Britain. As Thatcher pointed out in 1981, refugees from Communist countries were numerous, whereas 'the

---

[181] I. F. Clarke, *The Pattern of Expectation 1644–2001* (1979), 244.
[182] Quoted in B. Crick, *George Orwell: A Life* (1980), 396; cf. R. Williams, *Orwell* (1971), 76.
[183] J. Haffenden (ed.), *Novelists in Interview* (1985), 97.
[184] I. Q. Hunter (ed.), *British Science Fiction Cinema* (1999), 4–5.
[185] R. J. Wybrow, *Britain Speaks Out* (Basingstoke and London, 1989), 161.
[186] Callaghan, *Time and Chance*, 326. The moderately optimistic drift of this remark is captured in Castle, *Diaries 1974–6*, 221 (17 Nov. 1974), but becomes unduly pessimistic in Benn, *Diaries 1973–6*, 266 (17 Nov. 1974).

free enterprise democracies don't produce refugees—they're the places where refugees come'.[187]

Besides, the two-party adversarial system's anti-utopian impact is not necessarily regrettable: it ensures that all sections of political opinion are in with a chance, that nobody gets everything they want, and that change occurs relatively efficiently and humanely. The system usefully advertises the limits to the politician's capacities in a pluralistic society, especially in peacetime, and enlightens relatively painlessly those who expect too much from shifts in government's party composition. Scepticism about politicians, and about what they can achieve, denotes political maturity to the extent that it does not descend into cynicism. Political utopianism, by contrast, by over-simplifying problems and expecting too much of human nature, risks a disillusionment that leads to cynicism by a different and more dangerous route, contemptuous of the political system itself. Settling for gradualist incrementalism acknowledges that lasting change in human affairs normally occurs not through large policy shifts as new people capture office, still less through dramatic moral or other transformations that occur in the twinkling of an eye—but slowly, unpredictably, and often in areas well beyond the politicians' reach.

5. FINDING A ROLE?

When Dean Acheson on 5 December 1962 claimed that 'Great Britain has lost an empire and has not yet found a role', he warmed up a debate about the UK's world-wide role that had been in progress for some time. By 1970 several of the candidates for a role already looked implausible,[188] yet even in the 1990s prominent politicians could still conduct high-flown rhetoric about the nation's collective purpose. 'I want Britain to be seen as the best', Major told Conservatives in March 1992, '—not only in our eyes, but in the eyes of others. First and first again—a world leader—that is where I want us to be, and to stay.' It is a sign of the limits to Blair's modernity that in his Labour Party conference speech on 30 September 1997 he could strike a similar note: 'I want to set an ambitious course for this country—to be nothing less than the model 21st-century nation, a beacon to the world. Old British values, but a new British confidence. We can never be the biggest. We may never again be the mightiest. But we can be the best. The best place to live. The best place to bring up children, the best place to lead a fulfilled life, the best place to grow old.'[189] By then, however, such attitudes seemed rather out of touch, both with the overall situation and with British opinion. Blair, in a substantial

---

[187] Interview on Radio 4's 'The World This Weekend', 4 Jan. 1981.
[188] Harrison, *Seeking a Role*, pp. xvii, 542–5.
[189] Major quoted in Seldon, *Major*, 274–5. Blair, *DT* (1 Oct. 1997), 8.

speech delivered from HMS Albion on 12 January 2007, felt no need to argue for the position he took up: 'there are two types of nations similar to our own today', he said: 'those who do war fighting and peacekeeping and those who have, efectively, except in the most exceptional circcumstances, retreated to the peacekeeping alone. Britain does both. We should stay that way.'[190] He might usefully have hearkened to the experienced diplomat Sir Brian Barder, writing several years before; after listing recent errors in British foreign policy (with more to come) and the resentment they evoked, he ventured to suggest that 'it might behove Britain to display more modesty in its national aspirations and claims, and less enthusiasm for offering the rest of the world lessons in how to manage itself better'.[191]

Did any of the six candidates for national myth that had been in play during the 1950s and 1960s survive into the new century? Britain's retreat from the first three (great power) roles had occurred before 1970.[192] Thatcherism and the USSR's collapse outdated the fourth myth of Britain as occupying the potentially reconciling 'middle ground' between capitalism and Communism, and while the UK's post-war cultural efflorescence rendered the fifth (the UK as cultural exemplar) more credible, the UK could hardly hope in this sphere to prevail against longer established rivals in continental Europe. Nor could the sporting variant of this role enable the UK to prevail over countries far larger and more affluent—though the English euphoria at the football World Cup victory of 1966 and the rugby-football World Cup victory of 2003 showed how widespread was the yearning for such a role. The sixth of Britain's potential roles, as moral exemplar, had often been claimed in the past, but after 1945 carried little credibility outside the British Isles. After the Falklands victory Thatcher claimed that 'Britain *has* now found a role. It is in upholding international law and teaching the nations of the world how to live',[193] but so small a war could hardly carry such a burden. Furthermore, the prolonged conflict in Northern Ireland undermined any UK role as exemplar of stable democratic government. As even Blair put it in 1998: 'time and time again, from Israel to Bosnia, we have had it thrown back into our face. "Don't lecture us", they say, "you have your own problems".'[194] Just when Northern Ireland seemed to be moving towards a peaceful settlement, the major misjudgements behind British involvement in the Iraq war of 2003 created a new distraction from any morally elevating role for the UK. That war conclusively undermined at least two hopes: that British diplomacy amidst collaboration could restrain American exuberance, and that their experience in Northern Ireland would lend the British a special tact, denied to the Americans, in handling the Iraqis.

[190] <www.number10.gov.uk/Page10735>.
[191] B. Barder, 'Britain: Still Looking for that Role?', *Political Quarterly* (July 2001), 371.
[192] Harrison, *Seeking a Role*, 543.   [193] Campbell, *Thatcher*, ii. 253.
[194] *FT* (11 Apr. 1998), 5.

A seventh candidate for a distinctive British role briefly appeared in the 1980s: Thatcher's revival of Britain as exemplar of the free market. The role never really caught on. Such an outlook had been powerful with the Victorians, if only because it associated Magna Carta with a period of remarkable world economic leadership. In 1979 Thatcher, too, linked its two major features. Freedom, she said, 'was Britain's greatest gift to the world', ensuring that 'because we were a free people, we became the first industrial nation, and also were the hope and inspiration for Europe in World War II'.[195] In the 1980s, however, Britain's free-market role did not go far beyond justifying particular reforms, and never won a strong domestic following for its own sake; nor, in the 1990s, was there any widespread British view that EU membership should be seen as an opportunity for cultivating such a role in Europe. Besides, in the world's free-market stakes the UK could hardly rival the USA. In truth, at the start of the new century the six roles that might earlier have carried credibility had lost it, and no plausible new roles had appeared. By the 1990s globalization had begun to convert national histories into variations on a shared international theme, and a more modest role for Britain had won widespread if sometimes reluctant acquiescence within the UK—though no such acquiescence could ever spirit away the remarkable story of how so small a nation could once have played so distinctive a role in the world.

National myths, flags, and symbols exert wide influence, but there are severe limits to how far any democratic government can usefully recommend any 'role' for its own nation, let alone for others—except perhaps in wartime crisis situations, and myth-making is necessarily involved even there. Democracy's essence lies in its capacity to ensure that citizens pursue many roles, simultaneously and autonomously; indeed, maturity may have arrived only when a nation-state feels no need for collective 'roles', let alone roles that pander to notions of national superiority. More than in any earlier period, the British people after 1945 made their own history, however readily their leaders set out to exhort, instruct, and persuade. Politicians might appeal for a return of the Dunkirk spirit, and government-inspired publicity campaigns might aim to marshal the public behind one cause after another: for the export drive, for productivity, for wage-restraint, for entrepreneurship, for the Commonwealth connection, and for Europeanism. But to these campaigns the British public responded slowly, if at all. There is a long twentieth-century resonance to the response of the Conservative statesman Benjamin Disraeli, then in the last year of his life, to the ardent socialist H. M. Hyndman: 'it is a very difficult country to move, Mr Hyndman, a very difficult country indeed'.[196] Heath cited Disraeli's remark in 1973 when complaining to industrialists about their

---

[195] *STel* (13 May 1979), 4, speech to Scottish Conservative conference, Perth.
[196] H. M. Hyndman, *The Record of an Adventurous Life* (1911), 244–5.

failure to invest.[197] Other countries might secure mounting prosperity with or without successful incomes policies and Euro-enthusiasm, but the response of the British people was characteristically sceptical. They wanted prosperity, but not quite strongly enough to embrace collective strategies for wealth creation with much warmth. 'Britain is a country that resents being poor', said *The Times* at the end of 1976, 'but is not prepared to make the effort to be rich'.[198] In these years, at least, politicians acquired the appearance of influence only by adjusting themselves to trends that emerged spontaneously from the people at large: in attitudes to the foreigner and the environment, in approaches to social hierarchy and race, in the size and power-structure of families, in patterns of work and leisure, in religious belief and styles of life. Tony Blair left office in 2007 with that holy grail, a world role for the UK, as elusive as ever, for the British people were fortunate enough to live within a political structure and culture that prescribed for them no collective role at all. Grand collective visions might be conjured up for them by others, but whether in action or in contemplation they remained free—as producers or consumers, partners or parents—to pursue the many individual roles that they chose for themselves.

[197] Whitehead, *Writing on the Wall*, 96–7.
[198] 'Twenty-Five Years on', *T* (31 Dec. 1976), 15.

The United Kingdom:
Chronology of Events: 1970–1990

Date	Political/International	Economic/Social	Cultural/Religious
1970	11 Jan. IRA splits: Provisional IRA formed 30 Jan. Conservative leadership conference at Selsdon Park Hotel, Croydon, acquires subsequent unjustified reactionary image Feb. Prince of Wales takes seat in House of Lords Mar. Queen, Duke, Prince of Wales, and Princess Anne visit Fiji, Tonga, New Zealand, and Australia Mar. Queen's first 'walkabout' in New Zealand, followed by her first 'walkabout' in the UK, in Coventry in June Apr. Ulster Defence Regiment replaces B Specials (police auxiliary force), which was then disbanded 18 June GENERAL ELECTION; Conservatives 330, Labour 287, Liberals 6, Others 7 19 June Heath becomes Conservative prime minister	Jan. Protests at cricket grounds get the South African cricket tour cancelled Apr. ILEA commits itself to implementing the Plowden recommendation against corporal punishment (on 26 Nov. 1971 ILEA announces that the cane will be banned from London maintained primary schools from Jan. 1973) 29 May Equal Pay Act, promoting equal pay for work of equal value, to be implemented on a voluntary basis till 1975 13 Oct. London Gay Liberation Front founded First Gay Pride Festival in London The pressure group 'Life' founded to curb abortion Robin Day presents the first national phone-in programme, *It's Your Line*	4 Apr. 'The Third Programme' becomes 'Radio 3' June *Oh, Calcutta!* first opens in London at the Roundhouse; transferred to West End on 3 Oct. 19 Sept. 1,500 attend the first Glastonbury festival, then named the 'Pilton festival' Nov. Queen opens first session of the Church of England's new General Synod Ministry of Education circular 10/70 reverses the 1965 policy on comprehensivizing secondary education E. P. Thompson's *Warwick University Ltd* exposes industrialists' influence over the newly founded university University of East Anglia launches its course in creative writing Penguin Books sold to the Longman Pearson Group, a commercialized conglomerate

Date	Political/International	Economic/Social	Cultural/Religious
1970	20 July Iain Macleod dies, Anthony Barber succeeds him as Chancellor of the Exchequer	Standing Conference for the Advancement of Counselling established, later renamed British Association for Counselling and Psychotherapy	
	23 July Two CS gas bombs thrown into House of Commons to remind MPs of conditions in N. Ireland	Trust Houses merge with Forte Holdings	
	July Queen, Duke, Prince of Wales, and Princess Anne visit Canada		
	21 Aug. Social Democratic and Labour Party founded in N. Ireland		
	28 Oct. House of Commons votes by 356 to 244 for EEC entry		
	29 Oct. Lord Rothschild becomes head of the Central Policy Review Staff to advise the cabinet		
	1 Nov. Ministries of Health and Social Security merge into Department of Health and Social Security (DHSS)		
	2 Nov. Prices and Incomes Board wound up		
	15 Dec. Industrial Relations Bill passes second reading debate by 324 votes to 280		

Date	Political/International	Economic/Social	Cultural/Religious
1971	12 Jan. Angry Brigade bomb explodes at the Barnet home of Secretary of State Carr	15 Feb. New decimal currency comes into circulation	Jan. First Open University broadcast
	6 Feb. First British soldier killed in Belfast	25 Feb. Rolls–Royce nationalized following bankruptcy	23 Feb. Student occupation of North Western Polytechnic sets the tone for many subsequent disruptions
	Feb. Central Policy Review Staff (CPRS) established to advise the cabinet (discontinued after 1983 general election)	29 Mar. Trade unions first fined by National Industrial Relations Court	1 June Pinter's *Old Times* first performed at Aldwych Theatre
	20 Mar. James Chichester-Clark resigns as N. Ireland premier (Brian Faulkner succeeds him on 23 Mar)	30 Mar. Barber's budget replaces selective employment tax and purchase tax with Value Added Tax (VAT, introduced 1 Apr. 1973)	20–4 June 12,000 attend Glastonbury Fair for pop music, next held in 1979
		Mar. Prices and Incomes Board disbanded	June 26-day *Oz* (obscenity) trial begins
	8 June Upper Clyde Shipbuilders liquidation; work-in starts 29 July led by Communist shop stewards Jimmy Reid and Jim Airlie	Apr. Government agrees with tobacco industry to put health warning on cigarette packets	July Richard Handyside found guilty for publishing *The Little Red Schoolbook*
	5 Aug. Royal assent to Industrial Relations Act	20 Aug. First auction of North Sea oil concessions	25 Sept. Festival of Light rally in Trafalgar Square, followed by march to Hyde Park
	9 Aug. 342 men arrested in N. Ireland in preparation for internment without trial	23 Aug. Pound partially floated	15 Oct. *Times Higher Education Supplement*'s first issue
	14 Sept. Ian Paisley and Desmond Boal form the Democratic Unionist Party	Huge size of the Forties oil field in the North Sea first revealed, 400 feet deep	10 Dec. ITV serial *Upstairs, Downstairs* launched (25 episodes, ending 21 Dec. 1975)
	Oct. House of Commons votes to join EEC	CAMRA (Campaign for Real Ale) founded	Raymond Erith and his former apprentice Quinlan Terry build King's Walden Bury (Palladian-style country house) for Sir Thomas Pilkington
		Separate taxation of husband's and wife's earnings, if applied for	

Date	Political/International	Economic/Social	Cultural/Religious
1971	Oct. Emperor Hirohito pays state visit to London Oct. Queen pays state visit to Turkey 1 Nov. IRA bomb explodes near London's Post Office Tower 17 Nov. Roy Jenkins re-elected Labour deputy leader in 2nd ballot with 140 votes to Foot's 126 Nov. Princess Anne is voted BBC sports personality of the year Dec. House of Commons votes for civil list increase from £475,000 to £980,000 a year Immigration Act gives those described as 'patrial' the 'right of abode' in UK (comes into force in Jan. 1973)	Government subsidizes foundation of Action on Smoking and Health (ASH) by Royal College of Physicians	Barbican Centre for Arts and Conferences construction begins (Queen opens it on 3 Mar. 1982) Methodist Conference votes almost unanimously to ordain women (first women ordained 1974) Stanley Kubrick's *Clockwork Orange* (based on Anthony Burgess's novel of 1962) evokes controversy, and is withdrawn in 1973
1972	22 Jan. Heath signs Treaty of Accession, formally joining EEC 30 Jan. 'Bloody Sunday': parachute regiment shoots dead 13 marchers in Londonderry	20 Jan. Official unemployment reaches a million 9 Feb. State of Emergency declared as result of seven-week NUM strike (first since 1926) over pay. Mass picketing closes Saltley gates 10 Feb.	Jan. Government ends all restraints on hours of broadcasting (raised between 1955 and 1960 from 40 to 60 hours per week) May Church of England Synod rejects scheme for reunion with Methodists

Date	Political/International	Economic/Social	Cultural/Religious
1972	Jan. Queen's state visit to Thailand, and tours SE Asia and Indian Ocean 17 Feb. Government carries 2nd reading of Bill for entry into EEC by 309 to 301; 15 Conservative MPs vote against and 4 abstain (16 oppose and 4 abstain on 3rd reading on 13 July) 24 Mar. British government prorogues Stormont parliament and introduces direct rule 10 Apr. Roy Jenkins resigns as Deputy Leader of Labour Party at shadow cabinet's decision to hold a referendum on EEC entry Apr. Queen Juliana of the Netherlands pays state visit May Queen's state visit to France, and visits Duke and Duchess of Windsor (Duke of Windsor dies in Paris, aged 77, nine days later, 28 May) 26 June IRA ceasefire (IRA withdraws 9 July); Provisionals and IRA henceforth distinct	19 Feb. Major defeat for government's pay policy when NUM pushes it into conceding better terms after Wilberforce court of inquiry recommends 22% pay increase 28 Feb. Government announcement of £35m financial aid to UCS yards ends successful work-in there 17 Apr. Sir Robert Mark takes office as Metropolitan Police Commissioner 24 May 'Spaghetti junction' linking M5 and M6 motorways near Birmingham opened 23 June Pound floated freely against other currencies 6 Nov. 90-day freeze announced on wages, prices, rents, and dividends Gay News, Britain's first newspaper for homosexuals, founded NatWest, Midland, Lloyds, and Glyn's banks join to issue ACCESS credit cards, challenging Barclaycard's monopoly	21 Sept. Report from Lord Longford's private commission on pornography published 5 Oct. English Congregationalists and English Presbyterians coalesce into United Reform Church Independent Schools Information Service (ISIS) launched to coordinate information about private education, and act as pressure group for the public schools British Dyslexia Association founded Sound Broadcasting Act legalizes commercial radio (LBC and Capital go on air in Oct. 1973) National Council for Educational Standards founded

Date	Political/International	Economic/Social	Cultural/Religious
1972	7 July Whitelaw's fruitless meeting in Chelsea with Provisional IRA leaders to discuss peace terms	Concern about oil and fishing rights causes parliament formally to incorporate the island of Rockall (annexed into the crown dominions 1955) into the UK	
	18 July Maudling resigns as Home Secretary over his links with the Poulson corruption case	People Party (soon renamed Ecology Party, from 1985 Green Party) formed	
	21 July 'Bloody Friday': Provisional IRA's Belfast brigade detonates 22 bombs in the city centre, killing 11 and injuring 130		
	31 July In 'Operation Motorman', army and RUC end the Catholic areas' no-go status in Londonderry		
	3 Aug. State of Emergency declared: empowers government to move essential goods held up by dock strike		
	4 Aug. Expulsion of Asians from Uganda; main UK influx begins 18 Sept.		
	4 Sept. TUC confirms suspension of unions registering under the Industrial Relations Act		

Date	Political/International	Economic/Social	Cultural/Religious
1972	Nov. Queen and Duke celebrate silver wedding with thanksgiving service at Westminster Abbey and lunch at Guildhall 6 Dec. Four Angry Brigade leaders convicted and imprisoned Ray Belissario, intrusive royal photographer, publishes his collection *To Tread on Royal Toes*		
1973	1 Jan. Britain joins EEC 27 Feb. First strike in civil service history 1 Mar. Dick Taverne re-elected (as independent) in Lincoln by-election 8 Mar. N. Ireland poll (59% turnout): 591,820 vote to remain in UK, 6,463 oppose 8 Mar. IRA open bombing campaign in England, two bombs in central London kill one person and injure 200 Apr. President de Echeverria of Mexico pays state visit	6–7 Jan. Maria Colwell killed by her stepfather, with major impact on childcare administration. Report prompted by Sir K. Joseph's intervention published Sept. 1974 Mar. London Stock Exchange admits its first women members 1 Apr. Stage 2 of prices and incomes policy comes into effect; pay increases limited to £1 plus 4% 1 Apr. VAT introduced	16 June Britten's last opera, *Death in Venice*, first performed Sept. School-leaving age raised from 15 to 16 'Public' schools redesignate themselves 'independent' schools Association for Industrial Archaeology founded Jacob Bronowski's TV popular science series and book, *The Ascent of Man*

Date	Political/International	Economic/Social	Cultural/Religious
1973	11 July Duchess of Windsor pays a private visit to the Duke's grave	23 Oct. Maplin Development Bill authorizes £1bn to build 3rd London airport	
	18 July Parliament of N. Ireland abolished: Secretary of State empowered to appoint an executive	1 Nov. Stage 3 of incomes policy comes into effect for prices (for wages, 7 Nov.). Pay increases limited to 7% or £2.25 per week.	
	31 July N. Ireland Assembly's first meeting		
	1 Sept. Iceland unilaterally extends territorial waters to 50 miles	Dec. Betty Westgate founds the Mastectomy Association, from Jan. 1994 Breast Cancer Care	
	Oct. Queen opens Sydney Opera House		
	12 Nov. Miners start overtime ban	E. F. Schumacher's *Small is Beautiful* published	
	13 Nov. State of Emergency declared due to energy crisis		
	22 Nov. Unionist Party, SDLP, and Alliance Party form power-sharing executive for N. Ireland (takes up office on 1 Jan. 1974)	Crash helmets compulsory for all driving two-wheeled vehicles	
		Preparatory works begin on the Channel Tunnel, unilaterally abandoned by British government in Jan. 1975 because of economic uncertainty	
	Nov. Princess Anne marries Captain Mark Phillips at Westminster Abbey		
	6–9 Dec. Sunningdale talks on N. Ireland	Badger Act the first legislation protecting badgers (strengthened 1991)	
	13 Dec. Three-day week announced with effect from 31 Dec. to save electricity	Ombudsman system extended to the hospital system by appointment of the Health Service Commissioner	
	Dec. President Mobutu of Zaire pays state visit to London		

Date	Political/International	Economic/Social	Cultural/Religious
1973	Labour's NEC abolishes Labour's list of proscribed organizations, thus facilitating 'entryism'	Historic Houses Association founded for mutual help among owners continuing to live on the premises, Lord Montagu of Beaulieu first President	
1974	Jan. Queen leaves for Australasian tour 5 Feb. NUM executive call all-out strike, to begin on 9 Feb 23 Feb. Enoch Powell first hints that electors should vote Labour (sat as Ulster Unionist MP Oct. 1974–Dec. 1985) 28 Feb. GENERAL ELECTION; Labour 301, Conservatives 297, Liberals 14, Ulster Unionists 11, SNP 7, Plaid Cymru 2, Others 3 2 Mar. Heath invites Liberals to join in a coalition, but Liberals refuse on 3 Mar 4 Mar. Heath resigns as prime minister 6 Mar. Miners' strike settled 20 Mar. Princess Anne escapes kidnap attempt in Mall Mar. Queen's state visit to Indonesia	1 Jan. New Year's Day first becomes an additional bank holiday in England, Wales, and N. Ireland, and Boxing Day becomes an additional bank holiday in Scotland Jan. Squatters' symbolic two-day occupation of London's Centre Point, empty since completion in 1963 Jan. Manpower Services Act (1973) launches Manpower Services Commission 26 Mar. Healey's first budget first introduces an upper limit (£25,000 per borrower) on house-value for mortgage interest tax relief (raised to £30,000 per borrower in 1983, restricted in 1988 to £30,000 per property, abolished 2000)	7 June Anonymity ceases in *Times Literary Supplement* Controversy at William Tyndale junior school, Islington, about its teaching methods Roy Strong succeeds Sir John Pope-Hennessy as Director of the Victoria & Albert Museum Pinter's *No Man's Land* John Le Carré publishes *Tinker, Tailor, Soldier, Spy* (*Smiley's People* 1980) First Stonehenge Free Festival (70,000 attending by 21 June 1984)

Date	Political/International	Economic/Social	Cultural/Religious
1974	Apr. Lord Snowdon's maiden speech in House of Lords Apr. Queen Margrethe of Denmark pays state visit to London 1 Apr. EEC renegotiation begins 14 May Ulster workers' strike begins 28 May Brian Faulkner and the N. Ireland power-sharing executive resign, direct rule restored 29 May 13 June Prince of Wales's maiden speech in House of Lords June Centre for Policy Studies founded 5 Oct. Bombs explode in two Guildford pubs, five people killed 10 Oct. GENERAL ELECTION; Labour 319, Conservatives 277, Liberals 13, SNP 11, Ulster Unionists 11, Plaid Cymru 3, Others 1 19 Oct. Sir K. Joseph's Birmingham speech on birth control ends his chance to become party leader 7 Nov. Bomb thrown into Woolwich pub: two killed	Mar. Ordnance Survey maps abandon the inch for decimal distance measures 26 July Pay Board abolished and all statutory wage controls end 23 Aug. Royal Commission on the Distribution of Income and Wealth appointed, Lord Diamond as chairman London Gay Switchboard founded Jan Morris publishes autobiographical *Conundrum*, describing her sex change (surgery occurred in 1972) Passport Office first recognizes 'Ms' as designation for women	

Date	Political/International	Economic/Social	Cultural/Religious
1974	19 Nov. Prevention of Terrorism Bill, enacted in two days, empowers police to hold suspects for five days and deport them to Ireland 21 Nov. 21 killed, 161 injured when IRA plants bombs in crowded Birmingham city-centre pubs; 'Birmingham Six' convicted on 16 Aug. 1975 21 Dec. IRA bomb explodes in Harrods store, London 22 Dec. IRA announces ceasefire from 22 Dec. 1974 to 16 Jan. 1975 Tunnelling begins on Channel Tunnel scheme, but Wilson government abandons it on expense grounds in 1975		
1975	4 Feb. Margaret Thatcher beats Heath in 1st ballot for Conservative leadership by 130 to Heath's 119 10 Feb. Thatcher elected leader on 2nd ballot with 146 votes to Whitelaw's 79 19 Feb. Iceland breaks off diplomatic relations with UK over fisheries dispute	Jan. Work begins on building the Thames barrier 1 Mar. National Women's Aid Federation formed in Manchester to coordinate help for battered women	Aug. George Kohler and Cesar Milstein's hybridoma technique for producing monoclonal antibodies first published in *Nature*

Date	Political/International	Economic/Social	Cultural/Religious
1975	24 Feb. House of Commons votes by 354 to 182 to allow radio broadcasts but rejects TV by 275 to 263 (first radio broadcast of House of Commons 4 June) Feb. Queen pays state visit to Mexico Feb. House of Commons votes for civil-list increase 26 Apr. Special Labour conference calls for a 'no' vote in EEC referendum Apr. Queen attends Commonwealth Prime Ministers' Conference in Jamaica May Queen pays state visit to Japan 5 June 67.2% vote 'yes' in EEC referendum July King Carl XVI Gustaf of Sweden pays state visit to Edinburgh 3 Sept. Princess Anne the first senior member of the royal family to participate in a radio phone-in (Radio 4) 22 Oct. Old Bailey trial of the Guildford Four ends in a guilty verdict, all four imprisoned for life	15 Apr. Healey's budget cuts food and housing subsidies and increases direct and indirect taxes 18 June First landing of North Sea oil 11 July Government and TUC announce voluntary incomes policy (phase 1) on the basis of a £6 per week wage increase 14 July Unemployment figure (unadjusted) passes 1 million for the first time since 1940 22 July *Johnny Go Home* television film advertises plight of young people running away to London 19 Sept. Television sitcom *Fawlty Towers* (6 episodes in 1975, 6 in 1979) Oct. Job Creation Programme introduced to provide temporary jobs for the unemployed 29 Dec. Equal Pay Act (1970) comes into force *Him* 1st published, becomes *Gay Times* 1984	Victoria & Albert Museum exhibition on 'The destruction of the country house, 1875–1975' Keith Jacka et al., *The Rape of Reason*, on student disruption at North London Polytechnic, published Malcolm Bradbury's *The History Man* (broadcast as television serial, 1981) Norman Foster's head office for Willis Faber & Dumas, Ipswich

Date	Political/International	Economic/Social	Cultural/Religious
1975	Nov. President Nyerere of Tanzania's state visit to London 12 Dec. IRA Balcombe St terrorist four arrested (found guilty on 10 Feb. 1977) 30 Dec. 14 prison warders charged with assaulting the Birmingham Six (acquitted 15 July 1976)	British Leyland Motor Corporation nationalized and renamed 'British Leyland' Children Act gives priority to child's welfare where parents' interests conflict with this Sex Discrimination Act establishes Equal Opportunities Commission	
1976	6 Jan. Roy Jenkins becomes President of the European Commission 19 Jan. Thatcher makes the anti-USSR speech which leads the USSR to label her 'iron lady' 16 Mar. Harold Wilson resigns as Labour leader Mar. Princess Margaret and Lord Snowdon separate (divorced May 1978) 6 Apr. Healey's 'conditional' budget: income-tax cuts if pay-limit of c.3% agreed	1 Jan. Advisory and Conciliation Arbitration Service (ACAS, set up by Employment Protection Act Nov. 1975) established as an independent statutory body. 10 Mar. Brent Cross, the United Kingdom's first covered shopping mall, opened May Healey agrees with the TUC the terms of incomes policy phase 2 on the basis of a 5% increase for those at or near national average wage-levels	Sept. Jeffrey Archer's *Not a Penny More, Not a Penny Less* published in England 18 Oct. Callaghan's Oxford speech launches 'great debate' on education policy, followed up in Feb/Mar. 1977 by eight one-day regional conferences organized by the DES National Theatre (construction begun 1969) opens

Date	Political/International	Economic/Social	Cultural/Religious
1976	10 May Jeremy Thorpe resigns as Liberal leader after allegations by Norman Scott; Steel the first Liberal leader elected (7 July) in ballot of all the Party members	28 Sept. Healey at Heathrow abandons his trip to the IMF's annual conference in Manila	*Daily Mirror* provokes heated controversy by opposing the Tate Gallery's acquisition of 'Equivalent VIII' (1966), USA sculptor Carl Andre's arrangement of bricks
	26 May Wilson's resignation honours list published	29 Sept. Britain applies to IMF for $3.9bn support, the largest sum ever requested	Manchester Grammar School declares itself independent after Education Act withdraws state funding from direct-grant schools
	May Queen's state visit to Finland	Sept. Work Experience Programme takes over from the Job Creation Programme in providing young people with work	Nottingham's *Evening Post* first British newspaper to introduce journalists' direct input
	June President Giscard d'Estaing of France pays state visit to London	Mini-roundabouts introduced	
	July Queen's state visit to USA	Greenpeace founded, a splinter-group from Friends of the Earth	
	July Princess Anne competes in Olympic Games		
	21 Aug. Grunwick dispute on union recognition begins		
	10 Sept. Roy Jenkins resigns as Home Secretary		
	15 Sept. Republican prisoners begin Blanket Protest against removal of special category status		
	22 Nov. Race Relations Act substitutes Commission for Racial Equality for Race Relations Board and Community Relations Commission		

Date	Political/International	Economic/Social	Cultural/Religious
1976	29 Nov. Government withdraws from commitment to introduce a wealth tax in this parliament		
1977	Jan.–Feb. Trial of Balcombe St IRA terrorists, one of whom exculpates in court the 'Guildford Four' as having been wrongly convicted Feb. Queen and Duke visit Pacific Islands, New Zealand, and Australia 19 Feb. Crosland, Foreign Secretary, dies. David Owen replaces him as Foreign Secretary (21 Feb.) 22 Feb. Government defeated on guillotine vote for first devolution bill 23 Mar. Lib–Lab pact saves government on confidence vote Mar. Princess Anne visits N. Ireland, trial run for her mother's visit in Aug. 13–24 June Climax of Grunwick mass picket	14 June Rooker–Wise amendment to Finance Bill requires governments to raise personal tax allowances annually in line with inflation, except when the Finance Act makes specific exceptions 4 July Gay News prosecution for blasphemy opens at Old Bailey, Mrs Whitehouse wins, Court of Appeal quashes suspended jail sentence for the editor (Denis Lemon) Mar. 1978, but his appeal fails in House of Lords Feb. 1979 7 July Bristol cycle enthusiasts create 'Cyclebag', which grew into Sustrans, creator of the national cycle network 15 July Healey outlines phase 3 of incomes policy on the basis of a 10% norm for wage increases	Richard Rogers's Pompidou Centre building in Paris (begun 1971) completed Death duties force dispersal of Mentmore's huge art collection, and Victoria & Albert Museum fails to get it made an out-station

Date	Political/International	Economic/Social	Cultural/Religious
1977	June Silver jubilee week, thanksgiving service in St Paul's and Guildhall lunch	26 Sept. Laker's first Skytrain (first low-cost, no-frills) walk-on flight from Gatwick to New York	
	9 Oct. Reg Prentice quits Labour to join Conservatives	26 Oct. Shopfloor rebellion at Longbridge against shop steward Derek Robinson ('Red Robbo') ends British Leyland strike for a 47% wage increase	
	10 Oct. Nobel Prize for Betty Williams and Mairead Maguire, founders of the Peace People in N. Ireland	1 Nov. Sir Michael Edwardes arrives for five-year term as Chairman at British Leyland	
	Oct. Queen and Duke visit Canada and Caribbean	*Good Hotel Guide* first published	
	14 Nov. Devolution bills for Scotland and Wales get second reading on successive days	2m skateboards sold, and skateboarding craze takes off among the young	
	Robert Lacey's *Majesty* strikes a new matter-of-fact tone in writing about monarchy		
1978	12 Jan. Firemen's strike defeated	1 Apr. Youth Opportunities Programme (for 16–18 year-olds continuously unemployed for 6 weeks) replaces earlier programmes	8 Feb. Children's TV programme *Grange Hill* first screened
	18 Jan. European Court of Human Rights rules that interrogation methods in N. Ireland on internees were 'inhuman and degrading' but not torture		8 Mar. First episode of *The Hitch-Hiker's Guide to the Galaxy*
			25 July Louise Brown, the world's first test-tube baby, born

Date	Political/International	Economic/Social	Cultural/Religious
1978	21 Jan. Special Liberal assembly endorses Lib–Lab pact 30 Jan. Thatcher refers on TV to 'swamping' by immigrants 29 Mar. Moss Evans succeeds Jack Jones as TGWU General Secretary Mar. Saatchi & Saatchi win the Conservative Party advertising account 3 Apr. Regular broadcasting of parliament starts May Prince of Wales announces that Silver Jubilee Appeal raised £16m May Queen's state visit to Federal Republic of Germany June State visit of President Ceaucescu of Romania 14 July Grunwick workers abandon their strike for union recognition after 591 days Aug. Callaghan at TUC disappoints trade unions by failing to announce autumn general election	May First Monday in May in England, Wales, and N. Ireland, and last Monday in May in Scotland, become additional bank holidays 21 July White paper on incomes policy sets out a 5% limit for phase 4 2 Oct. Labour Party conference rejects 5% wage limit	July *The Black and White Minstrel Show*, controversial for its alleged racism since the 1960s, ceases to be televised 1 Dec. Times Newspapers cease producing *Times* and *Sunday Times* after trade unions won't cooperate to improve labour relations (dispute ends 21 Oct. 1979) M. M. Kaye's best-selling epic of war and romance set in 19th-century India, *The Far Pavilions* published, television series 1984

Date	Political/International	Economic/Social	Cultural/Religious
1978	5 Sept. Queen opens XIth Commonwealth Games in Edmonton, Alberta 21 Sept. Ford workers' strike against 5% wage offer begins Sept. Eric Hobsbawm's lecture on *The Forward March of Labour Halted?* (1st publ. in *Marxism Today*) urges the British left to counter Conservatism by broadening its range of allies 5 Dec. Britain opts out of European Monetary System at Brussels summit Wales Act and Scotland Act enacted, subject to referendum		
1979	3 Jan. Lorry drivers' strike begins 10 Jan. Press headlines Callaghan's remark on return from Guadeloupe summit as 'crisis, what crisis?' 22 Jan. Public employees' 'day of action', followed by six weeks of strikes Feb. Queen and Duke go on three-week visit to Middle East	12 June Howe's first budget cuts basic rate of income tax from 33p to 30p in £, top rate down from 83 to 60%, VAT raised to unified level of 15% 5 July UK removes exchange restrictions on non-bank use of sterling to finance third-country trade	21–3 June Revived Glastonbury Festival attended by 12,000, making a large loss 12 Sept. BBC documentary on Westminster School attracts 12m viewers (further film, 1980, on Radley College)

Date	Political/International	Economic/Social	Cultural/Religious
1979	1 Mar. Devolution rejected by 4–1 in Welsh referendum. Fewer than 40% vote 'yes' in Scottish referendum	18 July UK removes exchange restrictions on outward direct investment and on portfolio investment in securities in EEC currencies or from international organizations	Nov. Thirties Society (renamed Twentieth Century Society 1992) founded to defend inter-war architecture from destruction, with its brief later extended
	13 Mar. European Monetary System (EMS) comes into operation without the UK	31 July Price Commission abolished	Heseltine commissions Quinlan Terry for his summerhouse at Thenford House
	28 Mar. Government defeated by 311 to 310 in no-confidence vote	1 Aug. Clegg Commission recommends pay rises of up to 25.8%, half to be paid at once, half from Apr. 1980. Thatcher accepts recommendation, then abolishes Commission	Public lending-right campaign gets legislation to benefit authors loaned at public libraries (first payments made Feb. 1984)
	28 Mar. Serious accident at Three Mile Island nuclear power plant, Pennsylvania		Viv Anderson the first black footballer to play for England
	30 Mar. Airey Neave killed by INLA bomb in House of Commons car park	27 Aug. IRA assassinates Earl Mountbatten at Mullaghmore, Co. Sligo (funeral 5 Sept.)	Edward Norman's controversial Reith Lectures, *Christianity and the World Order*
	5 Apr. Jeremy Thorpe acquitted in trial for conspiracy to murder	4 Oct. Engineering unions breach the 40-hour week barrier with a settlement for a standard working week of 39 hours plus an extra week's annual holiday	
	3 May GENERAL ELECTION; Conservatives 339, Labour 269, Liberals 11, Others 16		
	8 May Sir Derek Rayner (Marks & Spencer) appointed to head Whitehall efficiency drive	23 Oct. Howe announces immediate abolition of remaining exchange controls	
	15 May First 'Dear Bill' letter in *Private Eye*		

Date	Political/International	Economic/Social	Cultural/Religious
1979	19 May Heath rejects offer of post as ambassador to USA	23 Oct. Nott allows referral of the London Stock Exchange's rule book to the Restrictive Practices Court, thereby initiating the move towards 'big bang'	
	7 June EUROPEAN ASSEMBLY ELECTIONS: 60 Conservatives, 17 Labour, 2 Ulster Unionists, 1 SNP, 1 Irish SDLP	Nov. Shop steward Derek Robinson ('Red Robbo') sacked from British Leyland at Longbridge	
	27 Aug. Warren Point explosion kills 18 soldiers	Closure, after long decline, of toy manufacturer Meccano	
	10 Sept. Lancaster House conference on Rhodesia starts (agreement 21 Dec.)	Freedom Organisation for the Right to Enjoy Smoking Tobacco (FOREST) set up, with donations from the five main tobacco companies	
	29 Sept. Pope John Paul in speech at Drogheda begs the IRA to forsake violence	Radicalized Voluntary Euthanasia Society rechristens itself EXIT	
	10 Nov. Thatcher calls for £1,000 million cut in Britain's EEC contribution	Legislation bans beating of children in state schools with effect from 1 Jan. 1987	
	15 Nov. Art historian Anthony Blunt is exposed as the 'fourth man' in Soviet spy network		
	22 Nov. Roy Jenkins in Dimbleby lecture calls for electoral reform and a 'politics of the centre'		
	Nov. State visit of President Soeharto of Indonesia		

Date	Political/International	Economic/Social	Cultural/Religious
1979	21 Dec. Lord Carrington signs the Lancaster House agreement on Rhodesia/Zimbabwe 25 Dec. USSR invades Afghanistan		
1980	2 Jan. Steel strike begins (called off on 3 Apr.) 4 Mar. Mugabe becomes prime minister of Zimbabwe 17 Mar. USSR's invasion of Afghanistan prompts House of Commons to recommend UK boycott of Moscow Olympic games by 315 votes to 147; games open 19 July 25 Mar. British Olympic Association defies government on Olympics participation 2 Apr. Riots against the police in St Paul's area of Bristol 5 May SAS ends terrorist siege of the Iranian embassy, Princess Gate, Kensington	Jan. Magdi Yacoub performs his first heart transplant at Harefield, weeks after Britain's first by Sir Terence English at Papworth Hospital Cambs. Jan. Barbara Woodhouse's first BBC TV dog-training programme 26 Mar. Budget announces Medium Term Financial Strategy June Britain becomes a net exporter of oil June EXIT publishes its booklet Guide to Self-Deliverance, but legal advice subsequently deters it from distributing it; in 1982 EXIT resumes its earlier name 11 Aug. First section of Newcastle metro line opens (Haymarket–Monkseaton–Tynemouth)	25 Feb. First episode of the TV serial Yes Minister broadcast (first broadcast episode of Yes Prime Minister 9 Jan. 1986) Aug. Trafalgar House hastily anticipate listing proceedings by demolishing the art deco Firestone Building, Great West Road 31 Oct. Evening News closes. Evening Standard henceforth London's sole evening paper

Date	Political/International	Economic/Social	Cultural/Religious
1980	15 July Service in St Paul's cathedral to celebrate Queen Mother's 80th birthday 22 Sept. Iran–Iraq war begins 10 Oct. Thatcher's 'the lady's not for turning' party conference speech 15 Oct. Callaghan retires as Labour leader (Foot beats Healey on 2nd ballot, 10 Nov., by 139 to 129) 27 Oct. First hunger strike by H-block prisoners began in the Maze prison in support of the right to wear their own clothing (called off 18 Dec., with one IRA prisoner critically ill, resumed 1 Mar. 1981) Oct. Queen's state visit to Italy 4 Nov. Reagan defeats Carter in US presidential election (Reagan re-elected 6 Nov. 1984) Nov. State visit of King Birendra of Nepal Old-age pensions henceforth decoupled from average earnings and linked only to prices	3 Oct. First British 'Telethon' (televised charity fund-raising) which, with four more broadcasts up to 1992, raised £66m 25 Nov. Seasonally adjusted unemployment figures for UK adults above 2 million Bourn Hall (infertility) Clinic founded	

Date	Political/International	Economic/Social	Cultural/Religious
1981	5 Jan. N. St.John-Stevas the first 'wet' to be dropped from cabinet	7 Jan. Thatcher appoints Professor Alan Walters as her personal economic adviser	13 Feb. Murdoch's News International acquires *Times* and *Sunday Times*
	24 Jan. Labour's Wembley conference substitutes election of party leader by conference for election solely by PLP (trade unions have 40% of the vote, cut to 33.3% in 1993)	18 Feb. Government, threatened by national coal strike, withdraws plans to close 23 pits and increases aid	19–21 June 18,000 attend Glastonbury Festival, financially successful, with £20,000 donated to CND
	25 Jan. Council for Social Democracy announced	Feb. Government sells off 51.6% of British Aerospace (then 48.4% in May 1985)	Waugh's *Brideshead Revisited* serialized in John Mortimer's TV version
	10 Feb. NCB announces plans to close 23 pits but withdraws them on 18 Feb. after local strikes	29 Mar. First London marathon	The 'assisted places scheme', to subsidize poor but able children at independent schools, first comes into operation
	25 Feb. 25th-anniversary dinner at Mansion House for Duke of Edinburgh's award scheme	30 Mar. 364 economists write to condemn Howe's deflationary policy	Seifert's Natwest high-rise tower in the City opened
	1 Mar. Second IRA hunger strike begun by Bobby Sands (elected MP 9 Apr. in a by-election, dies 5 May). Ends 3 Oct. after 10 deaths	17 July Queen opens Humber bridge	
	26 Mar. Social Democratic Party launched. Alliance with Liberals formed 16 June	27 July British Telecommunications Act splits telecommunications activity from Post Office	
		July First neighbourhood watch scheme in UK, at Mollington, Ches.	
		ct. Government sells off 49.4% of Cable & Wireless (27.9% more in Dec. 1983)	
		Conservatives set up the first group of Urban Development Corporations (the last of the twelve eventually created were wound up on 31 Mar. 1998)	

Date	Political/International	Economic/Social	Cultural/Religious
1981	Mar. State visit of President Shehu Shagari of Nigeria	Last London dock closures (Royal docks)	
	11–14 Apr. Brixton riots	Peter Sutcliffe ('Yorkshire Ripper') arrested and sentenced for life for murdering 13 women since 1975 and for attempting to murder 7 more	
	6 May Ken Livingstone becomes GLC chairman		
	May Queen's state visit to Norway		
	June State visit of King Khalid of Saudi Arabia		
	3 July Southall riot		
	4–8 July Toxteth and Moss Side riots: CS gas used for first time		
	20 July Heseltine leads task force to Merseyside		
	29 July Prince of Wales marries Lady Diana Spencer in St Paul's cathedral		
	29 Aug. Civil service strike ends after 21 weeks		
	10–11 Sept. Thatcher and Mitterrand agree to commission joint Anglo-French study of the options for a Channel Tunnel		
	14–15 Sept. Gilmour, Carlisle, and Soames dropped from cabinet		

Date	Political/International	Economic/Social	Cultural/Religious
1981	27 Sept. Healey beats Benn for deputy leader at Labour Party conference		
	28 Sept. Labour Party conference votes for mandatory constituency-party re-selection of MPs		
	Sept. Queen and Duke tour Australasia and Sri Lanka		
	Oct. Prince and Princess of Wales tour the Principality		
	12 Nov. Thatcher announces abolition of Civil Service Department, its powers to return to the Treasury		
	19 Nov. Benn is voted out of shadow cabinet		
	25 Nov. Lord Scarman's report on Brixton riots calls for positive discrimination in favour of black and Asian youth		
	26 Nov. Shirley Williams wins Crosby by-election for SDP by 19,272 majority		
	8 Dec. Scargill elected President of NUM		
	Women's Peace Camp is established outside cruise missile base at Greenham Common		

Date	Political/International	Economic/Social	Cultural/Religious
1981	Nationality Act ends commitment to Commonwealth residents on immigration rights		
1982	25 Mar. Roy Jenkins wins Glasgow Hillhead by-election for SDP	4 Jan. Young Workers Scheme starts, subsidizing employers of under-18s earning less than £40 per week	1 May Last *Times* issue made up partly through hot-metal printing. Thenceforward *Times* the first national broadsheet set entirely by photocomposition
	2 Apr. Argentines take Port Stanley in Falkland Islands	26 Jan. Unemployment passes 3m	
	5 Apr. Pym replaces Carrington as Foreign Secretary. Task force sails	Feb. Management buyout of National Freight Corporation	2 May *Mail on Sunday* launched as first photocomposed British national newspaper
	25 Apr. South Georgia recaptured	Feb. Amersham International privatized	
	Apr. Queen proclaims new Canadian constitution in Ottawa	26 May Queen opens Kielder reservoir, largest man-made lake in Western Europe	28 May–2 June First visit ever to Britain by a Pope
	2 May *General Belgrano* sunk		11 Oct. Henry VIII's *Mary Rose* (sunk 1545) raised from the Solent
	4 May Exocet hits HMS *Sheffield*	4 July The homosexual Terence Higgins dies from AIDS; Terence Higgins Trust formed in Nov. to promote education and research on AIDS	Nov. Channel 4 launched
	21 May UK forces land at San Carlos		14 Dec. Prince of Wales first addresses BMA in support of alternative medicine
	May Queen entertains Prime Minister of Zimbabwe at Buckingham Palace	31 Oct. All the Thames barrier gates are raised and the first full closure achieved	
	14 June Port Stanley recaptured; Argentine garrisons surrender	Isle of Dogs enterprise zone established in London	

Date	Political/International	Economic/Social	Cultural/Religious
1982	June Labour Party report on Militant Tendency recommends the Party to administer through the NEC a register of non-affiliated groups allowed to operate within it	Gerald Whent gets Racal to bid (successfully) for the first cellular licence in the UK, and sets up Racal Telecom (later Vodafone)	Secretary of State for Education Sir K. Joseph removes the word 'science' from the designation of the 'Social Science Research Council'
	June Queen entertains President Reagan at Windsor	Petrol first sold by the litre	Richard Attenborough's film *Gandhi*
	2 July Roy Jenkins defeats Owen in contest for SDP leadership	Government introduces 'claimant count' method of measuring unemployment	
	20 July 8 British soldiers killed and 51 people injured in two IRA bomb attacks in London	Barclays Bank reintroduces Saturday opening to high streets, followed by its rivals over the next three years	
	26 July St Paul's thanksgiving service for Falklands victory		
	Oct. Queen visits Australia and Pacific Islands		
	Oct. Princess Anne tours Africa for Save the Children Fund		
	Nov. State visit of Queen of the Netherlands		
	6 Dec. 17 people, including 11 British soldiers, killed by INLA bomb at Ballykelly		

Date	Political/International	Economic/Social	Cultural/Religious
1982	Church of England working party, chaired by the Bishop of Salisbury, produces the anti-nuclear statement *The Church and the Bomb*		
1983	8–12 Jan. Thatcher visits Falklands 18 Jan. Franks Committee clears government of Falklands negligence Feb. Queen and Duke visit Caribbean, USA, and Canada May State visit to Sweden 9 June GENERAL ELECTION; Conservatives 397, Labour 209, Alliance 23 13 June R. Jenkins resigns as SDP leader; Owen replaces him on 21 June 16 June Central Policy Review Staff disbanded 25 Sept. 38 IRA inmates break out from Belfast's Maze prison 2 Oct. Neil Kinnock is elected Labour leader, with Hattersley as his deputy	Feb. 51.5% of Associated British Ports sold off (48.5% more in Apr. 1984) Mar. British Rail Hotels sold off by private sale Apr. Youth Training Scheme (YTS), one-year work experience and training under-18s, replaces YOP; comes fully into operation in Sept. Aug. Enterprise Allowance Scheme, launched in five pilot areas early in 1982, extended nationwide Mountain bikes first reach UK, with a sporting image and glamorous Californian pedigree Seat belts compulsory for front-seat passengers in road vehicles (saves *c.*370 lives p.a.)	9 Jan. First broadcast in television series *Jewel in the Crown* Glasgow's annual mayfest arts festival launched Eddie Shah (Messenger Group Newspapers) invokes the 1980 and 1982 trade union legislation and defeats the NGA closed shop Technical and Vocational Education Initiative (TVEI) pilot schemes launched to encourage LEAs to promote vocational education

Date	Political/International	Economic/Social	Cultural/Religious
1983	3 Oct. Labour Party conference in private session confirms expulsion of five leading Trotskyite Militants		
	3 Oct. Griffiths report on NHS recommends appointment of 'general managers'		
	14 Oct. Cecil Parkinson, Trade and Industry Secretary, resigns after Sara Keays, his pregnant secretary, says he has broken his promise to marry her		
	25 Oct. USA forces invade Grenada (in Commonwealth), without consulting Britain, to ward off danger to USA residents from the new Marxist regime		
	11 Nov. First missiles arrive at Greenham Common		
	Nov. State visits to Kenya, Bangladesh, and India		
	8 Dec. 30,000 women demonstrate at Greenham		
	17 Dec. 6 die and 80 injured in IRA bombing at Harrods		

Date	Political/International	Economic/Social	Cultural/Religious
1984	25 Jan. Howe announces ban on trade union membership at GCHQ	12 Apr. Bill to privatize British Telecom enacted	26 Feb. First *Spitting Image* (TV puppet serial) broadcast, ending 18 Feb. 1996
	2 Feb. Thatcher arrives in Hungary to launch what became the distinctive British diplomacy towards Eastern Europe	7 June BBC1 TV series *Crimewatch* first broadcast	Feb. First payments made under Public Lending Right (enabling bill passed 1979)
	Feb. Princess Anne tours Africa for Save the Children Fund	5 July Death of 4-year-old Jasmine Beckford, starved and battered to death by her stepfather	Mar. James Stirling's extension to the Stuttgart Staatsgalerie (commissioned 1977) opened
	8 Mar. Miners' year-long strike starts from Yorkshire on a regional basis, spread by 'flying pickets'	July Sealink Ferries sold off by private sale	Apr. York's influential Jorvik tourist centre opens
	23 Mar. Sarah Tisdall jailed for leaking to *Guardian* plans for Cruise missile arrival	July Jaguar Cars spun off from British Leyland and sold	29 May Prince of Wales attacks National Gallery extension plans as a 'monstrous carbuncle'
	Mar. Queen entertains Crown Prince of Japan at Buckingham Palace	1 July Office of Telecommunications, modelled on Office of Fair Trading, set up	12 July Robert Maxwell buys Mirror Group of newspapers
	Mar. Queen's state visit to Jordan	28 Nov. British Telecom share issue (floated 20 Nov.) heavily oversubscribed	3 Dec. Conservative backbench revolt prevents Keith Joseph making rich parents pay more towards student grants
	17 Apr. Libyans open fire from their London embassy on anti-Gaddafi demonstrators, killing policewoman Yvonne Fletcher	Nov. Mitterrand and Thatcher issue joint statement that a fixed cross-Channel link would be in the interest of both countries	tabloid attacks during 1983 against 'video nasties' prompt Video Recordings Act (1984)
	Apr. State visit of Emir of Bahrain	Police Complaints Authority set up	
		'Help the Hospices', the first nationwide hospice structure, founded to raise funds	

Date	Political/International	Economic/Social	Cultural/Religious
1984	29 May In police/miners battle at Orgreave Coke Works, 64 injured, 84 arrested 14 June EUROPEAN ASSEMBLY ELECTIONS: 45 Conservatives, 32 Labour, 2 Ulster Unionists, 1 SNP, 1 Irish SDLP June Queen entertains President of USA at Buckingham Palace 10 July National dock strike (ends 20 July) 26 July Trade Union Bill enacted removing legal immunity for unions who hold a strike without a ballot; secret ballots enforced for union officers 18 Aug. Clive Ponting from Ministry of Defence is charged with leaking *Belgrano* documents (acquitted 11 Feb. 1985) 24 Aug. Second national dock strike (ends 18 Sept.) 4 Sept. Norman Willis succeeds Len Murray as TUC General Secretary Sept. Queen and Duke visit Canada	Chris Smith the first MP to disclose himself as homosexual (appointed Heritage Secretary 1997)	

Date	Political/International	Economic/Social	Cultural/Religious
1984	12 Oct. IRA bomb at Grand Hotel Brighton kills four and seriously injures Norman Tebbit 18 Oct. Nottinghamshire miners vote to set up breakaway union (UDM) 3 Dec. The world's worst industrial disaster, the Union Carbide gas leak at Bhopal, India, kills tens of thousands 11 Dec. Rate-capping of 13 councils announced 15 Dec. Mr and Mrs Gorbachev visit Chequers (Gorbachev elected Soviet leader 11 Mar. 1985)		
1985	25 Jan. Televising of House of Lords starts 5 Mar. NUM delegate conference votes by 98 to 91 for return to work Mar. Queen's state visit to Portugal 13 July 100m TV audience sees the Live Aid concerts at Wembley and Philadelphia to raise money for Ethiopia, raises £45m	2 Apr. Direct Line (founded by Peter Wood in 1981) first UK insurance company using telephone as main medium, initially for motor insurance, later diversifying; has 12% of UK private motor insurance market by 1990 Apr. Nissan signs single-union no-strike agreement with AUEW for its Washington factory	Mar. Quinlan Terry's Richmond Riverside classical revival development begins June Police forcibly prevent 11th Stonehenge festival from being held (revived 2001) 1 Dec. Church of England's *Faith in the City* report on urban deprivation Britain's first multiplex cinema opened, prompting greater attendance

Date	Political/International	Economic/Social	Cultural/Religious
1985	16 July Local Government Bill abolishes GLC and metropolitan authorities with effect from 1 Apr. 1986	11 May 56 spectators die in fire at Bradford City stadium	Inquiry rejects Peter Palumbo's plan to erect a Mies van der Rohe tower block near the Mansion House
	2 Sept. Tebbit becomes Conservative Party chairman in cabinet reshuffle	29 May Liverpool vs. Juventus in European Cup Final at Heysel Stadium (Brussels). Crowd fighting prompts a stampede in which 39 died	
	9–10 Sept. Serious Handsworth riots in which 400 youths attack police; 2 Asians killed	Pudding Club founded at Mickleton, Glos., to preserve British pudding recipes	
	24 Sept. Peter Mandelson selected Labour's Director of Campaigns and Communications		
	28–9 Sept. Brixton riots (220 arrests)		
	1 Oct. Kinnock infuriates the left by bitterly attacking Militant members of Liverpool council at Labour Party conference		
	6 Oct. Broadwater Farm (Tottenham) riots (PC Blakelock murdered)		
	16–25 Oct. Thatcher at CHOGM in Nassau strongly opposes sanctions against South Africa		
	18 Oct. Notts miners form Union of Democratic Mineworkers (UDM) to rival NUM		

Date	Political/International	Economic/Social	Cultural/Religious
1985	15 Nov. Anglo–Irish agreement signed at Hillsborough: no change in N. Ireland's status without consent of the majority of its people 13 Dec. Westland helicopters controversy erupts Data Protection Act gives citizens access to computer records on themselves		
1986	9 Jan. Heseltine unexpectedly resigns from cabinet over Westland 20 Jan. Thatcher and Mitterrand announce at Lille the decision to build a Channel rail tunnel. Treaty signed soon afterwards at Canterbury 24 Jan. Leon Brittan resigns, replaced at Trade and Industry by Paul Channon 3 Feb. Government considers, then drops, sale of Land Rover and BL Trucks to US bidders 10 Feb. House of Commons approves white paper on Channel Tunnel by 268 votes to 107	Jan. Pilot scheme for Restart (scheme for interviewing the long-term unemployed) begins 18 Mar. In Lawson's budget, income tax basic rate falls from 30 to 29% 25–6 Apr. Chernobyl nuclear disaster in Ukraine Apr. The New Workers Scheme, a two-year scheme for 16-year-olds, with opportunity to gain vocational qualification, is built on to the YTS 12 June Seasonally adjusted unemployment count peaks at 3.2 million	25 Jan. Sunday Times first produced at Wapping, first Times 26 Jan. 26–7 Jan. News International moves to Wapping (first mass picket there, 8 Feb, violence 3 May, dispute ends 5 Feb. 1987) 4 Mar. Eddie Shah launches Today, first national colour newspaper, produced with new American computer technology (ceased 17 Nov. 1995) 7 Oct. Independent launched, Independent on Sunday on 28 Jan. 1990

Date	Political/International	Economic/Social	Cultural/Religious
1986	28 Feb. Single European Act signed, for implementation on 1 July 1987	July Car production begins at Nissan's Washington plant (officially opened 8 Sept.)	Dec. Scientists identify bovine spongiform encephalopathy (BSE) as a new animal disease
	15 Apr. USA planes set off from UK bases to bomb Libya in retaliation for Gaddafi's support for terrorism	July Job Start Scheme expands from nine pilot areas (launched in Jan.) nationwide	Save British Science movement founded to oppose cuts in state funding for basic science
	4 May Biffen calls for Conservatives to fight next election on 'balanced ticket'	10 Oct. Trustee Savings Bank sold to public	Stowe Garden Buildings Trust set up, National Trust assumes responsibility for the gardens 1989
	21 May K. Baker replaces K. Joseph as Education Secretary	27 Oct. 'Big Bang' in the City of London	Richard Rogers's Lloyds Headquarters building, City of London (commissioned 1978), completed
	25 May 20m participate in worldwide 'race against time' raising funds for African famine victims	29 Oct. M25 opens	
	12 June Labour Party expels Militant Derek Hatton	30 Oct. 50,000 calls received in the 24 hours after Childline launched on television to tackle child abuse (200,000 calls and 23,000 children counselled in its first year)	National Council for Vocational Qualifications set up
	24 Sept. Liberal conference rejects David Steel's defence policy	Oct. Preliminary work on the Channel Tunnel at Sangatte (French side)	O level and Certificate of Secondary Education amalgamated into General Certificate of Secondary Education
	28 Oct. IRA in South Armagh first uses Libyan Semtex against the British army	Nov. Dr J. D. Carr, who had enabled his cancer patient to 'die with dignity', acquitted at Leeds (cf. acquittal of Dr Lodwig of Battle Hospital in 1990)	
	Oct. Labour Party conference adopts the red rose symbol	2 Dec. British Gas successfully privatized after mass advertising campaign	
	25 Nov. Labour Party expels Liverpool's Derek Hatton	Unleaded petrol goes on sale	
	Student pressure induces Barclays Bank to sell its South African interests		

Date	Political/International	Economic/Social	Cultural/Religious
1986		BL renamed 'Rover Group' Britain's second and third shopping mega-malls (Metrocentre, Gateshead; Merryhill, Dudley) opened Building Societies Act allows building societies to diversify beyond the savings and mortgage markets into banking services, prompting a wave of mutualizations National Osteoporosis Society founded	
1987	28 Mar. Thatcher visits Moscow in her successful five-day visit to USSR 11 June GENERAL ELECTION; Conservatives 375, Labour 229, Alliance 22, Others 24 19 June Royal *It's a Knockout* TV tournament discredits the younger royals 16 Sept. Thatcher's 'Walk in the Wilderness', Stockton-on Tees 6 Oct. Conservative Party conference votes for immediate implementation of poll tax	Feb. British Airways privatized 6 Mar. Townsend Thoresen's *Herald of Free Enterprise* ferry capsizes with 600 on board, 188 of them die 17 Mar. Lawson's budget cuts income tax standard rate from 29 to 27% May Rolls-Royce privatized 18 June Official unemployment figures fall below 3 million for the first time since June 1983	1 Apr. Queen opens James Stirling's extension to the Tate Gallery, begun 1983 *Palliative Medicine*, the first British journal concerned with palliative care, launched

Date	Political/International	Economic/Social	Cultural/Religious
1987	19 Oct. Charles Saatchi resigns the Conservative Party advertising account 5 Nov. Australian spy case begins 8 Nov. IRA bomb at Remembrance Day parade in Enniskillen kills 11 and injures 63 1 Dec. Excavation for the Channel Tunnel begins 8 Dec. USA and USSR leaders sign the Intermediate-Range Nuclear Forces (INF) Treaty to eliminate ground-based, medium-range nuclear missiles stationed in Europe	1 July Lawson tells NEDC it will henceforth meet only quarterly, and that he will chair it only once a year, with associated cutbacks in committees (NEDC abolished 1992) July British Airports Authority privatized 15 Aug. Child-beating banned from all state schools 19 Aug. Michael Ryan kills 16 people in Hungerford random shooting 31 Aug. London Docklands Light Railway and Airport opened Aug. Preliminary work on Channel Tunnel at Shakespeare Cliff (UK side) 15/16 Oct. Great storm damages the woodlands of southern Britain more seriously than any since 1703; 15m trees blown down 19 Oct. Big Stock Exchange slump ('Black Monday') Thatcher lays foundation stone of the Canary Wharf project for redeveloping London's dockland as an office area (in 1988 drove in the first pile)	

Date	Political/International	Economic/Social	Cultural/Religious
1987		Debit cards (Switch and Visa Delta) introduced, and overtake credit cards in number of transactions for the first time in 1994 Judge Tumim appointed Chief Inspector of Prisons for England and Wales (served till 1995)	
1988	10 Jan. Whitelaw resigns due to ill health 9 Feb. House of Commons votes by 318 to 264 to be televised 2 Mar. Liberals vote 87.9% for merger, SDP 65.3%, so SLD launched 3 Mar.; Owen launches continuing SDP on 8 Mar; SLD vote to call themselves Democrats on 26 Sept.; SLD ballot changes name to Liberal Democrat 16 Oct.1989 6 Mar. SAS shoot three IRA members dead in Gibraltar 8 Mar. D. Owen launches continuing SDP 21 Apr. Thatcher addresses General Assembly of Church of Scotland	15 Mar. Standard rate of income tax cut to 25%, top rate to 40% 6 July 167 killed in Piper Alpha oil-rig disaster, 100 miles south-east of the Orkneys 17 July Alan Walters returns as economic adviser to Thatcher 1 Oct. Midland Bank launches telephone banking with First Direct (650,000 customers by Nov. 1996) Nov. British Steel Corporation returns to private sector as 'British Steel' (renamed 'Corus' after merger in 1999 with Hoogovens of the Netherlands)	June *New Society* merged with the *New Statesman* Sept. First of the City Technology Colleges, government-fostered but independent and run by educational trusts with industrial links, opens at Solihull 9 Nov. Student loans announced Hay-on-Wye literary festival launched

Date	Political/International	Economic/Social	Cultural/Religious
1988	2 June *Spycatcher* case finally rejected in Australia	Employment Training Act creates employer-dominated, American-influenced Training and Enterprise Councils (TECs) to administer government training of the unemployed	
	8 July EETPU suspended by TUC (expelled 5 Sept.)		
	25 July DHSS split into DSS and Department of Health	British Aerospace buys Rover Group (sold to BMW in 1994)	
	28 July Ashdown elected leader of Liberal Democrats	Local Government Bill's clause 28 prohibits local authorities from 'promoting' homosexuality (clause repealed 2003)	
	20 Sept. Thatcher's Bruges speech		
	19 Oct. Ban on broadcasting IRA and Sinn Fein spokesmen live	London Underground and British Airways (on domestic flights) ban smoking	
	28 Oct. Prince of Wales's televised documentary on architecture		
	2 Nov. Thatcher begins three-day visit to Poland		
	2 Dec. Charter 88 launched		
	21 Dec. Pan Am bomb at Lockerbie kills 270		
1989	14 Feb. Ayatollah's *fatwa* against Salman Rushdie	Feb. Society of Teachers Opposed to Physical Punishment (STOPP) wound up, its aim almost achieved	30 Aug. Uppark, Sussex, gutted by a serious fire, followed by elaborate and costly restoration
	1 Apr. Poll tax introduced in Scotland		

Date	Political/International	Economic/Social	Cultural/Religious
1989	5 Apr. Gorbachev's three-day visit to UK begins	15 Apr. Sheffield Hillsborough stadium football crowd disaster	Tesco buy the Hoover art deco factory in Perivale, begin redevelopment in Jan. 1992 (completed in just under a year)
	13 May D. Owen indicates that SDP can no longer function as a national party (vote to suspend its activities by 17 to 5 on 3 June 1990)	12 July Abbey National Building Society floated on Stock Exchange	Education Reform Act removes polytechnics from LEA control to become independent corporations (41 get university status in 1992, ending the 'binary divide')
	15 June EUROPEAN ASSEMBLY ELECTIONS: 13 Labour gains, Greens get 15% of vote	Dec. Regional water companies privatized First wheel clamps appear in London streets	
	24 July Howe becomes Lord President and Leader of House of Commons in cabinet reshuffle, John Major succeeds him as Foreign Secretary	Stonewall founded Bunty Lewis revives Queen Charlotte's Ball, the high point of the London Season which had lapsed in the 1970s	
	22 Sept. IRA bomb kills nine army bandsmen and one civilian at Deal		
	16 Oct. Madrid summit: Britain agrees to enter ERM when three conditions met		
	19 Oct. Judges quash all convictions against the 'Guildford Four', who are freed. Blair apologizes to the families 9 Feb. 2005		

Date	Political/International	Economic/Social	Cultural/Religious
1989	26 Oct. N. Lawson resigns as Chancellor of the Exchequer, Major succeeds him, Hurd becomes Foreign Secretary 9 Nov. East Germany opens its border with West Germany. Berlin wall demolished from 10 Nov. 21 Nov. Televising House of Commons begins 5 Dec. In leadership ballot Thatcher defeats Sir A. Meyer by 314 to 33 (24 spoilt ballots, 3 abstentions)		
1990	31 Mar. Poll tax riots (poll tax starts in England 1 Apr.) 3 May. Labour gains 300 local council seats, but Conservatives win Wandsworth and Westminster 14 July Trade Secretary N. Ridley resigns after *Spectator* interview 30 July IRA bomb kills Conservative MP Ian Gow 2 Aug. Iraq seizes Kuwait. Operation Desert Storm liberates Kuwait Feb. 1991	26 Jan. Great storm causes damage from Isles of Scilly across southern England to Norfolk 1 Apr. Strangeways prison riot begins (last prisoners surrender 25 Apr.) 8 Aug. Queen opens Kennet and Avon Canal, navigable from Bristol to Reading 4 Sept. Britain's fourth shopping mega-mall opens (Meadowhall, Sheffield)	28 Jan. *Independent on Sunday* launched Aug. BBC Radio 5 launched 70,000 attend Glastonbury Festival for Contemporary Performing Arts, renamed to reflect its diversity Human Fertilization and Embryology Act (1990) lowers upper time-limit for termination of pregnancy from 28 weeks to 24

Date	Political/International	Economic/Social	Cultural/Religious
1990	8 Oct. UK joins ERM 30 Oct. Channel Tunnel: meeting of the undersea service tunnels from French and English ends (Channel Tunnel opens 1994) 1 Nov. Howe resigns from government (resignation speech, 13 Nov.) 20 Nov. 1st ballot for Conservative leadership election: Thatcher 204, Heseltine 152 22 Nov. Thatcher tells her cabinet she will quit 27 Nov. Conservative leadership ballot: Major 185, Heseltine 131, Hurd 56. Major's rivals withdraw in his favour 10 Dec. Communist rule ends in Czechoslovakia 22 Dec. Ceaucescu overthrown in Romania 23 Dec. Provisional IRA declares a three-day ceasefire, the first in 15 years	25 Oct. Britain's fifth shopping mega-mall opens (Lakeside, Thurrock, Essex) Dec. Electricity distribution companies privatized OutRage, homosexual direct-action group, founded	

Bibliography

GENERAL

For British history after 1970 the secondary literature is growing fast, and the primary sources still more so. Here, as with *Seeking a Role*, a short bibliographical introduction must suffice.

K. O. Morgan, *The People's Peace: British History 1945–1990* (2nd edn. 1999) is the best single-volume study. For this period synthesis and analysis often grow out of media programmes—for example, P. Whitehead, *The Writing on the Wall: Britain in the Seventies* (1985). J. Paxman, *Friends in High Places: Who Runs Britain?* (1990) is comprehensive and penetrating. A. H. Halsey had much of interest to say in his *Change in British Society: Based on the Reith Lectures* (Oxford, 1978). Wide-ranging successive snapshots of Britain published by the well-informed journalist Anthony Sampson include *The Changing Anatomy of Britain* (1982) and *The Essential Anatomy of Britain* (1992). B. Brivati, J. Buxton, and A. Seldon (eds.) *The Contemporary History Handbook* (Manchester, 1996) offers a wealth of guidance, stimulus, and information.

Reference works are increasingly now best consulted on the internet, most notably the *Oxford English Dictionary* and the *Oxford Dictionary of National Biography*. Important reference works in book format include P. Catterall's remarkably detailed *Bibliography of British History 1945–1987: An Annotated Bibliography* (Oxford, 1991) and K. Robbins, *A Bibliography of British History 1914–1989* (Oxford, 1996). G. Foote's *A Chronology of Post War British Politics* (1988) is useful. Essential is *British Political Facts*, edited by D. E. Butler and others; it went through eight editions between 1963 and 2000, complemented by D. and G. Butler's *British Political Facts since 1979* (Basingstoke, 2006). See also I. Crewe, A. Fox, and N. Day, *The British Electorate 1963–1992: A Compendium of Data from the British Election* Studies (Cambridge, 1995). There have been three editions, all of continuing value, of the essential statistically based collaborative study edited by A. H. Halsey: *Trends in British Society since 1900: A Guide to the Changing Social Structure of Britain* (London and Basingstoke, 1972); *British Social Trends since 1900* (London and Basingstoke, 1988); and *Twentieth-Century British Social Trends* (London and Basingstoke, 2000).

Valuable **sources on opinion** include G. Gallup, *The Gallup International Public Opinion Polls: Great Britain 1937–1975* (2 vols. New York, n.d.); A. King (ed.), *British Political Opinion 1937–2000: The Gallup Polls* (2001); and R. J. Wybrow, *Britain Speaks Out, 1937–87: A Social History as Seen through the Gallup Data* (Basingstoke and London, 1989). Newspapers, parliamentary and government documents are increasingly becoming available on the internet, and this enhanced accessibility will eventually transform research possibilities. Back numbers, too, are being made accessible in this way, including those of the *Times, Times Literary Supplement, Observer*, and *Guardian*. There is also growing internet access to Hansard's *Parliamentary Debates*. Parliament remains the focus of opinion, and House of Lords debates are in some respects superior to House of Commons debates as a historical source: wider ranging, more expert, and less preoccupied with scoring party points.

Several **periodicals** are valuable. For a rich collection of government statistics, see the *Annual Abstract of Statistics* published by the Central Statistical Office and its successors. For specialist aspects see *Economic Trends* (1953–), *Abstract of Regional Statistics* (1965–), *Local Government Financial Statistics* (1953–; from 1981 *Local Government Comparative Statistics*), *Local Government Trends* (1973–), *Trends in Education* (1966–), *Social Trends* (1970–), and the DHSS's *Social Security Statistics* (1972–). For London see Greater London Council, *Annual Abstract of Greater London Statistics* (1966–86). For secondary writing see the journals *Twentieth Century British History* (1990–), and the Institute of Contemporary British History's *Contemporary Record* (9 vols. 1987–95), continued from volume 10 as *Contemporary British History* (1996–); the latter has energetically accumulated a wealth of empirical as well as interpretative material.

Diaries bring the past to life by showing how it seemed at the time. See especially the three relevant, highly prejudiced, and eminently readable volumes of James Lees-Milne, strong on architectural and aristocratic aspects: *A Mingled Measure: Diaries 1953–1972* (1994), *Ancient as the Hills: Diaries 1973–1974* (1997), and *Through Wood and Dale: Diaries, 1975–1978* (1998), and the four relevant volumes edited by M. Bloch: *Deep Romantic Chasm: Diaries, 1979–1981* (2000), *Holy Dread: Diaries 1982–1984* (2001), *Beneath a Waning Moon: Diaries 1985–1987* (2003), and *Ceaseless Turmoil: Diaries 1988–92* (2004). A very different angle comes from K. C. Williams, *The Kenneth Williams Diaries* (ed. Russell Davies, 1993), covering the years 1942–88. It can be supplemented by his *Letters* (ed. Davies, 1994) from 1947 to 1988, and by his autobiographical *Just Williams* (1985). Also valuable is N. Henderson, *Mandarin: The Diaries of an Ambassador 1969–1982* (1994). Collections of correspondence resemble diaries in their bird's-eye-view usefulness. J. Betjeman, *Letters* (ed. C. Lycett-Green), ii (1995), for example, covers the years 1951–84; see also *The Selected Letters of Philip Larkin, 1940–1985* (ed. A. Thwaite, 1992).

I. THE UNITED KINGDOM AND THE WORLD

D. Sanders's *Losing an Empire: Finding a Role. British Foreign Policy since 1945* (London and Basingstoke, 1990) provides an important overall analysis. See also D. Maguire, 'When the Streets Begin to Empty: The Demobilisation of the British Peace Movement After 1983', *West European Politics* (Oct. 1992); A. H. Brown, 'The Change to Engagement in Britain's Cold War Policy: The Origins of the Thatcher–Gorbachev Relationship', *Journal of Cold War Studies*, 10/3 (Summer 2008), 3–47.

For **internationalism** in its cultural dimension see B. King (ed.), *The Oxford English Literary History*, xiii. *1948–2000: The Internationalization of English Literature* (Oxford, 2004); B. Brothers and J. M. Gergits (eds.), *British Travel Writers, 1940–1997* ('Dictionary of Literary Biography', 204; Detroit, 1999). See also D. Crystal, *English as a Global Language* (Cambridge, 1997); B. King (ed.), *Literatures of the World in English* (1974) and his *The New English Literatures: Cultural Nationalism in a Changing World* (London and Basingstoke, 1980). B. McCallen's *English: A World Commodity. The International Market for Training in English as a Foreign Language* (1989) is informative.

G. C. Staple (ed.), *Telegeography 1992* (n.pl., 1992) illuminates the UK's worldwide telecommunications links as at 1990. For the globalized economy see J. Stopford and L. Turner, *Britain and the Multinationals* (Chichester, 1985); J. H. Dunning, *Japanese Participation in British Industry* (1986); N. Oliver and B. Wilkinson, *The Japanization of British Industry* (Oxford, 1989).

On **tourism** the British Tourist Authority's periodic *Digest of Tourist Statistics* provides valuable statistics. See also A. J. Burkhart and S. Medlik's informative *Tourism: Past, Present and Future* (1981).

The recent history of **the armed forces** is transcending antiquarian chronology only slowly, but for the Falklands war see L. Freedman, *The Official History of the Falklands Campaign* (2 vols. 2005), and O. Franks et al., *The Franks Report: Falkland Islands Review* (1983, reprinted 1992 with introduction by A. Danchev). P. M. Hammond and G. Carter, *From Biological Warfare to Healthcare: Porton Down, 1940–2000* (Basingstoke, 2001) is important, and A. Gilchrist, *Cod Wars and How to Lose Them* (Edinburgh, 1978) chronicles a significant and unadvertised defeat.

On the **European Union** H. Young's *This Blessed Plot: Britain and Europe from Churchill to Blair* (1998) comes from an enthusiast, but is splendidly clear and synoptic. An admirable reference work is T. Bainbridge with A. Teasdale, *The Penguin Companion to European Union* (corrected edn. 1996). D. E. Butler and U. Kitzinger, *The 1975 Referendum* (1976) is important not only for the EEC but for documenting a significant constitutional innovation.

For the **empire/Commonwealth** see W. D. McIntyre, *The Significance of the Commonwealth* (Basingstoke and London, 1991), and W. G. F. Jackson, *Withdrawal from Empire: A Military View* (1986). On race in South Africa see R. Fieldhouse, *Anti-Apartheid: A History of the Movement in Britain. A Study in Pressure Group Politics* (2005). For **overseas aid** see M. Black, *A Cause for our Times: OXFAM. The First Fifty Years* (Oxford, 1992).

2. THE FACE OF THE COUNTRY

On **agriculture** see the Ministry of Agriculture and Food's *Agricultural Statistics, United Kingdom* (1867–), continued from 1991 as *Digest of Agricultural Census Statistics: UK*. Also valuable are D. Grigg, *English Agriculture: An Historical Perspective* (Oxford, 1989); T. Beresford, *We Plough the Fields: Agriculture in Britain* (Harmondsworth, 1975); B. Hill, 'Agriculture', in P. Johnson (ed.), *The Structure of British Industry* (1988); R. H. Best, *Land Use and Living Space* (1981); M. Robinson and A. C. Armstrong, 'The Extent of Agricultural Field Drainage in England and Wales, 1971–80', *Transactions of the Institute of British Geographers*, 1988; B. Burkitt and M. Baimbridge, 'The Performance of British Agriculture and the Impact of the Common Agricultural Policy: An Historical Review', *Rural History* (Oct. 1990).

For **archaeology** see the informative I. Longworth and J. Cherry, *Archaeology in Britain since 1945: New Directions* (1986). See also T. Gregory's influential article 'Metal-Detecting in Archaeological Excavation', *Antiquity*, 58 (1984), and C. Dobinson and S. Denison's informative *Metal Detecting and Archaeology in England* (London and York, 1995).

On **woods and forests** there is lively debate. G. F. Peterken's *Woodland Conservation and Management* (2nd edn. 1993) is historically aware and valuable. See also R. H. Grove, *The Future of Forestry: The Urgent Need for a New Policy* (Cambridge, 1983); R. Miller, *State Forestry for the Axe: A Study of the Forestry Commission and De-Nationalisation by the Market* (Institute of Economic Affairs Hobart Paper, 91; 1981). O. Rackham's *Trees and Woodland in the British Landscape* (rev. edn. 1996) is wide-ranging and very well informed. See also G. Hill, *Hurricane Force: The Story of the Storm of October 1987* (1988), and A. M. Whitbread, *When the Wind Blew: Life in our Woods after the Great Storm of 1987* (1991).

On **the environment** the aerial photographs in L. Gardiner's *The Changing Face of Britain from the Air* (1989) illustrate change between the 1930s and 1980s in, for example, urban sprawl and coastline erosion; see also A. W. Gilg, *Countryside Planning: The First Three Decades 1945–76* (1979); and the Department of the Environment's *This Common Inheritance: Britain's Environmental Strategy* (1990). J. Hassan introduces a neglected historical topic with his *A History of Water in Modern England and Wales* (Manchester, 1998). Path-breaking was the committee chaired by Sir A. Wilson on the Problem of Noise; see its admirable *Final Report* (1963, Cmnd. 2056).

For **transport** the Ministry of Transport's periodic compendia *Transport Statistics* are valuable, and see M. A. Cundill and B. A. Shane, *Trends in Road Goods Traffic 1962–77* (1980); W. H. Newton, *Trends in Road Goods Transport 1973–1983* (Crowthorne, 1985); B. A. Frith, *Trends in Road Goods Transport 1983–1991* (Crowthorne, 1994). G. Charlesworth's *A History of British Motorways* (1984) and his *A History of the Transport and Road Research Laboratory 1933–1983* (Aldershot, 1987) are valuable, as is J. Wardroper's *Juggernaut* (1981), an important subject. Valuable raw material has been collected by the Motorway Archive; see especially its first three volumes, generously illustrated: P. and R. Baldwin (eds.), *The Motorway Achievement*, i. *The British Motorway System: Visualisation, Policy and Administration* (2004); R. Bridle and J. Porter (eds.), *The Motorway Achievement*, ii. *Frontiers of Knowledge and Practice* (2002); and W. J. McCoubrey (ed.), *The Motorway Achievement*, iii. *Building the Network* (2009). From the opposite side see J. Tyme's *Motorways versus Democracy: Public Inquiries into Road Proposals and their Political Significance* (1978). Historians have yet to give the motorway system's impact due attention. Good books on the recent history of canals, air travel, motorways, and commercial seafaring are much needed, and a good history of the telephone in the UK since 1945 has become urgent. See, however, H. Banks, *The Rise and Fall of Freddie Laker* (1982) and R. W. Squires, *Canals Revived: The Story of the Waterway Restoration Movement* (Bradford-on-Avon, 1979). T. R. Gourvish has published a huge 2-volume history of British Rail—*British Railways 1948–73: A Business History* (Cambridge, 1986), and *British Rail 1974–97: From Integration to Privatisation* (Oxford, 2002). See also M. R. Bonavia, *The Channel Tunnel Story* (Newton Abbot, 1987), and D. Hunt, *The Tunnel: The Story of the Channel Tunnel 1802–1994* (Upton-upon-Severn, 1994). For motor-cycling see S. McDonald-Walker's two articles, 'Driven to Action: The British Motorcycle Lobby in the 1990s', *Sociological Review* (May 2000), and 'Fighting the Legacy: British Bikers in the 1990s', *Sociology* (May 1998).

On **towns and cities** E. Edwards, R. Golland, and S. Leach's well-annotated *Urban Riots and Public Order: A Select Bibliography 1975–1985* (1986) focuses on the riots of 1981 and 1985, together with H. Tumber's informative *Television and the Riots* (1982). See also A. Cox, *Docklands in the Making: The Redevelopment of the Isle of Dogs, 1981–95* (1995), and for architects see W. J. R. Curtis, *Denys Lasdun: Architecture, City, Landscape* (1994), and M. Girouard, *Big Jim: The Life and Work of James Stirling* (1998). For determined traditionalists regardless, see L. Archer, *Raymond Erith: Architect* (Burford, 1985) and C. Aslet, *Quinlan Terry: The Revival of Architecture* (1986).

On **housing** J. Newton, *All in One Place: The British Housing Story 1971–1990. A Compilation of Housing Statistics* (1991) conveniently collects relevant statistics. Valuable is the Building Societies Association's *Compendium of Building Society Statistics* (6th edn. 1986); the Association also published *Facts and Figures*, a *Bulletin*, and a *Yearbook*. R. H. Duclaud-Williams, *The Politics of Housing in Britain and France* (1978) is illuminating on the period 1965–72; A. A. Nevett's *Housing Taxation and Subsidies: A Study of Housing in the United Kingdom* (1966) explains thoroughly how the system then worked. See also J. Doling, 'British Housing Policy: 1984–1993', *Regional Studies*, 27/6 (1993). For the 'modern style' see the lavishly illustrated volume by M. Glendinning and S. Muthesius: *Tower Block: Modern Public Housing in England, Scotland, Wales and Northern Ireland* (New Haven and London, 1994).

For **non-English nationality and culture** see A. H. Birch, *Political Integration and Disintegration in the British Isles* (1977); R. Rose, *Understanding the United Kingdom: The Territorial Dimension in Government* (1982). For Scotland see R. Parry, *Scottish Political Facts* (Edinburgh, 1988); the *Scottish Abstract of Statistics* (1971–); J. G. Kellas, *The Scottish Political System* (Cambridge, 1973). For social and environmental trends in Wales with supporting statistics, see *Welsh Social Trends* (1977–). J. Aitchison and H. Carter's *A Geography of the Welsh Language 1961–1991* (Cardiff, 1994) is well informed, and M. Watson tackles the important subject of *Being English in Scotland* (Edinburgh, 2003).

For **Northern Ireland** see P. Buckland, *History of Northern Ireland* (Dublin, 1981) and S. Elliott and W. D. Flackes, *Northern Ireland: A Political Directory 1968–1999* (5th edn. Belfast, 1999); P. Compton's 'The Demographic Background', in D. Watt (ed.), *The Constitution of Northern Ireland: Problems and Prospects* (1981) fills in important context. For 'the troubles' see S. Bruce, *God Save Ulster: The Religion and Politics of Paisleyism* (Oxford, 1989); S. Bruce, *The Red Hand: Protestant Paramilitaries in Northern Ireland* (Oxford, 1992); V. Feeney, 'The Civil Rights Movement in Northern Ireland', *Eire-Ireland*, 9 (Summer 1974); and P. Bishop and E. Mallie, *The Provisional IRA* (1987). R. English, *Armed Struggle: The History of the IRA* (2003) is excellent on the IRA's thought processes. Maria McGuire's *To Take Arms: A Year in the Provisional IRA* (1973) exposes the Provisional IRA from within during her year (1971–2) of bombs, romance, and faction-fighting before leaving in disillusionment The photographs in J. Olley's *Castles of Ulster* (Belfast, 2007) vividly evoke the air of menace attending the strange buildings the security forces erected. It is too early for measured analytic assessments of order-keeping in Northern Ireland, but see R. Faligot, *Britain's Military Strategy in Ireland: The Kitson Experiment* (1983). For injustices that resulted, see K. D. Ewing and C. A. Gearty, *Freedom under Thatcher: Civil Liberties in Modern Britain*

(Oxford, 1990); Gerry Conlon's *Proved Innocent* (1990); and Paul Hill's *Stolen Years: Before and after Guildford* (1990).

3. THE SOCIAL STRUCTURE

For the **monarchy**, B. Pimlott's *The Queen* (1996) is the best of several on Elizabeth II. Also valuable is J. Dimbleby, *The Prince of Wales* (1994). P. Hall, *Royal Fortune: Tax, Money and Monarchy* (1992) is hostile but well researched on an important subject. See also J. Walker, *The Queen Has Been Pleased: The British Honours System at Work* (1986); and S. Martin, *The Order of Merit: One Hundred Years of Matchless Honour* (2007).

For the **upper classes** F. M. L. Thompson's four excellent essays on 'English Landed Society in the Twentieth Century' in successive volumes of the *TRHS*, should have appeared in book form: 'Property: Collapse and Survival' (1990); 'New Poor and New Rich' (1991), 'Self-Help and Outdoor Relief' (1992); 'Prestige without Power?' (1993). On the distribution of wealth see W. D. Rubinstein, *Wealth and Inequality in Britain* (1986); C. H. Feinstein, 'The Equalizing of Wealth in Britain since the Second World War', *Oxford Review of Economic Policy*, 12/1 (1996). On lifestyle see J. M. Robinson, *The Latest Country Houses 1945–83* (1983), and M. Girouard, 'Country House Crisis', *Architectural Review* (Oct. 1974).

There is all too little historical treatment of the **middle classes** for this period, though see Paul Halmos's interesting and somewhat neglected *The Faith of the Counsellors* (2nd edn. 1978); the retreat of poverty and class consciousness in these years made it seem less important to explore the working class. On **poverty**, however, see P. Townsend's massive *Poverty in the United Kingdom: A Survey of Household Resources and Standards of Living* (1979); and Frank Field's very detailed *Losing Out: The Emergence of Britain's Underclass* (Oxford, 1989). J. Welshman's *Underclass: A History of the Excluded 1880–2000* (2006) is a valuable synthesis on a neglected subject.

The **trade unions** were prominent enough in public life till the 1980s to ensure full attention. R. Taylor provides a valuable synthesis in his *The Trade Union Question in British Politics: Government and Unions since 1945* (Oxford, 1993), and see P. A. J. Waddington, 'Trade Union Membership Concentration, 1892–1987: Development and Causation', *British Journal of Industrial Relations* (Sept. 1993). For personalities see E. Silver, *Victor Feather, T.U.C.* (1973), General Secretary of the TUC 1969–73; perhaps significantly, his successors have not as yet received biographies. See also E. Hammond and C. Leake, *Maverick: The Life of a Union Rebel* (1992), a disappointing autobiography of Eric Hammond, but very detailed on disputes of the 1980s between trade unions. J. Gormley's autobiographical *Battered Cherub: The Autobiography of Joe Gormley* (1982) concerns the NUM's President (1971–82); S. Weighell's *On the Rails* (1983) is by the NUR's General Secretary (1975–82), and Jack Jones's *Union Man* (1986) portrays the TGWU's formidable General Secretary (1969–78).

For **immigrant/minority groups** see T. Modood and R. Berthoud (eds.), *Ethnic Minorities in Britain: Diversity and Disadvantage. The Fourth National Survey of Ethnic Minorities* (1997), and the three volumes in the series *Ethnicity in the 1991 Census* (1996) edited by D. Coleman and J. Salt (on demographic characteristics), C. Peach (on the ethnic minority populations), and P. Ratcliffe (on the social geography of ethnicity). See also articles by J. Haskey, 'Families and Households of the Ethnic Minority and White Populations of Great Britain', *Population Trends* (Autumn 1989); D. Coleman, 'Ethnic Intermarriage in Great Britain', *Population Trends*, 40 (Summer 1985); M. G. Marmot *et al.*, *Immigrant Mortality in England and Wales 1970–78: Causes of Death by Country of Birth* (Office of Population Censuses and Surveys, Studies on Medical and Population Subjects, 47; 1984). For racist hostility to immigrants see C. T. Husbands, 'Extreme Right-Wing Politics in Great Britain: The Recent Marginalisation of the National Front', *West European Politics* (Apr. 1988), and Lord Scarman, *The Brixton Disorders 10–12 April, 1981: Report of an Inquiry* (1981).

For particular minorities, see D. Garvey, 'The History of Migration Flows in the Republic of Ireland', *Population Trends* (Spring 1985). S. Waterman and B. Kosmin, *British Jewry in the Eighties* (1986) has valuable statistics. For Poles see K. Sword's excellent *Identity in Flux: The Polish Community in Britain* (1996), and P. D. Stachura (ed.), *The Poles in Britain, 1940–2000: From Betrayal to Assimilation* (2004). G. Dench, K. Gavron, and M. Young, *The New East End: Kinship, Race and Conflict* (2006) illuminates patterns of Bangladeshi settlement and local attitudes to it. For Chinese settlers see the three volumes of the House of Commons Home Affairs Committee's report on *The Chinese Community in Britain . . . Session 1984–85* (HC102-III, 1985), and D. Jones, 'The Chinese in Britain: Origins and Development of a Community', *New Community* (Winter 1979).

4. FAMILY AND WELFARE

D. A. Coleman and J. Salt's fine *The British Population: Patterns, Trends, and Processes* (Oxford, 1992) is essential for all demographic aspects. Many articles by J. Haskey in *Population Trends*, cited in numerous footnotes, almost always shed a flood of light on demographic issues. M. Anderson's classic article, 'The Emergence of the Modern Life Cycle in Britain', *Social History* (Jan. 1985), is admirably and concisely informative on major issues. See also M. Britton and N. Edison, 'The Changing Balance of the Sexes in England and Wales, 1851–2001', *Population Trends* (Winter 1986).

For **women at work** see S. Duncan's interesting 'The Geography of Gender Divisions of Labour in Britain', *Transactions of the Institute of British Geographers* (1991). On part-time working see O. Robinson and J. Wallace, *Part-Time Employment and Sex Discrimination Legislation in Great Britain: A Study of the Demand for Part-Time Labour and of Sex Discrimination in Selected Organizations and Establishments* (Department of Employment Research Paper, 43; 1984); C. Marsh, *Hours of Work of Women and Men in Britain* (1991) and C. Hakim's important studies: 'Explaining Trends in Occupational Segregation: The Measurement, Causes, and Consequences of the Sexual Division of Labour', *European Sociological Review* (Sept. 1992); 'The Myth of Rising Female Employment', *Work, Employment and Society* (Mar. 1993); 'A Century of Change in Occupational Segregation 1891–1991', *Journal of Historical Sociology* (Dec. 1994); and 'Five Feminist Myths about Women's Employment', *British Journal of Sociology* (Sept. 1995). The Equal Opportunities Commission's *Health and Safety Legislation* (1979) is informative on women and shift work.

For a concise digest of trends in **the family** see J. Haskey's two articles: 'Trends in Marriage and Divorce in England and Wales: 1837–1987', *Population Trends* (Summer 1987); and 'Population Review: 6: Families and Households in Great Britain', *Population Trends* (Autumn 1996). M. Murphy and A. Berrington's 'Household Change in the 1980s: A Review', *Population Trends* (Autumn 1993) is usefully synoptic. See also B. J. Elliott, 'Demographic Trends in Domestic Life, 1945–87', in D. Clark (ed.), *Marriage, Domestic Life and Social Change: Writings for Jacqueline Burgoyne (1944–88)* (1991); M. Young and P. Willmott, *The Symmetrical Family: A Study of Work and Leisure in the London Region* (1973); Department of Health and Social Security, *Report of the [Finer] Committee on One-Parent Families* (1974, Cmnd. 5629); J. Bradshaw and J. Millar, *Lone Parent Families in the United Kingdom* (Department of Social Security Research Report, 6; 1991); and R. M. Moroney, *The Family and the State: Considerations for Social Policy* (1976). On legal aspects the essential work is S. Cretney, *Family Law in the Twentieth Century: A History* (Oxford, 2003). M. Durham, *Moral Crusades: Family and Morality in the Thatcher Years* (New York, 1991) explores political aspects.

On **sexuality** see, for single-sex relations, J. Weeks, *Coming Out: Homosexual Politics in Britain from the Nineteenth Century to the Present* (rev. edn. 1990); B. Cant and S. Hemmings (eds.), *Radical Records: Thirty Years of Lesbian and Gay History, 1957–1987* (1988); D. Fernbach, 'Ten Years of Gay Liberation', *Politics and Power* (1980); A. Grey, *Quest for Justice: Towards Homosexual Emancipation* (1992); and R. McMullen, *Male Rape* (1990). For transsexuals, see J. Morris, *Conundrum* (1974), with introductions to several later editions. For pornography see Home Office [Williams] Committee on Obscenity and Film Censorship, *Report* (Cmnd.7772, 1979).

For **birth control** see L. V. Marks's wide-ranging and cross-cultural *Sexual Chemistry: A History of the Contraceptive Pill* (New Haven, 2001); A. Cartwright, *Recent Trends in Family Building and Contraception* (1978); P. Babb, 'Teenage Conceptions and Fertility in England and Wales, 1971–91', *Population Trends*, 74 (Winter 1993). B. Botting's 'Trends in Abortion', *Population Trends*, 64 (Summer 1991) is informative. See also J. Keown, *Abortion, Doctors and the Law: Some Aspects of the Legal Regulation of Abortion in England from 1803 to 1982* (Cambridge, 1988); E. Lee (ed.), *Abortion Law and Politics Today* (London and Basingstoke, 1998).

For **children** see B. Botting, 'Population Review (7): Review of Children', *Population Trends*, 85 (Autumn 1996). C. Hardyment's *Dream Babies: Childcare Advice from John Locke to Gina Ford* (2nd edn. 2007), broad-ranging in time and space, tackles neglected territory; it lacks adequate context, however, and concerns attitudes more than conduct. On the naming of children see S. Wilson, *The Means of Naming: A Social and Cultural History of Personal Naming in Western Europe* (1998); L. A. Dunkling, *First Names First* (1977); and E. Merry, *First Names. The Definitive Guide to Popular Names in England and Wales 1944–1994* (1995). B. Crowe covers important ground in *The Playgroup Movement* (4th edn. Hemel Hempstead, 1983); see also B. and S. Jackson, *Childminder: A Study in Action Research* (1979); C. J. Prynne et al., 'Food and Nutrient Intake of a National Sample of Four-Year-Old Children in 1950: Comparison with the 1990s', *Public Health Nutrition* (Dec. 1999); and D. Buckingham, H. Davies, K. Jones, and P. Kelley et al., *Children's Television in Britain: History, Discourse and Policy* (1999). In the 'Dictionary of Literary Biography' series see C. C. Hunt (ed.), *British Children's Writers since 1960*

(Vol. 161; Detroit, 1996). On violence to children see, for a helpful overview, N. Parton, *The Politics of Child Abuse* (1985); see also Select Committee on Violence in the Family, *Violence to Children: First Report* (1977). Valuable is K. Kiernan, 'Leaving Home: Living Arrangements of Young People in Six West-European Countries', *European Journal of Population* (Oct. 1986).

For **health and disability** V. Berridge's *Health and Society in Britain since 1939* (Cambridge, 1999) provides an excellent introduction. See also Office of Population Statistics and Surveys, *Mortality Statistics* (1977–); Department of Health and Social Security, *Health and Personal Social Services Statistics for England (With Summary Tables for Great Britain)* (1977). For a short introduction to political aspects see C. Webster, *The National Health Service: A Political History* (Oxford, 1998). Ampler is the second volume (1996) of his *The Health Services since the War*, covering the years 1958–79. Also valuable is J. P. Martin, *Hospitals in Trouble* (Oxford, 1984). I. Loudon, J. Horder, and C. Webster (eds.), *General Practice under the National Health Service 1948–1997: The First Fifty Years* (Oxford, 1998) tackles important territory not covered elsewhere. For private medicine, see J. Higgins, *The Business of Medicine: Private Health Care in Britain* (Basingstoke and London, 1988), and D. G. Green and D. Lucas, 'Private Welfare in the 1980s', in N. Manning and R. Page (eds.), *Social Policy Review*, iv (1992). For a well-publicized critique of the medical profession see I. Kennedy's Reith lectures, *The Unmasking of Medicine* (1981).

On the incidence of disease, M. J. Gardner et al. in their *Atlas of Mortality from Selected Diseases in England and Wales, 1968–1978* (1984) discuss regional factors. See also J. Charlton and M. Murphy (eds.), *The Health of Adult Britain 1841–1994* (2 vols. 1997), and I. Knight, *The Heights and Weights of Adults in Great Britain: Report of a Survey Carried Out on Behalf of the Department of Health and Social Security Covering Adults aged 16–64* (1984). For ethnic groupings see M. G. Marmot, A. M. Adelstein, and L. Bulusu, *Immigrant Mortality in England and Wales, 1970–78: Causes of Death by Country of Birth* (1984). For the disadvantaged generally, see P. Townsend's collection of essays, *The Social Minority* (1973), with contributions on the old, the poor, the disabled, the mentally ill, the institutionalized, the lonely. For disability see T. Shakespeare (ed.), *The Disability Reader: Social Science Perspectives* (1998); A. I. Harris, E. Cox, and C. R. W. Smith, *Handicapped and Impaired in Great Britain* (1971); and P. Hunt, *Stigma: The Experience of Disability* (1966).

On **old age** generally see P. Thane, *Old Age in English History: Past Experiences, Present Issues* (Oxford, 2000). M. R. Miller's valuable Kent Ph.D. thesis: 'The Development of Retirement Pensions Policy in Britain from 1945 to 1986: A Case of State and Occupational Welfare' (1987) covers neglected territory. For growing longevity see A. R. Thatcher's two articles: 'Trends in Numbers and Mortality at High Ages in England and Wales', *Population Studies*, 40 (1992); and 'The Demography of Centenarians in England and Wales', *Population Trends* (Summer 1999). See also P. Laslett, 'The Emergence of the Third Age', *Ageing and Society*, 7/2 (June 1987). For welfare aspects see P. Johnson and J. Falkingham, 'Intergenerational Transfers and Public Expenditure on the Elderly in Modern Britain', *Ageing and Society*, 8/2 (June 1988). For geographical aspects see C. M. Law and A. M. Warnes, 'The Changing Geography of the Elderly in England and Wales', *Town Planning Review* (1976); A. M. Warnes and

R. Ford, *The Changing Distribution of Elderly People: Great Britain, 1981–91* (King's College, London, Department of Geography and Age Concern Institute of Gerontology Occasional Paper, 37; 1993); and R. King et al., *Sunset Lives: British Retirement Migration to the Mediterranean* (Oxford, 2000).

There is no good overall study of changing **attitudes to death**, but see (for hospices) S. Du Boulay, *Cicely Saunders: Founder of the Modern Hospice Movement* (1984); and C. Saunders, *Selected Letters 1959–1999* (Oxford, 2002). For euthanasia N. D. A. Kemp's *'Merciful Release': The History of the British Euthanasia Movement* (Manchester, 2002) is the only serious historical treatment. See also L. Bulusu and M. Alderson, 'Suicides 1950–82', *Population Trends*, 35 (Spring 1984).

5. INDUSTRY AND COMMERCE

A. Cairncross, *The British Economy since* 1945 (Oxford, 1992) provides a lucid introduction. R. Floud and D. McCloskey (eds.), *Economic History of Britain since 1700* (2nd edn. 1994), iii, and R. Floud and P. Johnson (eds.), *The Cambridge Economic History of Modern Britain*, iii. *Structural Change and Growth, 1939–2000* (Cambridge, 2004) contain important essays on many aspects of economic history. An essential reference work is D. J. Jeremy (ed.), *Dictionary of Business Biography: A Biographical Dictionary of Business Leaders Active in Britain in the Period 1860–1980* (5 vols. and supplement, 1984–6); P. Johnson (ed.), *The Structure of British Industry* (1988) collects much useful information, and for particular industries see T. Kelly, *The British Computer Industry: Crisis and Development* (1987); B. M. D. Smith, *The History of the British Motorcycle Industry 1945–1975* (University of Birmingham Centre for Urban and Regional Studies, Occasional Paper, 3; Oct. 1981); W. M. Ashworth, *The History of the British Coal Industry*, v. *1946–1982: The Nationalised Industry* (Oxford, 1986); G. C. Band, 'Fifty Years of U.K. Offshore Oil and Gas', *Geographical Journal* (July 1991); K. Chapman, *North Sea Oil and Gas: A Geographical Perspective* (1976); M. Jenkin, *British Industry and the North Sea: State Intervention in a Developing Industrial Sector* (1981). See also M. Finniston (Chairman), *Engineering our Future* (1980); G. Jordan, *Engineers and Professional Self-Regulation: From the Finniston Committee to the Engineering Council* (Oxford, 1992). For nuclear power see T. Hall, *Nuclear Politics: The History of Nuclear Power in Britain* (Harmondsworth, 1986).

For **regional economic contrasts** see G. Manners and D. Morris, *Office Policy in Britain: A Review* (Norwich, 1986); R. Martin, 'The Political Economy of Britain's North–South Divide', *Transactions of the Institute of British Geographers* (1988); and R. Saville (ed.), *The Economic Development of Modern Scotland 1950–1980* (Edinburgh, 1985).

On **economic policy** see A. Britton, *Macroeconomic Policy in Britain 1974–87* (Cambridge, 1991); C. Thain and M. Wright, *The Treasury and Whitehall: The Planning and Control of Public Expenditure, 1976–93* (Oxford, 1996); and K. Burk and A. Cairncross, *'Goodbye, Great Britain': The 1976 IMF Crisis* (New Haven, 1992). J. Tomlinson's *The Politics of Decline: Understanding Post-War Britain* (Harlow, 2000) and 'Inventing "Decline": The Falling Behind of the British Economy in the Postwar Years', *Economic History Review* (Nov. 1996) tackle the important and interesting subject of changing attitudes to the economy. N. F. R. Crafts, *Britain's Relative Economic Decline, 1870–1995: A Quantitative Perspective* (1997) documents the statistical realities.

For **incomes policies** see W. H. Fishbein's neglected but valuable *Wage Restraint by Consensus: Britain's Search for an Incomes Policy Agreement, 1965–79* (1984); S. Brittan and P. Lilley, *The Delusion of Incomes Policy* (1977); B. Harrison, 'Incomes Policies in Britain since 1940: A Study in Political Economy', in K. Bruland and P. O'Brien (eds.), *From Family Firms to Corporate Capitalism: Essays in Business and Industrial History in Honour of Peter Mathias* (Oxford, 1998). H. A. Clegg's *How to Run an Incomes Policy and Why We Made a Mess of the Last One* (1971) concisely explains how it seemed at the time.

For **exchange control** see two articles in *Journal of International Financial Markets: Law and Regulation* (2000): D. Kynaston, 'The Long Life and Slow Death of Exchange Controls', in 2/2 (May), and R. Roberts, 'Setting the City Free: The Impact of the U.K. Abolition of Exchange Controls', in 2/4 (Aug.).

Privatization has yet to receive much attention from historians, but see L. Hannah, 'A Failed Experiment: The State Ownership of Industry', in R. Floud and P. Johnson (eds.), *The Cambridge Economic History of Modern Britain*, iii. *Structural Change and Growth, 1939–2000* (Cambridge, 2004), 84–111, and K. Newman, *The Selling of British Telecom* (1986).

Youth employment is clearly introduced in K. Roberts's *Youth and Employment in Modern Britain* (Oxford, 1995); see also P. G. Chapman and M. J. Tooze, *The Youth Training Scheme in the United Kingdom* (Aldershot, 1987).

On **banking and finance** R. C. Michie, *The City of London: Continuity and Change, 1850–1990* (London and Basingstoke, 1992) is invaluable. See also J. Plender and P. Wallace, *The Square Mile: A Guide to the City Revolution* (1985); D. Kynaston, *The City of London*, iv. *A Club No More 1945–2000* (2001); R. Roberts and D. Kynaston (eds.), *The Bank of England: Money, Power and Influence 1694–1994* (Oxford, 1995); and A. Leyshon and N. Thrift, 'South Goes North? The Rise of the British Provincial Financial Centre', in J. Lewis and A. Townsend (eds.), *The North–South Divide: Regional Change in Britain in the 1980s* (1989). For the social consequences of the City's growth in the 1980s see A. Leyshon and N. Thrift, *Money/Space: Geographies of Monetary Transformation* (1997).

For **consumerism** J. Benson and G. Shaw (eds.), *The Retailing Industry*, iii (1999) is edited too lightly, but it usefully collects informative essays on many aspects of retailing, including co-ops, discount stores, and out-of-town superstores. R. Coopey, S. O'Connell, and D. Porter's *Mail Order Retailing in Britain: A Business and Social History* (Oxford, 2005) is admirable for integrating social with business history. See also J. Obelkevich's 'Consumption', in J. Obelkevich and P. Catterall (eds.), *Understanding Post-War British Society* (1994); S. Bowden and A. Offer, 'Household Appliances and the Use of Time: The United States and Britain since the 1920s', *Economic History Review*, 47 (1994); and D. West, 'Multinational Competition in the British Advertising Agency Business, 1936–1987', *Business History Review* (Autumn 1988). On diet C. Driver's *The British at Table 1940–1980* (1983) was a pioneering work. See also D. H. Buss, 'The British Diet since the End of Food Rationing', in C. Geissler and D. J. Oddy (eds.), *Food, Diet and Economic Change Past and Present* (Leicester, 1993), and the Ministry of

Agriculture, Fisheries and Food's *Fifty Years of the National Food Survey 1940–1990* (1991), which contains ample statistics on dietary change. There is no good book on the history of vegetarianism. J. A. Spring and D. H. Buss, 'British Drinking Patterns for the Last 300 Years', *Nature* (1977) provides a wide perspective. See also P. Wilson's DHSS research, *Drinking in England and Wales* (1980) and T. R. Gourvish and R. G. Wilson, *The Brewing Industry 1830–1980* (Cambridge, 1994).

6. INTELLECT AND CULTURE

On **religion**, for statistical aspects see R. Currie, A. Gilbert, and L. Horsley, *Churches and Churchgoers: Patterns of Church Growth in the British Isles since 1700* (Oxford, 1977); P. Brierley, *A Century of British Christianity: Historical Statistics 1900–1985 with Projections to 2000* (1985); and Statistical Unit of the Central Board of Finance, *Facts and Figures about the Church of England* (1962). G. Davie, *Religion in Britain since 1945: Believing without Belonging* (Oxford, 1994) provides an overview. A. Hastings, *A History of English Christianity 1920–1985* (1986) is fair-minded and wide-ranging, strongest on the Catholic tradition. See also D. Jenkins, *The British: Their Identity and their Religion* (1975); P. Badham (ed.), *Religion, State and Society in Modern Britain* (1989); and A. Howard, *Basil Hume: The Monk Cardinal* (2005). H. Carpenter's gloriously indiscreet and therefore illuminating *Robert Runcie: The Reluctant Archbishop* (1996) has an informative preface in its paperback (1997) edition.

On **schools** the Department of Education's regular publications of examination results represent a rich resource that historians and sociologists have yet to exploit. For the 'public' (from 1973, 'independent') schools J. Rae, *The Public School Revolution: Britain's Independent Schools. 1964–1979* (1981) is illuminating. His *The Old Boys' Network: A Headmaster's Diaries 1972–1986* (2009) entertainingly yet seriously illuminates the delicate balancing act the public-school headmaster then had to perform as between pupils, teachers, parents, and school governors. See also G. Walford (ed.), *British Public Schools: Policy and Practice* (1984). An objective historical appraisal of the Assisted Places Scheme is much needed.

On **universities**, for a short introduction see R. Anderson, *British Universities Past and Present* (2006). See also the annual *University Statistics* (1980–). There are many histories of individual universities, most notably R. Dahrendorf, *LSE: A History of the London School of Economics and Political Science 1895–1995* (Oxford, 1995); M. Moss, J. F. Munro, and R. H. Trainor (eds.), *University, City and State: The University of Glasgow since 1870* (Edinburgh, 2000); and M. G. Brock's contribution to the collaborative *The History of the University of Oxford*, viii. *The Twentieth Century* (ed. B. Harrison, Oxford, 1994). Useful also is J. Tunstall (ed.), *The Open University Opens* (1974). J. Carswell, *Government and the Universities in Britain: Programme and Performance, 1960–1980* (Cambridge, 1986) is invaluable on governmental aspects. R. Simpson, *How the Ph.D. Came to Britain: A Century of Struggle for Postgraduate Education* (Guildford, 1983) collects important information on postgraduate study. The contributors to R. Finnegan (ed.), *Participating in the Knowledge Society: Researchers Beyond the University Walls* (Basingstoke, 2005)—especially A. J. Hunt, J. J. D. Greenwood, D. Cummings, F. Webster, and Finnegan herself—provide a salutary reminder that much research occurs outside universities. See also P. B. Dematteis, P. S. Fosl, and L. B. McHenry (eds.), *British Philosophers, 1800–2000* ('Dictionary of Literary Biography', 262; Farmington Hills, Mich., 2002) and R. J. Johnston's informative *Geography and Geographers: Anglo-American Human Geography since 1945* (1997). For an introduction to long-term themes in intellectual life see B. Harrison, 'Professionalism and Populism in British Intellectual Life since 1945', in J. E. Myhre (ed.), *Intellectuals in the Public Sphere in Britain and Norway after World War II* (Oslo, 2008), 35–78.

To **literary history** the best short guide is R. Stevenson's *The British Novel since the Thirties: An Introduction* (1986). Also valuable is B. Ford (ed.), *The New Pelican Guide to English Literature*, viii. *From Orwell to Naipaul* (1st publ. 1983, rev. edn. 1995). See the 'Dictionary of Literary Biography' series volumes: J. L. Halio (ed.), *British Novelists since 1960* (Vol. 14; Detroit, 1983); M. Moseley (ed.), *British Novelists since 1960, Second Series* (Vol. 194; Detroit, 1998); *Third Series* (Vol. 207; Detroit, 1999); and *Fourth Series* (Vol. 231; Detroit, 2001); M. Moseley (ed.), *British and Irish Novelists since 1960* (Vol. 271; Farmington Hills, Mich., 2003); M. R. Molino (ed.), *Twenty-First-Century British and Irish Novelists* (Vol. 267; Farmington Hills, Mich., 2003); D. Baldwin (ed.), *Short-Fiction Writers* (Vol. 139; Detroit, 1994); C. A. and D. Malcolm (eds.), *British and Irish Short-Fiction Writers, 1945–2000* (Vol. 319; Farmington Hills, Mich., 2006); V. B. Sherry, *Poets of Great Britain and Ireland since 1960* (Vol. 40, 2 parts; Detroit, 1985); S. Serafin (ed.), *Twentieth-Century British Literary Biographers* (Vol. 155; Detroit, 1995); D. Harris-Fain (ed.), *British Fantasy and Science-Fiction Writers since 1960* (Vol. 261; Farmington Hills, Mich., 2002); and G. Macdonald (ed.), *British Mystery and Thriller Writers since 1960* (Vol. 276, Farmington Hills, Mich., 2003). Valuable biographies include A. Motion, *Philip Larkin: A Writer's Life* (1993), complemented by *The Selected Letters of Philip Larkin, 1940–1985* (ed. A. Thwaite, 1992); and M. Drabble, *Angus Wilson: A Biography* (1995).

J. A. Sutherland's publications almost single-handedly tackle the serious study of **publishing** history, but he needs more helpers. See his *Fiction and the Fiction Industry* (1978), and *Reading the Decades: Fifty Years of the Nation's Bestselling Books* (2002). M. Crick's *Jeffrey Archer: Stranger than Fiction* (rev. edn. 1996) straddles, like its subject, the boundary between popular novels and Conservative politics. For **libraries** see A. Black, *The Public Library in Britain 1914–2000* (2000); for controversy about them see the Adam Smith Institute's *Ex Libris* (1986), by D. C. Mason. See also Mason's *Expounding the Arts* (Adam Smith Institute, 1987), and T. Coates, *Who's in Charge? Responsibility for the Public Library Service* (Libri, n.pl., n.d.).

Writing about the **history of the arts** in these years has yet to transcend the connoisseur and the enthusiast, and Robert Hewison's labours are much needed in this later period, though his *The Heritage Industry: Britain in a Climate of Decline* (1987) stakes out important ground. R. Strong's *Diaries 1967–1987* (1997) provide a rare glimpse inside the world of art, galleries, and museums; more such glimpses are much needed. On design see A. Forty, *Objects of Desire: Design and Society 1750–1980* (1986). For sculpture see R. Berthoud, *The Life of Henry Moore* (1987). For amateur music-making see Ruth Finnegan's brilliant *The Hidden Musicians: Music-Making in an English Town* (Cambridge, 1989). There is a serious lack of intelligent books about **popular** music; most are introverted, and many incoherent, but K. Negus's 'The Discovery and Development of Recording Artists in the Popular Music Industry' (Department of Social Science, Southbank Polytechnic, London, Ph.D. thesis 1991) is excellent, and D. Hesmondhalgh, 'The British Dance Music Industry: A Case Study of Independent Cultural Production', *British Journal of Sociology* (June 1998) is penetrating. See also S. Cohen, *Society and Culture in the Making of Rock Music in Merseyside* (Oxford, 1987); I. McDonald, *Revolution in the Head: The Beatles Records and the Sixties* (2nd rev. edn. 2005); and H. Davies, *The Beatles* (rev. edn. 1985). P. Norman's *John Lennon: The Life* (2008) and *The Stones* (updated edn. 2001), and A. Clayson's *Mick Jagger: The Unauthorised Biography* (2005) are comprehensive and fact-packed, but unreflective. Also relevant are M. J. Clarke *The Politics of Pop Festivals* (1982), and M. Hung and E. G. Morencos (eds.), *World Record Sales 1969–1990: A Statistical History of the World Recording Industry* (1990); the latter has valuable statistics.

On the theatre, M. Billington's informative synopsis, the unfootnoted and oddly titled *State of the Nation: British Theatre since 1945* (2007), is self-confessedly partisan, at times autobiographical, and racily readable. Its laudable aim of relating theatre history to contemporary socio-political events, however, could succeed only if tied to something more than the analysis of plays and plots—that is, if linked to the sociology and even the business history of the theatre which he does not supply. Billington's *Life and Work of Harold Pinter* (1996) is a fine biographical study. See also M. Darlow, *Rattigan: The Man and his Work* (rev. edn. 2000). In the 'Dictionary of Literary Biography' see S.Weintraub's four volumes: *Modern British Dramatists* (Vol. 10, 2 parts; Detroit, 1982), *British Dramatists since World War II* (Vol. 13, 2 parts; Detroit, 1982); and J. Bull's two volumes: *British and Irish Dramatists since World War II: Third Series* (Vol. 245, Detroit, 2001); *Fourth Series* (Vol. 310; Farmington Hills, Mich., 2005). See also J. Croall, *Gielgud: A Theatrical Life 1904–2000* (2001).

Important for the history of the press are J. Cunningham, 'National Daily Newspapers and their Circulations in the UK, 1908–1978', *Journal of Advertising History* (Feb. 1981); and Anthony Sampson, 'The Crisis at the Heart of our Media', *British Journalism Review* (1996). K. Sisson, *Industrial Relations in Fleet Street: A Study in Pay Structure* (Oxford, 1975) is good. See also M. Leapman, *Treacherous Estate: The Press after Fleet Street* (1992); H. Henry, *Key Regional Newspaper Trends: An Analysis of Circulations and Revenues during the Past Decade* (Henley-on-Thames, 1990); A. Smith (ed.), *The British Press since the War* (Newton Abbot, 1974). There are several histories of individual newspapers and periodicals, including *The History of 'The Times'*, vi (1966–81, by J. Grigg, 1993); D. Kynaston's *The 'Financial Times': A Centenary History* (1988); and R. Dudley Edwards, *The Pursuit of Reason: The 'Economist' 1843–1993* (1993).

Essential for the media is the fifth volume in A. Briggs's history of the BBC: *Competition* (Oxford, 1995), covering 1955–74. H. Carpenter's *The Envy of the World* (1996) covers the first fifty years of the Third Programme/Radio 3. The series 'Independent Television in Britain' is heavily administrative in emphasis: J. Potter's two volumes on 1968–80 are thematically divided into *Politics and Control* (1989) and *Companies and Programmes* (1990); P. Bonner's is the fifth volume in the series, *ITV and IBA, 1981–92: The Old Relationship Changes* (1998). M. Cockerell, *Live from Number 10: The Inside Story of Prime Ministers and Television* (1988) takes a broad sweep from Churchill to Thatcher and is invaluable on the political side. Among the useful contributions to J. Corner (ed.), *Popular Television in Britain: Studies in Cultural History* (1991) are those by Corner, P. Goddard, A. Medhurst, and G. Whannel. For changing attitudes to privacy see B. Harrison, 'The Public and the Private in Modern Britain', in P. Burke et al. (eds.), *Civil Histories: Essays Presented to Sir Keith Thomas* (Oxford, 2000).

Sport history received a welcome injection of reflectiveness in A. Guttmann's *From Ritual to Record: The Nature of Modern Sports* (New York, 1978), and in the UK the subject has recently begun to transcend antiquarianism, owing much to the *British Journal of Sports History* (1984–6), continued from 1987 as the *International Journal of the History of Sport*. See also R. W. Cox, *A Bibliography of British Sports History, 1800–2000* (3 vols. 1991). Valuable are Henley Centre for Forecasting, *The Economic Impact and Importance of Sport in the United Kingdom: A Study Prepared for the Sports Council* (1985); S. Dobson and J. Goddard, 'Performance, Revenue, and Cross Subsidization in the Football League, 1927–1994', *Economic History Review* (Nov. 1998); and R. Holt and T. Mason, *Sport in Britain 1945–2000* (Oxford, 2000), which maps out the territory. See also H. Richards, *A Game for Hooligans: The History of Rugby Union* (updated edn. Edinburgh, 2007); and J. Bryant, *The London Marathon* (2005). K. F. Dyer, *Catching Up the Men: Women in Sport* (1982), and E. Cashmore, 'Women's Greatest Handicaps: Sex, Medicine and Men', *British Journal of Sports Medicine*, 33/2 (Apr. 1999) open up an important dimension.

For **humour** see D. Nathan, *The Laughtermakers* (1971), a first-rate study of British humour 1940–70 with valuable interview material. Also valuable are B. Took's *Laughter in the Air: An Informal History of British Radio Comedy* (1981), and R. Wilmut's two books *Kindly Leave the Stage: The Story of Variety 1919–1960* (1985) and *From Fringe to Flying Circus: Celebrating a Unique Generation of Comedy 1960–1980* (1980). See also P. Goddard, ' "Hancock's Half Hour": A Watershed in British Television Comedy', in J. Corner (ed.), *Popular Television in Britain: Studies in Cultural History* (1991). For biography see Max Wall's autobiographical *The Fool on the Hill* (1975); M. Freedland, *Kenneth Williams* (1989); B. Took, *Star Turns. The Life and Times of Benny Hill and Frankie Howerd* (1992); P. Oakes, *Tony Hancock* (1975); and H. Thompson's excellent *Peter Cook* (1997).

7. POLITICS AND GOVERNMENT

On the constitution V. Bogdanor (ed), *The British Constitution in the Twentieth Century* (Oxford, 2003) gathers a wealth of material. Bogdanor's 'Britain: The Political Constitution', in Bogdanor (ed.), *Constitutions in Democratic Politics* (Aldershot, 1988) is excellent, as is his characteristically lucid and trenchant *The New British Constitution* (Oxford, 2009). On the executive see P. Hennessy, *Cabinet* (Oxford, 1986); A. King (ed.), *The British Prime Minister* (1st publ. 1969, 2nd edn. 1985). On the civil service see P. Hennessy, *Whitehall* (1989), compendious and informative; P. Kellner and Lord Crowther-Hunt, *The Civil Servants: An Inquiry into Britain's Ruling Class* (1980); G. Drewry and T. Butcher, *The Civil Service Today* (2nd edn. 1988). For the strains British government experienced under corporatism see A. King, 'Overload: Problems of

Governing in the 1970s', *Political Studies* (1975). C. Foster's 'The Encroachment of the Law on Politics', *Parliamentary Affairs* (Apr. 2000) provides valuable recollections on the changing relationship between ministers, civil servants, and lawyers when drafting legislation.

On **parliament** S. A. Walkland (ed.), *The House of Commons in the Twentieth Century: Essays by Members of the Study of Parliament Group* (Oxford, 1979) collects abundant material. A. King, 'The Rise of the Career Politician in Britain—and its Consequences', *British Journal of Political Science* (1981) is important. See also S. A. Walkland and M. Ryle (eds.), *Parliament in the 1970s* (1977); P. Norton (ed.), *Parliament in the 1980s* (1985). There is no historical study of the House of Lords for this period.

Local government is best approached through K. Young and N. Rao, *Local Government since 1945* (Oxford, 1997) supplemented by T. Byrne's admirable reference work, *Local Government in Britain: Everyone's Guide to How it All Works* (5th edn. 1990). See also G. C. Baugh, 'Government Grants in Aid of the Rates in England and Wales, 1889–1990', *Historical Research* (1992); W. A. Hampton, *Local Government and Urban Politics* (2nd edn. 1991); and D. E. Butler et al., *Failure in British Government: The Politics of the Poll Tax* (Oxford, 1994).

For **police and judiciary** see T. Morris, *Crime and Criminal Justice since 1945* (Oxford, 1989); D. Pannick, *Judges* (Oxford, 1987). The Policy Studies Institute's four volumes on *Police and People in London* (1983) are valuable, especially vol. ii (edited by S. Small, on attitudes among a group of young blacks) and vol. iv (edited by D. J. Smith and J. Gray, which provides rich qualitative information on police structure and attitudes). See also S. Holdaway, *Inside the British Police: A Force at Work* (Oxford, 1983). For private policing see T. Jones and T. Newburn, *Private Security and Public Policing* (Oxford, 1998).

The legal and penal system in the modern period has yet to find historians who can cope with the jargon and yet also escape the system's introversion, so as fully to exploit the ample raw material that is available. See *Criminal Statistics*, which from 1950 continued the earlier *Judicial Statistics*. S. Field in his *Trends in Crime and their Interpretation: A Study of Recorded Crime in Postwar England and Wales* (1990) does his best to interpret them. See also T. Morris and L. Blom-Cooper, *Murder in England and Wales since 1957* (1979). R. Mark's *Policing a Perplexed Society* (1977) and *In the Office of Constable* (1978) show an intelligent policeman conducting a rare dialogue with the public. On prisons there are no good secondary works, but see Lord Woolf and S. Tumim, *Prison Disturbances April 1990: Report of an Inquiry* (1991, Cm 1456). For a prisoner's account see R. Caird, *A Good and Useful Life: Imprisonment in Britain Today* (1974). For criminology's limited usefulness see D. Downes, 'Promise and Performance in British Criminology', *British Journal of Criminology* (Dec. 1978).

The most sustained historical and comparative study of **pressure groups** is K. Middlemas's three-volume *Power, Competition and the State* (1986–91), which covers analytically the period from 1940 to the 1980s; the second volume takes the analysis up to 1974, the third (which rather runs out of steam) to the end of the 1980s.

For **political parties** see S. E. Finer, *The Changing British Party System 1945–1979* (Washington, DC, 1980); and S. E. Finer (ed.), *Adversary Politics and Electoral Reform* (1975). On the interaction between policy and the two-party system see B. Harrison, 'The

Rise, Fall and Rise of Political Consensus in Britain since 1940', *History* (Apr. 1999). M. Pinto-Duschinsky, *British Political Finance 1830–1980* (Washington, DC, and London, 1981) covers important ground. The three volumes of party manifestos edited by I. Dale are invaluable: published in 2000, and divided by party, they cover all party manifestos from 1900 to 1997.

On the **Conservative Party** see R. Blake's *The Conservative Party from Peel to Thatcher*; this valuable introductory textbook, first published in 1970, went through several editions before reaching its final form in 1985. A. Seldon and S. Ball (eds.), *Conservative Century: The Conservative Party since 1900* (1994) provides an ampler and collective long run-in to the subject. John Ramsden's second volume in the party's history, *The Winds of Change: Macmillan to Heath, 1957–1975* (1996), provides rich detail. M. Walker's *National Front* (1977) is an able journalist's account of political groupings further right; for a sociologist's view, energetically probing the Front's 'ideology', see N. Fielding, *The National Front* (1981).

Among biographical studies, J. Campbell's *Edward Heath* (1993) is far superior to Heath's relentlessly self-justificatory autobiography, *The Course of my Life* (1998). See also S. Ball and A. Seldon (eds.), *The Heath Government 1970–74: A Reappraisal* (1996); A. Douglas-Home, *The Way the Wind Blows* (1976); D. R. Thorpe, *Alec Douglas-Home* (1996); R. Maudling, *Memoirs* (1978); L. Baston, *Reggie: The Life of Reginald Maudling* (2004); and S. Heffer, *Like the Roman: The Life of Enoch Powell* (1998). For Quintin Hogg, Lord Hailsham, see his second autobiography, *A Sparrow's Flight* (1990), and G. Lewis, *Lord Hailsham* (1997). On Thatcher, it was a remarkable feat for Hugo Young, in his *One of Us* (final edn. 1993), to compile as a busy journalist a biography so penetrating and so early of a subject that he disliked. Like almost all political autobiographies, Thatcher's sees the world primarily from the author's point of view, but her two volumes—*The Path to Power* (1995) and *The Downing Street Years* (1993) are important because unusually wide-ranging, thorough, and analytic; see also her *Collected Speeches* (ed. R. Harris, 1997). H. Young and A. Sloman, *The Thatcher Phenomenon* (1986) and J. Ranelagh, *Thatcher's People: An Insider's Account of the Politics, the Power and the Personalities* (1991) are also important. John Campbell's two-volume *Margaret Thatcher* (2000, 2003) is a biography built to last. It lacks Young's eloquence, but matches Thatcher's autobiography in range, and justifiably questions many of its details. Surpassing it in nuance, balance, and objectivity, it is formidable in its penetration and depth of research.

For the shift in ideas that fuelled 'Thatcherism' see R. Cockett, *Thinking the Unthinkable: Think-Tanks and the Economic Counter-Revolution 1931–1983* (1994); R. M. Hartwell, *A History of the Mont Pelerin Society* (Indianapolis, 1995); W. Eltis, 'The Failure of the Keynesian Conventional Wisdom', *Lloyds Bank Review*, 122 (Oct. 1976); H. Johnson, 'The Keynesian Revolution and the Monetarist Counterrevolution' (1970) in his *On Economics and Society* (Chicago and London, 1975); J. Hoskyns, *Just in Time: Inside the Thatcher Revolution* (2000); and B. Harrison, 'Mrs Thatcher and the Intellectuals', *TCBH* 5/2 (1994). On Thatcher's impact, see D. Kavanagh, *Thatcherism and British Politics: The End of Consensus?* (1st publ. 1987, 2nd edn. 1990), and D. Kavanagh and A. Seldon (eds.), *The Thatcher Effect* (Oxford, 1989), for a multi-dimensional approach. S. Letwin, *Anatomy of Thatcherism* (1992) was a pioneeringly probing analysis.

Although no significant diaries emerged from the Heath and Thatcher governments, there was a good crop of autobiographies. N. Lawson's *The View from No.11: Memoirs of a Tory Radical* (1992) is the most substantial autobiography of a Chancellor of the Exchequer (1983–9) that we possess; its length caused reviewers to grumble, but is fully justified. N. Fowler's *Ministers Decide: A Personal Memoir of the Thatcher Years* (1991), by an experienced and able cabinet minister, has received unjustly slighting comment, and is also valuable. Informative too is K. Baker, *The Turbulent Years: My Life in Politics* (1993). Other biographies are P. Carrington, *Reflect on Things Past: The Memoirs of Lord Carrington* (1988); I. Gilmour, *Dancing with Dogma: Britain under Thatcherism* (1992); M. Heseltine, *Life in the Jungle: My Autobiography* (2000); G. Howe, *Conflict of Loyalty* (1994); C. Parkinson, *Right at the Centre: An Autobiography* (1992); J. Prior, *A Balance of Power* (1986); N. Ridley, *'My Style of Government': The Thatcher Years* (1991); N. Tebbit, *Upwardly Mobile* (1988); P. Walker, *Staying Power* (1991); W. Whitelaw, *The Whitelaw Memoirs* (1989); and D. Young, *The Enterprise Years: A Businessman in the Cabinet* (1990). The many biographies include M. Garnett and I. Aitken's *Splendid! Splendid! The Authorized Biography of Willie Whitelaw* (2002). Neither M. Halcrow, *Keith Joseph: A Single Mind* (1989) nor A. Denham and M. Garnett, *Keith Joseph* (Chesham, 2001) do full justice to their important subject. Alan Clark is one of the few recent Conservative politicians to risk a career by publishing a diary: his *Diaries: Into Politics* (2000) cover 1972–82, and his *Diaries* (1993) cover 1983–91.

For the **Labour Party** see B. Pimlott's *Harold Wilson* (1992) and Wilson's last autobiographical volume, *Final Term: The Labour Government 1974–1976* (1979). Also illuminating is Joe Haines's remarkably frank *Glimmers of Twilight: Harold Wilson in Decline* (2003). Three Labour diarists provide invaluable first-hand insights: Barbara Castle's *The Castle Diaries 1974–76* (1980) is as good as her first volume. B. Donoughue, *Prime Minister: The Conduct of Policy under Harold Wilson and James Callaghan* (1987) is valuable, and still more so are the two volumes of his *Downing Street Diary* (2005, 2008), a sympathetic yet shrewdly critical commentary from the inside on Wilson's last two governments (1974–6) and on Callaghan's (1976–9). Donoughue supplements his diaries with his autobiography, *The Heat of the Kitchen* (2003). Four of Tony Benn's eight volumes of diary are relevant—for 1968–72 (1988), 1973–6 (1989), 1977–80 (1990), 1980–90 (1992); diminishingly ministerial in emphasis, they are all edited by Ruth Winstone. Valuable biographies or autobiographies include J. Barnett, *Inside the Treasury* (1982); C. Bryant (ed.), *John Smith: An Appreciation* (1994); J. Callaghan, *Time and Chance* (1987); K. O. Morgan's *Callaghan: A Life* (Oxford, 1997) and *Michael Foot: A Life* (2007); E. Dell, *A Hard Pounding: Politics and Economic Crisis 1974–1976* (Oxford, 1991); and D. Healey, *The Time of my Life* (1989). M. Westlake's *Kinnock: The Biography* (2001) is too long, but it is serious, and valuable for illuminating Labour's internal changes during the 1980s. For signs of rethinking in the party in the early 1980s, see M. Jacques and F. Mulhern (eds.), *The Forward March of Labour Halted?* (1981), where significant talent on the left was deployed.

In these years the **Liberal Party**'s history is bound up with the history of the Labour Party. See D. Steel, *Against Goliath: David Steel's Story* (1989), and A. Michie and S. Hoggart, *The Pact: The Inside Story of the Lib-Lab Government, 1977–8* (1978). A more powerful long-term source of Liberal strength was its pact with the **Social**

Democratic Party, of which the essential (and fine) study is I. Crewe and A. King, *SDP: The Birth, Life and Death of the Social Democratic Party* (Oxford, 1995). R. Jenkins's stylish autobiography, *A Life at the Centre* (1991) views its subject self-critically and in broad perspective; it is fair-minded, skilful at avoiding hindsight, and concludes appropriately with judicious and measured reflections on his career.

On **electoral behaviour**, D. E. Butler has performed the remarkable feat of writing or co-writing a book on every British general election between 1951 and 2005, and on **privacy and publicity** M. Cockerell's *Live from Number 10: The Inside Story of Prime Ministers and Television* (1988) is invaluable on the political side.

Index